THE JUSTICE FROM BEACON HILL

Oliver Wendell Holmes, c. 1910. *Library of Congress Collections.*

THE JUSTICE FROM BEACON HILL

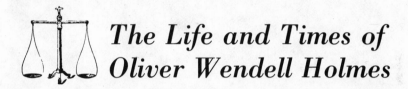

The Life and Times of Oliver Wendell Holmes

LIVA BAKER

HarperCollins*Publishers*

FIRST EDITION

Designed by Helene Berinsky

Library of Congress Cataloging-in-Publication Data

Baker, Liva.
  The justice from Beacon Hill / the life and times of Oliver
Wendell Holmes / Liva Baker.—1st ed.
     p. cm.
  Includes bibliographical references and index.
  ISBN 0-06-016629-0
  1. Holmes, Oliver Wendell, 1841–1935. 2. Judges—United States—
Biography. I. Title.
KF8745.H6B35 1991
347.73'2634—dc20
[B]
[347.3073534]
[B]   90-42380

---

91 92 93 94 95 MV/RRD 10 9 8 7 6 5 4 3 2 1

To

Judy and Sid Baker
Sheila Gellman
Barbara Germond
Marilee and Jack Reiner
Pat and Phil Robbins
Jane Anne and Jim Spellman

They were always there.

CONTENTS

Part VIII BENEDICTION

Illustrations follow page 274.

ACKNOWLEDGMENTS

Anyone who writes about Oliver Wendell Holmes owes an enormous debt to the late Mark DeWolfe Howe. His scholarship has helped all of us penetrate the impenetrable.

I would also like to thank

at Harvard Law School, Erika Chadbourn and Judith W. Mellins, who made research a pleasure;

at the Harvard Law School Art Collection, Bernice Loss for her patience;

at the Library of Congress, Suzanne E. Thorin, Victoria C. Hill, and Bruce Martin; the study facilities make serious scholarship possible; the staff of the manuscript room, as well as that of the rare book room, especially Peter M. Van Wingen and his musclemen, Robert R. Shields, Clark Evans, and Anthony Edwards; the staff of the law library, especially Robert N. Gee, who is at least partly responsible for the length of the bibliography, and Charles F. Brookes, Jr., who unsnarled many a legal knot;

Bernard and Emily Mehlman for their generous and warm hospitality; every writer ought to have Mehlmans to come home to after a hard day in the archives; old friends Nat and Howard Allen, who exposed me to Boston's and Brookline's more interesting restaurants, and, along with their daughter, Emily Allen Farnham, tracked down local obscurities;

Charlie Ball, who made me laugh;

Jane Anne Spellman, who introduced me to Wendell Holmes;

Mrs. Adell Wade, whose support and steadfastness made many things possible; all those who tramped wearily through the manuscript in whole or in part: Maxwell Bloomfield, Miles Bradbury, Sylvia Frey, Sheila Gellman, Gerald Gunther, Morton Lebow, Dorothy Naor, Russell Neuswanger, the late Anne Radilof, and David Wigdor;

at HarperCollins, M. S. Wyeth, Jr., and his assistant, Cynthia Barrett—in the jargon of the day, "caring" editors; my son, David Baker, also a four-star editor, and my daughter, Sara Baker, friend and helpmate; they have a unique understanding of the Fourth Commandment.

Thanks are due also the Trustees of the Boston Public Library, Harvard University Archives, Harvard Law School Archives, and Houghton Library for permission to cite materials in their possession.

Part *I*

 *SAINT*

When Americans gather to honor those who have gone before, they come, in a sense, to honor themselves. For what we do when we sing the praises of a great American is acclaim the virtues of the Nation as they were reflected in his life and his accomplishments. In doing this we honor our own aspirations if not our own achievements.

—Speech given by Mark DeWolfe Howe,
May 14, 1958, in Chicago

CHAPTER *1*

"The Magnificent Yankee"

THE CANONIZATION OF Justice Oliver Wendell Holmes of the United States Supreme Court took place over the CBS radio network at 10:30 P.M. on Sunday, March 8, 1931, his ninetieth birthday. He was the most distinguished Harvard Law School graduate in public life at the time, and five hundred people had gathered in Langdell Hall to hear the broadcast, after which Eugene Wambaugh, professor emeritus, reminisced of Holmes's long life in the law. The chief justice of the United States, Charles Evans Hughes, participated in the broadcast itself, as did Charles A. Boston, president of the American Bar Association, and Charles E. Clark, dean of the Yale Law School.

They quoted from his speeches and decisions. They called him "America's most respected man of law," and the "best company in Washington." Chief Justice Hughes said Holmes was a "constant contradiction of all that great age usually implies," and described Holmes's life as one "unmarred, unified by intelligent purpose and uninterrupted accomplishment, blessed by great talent employed in the worthiest activities, with deserved fame never dimmed and always growing. . . . We honor him, but, what is more, we love him. We give him tonight the homage of our hearts." Hughes and the others had struck just the right chords, found exactly the right words to satisfy Holmes's hunger, requite his ambition. Recognition of his achievement had not been as swift as Holmes would have liked, and throughout his life, he had indulged in bouts of bitterness whenever he had thought his work passed unappreciated.

This ninetieth birthday celebration had begun two days before, on Friday, March 6, when news photographers, anticipating the event, approached Holmes as he was leaving the Supreme Court for the noon recess.

"Not now," the justice had protested. "I'm going to have my victuals first."

Then, luncheon over, he and Chief Justice Hughes donned judicial robes and posed together. The years between youth and ninety showed mostly in Holmes's posture. His six-foot-three frame was somewhat stooped now, and his slim figure made him look more gaunt than lean. His constitution was remarkable for a man of ninety. He had always taken good care of himself. He drank little—practically nothing now— had given up cigars, and napped regularly, more now that he was old. Prostate surgery a decade before, periodic onsets of asthma, a family affliction, and attacks of lumbago were about the sum of his physical sufferings.

The years showed, too, in the whiteness of his thick hair and still luxuriant mustaches. But his blue-gray eyes still sparkled, and his skin was still pink. He could still mask his embarrassment with a fierce glare, and his face still was prepared to break into the familiar smile. His hand was still firm, his wit quick.

But he rarely if ever ventured out to social events now, and he had missed President Herbert Hoover's recent annual dinner for the Supreme Court justices. The current term of the Court had been the most exhausting he had known, and he wondered whether he ought to continue on the Court. Were the weaknesses of old age preventing him from doing his full share of the work? He worried about that, although the brethren had given no outward sign that they thought he ought to resign. Not yet, anyway.

Later that afternoon, Holmes's friend and admirer, Professor Felix Frankfurter of Harvard Law School, presented him with a volume of essays, *Mr. Justice Holmes,* containing tributes from some of his distinguished friends: Judges Learned Hand of the United States Court of Appeals for the Second Circuit and Benjamin Cardozo of the New York Court of Appeals, philosophers Morris Cohen and John Dewey, former dean of Northwestern University Law School John H. Wigmore, writers Walter Lippmann and Phillip Litell, the English political economist Harold Laski, and Frankfurter himself.

On Sunday morning, Holmes's actual birthday, the *New York Times* described him on the editorial page as "the greatest of living judges," and "a great personality—man as well as judge."

A cloudburst of congratulatory letters, telegrams, and tributes from world leaders, including President Hoover, as well as friends, acquaintances, and even strangers was threatening to drown him in affection. Lincoln's Inn, London, whose members included William Pitt, Oliver Cromwell, Benjamin Disraeli, and William Gladstone, had elected him to honorary membership. The Tavern Club of Boston, the only club to which Holmes still belonged, and the General Assembly of Rhode Island marked his birthday with congratulatory resolutions. The March 1931 issues of the Yale, Harvard, and Columbia law reviews had honored him, and Robert Marshall, exploring in Alaska, named, as his birthday gift, a previously undiscovered mountain after Holmes.

The adulation pleased the old man, "for," he said, "we don't get rid of interest in ourselves even when Self is so near vanishing."

There was this year, however, no sentimental gathering of the justice's former secretaries as there had been on previous birthdays. The young men felt that "the presence of all of them would put an undue strain on the justice with the other excitement of that day." They sent their "reverence" by mail and promised to call on him the following week, at which time they flattered him once more by asking him to sit for a portrait they had commissioned.

Holmes had dreaded the "plunge into the unknown radio." He had declined all such invitations for years, but this time he had found himself unable to resist the proposal presented by the law schools of Columbia, Yale, and Harvard to broadcast the ninetieth birthday greetings. At the same time, he had been reading a book of Latin poetry, and, equally unable to resist a good punch line, he explained, "what made me not positively refuse to take part in the radio talk was the thought of a line from the volume with which I could wind up—'Death, plucking my ear, says, "Live—I am coming."' "

He sat at a microphone which had been installed two days before in the second-floor study of his home at 1720 I Street, in the northwest quadrant of Washington. He recently had recovered from a cold, and he cleared his throat in a tentative sort of way before he spoke. At ninety, his voice was reedier than it had been formerly, but the cultivated Boston-British accent was as clear as ever, and he touched the hearts of all his admirers with his message:

> In this symposium my part is only to sit in silence. To express one's feelings as the end draws near is too intimate a task.
>
> But I may mention one thought that comes to me as a listener-in. The riders in a race do not stop short when they reach the goal. There is a little finishing canter before coming to a standstill. There is time to hear the kind voices of friends and to say to one's self, "The work is done."

But just as one says that, the answer comes, "The race is over, but the work is never done while the power to work remains."

The canter that brings you to a standstill need not be only coming to rest. It cannot be, while you still live. For to live is to function. That is all there is to living.

And so I end with a line from a Latin poet who uttered the message more than fifteen hundred years ago: "Death plucks my ear and says, 'Live— I am coming.' "

As Holmes undoubtedly had known it would, the quotation sent scholars scrambling for their anthologies. Their searches revealed the line had come from *Copa Surisca,* an ode to a Syrian girl who danced to castanets in some ancient tavern; it is usually but not certainly attributed to Virgil.

When the broadcast ended, the CBS engineer collected the microphone. Holmes settled in a chair by the fire. It was a comfortable room, with upholstered leather chairs and a high stand-up desk that had belonged to Holmes's maternal grandfather, Charles Jackson, judge of the Massachusetts Supreme Judicial Court during the early years of the nineteenth century. Books lined the walls from floor to ceiling—some fourteen thousand volumes in all, neatly arranged by subject. It was the library of an intellectual whose interests embraced nearly every field of human knowledge. Holmes read almost obsessively all his adult life: detective stories, adventure tales, risqué French novels, Greek philosophy, legal history, political treatises, memoirs, biographies. Beginning on his return from Europe in 1866, he listed, as if he were to be graded at the end of the year, every book he read—for the first years in the back of old diaries; later, beginning in 1876, in a special folio-sized volume of 159 pages which he called the Black Book. If his eye was on posterity, it is not apparent. He noted the risqué French novels as prominently as the Greek philosophy.

Holmes's young friend Harold Laski was sitting with him on this birthday night. At first the old man's eyes seemed far away and dreamy. Then, after a minute or two, they suddenly flashed and the familiar smile played over Holmes's still handsome face. "When I came back from the Civil War," he mused, "my father asked me what I was going to do and I told him I was going to the Harvard Law School." " 'Pooh!' " the elder Holmes, who perhaps already recognized the intensity of his son's ambition, had replied. " 'What's the use of going to the Harvard Law School? A lawyer cannot be a great man.' " The justice added, a little wistfully, "I wish that my father could have listened tonight for only two or three minutes. Then I could have thumbed my nose at him."*

High honors had been heaped upon Holmes for some years: honorary degrees from Yale (1886), Harvard (1895), Oxford (1909), University of Berlin (1910), Williams (1912), and Amherst (1922). Just the year before, on his eighty-ninth birthday, the United States Senate had taken time out to praise his "clarity of vision," the "tolerance and broadmindedness of his outlook." The fan mail on that occasion, too, had "swamped" him so that he had finally agreed to allow his secretary—Alger Hiss that year—to answer "(1) Those of whom he'd never heard (2) Those whom he knew but slightly and, as it were, officially (3) Those whom he knew so well that he was sure they'd rather save him trouble than hear from him personally." A few days later, on March 20, 1930, Harvard Law School had celebrated, with no little ceremony, the formal presentation of Holmes's portrait, to be hung in Langdell Hall opposite the bust of John Marshall. Holmes himself had been too infirm to make the trip in mid-Court term. He had, however, been deeply moved by the gesture and in his regrets had explained: "My emotion, were I able to be at the presentation . . . would be embarrassing . . . fortunately for my composure I cannot leave Washington."

Now at ninety, he was looking forward to receiving in September the American Bar Association's medal for conspicuous service and in October to publication of *Representative Opinions of Mr. Justice Holmes,* companion volume to *Dissenting Opinions of Mr. Justice Holmes,* published in 1929.

Few Americans of stature have had less contact with the public. He was in fact a snob. He lived largely inside himself where he followed a routine of reading, thinking, and philosophizing. He did not participate in popular causes, and after he took his seat on the United States Supreme Court, he rarely made a public speech. Nevertheless he had become a popular legend in his own lifetime. Who in America could not repeat his quotable quotes? "Oh, to be seventy again!" on sighting a pretty girl long after he had passed that comparatively youthful age had

* There are two versions of the reasons behind Holmes's enrolling in Harvard Law School: Laski's, described above, and that of Felix Frankfurter, who reported in 1932 that Holmes had told him: "After all I was kicked into the law by my governor. When I came back from the Civil War my head was full of thoughts of philosophy and in a vague way I thought of medical school. But my governor would not hear of that, and put on the screws to go to the Law School." Both versions rely on the memory of a very old man. Given the elder Holmes's well-known distaste for law—he himself had briefly gone to Harvard Law School—and lawyers, as well as his own preference for medicine as a profession, Laski's version, despite Laski's reputation for yarn spinning, has the truer ring. The younger Holmes in fact had begun reading in the law and had declared his intention of entering law school before he went into the Civil War.

endeared him to all. "I really like to pay taxes. It is buying civilization" may have been less endearing in a Depression-savaged America, but it was equally well known.

His patrician genealogy, his influence on American legal thought and jurisprudence, his sharply worded opinions read from the United States Supreme Court bench, particularly the dissents, even his more or less regular trips to a Washington burlesque house, had acquired a larger-than-life quality. It was said at the time that if you asked your neighbor to name the justices of the Supreme Court, he might name the chief justice, he might think of Louis Brandeis, but surely he would name Oliver Wendell Holmes. Holmes's birthdays were celebrated on the front pages of the *New York Times.* There was an Oliver Wendell Holmes Parent-Teacher Association in Cleveland, Ohio. And in 1946, Emmet Lavery wrote the popular Broadway play *The Magnificent Yankee;* Holmes was the first Supreme Court justice to be so portrayed.

It is unusual for a judge to capture the imagination and affection of the American people, to translate into a genuine folk hero. Judges in the popular mind wear somber black robes, stand aloof, symbolize sobriety, propriety, perhaps pomposity, are deferred to like royalty, and more often than not write with little regard for the public's ability to understand their words. Such men do not become popular heroes, and no one ever heard of a Willis Van Devanter Parent-Teacher Association; who except his intimates would have recognized William R. Day crossing the street? Holmes, however, was different.

His friends and admirers had made him accessible to all, although in their zeal they had made him a demigod, and he suffered almost as much at their hands as at those of his enemies. Dr. Holmes himself first made the future justice fit for inclusion in contemporary hagiography when he wrote for the *Atlantic Monthly* his sentimental account of his search for his wounded son following the Battle of Antietam in 1862. It was called "My Hunt After the Captain" and its memory never ceased to embarrass its subject. Although the justice had "tried a little to turn her from the plan," in 1926, Elizabeth Shepley Sergeant had drawn his figure larger than life, a man "touched with fire," for the *New Republic;* she included her portrait, which focused on Holmes's personality, in her later book, *Fire Under the Andes.* Publication of Holmes's opinions and the hoopla surrounding the ninetieth birthday celebration drew the public's attention once more and set the forces of adulation in motion.

The first full biography, *Justice Oliver Wendell Holmes,* appeared in 1932, shortly after he left the Court and three years before his death. It was written by Silas Bent, a journalist, who saw Holmes as a true democrat who had discarded the trappings of his aristocratic origins. Bent's book was followed by a spate of work by Holmes's friends and disciples, Felix Frankfurter and Harold Laski, who idolized and idealized him. The former an immigrant Viennese Jew, the latter a product of the Manchester, England, ghetto, they doted on Holmes's patrician background and upbringing. They hung on his every utterance and gesture, turned him into a judicial ancestor of the New Deal and dedicated civil libertarian, neither of which he was. But their outspoken veneration inspired others, and Morris Cohen, columnist Max Lerner, and Francis Biddle, former secretary to Holmes and later United States attorney general, soon joined the cult of Holmes's admirers. Writing in the professional journals, they focused on the liberalism they had found in Holmes's jurisprudence, a liberalism they also happened to embrace. In the popular press—*Atlantic Monthly, New Republic, Harper's*—they disseminated the wit and wisdom of the man. In their books they attempted to capture the essence of both man and judge. Alexander Woollcott included an appealing little section on Holmes in his 1943 memoirs. Edmund Wilson further immortalized him in *Patriotic Gore,* Wilson's study of men and women who acted various roles in the Civil War drama. Catherine Drinker Bowen semifictionalized the entire Holmes family in her worshipful and sentimental book *Yankee from Olympus.*

These people cast Holmes in marble, a serene immortal figure that never really existed wholly the way they saw him. They chiseled in the parts of him they admired, but ignored the contradictions in his nature, his Malthus-inspired pessimism and frustrations, his egotism, an ambition so intense he sometimes alienated his best friends, his cosmic confusions, his infidelities, the strong sense of isolation that runs through his writings, his wariness of intimacy in human relations, his general aloofness from the mainstream of human life.

Over the years, people tended to discover in Holmes statements of their own ideals and aspirations, and divergent schools of jurisprudence claimed him as one of their own. The legal realists appropriated him for his then-shocking thesis that law, "really," was what the judges said it was; pragmatists, for his thesis that law developed out of experience rather than logic or tradition; positivists for his persistent objectivity; utilitarians for his determination to separate law from morality, to distinguish between what the law *is* and what it *ought to be.*

Political liberals mistook his judicial detachment for liberalism— Holmes prided himself on his ability to "regard Montague and Capulet with equal detachment." He was the darling of the Progressives who mistook his judicial tolerance of their social reformers' schemes for political comradeship. During the last years of Holmes's life and the first years following his death in 1935, when his reputation was at its peak, it was said in some academic circles that generous quotation from Holmes's writings was a prerequisite of a successful article or speech.

Then in the 1940s, as Hitler's hordes threatened to destroy what men who had been constructing it for at least five thousand years called civilization, a cult of detractors, led by a group of Jesuit professors scandalized by Holmes's lack of religious faith, formed to demythologize him. When they were through, his democratic sensitivities, his scholarship, and his standards were all found wanting, his work the mechanistic mischief of a materialist. In their zeal to create a modern Antichrist, these critics, like Holmes's admirers, also had distorted the picture.

In an easy effort of transference, Holmes's capacity for deferring to legislative enactment as an expression of majority will became an expression of authoritarianism, might makes right. Supported by an occasional secular scholar, this group created out of Holmes's writings a judicial monster whose jurisprudence came closer to the philosophy of the German dictator than to that of America's Founding Fathers. From the professional journals, their ideas seeped into the nonacademic media. A heated debate was carried on in the American Bar Association *Journal* in the mid-forties. *Catholic World* popularized what the Jesuits had started. Commentator Westbrook Pegler took up the cry, calling Holmes a "cynical and senile brutalitarian" and the "God of an evil cult." And publisher Henry Luce, speaking in 1951 to a regional convention of the American Bar Association in Dallas, Texas, urged that Holmes be reversed "for the sake of the law itself, the American people and our own peace of mind."

More recently, critics have taken Holmes to task for his extraordinary detachment and what is viewed as a lack of humanity, for a relativism that negated all universal values, for an apparent indifference to civil liberties and civil rights, and for his want of a fighting faith, a kind of jurisprudential inconstancy. The late Grant Gilmore of Yale, chosen by Holmes's executors to write Holmes's biography following the death of Mark DeWolfe Howe, their first choice, never completed the project; he said about his subject:

> Holmes is a strange, enigmatic figure. Put out of your mind the picture of the tolerant aristocrat, the great liberal, the eloquent defender of our liberties, the Yankee from Olympus. All that was a myth, concocted by Harold Laski and Felix Frankfurter. . . . The real Holmes was savage, harsh, and cruel, a bitter and lifelong pessimist who saw in the course of human

life nothing but a continuing struggle in which the rich and powerful impose their will on the poor and weak.

It is possible to find in Holmes's thought currents consistent with positivism, realism, and pragmatism—he was realistic but not strictly a realist, pragmatic but not strictly a pragmatist. It is also possible to find ideas consistent with utilitarianism, sociological jurisprudence, evolutionism, authoritarianism, and totalitarianism. Threads of liberalism and progressivism add more color to the tapestry. It is not possible to reduce his work to any one system. He distrusted the absolute beliefs on which all systems were based—"rum things" he thought they were, hopelessly vulnerable to forceful intellectual assault. Truth was only what he couldn't help thinking on the basis of observation and experience, and his only absolute was an absolute abhorrence of absolutes. His concept of law was based on the principle that economic, political, and social premises—all life—were in a constant state of flux and required matching changes in the law, which was an expression of that life. The appropriate flexibility had been built into the Constitution, which had been meant not just for a few million people scattered along the eastern seaboard in the late eighteenth century but for the billions for all time.

The usual conflicting currents that complicate human life had been present in Holmes's, and he had been battered by simultaneous urges toward intellect and emotion, conformity and rebellion, filial love and competition, fidelity and inconstancy. Made up of the usual human ingredients of ego and id, body and spirit, blood and brain, he had responded to these pressures in the usual way, incorporating idealism and cynicism, indifference and involvement, vanity and modesty, awe and irreverence, liberalism and conservatism, intimacy and distance, insularity and cosmopolitanism, savagery and soaring statements of the spirit. He could heap scorn on his secretary for the young man's improvidence in buying a package of Life Savers—Holmes looked at the five-cent expenditure as a year's interest on a dollar—then turn around and treat a troop of his young friends to a bottle of champagne. He could weep over an etching of a poor family's supper—a bowl of milk and a few crusts—and in the next breath condemn with all his soul the "passion for equality." For every lovable quality Felix Frankfurter discovered, an equally disagreeable trait lurked in the shadows. Oliver Wendell Holmes was a complex and often inconsistent man. But he *was* a man. Not a myth.

* * *

AT NINETY, HOLMES had outlived father, mother, younger sister, and younger brother. He had outlived his Fanny, whom the world had known as an enigmatic recluse but whom he had known as a talented and serious artist, a devoted and understanding wife, a woman of clear judgment and strong will; her fires were inner. Whatever difficulties had arisen in their marriage, if Holmes's commitment had been less than total, if Fanny had suffered disappointments, they nevertheless had stayed together in a relationship that amounted to much more than mutual amity but perhaps less than mutual ecstasy, and Fanny had taught him, Holmes said, "how many poems and pictures are to be seen all about one, if one looks." Following her death in 1929 he told friends she had made his life "poetry" for nearly sixty years, and he visited her grave at Arlington National Cemetery regularly, slowly tracing the characters on her tombstone with his long slender fingers.

He had outlived, too, his Clare, his "Beloved Hibernia," to whom he had committed briefly another part of himself and whose grave at Doneraile Court, in County Cork, Ireland, he never would visit.

He had outlived friends: Pen Hallowell, with whom first he had shared the rigors of Harvard College and with whom later he had shared the blood-soaked floor of a Maryland farmhouse while they waited together for medical attention to their wounds following the Battle of Antietam. He had outlived William James, with whom he had shared his gaslight and whiskey when as young men they had "twisted the tail of the cosmos" together; and John Chipman Gray, who had helped him cram for his bar examinations, chosen his secretaries, and remained an intellectual intimate until Gray died in 1915. He had outlived Henry Adams, who had given Holmes his books on German law at a critical juncture in the latter's intellectual life. Now, cousin Johnny Morse, with whom Holmes had roved Boston Common as a boy and whose friendship he still cherished, was about the only one left who called him by his first name.

Holmes had outlived all the justices with whom he had sat on the Massachusetts Supreme Judicial Court for twenty years (1882–1902), and he had outlived all those justices with whom he had begun on the United States Supreme Court in 1902. Governor John D. Long, who had appointed Holmes to the Massachusetts court was dead, as was President Theodore Roosevelt, who had appointed him to the federal bench.

His ninetieth birthday came near the height of the Great Depression. It was the fifth (1857, 1873, 1893, 1907) national financial crisis he had experienced.

Holmes had been born on March 8, 1841, during William Henry Harrison's brief tenure in the White House. The twelve years of Democratic administration under Andrew Jackson and his protégé Martin Van Buren had just come to an end. Abraham Lincoln was a young Springfield, Illinois, lawyer. Former President John Quincy Adams was looking after Massachusetts's affairs in the House of Representatives at Washington. Twenty-six states—nearly half of them slave—made up the Union; Texas was an independent republic.

Only a few weeks before, Henry Clay and Daniel Webster had argued *Groves* v. *Slaughter,* one of several cases involving slavery issues decided by the Supreme Court along the way to civil war. In this case a splintered Court decided the case on the narrowest of grounds and sidestepped the potentially flammable questions involving state and federal power then dividing North and South. Eighty-six years later, Holmes himself, though his judicial record on blacks' civil rights was none too distinguished, wrote the same Court's unanimous and unequivocal opinion declaring Texas's white primary law unconstitutional (*Nixon* v. *Herndon*). Federal supremacy had come of age.

When Holmes was born, fewer than 100,000 people lived in Boston, fewer than 400,000 in New York City, and the journey between them by coach required two days. The journey from coast to coast required between four months and a year. Two weeks after his eighty-seventh birthday, Holmes brushed gravel from his coat as he watched Colonel Charles A. Lindbergh take off in a cloud of flying debris from Bolling Field near Washington in a demonstration of the skills that had enabled him to fly the Atlantic in thirty-three hours, thirty-nine minutes the year before.

During the intervening years, as rapidly developing technology accelerated the relandscaping of America, social, economic, and political institutions which Holmes had inherited were subjected to severe strain. Similarly, the truths that were his legacy were sharply challenged, as Karl Marx, Charles Darwin, Herbert Spencer, and Sigmund Freud expanded the horizons of men's thought far beyond what was considered either possible or proper.

Conflict between vested interests and revolutionaries constituted a large part of Holmes's ninety years. During his boyhood, Bostonians lived "in the atmosphere of the Stamp Act, the Tea Tax, and the Boston Massacre" as abolitionists and Cotton Whigs clashed. In the late 1850s, Holmes, then an undergraduate at Harvard, watched his little world react to Darwin's discoveries in science which threatened men's most ancient and cherished beliefs and dictated the setting of new standards for investigation, not only in the physical sciences, but also in the social sciences, in history and economics, and even law.

The conflicts of the early 1860s were largely political, and Holmes himself participated in the clash between North and South. Then while he prepared for his profession at Harvard Law School in the mid-sixties, Congress passed and submitted to the states for ratification the Fourteenth Amendment to the Constitution, intended to challenge the political shibboleths of race and ultimately to resolve the social conflicts associated with it. Actually, however, the amendment, used more often to sanctify the shibboleths of laissez-faire, had only intensified the conflict. As the 1870s opened and the young lawyer was busy at the bar, the new labor was challenging capital's power. At the same time, modern methods of production, distribution, and capitalization were punching holes in the old economics, and the urban dwellers, many of them immigrants who had come to man the new machines, were beginning to challenge the bankers and merchants of the old aristocracy for political power and social advantage.

In his half century of judging, 1882 to 1932, Holmes found himself resolving the disputes arising out of the political, social, and economic conflicts that had dominated his first forty years. He was one of the few Americans in a position of power at the time who understood the inevitability—if not necessarily the desirability—of change. Much of the time his heart was with the traditionalists, but his head perceived the futility of attempting to stop the clock. He recognized that the country into which he had been born was in a constant state of flux and development, unfinished, a utopia in the making. Its policies were as unsettled as its people, a restless tribe, always struggling toward some social or economic Nirvana where position and wealth would be distributed differently. He was one of the few in a position of power to argue for a system of law responsive to the changing needs and circumstances of the society it reflected, and he was one of the few in a position of power to risk putting his trust, though sometimes reluctantly, in the democratic majority.

OLIVER WENDELL HOLMES, Jr.—he retained the "Jr." until after his father's death in 1894—was born into the most traditional of families in the most traditional of American cities, Boston. He had not been born to great wealth. The thrill of the regattas off the North Shore and the camaraderie among the local merchants who met each day to discuss financial developments were equally foreign to him. He had not, however, been born in a log cabin, either. He came from good solid family, Brahmins all, with all the advantages, privileges, and prejudices the term implied. The royal blue blood not only of Olivers, Wendells, and Holmeses flowed through his veins, but also that of Quincys, Cabots, Jacksons, Lees, Eliots, and Bradstreets."Nature," he once said, "is an aristocrat or at least makes aristocrats, e.g., the cat—and one recognizes certain bloods that generation after generation turn out superior men with here and there a genius."

His father, Dr. Oliver Wendell Holmes, physician, professor, poet, essayist, novelist, and biographer, was a prominent member of the New England intellectual aristocracy during its finest flowering, the middle of the nineteenth century, and young Wendell, as he was called, had grown up in the presence of the local literary peerage: James Russell Lowell, Henry Wadsworth Longfellow, Ralph Waldo Emerson, Nathaniel Hawthorne—all members of his father's coterie. He remembered Herman Melville as a summer neighbor at Pittsfield. Far into his old age, Holmes continued to acknowledge his intellectual debt to Emerson.

Had he allowed it, Boston might have stifled him. The city was old, staid, static, conformist, insular, intellectually conventional, passionless, and self-defensive. Its introverted and traditional conservative character belied the fact that the struggle for American political independence had begun within its environs, that the shot heard round the world had been fired only a few miles from where Charles Bulfinch's gold-domed State House would rise before the century ended, that it had been Bostonians who had defied their royal masters and dumped British tea into the harbor. George Apley was a fictional metaphor for the nineteenth-century city, which alienated Henry James and turned Henry Adams melancholy.

Although he lacked Adams's pessimism and James's sense of shame for his country's rampant materialism and lack of manners, Holmes was as much expatriate as his two contemporaries. An unarticulated but nonetheless real ambivalence about his heritage stalked Holmes lifelong. His natural inclination was to look at the world from the perspective of a typical nineteenth-century provincial Bostonian, to apply the standards of the genteel tradition. At the same time, a more cosmopolitan creature struggled within him for dominance.

The Boston Brahmin's stiffness, formality, and reserve characterized his manner, and his summer home at Beverly Farms was about the only place where he could relax in what he referred to as a soft shirt. But there was another side of him, the Holmes of the twinkling eye and ready, if sometimes bawdy, wit, that loved a lark even if he had to have it in a starched collar. He lived by the social code of Boston gentlemen and he chose many of his friends from among them. But another side of him could not "breathe freely in [the] company" of the Wigglesworths who believed "too much in a phraseology of conventional virtues." This side of him reached out to the traditional outsiders—the Felix Frankfurters, Harold Laskis, Louis Brandeises, the John Wus, the Kentaro Kanekos, the Patrick Sheehans. A part of him resisted change; another part of him was willing to tolerate it. Emotionally, he clung to the introverted world his forebears had created; intellectually, he was questing, catholic, adventurous.

And Boston, whose natural product was a Johnny Morse, clubman, lawyer, literary bon vivant, and upholder of the genteel tradition, was ambivalent about Holmes. It could not always understand his wide-ranging intellectuality. There were some who cherished Holmes's friendship. There were others who undoubtedly accepted him because his name was Holmes. There were still others who believed Holmes had sacrificed them to his own ambitions. And there were also those who resented what they regarded as his sellout to liberalism. Overall, contemporary Bostonians seemed to distrust him slightly, wished he "wouldn't play with his mind."

The products of Holmes's adventurous intellect are numerous. Fifty years of judging begat volumes of his opinions; his many speeches filled in whatever voids were left. But the products of his emotional life are scarce—deliberately so. Even his private correspondence asks more questions than it answers. Holmes revealed himself to few, as if revelation conferred some mystic power over him upon the person who received it. Only his closest friends were aware of the sadness and sense of isolation that lurked beneath the gay and charming exterior.

He must have been one of the most prodigious correspondents of all time. Year after year, in the eighteenth-century tradition, he kept up running conversations with Sir Frederick Pollock, Harold Laski, Lewis Einstein, and Canon Sheehan, less often but nonetheless faithfully with Felix Frankfurter, whom he saw frequently in Boston and Washington, and with several women, including Alice Stopford Green, Ethel Scott, Nina Gray, Clara Sherwood Stevens, Ellen Curtis, Baroness Charlotte Moncheur, and, of course, Lady Clare Castletown, his Beloved Hibernia. A good many of these he wrote from the bench while he waited for counsel to come to the point. Such industry, he liked to say, made him look attentive.

By modern standards, Holmes's letters to men as well as women were flowery, and he seemed to want to make each correspondent feel that he or she ranked first in Holmes's affections. In his letters to Laski, he was urbane and charming, more literary than legal. Pollock was his legal confessor. To Frankfurter he was friend, one with whom he could share details of his work on the Court, and to John Wu he was father. He gossiped and flirted—harmlessly—with most of the women, all except Clare Castletown, with whom his relationship was substantially more intimate. However, life, literature, and law being the major components of his correspondence, his letters—always except those to Lady Castletown—were almost interchangeable. No great misunderstanding would have occurred if a letter to Laski had been missent to Alice Green or even Felix Frankfurter. His idea of intimacy was strictly intellectual, as if he preferred intellectual concerns to dominate his life, as if he thought perhaps he could escape emotional engagement by focusing on matters of the mind.

It was as if he had taken to heart a column Dr. Holmes had once written for the *Atlantic Monthly:*

> Every person's feelings have a front-door and a side-door by which they may be entered. The front-door is on the street. Some keep it always open; some keep it latched; some, locked; some bolted,—with a chain that will let you peep in, but not get in; and some nail it up, so that nothing can pass its threshold. This front-door leads into a passage which opens into an ante-room, and this into the interior apartments. The side-door opens at once into the sacred chambers. . . .
>
> Be very careful to whom you trust one of these keys of the side-door. The fact of possessing one renders those even who are dear to you very terrible at times. You can keep the world out from your front-door, or receive visitors only when you are ready for them; but those of your own flesh and blood, or of certain grades of intimacy, can come in at the side-door, if they will, at any hour and in any mood. Some of them have a scale of your whole nervous system, and can play all the gamut of your sensibilities in semitones,—touching the naked nerve-pulps as a pianist strikes the keys of his instrument. . . . Be very careful to whom you give a side-door key; too many have them already.

And careful he was. The private Holmes was so private that he listed his telephone under Fanny Holmes "to keep off strangers," and folded letters "queerly to have nothing private legible through the envelope." He did his "best to destroy" all "illuminating documents" and admonished his correspondents to do likewise with his letters. Aware of the price of fame, Holmes practically made such destruction a condition of his continuing friendship. "I forget," he warned Felix Frankfurter in 1921, "what I have written to you about my letters, but if you have not burned them I should feel easier if you would assure me that none of them should be published after my death. I print what I want printed and write to you with a feeling of absolute freedom which could not be if there were such a possibility. Also I am not proud of my epistolary performances. They often come from a languid pen and are written so to speak in dressing gown and slippers."

He wrote similarly to Harold Laski, who pledged his "solemn word that no letter of yours that I have shall be published." Laski asked, however, that he might be permitted to keep his friend's letters. "There's too deep a delight for me," he explained, "in re-reading them, and I cherish their possession as a monument to the greatest friendship I can ever hope to have."

Fortunately for the claims of history, Holmes's correspondents defied him. Edited by Mark DeWolfe Howe, Holmes's correspondence with Laski was in fact published after Laski's death in 1950. Several volumes of his correspondence with others—Frederick Pollock, Patrick A. Sheehan, Franklin Ford, Lewis Einstein—also have been published.

What follows includes the harvest from all those correspondents with whom he relaxed "in dressing gown and slippers."

Part *II*

 *BRAHMIN*

I am the sort of man I am because environment prevented my being anything else.

—John P. Marquand, *The Late George Apley*

CHAPTER 2

Family

"THERE IS . . . IN New England," wrote Dr. Oliver Wendell Holmes in 1861, "an aristocracy, if you choose to call it so, which has a character of permanence. It has grown to be a *caste*—not in any odious sense,—but, by the repetition of the same influences, generation after generation, it has acquired a distinct organization and physiognomy. . . ." Representative of this group, he continued, thinking perhaps of his own twenty-year-old son and namesake, was a young man "commonly slender,—his face is smooth, and apt to be pallid,—his features are regular, and of a certain delicacy,—his eye is bright and quick,—his lips play over the thought he utters as a pianist's fingers dance over their music,—and his whole air, though it may be timid, and even awkward, has nothing clownish."

Dr. Holmes was describing what he called the Brahmin caste of New England, the name for the highest, or priestly, caste of Hindus, worshipers of Brahma, which he had adapted to designate nineteenth-century Boston's intelligentsia, of which he himself was one: landlords, bankers, merchants, mill owners, educators, professional men, and philanthropists—all the local elite. They comprised, he said, a "harmless, inoffensive, untitled aristocracy" that had behind it "four or five generations of gentlemen and gentlewomen," family portraits by Copley, a good supply of family silver, love of the classics, and an aptitude for learning.

These Brahmins thought of the State House as the "hub of the solar system." They carried "the Common in [their] head as the unit of space, the State House as the standard of architecture, and measure[d] off men in Edward Everetts as with a yardstick." New York was older and more cosmopolitan. Chicago was more virile, and one could make a case that Philadelphia had more history. But Bostonians had a way of persuading themselves—and others—that America had begun in New England, and that they were the custodians of American commerce and culture. After all, until the twentieth century, young men came tò Harvard from New York, Chicago, and Philadelphia, but not many Bostonians went to Columbia, the University of Chicago, or Pennsylvania.

Dr. Holmes did not discuss this little aristocracy's rigid homogeneity. It was essentially English and Protestant, a people bound together from its seventeenth-century beginnings in the great Puritan migrations by the same language, religion, manners, and style of government. Elitist in its social assumptions, which were largely derived from Puritan concepts of an elect, as well as from its self-styled preeminence in the New World, it rarely if ever admitted a Kelly, a Cohen, or a Minnelli to its august drawing rooms, although the aliens were welcomed to the kitchens, textile mills, and foundries. Boston cared, as one commentator put it, "more about quality than about equality."

When Bostonians traveled, the first thing they did was seek out other Bostonians on the same train or packet. Dr. Holmes as a young medical student in Paris filled his correspondence with the adventures he was sharing with his little crowd of fellow Bostonians—a Bowditch, a Jackson, a Warren, and a Hooper. During the Civil War, the roster of the Twentieth Massachusetts Regiment of Infantry read like a roster of shareholders in the Athenaeum, an exclusive Boston library, and Captain—later Justice—Holmes filled *his* letters home with tales of adventures he had shared with a Whittier, a Bartlett, Reveres, an Abbott, Lowells, and a Cabot.

The first thing Bostonians did when a political position opened was look around for a fellow Bostonian to fill it, a custom even the generally unpolitical Justice Holmes honored. Recommending an acquaintance for a federal judgeship in 1931, he wrote President Herbert Hoover: "His mother a very old and dear friend of mine has asked me to say a word for him. It gives me pleasure to say that I believe him to be a remarkably able man far above the average available for such appointments. His brother whom I know better than I do him, is his partner, and was put upon the corporation of Harvard University at a very early age. My only motive for making this statement is affection for the family and my conviction that Mr. [Richard Cary] Curtis would be an appointment much above the average."

Quincys, Cabots, Lodges, Lees, Lowells, Curtises, Higginsons, and Holmeses banded together. They lived in the same neighborhoods, went to the same schools, read the same books, shared the same ignorances as well as knowledge, belonged to the same clubs, dined at the same houses, donated to the same charities, and married their cousins. They marched together in lockstep, whether bound for a cotillion, a court, or a war.

Wealth—commercial, cultural, and charitable—was consolidated in the same hands, or, as one commentator put it, Boston institutions were a self-perpetuating series of "interlocking directorates." The same group of men ran the Suffolk Bank, the Hospital Life Insurance Company, the great shipping lines, the textile mills, Massachusetts General Hospital, the Athenaeum, the Natural History and Massachusetts Historical societies, and, of course, Harvard University. Confident in the correctness of their beliefs, they tended the city's institutions as if they were family affairs, a proprietorship that inevitably bred some arrogance. Holmes used to say that "the way some of the ladies in Beacon Street treated their servants and employees was enough to start a socialist revolt."

These Bostonians were as orthodox as they were clannish. In the seventeenth century, they had accused dissenters of witchcraft and had sent Roger Williams and his Quakers packing. They had regarded the War of 1812 as an inconvenient interference with local shipping rather than an arrogant British affront to the new nation. Mid-nineteenth-century Bostonians considered abolitionist Wendell Phillips, a distant cousin of the Holmeses, a traitor to his class.

Social customs originated on Beacon Hill, economic policy on State Street, and political wisdom in the Federalist Party (later the Whig, 1830s–1850s, and after 1860, the Republican Party). Unsympathetic to, skeptical of, and sometimes baffled by the various reform movements and radical political currents abroad at the time, Brahmins, like the English from whom they were descended, respected the authority of the past and shared the conviction that white, Protestant, conservative Boston, its eighteenth-century heart still beating steadily, represented social and political perfection. They sincerely believed Jacksonian democracy contemplated the ruin of New England, and they agreed in principle with the social critic and Harvard professor Charles Eliot Norton that meaningful political reform would be accomplished not by extending more power to "the people," but through strong leadership by the "intelligent and prosperous classes"—democracy by noblesse oblige. They supported not only as sound economics but also as sound morals the twelve-hour day for workers in the textile mills, and in their drawing rooms they decried those who not only would shorten the working day but would clean up the prisons and insane asylums, give women the vote, and abolish, of all things, Southern slavery, on which New England's industrial prosperity depended. They had, they believed, inherited a perfect society, orderly, stable, and unsullied. They meant to preserve it intact and to pass it on with the family portraits and silver to their sons and daughters.

The justice's three distinguished New England names, which had required two centuries to combine, had guaranteed him a prominent place among these patricians whose tastes and traditions he shared. Olivers, Wendells, and Holmeses had been present alongside Cabots, Lodges, and Lowells at the creation of John Winthrop's New World utopia, his "City upon a Hill" upon which "the eies of all people" were expected to focus. They had fought in her wars, helped to create her government, dispatched her ships around the world, built her factories, preached from her pulpits, and contrived her culture. They had prospered, propagated, and achieved some local prominence. Their most persistent traits had survived the centuries and come to fruition in the last of the line, the second Oliver Wendell Holmes.

Olivers arrived first. The fifty-year-old surgeon and English Puritan Thomas Oliver came with his wife, Ann, and their eight children in 1632. Young (twenty-seven) Evert Janssen Wendell, progenitor of the wealthiest branch of Holmes's family, followed from Holland about ten years later, landing in New Amsterdam sometime in the early 1640s. His grandson Abraham took the Wendell name to Boston.

Dr. Holmes recalled that there had been a Dutch family Bible in the house during his boyhood. The first child to read a chapter in it was to have it for his or her own. The doctor, however, lost to his older sister, Mary. The Wendells, though, fed his class-consciousness and were a continuing interest of his:

> I suppose if I were there [in Holland] and found Mynheers of the name grand people I should claim their acquaintance, but if the descendants . . . were come to be poor devils,—I don't know just what I should do.

The doctor had no fears on that account regarding the American Wendells, however. He was in fact proud to "claim their acquaintance." Evert's grandson Jacob had followed his brother Abraham to Boston and united the Oliver and Wendell clans by marrying Thomas Oliver's granddaughter, Sarah. Sarah's mother, Mercy, was a Bradstreet. Mercy's grandmother had been Anne Bradstreet, one of America's first poets, *

* *The Tenth Muse Lately Sprung Up in America.* London, 1650.

and Anne's father had been a Dudley, an early governor of the Massachusetts Bay Colony. Jacob Wendell's marriage to Sarah Oliver had drawn the New Yorkers into the highest caste of New England's aristocracy. Ambitious and resourceful, Jacob had made it among the wealthiest. In 1760, he lost no fewer than forty buildings in the great fire.

His great-grandfather's losing all that property in the fire always made Dr. Holmes "feel grand, as being the descendant of one who had losses—in fact makes me feel a little grand now. . . . Most people's grandfathers in Boston, to say nothing of their great-grandfathers, got their living in their shirtsleeves."

The Holmeses, the real pioneers in the family, who lived on the outer edge of civilization for the first three generations in America, arrived in the New World in 1652. David Holmes, a Scotsman probably captured at the Battle of Worcester in 1651 and tossed aboard the *John and Sarah* as an indentured servant—the only indentured servant in Holmes's family's past—undoubtedly earned his living at least for a time working in his shirtsleeves. His second son, John, progenitor of the Holmes clan, was born in 1661 in Milton, Massachusetts.

At nearby Roxbury the population had outgrown its boundaries, and the selectmen had petitioned the colony government for a grant of land to the south in what recently had been Indian territory. In the spring of 1686, thirteen pioneers set out for the new colony. The following summer several more settlers arrived, including twenty-six-year-old John Holmes, who went along because the company needed a surveyor. The new settlement was called New Roxbury; in 1690 it was renamed Woodstock. Originally a part of Massachusetts, it later became part of Connecticut.

Holmeses, each in his or her own way right on down to the last of the line, seemed to seek out the uncharted waters, to find themselves adrift in a "black and frozen night." John Holmes provided inspiration. Cut off from friends, family, and the companions of civilization they had known back in Massachusetts, these settlers relived many of the experiences of the first American colonists. Indians still threatened, and a family at nearby Oxford was actually massacred in 1696. Dr. Holmes imagined his ancestor "probably carried an axe on his shoulder, and thought himself lucky if he could keep his scalp on his crown." Nature was no friendlier. Wolves, bears, and rattlesnakes lurked in the woods. Inclement weather threatened health, even lives.

The colonists, however, seemed to thrive on adversity. "Boundary squabbles sharpened the settlers' wits," Dr. Holmes wrote, "religious differences kept their enthusiasm alive, political division helped to shape their characters as citizens. They were strengthened by struggles with the wilderness and its tenants, and trained to thought and action in public meetings and committee."

The Holmeses remained in Connecticut for more than a century. Old John Holmes's brother, David, was killed by Indians in King Philip's War, and his grandson, David, marched in the French and Indian Wars. As soon as the latter heard the news of Lexington and Concord, he joined the Continental Army, although he was more than fifty years old at the time; he was taken prisoner at the Battle of Brooklyn, later exchanged, and returned to his regiment. Hardships, fatigue, and wounds, however, forced him to resign his commission, and he died at home in Woodstock before the war ended. His great-grandson the justice, another soldier in the family, long treasured a tomahawk David Holmes had brought back from the French and Indian Wars.

It was David Holmes's son Abiel, second of his eight children and paternal grandfather of Justice Holmes, who was to bring Olivers, Wendells, and Holmeses together in one family, and it is in this generation that later Holmes patterns of thought and behavior begin to be visible. Abiel Holmes was born the day before Christmas 1763, in Woodstock, Connecticut. At fifteen, he entered Yale College. He graduated in 1783, intending to make his way as a Calvinist clergyman.

His first posting was to Midway, Georgia. At Yale he had been a favorite student of President Ezra Stiles, and in 1790, he married Stiles's daughter, Mary. Neither the Midway pastorate nor the marriage lasted. In 1791, the hot, steamy climate forced him to leave Georgia, and in 1795, Mary Stiles Holmes died.

Several pastoral vacancies opened in the North in 1791, and in September, Abiel preached as a candidate at First Church in Cambridge, Massachusetts. They seemed ideally suited to each other. The congregation found Abiel's learning impressive, his Calvinist credentials satisfactory, and his kindly, handsome face appealing. Abiel found the congregation's dedication to traditional Calvinist principles admirable, and the 155-year-old church itself, where Harvard presidents had been inaugurated, George Washington had worshiped, and delegates had met in 1779 to frame the Massachusetts constitution, appealed to the historian in him. He was hired and installed on January 25, 1792.

For nearly three decades Abiel's life proceeded pleasantly. In March 1801, the same month that scalawag Thomas Jefferson, whose sympathies with the French Revolution had alienated patrician Boston, was inaugurated president of the United States, the thirty-eight-year-old Abiel remarried. Boston society was astonished.

Now, mama [wrote one young woman], I am going to surprise you. Mr. Abiel Holmes of Cambridge, whom we so kindly chalked out for Miss N.W. is going to be married, & of all folks in the world guess who to—Miss Sally Wendell! I am sure you will not believe it, however it is an absolute fact, for Harriot and M. Jackson told Miss P. Russell so, who told us; it has been kept secret for six weeks, nobody knows for what, I could not believe it for some time & scarcely can now.

This Sarah (Sally) Wendell was the granddaughter of Jacob and Sarah, née Oliver, Wendell. Her marriage to Abiel Holmes amalgamated the blood of the three families and guaranteed acceptance of the Connecticut Holmeses into Boston's aristocracy. Sarah and Abiel produced five children: three girls first, then two boys, including the first Oliver Wendell Holmes.

Sarah's life spanned the years between revolution and civil war. She never forgot her fright when at the age of six she had been hustled out of Boston, then occupied by the British, and taken to Newburyport, leaving her favorite doll behind. She lived long enough to sit for her photograph, a little old lady in white cap and wig.

She brought to the Oliver/Wendell/Holmes line a rare blend of Puritan severity and secular humanism. She had grown up among the worldly merchants of the city and tempered her Calvinism and the stern Westminster catechism, which she dutifully taught her children, with a natural vivaciousness, and dissipated the gloom of the old Calvinist hymns with lilting Irish melodies played on the piano she had imported from London. She even gave the children dancing lessons—generally taboo in strict Calvinist homes. Her ebullience complemented Abiel's calm and quiet nature. Although firm in his beliefs, his social nature had not been entirely chilled by their sternness, and contemporaries remembered him as urbane, courteous, and gentle if not "possessed of remarkably strong affections."

Abiel was another of the Holmeses who ventured into the unknown. His pioneering was intellectual, a trip into American time past, and the result was, like that of John Holmes before him and the two Oliver Wendell Holmeses after him, a new beginning. An avid historian as well as clergyman, he joined the Massachusetts Historical Society not long after he settled in Cambridge. In 1798, he published his *Life of Ezra Stiles*. In 1805, when most historians were still chronicling the lives of their local communities, he published his masterpiece, the two-volume *American Annals,* which contained the outline of American history from 1492 until the date of publication. An English edition appeared in 1816. A second American edition came out in 1829, appropriately updated. The two volumes had required ten years of research and writing, ten long years of isolation, inevitable discouragement, and doubt. The two volumes constituted, said Dr. Holmes, Abiel's older son, "a labor of love. To verify a doubtful legend; to disprove a questionable tradition by new testimony; to get at the absolute fact and let it tell its own story; and such labor as this was his highest literary pleasure."

Abiel Holmes's *American Annals* was a scholarly, copiously annotated chronological structure built by piling event upon event, fact upon fact. Causes and consequences he left to the philosophers. Despite the work's moralistic and sometimes pietistic tone, it was plain that the author had attempted to bring a degree of objectivity to it. He was no Livy or Tacitus, not even a George Bancroft, whose grandiose ten-volume national epic, *The History of the United States,* was to follow shortly and upstage *American Annals.* But Abiel Holmes's was an early attempt at a broad and sweeping yet orderly history of America, and, as such, a distinguished contribution to historiography.

Abiel Holmes, undoubtedly like Holmeses who had come before and certainly like Holmeses who came afterward, found himself in the midst of the quarrel between those who embraced tradition and those who urged change. In standing firm for what he believed, he provided an example for those later Holmeses who required at various points in their lives substantial quantities of steadfastness and resolution.

As Abiel's and Sarah's little brood was growing to adulthood, the winds of liberalism—Unitarianism—were picking up velocity, and the Calvinist grip on men's minds and souls was diminishing. New Englanders were reexamining the old Calvinist tenets of election and original sin and replacing them with tenets that emphasized God's beneficence over His cruelty and man's perfectability over his depravity. Harvard College converted to Unitarianism in 1805. The old religion had its tenacious defenders, including the Reverend Abiel Holmes, as well as the advantage of custom, and the battle of ideas that ensued was hard and long.

Abiel's upbringing, his training at Yale, headquarters of the old orthodoxy, and his experience urged him to keep the faith. His congregation, in which liberals outnumbered the orthodox by approximately two to one, urged him to come to terms with his times. He chose to spit into the wind.

He was no Jonathan Edwards, no Timothy Dwight. His theological influence was strictly local. His preaching was not impressive; he would bring about no revivals. He was, however, a sincere and pious man with a reverence for the Scriptures and an uncompromising faithfulness to the tenets of John Calvin.

For some time he had been exchanging pulpits on Sunday mornings with other clergymen in the area, including some of a more liberal stripe. Official Boston orthodoxy, however, was sharply critical of the practice, although it was common among local clergymen. Gradually the Reverend Abiel pulled back and began to limit his invitations to preach at First Church to clergy with sufficiently conservative credentials. His congregants were not pleased.

On July 20, 1827, a memorial signed by sixty-three church members was presented to the Reverend Abiel urging him to resume his former practice of inviting liberal preachers to First Church. Otherwise, they feared a "diminution of the numbers of your Church and Society, and the introduction of disagreement and disunion among those who constitute them." Abiel responded quickly and with conviction. He was, of course, unbending, pointing out the "difficulties and dangers" of the liberal presence at First Church. He deemed the shepherds, not the sheep, *the best judges of what is profitable for their hearers.* Abiel would listen to his heart and history. "The principles upon which *this* Church and Congregation were originally settled, and which have been uniformly maintained," he said, "are essentially the same as those of the first churches of New England; and these are the principles which I held and taught, at the time of my settlement here, and which I have never found reason to alter."

The controversy escalated, families were split, the Reverend Abiel standing alone against his parish, until neither pastor nor congregation could yield with any grace. Finally, unable to bend him to their wishes, the congregation terminated their pastor's contract. On June 7, 1829, Abiel preached his last sermon. The text was: "I have no greater joy than to hear that my children walk in truth."

However deep the hurt at his firing by the people whose children he had christened, whose young men and women he had married, whose old men and women he had buried for more than thirty years, Abiel neither compromised nor faltered. He and the orthodox among his parishioners established the Second Congregational Church, and on June 14, one week after his last sermon at First Church, he preached in the Cambridge courthouse on the text: "Beloved, think it not strange concerning the fiery trial among you, which cometh upon you, as though a strange thing happened unto you." He remained staunchly orthodox to the end, which came in 1837, at the age of seventy-four, as a result of a "paralytic affliction."

Abiel Holmes's fourth child and first son, Oliver Wendell Holmes the elder, author, physician, and father of the justice, was born in 1809. He liked to remind people it was the year that both Charles Darwin and Alfred Lord Tennyson also were born, each of whom represented a side of Holmes's nature struggling for dominance.

"I am just now agonizing," he once said, "between my patients clamorous for their morning doses, and a poem with which I have been saddled for an approaching medical dinner."

He was born in his father's house in Cambridge and died eighty-five years later in his own house on Beacon Street, Boston. His life moved largely within that frame. He always said a "man can see further . . . from the top of Boston State House, and see more that is worth seeing, than from all the pyramids and turrets and steeples in all the places in the world!"

By mid-nineteenth century, he had become one of the best-known writers of verse in America. He wrote about the homely, the familiar; the organ blower whose efforts to service the mechanical side of the church music went largely unheralded, his great-grandmother's portrait, love, friendship, the seasons, old age, the arrival of a new piano, local events and points of interest—all evoking feelings with which ordinary people could identify easily. To call his work poetry assigns to it a dignity and depth it does not possess. His verses are verses and no more. They are clever, often sentimental, graceful, precisely rhymed and metered. But poetry they are not.

He became, nevertheless, Boston's unofficial poet laureate and remained so for nearly half a century, his tongue as well as his pen eager and agile. No commencement, testimonial dinner, or local public celebration was complete without his presence. He sat at all the head tables, his poem at the ready. A little man—five feet three inches tall—he frequently stood on a chair to read it.

The characters he invented in his regular columns for the *Atlantic Monthly,* of which he was one of the founders in 1857, were "family" to Americans of all classes and castes. Presiding successively as autocrat, professor, and poet over his mythical boardinghouse breakfast table, he mixed, often poignantly, seriousness and humor in his lifelike pictures of the other boarders—a young astronomer (a thinly disguised portrait of his own eldest son), divinity student, school mistress, landlady, and other familiar Yankee characters—entertaining them with his poems, and expounding his own considered, and considerable, notions on life in general. In his three novels, he explored contemporary theological issues; in his medical essays he attempted to demolish contemporary medical humbug.

He had inherited his mother's sprightliness; he was as effervescent as his father was dour—one of Abiel's deacons at First Church accused the clergyman of feeding "his people sawdust out of a spoon." During the younger Holmes's boyhood, his father's gloomy Calvinism depressed him. The unalleviated oppressiveness of the Sabbath in his youth and the sepulchral demeanor of visiting preachers, one of whom "did more in one day to make a boy a heathen than he had ever done in a month to make a Christian out of an infant Hottentot," guaranteed early rebellion, and the first time he paid ten cents "for a peep through the telescope on the Common and saw the transit of Venus, [his] whole idea of creation [was] singularly changed." Later, as his intellect matured, distaste for the Calvinist God's representatives on earth took second place to his distaste for Calvinism's even gloomier dogma: predestination and original sin, along with all that flowed from them theologically. He could not and would not adopt a catechism that classified him, along with his brothers and sisters, as a "set of little fallen wretches, exposed to the wrath of God by the fact of that existence which they could not help." His father's quarrel with First Church while the younger Holmes was a Harvard undergraduate served only to reaffirm his nontraditional convictions, and in the end, he became a Unitarian, a pew holder at King's Chapel, local Brahmin bastion of Unitarianism, and a follower of the faith Abiel had stood so staunchly against.

Some of the theological pessimism that pervaded the parsonage was offset, however, not only by his mother's high spirits, but also by the Cambridge house in which he grew up. Known locally as the old gambrel-roofed house, it was an unpretentious country rectory with historical associations. Built in 1718, it stood quite near the street—not set back like the mansions on Tory Row—just north of Harvard Yard. There were sacred chambers for births and deaths, and there were garrets for ghosts.

It belonged to Judge Oliver Wendell, great-grandson of Evert Wendell and the sprightly Sarah's father, who had been a crony of the Adamses, Sam and John, during the Revolution, a political fighter behind the battle lines, and afterward a judge of the Suffolk County (Boston) probate court. He remembered the house as the meeting place for the Massachusetts Committee of Safety of which he had been a member, and he had bought it as a home for himself, his daughter, and her growing family.

Legend—a legend an imaginative boy was only too glad to appropriate—had it that the Battle of Bunker Hill had been planned there and that the dents in the floor had been made by the butts of the Continental militia's firelocks while it was billeted there. When the boy became a man he immortalized in verse the portrait of his great-grandmother, Dorothy Quincy Jackson—"Dorothy Q"—whose daughter had married Judge Wendell. Hanging there in the house, her

> Girlish bust, but womanly hair;
> Smooth, square forehead with uprolled hair;
> Lips that lover has never kissed;
> Taper fingers and slender wrist;

caught his eye every time he passed her and remembered that on the back of the portrait was written: "The holes in the canvas were made by the swords of British officers occupying the house prior to March 17, 1776."

Holmeses were a bookish lot, and in addition to ghosts, the gambrel-roofed house held the scholarly Abiel's library of some two thousand volumes, many of them theological, nearly all of them moralistic. Still, an intellectually adventurous youngster could discover less weighty distractions—enough history, biography, English literary classics, a multivolume illustrated encyclopedia, and piles of periodicals to ward off boredom or melancholy. The young Holmes became adept at sniffing out narratives and skipping the morals. He was eager to read anything but "what tasted of 'thou shalt' and 'thou shalt not'—'Be good and you will be happy.' " All his life books were his mainstay and salvation.

"I was born and bred among them," he said, "and have the easy feeling, when I get into their presence, that a stableboy has among horses."

His formal education—dame school where rule was by ferule, local secondary school, Phillips Andover, bastion of orthodox Calvinism, and Harvard—the usual for an upper-caste youth of his time and place—bored him. It was only in fact when he reached medical school that he converted his intellectual steam to power; until then he had dissipated it with gay abandon in mild flirtations and campus revelries. He was too small for sports and the local military unit, but he learned to compensate for his lack of height with sociability and wit, and he soon became known as an amiable fellow who sparkled at any sort of gathering.

In the spring of his junior year at Harvard, Holmes still had not decided what to do with his life. An indefatigable scribbler, he undoubtedly would have liked best to make his way as a writer. The first time he was "tempted . . . into print," he was thoroughly intoxicated. There was, he said, "no form of lead-poisoning which more rapidly and thoroughly pervades the blood and bones and marrow than that which reaches the young author through mental contact with type metal. *Qui a bu, boira,*—he who has once been a drinker will drink again, says the French proverb. So the man or woman who has tasted type is sure to return to his old indulgence sooner or later." Publication of a few verses, however, was one matter, a writing career another, and "it will have to be law or physick," he groaned to a friend, "for I cannot say that I think the trade of authorship quite adapted to this meridian."

He was, of course, the obvious choice for class poet when commencement exercises rolled around in the summer of 1829. Commented the *New England Palladium* on his performance:

Holmes, of Cambridge, has a very youthful appearance, and came forward with modesty and childlike innocence to beguile the audience with song. He has the elements of poetry in his nature, and his production on this occasion, though of a light and sarcastic character, was received with much applause.

Tentatively he entered Harvard Law School, though he continued to write his verses, which he had begun to have published in the Harvard *Collegian* and the *New England Galaxy*.

At the law school, Holmes found less than intoxicating the scholarship and backstage gossip of Justice Joseph Story, who taught at Harvard when the U.S. Supreme Court was not in session. (Few cases came to the Court in those days and sessions were short, allowing the justices to take on other responsibilities.) Holmes stayed only a year. He hated it. "I know not what the temple of the law may be to those who have entered it," he said, "but to me it seems very cold and cheerless about the threshold."

In the summer of 1830, as young Holmes was ending a term at the law school, his verse writing received substantial encouragement. He read in a Boston newspaper that the U.S.S. *Constitution*, forty-four-gun heroine of the War of 1812, now old and ailing, had come home to die in Boston, where she had been built in 1797. Fresh from Justice Story's lecture, Holmes retreated to his attic room at the parsonage and hastily penned the three familiar sentimental stanzas of his most famous work:

Ay, tear her tattered ensign down!
Long has it waved on high . . .

Next day "Old Ironsides" appeared in the *Boston Daily Advertiser* as well as other newspapers throughout the country to which the *Advertiser*'s editors had syndicated it. Legend has it—though it is only legend— that handbills printed and circulated in the streets of Washington and the subsequent outpouring of national indignation persuaded the secretary of the navy to rescind his euthanasia order, and the U.S.S. *Constitution* was saved by a poet.

Fame was exciting, but short-lived, hardly substantial enough to build a career on, and although Holmes continued to write, he also continued to pursue a learned profession. Disgusted with the law, he turned to medicine. "I know," he explained, "I might have made an indifferent lawyer,—I think I may make a tolerable physician—I did not like the one, and I do the other." Science became his religion, his salvation.

As became a Boston patrician, Holmes prepared for his career by means of the best education the country could offer at the time: Harvard Medical School for the theoretical side; the tutelage of a group of the city's most eminent physicians, who had established a private medical school, for the clinical side; and two years at Paris's Ecole de Médecine, where he was apprenticed to a famous French pathologist, M. Charles Louis.

Returning to Boston in 1835, Holmes finished off the requirements for his Harvard medical degree, was accepted into the Massachusetts Medical Society, and hung out his shingle at 2 Central Street, Boston, where he had boarded during his graduate years. His adventure into the private practice of medicine did not last, however.

He didn't even look like a doctor. Dr. Walter Channing of Boston liked to tell of taking young Dr. Holmes with him on a house call. As soon as the two men entered the sickroom, the patient sat up in her bed and said peevishly, "Dr. Channing, why do you bring that little boy in here? Take him away! This is no place for boys."

Nor did he, apparently, feel like one. Boston Brahmins sat on the boards of directors, but they saw little of the human suffering in the wards of Massachusetts General and the Lying-In hospitals for which they made important decisions and which they financed. Holmes's earliest experiences with the realities of sickness nearly finished him:

The white faces in the beds at the Hospital found their reflection in my own cheeks which lost their color as I looked upon them.

He did not faint, but he did not acquire a taste for clinical medicine, either. As a student, he dutifully followed his mentors from bed to bed, watching closely, listening, imbibing their wisdom. But when it was over, he shied away from actual contact with the white cheeks. He was not to be remembered for the brilliant diagnosis or the dramatic treatment of some savage disease or even as the kindly family doctor dispensing homely wit with his prescriptions. He removed himself as far as he could from the emotionally charged arena of the practicing physician.

At Harvard Medical School, where, beginning in 1847, he held the Parkman Professorship of Anatomy and Physiology for more than three decades, students remembered him as a tiny asthmatic figure bustling about the amphitheater, selecting plates, setting out specimens, arranging microscopes, but too squeamish to chloroform a rabbit required for a demonstration of a bone structure or nervous system. He had his assistant do the unpleasant work after he himself had left the room, and begged the fellow not to let the animal squeak.

The medical profession was to remember Dr. Holmes for his brilliant pioneering work on one of the deadliest scourges of his time: puerperal, or childbed, fever. From the beginning Dr. Holmes had inclined toward the theoretical side of his profession. From Paris he had written, not verses, but serious essays on medical subjects, winning Harvard's distinguished Boylston Prize for two of them. On his return home he founded, with two colleagues, a small informal medical school of his own, which ultimately was absorbed by Harvard Medical School. In 1838, he accepted a professorship of anatomy at Dartmouth College, which demanded only three months of the year, and he lectured at the Society for the Diffusion of Useful Knowledge, once again scribbling his verses, the demand for which on various public occasions was increasing steadily.

His medical essays have been all but overshadowed by his greater fame as the popular Autocrat of the Breakfast-Table, author of *Elsie Venner,* "The Chambered Nautilus," and "The Last Leaf," which President Lincoln could recite. Over a forty-year period, 1842–82, Dr. Holmes wrote, however, several such essays, all of them requiring close reasoning, the gathering of evidence empirically, the accurate weighing of it, and the presentation of arguments clearly, fairly, and forcibly.

When he began, in 1842 at age thirty-three, he was not a rebel. He was a Brahmin and unlikely to break the tribal rules, a hardworking young physician upwardly mobile professionally and not in a position to risk the public's disfavor. But he could not and would not tolerate the statistics of childbed fever, the cause, prevention, and treatment of which were unknown. All that was known was that women were dying of it in large numbers.

Beginning in June 1842, Dr. Holmes, whose own wife had been delivered safely only the year before and would within a matter of months be pregnant again, started down the lonely road to discovery; he began to study the statistics systematically, reading widely, discussing the subject with his colleagues, compiling evidence, building brick upon brick. He had learned as a medical student in Paris, he said, three principles that were to serve him in his work all his professional life: "not to take authority when I can have facts—not to guess when I can know—not to think a man must take physic because he is sick," an attitude of mind that did not stop with Dr. Holmes's generation.

The result of his researches was an unequivocal challenge to conventional medical wisdom; what it cost him can only be guessed at. Holmes concluded not only that childbed, or puerperal, fever was contagious, but that it was carried from patient to patient by germ-infested nurses, midwives, and attending physicians. Nearly two decades before Ignaz Semmelweiss of Vienna, generally considered *the* pioneer in the study of this disease, published his findings, young Dr. Oliver Wendell Holmes had surveyed the literature of childbed fever, assembled the recorded cases, systematized his findings, weighed the evidence objectively, and followed the trail to its logical conclusion.

In his article "The Contagiousness of Puerperal Fever," which he published first in the short-lived house organ of the Boston Society for Medical Improvement, of which he was a member, he named names, gave dates, and reported numbers of patients lost. The *American Journal of Medical Science* reprinted excerpts. The article immediately drew the attention and the brickbats of the vested interests. The physicians were not yet ready to scrub their hands and brush their nails before examining patients.

Letters to the editors, pro and con but mostly con, poured into the *Journal* for years afterward. The leading obstetricians in America, piqued at the accusation of negligence by a mere professor of anatomy, a man who didn't even practice medicine, who had never treated a case of childbed fever, took sharp issue with Holmes. Dr. Charles D. Meigs, professor of midwifery and the diseases of women and children at Jefferson Medical College in Philadelphia, urged physicians to disregard "the jejune and fizenless dreamings of sophomore writers who would thunder forth denunciations, and would mark . . . with a black and ineffaceable spot, the hard-won reputation of every physician." Dr. Meigs preferred to believe childbed fever the work of Providence or due to accident—concepts he claimed to understand—rather than caused by contagion, of which he said he had no clear idea. Hugh L. Hodge, professor of obstetrics at the University of Pennsylvania, published a book *On the Non-Contagiousness of Puerperal Fever* in 1852, refuting everything Holmes had said.

Hodge and Meigs were the two leading American authorities on the subject of childbed fever. Their entrance into the debate assured it of significance. The controversy raged in every medical society in the country, while the fevers continued to rage unabated in the wards, and women continued to die.

Despite the prestige of his detractors and the weight of the judgments against him, Dr. Holmes stood firm. His courage and determination throughout this controversy rank right up there with Abiel Holmes's during the confrontation with First Church. The doctor, however, was rewarded with success—his views ultimately prevailed. Abiel's did not.

Twelve years after its first publication, Dr. Holmes's essay was reprinted. To hard evidence of contagion, the doctor added passion:

I am too much in earnest for either humility or vanity [he wrote] but I do entreat those who hold the keys of life and death to listen to me also for this once . . . I beg to be heard on behalf of the women whose lives are at stake . . . let it be remembered that this is no subject to be smoothed over by nicely adjusted phrases or half-assent and half-censure divided between the parties. The balance must be struck boldly and the result declared plainly. . . .

Indifference will not do here; our journals and Committees have no right to take up their pages with minute anatomy and tediously detailed cases, while it is a question whether or not the "black death" of childbed is to be scattered broadcast by the agency of the mother's friend and adviser. Let the men who mould opinions look to it; if there is any voluntary blindness, any interested oversight, any culpable negligence, even in such a matter, and the facts shall reach the public ear; the pestilence-carrier of the ly-in-chamber must look to God for pardon, for man will never forgive him.

Gradually, a physician at a time, a country doctor here, a prominent practitioner there, succumbed to Dr. Holmes's logic. In 1856, the

American Medical Association added Holmes's 1855 essay to its list of recommended titles. The following year a reviewer in the *Boston Medical and Surgical Journal,* citing Dr. Holmes as the authority on childbed fever, criticized Dr. Meigs. Ultimately, Dr. Holmes's judgment was vindicated in the new science of bacteriology, and he was able to write in 1891: "Of course, the whole matter has been looked at in a new point of view since the *microbe* as a vehicle of contagion has been brought into light, and explained the mechanism of that which was plain enough as a fact to all who were not blind or who did not shut their eyes."

When asked whether his essay on the contagiousness of childbed fever satisfied him more than his verse writing, Dr. Holmes could not reply precisely or simply:

> I think oftenest of "The Chambered Nautilus," which is a favorite poem of mine, though I wrote it myself. The essay only comes up at long intervals. The poem repeats itself in my memory and is very often spoken of by my correspondents in terms of more than ordinary praise. I had a savage pleasure, I confess, in handling those two professors,—learned men both of them, skilful experts; but babies, as it seemed to me, in their capacity of reasoning and arguing. But in writing the poem I was filled with a better feeling—the highest state of mental exaltation and the most crystalline clairvoyance, as it seemed to me, that had ever been granted to me—I mean that lucid vision of one's thought, and of all forms of expression which will be at once precise and musical, which is the poet's special gift, however large or small in amount or value. There is more selfish pleasure to be had out of the poem—perhaps a nobler satisfaction from the life-saving labor.

Dr. Holmes's young literary friend William Dean Howells, at one time editor of the *Atlantic Monthly* and himself a clinger to the coattails of the New England renaissance, summed up Holmes in his memoirs: "He was not a prophet like Emerson, nor even a voice crying in the wilderness like Whittier or Lowell. His note was heard rather amid the sweet security of streets, but it was always for a finer and gentler civility. He imagined no new rule of life, and no philosophy or theory of life will be known by his name. He was not constructive; he was essentially observant, and in this he showed the scientific nature. He made his reader known to himself, first in the little, and then in the larger things. From first to last he was a censor, but a most winning and delightful censor, who could make us feel that our faults were other people's, and who was not wont 'To bait his homilies with his brother worms.' "

*　　*　　*

IN THE WINTER of 1830, the twenty-year-old Holmes had told a friend he never would be "contented" until he got "the undisputed mastery of a petticoat." A decade later, he had found the woman whose life was to "complement" his, to supply "the missing element in it which [he had] been groping after through so many friendships that [he had] tired of." On June 15, 1840, in King's Chapel, Boston, he married his distant cousin, Amelia Lee Jackson, third daughter of Judge Charles Jackson, niece of Holmes's former mentor, Dr. James Jackson, and descendant of that same "Dorothy Q" Jackson whose portrait hung in the gambrel-roofed house and whose daughter had married a Wendell.

Amelia's mother was a Cabot, her father one of the Newburyport Jacksons, who had arrived in the New World in 1643, about the same time as the Wendells—behind the Olivers but ahead of the Holmeses. No fewer than thirty-eight Jacksons had fought in the Revolution, and old Jonathan Jackson's privateers had harassed the enemy at sea. When the trade that had made Jacksons rich began to fall off, it was Patrick Tracy Jackson, Amelia's uncle, along with a few close friends, who organized the Boston Manufacturing Company, where for the first time in America all the operations for converting raw cotton into cloth were brought together under one roof. They thus invented New England's textile industry as well as the modern American factory system. It proved in time to be even more profitable than the China Trade had been.

Amelia had grown up in her father's big house on Bedford Place. His property, which included a garden with graveled walks, fine rosebushes, shrubs, and an old St. Michael's pear tree, covered the entire north side of the block. It might as well have been called Jackson Place. On the south side of the block stood the adjoining houses of the Henry Lees (Mary Jackson), the John Amory Lowells, the George Higginsons, the Charles Paines (Fanny Jackson), Miss Harriet Jackson, and Mrs. Henry Jackson. Later, Mr. and Mrs. Samuel T. Morse (Miss Harriet Jackson Lee) moved in.

Amelia's father, Charles Jackson, had made his money as an investor in his brother's textile mills and in the private practice of law, the last of the learned professions to be injected into the Holmes line. Following graduation from Harvard in 1793, he studied in the office of Theophilus Parsons, one of the commonwealth's most prominent attorneys and the mentor of John Quincy Adams. Parsons said of Jackson: "Of all my pupils, no one has left my office better prepared for his profession; he will prove himself the American Blackstone." Much later in his life,

Charles Jackson did produce a scholarly work on real actions, an arcane area of the law, and he read widely in legal history—his library, which Justice Holmes eventually inherited, included a number of legal antiquities. But he never fulfilled Parsons's prophecy. That awaited his grandson.

He did, however, build a very successful law practice. He was said to have been so fastidious about detail that whenever he took a marine insurance case, he obtained a model ship with every piece of timber labeled with its technical name. The financial rewards were commensurate with the effort. *Our First Men* (1846) estimated his worth at $150,000; *The Aristocracy of Boston* (1848) included his biography; *Rich Men of Massachusetts* (1852) estimated his worth at $200,000.

He was a public-spirited man who left his thriving practice in 1813 to serve ten years on the Massachusetts Supreme Judicial Court, where he made a reputation as the possessor of "profound legal knowledge," a "discriminating mind," "sound judgment," "great honesty and purity of purpose." In 1820, while still a sitting judge, he was appointed to the commission to revise the Massachusetts constitution, and he met at the State House with old (eighty-six) John Adams, young (thirty-eight) Daniel Webster, and four hundred or so other gentlemen of principle and property selected to protect the property against creeping agrarianism. In 1832, the governor appointed him to the commission to revise the public law.

As befitted a nineteenth-century New England man of means, he also assumed his philanthropic responsibilities. Jacksons began contributing to Harvard soon after they arrived in Massachusetts. Charles served as an Overseer (1816–25), and a Fellow of the Corporation (1825–34). He was also a prime mover in the founding of the Farm School on Thompson's Island, where mildly delinquent boys were taught a trade.

His personal characteristics were about what could be expected in a man of his professional stature and heavy civic responsibilities. He was a kindly man who treated young visitors to his study to gum balls, and a serious man who ranked high on a contemporary's scale of 0 to 7 for "Law Knowledge" (7), "Integrity" (7), "Practice" (7), "Talent . . ." (5), but low on the same scale for "Wit" (0).

His commanding presence, illustrated by his whirlwind courtship of his second wife, Amelia's mother, has come down through the years in Holmes family legend: He had known Frances Cabot, his late wife's cousin, for many years. One day as she sat shelling peas on the front porch of her father's house, Jackson, his year of mourning over, rolled through the iron gates in his chaise. The young lawyer wasted no time, but immediately proposed marriage and immediately was accepted. Years later, the second Mrs. Jackson described the incident to her daughter-in-law.

"How could you make up your mind so quickly?" asked the younger woman.

"My dear!" the heroine of the incident replied, "not marry Mr. Jackson!"

Mr. Jackson's second marriage had united Jacksons with the even more socially prominent Cabots. His daughter Amelia's marriage to Dr. Holmes extended the Holmes's connections, bringing financial Boston to what had been largely, except for some early Wendells, an intellectually oriented line. It was a marriage that assured their descendants of a rapport with and an understanding of merchants and industrialists as well as the physicians, clergymen, and lawyers who made up the learned professions.

At twenty, Amelia Lee Jackson was not a rebel, but there were moments when she chafed under the social restrictions imposed on nineteenth-century women. She had been educated at Miss Peabody's on Beacon Hill, and she longed for something more in her life than the daily regimen of sewing, berry picking, and visiting friends:

> I almost dread this winter [she complained to her cousin, Henry Lee, Jr.]. I think a girl's life at my age isn't the most pleasant by any means; she is in the most unsettled state: a young man can occupy himself with his business, and look forward to his life and prospects, but all we have to do is pass our time agreeably to ourselves. Not that we have not enough to occupy ourselves in carrying on our education, but I think everyone likes to feel the *necessity* of doing something, and I confess that I have sometimes wished I could be poor to have the pleasure of exerting myself.

Hers was a typical complaint of the pre-Victorian woman. Her life had an aura of time killing about it; while men could not possibly have enough time to fulfill their destinies, women had not nearly enough destiny with which to fill all the time at their disposal. Women of achievement outside the home were rare. For every Dorothea Dix there were a thousand women at home. Amelia's choices at twenty were few: she could marry or she could marry. Contemporary social conventions dictated that those women who did not—fewer than 13 percent in Massachusetts at the time, according to one study—would be lonely, intellectually unsatisfied, and professionally unfulfilled.

It was said of Amelia Jackson that her soul remained "more that of a woman of the world," and somewhere within, her elder son, Justice Holmes, detected a streak of melancholy which he said he had inherited from her and that seemed to afflict him when his career was not advancing on schedule or his work was not properly appreciated.

If she still ached for another life, wondered if she ever again would have use for her French and Italian dictionaries, yearned for another sort of self-validation, she did not advertise the fact, and her only grandson, the child of her second son, Ned, described her as "quiet, high-minded gentle unselfish and beloved." She appeared to have been the quintessential wife and mother in the genteel tradition, accepting of the prescribed functions of reproduction and nurture, entirely devoted to her family, and no less committed to a life-style dictated by contemporary custom and tradition. A neighbor noted she "absorbed her life in [her husband's], and mounted guard to make sure that interruption was impossible." Her nephew Johnny Morse pointed out "her delicate perceptions and quick sympathies that made her a delightful companion and a competent critic of her husband's prose or poetry." He looked forward to meeting them on their daily walks, "gaily chatting with each other or with a neighbor, or stooping to caress a little child." The most authoritative description of Amelia comes from Morse's *Life and Letters of Oliver Wendell Holmes.* Morse's book is authoritative in the sense that it was written by a close relative who knew the Holmeses well. It suffers, however, from a common complaint regarding nineteenth-century biography: that it is more hagiography than biography. Morse said about his aunt that she was

> an ideal wife,—a comrade the most delightful, a helpmate the most useful, whose abilities seemed to have been arranged by happy foresight for the express purpose of supplying his wants. She smoothed his way for him, removed annoyances from his path, did for him with her easy executive capacity a thousand things, which otherwise he would have missed or have done with difficulty for himself; she hedged him carefully about and protected him from distractions and bores and interruptions,—in a word she took care of him, and gave him every day the fullest and freest chance to be always at his best, always able to do his work amid cheerful surroundings. She contributed immensely to his success, as all knew who came near enough to have any knowledge of the household. . . . She eschewed the idea of having wit or literary or critical capacity; yet in fact she had rare humor and a sensitive good taste, which could have been infallibly counted upon for good service, if on any occasion these qualities could bring assistance to the doctor.

That Dr. Holmes appreciated his wife's devotion is apparent in his dedication of his last column of "The Poet at the Breakfast-Table":

To you, Beloved, who have never failed to cut the leaves which hold my record, who have never nodded over its pages, who have never hesitated in your allegiance, who have greeted me with unfailing smiles and part from me with unfeigned regrets, to you I look my last adieu as I bow myself out of sight, trusting my poor efforts to your always kind remembrance.

During the nearly half century Dr. Holmes and his wife spent together, their world did not substantially broaden. They were the most conventional of couples. They conformed to the principles and associated with the principals of the society which Olivers, Wendells, Holmeses, Jacksons, and their ilk had created for them and passed on to them. They fully expected to pass on what they had inherited to the next generation.

Part *III*

YOUTH

Trudging along the road or standing in some grimy wayside public house his elders spoke constantly of the subjects nearest their hearts, of Irish politics, of Munster and of the legends of their own family, to all of which Stephen lent an avid ear. Words which he did not understand he said over and over to himself till he had learnt them by heart: and through them he had glimpses of the real world that seemed drawing near and in secret he began to make ready for the great part which he felt awaited him the nature of which he only dimly apprehended.

—James Joyce, *A Portrait of the Artist as a Young Man*

CHAPTER 3

Beginnings

On March 9, 1841, Dr. Oliver Wendell Holmes scribbled a hasty note to his sister Mrs. Charles W. Upham:

> My dear Ann,—
>
> Last evening between eight and nine there appeared at No. 8 Montgomery Place a little individual who may be hereafter addressed as
>
> ———Holmes, Esq.
>
> or
>
> The Hon.———Holmes, M.C.
>
> or
>
> His Excellency———Holmes, President, etc., etc., but who for the present is content with scratching his face and sucking his right forefinger.

A few weeks later, the "little individual" was taken to King's Chapel, Boston, where his parents had been married exactly eight months and twenty-eight days before his birth, and christened Oliver Wendell Holmes, Jr.

In anticipation of his assuming his rightful place in society as imagined by Dr. Holmes at his birth, Wendell, as he was called, was pampered like a colt bred to run the Derby. He was groomed, petted, encouraged, tested, carefully surrounded with other boys of his social class, and fed a high-protein intellectual diet.

It mattered enormously in calculating his expectations that he had been born in a comfortable brick house on Montgomery Place and not among Irish immigrants in a South End tenement, that he lived during his youth around the corner from Cabots, not far from the Otis mansion on Beacon Street, and only steps away from the Common.* It mattered, too, that his great-grandfather had been Judge Oliver Wendell, that his grandfathers were Judge Charles Jackson and the Reverend Abiel Holmes, that his father was Dr. Oliver Wendell Holmes. It mattered that he belonged to that small group of elite Bostonians in whom generations of breeding had instilled an unself-conscious way of talking, walking, and dressing, who conversed easily with governors and senators and who never said "v'oo" instead of "view." Wendell would never have to press his face against the glass, his hot breath fogging the cold pane—he would always be on the inside looking out.

Dr. Holmes did not let it matter that the Holmeses possessed all the attributes of the Boston Brahmin except wealth. They were not rich; the big house on Montgomery Place had been part of Amelia Jackson's dowry. This dearth of financial resources, however, did not keep Dr. Holmes from providing his family with the wherewithal to carry on a proper life of the mind. When in 1843 he wished to join the Athenaeum, a relatively new (incorporated 1807) lending library on Beacon Hill which was popular among patricians, he bargained with the institution for a share, as memberships were—and still are—called, offering in place of the $300 fee a collection of books from his own library shelves: sixty-three issues of Marc Jean Bourgery's *Traité complet de l'anatomie* and twenty-four numbers—to the letter N—of Robert Todd's *Cyclopedia of Anatomy and Physiology*. The deal went through, and the Holmeses became members, joining Jacksons, Otises, Paines, and Saltonstalls. Membership in the Athenaeum, which was modeled on English "gentlemen's libraries," did not literally require distinguished family background or prominent connections, although shares, which passed from generation to generation, were sometimes scarce, but the $300 fee made membership prohibitive to the Fitzgeralds over in the North End, preoccupied with staving off starvation and unable to spare the time or work up the interest after a long day behind the grocery store counter to indulge in the luxury of reading.

Henry Adams, just three years Wendell Holmes's senior, and similarly burdened by the standards required of family names and similarly programmed for prominence, described in his autobiography, *The Education of Henry Adams,* his own sense of isolation and sadness that lurked behind his natural boyhood joy in adventure and camaraderie. Many

---

*Boston Common, established in 1634, is a forty-eight-acre plot of greenery in the heart of the city that has served as a pasture for cows, a temporary campsite for the militia, and the site of the local gallows, as well as a public park.

years later, and in retrospect, Wendell Holmes pronounced Adams's chapters "almost genius."

Whether he thought his undistinguished childhood was inappropriate to the image of eminence in his maturity, or whether his profound and lifelong sense of privacy silenced him, references to his own boyhood are scarce in Holmes's writings. He did not mention, for example, the snowball fights in Boston Common that had become a local tradition and which figure prominently in the memoirs of his contemporaries. Spectacular brawls they were, too—gang wars between Brahmins and the roughnecks, most of the latter Irish boys from the North and South ends, their heavy brogues contending against the carefully cultivated Anglo-Boston accents. The contests raged until dark, when it was easy to slip a stone or two inside the hard-packed snow. Boys were led from the field bleeding. In spring and fall mud substituted for snow. The Brahmins were usually outnumbered, outweighed, and out-maneuvered more or less in the same proportions as their parents were in local political combats, as Irish immigrants, fleeing famine in their native country, inundated the city and were threatening to wrest control from the older entrenched Bostonians.

The few boyhood adventures Holmes did recall later were of the kind he could enjoy alone. He remembered running "tiddledies" on the Frog Pond—jumping from ice floe to ice floe, each of which would hold a boy only so long as he kept jumping but sank immediately if he paused. He played "devil's tricks at back doors," and nearly ninety years later, the daughter of a former neighbor recalled how her mother had disliked the "little Holmes boy" because he hid behind trees, jumped out, and yelled "boo" at her. He fished with bent pins on the banks of Back Bay at the foot of Arlington Street and spent hours watching air bubbles perform in his father's microscope. But he had a tendency to "shrink from new things" and he could not bring himself to follow his contemporaries when they learned to skate and dance and ride.

He was already beginning to escape his programmers into the world of books, where he was surrounded by romantic heroes who had the power to dissipate his growing sense of isolation. When he outgrew the staples of the nursery such as *The Child's Own Book,* an anthology of children's stories which was his "dearest book when he was a child," and *Peter Parley's Short Stories for Long Nights,* which his mother gave him for his fifth birthday, he began to read his way through boyhood and adolescence. No one ever need worry what to give Wendell on his birthday or Christmas. From little Mary Brown's gift of illustrated Bible stories and children's prayer book on his fifth and sixth birthdays to

Emerson's essays on his seventeenth, books were standard fare. Father and mother, sister and brother, Grandmother Holmes, Grandmother Jackson, Aunt Lucy—they all fell in with Wendell's reading habits. History was welcome, as were the melodramas of America's first mass-production fiction writer, Sylvanus Cobb. Mayne Reid's *Rifle Rangers and Scalp Hunters,* along with Captain Marryat's *Children of the New Forest,* thrilled.

As boy and man both, Wendell Holmes relished "periodic wallows" in the novels of Sir Walter Scott, his heart pulsing at the noble exploits and aspirations of the author's purer-than-life heroes, the romantic side of him reveling in the temporary escape from the tedium of daily routine. However skeptical he professed to be in later years, however intellectually sophisticated, however urbane, "the old order in which the sword and the gentleman were beliefs" remained "near enough to me to make this their last voice enchanting in spite of the common sense of commerce."

Wendell's closest friend, the one who taught him "all the evil [he] knew as a boy," was his first cousin, John T. Morse, Jr., the son of Amelia Holmes's sister Lucy Cabot (Jackson) Morse. His ancestors were seventeenth-century settlers on the Morse as well as the Jackson side, his father was a merchant with an office on State Street, and he lived on fashionable Hamilton Place, the next street over from Montgomery Place. Known as Fatty, he told ghost stories so eerie they made Wendell, known as Leany, "afraid of the looking glass in [his] bedroom and the shadows on the front door."

It was with Johnny Morse that Wendell contemplated the moral dilemmas already present in his life. Roving the Common one day, Wendell asked Johnny whether any circumstances allowed the telling of a lie.

"Of course not," replied Cousin Fatty, a strict moralist at age eight, although he was not above a little swindling when Leany, a year younger and that much more gullible, had something Fatty wanted. But Johnny hadn't any doubt. A sense of doubt would not have been very useful to Johnny and, like many of his caste in Boston, he had been born without one.

"Suppose," Wendell persisted, "a man came running along here with terror in his eyes and panting for breath and hid in this thicket." He pointed dramatically at a nearby stand of trees. "Then the pursuers came along and asked us if we had seen him. Which would be better, to give the man away or to tell a lie?" That was the trouble with Wendell; he asked a lot of questions, then doubted everything. Johnny yielded this time, but he was always a little suspicious of his cousin, didn't always understand his intellectual gyrations.

That Wendell went to the right schools was imperative, whatever the condition of the family's finances. Boston respected learning, and a man's future success depended a good deal on what and whom he knew. Harvard set the standard, and preparation for Harvard began at the dame school, of which there were several around the Common, small selective schools more or less akin to the nursery schools of a later time, operated by genteel women from the best New England stock. As Irish boys and girls began to enroll in Boston's public schools in ever larger numbers, the result of increasing immigration, Brahmins sent more and more of their children to private schools; eventually they established a comprehensive private system that made academic contact with a "Paddy" practically impossible.

The dame schools were important for introducing Brahmin Boston's children to the rudiments of learning and equally important for introducing them to people with whom they later would spend their adult professional and social lives. There they sat at the little wooden benches: New England's future bankers and merchants, senators, governors, Harvard presidents, industrialists, lawyers, and judges, reciting in their childish lisps, cringing together in the face of the ferule, their faces scrubbed to a morning shine, their little bodies wriggling in enforced unemployment.

Despite Wendell's love for books and despite Dr. Holmes's expansive projections for the young man's future, Wendell's intellectual abilities and later achievements were not immediately apparent during his early years. If he was precocious, it has not been recorded. He was a decent student, not much more. At the neighborhood dame school, he seemed to be reasonably studious, articulate, and punctual. If there was any cause for complaint, it was that he "talks too much," a common complaint about him. His younger brother, Ned, used to grumble that at family meals, which were conversational free-for-alls, "Wendell ends every sentence with a but so as to hold the floor till he can think of something else to say."

Wendell's education began in earnest at the private grammar school for boys operated by Thomas Russell Sullivan in the basement of the nearby Park Street Church, where Johnny Morse was already a student. The sad-faced but kindly Mr. Sullivan, whose grandfather had been an early-nineteenth-century governor of Massachusetts and whose great uncle had been a general in the Revolutionary War, had New England roots every bit as deep and respectable as those of the Bigelows,

Parkmans, Jacksons, Holmeses, and Lodges who attended his school. He himself had begun his professional life as a Unitarian preacher in Keene, New Hampshire, and had been editor of a periodical called *The Christian Preacher,* sermons published for the purpose of dissipating the widespread hostility against the liberal Unitarian faith. In 1835, he left the ministry and moved to Boston, where he founded the little school at the northeastern end of the Common. Although he had abandoned his formal Christian ministry, he had not abandoned his personal affiliation with Christianity, and the essays of his young students were liberally laced with biblical references.

An unexpurgated, uncorrected, and entirely characteristic essay was written in November 1849, Wendell's second year at Mr. Sullivan's. He was eight and a half years old.

SCHOOL PLAN OF JOSEPH LANCASTER

The plan of Joseph Lancaster was to teach all the poor children. At last he got so many children that he had to divide the pupils into a great many classes, and set a boy at the head of them. When the King heard of this he sent for Lancaster and asked how he [could] teach so many children at once. Lancaster then explained his plan of which the King approved very much. And all thy children shall be taught of the Lord. Isa 54 13 Nov 10 1849.

The curriculum at Mr. Sullivan's appears, according to the subjects of the essays in Wendell's copybook, to have included American, English, European, and ancient history, current events, religion, and creative writing. Mary Trimmer's pre-Darwin (1849) *Natural History of Quadrupeds, Birds, Fishes, Serpents, Reptiles, and Insects,* "designed for youth in the United States," and discovered among Holmes's books, suggests that some sort of rudimentary zoology may also have been taught. The text was limited, however, to descriptive natural history; the author made no attempt to explain, or even to speculate on, the origins of the species she described.

Nonperformance provoked attacks of the ferule. Whether or not Wendell Holmes ever endured a whipping has not been recorded. But it was clear that the schoolmaster was fond of his young pupil, and when, at age ten, the boy was ready to move on to Epes Sargent Dixwell's private Latin school, where he would make his final preparations for Harvard College, Mr. Sullivan introduced him to his new headmaster:

O. W. Holmes, jr, the bearer, whom (like his cousin J. T. Morse,) I take delight in calling my young friend, has been for four years under my charge as a pupil. He has been uniformly docile, thoughtful, amiable and affectionate. Young as he is, his habits of application are confirmed, while his proficiency in all the English branches, and his love of study are remarkable for his age.

Ten-year-old Wendell Holmes became a member of one of the first classes at Mr. Dixwell's private Latin school. It was a new school, untried, but Mr. Dixwell had all the proper credentials to attract an elite clientele. He had graduated from Harvard in 1827, two classes ahead of Dr. Holmes, then had read law in the office of Wendell's grandfather, Charles Jackson, after the judge had retired from the bench. He had spent three years in a financially unsuccessful private law practice and in 1836 had been appointed, at the comparatively youthful age of twenty-nine, headmaster of the two-century-old Boston Latin School, the boys' grammar and high school on the English model where Boston's future social, civic, and business leaders traditionally prepared for Harvard and where his own grandfather had been headmaster. He stayed fifteen years, then left in the spring of 1851 when the Boston Common Council decreed that all who received salaries from the city, including teachers in the public schools, could no longer live in suburban areas but "must henceforth reside within the City's bounds." Mr. Dixwell, whose family had lived in nearby Cambridge for nine years, resigned rather than move. The following fall he fitted out the drawing rooms of a house at 2 Boylston Place in Boston with desks and blackboards, and opened his own private school for boys, which he operated for two decades. Applications soon outnumbered available places—fifty-five was the highest number of boys who attended at any one time—and Mr. Dixwell was able to be highly selective in his admissions.

Referred to as Dicky by his boys, Mr. Dixwell was a slight, bespectacled man, color-blind as well as nearsighted, and he appeared in the schoolyard each morning a few minutes before classes began clad in outlandish combinations of purple frock coat, green velvet waistcoat, and black-and-white-checked trousers.

He brought to his teaching a rare and vigorous classical scholarship, gentle manners, and the ability to maintain strict discipline without roughness. He compared an undisciplined school to an undisciplined army, and both to a disorganized mob, and he insisted on firm law and order. But he had little confidence in the benefits offered by corporal punishment, and during his years at Boston Latin, he avoided it except in clear instances of moral delinquency. By the time he opened his own school, he had abandoned it altogether—a substantial departure from local custom.

He was, however, less innovative in academic matters. He focused on training the memory and the will and left the mind to fend for itself. The curriculum was based entirely on the entrance requirements of Harvard, which "demanded yearly greater amount of knowledge both in breadth & depth." It included penmanship, drawing, French, algebra, plane geometry, and ancient history. But Mr. Dixwell's first love was classics: Greek and Latin grammars were thoroughly mastered, and the ancient authors read with diligence. American history, modern history of any sort, was "thought quite needless." The schoolmaster's record was enviable. His reputation for turning out well-schooled products preceded him to the Harvard examining board, and his boys, along with those of Boston Latin, seemed already to have a little edge when they applied to college.

Cousin Johnny Morse was first scholar at Mr. Dixwell's. Whether Wendell Holmes compiled as brilliant a record or whether he was just an average student is not known. His records have not survived. Nor is it known whether he found the headmaster "a delightful teacher of Latin and Greek," as did Charles W. Eliot, who had known Mr. Dixwell at Boston Latin, or whether, like Henry Adams, he felt stifled by the drillmaster's method of imparting knowledge. That Mr. Dixwell was a boyhood hero of Wendell's is evident in the headmaster's later recollection of the boy's waiting regularly after school to "walk along with me and talk of all topics."

Wendell developed a close relationship with the Dixwells outside the classroom long before he courted their daughter, Fanny. He used to stay with them when his parents left Boston for the summer before school was out, and in a letter he wrote Mrs. Dixwell just before he left to join his regiment in 1861, he addressed her as his "almost second mother."

Dr. Holmes could not afford summers in Nahant or Newport, where many of the Boston elite vacationed. He could, however, offer his family summers on a woodsy piece of old family land in western Massachusetts, two miles south of Pittsfield. Canoe Meadow it was called, named for an old Indian mark on the original deed.

The area was fast becoming a writers' colony. Hawthorne lived at nearby Lenox in a little red farmhouse that was to figure in *Tanglewood Tales* and *A Wonder Book*. Herman Melville, whom Wendell Holmes remembered seventy years later as a "gruff taciturn man," owned a little place called Arrowhead on the Lenox Road, where he worked on *Moby*

Dick. Feminist Catherine Sedgwick was writing novels and holding court for visiting literati at Stockbridge, and the Longfellows summered just down the Housatonic, within easy rowing distance of the Holmeses. Emerson, Lowell, Washington Irving, novelist G.P.R. James, and Harriet Beecher Stowe visited the area frequently. As if the Saturday Club, where they got together regularly in Boston for literary conversation, had been transplanted, they all gathered at Hawthorne's little cottage, on Melville's piazza, or climbed nearby Monument Mountain, their talk spirited, Dr. Holmes holding forth on the natural superiority of Englishmen, Hawthorne and Melville vigorously assailing his thesis.

Dr. Holmes's little 280-acre plot belonged to a "baronial" 24,000-acre purchase his great-grandfather, the wealthy Boston merchant Jacob Wendell, had made in 1835. All the town of Pittsfield, as it stood in mid-nineteenth century, except for a few thousand acres, had belonged to the doctor's ancestor, whose deed hung in the entry of the house to remind each Holmes, as he or she left to hunt arrowheads, pick huckleberries, or fish in the nearby Housatonic, that the family had sprung from America's early settlers. Jacob Wendell's son Oliver, Dr. Holmes's grandfather and the late owner of the gambrel-roofed house in Cambridge where the doctor had grown up, had added to the family's stature in the Pittsfield community when he donated a silver baptismal "bason" to the Union Parish Church.

"Don't you know," Dr. Holmes enthused in the summer of 1855, "I am the landlord of a great farm up here in Berkshire County, a hundred and twenty years in my family, with a mile of river running through it, a forest of trees of three and four hundred years' growth, and a meadow big enough to feed all the bulls of Bashan? Don't you know that, hey? Because if you don't, I tell you it is so."

Beginning in 1849, the Holmes family, which by that time included six-year-old Amelia and three-year-old Edward (Ned), spent seven summers at Canoe Meadow. They lived in a rambling house which the doctor had tried to build, along with a barn, on a $2,000 legacy of his wife's. Costs, however, had doubled and he had had to borrow funds.

Canoe Meadow was a perfect place for growing children to summer. It was set on a rolling plain of clover and wild flowers in cool, mosquitoless air 1,200 feet above sea level and less than a quarter of a mile from the river, a placid stream navigable even by little Amelia. Miles of fields and woods invited solitary wanderings, and each Holmes had a plot of garden to tend.

Standing five feet one inch as he entered his teens, Wendell was as tall as his mother and nearly as tall as Dr. Holmes. In a picture taken about 1855, at fourteen, his darkening ear-length hair is slicked close to his head. His lips are parted slightly in the beginning of a little expectant smile. His face has not entirely lost its baby fat, and the straight patrician nose in the classic patrician face that later became so familiar has not yet emerged.

During the five-month summers at Pittsfield, he did not abandon his beloved books but read and studied his Latin and French even then, still managing to be outdoors "almost all the time." He missed Johnny Morse and sent him a specimen of seed from a particular kind of wheat bred in Michigan, which the tenant farmer had given him. He rowed "a good deal," swam, shot, and fished until the family tired of pickerel. The imaginative and occasionally whimsical doctor liked to amuse his youngsters by picking out shapes—a lion, a chicken, General Andrew Jackson on horseback—among the distant hills and mountains, Hoosacs on the east, Taconics on the west.

Then in the waning hours of 1855's summer, the good times came to an abrupt end. The expenses of Canoe Meadow threatened to bankrupt the Holmeses. The house itself had cost twice as much as the architect had estimated. "Then," the doctor explained, "we had to build a barn; then we wanted a horse and carryall and wagon; so one thing led to another, and it was too far away for me to look after it, and at length, after seven years, we sold it."

The death of Amelia Holmes's father, Charles Jackson, in December 1855, did not add to the Holmeses' wealth as much as might have been expected. Mrs. Holmes realized only $5,400 in cash. As was the custom of the time regarding the estates of married women, whose property rights had not yet been legislated, the bulk of her inheritance—$30,000—had been put in trust "so secured as not to be liable for the debts of her husband" and only the income from it made available to her. Whether the sum was too small, came too late to save Canoe Meadow, or the Holmeses were simply tired of the financial drain, they sold the country house and most of the land—a small parcel belonging to Dr. Holmes's mother, Sarah, was retained and sold after her death in 1863—to Thomas F. Plunkett of Pittsfield for $18,250 in August 1856.

After he left it, Dr. Holmes, who had set out many of the younger trees near the house, who looked on the stately old maple at the gate and the solitary pine nearby as family, "couldn't bear to think of it or to speak of it for a long time." Nearly thirty years after he had sold it, he still felt its "very stones" were as "precious" to him as those "of Jerusalem to an ancient Hebrew."

Where he went to church mattered to a Bostonian as much as where he went to school and where he lived. Harvard had become officially Unitarian in 1805, and its divinity school was the official training ground for Unitarian ministers. By the time Abiel Holmes died in 1837, Unitarianism was the prevailing creed in Boston, and King's Chapel, where Dr. Holmes maintained a pew, was its cathedral. By 1850, about two-thirds of Boston's richest men were Unitarians, and only about one-tenth still clung to Abiel Holmes's old-fashioned Calvinism. Baptists, Methodists, and Catholics were déclassé. All Wendell remembered was the boredom. He got no "Hell talk" from his parents, but "Oh—the *ennui* of those Sunday morning church bells, and hymn tunes, and the sound of the citizen's feet on the pavement—not heard on other days." Sixty years later he had "hardly recovered from it."

A Bostonian's politics mattered, too. Although progressive in religious thought, the Holmeses were, like many Bostonians of high caste, social and political conservatives. Dr. Holmes had little sympathy for reformers of any ilk, and lumped what he called "dingy-linened friends of progress" with "come outers" in general. During his son's youth, it was the abolitionists, their methods too emotional for the scientist in him, their measures too extreme for the conservative in him, that unnerved the doctor.

The issue of abolition sharply divided Bostonians, and the threat of violence hovered constantly over the Common. Industrial, business, and banking Boston, whose mills relied on cotton picked by slaves and whose social theories were slower to change than circumstances, even in a national crisis, would save the Southern system. These "gentlemen of property and standing" one crisp October night in 1835 crashed into a meeting of the Female Antislavery Society, captured the fire-eating publisher of *The Liberator,* William Lloyd Garrison, and pulled him through the streets with a rope. Finally rescued, he had to be confined temporarily in the Leverett Street jail for his own protection. Two years later, these same gentlemen closed the doors of King's Chapel to antislavery meetings.

Intellectual Boston, its Puritan conscience stirred, turned the city into a center of abolitionist activism. The Unitarian preacher Theodore Parker, whose grandfather had led the minutemen on Lexington Green three-quarters of a century before and who as chairman of the Boston Vigilance Committee was translating the morality of his grandfather's war into the events of the 1850s, was a personal friend of Dr. Holmes's when Wendell was growing up. Wendell Phillips, son of Boston's first mayor and chief spokesman for the antislavery cause, whom Dr. Holmes called that "pestilent abolitionist," was a distant cousin to the Holmeses.

Close friends of the doctor—James Lowell, Waldo Emerson, Henry Longfellow, John Greenleaf Whittier—put their talents at the disposal of the abolitionists' cause.

Dr. Holmes did not. He marched with Brahmin-business Boston. No abolitionist sentiments were heard at 8 Montgomery Place. Wendell was a child of nine when Dr. Holmes, along with a thousand other Bostonians, signed a letter to Senator Daniel Webster supporting his famous Seventh of March speech, the main purpose of which was compromise with the South. If the boy was too young to understand fully the implications of his father's behavior, he was not too young to read the placards with which the abolitionists, following passage by Congress of the Fugitive Slave Act that same year, papered the city, warning the local black population to be wary of "kidnappers and Slave Catchers" lying in wait. He was not too young a year later to understand Bostonian concern when a mob of Negroes forcibly rescued a black man from the United States Courthouse and set him on the road to Canada and freedom. Two months later he listened to the church bells tolling for Thomas Sims, a fugitive slave captured in Boston, tried in federal court, and returned in chains to his owner in Savannah.

Wendell was thirteen in 1854 when all Boston turned out to see Anthony Burns led in chains down State Street to a U.S. revenue cutter waiting at the Long Wharf to return the fugitive slave to his master. To ensure law and order, local militia had been assigned to guard the streets through which Burns was to be marched. Cannon had been stationed in Court Square, and the lone unarmed black was flanked by two sections of lancers and two sections of United States Marines, each man armed with a saber and a brace of pistols. Two more sections of Marines stood ready at the rear of the square. Even the local merchants, their businesses dependent on Southern cotton, their minds long set against abolition, were at last moved to groans, curses, and hisses.

Dr. Holmes did not flinch. The following year, 1855, he inserted into an address to the New England Society of New York several paragraphs criticizing the extremists among the abolitionists, who, he believed, had done "great mischief . . . by violence and vituperation," and urging compromise with the South. His friends were disappointed. Theodore Parker and Wendell Phillips said so publicly. Emerson expressed his regret privately to his brother-in-law, who passed the sage's sentiments on to Dr. Holmes. Senator Charles Sumner sent the doctor a packet of pamphlets for his reeducation. And the newspapers howled. The *New York Tribune* suggested Dr. Holmes ought to have been lynched.

The argument moved closer to home when in 1856 one of the

Holmeses—the most likely candidate would seem to be young Wendell, who was fifteen at the time—checked out of the Athenaeum library the popular literary incendiary bomb *Uncle Tom's Cabin,* written by Dr. Holmes's friend Harriet Beecher Stowe.

On March 7, 1857, the U.S. Supreme Court decided that allowing the slave Dred Scott to go free would deprive his master of property without the due process of law guaranteed by the Fifth Amendment to the Constitution,* and the extremists among Boston's abolitionists smuggled firearms to their counterparts in Kansas, where John Brown was getting ready to wage his one-man war against the slave states.

Young Wendell, impressionable, sensitive, acutely observant, and curious, could not but have been torn between loyalty to his father and the humanitarian impulses and principles his father's friends supported and all Boston was debating, often fiercely. In one sense these must have been exciting times for a boy; in another sense, the pressures on him to choose a side had to have been difficult for an adolescent to cope with.

When the war, which had been predicted forty years before by his fellow Bostonian John Quincy Adams, finally came and Dr. Holmes's elder son marched off with his regiment, the doctor himself became a dedicated Unionist. He abandoned his Breakfast-Table characters and wrote—almost exclusively—war lyrics, patriotic pieces and verses for the *Atlantic Monthly,* and stirring addresses for those public occasions on which he was invited to speak. In 1863, while his son was at the front, he was appointed, along with Emerson, Longfellow, and Whittier, an honorary member of the committee on arrangements for the city's celebration of the issuing of the Emancipation Proclamation. In a Fourth of July address that same year, he declared:

> The struggle in which we are engaged was inevitable; it might have come a little sooner, or a little later, but it must have come. The disease of the nation was organic, and not functional, and the rough cirurgery of war was its only remedy.

In 1883, in reply to an invitation to attend the commemoration of the fiftieth anniversary of the American Anti-Slavery Society, Dr. Holmes wrote: "I regret that I cannot be present . . . I do not feel that I have any special right to be there, as I was later in waking to the day break of freedom than many of my less sleepy friends."

* *Scott* v. *Sandford.* 19 Howard 393 (1857).

*   *   *

HENRY JAMES, SR., on his return one evening from a dinner at the Saturday Club, remarked to his family that Dr. Holmes had asked him if his sons despised him and had seemed surprised when James said no.

"But after all," the doctor explained, "it is only natural that they should, for they stand upon our shoulders."

Dr. Holmes had developed a theory about embattled fathers and sons:

> Civilized as well as savage races live upon their parents and grandparents. Each generation strangles and devours its predecessor. The young Feejeean carries a cord in his girdle for his father's neck; the young American, a string of propositions or syllogisms in his brain to finish the same relative. The old man says, "Son, I have swallowed and digested the wisdom of the past." The young man says, "Sire, I proceed to swallow and digest thee with all thou knowest."

The relationship between Dr. Holmes and his older son was a little more complex than the one the doctor described, although elements of it were certainly present. At different times and under different circumstances it was loving, affectionate, proprietary, respectful, hostile, claustrophobic and competitive. Although Dr. Holmes "made it difficult for his son to be conceited," the son felt "lonely" when his father left to lecture away from home.

Different observers viewed the relationship differently. Wendell's later close friend William James reported after dining with the Holmeses that "no love was lost between W. *père* and W. *fils*," and Ned's wife's family, the Wigglesworths, believed Wendell "didn't care for [his] father and that Ned [was] the only genuine custodian of [Dr. Holmes's] name." Ned's son, also Edward Jackson Holmes, found the brilliant and energetic intellectual exchanges between his uncle and grandfather, which could not have occurred without a deep camaraderie and rapport, exhilarating and exciting.

They were both like and unlike, these two competing egos. The younger early on caught the elder's skepticism, the scientist's reluctance to depend on authority when he wanted facts, to guess when knowledge was available, and to rely on the old formulas handed down from generation to generation long after they had outlived their usefulness. These two Holmeses shared, as well as their name, a contempt for "come outers" and an aloofness that kept their pale Brahmin hands white, a chariness of human affliction; as the bedside did not suit the father, the role of advocate did not suit the son. They held in common, too, a ready wit and a way with words.

But they represented different generations, and the younger was more willing than the elder to face the inevitability of social change from one to the other. The elder Holmes was given to emotional outbursts, the younger's composure was rarely penetrated. The elder man flourished in his cocoon, the younger man chafed under its constraints.

In fact, the filial inclination to metaphorical patricide suggested by Dr. Holmes in his address was a dominant theme during the years father and son came into actual contact with each other, and Wendell continued to make occasional gestures of defiance long after Dr. Holmes's death in 1894. A man who called himself an autocrat could hardly have expected any other response.

Dr. Holmes himself had set the example when he rejected his own father's Calvinism, wounding the old clergyman where he was most vulnerable. The doctor's rebellion was complete. He joined the Unitarian Church, championed liberal religion in his columns for the *Atlantic Monthly,* and was principal speaker at the Unitarian Festival in 1859. And yet, just a little ambivalence remained. He never could get the "iron of Calvinism" entirely out of his soul. He could not bring himself to read novels on Sunday, and he often recalled with both pleasure and not a little longing the holy quiet time of the Sabbath eve. In his novels *Elsie Venner* and its sequel, *The Guardian Angel,* published in the 1860s, when Dr. Holmes was in his fifties, he was still in the process of "swallow[ing] and digest[ing]" the Reverend Abiel as he tried to work out the theological conundrums that had long taunted him.

A man who, like Dr. Holmes, so thoroughly and so proudly represented the insularity of a small region should hardly have been surprised when his elder son attempted to transcend the limitations of locale, although the son, too, remained always a little ambivalent. There were moments when class consciousness, conservatism, and conformity surfaced, moments when he was just as provincial and complacent as his father. And there were moments when he soared above convention, found release in creation, solace in the uninhibited convulsions of the intellect. One of Wendell's favorite books as boy and man—he first read it in translation as a youngster—was the *Prometheus* of Aeschylus, that powerful picture of Prometheus bound for all time to the rock of the past by his father, Zeus, for stealing fire, the future, for man. That story "always hit [him] where [he] lived."

Added to the natural antagonisms between the Holmeses, father and son, was the difficulty of being the offspring of a celebrity. Growing up as the first born son and namesake of a famous father and clocked by a Lowell, a Longfellow, and an Emerson, three of mid–nineteenth-century America's best judges of intellectual horseflesh, could not have been easy. In the autobiography he wrote for his Harvard Class Album, Wendell wrote of his three New England names with pride. But for a boy it wasn't easy to be an individual when he wore the name of another, especially a famous another. It could only have intensified the pressures to achieve what had begun in his crib. Schoolmaster Sullivan, in a poem prepared for his little pupils' sleighing party in January of 1850, publicly reminded Wendell, then nine, of his awesome burdens:

> While of versatile power in all paths to excel
> The inherited talent in Holmes we foretell.

Although Wendell stood in awe of his father, referred to him as "my guv'nor," he resented people who thought of him only as the son of an illustrious father; he was overheard to mutter about one woman who referred to him in that way, "the damned fool."

The same force that drove the two Holmeses apart could throw them together quickly when outsiders attacked. Wendell did not tolerate criticism of his father. On being introduced to the younger Holmes in London, the Scottish scholar, historian, and translator of Homer, Andrew Lang, opened the conversation:

"Are you the son of Oliver Wendell Holmes?"

Wendell admitted it.

"Well," said Lang, "I don't like him."

How Wendell "regretted that [he] was not quick enough with rapier or bludgeon to hand him one back before [Lang] vanished." He had to content himself with the pleasure of "think[ing] ill" of Lang's *Joan of Arc,* which he read on the way back to America.

The younger Holmes, for whom achievement in time became a moral commandment, was disappointed in his father's failure to achieve what he considered real greatness, in his father's squandering of a remarkable talent. The doctor, in his son's opinion, spread himself too thin. His father's strong point, Wendell explained, was "a fertile and suggestive intellect. I do not care," he continued, "as much as he would have liked me to for his poetry and novels—but I think he had the most penetrating mind of all that lot. After his early medical work, which was really big (the puerperal fever business) I think he contented himself too much with sporadic aperçus—the time for which, as I used to say, when I wanted to be disagreeable, had gone by. If he had the patience to concentrate all his energy on a single subject, which perhaps is saying if he had been a different man, he would have been less popular, but he might have produced a great work. I often am struck by his insight in things that he lightly touched. But, as I say, it is the last 5% that makes the difference between the great and the clever."

Conscious, however, of Dr. Holmes's position in American belles lettres, Wendell carefully preserved his father's books, and along with those of the elder Holmes's contemporaries, made a "little Shrine." A few years after the doctor's death, Wendell congratulated himself on performance of a "filial duty" when he put into "order and dignified form" a "confused mess" of his father's original manuscripts and had them bound. Later he presented, with some small fanfare, his father's copy of Shakespeare's works to the Folger Memorial Library in Washington and a thousand assorted volumes from the doctor's collection of books to the Berkshire Athenaeum in Pittsfield, near the Holmes's former summer place. The doctor, the son confessed, would have been surprised that Wendell "would take any trouble to do him honor, I not spending my time in adoring him when he was alive."

Long after Wendell had grown to manhood and as a Massachusetts Supreme Judicial Court judge into some local prominence, Dr. Holmes could not resist the impulse to tease his son publicly; it was not that he wanted to embarrass Wendell, it was just that he seemed unable to stop treating his son as a child; perhaps he feared the rivalry, required reassurance of filial dependency. Shortly after Wendell was appointed to the state court, the doctor, in response to a toast at a dinner of the Boston Bar Association, described the new judge's infancy:

> . . . The justice who, in gown and cap
> Condemns a wretch to strangulation,
> Has thrashed his nurse and spilled his pap
> And sprawled across his mother's lap
> For wholesome law's administration . . .

Four equally humiliating verses preceded, six followed. The doctor, who often included thinly disguised family incidents in his writing, especially his breakfast-table offerings, probably saw no breach of good taste in his poem. But it is not difficult to imagine the tall, handsome judge, new to his solemn responsibilities on the bench, mentally writhing as he tried to maintain his composure through the laughter at his expense.

The hills and valleys that complicated the relationship between Dr. Holmes and his son could not, of course, eliminate a natural father-son love, a love that time and worldliness could not suppress but whose sharp corners they may have smoothed. On Wendell's return from a trip abroad in 1889—the doctor was eighty, the son, forty-eight—Dr. Holmes told a friend:

> I look up to him as my magistrate, and he knows me as his father, but my arms are around his neck and his mustache is sweeping my cheek.

Amelia Holmes's presence in her son's later recollections is shadowy at best. Perhaps, like Henry James, he held the memory "too sacred." It is apparent, however, in the few clues that survive, that love and affection, only sporadically part of the relationship between Dr. Holmes and his son, more consistently dominated the relations between Wendell and his mother. No references to abrasiveness cloud what little Wendell had to say about Amelia Holmes. Stronger biological bonding no doubt made it easier for mother and son, however naturally reserved, to express their feelings. He gave without inhibition and she accepted with pleasure her golden boy's kiss when he "dance[d]" into the breakfast room each morning. "God bless you my darling I love you just as much as if I talked more with my mouth" was a typical peroration to Captain Holmes's letters to her during the Civil War. It was she who understood him and his need for privacy so well that she asked her to help him comb through his letters from the front for those that ought to be destroyed. Said she to Wendell, when she was forty-eight and he was twenty-five, "what does a woman of my age care as much for as her children, what they are and what they will be? I assure you that I give more thoughts to them than to anything else in the world . . . I suppose I bother you sometimes—but I love you very much."

She listened to him recite his grammar school lessons and later helped him prepare for his bar examinations. They took long walks together at Pittsfield, as the young teenager began to wonder about his place in the world. It is possible that as Wendell matured and his interest in serious intellectual matters developed, Amelia, an avid and sophisticated reader despite the domestic demands on her and although her opportunities for intellectual exchange may have been limited outside her home, found her elder son an intelligent and interesting companion.

Although Amelia appears to have conformed amiably enough to contemporary patterns for women born and bred in the genteel tradition, she was not a domestic drudge. It was her artistry that balanced the demands and desires of each family member, that soothed the tensions between the generations and the rivalries among the young, that provided the cement that held the five energetic Holmeses together.

She brought a love of books to her marriage and motherhood. She owned such works as Robert Southey's edition of William Cowper's works, the poetry of Samuel Taylor Coleridge, and various writings of François Fénelon. In the society in which she moved, a cultural perspective was a prerequisite to motherhood if her children were to assume their natural positions of leadership. Her role in fact required a broad knowledge and highly developed skills as well as a deep reservoir of love and affection if she was to mold the characters of her brood, develop their aesthetic tastes, cultivate their intellectual yearnings, and nourish their dreams as well as their growing bodies. Her role was significant if not as liberated as she might have liked.

Amelia Jackson Holmes, born October 20, 1843, and Edward Jackson Holmes (Ned), born October 17, 1846, completed the little family. Both siblings trod noiselessly through Wendell's life.

There is very little material with which to reconstruct the younger Amelia, as she followed Oliver, Wendell, Holmes, and Jackson women along the preordained path to marriage. The female side of the Holmes line tended to follow traditional patterns, whatever else they did. Even Anne Bradstreet, Amelia's poet ancestor, had a husband and eight children to attend to. Amelia had a local reputation as a chatterbox, the only woman who could outtalk Boston's popular new preacher, Phillips Brooks. Her letters to Wendell when he went abroad in 1866 were sprightly, full of family affairs and her flirtations, pleasantly teasing as if his absence affected her more than she wanted to admit.

Ned seems to have been a sharp contrast to Wendell, what the older generation called a "Buster": a practical joker, "red in the face, uproarious, aggressive, indomitable, loud in voice." Wendell, known as the "Favorite," the eldest, to whom the others were "children," seems only rarely to have noticed them in his preoccupation with trying to escape Dr. Holmes's shadow; even later, when Ned's persistent asthma required him to seek a setting with clearer air and he settled for a time in Lakewood, New Jersey, it was not Wendell, but Wendell's wife, Fanny, who wrote him regularly, offered encouragement and support, tried to tend his psychic needs from afar.

Family life during Wendell's youth seems to have proceeded as serenely as the life of a close-knit family ever does, punctuated by the usual milestones, storms, rivalries, disagreements, demonstrations of affection and solicitude. It was, as Mrs. Dr. Holmes once said, "as happy a little household as you will meet with."

Uncle John—John Holmes, the doctor's shy, chronically lame, though charming and witty younger brother—was the benevolent spirit that made the years of their youth joyful for the Holmes children. No less a Brahmin than the doctor—the right neighbors and friends, the right preparatory school, Harvard College, Harvard Law School, a prestigious law firm—his character had been tempered and his capacity for empathy heightened by an un-Brahmin-like rebelliousness. The practice of law did not suit him, and he went to sea for a brief period, following which he fell in love with a governess. His conventional brother and mother dissuaded him from such an unconventional marriage on grounds of social incompatibility, and the young woman had left town, then died before her suitor could follow her. Although he was said to have been the smarter, wittier, and more perceptive of the Holmes brothers, Uncle John had no further ambitions, and he retired to the gambrel-roofed former parsonage in Cambridge, where, having no fixed occupation, he cared for his mother, matriarch of the Holmes family, until her death in 1862, at the age of ninety-three.

Later he moved to a modest little house nearby in the Appian Way, where he presided over an inner circle of admiring cronies that included James Russell Lowell, the Hoar brothers, and James B. Thayer, professor of law at Harvard, and languished in the shadow of his famous brother—he liked to sign his name *frère de mon frère*.

But he was whimsical and humorous and imaginative and always ready to beguile a troop of young Holmeses with his amusing stories and impromptu monologues during their periodic visits to Grandmother Holmes. He taught them the joy of release in swearing. His entertaining letters—accounts of adventures experienced by an imaginary character named Goliath Tittle (the long and the short of it, the tittle being the name of a tiny punctuation mark in the Hebrew alphabet) in such remote outposts of civilization as the Island of Boogue and North Penny Royal West Parish Mass—followed them on each summer vacation, where they were awaited "with great eagerness." Every child should have an Uncle John. He acted as buffer between parent and child, confessor, comforter, and even, on occasion, fellow conspirator.

WENDELL HOLMES SAID much later in his life that "whatever atmosphere men are brought up in persists. Their first impressions largely determine what they revere and love—or hate." He absorbed some facets of his environment which he thought would be useful in his later life, and discarded those he thought would not.

He was, first of all, the child of a skeptical generation. His willingness to question became one of the characteristics that set Holmes off from, first Johnny Morse, then Harvard, then Brahmin Boston, and, lastly, the other judges of the United States Supreme Court.

As a youth he was surrounded by skepticism. The new democracy was challenging the platitudes of the old politics at the same time the new science was challenging the platitudes of the old faiths. The slavery question was one of several that presaged major transformations in American society during Wendell's formative years. Immigration—nearly three million in the 1850s, most of it from northern Europe, especially Ireland and Germany—urbanization, and industrialization were changing the way America voted and the way America lived. Jacksonian Democrats—Westerners with their egalitarian and anti-intellectual inclinations, newly enfranchised propertyless voters, some of them poor tenement dwellers—were questioning the conventional political wisdom and beginning to threaten the traditional leadership status of the elite. John Quincy Adams was the last president from New England for a century.

Although the leading scientists of Wendell's early youth were careful to square their theories with basic Christian theology, it was becoming clear that new developments and discoveries in paleontology, zoology, and geology, forerunners of Darwin's findings, would lead shortly to challenge of revealed truths.

At the same time, when most young people are being taught that the teacher is always right, that authority is to be obeyed, Wendell Holmes was learning, as well as the questing nature of scientific method, that those in charge are not always right. Dr. Holmes's defiance of medical authority in the matter of puerperal fever made a deep impression on him. He saw at first hand how important—if not particularly rewarding—it could be to question authority. Dr. Holmes set the example.

At home he was accustomed, too, to hearing Dr. Holmes challenge traditional theological principles—although not the fundamental principle on which all the principles were grounded; the doctor remained a lifelong deist. Much later in his life, his son expressed profound disappointment that the theologically liberal doctor, although brought up in the "scientific way of looking at the world," nevertheless harbored a "certain softness of attitude toward the interstitial miracle—the phenomenon without personal antecedents." That is, the doctor believed in God.

Wendell Holmes grew up in an atmosphere of and surrounded by the contagious sort of worldly success. He was the great-grandson, grandson, and son of achievers, and his own ambition, heightened by his rivalry with Dr. Holmes, was proportionately high. He was not on familiar terms with fishmongers and firemen. He heard few Irish brogues except from the butcher's boy and the serving girls. The black laundresses, stevedores, hairdressers, and waiters scattered through Boston's predominantly white population were strangers to him. He personally was not acquainted with business failures, wastrels, or malcontents. He had probably never seen the inside of an almshouse or an asylum. No open privies or contaminated wells marred the purity of Montgomery Place, to which poverty and its constraints were entirely alien.

The Holmeses themselves were as upwardly mobile as any other American family of the mid-nineteenth century. When by 1857 the house on Montgomery Place no longer met their needs, they moved to 21 Charles Street, prompting Dr. Holmes to remark, "We Americans live in tents." (The Montgomery Place house later was torn down and the street renamed Bosworth.) The new house stood on the river side of the Common, a new part of town developed on land filled in over the Back Bay swamps to accommodate similarly upward bound Bostonians. Some years before, the spot had been a small island in the Charles River estuary on which Dr. Holmes had then dreamed of owning a house. The new place offered a fine view of the river and western hills as well as a place for the doctor to moor his boats, in which he sculled mornings before breakfast.

During the first sixteen years of his life, Wendell saw his father make a reputation as a writer and the demand for his work increase. He saw the doctor's medical essays attract the attention of the profession nationally. As a boy of eleven, he had seen his father's excitement when the postman arrived at the Pittsfield house with the mail orders from the Athenaeum library or the local bookstore. He understood Dr. Holmes to be working that summer on a twelve-talk series about the English poets for the Lowell Institute, the most prestigious series in all New England. An experienced lecturer, Dr. Holmes had such a talent for making his scholarship appealing to a varied audience and drew such large crowds that the series had to be given twice in Boston, and parts were repeated in Cambridge, New York, and Louisville. With the rest of the family, from little Ned and Amelia to Uncle John and Grandmother Holmes, Wendell shared the joy in 1847 when Dr. Holmes was appointed Parkman Professor of Anatomy and Physiology as well as dean of the Harvard Medical School, the best in the country.

Wendell's father's friends were famous authors. His mother's family, the Jacksons, and their friends he recognized as powerful and wealthy members of the local business community. Everyone loved Uncle John, but no one would have suggested an ambitious boy follow his example.

Wendell's schoolmates came from the local elite. He knew no other life. Success at home and abroad surrounded him, goaded him, raised his expectations for himself and those of others for him. Since early childhood the men and women around him had hung on his every word, trying to detect signs of his literary inheritance, comparing him to his famous father.

Wendell was ambitious and anxious to get on with his life of achievement. He was not, however, materialistic, although the new industrialization that was putting more and more money in Bostonians' pockets was encouraging the unprecedented growth of materialistic values. As a boy of seven, he had written in his copybook for Schoolmaster Sullivan admiring portraits of historical figures in whom virtue (Socrates), courage (the Pilgrims), and a taste for adventure (Alexander the Great) played major roles, and he had stated flatly that "there are a great many things better than gold."

More attractive and congenial to the nature of a bookish boy was the intellectual and cultural awakening of New England which occurred during Wendell's formative years and of which his father's literary friends were so significant a part. Beginning about 1815 with the founding of the *North American Review* by a group of Harvard professors, and cresting about 1857 with the founding of the *Atlantic Monthly* by the local literati including Dr. Holmes—encompassing the more or less relaxed time between the wars—Boston was the hub of a humanist "renaissance."

Money to finance it was plentiful as profits from the nearby mill towns—Lawrence, Lowell, Lynn, Manchester—flowed into the countinghouses of local businessmen, who rather liked the idea of their city's becoming a cultural leader. After they had built their mansions and sat for Gilbert Stuart to paint them, the rich merchants and millowners rushed to endow local churches, chairs at Harvard, schools, public buildings, and benevolent institutions.

Local libraries—first the Massachusetts Historical Society library, established in 1791, followed less than two decades later by the Athenaeum, both supplemented by the Harvard libraries—contributed handsomely to the intellectual ferment.

The great names of nineteenth-century American intellectual endeavor lived and worked right there in Boston and its satellites. Most of them were friends of Wendell's father. A life of the mind could be contagious when you were surrounded by it.

The scholarly and engaging George Ticknor with his young partner, James T. Fields, who lived a few doors away from the Holmeses on Charles Street, operated Boston's preeminent publishing house. Emerson, of course, dominated intellectual matters and directions, along with his friend Henry Thoreau. Holmes and Longfellow were leading the way in popular poetry that expressed the ethos of a time and place. Hawthorne and Melville were reconstructing the novel; Francis Parkman and George Bancroft, American history. Aspiring young writers came to Boston to learn from the masters.

These giants, it appeared, were involved not primarily with money, but with the priceless matters of the mind. At the monthly meetings of the Saturday Club, they washed down their seven-course dinners with sauterne and good talk about life and nature and writing and art, things that really mattered.

The day of the professional writer had hardly begun. These men wrote for the love of it, supporting themselves in various other ways. Thoreau had, of course, taken a vow of poverty. Dr. Holmes's professorship at Harvard Medical School kept food on the table and his children in good schools. Hawthorne tried magazine editing, but his major support came from positions he held in the customhouses at Boston and Salem. After some years at sea, Melville tried lecturing, but in the end supported himself as a customs inspector in New York City. Longfellow had an endowed chair at Harvard, as did James Russell Lowell. All the time they were writing, writing, writing.

It was too early, of course, for Wendell to have chosen a profession, to know much at all about what directions his life would take, how all the disparate pieces would fall into a pattern. He was too young to do much more than absorb the atmosphere around him and try to imagine where he would fit in.

Youth for Wendell was a dormant time, of talent unutilized and energy untapped, "a weary time . . . of waiting for 'some divine far-off event,' " for real life to begin. An endless time of deferred gratification, a time of incapacity felt more deeply even than that of old age. That his destiny involved scaling heights seemed, in the light of his background, obvious and inevitable. That impatience should make him "melancholy and lonely," beset with "futile yearnings," was equally obvious and inevitable. Few surprises, he thought at the time, though he hoped for some, would spice his future. He knew that family pride promised him a thorough education. Family tradition assured him a good opening in a good firm; a place to which he would succeed as if to a title would be waiting when he was ready. Family reputation—the poetry and prose of Dr. Holmes was becoming known wherever English was spoken and in some places where it wasn't—practically guaranteed that he never would have to be introduced, never have to explain who he was. It seemed to be all planned, worked out in accordance with the traditional Brahmin blueprint for life.

But first there was Harvard, two-century-old bastion of learning, preeminent among American warehouses of the accumulated wisdom of the Western world.

CHAPTER 4

Harvard College

WALKING THE SHORT distance to the college from Mr. Danforth's boardinghouse where he was living, on Linden Street just off the Yard,* Wendell Holmes, aged sixteen and a half, looked very much the part he was about to play. The baby fat had disappeared from his face, and the patrician nose and chin, more Holmes than Jackson, that contributed to his mature classic good looks had emerged. His great height, his relaxed pose and half smile, his overall debonair appearance, masked perhaps the youthful doubts inevitably incurred as he confronted the "sadden[ing] and perplex[ing]" "riddles of life."

It was unthinkable for Wendell Holmes of Boston to have gone anywhere but Harvard. Grandfather Holmes had gone to Yale, but he was originally a Connecticut man and might be forgiven; besides, Harvard had given him an honorary degree shortly after he arrived in Cambridge. But hardly a generation of Olivers, Wendells, or Jacksons had passed lacking Harvard degrees. A few families made better showings. The Lowells, for instance, contributed five Fellows of the Corporation, as many Overseers, two professors, and a president over a century and a half. But by local standards, Wendell Holmes's kin were well represented among the ruling intelligentsia. Dr. James Oliver had been one of the five members of the class of 1680, Jacob Wendell had graduated in 1733, Oliver Wendell in 1753. Edward Jackson had been one of the university's earliest benefactors. Great-grandfather Wendell had been a

---

*What is called a campus by other colleges is called the Yard at Harvard. In the days when wolves and other predators roamed the Cambridge Common, local farmers brought their cattle into a protected area of town known as Cow-Yard Row. When part of the cow-yard as well as adjacent land was purchased for Harvard College in 1637–38, it was quickly named the College Yard to distinguish it from its original purpose.

Fellow of the Corporation, and Grandfather Charles Jackson had been both a Fellow and an Overseer. Dr. Holmes had been a member of the class of '29 and was now a member of the medical faculty. Harvard was a Boston Brahmin's duty.

Cambridge, which stood just across the Charles River from Boston and could be reached by horse car, was still a rural-looking town in those days, with vast fields of wild huckleberries and blueberries stretching beyond the garden gate and open space separating the houses along the streets. But the country atmosphere was deceptive. Harvard, then as later, was the major local industry and set intellectual standards for all. Its faculty inspired the community to various intellectual exercises and enterprises and drew scholars to it. Whole literary families—Wares, Danas, Channings, Lowells—settled there, and boys amused themselves by copying and translating the Latin inscriptions on tombstones in the local cemetery. Bret Harte once remarked that you "couldn't fire a revolver from your front porch without bringing down a two-volumer!"

That was one facet of the mid-nineteenth-century Harvard ambience. Van Wyck Brooks, in his Pulitzer Prize–winning *The Flowering of New England,* described another, equally important, one:

> The object of study was to form the mind, but this was to form the character; and Massachusetts knew what its character was and took a certain satisfaction in it. Everyone was aware of the best Boston and Cambridge type, the type that Josiah Quincy [member of Congress, mayor of Boston, president of Harvard] represented, or the late Chief Justice Dana, a strong distaste for nonsense, a steady composure, a calm and gentle demeanour, stability, good principles, intelligence, a habit of understatement, a slow and cautious way of reasoning, contempt for extravagance, vanity and affectation, kindness of heart, purity, decorum, profound affections, filial and paternal. A noble type, severely limited, which Boston celebrated in its marble busts. . . .
>
> This was the type, and almost the only type, the curriculum of Harvard contemplated. Whatever studies favoured its formation, whatever were the best ways to form it, these were the ways and studies that Harvard knew. Whatever studies did not favour it, or favoured the formation of other types that Boston did not like or had never heard of, these were no concern of Harvard, or its concern only to oppose them.

The university's mission had not changed since John Harvard had left it the wherewithal—his library and half his estate—to open in 1636. In the seventeenth century that mission had been to provide New England with a literate ruling class, especially clergymen, educated to Puritan truth and moral standards. The object of their studies, literary and scientific both, was knowledge of God. The institution was thoroughly orthodox and its first president, Henry Dunster, had been fired for heresy, although during his administration the university had achieved substantial growth. But he had had the audacity to argue publicly against scriptural authority for infant baptism and had refused to have one of his own children baptized. By the time Wendell Holmes entered the freshman class two centuries later, Unitarians had succeeded Calvinists, but the reformers had proven to be no more open-minded than their Puritan predecessors, and the institutional mission, directed largely by theologians, remained the same: to explain to students the mysteries of the universe rooted not in empirically arrived at truths but in inherited theological dogma, and to suppress disturbing questions. It seemed the most viable way, as Harvard—the members of whose governing boards had connections to financial, industrial, cultural, and medical Boston— looked at it, to initiate young men into the tribal mysteries and rituals of upper-middle-class America and to reproduce generation after generation of conventional young aristocrats prepared to assume their proper places among the leaders in politics, the professions, and in the boardrooms of the railroads, banks, and textile mills.

Intellectual humility was rewarded, aggressiveness was punished. Charles Eliot, class of 1853 and author, during his forty-year presidency of the university, of comprehensive curriculum reform, recalled that when he was a student, the mathematics professor, Benjamin Peirce, had reprimanded him:

> Eliot, your trouble is that your mind has a skeptical turn. Be on your guard against that tendency or it will hurt your career.

Henry Adams, Harvard '58, claimed never to have heard during his four years as a Harvard undergraduate the name of either Karl Marx or Auguste Comte, two of the nineteenth century's more flagrant disturbers of the peace.

The curriculum, passionless and calculated to stifle the exercise of passion, was for the most part an extension of the curriculum at Mr. Dixwell's. It had hardly changed since Dr. Holmes had studied at Harvard three decades before. Based on the idea that common knowledge of the ancient classics created a common culture, Wendell Holmes's course of study was hardly calculated to expand his intellectual horizons. Whether he liked it or not, in his freshman year he took Greek (Euripides' *Alcestis,* three books of Homer's *Odyssey,* a smattering of ancient history, and grammar), Latin (Livy, Horace's Odes, Cicero's *Tusculan Disputes,* grammar and exercises in writing), mathematics (algebra, trigonometry, and plane geometry), elocution (lessons in pronunciation—"Orthoepy"—and expression), and religious instruction.

Religious instruction was the official college statement of approved Christian dogma. The text used was the recently published *Introductory Lessons in Morals and Christian Evidence* by Richard Whately, Anglican archbishop of Dublin, the introduction to which happened to have been written by Harvard's own Frederic D. Huntington, D.D., Preacher to the University, Plummer Professor of Christian Morals, and instructor in the course. The tenor of Huntington's classroom theology, as extracted from the introduction he wrote for Whately's book, advocated Christian faith over scientific experiment, and the incorporation of Christian morality in the making of public policy—a convenient and perhaps reassuring message to instill in the receptive young minds of New England's future leaders, just then searching for philosophies of life to which they could adapt. The bulk of the volume was made up of "Lessons" in which Holmes and his fellow freshmen learned about relationships between conscience and Divine Will, how to apply scriptural morality to their daily lives, and "Cautions" against self-love and selfishness, deceit and falsehood, depravity and vulgarity. A section on "Christian Evidences" argued without apology the superiority and universality of Christianity. A former Oxford don, Archbishop Whately understood the youthful minds he was addressing. He himself thought of his students as "anvils" on which to beat out his ideas, but he did not burden them with labyrinthine metaphysical arguments or dogmatic treatises. He made his case simply and cogently on the basis of scriptural briefs, all applicable to the events and problems young men met every day.

It is unlikely that this year-long forced feeding of orthodox Christian dogma slipped down Wendell's throat easily, and in the fall of his sophomore year, he joined the recently established Christian Union, a liberal Christian student group that condemned discrimination on the basis of sect and required of its members only that they embrace the broadest principles of Christianity. The Christian Union was a liberal organization as opposed to the rival group, the Christian Brethren, which required of its members belief in the Trinity and in the doctrine of depravity and regeneration as well as evidence of "a saving change of heart"; Holmes joined the former not because he "considered [his] life justified in belonging to [it]," but because he wished to bear testimony in favor of a Religious society founded on liberal principles in distinction to the more "orthodox" and sectarian platform of the "Xtian [sic] Brethren."

His skepticism in fact prevented Wendell Holmes from adopting then or later the tenets of any formalized religion. Theological absolutes were repugnant to him. He might have preferred to embrace comfortable truths. He recognized and revered the mysteries of the universe, and seeking balm for his cosmic worries, he continually posed questions. But he never found satisfactory answers and looked on those who did as presumptuous.

Holmes's personal theology was a complicated and not always consistent melange of hypotheses he worked out that more or less satisfied him. In addition to skepticism of all rigid orthodoxies, it included agnosticism plus what he called "bettabilitarian[ism]"—if he could not positively *know* eternal truths, he could bet with some assurance on the recurrence of certain natural phenomena. Truth was relative, and "largely personal," only what "I can't help thinking."

He also felt strongly that man's place in the overall scheme of creation was not paramount, that the highest achievements in the evolutionary process were nothing but "cosmic ganglia," lacking any particular equipment for supremacy; he saw

> no reason to believe that a shudder could go through the sky if the whole ant heap were kerosened.

He found especially disturbing that the "humility of the Christian is based on the arrogant assumption that he has been let in on the ground floor by God—that he is privy to his ultimate judgments and a sharer in absolute truth."

Ultimately, Holmes's concept of mankind's less-than-exalted position on earth was much like that he assigned to the private soldier:

> I think one should accept one's (human) ultimates as governing one's life but not require assurance that they govern the universe. It is enough that one embodies one's little fraction of cosmic destiny—and I think one is wise to keep the humility of a soldier in the ranks and not ask to be told the final secrets of strategy, if there is any, or whether there is any.

He referred often to *"le Bon Dieu,"* but the references were casual, intended to embellish a story or make a collateral point. He revered his

Puritan ancestry, but only in a "filial" way; the "great currents of the world's life" had gone in other directions, and the future, Holmes believed, "lay in the hands of Bacon and Hobbes and Descartes." Comparing in conversation India as the home of religion and Europe of the steam engine, he was once heard to remark:

> On the whole I prefer the steam-engine as it stands for science.

Much later, Fanny, his wife, introducing herself to one of his secretaries, announced that the Holmeses were Unitarians:

> In Boston one has to be something and Unitarian is the least you can be.

Academically, Harvard's sophomore courses promised no more intellectual exhilaration than had freshman courses. Grammar, which included Anglo-Saxon, and botany and chemistry were added to the required Greek, Latin, elocution, and mathematics; French, if a student desired, could be taken as an "extra." Holmes, however, did not take it.

In the junior year, physics, rhetoric, Greek, and Latin constituted the required program; mathematics, botany, German, Spanish, and French, of which each student was required to choose at least one, were electives. Holmes chose German. In the senior year, philosophy (including political economy), rhetoric, physics, and history were required; among the electives, students could choose from mathematics, Greek, Spanish, Italian, modern literature, geology, zoology, and anatomy. Consistent with his lifelong interest in the humanities, which contributed to his lifelong neglect of—and ignorance of—science, Holmes took the course in Greek.

That so many mid-nineteenth-century Harvard graduates had been disenchanted during their undergraduate years has been attributed not only to the banality of the curriculum but also to the onerous and inane grading system which had been established by President Josiah Quincy (1829–45) and which prevailed for nearly half a century. Marks were determined on the basis of a complex Scale of Merit, which rated not only academic performance but also behavior. For example, a student received 8 points for a perfect recitation, 24 for a written exercise, 48 for a sophomore theme, 60 for a declamation, 72 for a forensic, and 96 for a junior or senior theme. He could, however, lose it all for infractions of the rules of conduct. Absence from daily prayers cost 2 points, absence from public worship, 32; absence from recitations and other official classroom programs cost 8 points, a "private admonition" cost 32, and a "public admonition," 64. The numbers accumulated from week to week, term to term, and year to year until graduation, when a student's total generally reached into five figures. Holmes's reached 18,681.

Such an environment lent itself conveniently to an educational system grounded in passionless rote learning, a system in which young men were required "to recite lessons from textbooks, and to write compulsory exercises. . . . The College proper," declared a disenchanted faculty member in 1866, "is simply a more advanced school for boys, not differing essentially in principle and theory from the public schools in all our towns . . . the principle is coercion. Hold your subject fast with one hand, and pour knowledge into him with the other."

Henry Adams, Wendell Holmes's friend and predecessor at Harvard by three years, characterized his own undergraduate experience as innocuous at best:

> Any other education would have required serious effort, but no one took Harvard College seriously. All went there because their friends went there, and the College was their ideal of social self-respect. Harvard College, as far as it educated at all, was a mild and liberal school, which sent young men into the world with all they needed to make respectable citizens, and something of what they wanted to make useful ones. . . . In effect, the school created a type but not a will. Four years of Harvard College, if successful, resulted in an autobiographical blank, a mind on which only a water-mark had been stamped.

The faculty was in general a homogeneous group, most of its members products of the system they were perpetuating. The majority were Unitarians and Harvard alumni; they further controlled the dispersal of knowledge by using their own textbooks and those of their Harvard colleagues in their classes.

Evangelinus A. Sophocles, A.M., who taught Wendell Holmes Greek, was one of the rare exceptions. It was, perhaps, Professor Sophocles' unorthodox teaching methods and magnetic personality that attracted Wendell to Greek courses and were responsible for the young man's proficiency in the language, a proficiency he cultivated lifelong. Among a group of men who shrank from personal relations with their students, Greek-born, spontaneous Professor Sophocles stood out because he clearly and openly loved his. Wendell remembered him later as "a beautiful fellow one of the most learned men in the world." His head was leonine, his hair white, his dark fiery eyes intense, his temperament Mediterranean, his heart large. He burned all the students' blue books. They were worthless for evaluating a man's progress. If a student did well in daily recitation, Sophocles reasoned, it was not fair to lower his grade on the basis of a poorly written examination; if he did well on the examination, it was obvious to the professor he had cheated. He appears not to have participated in the weekly recording of grades, and the records of the Greek classes during Wendell Holmes's years at Harvard are either haphazard or entered by one of the university proctors, John Noble. Sophocles liked to pose unorthodox questions, to open young minds to the less obvious, to expand the intellectual horizons of his young charges who, as he said, "know nothing," and in doing so, he often seemed out of place, though pleasantly so to a student like Wendell Holmes, among the dry and respectable schoolmasters who made up the Harvard faculty in mid-nineteenth century.

Joseph Lovering, on the other hand, Hollis Professor of Mathematics and Natural Philosophy, who taught Wendell Holmes physics, fit the Harvard mold perfectly. Eliot recalled Lovering's classroom manner some years later. "When he lectured he never showed the least emotion. . . . I can see him now, sitting like an inquisitor on an elevated chair overlooking the class, with his spectacles over the forehead, with the textbook to which he never referred, on the desk before him, and directing his questions to one man after another. . . . I . . . wonder at the feats of memory which enabled some of the class to repeat mathematical formulas, even differential equations, without the remotest intelligent knowledge of their meaning. . . . No direct instruction, not even any elucidation of the book, was ever attempted. We did learn the book so far as it was intelligible to us, but nothing more. . . . This formalism was the fashion in the education of the time, and the all but universal rule in the College." Lovering, with typical nineteenth-century Harvardian certitude, pronounced the growing interest in electricity "only a spurt."

Francis ("Fanny") Bowen, Alford Professor of Natural Religion—and editor of the *North American Review* on the side—under whom Wendell Holmes studied philosophy and political economy during his senior year, was Harvard's unofficial guardian of Christian truth, its philosophical bulwark against contemporary popular heresies. Weaving theology into justification of laissez-faire economics—"I have attempted," he declared, "to show that the causes of the increase of capital are moral rather than physical"—Bowen blatantly used the classroom to cultivate, convert if necessary, his students. He relied on his own textbooks—*The Principles of Metaphysical and Ethical Science Applied to the Evidences of Religion* and *The Principles of Political Economy*—to combat "the licentious and infidel speculations which are pouring in upon us from Europe like a flood," i.e., developments in science, contemporary revolutions in France and Germany, the vague emanations of transcendentalism. Professor Bowen's inclinations to dogmatism and Wendell Holmes's inclinations to skepticism could hardly have been compatible. Whether Holmes brought his increasingly sophisticated critical faculties to bear on the professor's orthodoxies or in some other fashion challenged Bowen's version of economic or philosophical truth is not known—Holmes did not refer in his writings to the cause of the trouble between them. But in the spring of his senior year, the Harvard faculty was provoked to admonish (minus 64 points) Holmes and another senior publicly "for repeated and gross indecorum in the recitation of Professor Bowen."

The ninety-five young men with whom Wendell Holmes entered Harvard were as unlikely to expand his understanding of the world around him as were his instructors. Harvard prided itself on being a national school, and in a geographical context it was. Although New Englanders predominated (eighty-three, of whom seventy-five came from Massachusetts, fifty-seven from the Boston metropolitan area alone), freshmen in 1857–58 came from Cleveland and Cincinnati, Philadelphia, and Racine, Wisconsin, and even from such remote places as Honolulu and Fayal in the Azores. Horatio Eustis of Natchez, Mississippi, and Christopher Memminger of Charleston, South Carolina, whose father was later a member of the Confederacy's cabinet, maintained the traditional close connection between commercial Boston and the plantation South.

Geographical diversity did not, however, imply social, political, or economic diversity. Preparation and cost separated the aristocrats from the commoners, and the Harvard student body was dominated by elitists. Most of the young men the sons of merchants, lawyers, doctors, educators, and clergymen, many of them the proud descendants of seventeenth-century settlers, economically respectable, ethnically what a later generation would call WASPish (forty-one Unitarians, all but two, a Roman Catholic and a Quaker, of the rest Protestant Christian), morally and educationally conservative, and politically Republican, the class of 1861 achieved the traditional Harvard self-perpetuating homogeneity. They had prepared at the same schools—Mr. Dixwell's (six), Boston Latin, Phillips Andover—and by the time they were seniors, they had coalesced into a typical group of Harvard alumni-to-be. Only one meant to go to sea, only one intended to farm; the rest proposed to join the traditional respectable professions where they would meet again shortly as clients and colleagues in the countinghouses, clinics, boardrooms, and law offices. Their differences were superficial, and the young men enjoyed a rapport they probably could not have established with other young men from their own hometowns, a few geographical but hundreds of cultural miles away.

The ennui of academic Harvard could only have heightened the naturally high spirits of the undergraduates, and the young men dissipated their stifled energies in a number of socially disapproved ways. Within the Yard in fact it was virtually a police state. "The whole spirit between the Faculty and the students," one of Holmes's contemporaries observed, "was one of war." Not long after he wrote that in his diary, he boasted he had broken his seventeenth window. Food fights—rice croquettes versus hunks of bread—settled a good many spats. Hazing of freshmen reached its height during Holmes's years at Harvard; eventually it became so dangerous it had to be abolished. The annual football fight—not a game (the game had been prohibited), but, literally, a fight— was a shin-kicking, shoving, pushing, rough-and-tumble affair in which serious injuries were often inflicted, and President Cornelius C. Felton noted, not with pride, in his annual report for 1860 that "it was a growing custom of scholars preparing to enter college to take lessons in sparring and boxing, by way of qualification for the football match at the opening of the term." The match had become, Felton complained, "no longer a manly trial of skill and strength, but a struggle of brute force."

Smoking, drinking, window breaking, stealing the clapper from the college bell were some of the most common offenses, although one student, in a burst of originality, was caught trying to imprison the mathematics tutor in his room by screwing the door shut.

Faculty minutes for mid-nineteenth-century years are dominated not by discussions of larger issues in higher education but by votes of fines and admonitions against students for what amount to petty crimes, and President Felton's correspondence involved no small number of letters beginning "Your son has probably informed you that he is in some trouble at college." Wendell's close friend Norwood ("Pen") Hallowell was suspended for eight months for hazing freshmen, and Cousin Johnny Morse was publicly admonished for "indecorum in the Recitation Rooms."

Wendell himself earned his share of demerits. In his freshman year he was fined twice ($1 each) for defacing the rooms of faculty members, privately admonished (minus 32 points) for "disturbance in the Yard after . . . examination" in the summer of his sophomore year, and in his senior year fined $10 and publicly admonished (minus 64 points) for breaking windows in a freshman's room. Privately, President Felton reminded Dr. Holmes that his son's behavior ordinarily would have been punished by dismissal from the college, but since the culprits had confessed and apologized, the faculty and administration were inclined to leniency.

His record for mischief making reflects Wendell's academic record: average but not outstanding. He was in fact an indifferent student. Those who looked for dazzling scholarship and enthusiasm from the son of the effervescent Dr. Holmes were disappointed. The faculty dealt with his indifference to the intricacies of geometry in his sophomore year by requiring him to study the subject during vacation. He was rarely absent from his classes prior to his enlistment in the Union army in the spring of 1861, but he was often late for recitations. He was reprimanded for "playing" in Latin class, for whispering in German class, and he frequently attended Professor Bowen's philosophy class unprepared.

His lethargy showed in his scholarship, as had his father's. Dr. Holmes, who had labored under similar conditions, had confessed to laziness and an inclination to neglect his studies as an undergraduate. Wendell's class ranking fell slightly below his father's achievement— not among the top scholars, but slightly above average: twenty-second in the freshman class, thirtieth in the sophomore, thirteenth in the junior, and fifty-second in the senior, the final drop accounted for by penalties incurred when he left the university and joined the Union army during the spring of his senior year.

Still, Wendell's undergraduate years were not without some small rewards and distinctions, his way of saying perhaps that he could when necessary cope with the tedium imposed by less imaginative intellects. He could do his duty; he would not disgrace his name. His overall record for his sophomore year entitled him to one of the thirty "deturs" awarded that year—books given to "meritorious" students. In recognition perhaps of his literary heritage, in his junior and senior years he was assigned to deliver disquisitions at two of the semiannual "exhibitions"; in May 1860, he talked on Socrates, and in May 1861, he was scheduled to give a talk on the Pre-Raphaelites, but army duties prevented his delivery of the latter, and it was published instead in the *Harvard Magazine* for June 1861. He was elected to Phi Beta Kappa, more of a society for literary and intellectual fellowship than an honor society in those days, and he shared with a classmate in his senior year the Bowdoin Prize for Latin and Greek composition—Johnny Morse had won it for *his* Greek prose two years before.

But it was difficult for a young man to concentrate on the classics and to listen every day to a man who considered the contemporary interest in electricity "only a spurt" when a whole new world was in the process of creation. All previous human understanding of the universe was changing as scientists, jettisoning centuries-old traditions and exposing the futility of metaphysical speculation, were demonstrating that it was observation and experiment that led to the discovery of truth.

What Wendell Holmes must have been hearing at home from Dr. Holmes, who kept up with developments in medical science—the doctor had been one of the first professors of medicine in America to insist that his students use the microscope—would have been enough to convince any young man with an inquiring mind that the methods of science were radically changing the way earthlings looked at their planet, and that the Harvard professors, with rare exceptions, were standing idly by.

But when Charles Darwin's *The Origin of Species,* assigning man unequivocally to the animal kingdom and entirely removing religion from the conditions of his development and survival, burst upon the Western world in November 1859—the first term of Wendell Holmes's junior year at Harvard—rocking the university and ultimately dooming the Bowens and Loverings to extinction, Harvard College was almost more than an intelligent young man could bear. Professor Bowen dismissed Darwin's work as a fad and tried to knead its conclusions into conformity with Christian principles. Josiah Parsons Cooke, Erving Professor of Chemistry and Mineralogy, with whom Wendell Holmes studied chemistry that year, fretted about Darwin's effect on undergraduate morals. Even the brilliant, internationally known Louis Agassiz, professor of zoology and geology in the Lawrence Scientific School, an adjunct of Harvard whose reputation had been established largely through Agassiz's work, publicly disavowed Darwin's disturbing conclusions. Which left only Asa Gray, distinguished botanist and friend of Darwin's, to champion this latest revolutionary advance in scientific knowledge. Gray, the distinguished Fisher Professor of Natural History under whom Wendell Holmes studied botany during his sophomore year, was the only one of his professors to take Darwin's side in what was one of the most profound upheavals in human thought in two thousand years. It seemed more difficult for Harvard to adapt to the changing scientific environment than it had been, say, for the otter to adapt to water.

The very fact that the Harvard ambience proved intellectually so inhospitable as well as undemanding in mid-nineteenth century may have been what made the four years as an undergraduate tolerable for Wendell Holmes. The juices he might have expended in a serious physics or philosophy course he could reserve for more interesting pursuits outside the required programs.

He envied, he said, the "noble philosophy" of the men of the fifteenth and sixteenth centuries, the certitude of their "simple and childlike faith" that defined for them a style of life and gave them the security to create their masterpieces. They could never, however, serve him as models. He had been born into an intellectually querulous civilization which was being taught by the new science that "all questions may be asked and that many venerable beliefs are not true." Skepticism was "in the air," and his own generation, he believed, was its beneficiary, "almost the first of young men who have been brought up in an atmosphere of investigation, instead of having every doubt answered." He was eager to join his contemporaries, to ask those questions, to test, to challenge the truths he had been handed.

It was the idea and methods of scientific inquiry that interested him, however, not the data discovered. He read *The Origin of Species*—an 1860 edition, with various pages noted inside the back cover, was found among his books after his death—but he read little else involving science. He knew next to nothing about biology and chemistry, or even mathematics, except where it crossed into philosophy. Literature, philosophy, and history were what drew and held his attention. In his ignorance of scientific fact, he overendowed the capacities of science, coming eventually to believe that the biologists and the chemists and the physicists, given enough time and resources, could and would apply their habits of orderly experimentation and observation to solve all the problems of humankind, social as well as physical.

The explosion of science in mid-nineteenth century was exhilarating to young Wendell Holmes, but it was not the only force to hit him where he lived. By the spring of his freshman year, he had discovered Ralph Waldo Emerson—not the mystical transcendental Emerson, with whom Wendell, who disbelieved in the cosmic significance of the human species, could not have established a rapport, but the courageous, intellectually independent, and scholarly philosopher who symbolized all that Wendell aspired to. Emerson was a doubter, too; small wonder Wendell felt a kinship with him.

Seventy years later, Holmes recalled with deep emotion Emerson as the "firebrand" of his youth. Long after he had forgotten the sage's precise words, he recalled the "spark [that] started a flame" in him. Spotting Emerson on the other side of the street one day, Holmes dashed across and genuflected verbally. "If I ever do anything," he said, "I shall owe a great deal of it to you."

It hardly could have been coincidence that on Wendell's seventeenth birthday—March 8, 1858, the second term of his freshman year at Harvard—his parents gave him Emerson's *Poems, English Traits, Representative Men,* and two volumes of *Essays.* Johnny Morse added to the pile a book of the great man's lectures called *Miscellanies.* Dr. Holmes already owned an autographed copy of *Nature* (1849), which included Emerson's most famous and perhaps his most eloquent speech, "The American Scholar."

By the time Wendell Holmes was a Harvard freshman, the speech was twenty years old, but its premises were as timely as ever and may well have been the catalyst that fueled the young man's discipleship. Even the imagery stuck in Wendell's mind. Compare Emerson's

[T]he best books . . . impress us with the conviction that one nature wrote and the same reads. We read the verses of one of the great English poets . . . with the most modern joy,—with a pleasure . . . which is in great part caused by the abstraction of all *time* from their verses. . . . But for the evidence thence afforded to the philosophical doctrine of the identity of all minds, we should suppose some preestablished harmony, some foresight of souls that were to be, and some preparation of stores for their future wants, like the fact observed in insects, who lay up food before death for the young grub they shall never see.

with Holmes's

I think it not improbable that man, like the grub that prepares a chamber for the winged thing it never has seen but is to be, that man may have cosmic destinies that he does not understand. (Address to the Harvard Law School Association of New York, 1913)

Compare Emerson's

Wherever Macdonald sits, there is the head of the table.

with Holmes's

> I once heard a man say, 'Where Vanderbilt sits, there is the head of the table. . . .' ("The Soldier's Faith," 1895)

"The American Scholar" was delivered to a packed hall at Harvard on the occasion of a Phi Beta Kappa Society's anniversary celebration. Dr. Holmes called it the American intellectual Declaration of Independence. It had appalled the old, thrilled the young, and established Emerson's reputation as a prophet of a new age. Its literary quality, its soaring ideas, its unconventional way of looking at scholarship at a time when Americans were still in thrall to the Old World in aesthetic and intellectual matters, and the author's courage in daring to speak of these national failures in the very fortress of convention could not help but stir. His pleas for truly independent scholarship—independent of the dead cultures of Europe, independent of the past, independent of accepted contemporary wisdom—the pleas for courageous, self-confident intellectual endeavors were enough to set afire the brain of a Harvard undergraduate, surrounded as he was by intellectual passivity and conventionality.

The long-faced Emerson was probably the first pedigreed New Englander of Wendell Holmes's acquaintance—descendant of seventeenth-century settlers and Revolutionary War patriots, alumnus of Boston Latin School, Harvard College, and Harvard Divinity School—who had had the nerve to challenge the Harvard theologians themselves, supreme authorities in local theological matters. In an address to seniors at the Harvard Divinity School, standing where *he* had stood less than a decade before, Emerson urged the clergymen-to-be to open their minds to new concepts of God, to discard the shackles of traditional Christianity, "to go alone; to refuse the good models, even those which are sacred in the imagination of men. . . . The imitator," he added, "dooms himself to hopeless mediocrity." Emerson was not invited to speak there again for twenty years.

Most of Dr. Holmes's literary friends were abolitionists in principle, but Waldo Emerson invited John Brown to his Concord home. He set aside a room in his attic in which to hide fleeing slaves, and kept his carriage ready to drive them to the train station.

No other New Englander of Wendell's social circle could write with the same deep conviction: "Whoso would be a man, must be a nonconformist."

In December of 1858, ten months after his family had added Emer-

son's works to Wendell's growing library, an unsigned—as was the custom—article entitled "Books" appeared in the four-year-old, mildly icon-
oclastic *Harvard Magazine,* which was a direct lineal descendant of the
Collegian, to which Dr. Holmes had contributed as a young man. Prim
in tone and stilted in style though it was, the article nevertheless
amounted to Wendell Holmes's version of "The American Scholar," his
own declaration of intellectual independence from the Harvard way of
education. What his defiance of authority cost him in emotional anguish
is not known. Whatever the price, he was not deterred.

While Cousin Johnny Morse, diligently practicing for his future role
in the local society, was writing for the same issue of the magazine on
the noble qualities of "The English Country Gentleman," always a favorite theme among Boston Brahmins, Wendell Holmes was taking to
task the authority worshipers and indulging in some Emersonian grumbling about the superficiality of the scholarship he saw around him. He
urged his readers not to avoid "books of an agitating tendency. We *must,*
will we or no," he wrote with all the forcefulness of an angry seventeen-
year-old, "have every train of thought brought before us while we are
young, and may as well at once prepare for it." Citing his hero as model,
and further defying the authority of tradition, he prodded readers to
sample the sacred books of Confucius, Zoroaster, and Buddha, which,
he declared, Americans wrongly "contemn on the authority of others
. . . and some of which . . . teach us lessons of love and forbearance
that, after eighteen hundred years have gone by, we have not yet granted
the New Testament to inculcate."

Dr. Holmes, who may not yet have been ready for his son's adulthood and possible rivalry, was less than pleased with Wendell's journal-
istic efforts. Although he himself had scribbled his way into college
publications as an undergraduate, he felt obliged to deprecate Wendell's
work. "I have not," he said, regarding the articles in the *Harvard Magazine,* "been anxious to have him appear in print, as he is forming opinions too fast to have much time to dress them up rhetorically."

Wendell ignored the criticism. Book reviews and editorials flowed
from his pen. He was chosen one of the editors in July 1860. In a major
article published the following October, the first term of his senior year,
he repeated his earlier assessment of conventional theology. "[T]he growth
of civilization," he wrote, "increases our faith in the natural man, and
must accordingly detract from the intense and paramount importance
attached in darker times to the form of the story embodying the popular
religion . . . nowadays we see that duty is not less binding had the
Bible never been written."

By January 1861, the *Harvard Magazine* had come under faculty scrutiny. It had published less than admiring comments about the Reverend Professor Frederic Huntington, D.D., official protector of Christian truth at the university, editorials demanding "free will in matters of religion," and Wendell Holmes had scandalized the authorities when he had written:

A hundred years ago we burnt men's bodies for not agreeing with our religious tenets; we still burn their souls.

Articles were appearing on such controversial contemporary issues as "Woman in College" (the author approved), abolition (the author also approved), and the strained relations between students and the administration (the author proposed an elective system, among other reforms). A faculty committee was appointed to consider whether the periodical should be allowed to continue. President Felton, who had been an undergraduate two years ahead of Dr. Holmes and had maintained a casual personal relationship with him, privately urged the doctor to discuss the matter with his son.

The problem was, said Felton, who confessed to never having read the magazine, that "the writers in it have from time to time made unbecoming allusions to gentlemen who are or have been members of the College government, and that they have assumed the liberty of criticizing the proceedings of the College &c &c., all of which, though it may not be wrong in itself, is considered incompatible with the relation of students to the College and cannot be allowed." Censorship was repugnant to the president, he hoped matters would not come to that; he realized the students would protest that such an action

interfer[ed] with liberty of thought, speech, and the press; but the Faculty will undoubtedly hold that it is simply a question of propriety and duty, inasmuch as these young men are the pupils and not the critics or judges of the College. . . . No one objects to criticism of course; but printed or oral acts of disrespect by students, are alike inconsistent with their relations to the College and the Faculty, and printed as well as oral acts of this description I am sure the government will not permit.

He hoped, he added, that the doctor would, "in a judicious manner, bring [his] son to see this matter rightly, and to influence his coadjutors to preserve the proper tone."

Dr. Holmes's reply to President Felton has not survived, nor has any record of the doctor's conversations with his son, if such occurred. The *Harvard Magazine,* to which some students subscribed *because* the faculty opposed it, survived, however, uncensored, its editors unchastened, and its tone unsoftened.

In an inoffensive little spoof "Concerning Philosophers" for the March 1861 issue of the *Harvard Magazine,* one of the regular contributors, Frank Hackett, wrote: "Plato, one of the most famous men of antiquity, is celebrated for his carefully prepared works on philosophy and kindred subjects; and for his having been a warm friend and personal admirer of Mr. R. W. Emerson."

Emerson was a dedicated Platonist, had included Plato among the demigods of *Representative Men,* which Wendell owned. Platonic concepts suffuse Emerson's work—his transcendentalism, his poetry, and his essays. It was Emerson who "fired" Wendell into reading the ancient philosopher's work in which, at seventeen, he expected "to find the secrets of life revealed." The young man consulted with Emerson himself.

"I'm going to study Plato," he announced.

Emerson cautioned him: When he read Plato, Emerson said, Wendell "must hold him at arm's length. You must say to yourself, 'Plato, you have pleased the world for two thousand years: let us see if you can please me.'" Those "secrets of life" might not be so readily available.

Beginning in 1859 and continuing into 1860, various editions of Plato's works were borrowed on the Holmes card from the Athenaeum library. The study of Plato soon broadened into an independent study of philosophy, a subject Wendell had not yet encountered in the Harvard curriculum. He seesawed between the commentators on ancient and contemporary philosophies, between metaphysics and empiricism: W. A. Butler on the ancient philosophers, G. H. Lewes on Auguste Comte, Comte on the philosophy of science, R. A. Vaughan on the mystics. For his eighteenth birthday, in March 1859, he received William Thomson's recently published treatise on logic. A few months later he bought *An Essay on Intuitive Morals.*

During the summer vacation between his junior and senior years, he wrote an essay on Plato for the *University Quarterly,* an intercollegiate magazine published in New Haven, Connecticut. His prose style had begun to mature in the two years between "Books" and "Plato," and occasionally effective imagery improved the literary quality of the latter. His critical faculties in philosophy were still developing, and parts of the essay are little more than a rewriting of Emerson.

"Plato," however, is young Wendell Holmes's most unequivocal—to date—statement of his preference for scientific views of the universe over traditional cosmologies, despite the sluggishness of the institution he was attending. The king of philosophers had not, as Emerson had suggested he might not, pleased Wendell Holmes. The ancient Greek's logic was faulty, his classification of ideas "loose and unscientific," his methods of investigation "vague and incorrect." In addition, Holmes had difficulty reconciling Plato's concept of a fixed order of the universe, logical and moral, with the new concepts of constant cosmic change without reference to values. But he concluded that this view of Plato was only in retrospect. The shortcomings were to be laid not to failure of Plato's intellect but to the fact that he "lived too early . . . it is only in these last days," declared Holmes, child of the new scientific age, "that anything like an all-comprehending science has embraced the universe, showing unerring law prevailing in every department, generalizing and systematizing every phenomenon of physics, and every vagary of the human mind." The Great Man "had done all that with his facilities was possible." If the construction of his republic was fault-ridden, it was because "he was laboring as vainly as one who should endeavor to find the successive actual positions of the moon from his mathematical knowledge, being ignorant of the solar perturbations, and the motions of nodes and apsides."

As soon as Wendell finished writing the essay, he "laid it at Mr. Emerson's feet."

"I have read your piece," said Emerson. "When you strike at a king you must kill him."

Emerson's criticism made the young scholar "feel damn bad at the time," nearly overshadowed the fact that his essay was judged the best one written by an undergraduate for the *University Quarterly* in 1860, for which he received a prize of $20. Reconsidering the older man's remark in later years, however, Holmes felt differently: "Weren't those fine things for the old fellow? . . . I always thought they were a model of what the old can do for the young."

In his continuing search for the secrets of life as a young man, Wendell also became deeply interested in art—a field considered neither quite manly nor quite scholarly at Harvard in mid-nineteenth century. He actually bought a set of etching tools, although it is doubtful he ever intended to make a career of it. Except for certain violent displays— storms at sea, for example—nature, the obvious interest of artists, for many years did not engage Holmes's emotions; he intellectualized nature as he intellectualized everything else. He preferred to think about rather than to see it, and the fact that he derived no "ecstacy" from nature served only to frustrate many of his artistic endeavors. He became proficient if not brilliantly creative, and much later he had one of his own prints framed for his library.

Intellectually, though, art—its history and standards of interpretation—attracted Holmes throughout his life. In later years he developed an educated appreciation of artistic endeavor; he put together a fine collection of etchings and, after he went to Washington in 1902, liked to spend an afternoon, whenever he could, in a good jaw with the curator of prints at the Library of Congress. But in his youth, spending "what my small pocket money would allow" on selections from local portfolios, his eye was not so discriminating, and he bought only "one or two good things and more rubbish."

Prints his father had bought as a student in Paris formed the nucleus of Holmes's collection. They also afforded him, he said, "the first breath of a different atmosphere from that of the Boston of my youth." He began to read intensively in aesthetic matters, books that took him as far from that very Boston as a young man could venture without a steamer ticket. In March 1857, his last year at Mr. Dixwell's, probably for his birthday, his mother and father had given him *Modern Painters* by John Ruskin, whose equating of art with philosophy in general and with Plato in particular may first have inspired the young Holmes aesthetically. A few months later, just before he entered Harvard, Wendell himself purchased Ruskin's *Elements of Drawing.* For his seventeenth birthday, in 1858, while the rest of the family was loading him down with Emerson's works, Ned gave him *Pre-Raphaelitism,* and Amelia gave him Ruskin's *The Political Economy of Art.* Other volumes by Ruskin, whom Holmes admired all his life, followed.

Records of the Holmes family's borrowings from the Athenaeum library indicate that during Wendell's undergraduate years books on the history and interpretation of art were taken out with approximately the same frequency as books on philosophy. Vasari's *Lives of the Painters,* Northcote's *Life of Titian,* Morgan's *Life of Salvatore Rosa,* Ruskin's *Stones of Venice,* Joseph Crowe's *Early Flemish Painters,* and T. Bosworth's *Poetry of Christian Art* carried him away from the sterile environment in which he was constrained to live and work.

The first fruit of his reading in aesthetics, "Notes on Albert Durer [sic]," appeared in the *Harvard Magazine* in October 1860, the same month his essay on Plato appeared in the *University Quarterly.* Following a detailed technical description of how engraving was done, Holmes soared into a philosophic discussion of Dürer's art derivative of the Emersonian and Platonic thought in which he had recently been immersed.

Upon reading "Notes on Albert Durer," William A. Holbrook, also a member of the class of 1861 and afterwards an Episcopal clergyman, submitted his reactions to Holmes's essay to the *Harvard Magazine,* of which Holmes was then an editor. Holbrook's article appeared in the issue of December 1860, without editorial comment. Holbrook accused Holmes of imitating Emerson and described his efforts to connect art and philosophy as "unscholarly" and "feeble" as well as blasphemous.

> Go on, if you will [Holbrook wrote], and talk about the "Eternal Truth," the "Absolute Virtue," the "ideal Good," "Objective and Essential Beauty,"— I do not comprehend you, nor can one practical mind in a thousand comprehend you. I prefer to take a humbler position with the humble learned and unlearned millions of the world, who still sit at the feet of the divine Nazarene, who taught not about the Absolute and the Infinite, but about doing His "Father's will, and finishing His work."

Whether Holmes was annoyed by his classmate's comments, amused, or perhaps even pleased to have offended Holbrook's pietistic sensitivities is not known.

He surely would have been pleased when nearly a century later, in December 1949, Wolfgang Stechow, critic and art historian, described Holmes's essay on Dürer as a "magnificent . . . piece of precocious writing" and in comparing Holmes with Ruskin on the same artist, Stechow declared the latter's comments "sound hazy and ephemeral when compared with Holmes's sure and methodical approach, his conciseness, deep understanding and modest restraint."

Life at Harvard College between 1857 and 1861 was not, of course, comprised of one intellectual and moral crisis after the other. For every editorial board meeting of the *Harvard Magazine,* for every hour spent gazing out the window while Professor Bowen or Professor Lovering droned on, for every hour spent in study, independent or prescribed, Wendell Holmes appears to have spent a corresponding number of hours satisfying the convivial side of his nature in the college social clubs where young men practiced for their future lives as Boston clubmen. At Harvard, the clubs men belonged to defined them as certainly as class standings did. Like his father before him Wendell belonged to the most prestigious: Hasty Pudding, founded in 1795 by members of the junior class who wanted to supplement the scanty fare in commons—Holmes was elected secretary in his junior year; Porcellian, older than Hasty Pudding by four years, established by a group of undergraduates who regularly dined on roast pig—to both of these Dr. Holmes also had been elected as a student, and for both of them he had written poems and songs; the Institute of 1770, originally a military organization; and Alpha Delta Phi (called the A.D. Club in 1861), which, unlike the others, kept up a fiction of serious literary interests. During Wendell Holmes's years, members frequently met in his room at Mr. Danforth's and listened to each other's essays "before the business of the bottle began."

Among other exhibitions of tomfoolery during Wendell's college years, Hasty Pudding, whose original commitment to sacred songs had diminished over the years, sponsored several variety shows each term. As juniors the class of 1861 staged two burlesques, *The Lady of the Lions* and *Raising the Wind,* in which Wendell played small parts. As seniors the same class outdid itself with a burlesque of *Othello* featuring "New Scenery! Novel Effects! Restoration of the Original Text!!!" Holmes played Ludovico. The following spring, despite the coming of war, '61 put on three more extravaganzas. Holmes, however, missed these; he and other members of the class already had left for guard duty at Fort Independence.

When in the spring of 1861 he joined the Fourth Battalion of Infantry and was shipped to Fort Independence in Boston Harbor, Wendell Holmes's four-year association with Harvard College as an undergraduate came to an end, as did the crucial postadolescent years. The questing and questioning, the intellectual adventures into art and philosophy, were over temporarily. The wide-roving mind would have to be submerged for a time while other facets of his nature rose to the surface, even dominated.

Whatever alienation from the rigidities of Harvard he had felt at the time he endured it, he remained intensely loyal to the institution. He was "Harvard to the bone." He soon suppressed his memories of individual faculty members, the uninspiring recitations, the silly grading system. The Harvard he remembered later in his life gave off an "aroma of high feeling, not to be lost on science or Greek," and "helped men of lofty natures to make good their faculties." The Harvard he remembered later was the "invisible Harvard" of his friend William James, an institution that existed "in the souls of her more truth-seeking and independent and often very solitary sons."

As a young lawyer, he served as an Overseer and spoke at commencements. Even into his old age, he went to reunions and sang the old songs at Alpha Delta Phi. Shortly after his resignation from the United States Supreme Court in 1932, seventy-one years after graduation from Harvard, the ninety-one-year-old Holmes exhibited an unaccustomed impatience to leave Washington for his summer place at Bev-

erly Farms north of Boston. He wanted, he at last explained, to lunch
with the Porcellians on Commencement day.

On the way home from the festivities, he was in a nostalgic mood,
pointing out to his secretary the houses where friends had lived, finally
reminiscing about his own and another Massachusetts Civil War regiment. He sat musing for a moment, then suggested that "the feeling
between those two regiments was quite a lot like the feeling between
Harvard and Yale."

"Don't you think," the secretary asked, "we all have that feeling
about things we've grown up with?"

Holmes sat bolt upright. His eyes flashed. "Why, Sonny," he said,
"you don't mean to say they feel that way at Yale."

ON THE SURFACE, the students' high spirits seemed during
Wendell Holmes's years at Harvard to reach the usual altitude. Yet a
pall hung over the Hasty Pudding rehearsals and the skating parties at
Fresh Pond. Every day the newspapers brought word of the deepening
chasm between North and South; every day their differences became
more and more irreconcilable. In the back of every young man's mind
lurked the question of where and when the national interest would
overtake his personal life.

At first the gathering storm did not interfere with the camaraderie
between North and South in the Harvard houses. Then, as the threat
of war intensified, Southern students began to leave for home.

Among the faculty, opinion was divided. Asa Gray was outspokenly
abolitionist. The late Reverend Henry Ware, former Overseer and professor at the Divinity School, had founded an antislavery society at the
university, for which the local press, allied with the bankers and merchants, had slapped his wrists; he had impaired, the editors said, his
professional usefulness and damaged the institution. Louis Agassiz's public
remarks on the inferiority of the black approached proslavery arguments
and were interpreted as a defense of it, especially in the South. Enthusiasm within official Harvard for the Union cause may be measured in
part by the fact that one member of the faculty, George A. Schmitt, a
German immigrant who had been Wendell Holmes's German instructor,
was its only contribution to the Union forces when war finally came.

Outside the Yard, Brahmin Boston's willingness to look the other
way when its Puritan conscience clashed with its economic self-interest—an economic self-interest not unlike that which, in living memory,
had raised the same group's opposition to the War of 1812—grew in

intensity approximately in proportion to the growth of sentiment for abolition. Households divided; brother cut brother dead in the street. Formerly popular writers found their books boycotted, and mobs gathered whenever William Lloyd Garrison or Wendell Phillips was scheduled to speak. The churches and lecture halls of Boston proper were closed to Mr. Emerson, and he had to take his outrage at slavery to the Concord green.

By the time Wendell entered his last term at Harvard, nearly all the Southern students had left, abolitionist John A. Andrew, who had defended John Brown in the Virginia courts, had been elected governor of Massachusetts, Abraham Lincoln had been elected president of the United States, and South Carolina had seceded from the Union, the last-named event prompting Dr. Holmes to memorialize it with the poem "Brother Jonathan's Lament for Sister Caroline"; it was a sincere expression of grief, and the doctor did not allude to the practices that had brought about Sister Caroline's alienation.

By this time Wendell was a "pretty convinced Abolitionist" and believed in the cause "devoutly." Any number of factors may have been responsible: the tragedies of the fugitive slaves he had witnessed as a boy; Mrs. Stowe's novel; the emotional oratory of Theodore Parker and Wendell Phillips, along with the appeals Mr. Emerson was making to the intellect and the sense of morality he was so sure resided in his audiences; the "belittling of a suffering race" in a black minstrel show he had seen in recent years; the fact that his best friend at Harvard, Pen Hallowell, embraced the cause, and Pen's older brother, Richard, a local merchant, was a member of a small group which acted informally as bodyguards against the mobs that at times harassed Wendell Phillips when he spoke in public. Rejecting the conservatism of his father and asserting his independence of the local ruling class, Wendell became an abolitionist.

He supported his conviction with a fifty-cent contribution to William Lloyd Garrison's *Liberator* on the twenty-seventh anniversary of the National Anti-Slavery Society, and he joined Richard Hallowell's little platoon of bodyguards when Wendell Phillips was scheduled to speak in an unusually hostile climate at Tremont Temple. Nearly seventy years later, he summed up in a single sentence the difficult choices he had had to make in connection with the controversy that was tearing Boston apart in his late youth: "I am glad I was and did."

But his experiences among the abolitionists "gave [him] a lasting disgust for come outers," who were "so cocksure on the strength of semi-education. They may be one of the disagreeable necessities of progress." He came in time to be suspicious and skeptical of all reformers, who he believed saw themselves as little gods who knew what was best for others, and in retaliation he founded an imaginary Society of Jobbists, "who were free to be egotists or altruists as their heart dictated on Sunday afternoons but who didn't bother about either while they were on their task." He often reproached himself "for not loving [his] fellowmen in general enough," but consoled himself "by thinking that if one does one's job as well as one can one achieves practical altruism and it doesn't matter so much how one feels about it. . . ."

Following Sister Caroline's departure from the Union in December 1860, agitation for secession among the planters and merchants in the South increased appreciably. Alabama, Florida, and Georgia followed in short order; Louisiana and Texas went next. In February 1861, delegates from the errant sisters met in Montgomery, Alabama, to organize the Confederate States of America. Compromise was tried but it was too late; minds had been made up. North and South were headed irretrievably on a collision course. Abraham Lincoln's inaugural on March 4, 1861, seemed to some observers more like a funeral.

The Confederates immediately began to seize the federal installations within what they considered their jurisdiction—by April they had taken over all except Fort Pickens in Virginia and Fort Sumter in South Carolina. The Confederacy's president, Jefferson Davis, demanded Sumter's surrender, but the Union's president decided to make his stand there and stood fast, dispatching food and supplies to the beleaguered fort, which was surrounded by Confederate cannon. On April 12, at 4:30 A.M., the Confederates fired on Sumter, and the Civil War began. Within hours, a little band of Southern marksmen had galvanized a badly splintered North into a fighting frame of mind, a feat years of political oratory had been unable to accomplish. The peace-loving, quiet, scholarly representative on earth of the Over-Soul, Ralph Waldo Emerson, spoke for a lot of people when he said calmly that "sometimes gunpowder smells good"; and even Dr. Holmes rejoiced in the new "sense of national life and unity throughout the free states . . . the most exulting, joyous triumphant feeling that our nation has ever known. . . . We have lived more true life in the last month than in all the years that have gone before it. There is absolute fusion of all parties, a complete unity of purpose throughout the whole north."

On April 17, Lincoln called for 75,000 volunteers. He could have doubled, tripled the figure, so enthusiastic was the response. Troops from Maine and New Hampshire as well as Massachusetts marched through the streets of Boston. On that very day, four Massachusetts regiments left for Washington, D.C., only to be attacked by the local citizenry as they marched between railroad stations in Baltimore. The usually conservative bank managers of Boston met and voted to lend 10 percent of their aggregate capital to the state treasury, a sum of about $4 million, and the Thursday Club met and voted to outfit a Massachusetts regiment with knapsacks.

Wendell Holmes already had abandoned Professor Bowen's recitation room and, along with Pen Hallowell, with whom he was to go through much of the war, had enlisted as a private in the Fourth Massachusetts Battalion of Infantry.

He never fully revealed his motives for doing it; undoubtedly, they were mixed. To a youth of twenty, even one as bookish as Wendell Holmes, Boston in the spring and summer of 1861 must have made enlistment in the military well nigh irresistible. Suddenly the city was aglow in torchlight parades, flag-waving, and war fever. Business was suspended, the streets filled with people, and troops were moving into town. Faneuil Hall was opened to receive them. Crowds cheered them as they marched from the railroad station. Bostonians hung out upper-story windows in the rain to wave flags and handkerchiefs. Troops had the right-of-way, and the horsecars stopped to let them pass. The crowds followed, surging alongside the columns and on into the hall. Military companies were organized in the schools, and boys compelled to drill. Cheers met every patriotic allusion at the theater. The war dominated discourse—in the streets, at the Adirondack Club, in the Harvard Chapel—and even the great Emerson was talking of the "whirlwind of patriotism." A quarter century later when he had had time to digest this period of his past, Holmes explained that "as life is action and passion, it is required of a man that he should share the passion and action of his time at peril of being judged not to have lived." That he considered slavery an intolerable evil and thought of the war as the "Christian crusade" of the century undoubtedly contributed to his decision to enlist. And there were other possible factors.

At Wendell's age, a young man's confidence in his own strength knows no limits—the only question is whether he will have the courage to use it—and he is too young to have contracted a fear of death. He craves adventure, requires tests of his manhood, and war reveals life at its most intense, represents the ultimate test. The literature of the day is rife with references to the "manly" course to follow, and Wendell Holmes's correspondence from the front—and even some of his later writings—is rife with references to the aristocrat's code of "manly" behavior, "duty," and "honor."

Youth also craves freedom, and the army provided obvious escape for a young man of twenty: escape from family, from the gubernatorial ministrations of Dr. Holmes, which had begun perhaps to seem oppressive on occasion, and escape from the still waters of academic life into the eddies of action.

Much later, after fifty years of intimate involvement in constitutional government as a judge, Holmes commented casually to one of his secretaries that he had joined the Union army in order to preserve "this unique government which his forefathers had created."

On April 25, 1861, he reported, with 123 others with whom he was to go through much of the war, to the Boylston Armory. From there they were marched in fatigues to Liverpool Wharf, where the *Nantasket* waited to take them to Fort Independence for guard duty and military training while Harvard authorities stewed about what to do with the delinquents.* The fort, which stood not far out in Boston Harbor, had long lacked a garrison; only one soldier, a sergeant, had been stationed there. Within a day or so, thirty more men followed, bringing the total force to over 150.

A mildly rigorous routine of drill, dress parade, and guard duty interspersed with training in the use of weapons and interrupted by visits from friends consumed Wendell's days for a month. Then on May 25, the Fourth Battalion, jaunty in new uniforms, was returned aboard the *Nellie Baker* to the Long Wharf, paraded again through the streets of Boston, reviewed on the Common, and disbanded at Boylston Armory where it had formed, the young men's dreams of glory dashed.

When he joined the Fourth Battalion, Wendell had expected to be sent south. Disappointed when the unit broke up, he applied to Cousin Henry Lee, aide to Governor Andrew, for a commission as lieutenant in the Twentieth Massachusetts Infantry. At the time, Lee told Wendell later, he could feel only "pity for your youth and delicacy" as they discussed the matter during a stroll across Harvard Yard.

But first there was time to return to Harvard to attend to the last rites of graduation.

Of those young men who had left Harvard to join the military that spring, Wendell Holmes was the only one who had failed to ask permission of the college authorities. Assuming he would be sent south, the

---

* By May, sixteen undergraduates had left Harvard for military service—ten to fight for the Confederacy, six to fight for the Union.

young man also assumed his enlistment ended his connection with the institution. He had been demobilized, however, before Commencement festivities began.

On June 10, the Harvard faculty voted to inform him he must return to college and pass the usual examinations if he wanted his degree. At the same meeting, the faculty voted to divide the annual prize for excellence in Greek prose composition between Holmes and John H. Dillingham of the junior class. Forfeiture of points because of class absences during his month with the army, however, cost Wendell his rank in the upper half of the senior class and deprived him of a part in the graduation exercises, punishments Dr. Holmes believed were both unexpected and unwarranted, and said so in a long letter to President Felton.

He wanted the president to understand, he said, that he had not heard a "word of complaint" from Wendell. The young man had left Harvard "suddenly, no doubt, but if he did not stop to kiss his Alma Mater, neither did many other volunteers stop to kiss their mothers and wives and sweethearts." The doctor believed his son had been treated unfairly by the university, that his patriotism had been penalized rather than rewarded.

> For his promptitude in offering his services [Dr. Holmes wrote] at the very close of his college life he is not only deprived of the honors which I know you personally wished him to obtain, as one who would not discredit the College, but is consigned to the inglorious half of the Class, standing forever on the College record as one not worthy to be named among those who had achieved a decent mediocrity.

President Felton patiently reiterated the university's position. Had Wendell troubled to make up the work he had missed, he undoubtedly would have been returned to his former rank in the class. "To enter on our scale a fictitious estimate," however, declared Felton, "would vitiate it entirely. More than that, it would work an injustice to those who stay and do all their duty as students." Wendell Holmes and his father would have to be satisfied with the degree alone.

The younger Holmes was permitted, however, to retain his position as official class poet, and to perform at the Class Day exercises. He had written in his sophomore year a sentimental ballad called "Alma Mater" to be read at the class supper. It was published in the *Harvard Magazine* in October 1860, the issue in which the somewhat more sophisticated

"Notes on Albert Durer" appeared. At the senior class meeting in March 1861, Wendell was elected class poet, the office to which his father had been elected by the class of 1829.

Between drills and dress parades that month at Fort Independence, he "patch[ed] up a Class Poem as quickly and as well as [he] could under the circumstances" and delivered it on Class Day "side by side with [his] friend Hallowell who was orator."

The Class Day program was held on June 21 in the First Church, Cambridge, where Grandfather Holmes had preached until his congregation evicted him. No complete copy of Wendell's poem survives, but according to an encapsulated version that appeared in the *Cambridge Chronicle,* he urged his classmates to

Be brave, for now the thunder rolls.

The *Boston Evening Transcript* described it as "excellent" and worthy of the applause it received. It was, however, one of the author's less original efforts, comparing as it did, according to the *New York Tribune,* the "student leaving college to a steamer leaving port." Both the exercises and the poem ranked considerably below the "spread" to which Dr. Holmes treated guests that afternoon, as was the custom on Class Day: "His ice cream," declared the reporter for the *Tribune,* "was like the Pyramids of Egypt, his wine like the overflowing of the Nile, his presence as joyous as Apollo. The very lobsters that did furnish his salads came voluntarily to the cooks, and said, 'Sacrifice us to the gods! A Poet and the son of a Poet. . . .' "

With the traditional smashing of hats into fragments at the end of the festivities, Wendell Holmes's affiliation with Harvard College as an undergraduate officially ended (Commencement on June 17 had preceded Class Day).

FOR A LOT of young Americans, including Wendell Holmes, the summer of 1861 was time suspended. The war progressed sluggishly. Following the shock of Fort Sumter, both sides, like street fighters, after the first impulsive jabs at each other, seemed to pull back, partly to prepare for the attack, and partly to reconsider the enormity of what they had started, substituting halfhearted and face-saving feints for real assaults. And the nation, like the crowds that gather to cheer the fighters on, shouted in frustration for blood. There was more fire in a Boston torchlight parade than there was on the battlefield.

Still, careers, marriages, personal plans were postponed, and the waiting began. While Lincoln waited in the White House for his generals to move, Wendell Holmes waited at home in Charles Street for a place in one of the new Massachusetts regiments then forming. Dr. Holmes was spotted waiting in the lobby of the Parker House to talk with a regimental commander about his son and at the State House waiting to talk with the governor. Longfellow's wife died, and the war receded temporarily.

Wendell finished writing his autobiography for the Class Album in which he announced his intention to "study law" if he lived. It was a brief, skeletal statement; he did not believe "in gushing much in these College Biog's and think a dry statement fitter." He checked John Austin's *Lectures on Jurisprudence* out of the Harvard Library and submerged his impatience in one of the early authors to apply scientific analytical methods to the law as well as to separate law from morality and theology. Austin had been "the only philosophy within reach" at the time, a felicitous accident. He appealed to Wendell Holmes; he made the law sound so logical.

The doctor and his son had a discussion about death and dying for nonbelievers, the doctor arguing that "death bed repentances generally meant only that the man was scared." Wendell, the doctor suggested, was ineligible; the young man could not so easily mask his unbelief.

Dr. Holmes went out to Readville, where Colonel William Raymond Lee (no relation to Henry Lee, the governor's aide and the doctor's cousin) was assembling the Massachusetts Twentieth Volunteer Infantry, and presented the regimental commander with a letter from his influential cousin indicating the governor had approved a commission for Wendell. The matter was settled then and there. The commission came through in late July, days after the abortive Battle of Bull Run.

Wendell was on his way home from the Athenaeum library with Thomas Hobbes's *Leviathan* under his arm. A friend tapped him on the shoulder and told him he had gotten his commission. The book went back unread to the library. First Lieutenant Wendell Holmes was ordered to report almost immediately to the Twentieth's camp, where he was mustered into a strange and uncertain world.

Life as he had known it for two decades was about to change abruptly. The rules as he had known them at home, at Mr. Sullivan's, at Mr. Dixwell's, and at Harvard, changed. He had no real sense of what lay ahead. He was proud, pleased, and inevitably not a little frightened. But it was the pride that emerged in the letter he wrote almost immediately to Mrs. Dixwell, his "almost second mother":

> I have received a First Lieutenancy in Lee's reg. and expect to go into camp in a day or two—The Rg.t will be a stunner—Hayes is my Captain & C. Whittier of '60 (Harvard) my 2nd Lieut. . . .

Part *IV*

SOLDIER

This day is call'd the feast of Crispian:
He that outlives this day, and comes safe home,
Will stand a tip-toe when this day is nam'd,
And rouse him at the name of Crispian.
He that shall live this day, and see old age,
Will yearly on the vigil feast his neighbors,
And say, Tomorrow is Saint Crispian:
Then will he strip his sleeve and show his scars
And say, These wounds I had on Crispin's day.
Old men forget; yet all shall be forgot,
But he'll remember with advantages
What feats he did that day: then shall our names
Familiar in their mouths as household words,—
Harry the king, Bedford and Exeter,
Warwick and Talbot, Salisbury and Gloster,—
Be in their flowing cups freshly remembered.
This story shall the good man teach his son;
And Crispin Crispian shall ne'er go by,
From this day to the ending of the world,
But we in it shall be remembered,—
We few, we happy few, we band of brothers;
For he to-day that sheds his blood with me

Shall be my brother; be he ne'er so vile,
This day shall gentle his condition:
And gentlemen in England now a-bed
Shall think themselves accurs'd they were not here,
And hold their manhoods cheap while any speaks
That fought with us upon Saint Crispin's day.

—Shakespeare, *King Henry V*, act 4, scene 3

CHAPTER *5*

Ball's Bluff

IN MIDSUMMER 1861, Wendell Holmes was a personable young man, described by his mother as "a very noisy boy," confident though not a swashbuckler, longing for adventure and heroic deeds which thus far he had encountered only in books. Oliver, Wendell, Holmes, and Jackson genes had combined to turn out a handsome product more than six feet tall with well-formed features, thinner but otherwise not unlike his famous father's. He was still clean-shaven, and except for the differences in age, bulk, and height—Dr. Holmes was fifty-two years old and only five feet three inches tall—they might almost have been mistaken for each other.

Although he carried the Boston into which he had been born to the grave, the years between 1861 and 1864 comprised the last great adventure Oliver Wendell Holmes, Jr., would share wholeheartedly with his fellow Bostonians. The harsh lessons learned during these years combined afterward with the restlessness of his outward-bound intellect to separate him from the mainstream of the Brahmin life he had been prepared for. The process was slow, to be sure, but it was nonetheless steady, continuous, serious, and sure.

To describe the next three years as quick-maturing is understatement. It was as if a high-voltage electric current were run through him, skewing all the carefully arranged perspectives and dismantling the equally carefully built structure of his comfortable existence. As Fanny Dixwell, who had known him before and married him after, put it, had it not been for the Civil War, Wendell would have been a "coxcomb."

Between the summers of 1861 and 1864, Wendell Holmes was either suffering the dangers and discomforts of the battlefield or recovering from wounds. He fought with the Army of the Potomac in most of the major campaigns in and around Virginia and Maryland except Gettysburg and was wounded three times, once almost mortally. In these three years he saw more of life—and death—than most people have seen at seventy. Terror stalked him daily without pity. Helplessly he watched as friends died at his side. He marched under incompetent, stupid, and drunken officers whose irresponsibility jeopardized the lives of their men. He endured vermin, disease, mud, hunger, thirst, and a fatigue he never before had known. It was only long years afterward and in rosy retrospect that he could recall the experience of war as "our great good fortune" and describe war's message as "divine."

Those of his letters home that survive* reflect an intense need to communicate to those closest to him all he was enduring as it happened. His war had few heroes. He made no pretensions to heroism himself, and there is nothing particularly heroic about his letters. He recorded the weather, the mud and dirt, the incompetence of his superiors, the anxieties of the moment, the movements of troops, and the trouble with his bowels. The horrors he related undramatically, the violence he understated. Although he was always an internal man, he had little time in these days for reflection, and his letters home contain very little of it. With certain exceptions toward the end, most of his letters are in a low key, limited to descriptive narrative.

He needed mother and father, brother and sister back in Boston to know, as Dr. Holmes gave his little impromptu violin recitals in the parlor in the evenings, that he was attentive to his duty, that he was a good soldier and would not disgrace the name of Holmes; the family had contributed soldiers to American causes from nearly every generation since its arrival in the New World. Perhaps most of all, he needed to reassure himself, as he slogged through the mud of southern Virginia and dodged the enemy's bullets at Antietam, that his family still existed, that the little world he remembered remained intact, warm and waiting for him. Writing to its inhabitants may have helped to confirm that world's continued existence.

For all their dry detail, Wendell's letters from the front reveal an

---

* Touched with Fire: Civil War Letters and Diary of Oliver Wendell Holmes, Jr., 1861–1864, edited by Mark DeWolfe Howe, was published in 1946 by Harvard University Press. While sizable, the collection is not complete. Apparently Holmes, with the assistance of his mother—notations on some envelopes are in Mrs. Holmes's hand—weeded out and probably destroyed a number of letters Holmes did not want others to see. A few remain in his Civil War scrapbook, which he put together in December 1864, following his return home; attached is the notation: "The enclosed letters to be burned at my death without fail."

affectionate side of him that a later reticence often suppressed. Living at last outside of Dr. Holmes's shadow had its advantages, but a young man, after all, needed to know that the love of his family continued, that the ties had not been irrevocably cut.

The early weeks of Holmes's life in the military were not so difficult as the later ones, however. The early weeks seemed more like summer camp. His regiment—the Massachusetts Twentieth Volunteer Infantry, one of the three-year enlistment units—had formed in the summer of 1861 at Camp Massasoit, a hurriedly assembled training center on a broad plain at Readville, about eight miles from Boston. It was under the command of Colonel William Raymond Lee, a classmate of Jefferson Davis at West Point, afterward a civil engineer in Roxbury, Massachusetts. His gray mustache, shaped like a shoe brush, and his close-shaved gray beard gave him the military bearing his slight figure—five feet six inches—and thinning gray hair might have concealed. His officers remembered him as pleasant-mannered and gentlemanly despite his extraordinary pluck and determination. Others in the regiment may have surpassed Lee in their knowledge of military tactics, but, Holmes said later, Lee gave the regiment its "soul." He "was the example of careless, generous gallantry. His 'Forward Twentieth' stirred us more than trumpets." His immediate challenge in the summer of 1861 was to train city boys for country living, habitual individualists for collective life, patricians for deprivation and frustration, and to mold young men into efficient killing machines.

The roster of officers, who took their commissions as their natural right, just as under normal circumstances they ultimately would have assumed the bank presidencies, judgeships, high political nominations, and leadership of the local community, read like a Boston social register: Palfrey, Revere (grandsons of the midnight rider, one killed at Antietam in 1862, the other at Gettysburg a year later), Curtis, Putnam (killed at Ball's Bluff, 1861), Abbott (killed in the Wilderness, 1864), Crowninshield, Holmes, Cabot (killed at Fredericksburg, 1863), Whittier. Englishmen off to Agincourt, Scots off to Bannockburn, Hectors all, characters in the American epic.

Although the Massachusetts Twentieth included men from all sections of the commonwealth, it was known as the "Harvard" regiment, and Lieutenant Colonel Francis Winthrop Palfrey, son of the New England historian John G. Palfrey and second in command of the Twentieth, was warned by a general officer that "the sooner you get this blueblood notion out of your head the better, for yourself and the regiment."

In his letters home, Holmes described his camaraderie with the same men he would have met in his Boston club, on State Street, at the courthouse.

Under normal circumstances, these young men were well-mannered, cheerful, and dependable; they were pleasant-looking, partly because life had done nothing to make them unpleasant-looking, partly through inheritance from ancestors to whom life also had done relatively little to make them unpleasant-looking. Their faces were unpinched by poverty, their bodies unstiffened by hard labor. Their beards had barely begun to darken, and the only shots they ever had fired had been aimed at squirrels and rabbits.

They were not at all prepared for the ordeal into which they were marching, for the fear and exhaustion and, yes, even boredom; for an enemy who was just as dedicated and was going to shoot back. Survivors of the Revolution, who could have told them something about blood-stained blankets, were rare in 1861. The modern realistic literature of war had not yet been written; Tolstoy was only thirty-three, Erich Maria Remarque, Stephen Crane, and Ernest Hemingway had not yet been born. These young adventurers of 1861 had been schooled on the sentimental novels of Sir Walter Scott in which honor and glory, not pain and fear, had dominated.

Although the Harvard men functioned socially as a little community within the regiment, their common background and experiences drawing them together, their motives for joining the Union forces varied, reflecting the national confusion that marked the general war effort. Pen Hallowell, who signed his letters "Thine, N. P. Hallowell," and whose Quaker family hid fugitive slaves in their Philadelphia barn, had allowed his loathing for slavery to overrule his doctrinal pacifism. When Philadelphia Friends later criticized him for his military service, Hallowell replied, "I told them that I only obeyed George Fox, who said, 'Mind the Inner light.' " More than half a century later, Holmes described his friend as a "savage abolitionist, a fighting Quaker who blushed at his own militancy, intolerant of criticism or opposition, but the most generously gallant spirit and I don't know but the greatest soul I ever knew."

Others of the Twentieth, like President Lincoln himself, fought to preserve the Union whole. Still others undoubtedly were afflicted with the war fever that was epidemic in Boston during the early days of the war and the president's subsequent—and timely—call for volunteers. A craving for novelty and adventure, the chance to prove themselves physically, to demonstrate their manliness, no doubt attracted some.

Several of Wendell Holmes's friends among the officers of the regiment nurtured strong doubts about the Union cause—W. F. Bartlett, Charles A. "Whit" Whittier. Henry L. "Little" Abbott, whose devil-may-care courage Holmes particularly admired, was an outspoken copperhead; he distrusted Lincoln and denounced military strategy. But they all shared their mess with and risked their lives alongside the fire-eating abolitionists like Pen Hallowell to whom Wendell also remained close. Shared backgrounds counted for more than politics.

The war demands of the military for materials and the government's extravagance in issuing contracts stimulated industrial America to record-breaking production, and while Wendell Holmes marched with the Massachusetts Twentieth into one kind of adventure, other youths, whom Holmes would later come to admire, satisfied their cravings elsewhere. Future industrial and financial moguls, whose machinations and manipulations would require Holmes's attention a half century later when he sat on the United States Supreme Court, were hiring substitutes for army service and were facing the early challenges of their careers as empire builders. J. Pierpont Morgan, only four years older than Holmes, was testing his financial reflexes in his father's New York City banking firm. James J. Hill, three years Holmes's senior, kept out of the war by an old eye injury, was exploring the bottom floor of the transportation field as a clerk for a Mississippi steamboat line. Jim Fisk, seven years Holmes's senior, was measuring his own commercial instincts by managing war contracts for Boston's Jordan Marsh and Company. Andrew Carnegie, a young man of twenty-seven, after a brief time in the War Department's military transportation section, was investigating management techniques as a member of the inner circle of the Pennsylvania Railroad. Theirs was no three-year enlistment, but a lifetime commitment to adventure in the new business and industry that would excite postwar America, and the more contemplative Holmes would come in time to admire these master builders enormously, at the same time that he despised the materialism they had sponsored.

LIFE IN THE new tent city of Camp Massasoit was not much more strenuous or even more serious than it had been back in May at Fort Independence. The gentle grass-covered slope was bordered on two sides by stately stands of old Massachusetts elms. Drills, inspections, and guard duty were punctuated with swimming in the nearby Neponsit River, visits from family and friends, and, until Major Revere put a stop to it, sociable glasses of beer at Klemm's in Mill Village. Less than a month after arriving, Holmes had his first bout with diarrhea, which was to land him in regimental hospitals periodically throughout the war. On August 30, the ladies of Boston, as was their custom for Massachusetts regiments, presented the Twentieth with a silk standard—a state flag with the coat-of-arms of the commonwealth on one side and the motto *Fide et constantia* on the other. And so the summer passed, the pleasant young men who made up the Massachusetts Twentieth being gently molded into a united fighting unit, alert and skilled in the arts of war, their former identities submerged as far as possible in the group persona.

The regiment had been put together hurriedly out of volunteers with little or no familiarity with the military. The rule generally followed was, the higher the officer, who often was a political appointment, the less his knowledge of the military. The captain knew less than the lieutenant, and the general knew least of all. Stories of blunders were rife among the men—of officers marching soldiers up a high wall before they could remember the order to stop. One of Holmes's fellow officers swore that when first he faced his company he saw the sergeant smile. He compared the "anxious moment" to the time he was first called on to recite in a college class. The feeling soon wore off, however, and after giving "two or three wrong orders," he "got on quite well."

Still, intimations of events less pleasant intruded in the warm summer air. The old smooth-bore rifles were abandoned for more modern Enfield rifles bought in England. The typical soldier's unspoken fear, not of death, but of the possibility that he might lack the courage to face it, that he might disgrace his name, that he might, after all, die a coward, plagued young Holmes, and he later confessed that he had consoled himself with the "reflection that armies were made up of average people, and that no more would be demanded of him than the general run of people could accomplish." And he began to wonder, too, as he sat at the long mess table in the camp at Readville, "how many of those who gathered in our tent could hope to see the end of what was then beginning."

At last, on September 2, the regiment received the orders for which it had been practicing: to proceed to Washington, D.C., and, ultimately, the front. April's patriotism had palled, and despite summerlong efforts at recruiting, the regiment remained at only about two-thirds of its capacity.

On September 4, the Massachusetts Twentieth—forty-one officers and 750 men (a full regiment was a thousand men)—boarded a train for Groton, Connecticut, where it transferred to a New York–bound steamboat. In New York, the Sons of Massachusetts stood the men to a dinner at the Park Barracks; Governor Andrew himself turned up for a last hurrah; some of the officers, however, including Holmes, preferred the fare and privacy of Delmonico's. Philadelphia treated the soldiers to breakfast at the old Cooper Shop. Baltimore, where previously Union regiments had been attacked by mobs, let the Twentieth pass through peaceably; women waved handkerchiefs and children cheered for the Union, although most of the men remained silent and inscrutable. And at last, on September 7, fifty-seven hours from Camp Massasoit, the regiment arrived in the nation's capital, where camps had been set up to receive the troops marching in from whatever states were left in the Union.

Later that day, the Massachusetts men marched down Pennsylvania Avenue, passing in review before Lieutenant General Winfield Scott, revered hero of the Mexican War but now too old and fat to command the Union armies then bedded down at Camp Kalorama on Georgetown Heights, about two miles from the center of the city. Later in the week, the regiment moved to Camp Burnside on Meridien Hill, overlooking the central city and the unfinished Capitol.

The passage, Holmes wrote his mother, had been "very long and there was little sleep or food." He had, however, "rather enjoyed it," even though a wagon wheel had smashed his trunk, and his brandy flask had been "pulverized."

Despite heat, dust, and confusion, army life was still more exhilarating than it was depressing. Holmes wrote home cheerfully from Camp Burnside, his sense of growing excitement evident: "We are right in the midst of the work now—all sorts of camps around us—military discipline—and a regular soldier's life." The officers at least were able to buy milk, eggs, fruit pies, and even a little meat now and again. In general, he said, they were having "a very comfortable time," he was feeling *very* well and in *very* good spirits."

Most of Holmes's early letters home from the front were dry and matter of fact, less expressive of his feelings beyond an occasional restlessness during a period of inactivity or a disappointment at an objective unrealized. They were also practically humorless. Hardly ever does the soldier's grim humor, the kind Bill Mauldin popularized nearly a century later, come from Holmes's pen.

On September 12, the day after Holmes wrote his mother, the regiment was ordered to break camp and proceed northward toward Poolesville, Maryland, thirty-five miles away. There it was to join General Charles P. Stone and his Corps of Observation assigned to watch Confederate movements along and across the Potomac River in the vicinity of Leesburg, Virginia.

Stone liked to boast that he was the first man in America to defend the Union against the Seceshers—he had been given the responsibility for maintaining law and order during Lincoln's inauguration. He was a strict disciplinarian and had been known to inspect the camps at all hours of the day and night. But when the time for battle came, he lacked the leadership qualities required. His preparations were meager and his knowledge of events in the field appallingly inadequate.

After three days of fording streams and climbing steep hills, the Massachusetts soldiers reached Poolesville, Maryland, their destination (September 14), where they settled down for five weeks of further training.

Here military life began somewhat more seriously; company drills every morning, battalion drill and dress parade every afternoon, with occasional reviews and brigade drills, and regular Sunday morning inspections. Every other night two companies were assigned outpost duty at the river along with other troops of the brigade. Skirmishing drill was begun and a school was opened for noncommissioned officers in tactics, bayonet exercises, and discipline. Daily drilling in platoon firing from noon to two o'clock began—many of the men, it had been discovered, shut their eyes when they pulled the trigger. Ambulance drills and first aid training completed the routine, all of which could only serve to key the men up, and they began to ache for a fight.

Still, it was not just drill, drill, drill. Maryland was not Massachusetts with its familiar boulder-strewn lunarlike hills and crisp cool September air. But it had a beauty of its own. The weather was cooler than Washington's had been, a welcome autumn breeze after the dust and heat of the march from the capital. The scenery was fine: low hills rolling into the Blue Ridge sixty or seventy miles away to the west. The campsite was so high that little dew fell at night and for once the blankets were not soaked by morning. There were cribbage and euchre, letter writing, and sociability in the evening, and, like pickets before and after, those of the Massachusetts Twentieth fraternized with their enemies across the river, trading tobacco, newspapers, conversation, and, occasionally, shots. Officers were treated to hearty meals at a neighboring farmhouse by a Confederate sympathizer who bartered her food for the Union's protection of her property. They could see men and horses across the river, even hear the Confederate drums, and one night they slept in their boots and kept their horses saddled, just in case, but mostly, Holmes said, "we sit & look & listen to their drums."

On October 7, Colonel Lee reported to Dr. Holmes on his son and other young men in the regiment: "They have been tried under all circumstances of duty, acquiring fortitude, patience, and cheerful submission to privation; their physical ability has been put to a severe test. You will be pleased to hear that they have passed all ordeals, manfully. . . . The boy officers . . . never flinch from duty . . . I have, myself, entire faith in their constancy put to most arduous service. I have within the last hour visited an outpost . . . where I was greeted by your soldier boy with one of his pleasant smiles."

The letter must have made the proud father smile in return. His oldest child, his namesake—in a sense, the substitute for himself in the war—was upholding the name of Holmes. Pride could alleviate a lot of parental anxiety.

And well might Wendell smile. Here, more than ever before—his superiors' reports to Dr. Holmes notwithstanding—he was on his own and out of his father's shadow, recognized for his own abilities, known for his own particular qualities. Here, for the first time in his life, he was living independently of his family—not just across the river in Cambridge, as he had in college, but really away, four hundred miles away in Maryland. Here, for the first time, he was neither dependent on nor accountable to the doctor but was responsible to and for himself, a man among men. It all seemed to be worth the occasional twinges of homesickness.

The idyll might have lasted a little longer except for the arrival in camp of a black teamster who had deserted from the Thirteenth Mississippi at Leesburg, Virginia, and told a tale of Southern weakness just across the Potomac. The Rebels at Leesburg, he reported, had begun to pack up and retreat south toward Manassas, Virginia, in the face of potentially aggressive Union troop concentrations in nearby Maryland. At about this time, General George B. McClellan, the popular thirty-five-year-old boy wonder to whom Lincoln had given command of the Army of the Potomac, having dispatched a division to a site near Leesburg, telegraphed General Stone to watch whether this new threat might drive the Rebels off; he added, somewhat vaguely, "perhaps a slight demonstration on your part would have the effect to move them."

Stone misinterpreted the suggestion as marching orders, and the result was the disaster known as the Battle of Ball's Bluff, a minor encounter, an unnecessary and deadly blunder that served only to carpet a few acres of Virginia soil high above the Potomac with the blood of young men needlessly, and to discredit the judgment and military abilities of the Union commander.

Whatever the prebattle speculations Holmes and his comrades of the Twentieth had indulged in, they could not have come close to the reality of this, their first fight: a disorderly, leaderless misadventure in which they were outmaneuvered, outnumbered, and outgunned. None of their training had prepared them for climbing a 150-foot-high bluff, only to be chased back down again in a confusion of blood and bullets. McClellan said later that his telegram to Stone in which he had suggested a "slight demonstration" had not contemplated "the making of an attack upon the enemy or the crossing of the river in force by any portion of Stone's command."

Nevertheless, on the night of October 20, 1861, five companies of the Fifteenth Massachusetts under the command of Charles Devens, with whom Holmes would later sit on the Massachusetts Supreme Judicial Court, crossed the Potomac from Maryland to the Virginia side. The next day other units, including sections of the Twentieth Massachusetts, followed. They were ferried across, a few men at a time, in a whaleboat that held only sixteen men and in two small boats that held only four or five each—all the boats that were available, thanks to advance planning. The men scaled the slippery 150-foot-high bluff and waited to engage the enemy who were forming in the surrounding protective woods.

"What a long morning it was," wrote Captain William F. Bartlett, most recently of Harvard College, to his mother. Bartlett was a tall slender officer more at home hunched over a billiard table or skating across a frozen pond in his native northland than he was standing on a high bluff in foreign territory, a ready target for Confederate bullets. He was also one of the copperheads of the regiment and had written in his diary during the frantic days of April 1861: "The Battalion has not been ordered out yet. I don't know what I shall do if it is. . . . It wd be fighting rather against my principles. Since I have stuck up for the South all along." Less than a year later he lost a leg in battle, yet continued in the service of the Union, ultimately rising to the rank of major general. Herman Melville immortalized him in the poem "The College Colonel."

A long morning it was indeed, as the men of the Twentieth awaited either reinforcements or an order to withdraw. Neither came. The men had had nothing to eat since dinner the day before. If they were typical soldiers, eagerness for battle alternated with apprehension. "My company being deployed as skirmishers," Bartlett continued in his letter home, "I had given the order 'Lie down,' I myself reclined on my elbow and dozed for half an hour. I woke up and found that nearly all my skirmishers lying down had taken the opportunity to go to sleep. . . . I couldn't bear to wake them until the first volley of musketry was heard from the woods near us."

Musket balls then flew "like hail," Bartlett said; the Rebels shot from the cover of nearby woods; Bartlett's men were fully exposed on the open plain. Any sense of corporate unity the Twentieth might have started with had dissipated. "An old German soldier," Bartlett recalled, "told me that he had been in a good many battles, but that he never saw such a concentrated fire before." The Southerners were skilled marksmen, and the Massachusetts men began to drop. "I felt," said Bartlett, "that if I was going to be hit, I should be, whether I stood up or lay down, so I stood up and walked around, among the men, stepping over them and talking to them in a joking way, to take away their thoughts from the bullets, and keep them more self-possessed. I was surprised at my own coolness. I never felt better, although I expected of course that I should feel the lead every second, and I was wondering where it would take me. . . . I remember Macy was lying where the grass was turned up, and I 'roughed' him for getting his coat so awfully dirty. . . . The different companies began to wilt away under this terrible fire. Still there was no terror among the men."

Inch by inch the Massachusetts men were driven back toward the edge of the bluff. The ground around Bartlett was smoking and covered with blood; the noise was eardrum-shattering. "Men," he said, "were lying under foot, and here and there a horse struggling in death. Coats and guns strewn over the ground in all directions."

What Bartlett did not include in his narrative was the story of mismanagement and confusion that decided the outcome of the Battle of Ball's Bluff. No order of battle was being followed by the Union troops; none of the officers seemed to know what to do. Colonel Edward D. Baker, a former senator from Oregon and intimate of the president, a romantic figure of a fellow who quoted poetry under fire, had been put in charge by General Stone. But Baker was killed early in the engagement, and no one took his place. The Union cannon were knocked out early. Two of the gunners were shot and one gun recoiled back to the edge of the bluff and fell over. The Rebels won only partly because superior strategy allowed them to fight from the cover of thick woods and from higher ground. They were victorious also because the Union troops were in such disarray.

Badly beaten, the Union troops scrambled down the high bluff in twilight, the enemy close behind, firing down on the men who were waiting to cross back to the safety of the Maryland shore in the only

four boats available—two of these small skiffs. One overloaded boat cap-
sized. As the men surfaced, "they looked," to the regimental historian,
"like a huge ball of men entangled together and holding on to each
other, rolling over and over in their desperate attempts to break apart
and swim ashore. It was a fearful and heartrending sight!" The odds in
favor of survival were not good. If Rebel bullets didn't find the swim-
mers, who carried their watches in their mouths and their swords high
over their heads, the icy water or the strong current defeated them, and
the return trip turned out to be too great a task for many a strong
swimmer.

"Here was a horrible scene," Captain Bartlett continued. "Men
crowded together, the wounded and the dying. The water was full of
human beings, struggling with each other and the water, the surface of
which looked like a pond when it rains, from the withering volleys that
the enemy were pouring down from the top of the bank." Temporary
hospital facilities were set up on Harrison's Island, in midstream, where
the regimental surgeons did their best to stanch the flow of young blood.

The battle had begun about 3 P.M. The Massachusetts Twentieth
had been posted in the open. Lieutenant Holmes had been too "keyed
up to meet the unknown" to be scared while he waited for his first
experience of battle, and "too busy once [he] got in to bother." He had
lasted about an hour before a spent bullet knocked the wind out of him.
The first sergeant and the colonel helped him to his feet, and the latter
ordered him to the rear. Holmes, however, was not ready to quit. He
rushed back to the head of his company and attempted once more to
lead his men into battle. He was hit almost immediately, and this time
it was much more serious.

"I felt as if a horse had kicked me and went over," he wrote in a
memorandum he compiled some time after the event—he had wanted,
he said, the intellectual in him emerging even then, to record "the rapidity of thought & queer suggestions which occur when one is hit."
His first sergeant caught him and pulled him to the rear a little way,
then opened the wounded man's shirt. "[E]cce the two holes in my
breast & the bullet, which he gave me." Holmes remembered next the
"sickening feeling of water in my face," of feeling faint, and seeing one
of the regiment's noncommissioned officers lying nearby, shot through
the head and covered with blood. "Then," he said, "the thinking began—Shot through the lungs? Lets see—and I spit—Yes—already the
blood was in my mouth." Books being the basis on which Holmes's
knowledge of life had developed so far, his associations naturally jumped

to a similar situation in his reading, to " 'Children of the New Forest' which I was fond of reading as a little boy, and in which the father of one of the heroines is shot through the lungs by a robber—I remember he died with terrible hemorrhages & great agony.* What should I do?" He felt in his waistcoat pocket for the bottle of laudanum he carried for just such emergencies, then decided not to take it; he would talk with a doctor first. He might not be dying after all. In any case, he would wait to take it until the pain began.

If indeed the wound should turn out not to be as bad as it looked, it was bad enough. Only a thin partition separated the cavity where the bullet lodged from heart and lungs.

Somehow—Holmes does not describe how—he got, or was gotten, to the bottom of the bluff where boats were being loaded with survivors. Still in a half-conscious state, he heard somebody groan, and the noble sentiments of the aristocrat's code penetrated through the haze; he thought, "Now wouldn't Sir Philip Sidney† have that other feller put into the boat first?" Holmes answered his own question, but not, even in his condition, without intellectualizing it.

"The question," he wrote afterwards, "as the form in which it occurred shows, came from a *mind* still bent on a becoming and consistent carrying out of its ideals of conduct—not from the unhesitating instinct of a still predominant & heroic *will*—I am not sure whether I propounded the question but I let myself be put aboard."

Pursued by Confederate bullets raining down from the bluff, the little craft reached Harrison's Island, where two men made a chair of their crossed hands and carried Holmes from the ferry to a makeshift hospital which had been set up in an abandoned house.

He was still conscious enough to be shocked by his first sight of wounded friends lying all about, their faces distorted in pain, their blankets red with blood. Nearby a surgeon was calmly cutting off a man's finger, the victim unanaesthetized. A fair-haired, rosy-cheeked youngster, "Willy" Putnam—William Lowell Putnam, whose grandfather, Judge John Lowell, had put the antislavery clause in the Bill of Rights of the Massachusetts constitution—between groans was arguing against surgery; he knew it was useless, that this wound was mortal.

---

*Holmes kept an 1855 London edition of Frederick Marryat's *Children of the New Forest* in a prominent place in his library ever after. On the title page he wrote in 1919 that the account of the man "shot in the lungs was the first thing I remembered when I came to at Ball's Bluff & supposed that I was shot in the same way."

†Sir Philip Sidney, mortally wounded at Arnhem in 1586, relinquished his water flask to a foot soldier being carried past, saying, "Thy necessity is yet greater than mine."

Afterwards friends remembered how he liked to shout "Scott's rousing verses as we played Highlanders and Lowlanders among the wooded rocks behind the house."

Presently one of the surgeons examined Holmes.

"How does it look, Doctor, shall I recover?" Holmes asked anxiously. "Tell me the truth," he begged, "for I really want to know."

The doctor hedged. "We-ell," he replied, "you *may* recover. . . ." It was believed the bullets had lodged in Holmes's lungs and he was bleeding at the mouth from the damage they had done.

"That means the chances are against me, don't it?" Holmes persisted.

"Ye-es," the doctor answered, "the chances are against you," and he picked a bit of flannel from one of the bullet holes.

Again Holmes felt for his bottle of laudanum, and again decided to wait until pain or sinking strength told him the end was near. "I didn't feel sure there was no chance," he explained, "and watching myself did not feel the hand of death upon me beyond hope—my strength seemed to hold out too well." He was not nearly ready to quit yet.

After that his recollections dissolved in a haze of semidelirium during which he alternately called on and rejected God. He recalled his discussion with his father and their agreement that a deathbed recantation "meant nothing but a cowardly giving way to fear." He cursed at his friends, flirted with appropriate philosophical concepts, asked a soldier to "write home and tell 'em I'd done my duty—I was very anxious they should know that"—and finally gave in to sleep.

He remembered Pen Hallowell, who had "fought like a brick," coming in and kissing him, he thought Whit (Lieutenant Charles A. Whittier) visited, and others. He thought bullets struck the house where he lay and he remembered hearing a rumor that the enemy was about to shell the island. But the recollections were "obscure" and the order in which they occurred "uncertain."

Much more vivid was his recollection of his state of mind, in which the notion he would proudly "die like a solder . . . shot in the breast doing [his] duty up to the hub" was uppermost.

Later, Holmes was carried across Harrison's Island in a blanket, then in a boat to the Maryland shore. There he was put into an ambulance whose "horses baulked and the man didn't know how to drive." He reached the hospital at the regimental campsite near Poolesville at early dawn, October 22. A steward looked at his wound, bandaged it, and "then," Holmes wrote, "left me uncomfortable but still exceedingly joyful, for he told me I should live—I could have hugged him for that—

After this—whiskey—lightheadedness—laudanum" and more laudanum.

Life and strength rejoined his battered body. By Wednesday, October 23, two days, a mere forty-eight hours, after the bullet had invaded his chest, Holmes could reassure his mother—who had received the news of his wound by telegram on the day of the battle—that although he was flat on his back, he was "pretty comfortable—so well that I have good hopes." With obvious pride he told her how he had passed the first test of manliness under fire, how he had "felt and acted very cool and did my duty I am sure." A visitor to the hospital shortly afterwards found Holmes "so patient, so cheerful and withal so full of manly spirit." He was content; he had done his duty.

On October 25, four days after the battle, Lieutenant Colonel Palfrey visited Holmes. He reported immediately to Dr. Holmes, assuring him that his son's conduct in the field had been "of a piece with that of the gallant band. . . . His first experience was a severe one but he was equal to the emergency." Palfrey added: "I found him smoking and deriving much satisfaction from the contemplation of the photographs of certain young ladies. He declared that to look at the portrait of Miss Agassiz was like having an angel in the tent." Wendell later confessed that one of the things that had made dying particularly difficult was the "recollection of several fair damsels whom I wasn't quite ready to leave."

Dr. Holmes tolerated his son's soldiering about the way most parents did—and do. He worried constantly. He even gave up his daily row on the Charles because he couldn't bear to be beyond call. But he was proud, too. He could hardly wait to boast to his friends that his son had been "on the right of the advance on the upper Potomac, the post of honor and of danger."

Others did not fare so well at Ball's Bluff. A foolhardy adventure to begin with, with no significant objective, no avenue of retreat, and no way to send reinforcements, the engagement, mismanaged from the start, cost much more than it was worth. Like other regiments involved, the Massachusetts Twentieth lost some of its best men: 40 killed, 36 wounded, and 113, including Colonel Lee and Major Revere, taken prisoner. General Stone attracted the attention of the Congress, which formed the Joint Committee on the Conduct of the War to keep the generals properly respectful, and General Stone himself, following a round of congressional hearings, was locked up in Fort Lafayette in New York Harbor for some months; it was late in the war before he was entrusted with another command.

The depleted Massachusetts Twentieth, its morale improved if not entirely restored by the resumption of normal prebattle routine including a dress parade on the night following the disaster, settled down once again at the campsite near Poolesville for four months.

Again the guns along the Potomac were silent while General McClellan, who had succeeded General Scott as commandant of all the Union armies, shrank from attack. Lincoln sat embarrassed in the White House, and the Congress, reflecting the frustrations of its constituencies, clamored for action.

It was not long before Holmes was strong enough to travel to Philadelphia, where Pen Hallowell's family had turned their Walnut Street home into a rest and rehabilitation center for their son's wartime comrades. He stayed a week, during which he was under the care of Dr. William Hunt. Hunt immediately wrote to reassure Dr. Holmes. Wendell's wound "has been represented as trifling and as far as constitutional symptoms are concerned it would appear to be so, for the patient has had very little pain scarcely any irritative fever and sleeps and eats well. I therefore anticipate nothing but a favorable result, but the wound is much more extensive and will be longer in healing than one would think, who formed an opinion without inspecting it." Speaking doctor to doctor, Hunt described the wound in some medical detail, then added: "you can judge . . . what a narrow escape your son has had from immediate death, and also that trouble may yet occur as the cavity I speak of is separated from important parts by a very thin partition. . . . However, so far, all has gone well, and I think will end well. . . . Your son is in all respects 'jolly.' . . . While I should be glad to see you there is no positive necessity as yet of your presence."

Wild horses, however, could not have kept the elder Holmes away. The day after delivering his introductory lecture for the academic term at Harvard, he was on the train for Philadelphia, where, he was pleased to inform his wife, he found Wendell "looking nicely—fat and in good spirits."

The doctor booked six seats on the return train trip to Boston in order to improvise a bed for the convalescent. Arriving there on November 9, he immediately summoned two of his medical colleagues for consultation. After a thorough probing of the wound, the prognosis was: "Wendell is in every respect excellently well."

From that point on, convalescence was one long party, as his friends and his family's friends vied with each other to honor the wounded hero. Whatever ghosts of the recent past haunted his memory had long since vanished, or been suppressed. Mrs. Holmes compiled a list of the young man's visitors, many of whom treated him to flowers, fruit, and ice cream. Miss Ida Agassiz, the "angel" of his hospital tent, was one of his earliest callers. She was followed by her father, the Harvard botanist Louis Agassiz. Senator Charles Sumner came twice. Even President Felton of Harvard, who so reluctantly had conferred on Holmes his B.A., called. Cousin Johnny Morse—a copperhead, he had not gone to war—came to visit and dress the wound. Fanny Dixwell, daughter of Holmes's former schoolmaster, called and brought flowers. Mrs. Holmes listed 133 visitors during the month of November, plus four bouquets from unknown donors. Dr. Holmes described his son in the winter of 1861 as "a great pet in his character of young hero with wounds in the heart, and receives visits *en grand signeur.* I envy my white Othello, with a semi-circle of young Desdemonas about him listening to the often told story which they will have over again." War, a cocky Wendell had told his worshipful audience, scandalizing as well as showing off to all about him, was an "organized bore"; he could hardly have flaunted his pride in his recent courage and gallantry, however he might have wanted to.

There was, too, leisure to read again. Philosophy, military strategy, biographies, art, John Stuart Mill on *Representative Government,* de Tocqueville's *Democracy in America* were some of the books withdrawn under the Holmes name from the Athenaeum library that winter.

On December 7, Wendell was well enough to go to breakfast at the home of a Charles Street neighbor, James T. Fields, editor of the *Atlantic Monthly.* Mrs. Fields commented then: "The young lieutenant has mostly recovered from his wound and speaks as if duty would recall him soon to camp. He will go when the time comes, but home evidently never looked half so pleasant before."

With the big battles that keep a fighting spirit alive in a national war effort not being fought in the winter of 1861–62, enthusiasm for fighting was flagging; enlistments were down, and the Union was desperately in need of men. Despite the early war fever, Massachusetts had provided only 32,177 of its 34,868-man quota following Lincoln's call for volunteers the previous May, and Wendell spent part of that winter recruiting soldiers in western Massachusetts—the Berkshire area where only a few summers before he had walked the woods with his mother and swum in the river with Ned and Amelia, and where now he "made love to all the available girls." Soon he was ready to return to his regiment.

In the brief but decisive encounter at Ball's Bluff, the young Wendell Holmes had begun the passage to the adult Wendell Holmes. His abilities as a military officer never were outstanding. He was not mentioned in dispatches and rarely in his fellow officers' memoirs—not like the Hallowells or Captain Bartlett or Little Abbott, all of whom figure much more prominently in regimental memories, and Holmes himself said that he had a "very modest" estimate of his own abilities. Sixty years later he told a youthful admirer who tended to write him worshipful letters: "Don't call me Hero. I trust I did my duty as a soldier respectably, but I was not born for it and did nothing remarkable in that way."

Ball's Bluff had tested Wendell's courage, which had passed, his sense of honor, which had survived intact, his physical stamina and constitution, which had proved virtually indestructible. And although he had learned there was more to battle than noble sentiments, the very real horrors seemed not yet to have penetrated his persistently romantic nature, which grasped at literature and philosophy when confronted with the possibility of death. War—and his hero's welcome home did nothing to disabuse him of the notion—was still an exciting adventure story in which he, Oliver Wendell Holmes, Jr., was cast as the lead character.

IF NOT *as* hard, the war was nevertheless hard on women, who could only wear away time with memories, regrets, and fears, then steel themselves to face the daily casualty lists in the newspapers. Being limited to kneeling in prayer while their men knelt in shooting position both frustrated and rankled. "I envy you your wound," a family friend told Wendell. "If women could only bear the pain and send the men back to battle to run new gamuts—but—alas! we must stay here and pray." All over the Union, they gathered in parlors and churches to ask what they could do.

The answer was not long coming. On November 28, 1861, while Wendell was still convalescing at home, Dr. Henry W. Bellows, president of the United States Sanitary Commission, arrived in Boston to promote the establishment of a New England branch of his organization, which in other sections of the country was collecting donations of dollars for the Union cause and disbursing clothing, stores, books, and bandages to the men in the field. Most of the work was being done by women in their sewing circles and their fairs. Bellows met in a private parlor with a group of Boston's most prominent women, who responded to his requests with much the same patriotic fervor as those ancient Carthaginian women who offered their hair for their husbands' bowstrings.

Where suffrage and abolition both had failed, having a son at the front achieved. Amelia Jackson Holmes accepted the presidency after what must have been considerable inner struggle. Although she was the daughter of a public figure, she was a very private person even in Boston's terms. During the quarter century of her married life, she had been known as a "retiring" woman content to tend her nest in virtual seclusion, a gentle benevolent figure devoted almost exclusively to bringing up her children and ministering to the needs of her husband— quietly furthering his career and unselfishly catering to his vanities. Now for a brief moment, she, like her older son, was propelled by a public matter out of her isolation and persuaded to engage her faculties beyond her little domestic circle. At last she felt "the *necessity* of doing something," that lack she had complained of in her youth. She became in fact so deeply involved and gave so much of herself that Dr. Holmes was distressed, fretted over her health, and attempted to persuade her to curtail her hours.

A recently built store on Sumner Street was given rent-free for use as a local Sanitary Commission headquarters, and the work began. Like the officer corps of the Massachusetts Twentieth, the roster of the new organization contained the names of some of the city's best-known women: Holmes, Gray, Parkman, Eastburn, May. Fanny Dixwell and her friends made bandages, scraped lint, and sewed clothes. During one year the women shipped out 34,142 articles of clothing—bed sacks, quilts, sheets, pillowcases, cushions, wrappers, shirts, and drawers. They bought and sent more than $10,000 worth of food—farina, condensed milk, beef stock, tea, sugar, cocoa, jellies, fresh and dried fruit, wines, and syrups—plus hospital supplies such as surgical instruments, soap, sponges, tallow, cologne, bandages, fans, and handkerchiefs.

Of Amelia Holmes's participation it was later said, she "impressed us all as being strong, steady, clear and firm. There was not one among the whole body with whom we were so united as with her . . . she really had the executive ability and the clear mind, as well as the gentle and amiable spirit. . . . In counsel and advice she wooed to her side . . . she was far more capable than most, even as a manager."

Although her son returned to the front, she kept her anxieties to herself, scarcely ever alluding to the matter in public. In private she wrote to a friend: "It is very hard to have our sons and brothers go off, but we would not keep them at home if we could. . . . I only hope and pray that the war may go on till every slave is free, and that my child will always be ready to defend and struggle for humanity. I hate bloodshed . . . but I hate slavery more."

And when it was all over, the issue of slavery settled at last and the Sanitary Commission's work done, Amelia Holmes, having given unflinchingly and unsparingly of herself, returned to her Charles Street home and resumed her old domestic identity as if there had been no interruption. She had come out as far as she was able.

CHAPTER 6

Antietam

WITH RALPH WALDO Emerson's autograph, which Wendell had asked the sage to send, safely tucked away, his new captain's bars shining on his shoulders, and his father's "God bless you" still ringing in his ears, Wendell left Boston in late March 1862 to rejoin his regiment. No more than half a year passed before another telegram arrived at 21 Charles Street. It came from Hagerstown, Maryland. CAPT H_____ WOUNDED SHOT THROUGH THE NECK THOUGHT NOT MORTAL AT KEEDYSVILLE and the young man was home again to recuperate. Like the bullet that had felled him at Ball's Bluff, this second Rebel bullet, had it veered less than a quarter of an inch in its trajectory, would have destroyed some vital part: carotid artery, spinal cord, windpipe, food pipe, jugular—all lay within easy reach.

That six months between Holmes's rejoining the Massachusetts Twentieth and his return home wounded the second time was a far more severe and prolonged test of his abilities, of his will and determination to survive, and of his devotion to the ideals of manliness and honor than he would face ever again. Ball's Bluff had come as a sudden shock following several weeks of not unpleasant duties. The road to Keedysville was long and horror filled, mined with fear and exhaustion. His romantic optimism dissipated daily. He was a "devilish sight more scared" now than he had been at Ball's Bluff when he had been "keyed up to meet the unknown," and he later remembered days when he looked at the sun and said, "God why can't it go down faster so that we can rest."

This personal testing of the young Holmes reflected the condition of the young nation itself, then being tested similarly. The unity forged

after Fort Sumter was disintegrating, and its military capacities, determination to survive, willingness to live in a blood bath, and dedication
to its ideals were to be severely strained during the same six months.

By mid-January of 1862, General McClellan, Lincoln's supreme
commander still, had prepared, with the president's approval, a general
scheme for the year's operations against the Confederacy. In the west,
the Army of the Ohio was to rescue the Unionists in eastern Tennessee;
General Harry W. Halleck was building a fleet of armored river gun-
boats to support Union forces pushing down the Mississippi Valley; they
were to connect with a naval expedition to force a passage from the Gulf
of Mexico to New Orleans and Vicksburg. In the east, the Army of the
Potomac, of which the Twentieth Massachusetts was a part, was to
advance against Richmond under McClellan himself.

The Massachusetts Twentieth was but a small part in this mighty
military machine, fewer than a thousand men among more than a hundred
thousand. Holmes, of course, had little acquaintance with the grand
strategy; it was enough to advance objective by objective, earthworks by
earthworks, day by day.

McClellan's plans were only partially implemented. The young, newly
commissioned brigadier general, Ulysses S. Grant, attended to Tennessee for the Union, his victories restoring some measure of self-confidence to the North and challenging the Confederacy's reputation for
invincibility. Admiral David G. Farragut took New Orleans. Vicksburg
held out for some months; by July 1862, however, most of the Mississippi Valley had been subjugated.

Richmond, however, was another story.

On March 27, 1862, the Massachusetts Twentieth embarked by
steamer with the rest of the Army of the Potomac—110,000 well-drilled
and -disciplined troops—for Fort Monroe and Hampton, Virginia. Holmes
had been promoted to captain only four days earlier. The men disem-
barked at Hampton on March 31 and set up their bivouac within view
of the new little *Monitor* lying in port—a "most insignificant looking
affair," the regimental historian wrote later, "so much so that one would
laugh at the idea of her fighting the *Merrimac*. Her turret did not reach
up to the deck of a small ship."

Brigadier General John Sedgwick, commander of the division to which
the Twentieth was attached, described what war already had done to
Hampton. "The town presents the most desolate appearance you can
imagine; not a house standing, where formerly it contained a population
of perhaps three thousand people. It was . . . one of the oldest places

in the United States. There was a church standing here that was built in 1630, now in ruins."

This was to be the biggest campaign of 1862: George B. McClellan's Army of the Potomac against Robert E. Lee's Army of Northern Virginia. Richmond was McClellan's long-range objective. Reaching it required that the Union soldiers fight their way north through the peninsula formed by the York and James rivers until they faced the Confederate capital—before the summer heat set in, if they were lucky.

History had trod this ground before: Jamestown, Yorktown, Williamsburg, the Chickahominy River first explored by Captain John Smith.

Spring in Virginia that year was as sweet as spring in Virginia gets: bright, balmy, and budding. This spring, however, it was also to be bloody.

The siege of Yorktown alone required thirty days. "We are on the advance with . . . George B. in person," Holmes wrote home from his post on guard duty on April 7. "Our division is at center. . . . It's a campaign now & make no mistake—No tents, no trunks,—no nothing." It had, however, rained for about thirty-six hours. Whoever had told McClellan that the Virginia roads were sandy had misinformed him. The Virginia roads in this balmy spring of 1862 had been turned by the warm rains into mud. Slippery, slimy, gluey mud. Wagons and guns sank up to their axles, men sank up to their knees. One soldier reported seeing a mule sink up to its ears. Two or three thousand men a day were required to haul up supplies and maneuver the heavy artillery into position. "The men and officers are wet enough," Holmes continued, "but there is real pluck shown now as these are real hardships to contend with."

The Twentieth was camped within four miles of the enemy's fortifications. Reconnaissance missions took small groups of men within half a mile. Through the trees they could see the enemy's outworks during the day and the lights of his working parties at night, sometimes even overhear conversation punctuated by a sharpshooter's shot or a volley of musket shots. Constant false alarms turned out the men to battle positions nightly. And all through the working and watching, the rain fell.

"It is very unpleasant duty," Captain Bartlett complained. "No glory in being shot by a picket behind a tree. It is regular Indian fighting. . . . This is the hard part of a soldier's life; the battle would be a holiday as a relief from this." Four days later, Bartlett was in fact shot by a picket from behind a tree; his left leg had to be amputated.

Malaria swamps, exposure to the elements—"Regular officers and soldiers know how to make themselves comfortable on picket duty; volunteers do not," the medical director of the Army of the Potomac grumbled to General McClellan—the steady diet of salt pork and hardtack uninterrupted by fresh vegetables and fruit took a large toll of the troops. Scarcity of medical supplies worsened the effects. A third of the regiment was sometimes hospitalized at one time.

On May 2, Colonel Lee and Major Revere, who had been captured at Ball's Bluff, having finally been exchanged, reached the Twentieth's campgrounds. Heavy infantry fire during the night of May 3 brought the regiment to its feet early in the hot, clear morning of May 4. An aide-de-camp brought news that the enemy had evacuated, and ordered the Twentieth to advance. Colonel Lee gave the order. The men waded through a swamp, crossed a couple of ditches, and at 7:45 A.M. mounted the main redoubt. Colonel Lee called for the regimental flag, and in a few minutes it waved over the Confederate works at Yorktown. Lieutenant Henry Ropes looked back and caught a "glittering sight" as other regiments followed the Twentieth, "the glittering columns pouring out of the woods in all directions moving on the forts. The horse artillery galloped forward," and the siege was over.

The Twentieth missed the Battle of Williamsburg on May 5. On May 6, the regiment was ferried to West Point, about twenty-five miles northwest of Yorktown, after which the Massachusetts men moved through the month of May slogging about the peninsula until they met a substantial Confederate force at Fair Oaks on May 31 and June 1.

On June 2, Holmes wrote his parents from the battlefield that he was "nearly tired out with the constant labors of the last two days"; he only wanted, he said, to reassure them of his safety and "spirits." He seemed, however, unable to stop at that, but unwound by recounting the events of the engagement, shot by shot. A soldier cannot stop to dwell on the suffering around him while the battle rages. Holmes saw "no good in unproductive emotion that detracts from one's working force." Perhaps, though, it helped to write about it.

He described each scene in vivid detail without comment; the reader of his letter can almost hear the shingles of the house rattling "with the hail of Reb. bullets and many whistled by," almost see the "company of Rebs trying to pass out of the woods" and being "knocked to pieces." One stumbles with Holmes over the "swollen bodies already fly blown and decaying, of men shot in the head back or bowels—Many of the wounds are terrible to look at—especially those fr. fragments of shell." One hears the bullet's "most villainous greasy slide through the air" and the "smart rap" of Holmes's sword over the backsides of a soldier who cowered in the midst of an attack. He writes graphically of the most inhuman of horrors, and he describes the "indifference" with which he looks on "the dead bodies in gray clothes wh. lie all around—(or rather did—We are burying them today as fast as we can—)."

He still at times reverted to writing an adventure story in which he was the hero—"OWH in the front rank . . . handling a sword & pistol"—following the "manly" course. "I stood with my revolver & swore I'd shoot the first who ran or fired against orders."

He remained, he said, despite fatigue, privation, and severe anxiety, "in spirits."

At last, however, albeit in a kind of parentheses, he came to the fearful subject of his own mortality. "If I am killed," he said, "you will find a Mem. on the back of a picture I carry wh. please attend to. I must sleep a few minutes . . . God bless you both."

Fair Oaks was followed by the hardest work to date—"ten days of unceasing vigilance in the face of the enemy," Lieutenant James Jackson Lowell, Harvard '58, and a cousin of Holmes's, told a friend: "Rain or shine, night or day, we were under arms at the slightest alarm, and remained in line for an hour or two." For twelve days the men had no change of clothing. Exhaustion, lice, disease, hot weather: all took their toll. Then came the Confederate guns. The Seven Days' Battles: Allen's Farm, Savage's Station, Glendale, Malvern Hill. Holmes was safe so far, he told his mother, though "you can't conceive the wear & tear."

In Boston, Dr. Holmes was neglecting "almost everything in the tremulous interest" with which he was following the news from the South. He could hardly think of anything else.

Just before the battle at Glendale, as the advance was beginning, Captain Holmes glanced down the line of officers poised to attack at the head of their companies. He caught Lowell's eye. When Holmes next looked, Lowell was gone. He had been hit; he died in the hands of the enemy shortly afterwards.

Lest he be distracted from the main business of killing the enemy, however, Holmes could not stop to grieve, though he wrote in near anguish to his mother on July 4: "We have had hard work for several days—marched all night—lain on our arms every morn'g & fought every afternoon—eaten nothing—suffered the most intense anxiety—and everything else possible."

Allen's Farm, Savage's Station, Malvern Hill. But not Richmond. Lee had outgeneraled the young Napoleon, who had failed to attack the Confederate capital, although he had come within four miles of it—one unit got close enough to hear church bells ringing. Instead, he listened to his intelligence men who told him he was vastly outnumbered; he dallied and finally retreated. The suffering had been for naught.

Reassured of their invincibility, the Confederates rejoiced and prepared for the next round. In the North there was agony and frustration. The last chance for a short war had been lost, and the realization dawned on the Union that it was in for a long, agonizing struggle. The Peninsula Campaign was but prelude to the next three years, during which the country's will would be even more severely tested.

Lee having dispatched his troops north to invade Maryland and thus lure the Union forces away from Richmond, McClellan was ordered to withdraw his Army of the Potomac from the peninsula and to ship it up the Potomac to place it between Lee and the capital, thus to head off the Southerner's forward thrust. The Massachusetts Twentieth retraced its march of the past summer and spring and embarked at Newport News, Virginia, on the steamer *Atlantic* for Alexandria, arriving on August 28.

Wendell Holmes got the news then that while he was sailing up the Virginia coast, Grandmother Holmes—Judge Wendell's daughter and the Reverend Abiel's widow—had died at the age of ninety-three, "keeping her lively sensibilities and sweet intelligence to the end." But he could not stop to mourn while there was work to be done.

THE VALLEY OF the Antietam was one of Maryland's most beautiful and fertile in the fall of 1862. Languid herds of cattle grazed its rolling green hills. Heavily laden fruit trees awaited the harvest. Comfortable little farmhouses nestled in the shade of the orchards. The leaves had not yet turned to flame; their rich green added to the impression of lushness.

Despoiling the idyll, a hundred thousand Confederate troops had assembled along the banks of Antietam Creek to wait for the enemy. A Confederate victory on Northern soil, Lee reasoned, might attract badly needed English and French aid; such a triumph might also frighten Northern politicians into suing for peace.

After a brief stopover in Washington during which Holmes replenished his wardrobe and ate himself into a "plethora," the Massachusetts Twentieth, along with the rest of General Sedgwick's forces, reached Antietam Creek on September 15. Lee's General James Longstreet had watched them come. "The number increased," he said, "and larger and larger grew the field of blue until it seemed to stretch as far as the eye could see, and from the tops of the mountains to the edges of the stream gathered the great army of McClellan. It was an awe inspiring spectacle as this grand force settled down in sight of the Confederates, then shattered by battle and tiresome marches."

At 3 A.M. on the morning of September 17, keyed up by the approach of battle and apparently unable to sleep, Holmes wrote by candlelight—and with a bravado he perhaps did not feel—of the uncertainties that had begun to roil his youthful spirit: "Dearest Parents . . . All of us feel a deuced sight more like a fight than in that forlorn peninsula. I don't talk seriously for you know all my last words if I come to grief—You know my devoted love for you—those I care for know it—Why should I say any more—It's rank folly pulling a long mug every time one may fight or may be killed—Very probably we shall in a few days and if we do why I shall go into it not trying to shirk the responsibility of my past life by a sort of death bed abjuration—I have lived on the track on which I expect to continue travelling if I get through—hoping always that though it may wind it will bring me up the hill once more." Before his parents received this letter, the telegram informing them of his neck wound had arrived at 21 Charles Street.

Whatever romance war had held for Holmes had by this time dissipated in the smoke of realities. Just before the battle he had fantasized that "it would be easy after a comfortable breakfast to come down the steps of one's home putting on one's gloves and smoking a cigar, to get on a horse and charge a battery up Beacon Street, while the ladies waved handkerchieves from a balcony—but the reality was to face a night on the ground in the rain and your bowels out of order and then after no particular breakfast to wade a stream and attack the enemy."

The main thrust of the battle,* which began only a few hours after Holmes finished his letter to his parents, consisted of five desperate, uncoordinated attacks on the Confederates by as many different Union commanders. It resulted in what was regarded as a modest Union victory, with Lee retreating back into Virginia and Lincoln issuing the Emancipation Proclamation. After the battle, the nearby town of Sharpsburg was "one large hospital" for men wounded at Antietam. Every barn, house, and haystack formed the nucleus of a hospital.

Advance planning on a level with that before Ball's Bluff sent the Twentieth straight into a Confederate ambush where Rebel fire quickly cut men down. There had been, up to now, a proud tradition among

---

*In 1990, the Richard King Mellon Foundation of Pittsburgh gave the U.S. government 100,000 acres of land, much of it threatened by urban development. The gift included 3 tracts totaling 280 acres of the Antietam National Battlefield over whose future historians and environmentalists have been arguing with developers for some years.

the Massachusetts troops that they never had been hit in the back. After Antietam it was no longer true. Three decades later, Holmes, in a speech to the Regimental Association, said: "We have stood side by side in a line—we have charged and swept the enemy—and we have run away like rabbits—all together."

Holmes himself was hit in the back of the neck while he was "bolting" as fast as he could, he said, which, he added, was "all right—but not so good for the newspapers."

The day after the battle, he wrote again to his parents: "Usual luck—ball entered at the rear passing straight through the central seam of coat & waistcoat collar coming out toward the front on the left hand side—Yet it don't seem to have smashed my spine or I suppose I should be dead or paralyzed or something—It's more than 24 hours and I have remained pretty cocky, only of course feverish at times—& some sharp burning pain in the left shoulder. . . . Only one doctor . . . has yet looked—he glanced hastily yesterday & said it wasn't fatal." Thinking he might "faint and so be unable to tell who I was," Holmes scribbled a hasty note on a small card: "I am Capt. O. W. Holmes son of Oliver Wendell Holmes, M.D. Boston."

Pen Hallowell also was hit—his left arm smashed above the elbow—and the two old friends who had been through so much together huddled side by side in a farmhouse whose yard and floor were carpeted with the bodies of wounded soldiers. Later that afternoon ambulances carried them off to Keedysville, along with several jars of preserves which Hallowell purloined from the farmhouse shelves.*

Surgeons attending the wounded following the Battle of Antietam were not so sanguine about Holmes's prospects when they examined his wound. The first shook his head when he was asked to give the young man attention; he said his duty was to try to save those who had some chance of recovery. Holmes, he believed, had none.

Another medic, Captain William G. Le Duc, approached. "Tell me what to do for him," Le Duc said.

"Wash off the blood," the first replied, "plug up the wound with lint, and give him this pill of opium and have him keep quiet."

Le Duc led Holmes to the first available house in sight and comman-

---

*Some years later, in 1868, Hallowell and his bride made their wedding trip to Antietam. They found the farmhouse and the owners who in 1862 had been Union sympathizers and had fled as the armies approached. Pen asked what they had intended to do with all those jars of preserves; he was told that the owners' business was making and selling preserves, and that soldiers had stolen an entire batch in their absence. Hallowell confessed to the theft and persuaded them to accept $20 in compensation.

deered the owner's best feather bed.* He washed and bandaged the wound, gave Holmes the opium, and left him in charge of the family. Le Duc, on examining the wound, was amazed at Holmes's narrow escape from death, but counted on the young man's vitality to carry him through.

At about this time, Captain Le Duc sent Dr. Holmes the telegram announcing Wendell's wound. Rumors of the battle had been rife all day in Boston, and the streets had been thronged with people seeking news of the casualties as the lists came in direct from the battlefield.

The telegram arrived in the dead of night. Traveling on a safe-conduct pass from the Massachusetts surgeon general, Dr. Holmes set out "with a full and heavy heart" the following day on the 2:15 P.M. train to retrieve his son.

Too late, Wendell wrote that he did not wish "to meet any affectionate parent half way"; the doctor had already started. To the younger Holmes's eternal embarrassment, the elder Holmes fashioned the events of his search into the narrative "My Hunt After 'the Captain,' " to which he treated readers of the *Atlantic Monthly* in December of 1862, a sentimental story of a father's love for his son and his desperate fears for the young man's safety.

Dr. Holmes described his inner journey this way: ". . . many times my blood chilled with what were perhaps needless and unwise fears. . . . I broke through all my habits without thinking about them, which is almost as hard in certain circumstances as for one of our young fellows to leave his sweetheart and go into a Peninsula campaign. . . . I did not always know when I was hungry nor discover that I was thirsting. . . . I had a worrying ache and inward tremor underlying all the outward play of the senses and the mind."

On reaching Philadelphia, Dr. Holmes went immediately to the Hallowell home "where the Captain would be heard of, if anywhere in this region." There he found Pen Hallowell and his brother as well as Lieutenant Colonel Palfrey of the Twentieth recovering from their wounds, but no Wendell, although a fourth bed had been made ready for him.

Disappointed but not discouraged, Dr. Holmes slowly made his way by train and wagon to Keedysville, where he asked the mayor, whom he

---

*Holmes wrote sixty years later to Harold Laski: "I have just received a letter from the great granddaughter . . . of the old woman into whose house I was put after Antietam. . . . She suggests that her nursing saved my life. General Le Duc who put me there told me that he used some threats to force me upon an unwilling hostess."

found working in the rubble, the question he had traveled five hundred miles to ask:

"Where is Captain H.?"

The mayor could not answer—there were thousands of wounded in Keedysville—could only suggest the anxious father knock at every house. A medical officer appeared.

"Do you know anything of Captain Holmes of the Massachusetts Twentieth?" the doctor asked.

"Oh, yes," came the quick reply, "he is staying in that house. I saw him there, doing very well."

The doctor approached the cottage referred to.

"Captain H. here?" he asked the old woman who answered his knock.

"O, no, Sir,—left yesterday morning for Hagerstown—in a milk-cart." She gave, however, a good account of Wendell's condition; he had been able to get into the cart without assistance and was in good spirits. He had gone to Hagerstown to catch a train for Philadelphia, where the Hallowells awaited him.

He did not, however, arrive in Philadelphia. On the afternoon of Saturday, September 20, the Kennedy family of Hagerstown discovered him walking languidly along the street, a bandage around his throat. He told the Kennedys of his wound, that it was giving him pain, and that he was on his way home to Boston.

The Kennedys, although Union sympathizers, had opened their rambling old brick house to wounded soldiers of both sides throughout the war. They took Holmes in and nursed him until he was strong enough to travel.

Mrs. Kennedy dressed his wound every day, and it began to heal. Wendell gained in strength, but seemed somewhat loathe to leave; he was basking in Mrs. Kennedy's "womanly kindness and motherly tenderness." She had given him "a home when [he] most needed it and with it, all those charming attentions that make home what it is." He frolicked with the Kennedy children and flirted with Miss Ellen Jones, who was visiting from Philadelphia. She sang, played, and entertained him. When he complained that it hurt him to write, she wrote his letters for him. He once dictated a letter to his father in Latin; she knew Latin as well as he did and warned him that he was becoming too personal in his comments about her.

Meanwhile, Dr. Holmes was searching frantically for his son. Still he felt compelled to inspect the scene of the recent carnage before he left the Keedysville area. Soldiers now were washing their clothes in

Antietam Creek; women were combing the fields for trophies. Fresh mass graves had been dug at intervals in the cornfields. The ground was strewn with bits of abandoned clothing, haversacks, caps with bullet holes in them, canteens, bullets, cartridge boxes, even pieces of bread and meat. Dead horses, piles of lost muskets, and caked curdled pools of blood turned the doctor's stomach. For the first time, he saw through his own eyes what his son had endured. "It was like the table," he wrote, "of some hideous orgy left uncleared, and one turned away disgusted from its broken fragments and muddy heel-taps."

On finally reaching Baltimore, the doctor was disappointed that no news of his son awaited him. Again he set out for Philadelphia, certain Wendell would be waiting for him there. "Up a long street with white shutters and white steps to all the houses. Off at right angles into another long street with white shutters and white steps to all the houses. Off again at another right angle into still another long street with white shutters and white steps to all the houses. . . . This corner house is the one. Ring softly." But the fourth bed was still empty, and there had been no word from Captain Holmes.

"My heart sank within me," the doctor wrote, imagining all the horrors that come so naturally to a parent. "Had he taken ill on the road? . . . Was his life ebbing away in some lonely cottage, nay, in some cold barn or shed, or at the wayside, unknown, uncared for . . . I must sweep the hundred and eighty miles between [Philadelphia and Hagerstown] as one would sweep a chamber where a precious pearl had been dropped."

Once again he set off, inquiring along the way to Harrisburg for wounded officers, at the same time conscious of his "insane reliance on a very feeble reed." At Harrisburg, he heard his son had left that very afternoon on the train for Philadelphia.

"*Te Deum Laudamus!* . . . The dead pain in the semilunar ganglion (which I must remind my reader is a kind of stupid, unreasoning brain, beneath the pit of the stomach, common to man and beast, which surfaces in the supreme moment of life, as when the dam loses her young ones, or the wild horse is lassoed) stopped short. There was a feeling as if I had slipped off a tight boot, or cut a strangling garter,—only it was all over my system." A telegram went out as soon as possible to the Hallowells. The disappointing reply from Philadelphia: "I think the report you have heard that W. has gone East must be an error we have not seen or heard of him here."

Perplexity. Wendell had gone east but no one there had seen him.

Then came a second wire from Philadelphia. "W" had been seen the previous week at the home of a Mrs. Kennedy in Hagerstown. Dr. Holmes immediately wired Hagerstown.

The hours passed, but slowly. In the morning the doctor visited several local hospitals, churches, and schools where wounded men were being housed temporarily. In the afternoon he went in a rickety wagon to a nearby army camp. On his return to his hotel, he found no reply to his telegram. He had dinner. Still there was no reply.

Late that evening, minutes before the telegraph office closed, a message finally arrived: CAPTAIN H. STILL HERE LEAVES TOMORROW FOR HARRISBURG PENNA IS DOING WELL MRS. H. KENNEDY.

"We shall sleep tonight."

The train from Hagerstown was due in Harrisburg at 11:15 A.M. Dr. Holmes went to the station. The train was late. Fifteen minutes. A half hour. At last.

"In the first car, on the fourth seat to the right, I saw my Captain; there saw I him, even my first-born, whom I had sought through many cities.

" 'How are you, Boy?'

" 'How are you, Dad?' "*

---

*The exchange of greetings above is as reported by Dr. Holmes in his *Atlantic Monthly* article. Alexander Woollcott reported nearly a century later that the young Holmes actually replied, "Boy, nothing."

CHAPTER 7

Second Fredericksburg

SIX SPLENDIDLY LUXURIOUS weeks at 21 Charles Street, sleeping every night in a dry bed in a warm house, once again eating food fit for human consumption, wearing clean dry clothes, reading—the elder Holmes had given him John Stuart Mill's *Considerations on Representative Government;* Austin's *Lectures on Jurisprudence* was taken out of the Athenaeum library for rereading—walking in the cool, clear air of Boston, waited on by an adoring mother and proud father, basking in the attention of his friends, far from the killing fields, and the young warrior was ready, at least physically, to return to his regiment, then camped at Falmouth, Virginia.

Twenty-one years old at last, he cast his first ballot that November for the "Union Republican" ticket headed by the incumbent and abolitionist governor, John A. Andrew, against a coalition conservative ticket headed by General Charles Devens, protesting Lincoln's conduct of the war. Holmes's heart apparently was still with the crusade. In his head, however, he was beginning to doubt the capacity of the Union for winning.

A general malaise marked the Union war effort that winter and spring of 1862–63. The crowds were no longer lining the streets to cheer the soldiers as they marched into Boston. Even the number of soldiers had declined. The torchlight parades and flag-waving were over. Bostonians still talking about the war at the Adirondack Club were talking about reverses and misfortunes and the "eventual separation of the country." Those still talking about the war in the Harvard Chapel were mourning the dead.

Wendell had felt it and doubted the country would support the war another year. Nevertheless, he and Little Abbott, who had been home on sick leave, set out in mid-November 1862 for Washington and points south. The wartime capital, Holmes told his parents, "stinks of mean- ness—it's absolutely loathesome." He had decided on this trip that his democratic inclinations were limited, that in actuality he "loathe[d] the thick-fingered clowns we call the people—especially as the beasts are represented at political centers—vulgar, selfish & base." Finding the regiment was not only difficult but disheartening, for "everyone seems to hold that you are a nuisance for not having stayed at home as indeed but for honor I should suspect I was a fool." At last he was able to confess to a waning of enthusiasm for the war into which he had marched so eagerly, and he allowed himself to daydream: "I have in fancy today," he said, "been swelling on Beacon Street when I was in fact in beastly gov^t cars smoking a T.D. & plug tobacco."

A week out from Boston, Holmes and Abbott at last found the Twentieth—an exhausting week of trudging along muddy roads in the rain, listening to sneers of passing troops, never getting enough food or water, and wondering when "gurillas" "might pick us up." It was enough to wash the idealism and resolve out of any soldier. "I've pretty much made up my mind," a discouraged Holmes wrote to his sister the night he arrived at the Twentieth's camp, "that the South have achieved their independence & I am almost ready to hope spring will see an end—I prefer intervention to save our credit," but he could offer no hope of winning. "The Army," he explained, "is too tired with its hard, & its terrible experience & still more with its mismanagement." He predicted most people would soon realize that the efforts to subjugate "a great civilized nation" had been in vain. It couldn't be done, at least not by the military.

Following the Battle of Antietam, Lee's Army of Northern Virginia had retreated south, but McClellan had failed to pursue it and instead, in a fit of reorganizing, reoutfitting, and refilling the ranks, procrasti- nated until on November 7, 1862, the president, unable to endure the inaction any longer, replaced him with General Ambrose E. Burnside, a tall bewhiskered West Pointer—the very picture of a general—and former Rhode Island businessman who, unfortunately, had reached the acme of his military capacities at the rank of colonel. Holmes described him as "flabby as a dead jelly fish."

Burnside decided to approach Richmond via Fredericksburg, but the Confederates got there first and dug themselves in on the wooded hills above the town, "a stronger position for a defensive battle," the histo- rian of the Massachusetts Twentieth described it, "than any on which the world's great battles had been fought." The result was, of course, a virtual slaughter of Burnside's attacking army as well as, again according to the Twentieth's historian, "the mournful but unenviable notoriety of having reduced the spirits of the army to its lowest ebb."

Burnside had thrown his forces, the Massachusetts Twentieth in the vanguard, straight into the Confederate artillery which completely swept the open plain in front of the town. Whole platoons fell at a time. The Union lost upwards of 12,000 men; the Confederates, 5,000 (the Massachusetts Twentieth: 165 killed and wounded).

Holmes's recent traveling companion, Little Abbott, was the hero of Fredericksburg; his cool courage from that point on assumed the status of regimental legend. His first platoon was annihilated at once; all ten members of it fell together, almost as if they were carrying out an order. Did Abbott falter? Not for a moment. He quietly turned to the other half of his company and commanded: "Second platoon, forward!" And again he led his men into the enemy's fire, his sword "swinging from his finger like a cane."

Abbott's was the kind of courage Holmes clearly admired, then and later, the kind he undoubtedly yearned to demonstrate. In Emerson's essay on "Heroism," which Holmes had read during what must have seemed—and in many ways was—another life, Emerson had described Abbott's type as one which "feels and never reasons . . . [which] finds a quality in him that is negligent of expense, of health, of life, of danger, of hatred, of reproach. . . ." Ironically, owing to changes in the Twentieth's chain of command since Antietam, Holmes rather than Abbott should have been at the head of the first company across the Rappahannock.

Holmes, however, missed the battle entirely. He was "stretched out miserably sick" with dysentery and growing weaker each day. But the physical strain was nothing compared to the mental and emotional strains. He was angry, frustrated, and overwhelmed by guilt as he watched the regiment "going to battle while I remain behind—a feeling far worse than the anxiety of danger, I assure you." As weak as he was, the rage and disappointment and sense of failure engulfed him. And he cried— "yet knew that [his] hide was safe."

At one point he considered trying to join his comrades, but found that he was "too weak for the work." He could only wait in "helpless hopelessness." He had no books to distract him, so he tried to calm himself by drawing. He found he was strong enough to climb a nearby hill and watch the battle, but that only heightened his anguish—"a terrible sight when your Regt is in it but you are safe—Oh what self-reproaches have I gone through for what I could not help and the doctor, no easy hand, declared necessary."

He was perhaps in as much danger in the hospital as under fire. Poor sanitation, polluted water, dirt, poor nutrition, and downright negligence worsened the effects of any illness or wound and imposed heavy losses on Confederate and Union forces alike. In his depression, he listened to the moans of the wounded and watched the dead carried out without emotion. "It's odd," he reflected, "how indifferent one gets to the sight of death—perhaps, because one gets aristocratic and don't value much a common life—they are apt to be so dirty it seems natural—I would do anything that lay in my power but it doesn't affect my feelings."

Fredericksburg was one more disappointment in a generally discouraging year for the Union. The early high hopes and expectations that followed Antietam had long since vanished in the smoke of the guns. Union victories had been few and very expensive. The reality of all-out war had been disillusioning. Evidence of mismanagement at the top was abundant. Desertions were increasingly frequent. The year 1862 closed on the gloomiest note to date.

After his discharge from the hospital, Holmes secured a leave. Once more he went to the Hallowells in Philadelphia, where his mother and father visited him. He checked into the army hospital there, probably as an out-patient. He was listed as "convalescing" from January 1 to January 20, 1863. On his return to the regiment, he found that "in recognition of [its] brilliant services" at Fredericksburg, it had been assigned to what amounted to a winter of rehabilitation: duty as provost guard in the town of Falmouth, Virginia. Holmes was appointed provost marshal.

The winter passed somewhat less unpleasantly than had the past one. The Army of the Potomac was revitalized. General Burnside was replaced by the energetic if disagreeable General Joseph Hooker, who inspired somewhat more confidence. "[I]n a week," Holmes said, "men who had never seen him got a swagger on and believed they could do things."

The men of the Massachusetts Twentieth were issued new clothing, including white gloves and paper collars which they were required to wear on duty. Comfortable quarters were found in the vacant houses of Falmouth. There was beefsteak and beans with rice instead of dry and inedible field rations, enough to make a hungry man sick. Duties were time consuming, but not nearly so arduous as those during the preceding year: frequent drill and picket duty along the river. Little Abbott, now promoted to captain, instructed and drilled the men in street fighting, in which he had become an overnight expert. In the evenings the men sat around the fireplace to talk, play cards, or write letters home.

Holmes visited Charles A. Whittier at Sixth Corps headquarters, to which Whit had been transferred, and made the acquaintance of the commanding general, John Sedgwick, formerly commanding the division of the Second Corps to which the Twentieth was attached. Sedgwick liked Holmes and suggested to Whittier that his friend might like to transfer to the general's staff. Whittier, however, told the general that Holmes probably would not want to leave the Twentieth. Holmes in fact yearned for a staff position, but not so hard that he was ready to transfer—yet.

At the end of 1862, heavy Union losses encouraged the recruiting of black troops. Although it was not a popular notion, and its success by no means certain, Governor Andrew of Massachusetts was one of the first to respond, and Pen Hallowell, "drawn" by a "power as irresistible as fate," was one of the first white officers to accept a commission in the Massachusetts Fifty-fourth. The regiment was to be commanded by Robert Gould Shaw, Bostonian, Brahmin, and abolitionist. Governor Andrew was looking for more officers like Hallowell and Shaw, "gentlemen of the highest tone and honor," who would bring their names as well as their abolitionist principles to the leadership of the unusual regiment. Hallowell urged his friend Holmes to apply for the regiment majority.

Holmes's reply has not survived. If he applied, it is unlikely he was rejected. But he probably didn't apply. He would not shirk his duty, not ever, but after a year and a half of intense fighting and two near-mortal wounds, he was not prepared either psychologically or physically to assume the leadership of eager young troops, many of whom felt they had to prove the courage and reliability of their race. At least for the foreseeable future, Holmes remained with the Twentieth, and the Fifty-fourth marched bravely off to battle at Fort Wagner, South Carolina, where half the enlisted men and more than half the officers were killed, and Colonel Shaw, as the fort commander put it, was "buried with his niggers."

Despite the comparatively luxurious conditions of this winter of 1862–63, the war was beginning to tell on Holmes. It was painfully evident that very few men who had been at Readville that self-confident summer of 1861 still answered the roll call. The few that were left had changed, too, as the realization had dawned on the young adventurers that war held no glory, only everlasting grimness and sorrow and tedium. It required all the courage the young officers had expected it would, but it required also the greatest determination and the largest capacity just to endure. In the winter of 1862–63, Holmes was running short of these.

Dr. Holmes, on the other hand, while Wendell was withstanding the batterings of war, had turned from prewar nonbeliever to jingoist, and had written to an English friend in late 1862 with all the frankness and fervor of a convert: "We cannot get over the fact that you Englishmen have failed to give us of the North your entire and universal sympathy in our great struggle to prevent an empire devoted to breeding and colonization of slaves from taking our strongholds and our capital. . . . This revolution or rebellion of ours has waved its flambeaux over a great gulf. . . . It was born a moral sentiment manifesting itself in an organized attempt to check the expansion of Slavery. It has already practically broken up the clandestine slave-trade. It has made the Capital of the Country the home of Freedom instead of a slave-pen. It is getting on in the face of all obstacles to assert and maintain the rights of humanity."

Apparently, although his words have been lost, Dr. Holmes also had admonished his son for a lack of faith. The son, however, was no longer the pliant fellow he had been in the recent past. In some ways, perhaps, it was easier to confront the enemy's army than one's own father; nevertheless, Wendell replied in strong terms: "I never I believe have shown, as you seemed to hint, any wavering belief in the right of our case—it is my disbelief in our success by arms in wh. I differ from you . . . I think in that matter I have better chances of judging than you—I don't think you realize the unity or determination of the South. I think you are hopeful because (excuse me) you are ignorant." The young officer was, however, "heartily tired and half worn out body and mind by this life." His harshness of phrase must be understood for what it expressed. In the end, he added, "I believe I am as ready as ever to do my duty." Evidently Dr. Holmes persisted in his criticism and Wendell replied in kind. The argument has not survived, but on March 29, 1863, Wendell wrote "Dear Old Dad" that he had had his "blowoff" and "now let bygones be bygones—if *you* will." He feared he had been "in the mood wh. would have led to sass had [he] been at home." The matter was dropped, at least for the present.

In the same letter, Wendell guessed it was only a matter of days before the regiment moved out, a matter of weeks until it would fight again. He was not far wrong. On May 2, 1863, the Second Corps, to which the Massachusetts Twentieth was attached, was again ordered to take Fredericksburg, then to move on toward Chancellorsville, ten miles to the west.

Shortly after midnight the regiment broke camp and moved toward Fredericksburg and the very spot from which its suicidal attack had been launched less than six months before. Marching into town, the Twentieth passed the graves of the men who had fallen there the past winter, then turned along the River Road toward Chancellorsville. Not far out of town, a canal over which the bridges had been destroyed stopped the troops' progress. As they paused, fully exposed in an open field, Confederate artillery fire from the nearby hills peppered them, and the third war telegram—THE CAPTAIN HAS BEEN WOUNDED IN THE HEEL NOT SERIOUSLY—arrived at 21 Charles Street, Boston.

Holmes described his third wound in detail while he waited for the stretcher: "Pleasant to see a d'd gun brought up to an earthwork deliberately brought to bear on you—to notice that your Co. is exactly in range—1st discharge puff—second puff (as the shell burst) and my knapsack supporter is knocked to pieces . . . 2nd discharge man in front of me hit—3d whang the iron enters through garter & shoe into my heel—

"They have been firing hard ever since & as the stretcher is waiting for me I stop." Later, he added by way of reassurance, he had been chloroformed, the bone had been extracted, and he probably would not lose his foot.

What he did not tell his mother, but what he confessed seventy-one years later, was his ardent prayer that he might in fact lose the foot in order to have an irrefutable argument when his sense of honor and duty urged him to return to the front. The wound did, however, keep him out of Gettysburg that summer, where the Twentieth lost half its enlisted men and ten out of thirteen officers.

The regiment marched on from Fredericksburg to defeat at Chancellorsville and on to costly victory at Gettysburg. After the usual visit to Philadelphia, Holmes, his journey facilitated by a pair of crutches, went home to Boston and the longest period of home cooking since he had joined the army: six whole months.

Dr. Holmes predicted the wound would keep his son quiet for a time but probably would not leave any permanent lameness. "He lies on a couch," the doctor said, "and receives lots of pretty company, is very jolly and does not seem to think much about his past exposures."

Dr. William Hunt of Philadelphia, who had attended Wendell's wounds during the officer's previous visits at the Hallowells', cautioned Dr. Holmes that while the wounds suffered at Ball's Bluff and Antietam had been potentially life-threatening, the threat had been brief. Recovery from the wound in the foot was going to be "tedious." He felt compelled to advise "that the crutches be immediately removed from the reach of the young man, who will be certain to use them if he gets a chance. They were purchased for him as an aid in getting in and out of cars on his way home," and they had now outlived their usefulness.

To which Dr. Holmes replied that Wendell was "doing very well. . . . There has been very little pain, no mark of inflammation, nothing but what belongs to the healing process." A colleague, Dr. Henry J. Bigelow, had been called in to probe the wound and had found the patient's physical condition satisfactory.

At the same time, Dr. Holmes found his son's psychological condition equally satisfactory. If the young man suffered in other than physical ways, he kept it to himself. Perhaps it seemed a time to avoid confrontation, to tone down the arguments father and son had been having by letter. Wendell was "in excellent spirits," the doctor reported, "not at all nervous, as when he was last wounded, is very reasonably tractable, avoids stimulants, smokes *not* enormously, feeds pretty well, and has kept tolerably quiet until today, when Dr. Bigelow let him ride out, and is, on the whole, a quite endurable patient."

Dr. Bigelow's scheme for keeping the wound open involved plugging it with a bit of carrot. The device worked not only for the wound, but it fueled Dr. Holmes's irrepressible penchant for punning.

"I pinched W's heel the other day," he said, "and asked him into what vegetable I had turned his carrot. No answer.

" 'Why, into a Pa's nip' was my response."

The patient's reaction was not recorded. He later said, however, that during his convalescence he came to cringe in advance in anticipation of the "Ah! Achilles!" inevitably made by every visitor.

Once again convalescence offered Wendell time for catching up on serious reading. The books that came home from the Athenaeum library during the period are the usual potpourri of philosophy, sociology, military history, and biography. He also took riding lessons for the first time, thinking perhaps that horsemanship would be required for a promotion that would take him out of the line.

All the bad jokes, Platonic *Dialogues,* and canters through the serene Massachusetts countryside could not push the war away for long. The Army of the Potomac, including the Massachusetts Twentieth, had followed Lee to Pennsylvania and had seen some of the worst of it at Gettysburg. Little Abbott once again commanded where Holmes would have, had he been with the regiment.

And then the youngsters began to come home: Sumner Paine, Holmes's cousin, killed; Henry Ropes, who had boarded at Danforth's with Holmes, killed and "not in a state to be seen . . . a fearful wound in the region of the heart . . . a sad and shocking sight. Nothing of the face can be seen but the chin, round which is a handkerchief." Holmes was a pallbearer at Ropes's funeral. The regimental flags that had left the city so confidently were coming home bloodstained and tattered to ribbons.

Following Gettysburg, vacancies in the ranks of the Twentieth's officers put Holmes in line for lieutenant colonel. Although at first he suggested waiving the promotion in favor of Little Abbott, he in the end accepted it, and Dr. Holmes immediately boasted of the "stern trials and faithful service" that had earned the "honourable title" for his son.

When he returned to the regiment in January 1864, newly commissioned by the governor, he discovered that procedural difficulties and regimental politics barred his assuming his new rank, and the regiment already had too many captains. There was no room for him at the Twentieth. In addition, despite his long rest at home, his usefulness in the line in his present state of exhaustion had to be considered. A man, after all, has just so much courage, just so much adventurous spirit, just so much stamina, and Holmes had about used up his allotment. "I find myself," he confessed not long afterwards, "too weak from the previous campaigns to do the duties of an officer of the line properly." His stay with those who were left of his old comrades of the Twentieth was brief.

On January 29, General Sedgwick, now commander of the entire Second Corps, ordered Holmes to report for temporary staff duty at the headquarters of General Horatio G. Wright, soon-to-be commander of the Sixth Corps.

At last Holmes was willing to leave the Twentieth, which had been practically family. In 1864, it was not the same regiment in which he had fought and with whose officers he had marched and shared his mess and grown up. Many of his friends were dead. Others had resigned, been discharged, or transferred. The mix-up over his promotion undoubtedly lessened his feelings of loyalty, and he was readier to go than formerly.

The Union's fortunes had improved somewhat since Holmes had last seen action. Victory in July of 1863 at Gettysburg had been the turning point, although Congress's passage of the first American conscription act the same month promised that victory was not going to be left entirely in the hands of the gods. Shortly after Holmes's return to duty,

General Grant, whom Lincoln had made commander of all the Union forces in March 1864, succeeding a series of incompetents, was at Culpeper, Virginia, with the Army of the Potomac, planning the final assault on Richmond.

Holmes had said previously that he would like to be appointed to a staff position. If he thought it would demand less fortitude or that it would involve him less directly in the cruel events of the battlefield, he was mistaken. The best he managed was an orderly whom he trained to wake him up in the morning with a whiskey cocktail and a chew of tobacco. Even at this late juncture in the war, some of the biggest battles ever fought on the North American continent remained to be endured: the hideous massacres in the Wilderness, Spotsylvania, Cold Harbor; and the Sixth Corps fought through them all.

"Every battle grows worse," Little Abbott said, the pain propelling his pen, ". . . it makes me sad to look on this gallant regiment which I am instructing and disciplining for a slaughter to think that probably 250 or 300 of the 400 which go in, will get bowled out."

Afflicted with a severe case of combat fatigue, Holmes saw his morale was fast sinking. Only because he still considered the war the "Christian crusade of the nineteenth century . . . in the cause of the future of the whole civilized world," was he able to "keep the hand to the sword." At that point he expected to return to the Twentieth as lieutenant colonel. Within a month he decided instead to resign.

Sixth Corps veterans remembered him as a dashing officer riding along the marching line or pushing his horse to a gallop to the firing line, carrying the order to "go in." Holmes's diary and letters home, however, reveal an exhausted, frustrated, battle-weary, and sometimes misunderstood man whose former determination to see the war through to a victorious end was giving out with each engagement.

Grant's mighty Army of the Potomac (118,000 strong) and Lee's Army of Northern Virginia, smaller but more agile, met in May 1864 at a place in central Virginia known locally as the Wilderness: a large patch of dark forest, dense underbrush, and little meandering streams that could only impede a soldier's progress. Battle was not possible there; yet battle they did.

Shortly before dawn on May 3, the Army of the Potomac, which included the Sixth Corps, crossed the Rapidan River and marched toward the terrible confrontation on May 5. All order vanished as the men, blinded and choked by smoke, stumbled through tangled undergrowth and over the dead and dying. Several horses and men were hit at Sixth Corps headquarters, as artillery shells rained in from three directions.

On May 6, Little Abbott was killed. Abbott haunted Holmes for years, became a kind of polestar. Had Holmes not been down with dysentery at Fredericksburg. . . . Had Holmes been with his regiment at Gettysburg. . . . Had Holmes's promotion to lieutenant colonel materialized, it might have been he rather than Abbott commanding the Twentieth in the Wilderness. Abbott the copperhead, who didn't even believe in the goals of this war, yet died for them. His death was more than the loss of a personal friend, coming as it did at a time when Holmes's own zeal was flagging. Remembering later, Holmes the accidental survivor wrote a sentimental requiem to his fallen hero in which he paid his respect to Abbott's "noble heart . . . Lit by deeds that flamed across thy track," and hoped he had "vanished only as the morning star, Into the glory of a perfect day!" It appeared anonymously on the editorial page of the *Boston Evening Transcript* in the fall of 1864. Two decades later, Abbott was still "always present to [Holmes's] mind," and as he stood before the veterans in Keene, New Hampshire, on Memorial Day 1884, the memories of his friend came flooding back; he brought Abbott back to life in his moving words:

> He entered the army at nineteen, a second lieutenant. In the Wilderness, already at the head of his regiment, he fell, using the moment that was left to him to give all his little fortune to his soldiers. I saw him in camp, on the march, in action. I crossed debatable land with him when we were rejoining the army together. I observed him in every kind of duty, and never in all the time that I knew him did I see him fail to choose that alternative of conduct which was most disagreeable to himself. He was indeed a Puritan in all his virtues, without the Puritan austerity; for, when duty was at an end, he who had been the master and leader became the chosen companion in every pleasure that a man might honestly enjoy. In action he was sublime. . . . He was little more than a boy, but the grizzled corps commanders knew and admired him; and for us, who not only admired, but loved, his death seemed to end a portion of our life also.

"May 7: Up all night in the saddle—establishing new line . . . Cavalry sent up the road, but got stampeded & mizzled . . . Horse got his only feed for 36 hours in the A.M. . . .

"Not much except picket firing today—

"Orders to march at 8½ P.M. postponed to 9½ P.M. Were on the Road all night.

"This day was very fatiguing—my heart beat strangely . . .

"Lee started within an hour of the time we did, they say, & we taking all night to make Chancellorsville L. was enabled to get to Spott-sylv^a C^{t}H^s just ahead of us, marching by a parallel road . . . I think this was discreditable to us—

"May 9: . . . Sedgwick was killed—we had been with him a moment before—he was in an exposed angle . . . & had just been chaffing a man for ducking at the bullets of a sharpshooter; saying 'Why man they couldn't hit an elephant here at this distance'—he was struck on one side of the nose & sunk senseless & soon died . . .

"May 12:—Foggy—Rain & was soaked . . . Hard fighting . . . Firing sounds dull in fog . . . All day we have been fighting & are banging away still—bullets are now whistling round these H.Q. & meanwhile a flock of little chickens are peeping & cheeping—their mother no doubt being in the belly of some soldier . . . The firing had not ceased at 2 A.M. when I turned in . . .

"May 13: . . . The enemy has fallen back, we don't yet know how far—(They fell back very little) Day spent in straightening out Corps, burying dead, strengthening lines, &c. In the corner of woods . . . the dead of both sides lay piled in the trenches 5 or 6 deep—wounded often writhing under superincumbent dead—The trees were in slivers from the constant peppering of bullets."

Four days later, in a letter home, Holmes succumbed at last to his fatigue. No longer could he brush away the inner wounds which had been deepening for three years but recently at a greatly accelerated rate. "Before you get this," he advised, "you will know how immense the butchers bill has been . . . I have not been & am not likely to be in the mood for writing details . . . Enough that these nearly two weeks have contained all of fatigue & horror that war can furnish." Finally he came to the point. He intended to remain on General Wright's staff through this campaign and then, if he survived, he intended to resign. "I have felt," he explained, "for sometime that I didn't any longer believe in this being a duty & so I mean to leave at the end of the campaign . . . if I'm not killed before." Revealing his utter exhaustion, he added: "The duties & thoughts of the field are of such a nature that one cannot at the same time keep home, parents and such thoughts as they suggest in his mind at the same time as a reality—Can hardly indeed remember their existence—and this too just after the intense yearning which immediately precedes a campaign. . . ."

On May 29, the last remnant of Holmes's adventurous spirit emerged once again briefly when he was ordered to deliver an important dispatch from General Wright to Major General David A. Russell and instructed "not to spare [his] horse." He was attacked on the way by Confederate cavalry and escaped in the best swashbuckling style, "lying along the neck of my horse Comanche fashion," while Rebel bullets sought him out. He got through to General Russell, carried the answer back to General Wright, and confessed to a certain feeling of "triumph" in his success. But still the bitterness could not be suppressed, and he scribbled on the back of the envelope containing his letter: "It is still kill—kill—all the time."

Holmes's letters from his parents have not survived, but it seems apparent from his defiant answers during this time that he was being criticized for his decision to resign. Dr. Holmes had made his son and "substitute" a hero in the *Atlantic Monthly,* and it perhaps seemed to him there was something ignoble in quitting before the job was done. What would the doctor's friends say?

Dr. Holmes's sentiments not having survived, a passage from John P. Marquand's *The Late George Apley* may perhaps explain the doctor's reluctance for his son to leave the army. The time, at this juncture in the novel, is 1917, and Apley's son, John, has been shipped to France. Apley writes:

"Yet no matter what happens, I shall be able to hold my head high, I think, because John is with the Second Division at the Front . . . he went among the first as cheerfully as he might have gone to breakfast and certainly will be in the forefront of the battle. . . . I wish you and I were with him. We often used to speak about going to war, at the Club. There are not many men of my age to-day who can be as proud as I, because John is at the front. In a way, I think, I am making as great a sacrifice as he, for I cannot envisage life without him. Everything I have done would amount to nothing then. As for him, if he dies on the Field of Honour, . . . he may be saving himself a good deal of trouble, a good deal of disillusion, a good deal of difficulty with personalities. He will have died in the full vigor of his strength, and that is something. Yet, of course, he must come back. . . . I have tried to think what it is like out there, but none of us can know."

On May 30, the younger Holmes's hurt and resentment fully emerged. His facing the guns and trudging through the carnage for three years entitled him, he believed, to take charge of his own life. The heat of his letter may also indicate that he was still convincing himself his decision was the right one.

"I wish," he told his parents, "you'd take the trouble to read my letters before answering—I am sure I cannot have conveyed the idea, rightfully, that I intended resigning before the campaign was over (i.e.

next winter just near the end of my term of service)—then I probably shall for reasons satisfactory to myself—I must say I dislike such a misunderstanding, so discreditable to my feeling of soldierly honor, when I don't believe there was a necessity for it . . . If I am satisfied I don't really see that anyone else has a call to be otherwise . . . I am not the same man (may not have quite the same ideas) & certainly am not so elastic as I was and I *will not acknowledge the same claims upon me under those circumstances* that existed formerly."

A week later, shortly after the slaughter at Cold Harbor, he escalated the degree of determination: "The campaign has been most terrible," he told his mother, "yet believe me I was not demoralized when I announced my intention to leave the service next winter if I lived so long—I started in this thing a boy I am now a man and I have been coming to the conclusion for the last six months that my duty has changed—"

He had proven he could "do a disagreeable thing or face a great danger coolly enough when I *know* it is a duty—but a doubt demoralizes me as it does any nervous man—and now I honestly think the duty of fighting has ceased for me—ceased because I have laboriously and with much suffering of mind and body *earned* the right . . . to decide for myself how I can best do my duty to myself to the country, and, if you choose, to God." He hoped his parents would approve. He had, however, made his decision, and it was final. Holmes, even at twenty-three, was not accustomed to defying his father, and his determination must have cost him something. Once his decision was made, however, he did not falter.

There was no interruption in the "nasty" times—the carnage, the picket lines, the interminable marches, shellings and skirmishes, march and fight, forward and back, march and fight, forward and back, as Grant relentlessly pushed the Army of the Potomac toward the Confederate capital—"I tell you many a man has gone crazy since this campaign begun from the terrible pressure on mind & body," Holmes scrawled in pencil on bits of paper on June 24.

At last, on July 8, he told his mother to "prepare for a startler." He expected to leave the army on the seventeenth of that very month. The Massachusetts Twentieth, now at the end of the three-year life for which it had been created, and General Wright not being allotted enough aides to include Holmes much longer, it was, Holmes believed, time to quit. He had heard the bugler call for a charge as many times as he could stand it.

Before that magic date, however, the incident occurred which threatened to give secondary significance to the real exploits of the young Holmes as a genuine hero of the great American epic and to cast him forever as a minor character in the great American legend.

While "Butcher" Grant in the summer of 1864 was marching the Union forces toward Richmond, marking his trail with piles of bodies, his wily opponent, General Lee, attempted to divert attention from the Confederate capital by sending the indomitable and equally wily General Jubal Anderson Early from Lynchburg, Virginia, through the Shenandoah Valley to Frederick, Maryland, and ultimately to within sight of the Capitol dome at Washington itself.

In response, Grant dispatched General Wright and his Sixth Corps north to defend the thoroughly panicked federal city. The unit arrived at Fort Stevens at the head of the Seventh Street Pike—the main road between Washington and Maryland—on July 11. Early's troops had already arrived, and the fort was under siege.

The great American legend has it that on one of his regular visits to the fort to inspect the capital's defenses, President Lincoln stood up on one of the parapets to get a better view, his stovepipe hat enhancing his own visibility. As the Rebel bullets flew around the president, Captain Oliver Wendell Holmes took his commander-in-chief by the arm and led him to cover, shouting, "Get down, you damn fool, before you get shot." Afterwards, on leaving the fort, Lincoln is supposed to have remarked to Holmes: "I am glad you know how to talk to a civilian."

A whole scholarship has grown around this story. Alexander Woollcott was the first to make it public—in the *Atlantic Monthly* for February, 1938. He claimed to have heard it from Harold Laski. John Cramer, in his book *Lincoln Under Enemy Fire,* published in 1948, wrote somewhat skeptically of the yarn, although he admitted that the evidence either way was inconclusive. In assembling his book, he had queried Holmes's good friend the late Justice Felix Frankfurter. Frankfurter confirmed the story, saying he had heard it from Holmes himself, as did Holmes's niece, Miss Esther Owen, daughter of Fanny Holmes's sister. Carl Sandburg omitted it from *Abraham Lincoln: The War Years;* Bruce Catton omitted it from his *A Stillness at Appomattox;* Margaret Leech included it in her Pulitzer Prize–winning *Reveille in Washington.* Frederick C. Hicks debunked it in the September 1946 issue of the Journal of the Illinois State Historical Society. Mark DeWolfe Howe, one of Holmes's secretaries, wrote skeptically about it in *Justice Oliver Wendell Holmes: The Shaping Years.* In 1933, during Howe's year as secretary,

Holmes had taken the young man to Fort Stevens, had described his own arrival at the fort nearly seventy years before, including the presence of the president, but had not included the disputed exchange. Other clerks reported similar experiences. Which was the way Holmes usually presented Fort Stevens. Typically, he would take a visitor there and describe it as the place where "in '64 I saw my general walking up and down the earthworks, and President Lincoln standing within it, and the big guns going."

Alger Hiss, on the other hand, said he had heard the story from Holmes himself. Lincoln's secretary, John Hay, reported in his diary for July 11, 1864, that while the president stood exposed to enemy fire on the parapet, "a soldier roughly ordered him to get down or he would have his head knocked off." Neither Holmes's few surviving diaries nor his voluminous surviving correspondence make any mention of the incident. David Donald, professor of history and Pulitzer Prize–winning historian, has found tracking down the truth of this story a good "training exercise" for his graduate students.

In any case, what was really a minor skirmish at Fort Stevens appears to have been Holmes's last. Physically and mentally exhausted— the medical director of the Sixth Corps had recently told him that he "was not keeping up by the strength of his constitution now but by the stimulus of this constant pressure"—he was mustered out at Petersburg, Virginia, on July 17, 1864, and cheered on his way by a scribbled note from Whit, still with the Sixth Corps: "Citizen Holmes will proceed at once to Boston and take drinks accordingly. C.A.W."

He later indicated he regretted his decision to leave the military before the war was over. The Puritan in him made leaving any part of a job unfinished unnerving. At the time, however, it was all he could do to pack his things and catch the train for Boston.

Two days later he was home on Charles Street. The next night, July 20, 1864, he set out for Young's Hotel, where the Harvard Class of '61, or what was left of it—ten of its members had been killed or died of disease in the war—was holding a reunion dinner. Once again he had been asked to serve as class poet, and he wrote and read a few verses reeking of Tennysonian sentimentality. Soldiers in the audience would know what was left unsaid and men who had not gone to war would prefer conventional mid-nineteenth-century remoteness from the squalid details of reality:

> How fought our brothers, and how died, the story
> You bid me tell, who share with them the praise,

Who sought with them the martyr's crown of glory,
The bloody birthright of heroic days.

But, all untuned amid the din of battle,
Not to our lyric the inspiring strains belong;
The cannon's roar, the musket's deadly rattle
Have drowned the music, and have stilled the song.

Let others celebrate our high endeavor
When peace once more her starry flag shall fling
Wide o'er the land our arms made free forever;
We do in silence what the world shall sing.

These three little verses stand as Holmes's first attempt to romanticize the events of the past three years, to suppress the horrors and deal in heroics. It was not, however, his last.

CHAPTER *8*

Life Is War

THE CIVIL WAR still had eight bloody months to run before Generals Grant and Lee sat down together at Appomattox Court House, and Holmes missed the last several engagements. His own war still had seventy years to run; he never was mustered out psychologically. Despite the flagging of his faith and energies during the last months, in retrospect he considered the experience of war his "great good fortune."

An imaginary photograph album in which he had pasted the mental pictures of fallen comrades, the smoke of guns, men up to their knees in mud, bloodstained blankets, the battlefield stench, the brassy calls of the bugle, the feel of the sword in his hand seemed to have lain open across his lap nearly all the time for the rest of his life. The merest reminder set him to turning the pages eagerly, calling up the appropriate memories.

The sight of a couple of old soldiers hauling up a flag while a band played the familiar war songs could bring tears to his eyes. A military parade took him immediately back to White Oak Swamp and Antietam and the Jerusalem Road. A shot fired in the distance could stop his heart for a second, he would think, "The skirmishers are at it," and he would "listen for the long rolls of fire from the main line."

Meeting old army comrades recalled vividly "the moment when you are surrounded by the enemy, and again there come up to you that swift and cunning thinking on which once hung life or freedom—Shall I stand the best chance if I try the pistol or the sabre on that man who means to stop me? Will he get his carbine before I reach him, or can I kill him first?"

In 1912, nearly fifty years after Holmes left the military, he attended a ceremony honoring the men who had gone down with the *Maine* in 1898. He could not help but contrast the stirring scenes of caissons and strings of horses passing with what he considered the transitory issues that concerned Americans at the time: woman suffrage, former President Theodore Roosevelt's independent candidacy, the referendum and recall, the "iniquities of capital and the wrongs of labor." These questions could be settled in the legislatures and the courts and the voting booths. In war, however, he concluded, "you come down to Truth." He felt, as he listened to the jingle of the sabre and the sharp "command of the bugle," that he had "touched the blue steel edge of actuality for half an hour."

He began to collect diaries, songs, poetry, letters, memoirs, cartoons, and novels that dealt with war and other struggles involving individual heroism—the literature of manliness. Not *his* war; he didn't really like to read about that and hoped "someone stole it" when a friend loaned him Lord Charnwood's biography of Lincoln. He was pleased, though, when John Mosby, the former Confederate guerrilla leader who served in President Grant's Justice Department after the war, gave Holmes a copy of Stuart's *Cavalry in the Gettysburg Campaign*. Mrs. Mark Hanna gave him James Ford Rhodes's *History of the Civil War*, which, despite Holmes's dislike of "recur[ring] to Civil War times," he read "with pleasure." Stephen Crane's *Red Badge of Courage* and Walt Whitman's *The Wounddresser*, based on the latter author's Civil War experiences, were found among Holmes's books after his death, as were several volumes of memoirs, journals, and histories of "those days." He was not illiterate on Civil War matters and need not rely entirely on his memory for knowledge of the war's events.

Other classic tales of war and bravery—John Dos Passos's *Three Soldiers*, Erich Remarque's *All Quiet on the Western Front*, and many others—took their places next to Mill and Emerson and the volumes of art history. He especially liked Laurence Stallings's and Maxwell Anderson's play *What Price Glory?* because the soldiers talked "more or less as soldiers do—mainly profanity." In 1890, Holmes, probably with Fanny, who regularly read to him in the evenings, did Homer's *Iliad* aloud.

Explorers, particularly the polar explorers, Nansen, Scott, and Peary, and the heroism they were called upon to demonstrate moved Holmes perhaps more than any others, and he devoured their stories with gusto. Explorers of Africa, climbers of the Himalayas, sailors crossing the seas alone in small boats: their stories of struggle against high odds never ceased to captivate him. The higher the odds, the better he liked them. He admired Lindbergh as a "man who bets his life on his own courage and skill."

Of them all, the book that most realized "the terrors of the world [and] the abysses of the human spirit" involved another sort of combat: the pursuit of the great white whale of Herman Melville's *Moby Dick*. Holmes understood fear. Ishmael's terror of the huge and powerful animal was familiar to a man who had confronted Confederate armies. Ishmael's sense of isolation was not unknown to a man whose survival in battle depended on his own inner resources. It may also be that Holmes recognized in this tale of conflict between man and Nature that what he himself had been through was a similarly intense battle between a man and the bestial side of his own nature. Undoubtedly Holmes identified with Melville's hero at the end of the story, the sole survivor of the *Pequod*'s crew, alone on the sea supported only by a coffin. Willy Putnam, Henry Ropes, Little Abbott, General Sedgwick, the black regiment Holmes had not joined: their names and deeds were never out of his consciousness; he seemed to feel responsibility for keeping them alive, to compensate in some way for his own continued existence.

Still, his romantic side had not been entirely killed, and Holmes continued to read—and savor—Sir Walter Scott for the rest of his life, recalling perhaps the callow youth he had once been. After the war, manliness held a far different meaning from the one it had held that summer day in 1861 when he had marched off with confidence and anticipation.

In time, he began to mark wartime anniversaries in his correspondence: "Ball's Bluff 61 years ago yesterday—Oct. 22, 1922." On the anniversary of Antietam he might drink a glass of wine "(contrary to [his] custom when [he] was alone at home) to the living and the dead." When he was asked to contribute to Harvard's *Memorial Biographies*, he wrote with feeling and sensitivity of student-soldiers he had recently called friends.

After he moved to Washington, he took visiting dignitaries to tour Antietam, went himself to Arlington National Cemetery each year on General Sedgwick's birthday. In his daily drives around the area with his secretaries or his wife, he included Arlington, Ball's Bluff, and Fort Stevens at regular intervals.

He never missed, if he could help it, a military funeral, a war commemoration, the dedication of a soldier's monument, or a veterans' reunion. He was pleased that when he put on his old uniform in 1897, at age fifty-six, to attend the unveiling of a monument to Colonel Robert

Gould Shaw, killed leading his black regiment—the one Pen Hallowell had urged Holmes to join—he could still button it. He marched in their processions and spoke at their banquets.

He didn't talk much about the sleeplessness, the hunger or fatigue, the distorted faces of the dead and dying, all those "nights on the ground in the rain with your bowels out of order," the "terrible pressures of mind and body" of which he had complained at the time. They touched perhaps that private part of him he was reluctant to reveal, and the men in his audiences knew the realities; like him, they preferred perhaps to recall the myth.

He was more apt to present the typical antebellum intellectualized, romanticized, and sometimes sentimentalized version of war, in which all the sabers were gleaming silver, all the steeds noble, and all the fallen heroes died bloodless and gallant deaths—as if he had not actually been there at all but had assembled his information from books. No ideology colored his reflections. The exchange of gunfire had settled the political issues, answered the economic questions, simplified the social complexities.

The war undoubtedly had toughened physically this effete young man whose most strenuous prewar activities had been snowball fighting on Boston Common and dormitory roughhousing. But it had toughened him in other ways, too. He had returned from it a changed man. Oh, he still looked the same: tall, slender, handsome, his hair slicked down to conform to the fashion of the day, a wisp of a mustache beginning to sprout, the familiar wry half-smile lurking in the thin lips. Despite his ready surface charm and wit, though, there seemed something about him that was austere, reserved, even a little hard.

This "great good fortune" of his could not but have deadened emotions. To have seen what he saw, heard what he heard, felt what he felt could not but have distanced him from those who had not shared these experiences, and except in a few rare instances, he never afterward seemed to have much enthusiasm for intimacy with other human beings. It was as if gunfire still crackled in his head, and he feared to lose the friends of his manhood as he had lost those of his youth. If he turned his head to wave at a friend, the friend might vanish. The fears he had held during the war did not disappear at war's end. Much later, one of his secretaries complained that he had been in Holmes's service three months before the justice asked him a personal question.

A visible sign of Holmes's inner remoteness was a detachment that marked his utterances, public as well as private. His war experiences completed what the new scientific methods that came into vogue while

Holmes was in college had begun. The war had gradually "stripped away everything until nothing but victuals and soldiers were left," and he contracted a detachment that only a man who has had to go on fighting while his friends lay wounded or dying could contract, a detachment that could hardly be discarded in contemplation of financial loss to Swift & Company, should he decide to apply the Sherman Anti-Trust Act. He counted it a positive asset, "saw no good in unproductive emotion that merely detracts from one's working force," a natural result of growing up in a scientific age. Those who are astonished at the bloodlessness of his jurisprudence, however, might also look for its origins in Ball's Bluff and Fair Oaks and Malvern Hill. For a judge such detachment may be a great gift. For a man, if he is not careful, it can be isolating, inhibiting, emotionally petrifying.

Two young men who had not gone to war summed up their friend Wendell Holmes's and America's experiences. Henry Adams wondered

> whether any of us will ever be able to live contented in time of peace and laziness. Our generation has been stirred up from its lowest layers and there is that in its history which will stamp every member of it until we are all in our graves. We cannot be commonplace.

Henry James, in his biography of Nathaniel Hawthorne published in 1879, just fourteen years after the war ended, compared the national war experience to the eviction from Eden:

> [T]he Civil War marks an era in the history of the American mind. It introduced into the national consciousness a certain sense of proportion and relation, of the world being a more complicated place than it had hitherto seemed, the future more treacherous, success more difficult. . . . the good American . . . has eaten of the tree of knowledge.

Holmes and America had lost their innocence together.

For one brief moment, Holmes had belonged to the fraternity of fighting men that knows no political boundaries, that "happy few" of North *and* South whose common experiences in battle bonded them together in the strongest of brotherhoods, set them forever apart from ordinary men. He knew the emotions that prompted the Confederate generals to walk as pallbearers in Grant's funeral procession. They were his emotions, too.

He began to measure men by soldiers' standards, to see men in terms of battle. When, later, his law partner, George Shattuck, addressed a jury, his words, Holmes said, "carried everything before them like a victorious cavalry charge." Men he encountered in his professional life he saw as "soldiers" who awoke to the bugler's call and went forth to the "battle of the day." He defined them by their expenditure of energy in their "fight for mastery in the market or court." His opinion of a man often depended upon whether or not the fellow could "think under fire."

A man whose future, had it lacked the searing experiences of the war, might have been serene, even bland, Holmes began, too, to see battle as a metaphor for life. Darwin's concept of the constant struggle in nature had prepared him for it. In war, he saw the concept applied to the affairs of men. He concluded that "combat and pain" were the normal heritage of men, and "the struggle for life is the order of the world."

> [T]he measure of power [he told Harvard seniors on Memorial Day, 1895, in "The Soldier's Faith," probably the most frequently quoted of all Holmes's addresses] is obstacles overcome; to ride boldly at what is in front of you, be it fence or enemy; to pray, not for comfort, but for combat; to keep the soldier's faith against the doubts of civil life, more besetting and harder to overcome than all the misgivings of the battle-field . . . to love glory more than the temptations of wallowing ease, but to know that one's final judge and only rival is oneself, these things we learned from noble enemies in Virginia or Georgia or on the Mississippi, thirty years ago.

He had not far to go from that point to the recognition that inevitably in conflict, there must be a superior force, a victor, and Holmes afterwards associated force with the *"ultima ratio."* He could "see no remedy except force" between "two groups that want to make inconsistent kinds of worlds"—between father and son, North and South, labor and capital, the government and the trusts, the majority and the minority. All authority, he concluded, was vested in force.

Holmes went on illustrating his points with images of war long after most men had stopped talking about it; amused glances began to follow the perorations of his after-dinner speeches. Would the old duffer never stop talking about his war?

The old duffer, however, did not stop talking about his war. Spontaneous scribbles to his fellow judges were apt to refer to his "second line" or his "skirmishers." The most casual remark was apt to elicit a martial figure of speech. When a college president asked a simple note from Holmes to students anxious to honor the old judge on his ninetieth birthday, Holmes replied with an anecdote of a naval battle in which a little sloop was sunk by a large battleship. The smaller boat went down heroically, its flag flying high. "Fight to the end," the old soldier advised, "and go down with your flag at the peak. I hope that I shall be able to do it—and that your students may live and die by the same text."

He lived what he spoke. The continual and persistent pursuit of specific goals that war demands—one earthworks after another, Yorktown to Williamsburg to Allen's Farm to Savage's Station to Glendale to Malvern Hill—served to focus the postadolescent Holmes's ambitions which he had absorbed from drawing-room conversations as a youth on Montgomery Place, and to settle his future in a life of action. The common soldier concerned himself with the practical matters of the world, matters he undoubtedly hoped would be as meaningful as the events of the recent Peninsula Campaign. These three war years of concentrated action, allowing him neither the time nor inclination for the old familiar scholarly ventures, gave Holmes's life a sharpness of focus he could not have found in so short a time—perhaps ever—had he drifted into a Boston bank or law office. He had become a doer, an intellectual doer to be sure, but a doer nevertheless.

His yearnings, though, went beyond mere action. His survival had to have meaning. Action was the starting point, the foundation on which all else was based. But action was only a part of what he required. He wanted—desperately—a fullness to his life, what he himself might describe as "the unutterable," so full and challenging he could not define it precisely. He came closest with "putting out all one's powers as far as they will go" and "touch[ing] the superlative." A century later, Tom Wolfe, writing in *The Right Stuff* about U.S. Navy test pilots—this century's "fighter jocks"—called it "pushing the outside of the envelope." Out of the scenes of violent death, a voracious appetite for life, which he had learned was "a profound and passionate thing," had emerged.

Some of the men with whom Holmes associated in the ensuing years came to view his ambition, as he climbed the professional ladder with single-minded determination, as overreaching. "[T]he real anguish" for Holmes, as he looked back perhaps on fields strewn with young bodies, "is never to have your opportunity. I used to think of that a good deal during the war."

Part *V*

⚖ SCHOLAR

The scholar of the first age received into him the world around; brooded thereon; gave it the new arrangement of his own mind, and uttered it again. It came into him life; it went out from him truth. It came to him short-lived actions; it went out from him immortal thoughts. It came to him business; it went from him poetry. It was dead fact; now, it is quick thought. It can stand, and it can go. It now endures, it now flies, it now inspires. Precisely in proportion to the depth of mind from which it issued, so high does it soar, so long does it sing.

—Ralph Waldo Emerson, *"The American Scholar"*

CHAPTER 9

Harvard Law School

WENDELL HOLMES WAS not only to have his chance, but he was, over the years, to make the most of it. The practical problem that confronted him when he returned from the war was to choose which chance to seize, to settle on a profession. Although in July 1861 he had vowed to study law if he survived the war, in the summer of 1864, he was less certain of his inclinations. In the interim between making the resolve and carrying it out, he had grown from boy to man, and faced with the possibility of implementing his plan, he was faltering.

His head, he said, was "full of thoughts about philosophy," which would have satisfied the ascetic as well as the contemplative side of his nature. On his return from the war, however, some of the old fondness for philosophical speculation had given way to a hunger for the action to which he had become accustomed as a soldier.

Shortly after he was mustered out of the military, Wendell visited his hero, Mr. Emerson, at the latter's home in Concord. The young man seemed to be testing his new resolve: Would the philosopher's glowing talk seduce him once again? Or could he maintain the momentum? Emerson's discourse was, as always, captivating, but Wendell did not succumb. When he left Concord that night, he gave the door to a contemplative career a final slam—although he continued to admire the philosopher extravagantly. Mere speculative thought, as much as Holmes enjoyed it—and it would be an important part of his life always—could not satisfy him any longer. He required action.

If he had wanted to make a lot of money, commerce or industry was the place to be. The new machines and processes that had been developed during the war to feed, clothe, and arm soldiers were being converted to peacetime uses. The railroads, built in haste to transport troops, could now be adapted to carrying freight and passengers—35,000 miles of track already had been laid. Markets were expanding as men and women left the increasingly crowded eastern seaboard and struck out across the Mississippi River. Vast fortunes were there to be made. Commodore Vanderbilt was already a millionaire. J. P. Morgan was about to begin construction of his financial empire, and Jim Hill had just made his first contact with railroads as agent for the St. Paul and Pacific. Andrew Carnegie had resigned the previous year from the Pennsylvania Railroad in order to devote all his talents to the burgeoning iron industry. Although in 1864 America's economic future was discernible to a relatively few people, the next decade or so offered Americans their last chance to accumulate large sums of money unregulated by government and unharassed by labor. The predisposition to a life of the mind and a growing contempt for materialism that Wendell had absorbed during the years on Montgomery Place, however, would never have allowed him to join these individuals, although he always admired their enterprise. But it was not for the pursuit of mere money that he had survived two near-fatal wounds and uncounted close calls on the field of battle. Although his ambition was as large, Holmes's failure to appreciate great wealth would prevent him from building a financial or railroad empire.

He liked drawing very much, but he wasn't really good enough to make a living as an artist. He had been thinking "in a vague way" about medical school. Medicine could provide a life of action, but it would put him in competition with Dr. Holmes.

His association with Dr. Holmes and his work as class poet as well as contributor to and editor of the *Harvard Magazine* gave him some small taste of the demands of a literary career. But, like medicine, that would put him into competition with his father; a war veteran who had chafed under the autocrat's rule even before he joined the army, Wendell was not apt to choose to follow in the doctor's footsteps. In addition, as a writer, he would be only an observer, if a sensitive one, but it was action he required now. The clerical life was entirely out, since it demanded theological and moral certainties Wendell had not achieved. Of the respectable professions, it seemed only the law remained.

Oliver Wendell, his great-grandfather, although lacking formal training in the law, had achieved some distinction as judge of the Suffolk County probate court. Grandfather Jackson's contributions to the law of the commonwealth were recorded for all time in the *Massachusetts Reports*. Uncle John had studied law and practiced briefly before he retired to

Cambridge. The law seemed to be in the family genes, even though Dr. Holmes had a low opinion of lawyers, believed they had to "be watched perpetually by public opinion," that their profession had but "recently emerged from a state of *quasi* barbarism." There was nothing "humanizing about their relations with their fellow-creatures." Their morality was suspect. They went "for the side that retain[ed] them . . . defend[ed] the man they [knew] to be a rogue, and not very rarely [threw] suspicion on the man they [knew] to be innocent." No lawyer could ever be a great man in Dr. Holmes's estimation. Although the doctor was frequently absent from the tea table that summer—he was off giving lectures—he tried to discourage his son by playing to the young man's ambition.

Wendell did not yield. The study of law did not irrevocably commit a man to being a lawyer. It might in fact provide a springboard to another profession. Dr. Holmes's friend John Lothrop Motley had found his brief experiments with it helpful to a later career in diplomacy, and Lowell, to his in literature. But more than that, there were positive attractions in law. The law was action, drama, conflict; a soldier could feel at home there. The law was history; the annals of civilization were woven through its fabric. The law was philosophy; a scholar could feel at home there. What Wendell perhaps only dimly perceived at twenty-three, he was to rhapsodize on two decades later:

> And what a profession it is! . . . [W]hat other gives such scope to realize the spontaneous energy of one's soul? In what other does one plunge so deep in the stream of life—so share its passions, its battles, its despair, its triumphs, both as witness and as actor.
>
> But that is not all. What a subject is this in which we are united—this abstraction called the Law, wherein, as in a magic mirror, we see reflected not only our own lives, but the lives of all men that have been! When I think on this majestic theme, my eyes dazzle.

He sensed that a man could live greatly in the law. He recognized that the law was a profession in which a mark could be made, that he had the intellectual equipment to make it as well as the determination that would permit him to endure the long and lonely hours required for ultimate success.

In the summer of 1864, however, still feeling some ambivalence about his choice, he could only sigh:

> I suppose the law is worthy of the interest of an intelligent man.

Although he could not have known it then, he was taking, in the choice of the law as his profession, the first step in a natural progression. At the law school, he would learn what the law was. Within the decade, he would interpret what others thought it was. Within two decades, he was to find himself, as author of *The Common Law*, a distinguished American legal commentator telling others what he himself thought the law was. And before those two decades were up, he was to sit on the highest court of Massachusetts, deciding what the law was.

Law school for a Holmes could only mean Harvard Law School, established in 1817. Dr. Holmes's literary friend Thomas Gold Appleton, who was also one of Boston's most civic-minded and philanthropic citizens, had gone to Harvard Law School. So had Uncle John and his friend Judge Ebenezer R. Hoar, who was on the Supreme Judicial Court. In 1864, the school's distinguished alumni were serving on all the federal courts, including the United States Supreme Court, the courts of no fewer than twenty-seven states and territories, even on some Canadian courts and the International Court sitting in Egypt. Governors, senators, and leaders of the bar were scattered prominently through the alumni lists.

Although Dr. Holmes, when he entered Harvard Medical School in 1830, left his father's house and hung up his skeleton in a Boston boardinghouse—fruitful source for *Atlantic Monthly* material later—Wendell chose to live at home during the year and a half he spent at the law school. Perhaps after his recent experiences he still needed the warmth and domestic serenity of family surrounding him, his mother's unstinting love, his sister's affectionate teasing, an atmosphere of orderliness and predictability. Amelia was twenty-one now, a gregarious young woman with a local reputation for garrulousness, courted but not yet caught. Ned was eighteen, a Harvard undergraduate, and, like his older brother and father, a member of the right clubs: Porcellian and Hasty Pudding. Perhaps he and Wendell took the cars to Cambridge together on school days. In addition to lecturing, Dr. Holmes was teaching at the medical school, writing for the *Atlantic Monthly,* and holding court at the monthly dinner meetings of the Saturday Club, which just that past April had celebrated Shakespeare's three hundredth birthday; Dr. Holmes had, of course, written appropriate verses for the occasion. Wendell had found his prewar life right where he had left it.

Learning what the law was began one bright summer day in 1864. It was the custom on the first day of each twenty-week term in those days for the young men to assemble in the library to meet their fellow students and the faculty, and it was a mixed group when Wendell Holmes entered. The rise in student enrollment in 1864 already looked to the end of the war—back up to 138, the average number in prewar years. The school having built a national reputation during its short life, young men came from all over New England and the Middle Atlantic states, the midwest, and even the far west, but it would be another year before they would begin to return from Georgia and Louisiana. Some had B.A.s, others did not. There were no requirements for admission, no examinations, no standards of academic preparation. Students had only to be nineteen years old, able to afford the $50 tuition, and to "produce testimonials of good moral character."

The faculty, the men who set the tone of the law school between 1855 and 1868, consisted of three men from old respectable New England families. That all three were not trained academics but experienced practitioners and eminent in their field reflected the fact that in those days academic training in the law was still the exception, reading law in a working law office the rule. They brought the real world in all its apparent disorder into the law school. Such an approach gave students invaluable practical training. It denied them, however, acquaintance with the deeper historical, sociological, economic, and philosophical aspects of their chosen field. The Harvard faculty did not teach "perspective."

Emory Washburn, seventh-generation New Englander and still strikingly handsome at sixty-four, was the first Bussey Professor. He taught real property, sales, arbitration, bankruptcy, conflict of laws, criminal law, domestic relations, and wills and administration. Before he was appointed to the professorship, he had been elected to both houses of the Massachusetts legislature as well as a judge of the common pleas and governor of the state. Genial and frank, he kept the door to his office as well as that to his house on Quincy Street open to his students, who came for advice on personal as well as legal matters. Even Henry James, who more often spoke caustically of his instruction at the law school, thought of Washburn "with singular tenderness," and John Fiske was in the minority when he described the former governor as "detestable," his style as "clumsy, obscure, inelegant, ungrammatical . . . ambiguous," and his thinking as "little more lucid than his style." As a teacher, Washburn liked to illustrate his lectures with hypothetical cases—"now, Mr. X, suppose you marry my daughter"—one reason his students may have found his elucidation of the driest technical points minimally interesting. Undergraduates and students in other departments sat in on his lectures frequently. He did more for Holmes "than the learning of Coke and the logic of Fearne could have done without his kindly ardor."

Joel Parker, also descended from seventeenth-century settlers of New England, was the sixty-nine-year-old Royall Professor, holder of the law school's first endowed chair, and a kind of acting dean. He taught agency, equity, constitutional law, corporate law, bailments, pleading, evidence, and the jurisprudence of the United States. He had served in the state legislature and been chief justice of New Hampshire for nearly a decade before accepting the prestigious professorship.

As a lecturer on law, he was "dignified and judicial, and spoke as if by authority, never indulging in trivialities." His intention was to familiarize the student with the whole body of the law as a homogeneous entity capable of being organized logically and reasonably. Henry James thought Parker "represented dryness and hardness, prose unrelieved, at their deadliest." Joseph Choate, who was to emerge in time as perhaps *the* leading American lawyer of the late-nineteenth and early-twentieth centuries and who was to argue frequently before Holmes after the latter's appointment to the U.S. Supreme Court, found Parker as instructor "altogether too deep for me . . . too learned and profound for the average mind to follow." Holmes preserved his customary veneer of decorum in his later recollections of the law school faculty and did not commit criticisms of individuals to print. Years later, indulging perhaps in nostalgia, Holmes remembered Parker as "one of the greatest American judges . . . who showed in the chair the same qualities that had made him famous on the bench."

If Parker made "Chitty's Pleading about as interesting as Webster's Dictionary," sixty-seven-year-old Theophilus Parsons, son of Charles Jackson's mentor, in 1864 Dane Professor and third member of the law school's triumvirate, "made ample amends by making the Law of Contracts almost as fascinating as a Dime Novel." Like his two colleagues, he was the descendant of seventeenth-century settlers. He was also the son of a famous father: the first Theophilus Parsons, who had been chief justice of the Massachusetts Supreme Judicial Court, member of the Essex Junto, and a founder of the Athenaeum.

The younger Parsons taught Blackstone's and Kent's commentaries, contracts, evidence, the law of nations, admiralty, bills and notes, and partnerships. While Parker preferred to deal with the organic totality of the law, Parsons was known as a "case lawyer," a man to whom decisions rather than principles were more important. Such an approach perhaps came naturally to a man who had built a successful practice, specializing in admiralty, patent, and insurance law. His lectures were anecdotal and gossipy, his scholarly publications—his treatise on contracts was for some years the leading American work on the subject—charmingly literate as well as authoritative. Although he lacked the "profundity and deep learning" of Judge Parker, he had, Joseph Choate recalled, "essentially everything he knew at his tongue's end, and had a very happy faculty of imparting information and of impressing the common maxims of the law upon the minds of students and enforcing the same occasionally by an interesting story." It was perhaps natural that a teacher like Parsons would appeal to a man like Choate, who was to make his reputation and fortune in the practice of law, a man to whom decisions would matter more than principles. He would perhaps appeal less to a man like Holmes, whose mind habitually tried to separate out the general principle. At this stage in his life, however, when he was imbibing the details, the particulars upon which to build his principles, Holmes looked on Parsons as "almost if not quite a man of genius, and gifted with a power of impressive statement which I do not know that I have ever seen equalled."

If the life of an undergraduate at Harvard College had seemed overly constricted and rigid, the life of a student at the law school was casual by comparison. As if young men—some of them the same young men who as undergraduates had derived their pleasures from breaking windows, food fights, and other common crimes of youth—became suddenly mature and responsible when they first mounted the steps of the Greek templelike structure in the Yard known as Dane Hall, the law school had no regulations, either parietal or pedagogical. The course of study was based on the notion that bright young men would educate themselves in an atmosphere of freedom: free study, free discussion, free access to appropriate texts, and congenial talk with the experts—a faculty that combined scholarship with judicial and political experience and well equipped to assist the self-directed efforts of their students. Lacking admission requirements, the school did not always enroll the brightest young men—the money of the mediocre was just as good as that of the brilliant—and system, or lack of it, did not suit every student.

No course was required, no attendance taken at lectures. Courses could be taken in any order; prerequisites were suggested but not required. It was recommended, but not required, that students working toward admission to the bar enroll in the courses that embraced the various branches of the common law, equity, admiralty, commercial, international, and constitutional law, plus the jurisprudence of the United

States. Those students interested in preparing for a "mercantile profession" were advised to take courses in the various branches of commercial jurisprudence. An LL.B. was generally conferred after two years of study—in exceptional cases, in a year and a half—haphazard though that study may have been.

Despite the presence of an experienced and worldly-wise faculty, a conservatism dominated the law school as it had the college when Wendell was an undergraduate. What was good enough for Joseph Story, first Dane Professor (1829–45) and guiding light of the school at the same time he was writing his multivolume *Commentaries on the Constitution* and serving as associate justice of the U.S. Supreme Court, was good enough for Parker, Parsons, and Washburn. In the twilight of their lives, they were not interested in putting the law into the context of the social and economic currents that were reshaping society in mid-nineteenth century, but were content to present their knowledge as an isolated entity. When answers to new problems were required, they could be illumined from old doctrines and principles. For more than a decade, the reports of these three men, although assaulted on every side by change, reassured law firms that hired their graduates that they had made "no new arrangements in relation to the organization of the School or the course of instruction."

William Blackstone's century-old *Commentaries* on the English common law, along with James Kent's *Commentaries on American Law,* first published in 1826–30, both of which celebrated the universality and immutability of the divinely inspired natural-law principles, remained the cornerstone of the curriculum. Such an approach could hardly have been more appealing to the conservative triumvirate that operated the law school or less appealing to a skeptic like Wendell Holmes. Rooted in the philosophies of ancient Greece and Rome, reinforced by the medieval Christian Church, and adopted by the authors of the American Revolution, natural law had withstood the test of time. Originating in the very nature of the universe, natural law was rational, permanent, common to all men, moral, optimistic, simple, and backed by God himself. It offered a strong sense of security and order in a changing and disorderly world.

Contemporary efforts like John Austin's to bring the new methodology of the physical sciences to thinking about the social sciences, including the law, were virtually ignored. Change in the way men thought about the law at Harvard Law School, where students were being trained to carry on what were essentially the traditions of a medieval legal community, was as popular as change in the way men thought about their biological origins had been when Holmes was an undergraduate at Harvard College, where students were being trained to take their prescribed places in a traditional society. These matters had been settled at the Creation.

The faculty assigned appropriate readings in available legal texts to supplement the lectures. Although the period from 1830 to 1860 had been one of unprecedented productivity by writers of legal texts and commentaries, only about half of the latest texts appear on the law school's list of recommended reading. Several of those that do were homegrown: Washburn on real property, Parsons on contracts and other of his specialties, the sainted and prolific Story on whatever was left, including the Constitution. Holmes dutifully read his Blackstone and Story, his Parsons and Washburn, but, conforming to the patterns he had set as a youngster and confirmed as an undergraduate, he refused to be confined to the rigidities of the institution, and compensated for his disappointments and the drudgery with independent intellectual adventure, eagerly investigating what may have been considered "agitating" works, works that held the potential for supplementing the daily fare with meaning and perspective: he got so excited over Sir Henry Maine's seminal *Ancient Law,* in which the author considered jurisprudence from a historical viewpoint, that he persuaded Clover Adams to read it; he was less enthusiastic about, yet interested in *Defence of Usury* by Jeremy Bentham, whose radical concepts of legal reform had stirred up British intellectuals; and he read Austin's *The Province of Jurisprudence,* companion volume to *Lectures on Jurisprudence,* which he had found so provocative before the war, and which had not been included in the reading recommended by the law school faculty. He recognized that if he wanted to discover the secrets of life in the law, he would have to strike out on his own, be a legal pioneer.

Supplementing the formal prescribed course of study and giving the young men opportunities to practice thinking on their feet, one of a litigator's most valuable skills, were the weekly moot courts and student law clubs. Holmes got so excited before arguing in one of the moot courts before Professor Parker that neuralgia paralyzed the left side of his face—the trouble caused, he thought, by disturbance of a nerve injured at Antietam. Just the recollection made him "inwardly swagger."

If Holmes followed the faculty's curricular recommendations—there are no records to indicate whether or not he did—he attended in his first year Professor Parker's classes in agency, equity jurisprudence, pleading, and constitutional law; Professor Parsons's lectures on Blackstone and Kent, contracts, evidence, and the law of nations; and Professor Washburn's on law of real property, arbitration, wills and administration, and criminal law.

He found Blackstone "a very puzzling book to a beginner," although he realized the work was thought necessary to a legal education "just as two generations before when Blackstone was new and illuminating, Coke and Littleton [*sic*] was recommended by true conservatives."

The love for the profession he had entered that would cause him to rhapsodize over it years later was not evident during these early days. At first he was like a musician practicing his scales—over and over and over again. He viewed the law at first only as a "ragbag of details." The study of it "required blind faith—faith that could not yet find the formula of justification for itself." As he adjusted to the routine, he had an occasional opportunity to burst into song, and his morale improved. Midway in his first year, John Ropes spent a pleasant Sunday evening with him drinking gin toddies and smoking cigars. Ropes noticed how hard Holmes was working and "the fondness he has for talking over his points," concluding that his friend was "much interested in it." Overall, that first year satisfied Holmes, even exceeded his expectations "both as gymnastics and for its intrinsic interest."

The soldier's discipline was paying off. The unfamiliar was becoming the familiar. The tiresome waiting, the ennui of childhood, youth, and undergraduate life, which had been interrupted by the war that had heightened Holmes's taste for action, were nearly over now. Despite the fact that Professor Parker's lectures on agency were hardly more stirring than had been Professor Lovering's on mathematics, the regimen of professional training, carrying him each day closer to entering the professional world, was infinitely more tolerable.

Three decades later, with ten years as law scholar and seventeen years as judge behind him, he advised a young man aspiring to the law not to "forget actualities—Law is a practical thing. The first thing you want to aim at is to make it a practical weapon in your hands—not to begin by inventing a new jurisprudence or any of the fancy topics which amuse and delight the incompetent." He suggested beginning "with books nearest to everyday life and common modes of thought": a book on real property, evidence, and pleading, all supplemented by studies of cases. "All the pleasure of life is in general ideas," he explained. "But all the use of life is in specific solutions—which cannot be reached through generalities any more than a picture can be painted by knowing some rules of method. They are reached by insight, tact and specific knowledge. If you have fire enough in your belly you will give the high romantic turn to your work—but you will not do it as to so count unless you know the school of the soldier as well as the least aspiring private with whom you may be called on to fight."

Although the demands on a first-year law student might have discouraged another man, Holmes found time not only for that but also for other pursuits. Fanny Dixwell, oldest daughter of Wendell's former schoolmaster, was still unmarried and living at home on Garden Street in Cambridge. Fanny was a shy creature, but witty and playful once you got to know her. Friends did not forget her quick and vivid perceptions or her originality and charm. The victims of it rarely forgot her tart tongue. She was having trouble with her eyes at about this time, and the difficulty was keeping her from going into painting "in good earnest." The state of the relationship between Wendell and Fanny at this time is uncertain. She did not, however, lack for beaux. William James, a first-year student at Harvard Medical School, for one, was taking her out in his buggy. He pronounced her "decidedly A1, and (so far) the best girl I have known," but lamented that "that villain Wendell Holmes has been keeping her all to himself out at Cambridge for the last eight years."

It was during that first year after Wendell's return from the war that he and William James, whose Irish geniality drew people to him, struck up their long, though later more distant, friendship. As young men they had much in common, and they quickly became "Wendy" and "Bill." An unholmesian, though not so unjamesian—James was the more effusive of the two—affection marked their relationship. During these years, even Holmes, stiff detached Victorian that he appeared, could let himself go and address James as his "beloved" whom he "yearned after" when they were apart:

> I believe I shall always respect and love you whether we see much or little of each other.

How Holmes had "admired those brave, generous and magnanimous traits." He was "the better" for having known James.

They shared a profound interest in art, possessed expansive and speculative intellects, questing natures in search of philosophical verities, the need to come to terms with life. They were observant, perceptive, and articulate about their perceptions. Each chafed under a real or imagined paternal tyranny, Holmes struggling against the social and political orthodoxy of his father, James struggling against the *un*ortho-doxy of *his,* an unworldly man unusually permissive and indulgent with his four sons.

The Jameses were new to Boston. Originally from New York, they had lived abroad for most of the past two decades, and William, brought up in continental schools, as at ease in London and Paris as in New York and Boston, had a cosmopolitan air Wendell Holmes could only envy. Wendell, on the other hand, had survived a war, an experience James, with his weak eyes and mental instabilities, had not had: he remained psychically wounded, never quite forgiving himself for his failure.

In the fall and winter of 1864–65, until James left in April of 1865 for Brazil to collect zoological specimens in the Amazon basin with Louis Agassiz, he and Wendell wrangled in metaphysical discussion with un-inhibited affection and intimacy—twisting the tail of the Cosmos they called it. Holmes would stand beside the fireplace in his little gas-lit room at his parents' home, his elbow leaning on the mantelpiece, and the pair would discourse, over glasses of whiskey, on "the facetiously excursive, the metaphysically discursive, the personally confidential, or the jadedly *cursive* argumentative." When he returned from South America, James told a friend:

> The only fellow here I care anything about is Holmes, who is on the whole a first-rate article, and one which improves by wear. He is perhaps too exclusively intellectual, but sees things so easily and clearly and talks so admirably that it's a treat to be with him.

On July 21, 1865, just after the close of the war, Holmes donned his uniform once more to attend Harvard's Commemoration Day orga-nized to honor the university's war heroes, ninety-nine of whom had given their lives. As the chimes at Christ Church pealed a welcome to this day that was to mark the end of the bloodletting, to express offi-cially, publicly, and explosively the relief and thanks Bostonians were feeling, the returned veteran entered on a Yard all decorated with ban-ners and bunting, heard alumni and undergraduates shouting out fa-miliar college songs, watched while the formal procession headed by Governor Andrew marched at funeral pace into the Unitarian Church. There Major General William F. Bartlett, class of 1862, who had been at Ball's Bluff with Holmes and who afterward lost both an arm and a leg, waited to address the suddenly solemn audience, and James Russell Lowell stood ready to read his famous ode written especially for the occasion. Following the orchestra's playing of "America," Dr. Holmes, without whose participation a local commemoration surely could not succeed, read one of his soul-stirring lyrics celebrating the return of peace, following which a choir sang his "Union and Liberty" set to music. A final prayer of resignation, triumph, and supplication, offered by the young clerical sensation, Phillips Brooks, class of 1855, left believers breathless and unbelievers tearful.

Eleven days later, on August 1, 1865, Wendell Holmes, his friend John Chipman Gray, recently discharged from the Union army, and William James's twenty-two-year-old brother Henry, just beginning to publish his work, boarded a coach bound for North Conway, a popular resort in the White Mountains of New Hampshire—two action-oriented veterans who had proved their manhood on the firing line and a stay-at-home aesthete who had listened with acute emotion to his two youngest brothers' letters from the battlefield and was deeply aware of his failure to perform. The potential for disharmony must have haunted the little party. Fortunately their common intellectual interests transcended any disagreeableness that might have emerged, and they turned their vacation into an idyll that could be enjoyed only by young men at this stage in their lives, that murky stage of uncertainty and pain that lies between becoming and being.

They flirted with Minny Temple, James's cousin, who was staying nearby with her family, read Matthew Arnold aloud, and talked long hours together on subjects of mutual interest. Two years later, "Poor Richard," a short story by Henry James which appeared in the *Atlantic Monthly* in the summer of 1867, gave full expression to the author's feeling of inadequacy in the presence of the two military men. Still, in 1905, at the age of sixty-two, James returned to the scene and was able to recapture the best of that "splendid American summer," the "fraternising, endlessly conversing group of us gather[ed] under the rustling pines"—"our circle," he fondly called it. For a brief moment, these three young men had created their own "little world of easy and happy interchange, of unrestricted and yet all so instinctively sane and secure association and conversation, with all its liberties and delicacies, all its mirth and its earnestness protected and directed so much more from within than from without." He recalled with longing their "interplay of relation as attuned to that fruitful freedom of what we took for speculation, what we didn't recoil from as boundless curiosity—as the consideration of life, that is, the personal, the moral inquiry and adventure at large, so far as matter for them had up to then met our view."

Refreshed and relaxed, Holmes returned to the law school for the

1865–66 term. Again, if he followed the faculty's recommendations, he attended during the first term Professor Parker's classes in bailments, corporations, equity jurisprudence; Professor Parsons's lectures on Blackstone, shipping and admiralty, insurance; and Professor Washburn's on law of real property, domestic relations, bankruptcy and insolvency. He exuded a confidence and optimism rare for him before or after. He found the assigned material "going down like macaroni. You give a little suck and pwip! you've swallowed it and never known it." The law, he concluded, "which I once doubted, is now my enthusiastic pursuit."

Holmes's reading list that fall and winter was made up largely of what were probably assigned texts: Blackstone, Kent, and Story; Professors Washburn on real property and Parsons on contracts and mercantile law; legal examinations of pleading, equity, bills and notes, and the other subjects that were required for his courses. Still hungering for some philosophic sugar to make the tedious compilations of rules and cases go down, he substituted for the recommended legal histories works of his favorite philosophers, Comte, Spencer, and Mill, whose three-volume *Dissertations and Discussions* he received for Christmas, 1865, from Amelia and Ned. He admired Mill. Mill applied scientific methods to philosophy. Mill took no one's word for anything; he based his conclusions on observation and experience.

Although Holmes remained emotionally loyal to Harvard Law School and contributed to its fund drives for many years, even, at the age of eighty-nine, yearned for "one more glance" at it, intellectually he was dissatisfied as a student there. In 1870, an anonymous article on the law school, brief but disparaging, appeared in the *American Law Review,* of which Holmes was then co-editor, with Arthur G. Sedgwick, who had been a year ahead of Holmes at the law school. If Holmes did not write the article, he allowed it in his capacity as editor to be published. Ostensibly it was an announcement of curriculum changes, appointment of new faculty to replace Professors Parsons and Parker, who had resigned, and installation of written examinations as prerequisite to conferral of the Bachelor of Laws degree. The author applauded the reforms, but seized the occasion to savage the institution, calling it a "disgrace" to the state, injurious to "the profession throughout the country," and discouraging to "real students."

So long [the author wrote] as the possession of a degree signified nothing except a residence for a certain period in Cambridge or Boston, it was without value. The lapse of time insured its acquisition.

Worse than the haphazard system of granting degrees, however, the author concluded, was the school's failure to confer on the discipline its proper academic and philosophical foundation.

> The object of a law department [the author continued] is not precisely and only to educate young men to be practicing lawyers, though it will be largely used for that purpose. It is to furnish all students who desire it the same facilities to investigate the science of human law, theoretically, historically, and thoroughly, as they have to investigate mathematics, natural sciences, or any other branch of thought.

How much this last condition of the training at Harvard Law School had to do with Holmes's leaving before he completed the suggested two-year course of study he did not reveal. He only scribbled in his diary for 1866 that he had gone "to most of the lectures until end of 3rd term when I went into Robert Morse's [Harvard Law School, 1860, and a distant cousin of Johnny Morse] office toward end of 3rd term. Looked up some cases there." Surely it was the sort of situation that Holmes, who was in the habit now of investigating whatever subject he was studying, would find disturbing, perhaps even drive him away. His tolerance for the "ragbag of detail" may have been strained beyond endurance, or he may have decided he could absorb what was left just as well in a working lawyer's office.

Professor Parker, under whom Holmes had recently studied, furious that the institution he had served for two decades had been thus disparaged publicly and at the implied criticism of Parker himself, wrote a fifty-six-page rebuttal, *The Law School of Harvard College,* in which, although he claimed he did not know who wrote the law review article, he singled out the publication's editors as a pair of "illmanner[ed]" ingrates who within recent memory had "consented to receive the honors of the School in the shape of a degree of Bachelor of Laws, without insisting upon a preliminary examination to show that they deserved them. The extent," he added acidly, "of the injury to the Profession, thereby, is, perhaps, not yet ascertained."

Harvard Law School did in fact confer the Bachelor of Laws degree on Oliver Wendell Holmes, Jr., in the summer of 1866, despite his not having finished the prescribed work. But by that time, having learned a great deal of law but very little regarding its position in the grand scheme of man's relationship to man, the young lawyer already had sailed for Europe and the grand tour.

*   *   *

As HOLMES OFTEN would following a period of intense intellectual expenditure, he flung himself just as intensely into nonintellectual diversions. Dr. Holmes, as insular as he was, had been steeped in European art and letters in his youth, and had gone abroad when he had been but a year younger than Wendell was in 1864. Although he had gone mainly to supplement his medical studies, he had insisted on nourishing the humanist part of his nature in addition, and had not missed seeing the sights or indulging in the pleasures Europe offered young American travelers in the 1830s. How much Bill James's infectious cosmopolitanism had to do with Wendell's decision to travel abroad for the summer of 1866 is unknown, but on Monday, May 7, he arrived in Liverpool, England, aboard the *Persia.*

Boston's umbilical cord to the mother country never was entirely severed, nor was it ever intended to be. Upper-class Bostonians continued to maintain close ties to England, refusing to contribute their share to the United States's 1812 war effort, saturating themselves in British culture, traditions, and ideals. English "gentlemen's libraries" and "lecture institutions" inspired Boston's Athenaeum and Lowell Institute lectures, and it was hoped among Brahmins that their own Harvard would produce the same sort of high-caste cultural, social, and political leadership that came out of Oxford and Cambridge each year. The true Bostonian, Henry Adams said, "knelt in self-abasement before the majesty of English standards." And so it was only natural that Wendell Holmes should begin his trip in England carrying an armload of glowing letters of introduction from Boston's prominent to counterparts across the sea. Catering to British tastes, most of these letters described Wendell's gallantry during the Civil War.

His first impressions of the country the folks at home admired so extravagantly were not exalted. His hotel in Liverpool was "very poor." The country between Liverpool and London, which he glimpsed from the window of the train, was "much like vicinity of Boston." The Bath Hotel in London was a "beastly place—like a 2d rate Am." And the horse guards, Parliament houses, and Westminster Abbey "seemed an old story after the stereoscopes. Everybody tries to be a swell." He moved out of the Bath Hotel and into Mrs. Draper's on Sackville Street, and on May 9, his first full day in London, what did he hear but a boy whistling the familiar "When Johnny Comes Marching Home"? He also found that day "common people like ours—swells finer—2 types—saxon and dark—all dressed alike Lavendre gloves & sailors ties. Evg. whores stop you everywhere."

Wendell's having been friendly with the Adamses back home in Boston guaranteed him special treatment by the American minister, Charles Francis Adams, and his family. It was young Henry Adams, the minister's son, whose time as a Harvard undergraduate had briefly overlapped Wendell's, who was Wendell's first caller on his first full day in London. The following day they shared lunch, cigars, and a stroll in Hyde Park, which elicited this comment from Holmes: "Few of the gentlemen real ones—Ladies devilish frowsy in the hair—Ladies look best on horseback." It was the Adamses who took Wendell to London's great houses and introduced him to the local peerage. The Adamses were Boston, like Wendell. They shared not just a city but an attitude of mind, and it was the Adamses on whom Wendell tested his impressions and to whom he went for advice. Wendell found cultural and artistic London on his own, but it was the Adamses who showed him society and political London, adding a dimension to the young man's visit not often accorded young American tourists.

Thanks to his letters of introduction as well as the Adamses' sponsorship, the doors of the rich and titled opened at Wendell's first knock during his five-week stay in England. A Holmes was, after all, practically one of them. Although at one party, he confessed he "felt the wine and was too talky & loud," in general Wendell's youthful charms won friends wherever he appeared, and more invitations than he could take advantage of came to him at Mrs. Draper's. He saw England from the best tables, the best carriages, the best country houses, and the best London clubs. Londoners found him a "very intelligent, modest young man; as little military as needs be, and, like Coriolanus, not baring his wounds (if he has any) for public gaze."

Henry Cabot Lodge, who arrived in England after Wendell left and was entertained in the same rank in society, liked to describe Wendell's meeting at dinner with British General Sir Edward Bruce Hamley, author, veteran of the Crimean War, and almost as hostile to Americans as he had been to Britain's enemies.

"Colonel Holmes," the general blurted out, "could you train your men to fight in line?"

"Train our men to fight in line!" Wendell retorted. "Why, General Hamley, you can train monkeys to fight in line." Wendell described his antagonist in his diary as "stiff and pedantic seeming—but is funny I believe."

He met the dean of Westminster Abbey. He made the acquaintance of Sir Roundell Palmer, the attorney general, at a reception at the prime minister's, and even the prime minister took notice of him; he had "quite a long talk with the great Panjamdrum G [ladstone] himself whereat people stared—G. in considn of my wounds made me sit & I was a great gun." Ten days later, Gladstone entertained Holmes at a breakfast for a select group that included the American minister. The event, during which Gladstone paid Wendell the compliment of seating himself at the young man's right, was, said Holmes, "uncommonly pleasant," and Adams agreed that the talk of politics, philosophy, and literature "with hardly an exception . . . was the pleasantest thing of the sort he had seen since he'd been in London."

Holmes dined at the home of the lord chancellor, and when he appeared next day in his lordship's court, the older man spotted him immediately and "had me sit beside him. I did until adjournment." Looking "interested and intelligent," he watched the "bigwigs of the bar ask who the————is that? and drop their monocles with a smile."

He visited the House of Commons where he heard Gladstone and Disraeli speak and where he left his card and John Lothrop Motley's letter of introduction to John Stuart Mill, "who came out and was very civil." Four days later, Mill, whose *On Representative Government* Wendell had reread before he sailed and whose writings on philosophy were captivating American as well as English intellectuals at that time, took him to the Political Economy Club for dinner. A few days later, Mill entertained Holmes at dinner in the M.P.'s private dining room, along with psychologist Alexander Bain. Wendell was "struck with the absence of imaginative impulse esp. in Mr. Bain—excellent for facts and criticism but not open to the infinite possibilities—Eh?"

He met Robert Browning and Sir John Millais, whose Pre-Raphaelite movement he had discussed in the *Harvard Magazine* as an undergraduate. He heard Charles Dickens read and strolled more than once through the National Gallery, where he "was at once at home." Law school had not adversely affected his interest in art, and he made the rounds of London's galleries, jotting down for his diary his impressions of the moment. Digestion was not possible in such haste. The French gallery "disappointed" him; the Holbeins at the Kensington Portrait Gallery, on the other hand, "delighted" him; he found some "fine Turners, Reynoldses, Gainsboroughs, and a Holbein of Henry VIII" at the Vernon Gallery.

Although kept uncommonly busy shuttling between the houses of Brahmin London, Wendell nevertheless managed to include in his itinerary the usual tourist sights: the Tower of London, Windsor Castle, a cricket match, Ascot, the Botanical Gardens at Kew, Covent Garden (for Gounod's *Faust*), and Oxford, where he spent a particularly delicious time with Benjamin Jowett, classical scholar, theologian, and one of the nineteenth century's greatest teachers. Jowett was just then entering the final years of his translation of Plato's *Dialogues*, which he had begun about the time Wendell Holmes was born and would publish in 1871.

In his first letter home, Wendell apologized for his failure to keep his family informed of his activities. He was, he explained, keeping "a record of each day's doings in a little book," which was all he had time for. "Suffice it to say," he told his mother, "I am for the moment a society man and see the illustrious swells of politics, of war—&c &c."

Letters for him from home, however, were planned to arrive about every seven days, the doctor, Mrs. Holmes, and Amelia each taking a weekly turn. Ned, still a Harvard undergraduate, seems to have been otherwise occupied, first with his final examinations and later on vacation in the White Mountains; he apparently did not contribute to the family's letter-writing pool. Amelia—who opened one of her letters with "Well Favorite how are you:"—was clearly enjoying her older brother's absence, finding herself "much more noticed by my family." Dr. Holmes kept his son up to date on local events such as the Harvard-Yale regatta and such national events as the laying of the Atlantic cable. He considered offering his son advice, but forbore; Wendell, he assumed, was "too busy to read it."

Mrs. Holmes, who waited anxiously for the steamers that carried the mail to arrive and fretted when too much time elapsed between letters from Wendell, worried enough for everybody. At the same time she encouraged him to see all of Europe he could, not to miss Rome, to go to Holland and "all over Switzerland"; she showered her anxious affection on him, begged him not to forget his "little mother at home," and wondered how she would get through the Fourth of July holiday "without you my beloved child." She also teased him about Fanny Dixwell, with whom he apparently was corresponding. Fanny, she said, was "living quietly in Cambridge with the exception of visits from Bill James, who appears to go there at any time from 9 o'clock in the morning—I told her to let me know how the flirtation got on—she says he is a person who likes to know his friends very well—I had a little fun with her, about him, & told her I should write to you about it."

He himself had not exactly taken a vow of celibacy, and the entries in his diary, beginning with his frequent mention of Mary Adams, the

American minister's youngest daughter, whom he described as "each time prettier and more charming than the last," are spiced with his comments on the women he met. Throughout his life, even into old age, Wendell Holmes reveled—he may even have paraded it a little—in the society of bright and beautiful women to whom he offered his affection in varying degrees and to whose dashing good looks, courtliness, and urbanity they responded in kind. He was, as one of his contemporaries put it, "a dangerous flirt."

Wendell stayed in London about five weeks, until the fourteenth of June. Dr. Holmes compared the social whirl in which his son was engaged to "the Peninsular campaign in wear and tear." Much of his time was spent also with visiting Americans who, like Wendell, periodically checked in at the American legation where the Adamses had established a London branch of Boston's Brahmin society. Americans met each other there and Englishmen met Americans there. The list of dinner guests just after the Civil War included John Hay, formerly Lincoln's secretary, congressmen, senators, war heroes, and other eminences.

Wendell had met Leslie Stephen three years before in Boston. In the summer of 1863, it was Dr. Holmes that Stephen had come to see in Boston, and meeting Wendell, just then recovering from the wound he had received in the heel at Fredericksburg, proud to exhibit the scar from his wound at Ball's Bluff, was peripheral to Stephen's purpose. At the time, Stephen suggested a visit to the Alps as an aid to complete recovery. Now, in London in the summer of 1866, they met as equals.

Stephen, tall, slim, not unlike the young Lincoln in appearance, was exactly the sort of person to whom Wendell was drawn. Still youthful at thirty-three, he had not yet become the moody and insensitive man, the Mr. Ramsey, that his daughter, Virginia Woolf, later caricatured in her autobiographical work, *To the Lighthouse*. He came from a family of distinguished British intellectuals. His father, Sir James Stephen, had been one of the great British colonial administrators and later a noted historian at Cambridge. His older brother, Sir James Fitzjames Stephen, was in 1866 en route to becoming an eminent legal historian and jurist; his *General View of the Criminal Law of England* was already three years old. Leslie Stephen himself had been educated at Cambridge. He had been ordained in 1859, but his study of contemporary philosophy had cost him his faith, and he had abandoned it. Questions, however, remained unanswered, and his nature was as cerebral and questing as was Holmes's. Like Holmes in 1866, he was still becoming. The books were still to be written, the work for which he was preparing remained to be done.

At the same time his complex nature required physical satisfaction, and in 1866, Stephen was president of the London Alpine Club and sports hero to upper-middle-class Victorian youth who, lacking a war at the time, were spending their manly energies and talents on conquest of the Alps. Stephen, as one of his biographers put it, loved the Alps "as if they were his native home—as if they were the Delectable Mountains where the Pilgrim might at last find blessedness and rest." These slippery, rocky, impossible mountains also held conflict—the eternal conflict of man against Nature and against his own inner nature—and their conquest held the thrill of mortal risk overcome. Some of what the war had meant to Wendell may have attracted Stephen to the mountains, and he often wrote and spoke in the metaphor of mountain climbing in much the way Holmes wrote and spoke in the metaphor of war. When his brother Fitzjames was made a judge, Leslie Stephen wrote Holmes: "[T]here he is on top of the pass, long got over the bergschrund and up the snowslope, and he has a nice bit of tableland before him."

The two congenial young men met three or four times during that summer in London, sometimes in company with Fitzjames. Two nights before Wendell left England for the Continent, Leslie Stephen took him to dine with the Alpine Club at a "pothouse" near Leicester Square. Wendell knew something of courage himself, and he admired it extravagantly in others—in the soldier, the explorer, the mountain climber. The "sword-slashed faces" of the students at Heidelberg inspired his "sincere respect"; he "gaz[ed] with delight" on polo players, "rejoic[ed] at every dangerous sport" he watched, so that it is not surprising that the young men with whom he dined struck him as heroic. He was especially impressed when he "saw one of those who tumbled down the Matterhorn."* Stephen and Holmes planned to meet again in Paris in early July, from where they would journey together to Switzerland and views of Alpine grandeur from the top that Holmes would describe in awe and wonder to friends for the rest of his life.

In the meantime in London, he bought a "travelling bag" at a shop

---

*Holmes referred to Edward Whymper, the only English survivor of a climbing party that had attempted the Matterhorn the previous summer. Four Englishmen, including nineteen-year-old Lord Francis Douglas, all members of the Alpine Club, along with three Swiss guides had ascended to the summit with little difficulty; on the descent, however, Lord Douglas slipped. The violence of the pull on the rope that held the party together felled those behind him. As all were pulled toward a precipice four thousand feet deep, the rope broke. The first four in the line plummeted to their deaths. The last three, Whymper and two of the guides, survived.

in Trafalgar Square, paid a final visit to the National Gallery, went to a "nasty little Am. party for purpose of having a talk with Miss A. which I done it," said his good-byes to his new British acquaintances, to the Adamses who had treated their fellow Bostonian almost like family, and on June 14, five weeks after landing in Liverpool, caught the boat train for New Haven. He enjoyed a "smooth passage" across the Channel. Aboard the ferry he spoke "French to a pretty French girl and English to ugly English do." On arrival he took the train to Rouen, where he stayed the night. He toured the city the next day and missed, because he waited for friends to catch up, the 5:30 train for Paris: "rage unutterable and forgot my French proportionately—prevented by presence of the lady from resorting to the potent Saxon." At last he reached Paris at 11 P.M. on the night of June 15, and settled himself at the Pavillon de Rohan on the Rue de Rivoli, conveniently just opposite the Louvre.

Holmes's experiences on the Continent bore little resemblance to those in London. The American minister in France, John Bigelow, was not only a New Yorker but a Free Soil Democrat. The Boston connection had broken, and the American legation did not serve as the young traveler's second home, as that in London had. People like those who had welcomed Wendell in London did not even know of his existence in Paris. The brilliant court of Napoleon III were strangers to him. He wandered alone a good deal, read some in the evenings, and instead of dining with dukes and duchesses, he dined with Higginsons and Crowninshields. He made the acquaintance of John Hay, who was in the summer of 1866 secretary to the American legation in Paris and near the end of the century would be appointed secretary of state by President William McKinley. He called on his father's former mentor, M. Charles Louis, who invited him to dinner. He went to the theater and the opera. But he made no solid French connections, and his most constant companion was Frank Higginson from Boston, who moved into Holmes's hotel shortly after the latter's arrival in Paris.

During his two weeks in Paris, Holmes haunted the Louvre, soaking up the pictures he so loved. Here he was not a tourist but an aficionado. Nearly every day included a trip there, and his enthusiasm for what he saw—"sensation when the Venus of Milo shone before me"—contrasts sharply with his disappointment in the art London had offered.

On July 2, Leslie Stephen arrived in Paris, and the two young men boarded the night train to Basel, where they arrived in time for breakfast on the third. Holmes's observation following his first sight of the mountains: "This is not the place for squirts."

For nearly two weeks, July 6 to July 19, Holmes climbed with Stephen, who was known as one of the fastest climbers in the alpine fraternity. To have been invited to climb with Stephen was considered a "signal" honor, but it was probably not the American's climbing skills which earned it. Rather, Stephen, then "in labor" with his *History of English Thought in the Eighteenth Century,* was more likely attracted by Holmes's intellectual compatibility, and Holmes's diary for those days notes their discussions of metaphysics along with the rigors of their climbs. They began with the Balmhorn (12,175 feet), crossed the Tschingel Pass (9,265 feet) to Lauterbunnen, from which they made their way to Grindelwald. Ascent of Mönchjoch (11,870 feet) and Mönch (13,465 feet) followed. For Stephen, their climbs, adapted to Holmes's inexperience, were easy. For Holmes, testing himself against these heights as he had been tested previously only by war and as he never would be so tested physically again, these days were thrilling beyond his expectations. He never forgot "the silence of the peaks" which he had found "one of the great sensations of life." His face sun- and wind-burned "horribly" despite daily applications of cream, his feet, which had troubled him even as he tramped the streets of London and the corridors of the Louvre, "hurting . . . badly," feeling the "unpleasant creeping" of fear in his backbone at the sight of a "yawning gulf" beside which he picked flowers, Holmes nevertheless, doggedly and swearing furiously all the way, followed his companion as Stephen bounded over snowfields, picked his way up moraines, and crawled over rocks.

It was not, however, the rigors of the climbs that Holmes remembered later. He romanticized the mountains just as he had the war. He admired, as he viewed the peaks in whose awesome midst he found himself, the supreme creations of nature in a way he rarely admitted to. His diary entries written in London and Paris are terse little paragraphs, limited to highlights, generally nondescriptive, and not very illuminating. His diary entries during the fortnight he spent in Switzerland on the other hand indicate a substantially deeper degree of engagement. "When we were nearly up," he wrote early in the expedition, "the finest sight I ever saw burst upon us—beyond the precipice—vast rolling masses of cloud and above & beyond that a panorama of the greatest alpine peaks. . . . Stephen said he never'd seen the like." The clear air, the colors on the snow and rocks, particularly during the rising and setting of the sun when it was night below and day above, struck Holmes with particular intensity. Not even in his beloved Louvre was there anything to match them. Something of the eternal in the mountains touched him deeply. "When one first sees an Alp in the distance," he also wrote in his diary, ". . . there is something very human or rather diabolic in the gleaming reaches of snow." Three decades later he had not forgotten a minute of it. "[T]he romance of the mountains," he said, "is in my soul forever. The great experiences of life are war women a storm at sea and the mountains. . . . It would not be the silence of the snow or the passion of the return to life when one first hears running water on the descent, but slanting meadows full of flowers and woods haunted by the past, and a medieval castle and, oh, la la." No mere book on philosophy could ever be so satisfying.

Holmes and Stephen said good-bye at Gandegg sometime after midnight on Thursday, July 19, Holmes to make his way back to Paris, Stephen to meet at Zermatt an English party that included the daughters of William Thackeray, the younger of whom, Harriet Marian ("Minny"), Stephen was to marry. Their time together had been brief but intense. They "understood each other," Stephen said, and Holmes "showed remarkable penetration in some observations upon" Stephen's "character which most people misunderstand." An interlude under circumstances of detachment that invited communion. Stephen continued to climb, Holmes never climbed again, although Stephen got him elected to the Alpine Club on the strength of the climbs he made in the summer of 1866. It was the second fraternity of courage to which Holmes had earned the right to membership.

A week later, having viewed en route Mont Blanc by starlight— "pale and unearthly"—and other wonders of the Alpine world, Holmes was again briefly in Paris where he "was stared at [he] was so burned." Back in England by the end of July, he spent his final four weeks basking in the traditions and luxuries of titled English country life, first as the guest of Sir John Kennaway at his estate in Devonshire, then as the guest of the Duke of Argyll at Inverary Castle, the duke's ancestral home in Scotland, giving, as Leslie Stephen put it teasingly, "the sanction of your presence to the system of primogeniture." On September 1, Holmes sailed for home aboard the *China,* where his tablemates were a Perkins, a Lowell, and a Jackson. He ate for breakfast one of the grouse he had shot in Scotland, and sent the other to the captain. As the ship steamed westward, the events of the summer receded from reality—though not from memory.

In one sense, he had never left home. The men and women he had met abroad had had the same books in their libraries, the same family portraits on their walls, the same silverware on their tables as did the people with whom he always had associated in Boston. They shared intellectual, professional, and political commitments as well. If their customs or traditions differed, it was only superficially. One can only imagine Holmes's reflections on his summer-long fling as the New England coastline loomed ahead, and he faced the prospect momentarily of settling down and earning a living.

CHAPTER *10*

Lawyer/Scholar

BY 9 O'CLOCK on the morning of October 18, 1866, twenty-five-year-old Wendell Holmes was hunched over a pile of books at one of the long tables in the Social Law Library, a courthouse facility serving Boston's legal community. Still a neophyte in practical legal matters, his knowledge of them more or less limited to recognizing the difference between writs of assumpsit and trover which he had acquired during his brief stay in Robert Morse's office, he was assigned to make abstracts of "endless cases on precatory trusts" for George Otis Shattuck, chief litigator, and James Bradley Thayer, junior partner, in Chandler, Shattuck, and Thayer, who were preparing to argue a complicated wills case—*Warner* v. *Bates*—in the Massachusetts Supreme Judicial Court in November (the decision, a year later, upheld the claim of the Chandler firm's clients).

Within a month after Wendell's return from his triumphal march through England and the Continent, he had become one more obscure young lawyer in a large and busy professional world. His entry had been unheralded, his presence, at least at first, unnoticed. If the let-down disheartened him or sapped his self-confidence, it is not evident. That first day he stuck it out for five hours, researching, with his customary intensity, questions of inheritance, then left to dress for the 5 o'clock wedding of Esther Dixwell, his future sister-in-law.

So passed Wendell Holmes's first day of work for Chandler, Shattuck, and Thayer, which he had joined to prepare for his bar examination. It was one of Boston's best, pure Brahmin, counting among its clients the National Bank of America, the Boston Railroad Company, the Boston Water Power Company, the Broadway Horse Railroad Company, the Merchants' Steam Ship Company, Etna Insurance Company, the Grand Trunk Railway Company, and the National Tube Works. Peleg Chandler, the senior partner, had been known as one of Boston's leading litigators until deafness kept him out of the courtroom. Since then, George Shattuck had taken over much of Chandler's trial practice. The erudite Thayer, a friend of Uncle John's, was later to become one of Harvard Law School's most distinguished professors and one of America's foremost commentators on constitutional history and law.

The scholarly Thayer, ten years Holmes's senior, would seem to have been the most compatible with Holmes. Ultimately, however, they proved to be ethically incompatible, and of the three partners, Shattuck—Harvard College, 1851; Harvard Law School, 1854; descendant of seventeenth-century settlers and grandson of Revolutionary War heroes—was the partner who provided the mainspring in Holmes's professional life, a kind of father figure, taking over where Emerson had left off. Shattuck, twelve years older than Holmes, had been a member of the bar since 1855. The two lawyers, the older man and the neophyte, soon began taking long walks together, occasionally dined together, and talked of law and life together. The younger man helped the older work up his cases, accompanied him into court, and sat beside him when he testified at legislative hearings. He absorbed Shattuck's trial techniques and his modes of reasoning. The older man complimented the neophyte by trusting the latter to put a case together and by soliciting suggestions for his own briefs. Holmes found his mentor not only "a master in the argument of questions of law," but also a "true and generous friend." Their association illustrates serendipity at its best. "Young men in college or at the beginning of their professional life," Holmes said, "are very apt to encounter some able man a few years older than themselves who is so near to their questions and difficulties and yet so much in advance that he counts for a great deal in the shaping of their views or even of their lives. Mr. Shattuck played that part for me."

These next fifteen years, until he was appointed to the Massachusetts Supreme Judicial Court in 1882, provide a kind of table of contents to the Holmes of history. His varied experiences during these years afforded him the opportunity to originate ideas, to test them for both workability and logic, case by case, treatise by treatise, and to develop his own individual approach to the law.

During these fifteen years, Holmes's professional life was divided between the duties and demands of the practicing lawyer and those of the legal scholar. He tried advocacy, teaching, and independent scholarship. He argued cases in the federal courts, including the U.S. Supreme Court, never dreaming then he would actually sit on it one day himself. He argued in the state courts—thirty-two cases before the Massachusetts Supreme Judicial Court, some as co-counsel, some alone. He taught constitutional law at Harvard, and published the fruit of his scholarship.

His devotion to advocacy he doubted from the very beginning, never quite embracing it with his whole soul. He hated business and disliked practice "apart from arguing cases," which tested his combat skills. People's trivial problems did not interest Holmes; he preferred to deal in ideas, challenges to his intellect. Too, the personal intimacy with clients that a law practice demanded must have been disturbing. And the damage suits that were the daily fare of lawyering only served to remind him of the gross materialism closing in about him.

He worried about honor. Were honor and success compatible? Was it "permissible in a duel to grasp the antagonist's sword"? Confronting a recalcitrant witness one day, he pressed too hard and was stopped by Shattuck:

> It was a lesson on how to behave in the dark on the picket line, when no one can see you and the enemy is close at hand.

Overall, his years as a member of the Boston bar were unpleasant and unsatisfactory.

Teaching he enjoyed. But in the end he concluded that "academic life is but half life . . . withdrawal from the fight in order to utter smart things that cost you nothing except thinking them from a cloister."

In contrast, he brought to his scholarly pursuits an eagerness and intensity that amused his colleagues and frightened his friends. He criticized his friend Henry James for the intensity James brought to *his* work and claimed there were times when "a bottle of wine, a good dinner, and a girl of some trivial sort" enhanced his own leisure hours. But Holmes's friends knew better; glimpses of Holmes indulging himself in such relaxation were rare indeed. Boston's most eligible bachelor had taken himself nearly out of circulation for a time.

From Great-great-grandmother Temperance Hewet (Abiel's grandmother) who had laboriously translated works of Virgil's with a minimum of instruction and the aid only of a dictionary, and from Great-grandmother Temperance Holmes (Abiel's mother) who had a reputation for disdaining "the bread of idleness," Wendell Holmes had inherited the "Puritanical feeling" that, life being short, he "should make the most of time and that . . . [he was] not doing what he should unless [he had] some serious and more or less difficult work on hand."

Partly out of Puritanical compulsions and partly because he wanted to be sure that a hundred years hence, "men who never heard of him" would be "moving to the measure of his thought," Holmes as judge and justice wrote as many opinions as he could legitimately get his hands on, regularly relieving others of their burdens. Even as an old man, he was happiest when he was "hard at work, was absorbed in doing his duty." A good murder mystery, a story by P. G. Wodehouse allowed him to relax for a little while, but "what satisfied his New England sense of duty, deep in his nature, was 'a good dull improving book of six hundred closely printed crown octavo pages.' "

Any prolonged pursuit of pleasure gave him a stomach-ache, as if he had eaten too many chocolates. Some feeling of accomplishment was necessary to his well-being—without it, he felt "as if it were time for me to die."

As a young lawyer in mid-nineteenth century, Holmes explored the legal universe with an un-Bostonian fervor more often observed in searchers after religious truths. He needed to know from what material the law had been fashioned, what its nature was, what were its objects and ends, its capacities and limitations, its sources and sanctions, however lonely the remote reaches of legal scholarship.

FOR THE FIRST six months after he joined Chandler, Shattuck, and Thayer, he was preparing for his bar examination, in addition to carrying out assignments in the office and generally familiarizing himself with the way law was practiced in Boston, Massachusetts, in mid-nineteenth century. He was absorbed in mastering state law and attacking various technical legal problems involved in the Chandler clients' cases: admissibility of evidence in court, assignment of liability for accidental injury or death, the law as it applied to local utilities. He was drafting deeds and wills, including those of Dr. and Mrs. Holmes, annotating statutes, observing arguments in Superior and Supreme Judicial courts, taking notes for Chandler—"writing as hard as ever I could"—and meeting some of the local lawyers. He was particularly thrilled to meet Sidney Bartlett, a preeminent member of the Boston bar to whom he ventured a suggestion regarding a case Bartlett was then arguing. Bartlett "thanked me. I felt proud," Holmes confided to his diary.

Older members of the bar sometimes patronized him. William Crowninshield Endicott, a leader of the Essex bar, engaged Holmes to assist in a complicated case involving building construction. Holmes never did completely understand the case and claimed to have been of little help. But he learned from Endicott about "thoroughness of preparation," about the calm and methodical approach to untangling the snarls of complex matters, and about presenting one's views to a jury, all invaluable abilities in a lawyer, young or old.

His days were filled with the practical applications of the law, his nights more often than not with the theoretical, the historical, or the philosophical. His idea of "debauch[ery]" was an evening with Mill's *System of Logic* or *Political Economy,* his recent personal acquaintance with the author undoubtedly adding zest to his reading.

The social pressures of the Christmas season, which he opened with the reading of "Dickens' new Xmas story," forced him, at least temporarily, out of his monastic existence. On the evening of December 7—although not, of course, before reading some Kent—he went to a party "*(mirab. Dictu)*" given for Miss Clemence Haggarty of New York (afterwards Mrs. James Mason Crafts, wife of the president of Massachusetts Institute of Technology) "with whom I divided winged words and walked home with her & sat on door step & talked till Mr. Dorr came after to let her in." A few days later, on December 12, he went to Cambridge for Fanny Dixwell's twenty-sixth birthday. Although references to "FBD" predominate in Holmes's diary during this period, she was still only one of several young women, the daughters of Holmes family friends, to whom Holmes was paying particular attention: Clover [Marian] Hooper, soon to marry his friend Henry Adams, Lily Winsor, Cora Crowninshield, and he was apt, too, to call on Minny Temple whenever she visited the Jameses. On December 14, he took time off to attend a Hasty Pudding Club performance to see Ned, a Harvard senior, "dance clog dance." In a melancholy aside to his diary, he added:

> But the delights of Playnight have vanished—I am growing older.

On Christmas eve he called on the Dixwells and the Jameses, following a tedious day at the office. Characteristically, the Christmas present he liked best was a set of Edmund Burke's works. He walked with Clover Hooper as he had the last couple of Christmases. After dinner at 3, he put his room "to rights"—he was still living at home with his parents—and by evening his nose was back in his law books.

Socially speaking, December had been an exceptional month. Wendell's usual evening fare, when he could spare any time at all from his study, was a bout with young men of his social circle who shared his world of intellectual abstractions: William or Henry James, John Gray, beginning, like Holmes, to make his way in the legal profession, or Henry Bowditch, cousin to Fanny Dixwell, fellow student at Mr. Dixwell's school and Harvard College, later one of America's foremost physiologists. Despite the approach of the bar examination for which Holmes was now cramming, he still liked an occasional "bender" with John Gray or a heated discussion with Bill James. Just over a week before the fateful day, the two intellectual sparring partners "had the Cosmos hot and heavy til half past eleven." He seemed to enjoy these young intellectuals whose temperaments were somewhat similar to his own, but, as was his custom then and later, he kept his distance, unable or unwilling to communicate on any but an intellectual level, at the same time grieving that "in spite of my many friends I am almost alone in my thoughts and inner feelings."

As the date for Holmes's bar examination approached, Gray and his law partner, John Ropes (also Harvard Law School), who was to distinguish himself as a military historian, coached him, questioning him with particular intensity on the law of the state in which he intended to practice. *Allen's Reports*—ten volumes at a gulp—the *Massachusetts Digest*, he swallowed them all, then regurgitated what he had read, first to his mother, then to Ropes and Gray.

Holmes had hoped to have John Gray's half brother, Chief Justice Horace Gray of the Massachusetts Supreme Judicial Court, examine him for the bar, but on the day he appeared for examination, Saturday, February 23, 1867, the chief justice was unavailable. "Nervous" and unwilling to wait, Holmes scurried around for a substitute. Deadlines always unnerved Holmes. As a young lawyer he worried and fussed over court schedules; as a judge he worried and fussed until he had finished every opinion assigned to him.

Judge Otis P. Lord, then of the Superior Court, later of the Supreme Judicial Court and the man Holmes was to succeed there fifteen years in the future, appointed examiners, and Holmes reappeared on the following Monday. Unable to find them, however, he "wandered restless all day." Finally, on Tuesday, February 26, Asaph Churchill, whom Holmes later described as "a wise and good man" for whom he developed in that brief time of examination "a sense of quasi-filial deference and respect such as one naturally feels for his sponsor in grave affairs," tested him with "satisfactory" results. On Saturday, March 2, Holmes appeared before the second examiner Judge Lord had appointed, making, he feared, "a devilish poor show I thought." It could not have been too poor, for on the following Monday, March 4, at 2 P.M., Peleg

Chandler, senior partner in Chandler, Shattuck, and Thayer, moved in Superior Court that Wendell Holmes be admitted to the Suffolk County bar. Holmes paid $5 for his certificate and the following day began life as a lawyer, inauspiciously, he may have thought, as he wryly told his diary, "the rush of clients postponed on account of weather."

Following the bar examination, Holmes relaxed some, as he characteristically did after a period of intense demands on his energies. He went to the opera, took a two-week trip to Maine where he fished for landlocked salmon, and attended the events connected to Ned's graduation from Harvard College. Dr. Holmes's latest novel, *The Guardian Angel,* was running in the *Atlantic Monthly* that spring and summer, and the son devoured each installment as it appeared. The *Nation* served him his "weekly dose of politics." He even "cut the shop for Nahant" one hot July day and sat up talking until dawn with George Shattuck and others visiting the summer resort.

Although Holmes continued to walk with and call on "Miss Clover" and Cora Crowninshield and Anna Hallowell, Fanny Dixwell's name began to appear in his diary with increasing frequency, and when she went off to Hartford, Connecticut, for a fortnight, he wrote her. Following a "farewell session" of "evolv[ing] cosmos out of chaos for positively the last time," Bill James left in April to study and try to recover his health in Germany, leaving his brother Henry, with John Gray and John Ropes, to keep Holmes's mind engaged.

Although his brief brush with the day-to-day routine of the legal profession had not persuaded Holmes that he had found his niche in the usual kind of lawyering, he was not unwilling to give it his best shot. During a bout with flu in November 1866, while he was still preparing for his bar examination, he finished Mill's *Logic* "by way of removing an old incubus before endeavoring to immerse myself in law completely." Shattuck had told him he must do that at some period of his career "if he would be a first rate lawyer," although at the time Holmes "despair[ed] of achieving that distinction."

A little more than a year later, he was reconciled but still unsatisfied. He no longer "debauched o'nights in philosophy." Now it was nothing but "law—law—law." Shattuck had convinced him that total immersion was indeed necessary, however distasteful it might be. When a man "chooses a profession," Holmes at last concluded,

he cannot forever content himself in picking out the plums with a fastidious dilettantism and give the rest of the loaf to the poor, but must eat his way manfully through crust and crumb—soft, unpleasant inner parts which, within one, swell, causing discomfort in the bowels.

He complained that wrinkles were "deepening in my face and a stoop settling in my back." Although he "yearned after" his "beloved" Bill, by April of 1868, Holmes was almost glad his friend was absent and could not see the slippage of his philosophical interests, which had had to yield to professional demands.

He complained of working for "filthy lucre" and that "the men who really care more for a fruitful thought than for a practical success are few Everywhere." And indeed, the America of the late sixties and seventies in which Wendell Holmes was setting out in a new career was not the one in which he had grown to manhood. The Adams family, returning home in the summer of 1868 after ten years in the American legation in London, could scarcely believe what they saw. "Had they been Tyrian traders of the year B.C. 1000, landing from a galley fresh from Gibraltar," said young Henry, who never did make his peace with the dynamo, "they could hardly have been stranger on the shore of a world, so changed from what it had been ten years before."

It was a political jungle out there, as ruthless and bloodthirsty as anything Charles Darwin had found in nature. Adamses and the idealism they represented had gone out of fashion, seemingly unable to adapt to the new environment, and two of Henry's brothers were shortly to lose elections to the state legislature. In vogue now was the political opportunism of the James G. Blaines, Mark Hannas, and Thomas C. Platts.

In the commercial world, a similar dog-eat-dog mentality was soiling the prosperity rapid wartime industrialization had wrought. Jim Hill, one of the most aggressive of them all, was hip deep in the coal business, supplying fuel to the railroads that were sewing the continent together at the same time they were gaining a tight control over continental transportation. Andrew Carnegie had resigned from the Pennsylvania Railroad and organized the Keystone Bridge Company, recognizing the importance of iron and steel in the construction of railroad bridges. His entrance into the steel industry proper within the decade would bring him one of the largest fortunes in America at the same time it began construction of one of the most powerful monopolies. J. P. Morgan, having wrested control of the Albany & Susquehanna Railroad from Jim Fisk and Jay Gould, was beginning to make a reputation in the field of high finance. The New England textile mills were setting production records. Americans were making millions. Immigrants were swarming in as fast as the steamers could carry them to tend the machines.

All this industrialization, concentration of wealth, and urbanization were creating a class of poor people, and slums were elbowing the sedate tree-lined avenues of yore. Irish brogues began to be heard in Boston's old established neighborhoods, and the Brahmins began to huddle together against the aliens.

Despite the risks, ambition and optimism were epidemic, and not even staid and complacent old Boston, which had become the sixth most populous city in America, was immune. Dreams of wealth and adventure elsewhere, stimulated by the Homestead Act's promise of land and the opening of the west, were siphoning off many of Boston's best and brightest who a decade or two previously might have stayed at home, perhaps lived quietly and unostentatiously on a China trader's or lawyer's income, perhaps would have written poetry and novels or articles for the *Atlantic Monthly*. Louis Agassiz's son, Alexander, ruined his health accumulating a mining fortune before he returned to Harvard and oceanography. Henry Lee Higginson, Mrs. Holmes's cousin, went west to the oil fields. Two of the four James boys, Garth and Robertson, mustered out of the Union army, traveled south to Florida to cultivate oranges.

Such adventures held no appeal for Wendell Holmes. He did not worship "the bitch-goddess, Success," his friend William James's contribution to the American language. He was as ambitious, determined, and optimistic as any of his contemporaries and equally hard-working, but it was desire not for financial gain but for influence on the law that moved him. Even at this early period of his professional life, he perceived the vehicle for his ambition to be the judiciary and had already told a distant cousin whom he chanced to meet occasionally at the Social Law Library that he was aiming for the chief justiceship of the Massachusetts Supreme Judicial Court and "eventually, impossible as it might seem," a justiceship on the U.S. Supreme Court.

He gravitated to those young men who shared the same values. He belonged to a small informal dinner club organized, like the Saturday Club to which Dr. Holmes belonged, for intellectual adventure, although later, also like the Saturday Club, it became "hopelessly swamped in its buttoned-up Boston respectable character." In its early days, the membership consisted of young Boston's best and brightest: Holmes's cousin, Johnny Morse, by this time a practicing lawyer with literary inclinations; Henry James, publishing regularly now in the *Atlantic*

Monthly, the *Nation,* and the *Galaxy,* although emotionally already an expatriate; his brother William, who had returned in 1868 from Europe and again was living with his parents following completion of his medical degree; Moorfield Storey, young lawyer-about-town; John Ropes, John Gray, Henry Adams, recently appointed assistant professor of (medieval) history at Harvard College, and others of that ilk. Holmes "scarcely ever failed" to show up for club dinners, one of the rare social gatherings he found time for now, and anyone who wanted to talk with him could count on finding him there.

When William James returned from Europe, he and Holmes had resumed twisting the tail of the cosmos. James, however, regretted that his friend "should be getting more and more absorbed in legal business and study whereby the sympathies we have in common are growing very narrowed." James had detected an unaccustomed coolness to his ideas in his friend, a coolness that was in time to lead to intellectual divorce. The rift was to go much deeper than superficial resentment of Holmes's immersion in the law. James began to discern an intellectual heartlessness in Holmes at about the same time Holmes began to discern in James an inclination to inject moral and religious concepts into otherwise hardheaded philosophical thought. Their early intimacy slowly began to dissolve. William was plainly upset:

> The more I live in the world, the more cold-blooded, conscious egotism and conceit of people afflict me. . . . All the noble qualities of Wendell Holmes, for instance, are poisoned by them, and friendly as I want to be towards him, as yet the good he has done me is more in presenting me something to kick away from or react against than to follow and embrace. I have seen him sparingly since the spring, but expect he will be here tonight.

John Ropes and John Gray, two of postwar nineteenth-century Boston's most promising young legal talents as well as Wendell's friends and coaches, were co-editors of the *American Law Review,* a new quarterly which they themselves had established to keep practicing lawyers *au courant* with developments in American and English law. It was a kind of *Saturday Evening Post* for lawyers—a little something for every breed. The first issue had appeared in 1866. Being scholarly men themselves, Ropes and Gray were not inhospitable to essays on legal theory, and their publication was to become one of the more influential among American legal periodicals.

One otherwise bleak November day in 1866, while he was still preparing for his bar examination, Wendell Holmes returned from work with a copy of the sixth edition (1866) of Henry Roscoe's *Digest of the Law of Evidence in Criminal Cases*. Ropes and Gray had given it to him as "plunder" if he would review it for the next issue of their journal.

His unsigned review appeared in the January 1867—the second— issue of the *American Law Review*. The *General View of the Law of England* by his recently acquired English friend Fitzjames Stephen—Leslie Stephen's brother—which he had read after his return from abroad, had provided valuable background. Holmes's review, containing a brief essay on the superiority of British and American standards of evidence as compared to the French, was philosophical in tone and scientific in approach, mirroring the interests of the author. He clearly admired Roscoe's ability to organize his material in a logical, even scientific fashion, but complained that references to several "familiar" American cases had been omitted. In the same issue, he reviewed *A Manual of Medical Jurisprudence* by Alfred Swaine Taylor, M.D. (1866), finding its science inadequate for a medical audience and its law inadequate for a legal one.

Ropes and Gray, although perhaps neither they nor Holmes realized it at the time, had opened a door. Holmes's career in the law need not, after all, be all deeds and wills, brokers and stock liens, the "ragbag of details" he had encountered in law school and in the early months of practice. Legal writing offered a man with a philosophical and speculative mind infinite opportunities for exploration. Was it possible that here, rather than in Plato, he might discover answers to the questions that haunted him? Too early to tell, perhaps, but there was cause for optimism. Following his study at Harvard Law School of what the law was, the second step in his investigations—study of what others had to say about it—was already proving to be of interest, and during the next three years he contributed regularly to the journal, writing digests of developments in English law and American state law, and book reviews, or "notices" as they were called in the *Review*. For the issues of April and July 1868, having solicited material from Senator Charles Sumner, he put together a long descriptive—and largely detached—two-part piece on the impeachment proceedings of President Andrew Johnson which were dividing, disrupting, and disgracing the country during the early months of 1868.

In his legal writing, themes from his later work were just beginning to surface. He was already critical of judicial "moralizing, which is notably out of place among the rules and precedents of courts." He had begun to see relationships between law and life, to perceive law as a living organism, susceptible less to the rules of logic than to social and economic imperatives. Reviewing the latest volume of the *Iowa Reports,* he congratulated the westerners on "adapting the law to modern requirements" and their rejection of the "ancient ways."

During the summer of 1867, Holmes tried to write an essay on "Damages." When he had what he thought was a good rough draft, he read it to Thayer; Thayer, however, didn't like it, said Holmes was trying to cover too much ground, and it wasn't published.

At the same time Holmes was writing for the *American Law Review,* he was putting in full days at the law office and still reading heavy legal tomes at night, sometimes leavened by Spinoza or Descartes, sometimes not. John Ropes commented that he had "never known of anyone in the law who studied anything like as hard as Wendell. (This must lead to Chief Justice, U.S. Supreme Court.)" If he was not to be entirely consumed by his subject, he must, he perhaps concluded, take occasional vacations.

That same summer of 1867, not only did he spend two weeks fishing in Maine, but later, in August, he returned to North Conway in the White Mountains where he had spent a similar period in 1865, between his first and second years at Harvard Law School. Again, his companions were John Gray, Henry James, and James's cousin, Minny Temple. Coincidentally, that very month the third installment of James's "Poor Richard," which James had written following the previous sojourn at North Conway and which involved two Civil War veterans and a stay-at-home all in love with the same heiress, was concluding in the August issue of the *Atlantic Monthly.* Last time it was the intellectual gambols the participants remembered. This time it was the charming presence of a pretty little girl of ten or eleven.

Olivia Murray was spending the summer of 1867 with her family in North Conway. One morning she encountered Holmes and his party on their way to climb Mount Kearsage. Holmes liked children and children liked him. In this case the tall handsome lawyer and winsome child "adored each other" at first sight. Perceiving the youngster's longing to join the group, Holmes approached her mother.

"Mrs. Murray," he asked, "will you let Olivia come with us? I will take care of her."

Mrs. Murray consented, and Holmes kept Olivia at his side throughout the day, amusing her with stories. She remembered especially one about a green-eyed monster which, young as she was, she recognized as a story of his devotion "to a beautiful young lady of the party and his envy of those he thought more favored."

Holmes's holiday ended, and he returned to Boston "very much exhausted." But he kept in touch with little Miss Murray for a time. She "adored him; he was her hero and the acme of perfection." She made for him a bookmark, "scarcely daring to hope that he would use it."

They did not meet again for many years. Then they ran into each other at a reception at the British Embassy in Washington. She was Mrs. Bayard Cutting now; he was Mr. Justice Holmes. "Why, Olivia Murray," the ever-gallant Holmes exclaimed, "you are my oldest friend; come right over to that sofa with me and we'll start where we left off." To another friend he confided that the charming child he had known was now a grandmother. "Grandmothers," he said, grinning perhaps as he wrote, "ain't so old as they used to be."

Again some years later they met in Washington, and the justice invited her to tea. He took her up to his study; he wanted to show her his books, he explained. He directed the secretary to find a particular book, and from it he took the bookmark his guest had made those many years ago.

THE HIGH POINT of Holmes's work for Chandler, Shattuck, and Thayer was undoubtedly the first time he argued a case before the Massachusetts Supreme Judicial Court: November 11, 1867. He had defended in Municipal Court a Mrs. Gallagher who had been accused of spitting in Mrs. Allen's face—for which he had charged Mrs. Gallagher $2 plus costs and "magnanimously didn't charge her anything for my private pocket." But he had never before faced the judges of the state's highest court where Grandfather Jackson had so distinguished himself. Then and ever after, he had the same nervous feeling before trying a case that he had had before going into battle in the war.

The technological advances that were making Americans rich in the second half of the nineteenth century were also injuring and killing them. The laws governing recovery for injury and death were as new as the situations that had created them. They differed from state to state and left many questions unsettled. *Richardson* v. *New York* involved the question of whether a suit could be brought by a citizen of Massachusetts in a Massachusetts court for the death of a passenger on a train in New York and thus covered by a New York statue. Holmes had been reading for it for a year. He and Shattuck argued for the widow Richardson that it could.

Shortly after Holmes had appeared in the state supreme court, Justice Ebenezer Rockwood Hoar of that court, Uncle John's good friend, described Wendell's performance to Dr. Holmes:

I have just had the pleasure of hearing your son make his first argument before our court—and found it very curious to notice the general Jackson style and manner (I don't mean Gen. Jackson, by the by, as I see how I have written it) with your expression now and then coming over it or out of it. He made a very creditable appearance—had a case a little savoring of experimental philosophy, but none the worse as a test of capacity on that account; and I rather think will in the long run show that the material of a good lawyer which Judge Jackson's grandson inherits have not been crowded out of his composition by your poetry and anatomy—whether of mirth or melancholy.

However impressed Judge Hoar had been with Wendell's demeanor, he was not persuaded by the argument for the plaintiff. Although he publicly complimented Holmes and Shattuck on presenting an "ingenious and impressive" argument, Mr. Justice Hoar nevertheless decided against them.*

In the summer of 1868, Holmes went with Henry Cabot Lodge, then a Harvard undergraduate, to shoot prairie chickens in Illinois. Henry James had invited him back to the White Mountains, but Holmes, pleading the pressures of his work, declined. The summer of 1869 found him visiting briefly—in the company of John Gray—the James family at Pomfret, Connecticut. Mrs. James described him as "charmingly fresh and boyish," although looking "as if he needed recreation." And William remarked that his two guests seemed "in very jolly spirits at being turned out from their Boston pen. I should think Wendell worked too hard." Gray was taking a two-week vacation, but Holmes intended to take none. He did, however, take the opportunity to "go and shed a tear" over the grave of his great-grandfather, Captain David Holmes, who had lived in the town of Woodstock, about five miles away.

THE YEARS FROM 1870 until 1873, coinciding with Holmes's early thirties, were as hectic for him as the previous three years. He did not ease up in his routine, but continued the day-to-day practice of law—drafting documents, counseling clients, and appearing in court— which was all very well for earning a living, but it offered little opportunity to Holmes's intellectual ambitions, and at the same time he was

---

*Judge Hoar's was not the final word. The issue made its way to the U.S. Supreme Court just over a decade after Holmes had argued it in Massachusetts, counsel for the defendant railroad citing *Richardson* in support. That court, however, decided for the plaintiff and overruled *Richardson* specifically by name (*Dennick* v. *Central Railroad.* 103 U.S. 11, 21, 1880).

arguing cases, he was deepening his commitment to legal scholarship, teaching constitutional law at Harvard, reading and writing in law and philosophy, twisting the tail of the cosmos with William James and other questing young men, and courting Fanny Dixwell, all at the same time. He was structuring his professional life in the same design he had constructed his life as an undergraduate, alternating the required drudgery with the pleasures of independent scholarship, bounding from the demands of client, case, and courtroom to the nether regions of intellectual adventure. It was like playing tiddledies on the Frog Pond, jumping from ice floe to ice floe, fearing that if he stayed too long on one, he would sink. He was steaming along but had no sense of destination yet, and sometimes he did not seem—to others or even to himself—to be getting anywhere. His early thirties was still too early perhaps to realize that he was in fact preparing for future tasks, even though he did not know precisely what these were.

The first case in which Holmes appeared before the Massachusetts Supreme Judicial Court alone, without Shattuck, *Brooks v. Reynolds,* was an uncomplicated action for obstruction of an easement. He argued it in the November Term, 1870, and won. Most of his briefs during this period were straightforward, short, and authoritative. There was no fancy figure skating, no innovative interpretation of rules and precedents. Lawyerlike and conventional, they did not hint that their author was aggressively intellectual and ambitious, that he spent his leisure in scholarly investigations.

In 1870, Ropes and Gray handed down the editorship of their *American Law Review* to Holmes and Arthur G. Sedgwick, who had fought alongside Holmes as an officer of the Massachusetts Twentieth, sat with Holmes in the lectures at Harvard Law School, and worked with Holmes in the office of Chandler, Shattuck, and Thayer. Complementary in nature—Holmes inclined to legal philosophy, Sedgwick to editorial matters—the two young men made an effective production team. Brahmins both, however, they tended to write for lawyers from similar backgrounds—to Holmes, at least, a "manual laborer" didn't "matter"—and the *United States Jurist,* a competing journal, accused them of "play[ing] the fop in matters legal" and of condescending to the "rural bench and bar."

In addition to his editorial duties, Holmes continued to write for the *American Law Review:* some sixty book reviews, and editorial comments and digests of law reports—which is what made the *American Law Review* valuable to a practicing lawyer who could probably do without the abstract essays Holmes wrote. What appeared in the *American Law Re-*

view was the still-maturing result of Holmes's early forays into legal history and philosophy in which he had been involved since he had first checked John Austin's *Lectures on Jurisprudence* out of the Harvard College library in the spring of his last year as an undergraduate. He was beginning to try out definitions, systems, methods at the same time he was still learning what the law was from others. The articles Holmes wrote were arcane, of interest largely to other legal scholars. Familiar Holmesian concepts and phrases nonetheless began to take their assigned places in his legal cosmology gradually forming out of the void.

The first major essay, "Codes, and the Arrangement of the Law," appeared in October 1870. Austinian in style, analytical in tone, it addressed one of the contemporary legal culture's most timely issues, codification; at the same time it anticipated the later, pragmatic Holmes.

By 1870, the flood of case law had become virtually unmanageable. Relationships between management and labor were changing rapidly in a period of high-speed industrialization. The lines between negligence, malice, and error of judgment were blurring during a time when new modes of transportation were proliferating, accompanied by an increase in the number of accidents. Unfamiliar situations created by the new financial structures daily challenged traditional legal structures. The opening of the West and the accompanying disputes over grazing lands and water rights were defying the old property rules Americans had grown up with. Lawyers and judges were hard pressed to keep pace with the ever-multiplying decisions out of which new precedents were being established.

The common law—that body of law derived from judicial decisions, or precedent, whose roots had been planted in Norman England and to which remnants of feudalism still clung—had grown into a large and shapeless mass: disorderly, obscure, and, worse, many people believed, antidemocratic, its potential for judicial manipulation through misinterpretation a serious threat to American institutions.

During the latter part of the nineteenth century, a movement to codify the law swept America. Reformers who looked to legislation as the panacea for all society's ills believed the nearly impenetrable forest of precedent, the raw material of contemporary judicial decisions, ought to be collected, translated into logically arranged general principles, and given the force of statutory law. Codification was intended to clarify meanings and illumine obscurities at the same time it ensured judicial conformity to firmly established principles. A natural by-product would be the assembling of the laws into logically convenient categories, so that a lawyer who needed to know, for example, the rules regarding admission of evidence in court could find out easily without plowing through the unwieldy and unorganized tomes of reports and records, the only sources available to him at the time. The purposes of codification were not unlike those of lexicography, the one to bring order out of legal chaos, the other to bring it out of linguistic chaos, and both to make a body of knowledge accessible to all, a brake on tyranny of the elite.

The opposition to codification argued that it would stultify the law, prevent improvement and development, and they feared that transferring power from judges to the legislature—the code-making body—replaced experts with less knowledgeable members of an essentially short-sighted and politically malleable institution. Nevertheless, when Holmes sat down to write his article for the *American Law Review,* British and American lawyers were deeply involved in discussions regarding codification.

Suspicious of reformers, Holmes agreed on the whole with the opposition. Illustrating his points in considerable detail, he said he felt the structure the judges had built over the ages was sturdy, if complex, and he didn't think the complexities would submit easily to generalization. He liked the idea that several cases were required to formulate a general principle. He liked the fact that a "well-settled legal doctrine" was the work of "many minds," had been "tested in form as well as substance by trained critics." He liked the fact that the common law was constantly becoming, that it was never static but always developing. It moved too fast for rule-makers to keep up; the minute a principle was stated, new cases would arise, "elud[ing] the most carefully constructed formula." Properly compiled in a broad philosophical arrangement that allowed also for "practical convenience," Holmes thought, a code might be useful for training the mind of a student "to a sound legal habit of thought" and for removing "obstacles from his path which he now only overcomes after years of experience and reflection." He did not really believe, however, a viable code could be constructed; those with which he was familiar, certainly, he had found far from "remarkable."

The editors of the *Albany Law Journal* pronounced Holmes's article "about as vague, indefinite, and unsatisfactory as we care ever to read." They had "waded through it twice in the hope to discover what it was all about, but could only say with 'truthful James,' that 'for ways that are dark and for tricks that are vain,' the writer of that article is 'peculiar.' "*

---

*Nearly three decades later, Sir Frederick Pollock, noted English legal scholar and by that time Holmes's friend, acknowledged in the introduction he wrote for the 1897 edition of the *Encyclopedia of the Laws of England* his own debt to Holmes's *American Law Review* article.

Holmes was always disappointed when he felt misinterpreted, but he was professional enough to understand he could not allow a critical review to retard his studies. He was playing with formulating a definition of law, thinking perhaps it had something to do with courts and what they enforced. He was beginning to see, too, that if he wanted to find the source of nineteenth-century legal springs, he would have to trace them all the way back to antiquity.

In addition to his editorial duties for the *American Law Review* and his independent scholarly adventures, Holmes was still practicing law. He had left Chandler, Shattuck, and Thayer, and for two years shared offices at 7 Pemberton Square with his brother, Ned. Ned had graduated from Harvard Law School in 1869 and had distinguished himself by winning a first prize of $60 for his dissertation, "The Growth and Progress of the Common Law, as a Science, as Illustrated in History." He had then spent a year or so in Washington as private secretary to Senator Sumner and as clerk to the U.S. Senate Committee on Foreign Relations. In March 1871, he had returned to Boston to practice his profession. In October, a few months after Amelia married widower and fellow Brahmin John Turner Sargent, he had married Henrietta Wigglesworth, from one of Boston's best families, leaving Wendell home alone with Dr. and Mrs. Holmes. Records of the Holmes brothers' law practice amount to little more than the briefs of a couple of cases* they argued—and lost—as co-counsel in the Massachusetts Supreme Judicial Court. Asthma, which he apparently had inherited from Dr. Holmes, soon forced Ned to abandon his law practice, and he thereafter spent his energies studying antiquities and his time traveling abroad from country to country, climate to climate, in search of a place where he could breathe.

Wendell, on the other hand, was becoming a man of some stature among legal scholars, and, recommended perhaps by mutual friends in the local legal community, had attracted the attention of Charles William Eliot, who had been warned as an undergraduate not to think too much, who had been a lowly tutor of mathematics to young Holmes at Harvard College, and who in 1869 had been chosen president of the university. Harvard had not been expanding with the country as Yale and Princeton had been. Tradition bound and dominated by old men, Harvard was losing the competition for young men to the new engineering schools and institutes of technology, more representative of the age. Eliot was engaged to reverse the trend.

---

* *Woodward* v. *Boston.* 115 Mass. 81 (1874); *Temple* v. *Turner.* 123 Mass. 125 (1877).

In an astonishingly short time, Eliot had, according to Dr. Holmes, Parkman Professor of Anatomy and Physiology, "turned the whole University over like a flapjack." He immediately had shown himself to be a take-charge sort of president with "an organizing brain, a firm will, a grave, calm, dignified presence, taking the ribbons of our classical coach and six, feeling the horses' mouths, putting a check on this one's capers and touching that one with the lash,—turning up everywhere, in every Faculty . . . on every public occasion, at ever dinner *orné,* and taking it all as naturally as if he had been born President."

His funereal voice was offset by a placid smile, and Dr. Holmes and others of the senior faculty were amused at the determination of "this cool, grave young man proposing in the calmest way to turn everything topsy-turvy, taking the reins into his hands and driving as if he were the first man that ever sat on the box." He doubled the number of faculty meetings per month, kept professors in discussion until midnight. He showed "an extraordinary knowledge of all that relates to every department of the University and presided with an *aplomb,* a quiet, imperturbable, serious good-humor, that it is impossible not to admire." Some of the men thought he was in too much of a hurry with his innovations—he had immediately jettisoned the antiquated recitation system, for which he substituted lectures and written examinations—but he had a good deal of time to make up, if he was to turn Harvard into a modern university, to rev up long-dormant engines. Young Wendell Holmes, engaged to teach constitutional law, was part of that modernization.

The Overseers, knowing "little or nothing of Wendell's fitness for so deep and grave a subject," had been skeptical of his appointment, preferring a "man of mature experience, professional and political," or a teacher. But they feared that such a person, who also must be willing to move to Cambridge for a term, could not be found. And "as between a hack tutor, and an ambitious, hard-working youth, taken from real life," they decided Eliot had "judged wisely" and confirmed Holmes's appointment. While it was unlikely to bring him any "increase of business," his co-editor at the *American Law Review* gossiped to Henry James, the appointment surely enhanced Holmes's reputation as a legal scholar and "must—sooner or later, redound to his advantage." In the same crop of teaching appointments were Holmes's friend, John Gray, as lecturer in the law school and Christopher Columbus Langdell as dean of the law school. The latter, who like Holmes and Gray was a product of the old law school's Parker, Parsons, and Washburn triumvirate, was to introduce at this time Harvard Law School—and America—to an entirely new method of learning the law.

Holmes accepted, reiterating what he understood to be the president's terms: "I am to teach the Juniors Constitutional law from a small text book—asking questions enough to mark them and telling them such matters as I think likely to be interesting and instructive . . . I am, I suppose, under the control of nobody but yourself." He was to teach from 8 to 10 A.M., Mondays and Saturdays through the spring term. He was to be paid $300.

He had 158 students divided into four sections—the usual contingent of young Brahmins: an Aiken, an Amory, a Bigelow, Charles J. Bonaparte, who later was to argue as Theodore Roosevelt's trust-busting attorney general before U.S. Supreme Court Justice Holmes, Henry Cabot Lodge, who as a U.S. Senator and confidant of Roosevelt's was to be the mainspring in Holmes's appointment to that Court three decades later, a Lyman, a Minot, a Story, a Thayer, a Ware, and a Warren.

The college faculty was mixed. Men who had taught Holmes as an undergraduate—Francis Bowen, Evangelinus Sophocles, Josiah Cooke—and some of their contemporaries were still there. The new blood—Holmes, Charles Peirce, John Fiske, Thomas Sergeant Perry, a few other younger men—was being injected gradually.

The text Holmes used—*The Science of Government in Connection with American Institutions* by Joseph Alden, D.D., LL.D.—was as pietistic as anything Francis Bowen could have cooked up. Its major premise was that "Government is a divine institution—is of divine origin," that "God made men to live together in a social civilized state," and that "God is the author of man's nature." It seems perhaps an unlikely textbook for a non-believer who looked at the law empirically to choose, especially when other, secular textbooks—Thomas M. Cooley's *Constitutional Limitations,* for example—were available. Coming to Harvard late in the academic year, Holmes may have had it chosen for him. Having the option to present "such matters as I think likely to be interesting and instructive," it is also possible that he confined Alden's book largely to use as a reference source, for which, despite its theistic tone, it was well adapted, and elaborated in his lectures on the whys and hows of constitutional law as he saw them. The examination he gave his students in June 1870, which probed the students' grasp of constitutional provisions, concepts of political powers and federal jurisprudence, indicates a thorough and thoughtful consideration of American constitutional government.

Holmes found it "delightful and stimulating to expound to a lot of intelligent young men old enough to have serious opinions." The pleasure was mutual. One of the Lawrences, later Bishop William Lawrence, who took the course, recalled some years later "the ease with which he spoke and the familiarity with which he treated us, so different from the more formal method of professors of those days."

The Committee to Visit the Academical Department reported to the Harvard Board of Overseers that Holmes had been "very successful with his pupils," and his appointment was renewed in February 1871 for the current term. In April of the same year, he was appointed University Lecturer on Jurisprudence for 1871–72; it was a new category of instruction to be given by distinguished scholars through which Eliot hoped to attract graduate students; Harvard graduates seeking advanced degrees had to look elsewhere at that time. When the scheme failed, the University Lecturers were given new titles and reappointed to the appropriate professional schools—law, divinity, medicine. Holmes was reappointed for the 1872–73 term to the law school faculty where he taught jurisprudence under the new dean, Langdell; his salary was increased to $500 for eighteen lectures.

As dean (1870–95), Langdell stiffened the admissions requirements, built up the library, and began to assemble a distinguished faculty. He also introduced an original system of legal instruction which became known shortly as the case method.

Coinciding with the explosion of discoveries in the natural and physical sciences, Langdell's method rested on the concept that the law could be scientized as neatly and efficiently as chemistry or biology. If one could isolate gases, observe their properties, and draw conclusions from which scientific principles could be developed, one ought to be able to bring the same logic to legal precedents, reach back into time for the earliest applicable cases and trace their progress, observe the properties of each, and from them develop constant legal principles, or, as Holmes once put it:

> The common law training (e.g. in our law school) is to keep a student at the solution of particular cases. Just as Agassiz would give one of his pupils a sea urchin and tell him to find all about it that he could.

It was all too coldly logical for Holmes, to whom the law was much more than isolated cases considered in a vacuum and could not be divorced from the political and social realities of its time. He pronounced Langdell's eight-volume casebook on contracts a "misspent piece of marvellous ingenuity" representing the "powers of darkness." He thought the author narrowly focused, nearly illiterate in history, and "wanting in horse sense." Chafing under the strictures of the new method of instruction, Holmes stayed at the law school only a year.

THE LAW HAD changed since New York State Chancellor James Kent, the American Blackstone, had published the first edition of his four-volume *Commentaries on American Law* between 1826 and 1830. Large departments had been created; others had increased in importance; some had diminished. Conflicts of interpretation were growing in number. In the winter of 1869–70, the chancellor's grandson, also named James Kent, had arranged for the editing of a twelfth edition of the chancellor's work with James B. Thayer, junior partner in Chandler, Shattuck, and Thayer, for whom young Holmes had done donkey work following graduation from Harvard Law School. By 1870, Thayer was one of Boston's best-known young practitioners and legal scholars, soon to be appointed to Langdell's growing law school faculty. Kent undoubtedly believed he would add to the prestige of the project. Thayer in turn invited Holmes to help him. Holmes was interested, though he already had too much to do.

Holmes spent all his afternoons and most of his mornings for three weeks annotating a sample section of the commentaries, which consisted of sixty-eight lectures, in order to discover what the project would involve. He feared it would "prove impossible" to do it thoroughly "in the time allowed," and he refused to have his name associated with "slopwork." He agreed that rhetorical "continence" was a virtue. He could not but think, however, that the editors should be "somewhat full," especially on "points which are the present fighting ground of the law," if they were to be "of service to the working lawyer." Kent's immediate response to his editors' concerns has not survived. That the work went forward indicates at least some degree of consensus among the three men.

His Puritan instincts for hard labor surfacing, Holmes submerged himself in the sea of legal precedent and analysis to the exclusion of virtually everything else. Brooks Adams, Henry's brother, knew he could find his friend at almost any hour of the day bent over his books at one of the long wooden tables in the Social Law Library. He neglected his law practice and cut himself off from his friends. The Poet of the Breakfast-Table complained, in a thinly disguised description of his son in the *Atlantic Monthly,* that Wendell was too much given to lonely study, to self-companionship, to all sorts of questionings, to looking at life as at a solemn show where he is only a spectator.

Wendell began carrying his growing manuscript with him and subjected the entire Holmes household to a monthly fire drill designed to instill in each member the duty to rescue the green bag above all.

Mrs. Henry James was shocked at his appearance when he came to dinner toward the end of the project:

> His whole life, soul and body, is utterly absorbed . . . his pallid face and this fearful grip on his work makes him a melancholy sight.

Outwardly he seemed cheerful enough, but revealed his tenseness in his watchfulness over the manuscript, which he never lost sight of. He took it with him to the washroom and when Mrs. James inquired whether he wouldn't like to take it in to dinner, he replied that he would, he always did so at home.

Holmes and the late chancellor, however, were not particularly compatible. The latter, who deduced his legal principles from natural-law models, was a self-proclaimed conservative in whom the French Revolution had created "an aversion to innovation." As a judge in New York, he spoke for many of his legal generation when he declared that "our system of jurisprudence will be best preserved by resisting innovation." * In his commentaries he was inclined to ignore historical legal developments and to mix biblical and other moral authority with his law. Holmes constantly had to fight the temptation to rewrite the chancellor and chafed under the restrictions imposed, finally complaining because he had to

> keep a civil tongue in my head while I am his valet. But his arrangement is chaotic—he has no general ideas—except wrong ones—and his treatment of special topics is often confused to the last degree. Still he has merits and there is lots of law in his book if you can find it.

When he considered the time and energy consumed in the project, Holmes added, he himself "could have almost easier made a new book." He almost did. He had deleted, with only a few exceptions, all notes written since Kent's death and replaced them with new ones. He had com-

---

* Post v. Neafie. 3 Caines 22 (1835).

pared Kent's original notes with the best edition available "to restore them to purity and correct error."

The work required, of course, not two years but three, winding down in the spring of 1873. When it was published in December of that year, it was discovered that Holmes not only had updated the cases in the usual way but also had written little summaries on how the law had developed since Kent's day and incorporated into his annotations little essays on the influence of such modern legal scholars as John Austin and Henry Maine. He had turned the menial chore of collecting cases into his own individual commentary on the origins of the law.

It was also discovered on publication that Wendell Holmes as editor, and not James Kent as anticipated, appeared on the title page, that Holmes had written and signed the preface, and that James B. Thayer, the prestige of whose name Kent had wanted for the work, was reduced to an acknowledgment, an important one, but still an acknowledgment. Neither Kent nor Thayer was pleased with Holmes's arrogance; Thayer in fact resented it for many years. But the ambitious young man who had done virtually all the work was not eager to share the credit.

The reviews singled out Holmes, congratulating him on his "abundance of knowledge" marked by "large resources of reading and reflection." Wendell Holmes, it seemed, was a true legal scholar, "a rare specimen among our active and busy people." He possessed "a natural aptitude for study and research, for the patient collecting and sifting of abundant material." The establishment of a fundamental principle was "his especial delight."

The *North American Review,* in whose pages such arcane subject matter rarely appeared, made an exception for the twelfth edition of Kent's *Commentaries on American Law.* The editors recognized the respect in which Kent was held among the general public in America. They also recognized achievement when they saw it.

> The immense size of the field which has been searched for authorities [the editors rhapsodized], the discretion with which they have been selected, and the extreme conciseness with which their result is stated, are apparent on a very little use of the book and calculated to inspire confidence in the soundness of the original views which are sometimes taken, and which it must have required some self-denial not to expand into a larger proportion of the whole space.

Holmes had come a long way from "Books," his first article for the *Harvard Magazine* in 1858 and his first attempt at independent work. It was clear as 1873 faded into 1874 that with his editing of Kent, Holmes had established his scholarly credentials. Perhaps the next time an editor was wanted, he would have at least an equal chance with Thayer. His annotations had all the attributes scholarship demanded: substance, maturity, and originality. He had arrived, at age thirty-two, and the twelfth edition of Kent's *Commentaries* was long afterward recognized as the standard edition. Charles M. Barnes, editor of the thirteenth edition, published in 1884, commented in his own preface on the "thoroughness" of Holmes's work and remarked that Holmes had left only the bare bones of recent legal developments for him to add.

The editors of the *North American Review* had pointed out that Holmes leaned toward modern schools of legal interpretation. They had then added, presciently, "if, indeed, he be not, as some of his other writings tend to show, the prophet of one yet newer."

THE EDITING OF Chancellor Kent had occupied a large share of Holmes's intellectual agenda over the first three years of the 1870s, but he was able to recycle many of his ideas and examples and use them again as foundation stones for his articles, which continued to appear in the *American Law Review*. He had no doubts about the role of historical forces in legal development. He had been reading more widely; it was not all "law—law—law" now, and anthropology and history texts were taking their places beside Austin's *Province of Jurisprudence* which he continued to reread and use in his articles, English case law, and Justinian's *Institutes*. Allusions to primitive marriage customs and Roman social mores were an integral part of his scholarly repertory now.

For his second major *American Law Review* article, "Misunderstandings of the Civil Law," which appeared just a year after "Codes, and the Arrangement of the Law," Holmes traced to its source in Roman law an old rule that a man born deaf and dumb was mentally incompetent to make a contract and explained how ignorance of the rule's origin had led to confusion and allowed it to be "swerved" from its original purpose. He found it had probably begun as a simple real estate deal between two ordinary Roman citizens, one of them deaf and dumb. When the handicapped one was unable to participate in the oral question-and-answer session that constituted the sealing of a contract at the time, the deal had to be called off, and disqualification of the deaf and dumb to make contracts found its way into Justinian's *Institutes*. Over time, the incorrect translations of the Latin and misinterpretations of the rule by English text writers had transformed a man with the specified disqualifications into an "idiot" or a "lunatic." Similar examples had proliferated throughout the body of laws, and Holmes briefly described a few, warning that

> A rule of law that has been gradually developed can only be understood by knowing the course of its development.

Understanding in the instances he had chosen to discuss, the failure of which had assured they would be "the source of . . . great injustice," was of more than "antiquarian interest." In his third major essay for the *American Law Review,* "The Arrangement of the Law: Privity," Holmes searched history for explanations of contemporary rules of privity. Where his texts were primarily analytical, as in his fourth—and last before he had to return to the almost exclusive practice of law—essay, "The Theory of Torts," published in July 1873, he nevertheless pressed history into service as a tool of analysis. The naked facts of history could, however, explain only so much. Environmental pressures—corrupt Latin translations, misreadings and misinterpretations of legal inheritances, as well as political factors and social climate—counted, too. Pieces of the puzzle, disjointed and disconnected at first glance, were falling into place. The law was emerging in Holmes's mind, more rapidly now, as an evolutionary body. Darwin's principle of natural selection was hard at work on the law as well as on the horse.

Although investigation of legal architecture drew Holmes's special attention at this time, notice of contemporary events did not escape him or his agile pen. In the April 1873 issue of the *American Law Review,* Holmes wrote a brief but revealing and prophetic commentary on the London gas-stokers' strike that had plunged the city into semidarkness for several nights the previous December. English liberals had been aroused when the gas company prosecuted the strike's five leaders, all union members, for conspiracy in restraint of trade, and the court had sentenced them to a year each in prison—a common occurrence at the time, as new labor combinations, still largely unprotected by the law, began to threaten the old established power of capital, which could still rely on judges' partisanship. The English reformers and commentators were urging changes in the law, a redistribution of power which they believed was unfairly weighted in favor of the masters against the workers. All these sentimentalists made Holmes a little sick; didn't they realize that legislation was only a means by which a body, having the power, puts burdens which are disagreeable to them on the shoulders of somebody else.

Darwin had got it right about the monkeys, and Herbert Spencer, translating monkeys into contemporary men and women, had got it right about human society. Holmes had learned a lot from Spencer:

> The struggle for life . . . is mitigated by sympathy, prudence, and all the social and moral qualities. But in the last resort a man rightly prefers his own interest to that of his neighbors. And this is as true in legislation as in any other form of corporate action. All that can be expected from modern improvements is that legislation should . . . modify itself in accordance with the will of the *de facto* supreme power in the community, and that the spread of an educated sympathy should reduce the sacrifice of minorities to a minimum.

But utopia? Equality? An end to suffering? Out of the question.

> The more powerful interests must be more or less reflected in legislation; which, like every other device of man or beast, must tend in the long run to aid the survival of the fittest.

This Communism intellectuals were all talking about "would no more get rid of the difficulty than any other system." In a class war, nobody won. The fault did not lie in systems. The fault lay in the soft-hearted assumption that happiness for everyone could or would be enacted into law. All this talk about legislating "the greatest good of the greatest number" was humbug. The premise was all wrong. If it was social improvement that was wanted, he hinted that perhaps a little breeding out of the unimproved would not be amiss:

> Why should the greatest number be preferred? Why not the greatest good of the most intelligent and most highly developed? The greatest good of a minority of our generation may be the greatest good of the greatest number in the long run.

In 1868, WILLIAM JAMES had written Holmes from Berlin:

> When I get home let's establish a philosophical society to have regular meetings and discuss none but the very tallest and broadest questions—to be composed of none but the very topmost cream of Boston manhood. It

will give each one a chance to air his own opinion in a grammatical form, and to sneer and chuckle when he goes home at what damned fools all the other members are—and may grow into something very important after a sufficient number of years.

Such a society did in fact flourish in the early 1870s. It was called the Metaphysical Club—the members' wry little private joke on metaphysics which, forced to yield to science, had gone out of fashion, or, as one of its members put it, "a name chosen to alienate such as it would alienate." The founders were Holmes, James, and Charles Sanders Peirce, son of Professor Benjamin Peirce of Harvard who had warned Charles Eliot against further cultivation of his skeptical habits of mind. Despite the father's intellectual conservatism, the son possessed one of the most original minds in nineteenth-century America. For the moment, however, he was principally employed as an assistant in the Harvard observatory, and, like Holmes, working during his off hours on satisfaction of his intellectual inclinations.

Six of the "very topmost cream of Boston manhood" comprised the core of the membership: in addition to Holmes, James, and Peirce, there were Chauncey Wright, writer and lecturer on scientific subjects; Nicholas St. John Green, a bright young Boston attorney; and Joseph Bangs Warner, a student of Green's at the law school and at twenty, the youngest member of the club. All but James were educated at Harvard College. The thread that tied them together was their common interest in trying to make sense of a universe turned upside down by Darwin.

The club had no by-laws, no officers, and no clubhouse. The young men met in each other's homes, an arrangement that sorely tried James's mother's tolerance for "late hours and tobacco smoke." Wright, one of the older members (early forties), was known as the "boxing master" who "severely pummelled" the assembled intellectual athletes as they sparred at their Sunday meetings, settling "the highest questions forever." Henry James characterized the group as a collection of "longheaded youths" who "wrangle grimly and stick to the question." It gave him a "headache merely to know about it."

William James's original hope that the Metaphysical Club might "grow into something very important after a sufficient number of years" did materialize in a limited way. The little society, so informal that reconstruction of its history has defied some of the most determined scholarship, lasted only four or five years at most. But out of the tobacco smoke and the set-tos, something important to the development of American intellectual history did grow. It was here that "Boxing Master" Peirce, in a paper he read to the Metaphysical Club in 1872, breathed life into a philosophical concept that had been hanging in the air for some time. He called it pragmatism; the name came from a Greek word meaning action; close kin were the English words practice and practical.

An outgrowth of the nineteenth century's enthusiasm for scientific methods and subsequent revolt against formalistic and mechanical systems of knowledge, pragmatism is that distinctively American philosophical school that requires ideas, like engines, to be useful, workable, and practical if they are to be believed, if they are to have merit. It relies on experiment for truth and on action for justification. Its natural allies are skepticism and evolutionary change. Truth can never be final. Ideally, moral and metaphysical considerations have no place in pragmatism. Concrete results and consequences are the stuff of reality, the only acceptable test of an idea's or a policy's worth.

The young men had argued and reargued their propositions, far into the long northern nights. Fixed principles fell, absolutes vanished, abstractions took second place to facts. Education, economics, religion, philosophy: all succumbed to their premises. That the others nurtured so many notions similar to his own could not but have bolstered Holmes's confidence in the speculations he had been advancing, the theories he had dreamed up, some gleaned from his reading, others derived from his experiences in court—which were which may have been difficult to say at this point.

He had been thinking toward a pragmatic theory of law for some time. In his first major essay for the *American Law Review* in 1870, "Codes, and the Arrangement of the Law," he had ventured to state that law had nothing to do with divine will or morals or intentions or any of the other subjective ingredients that were always intruding on hard-headed intellectual endeavors. Law, he had said then, was what worked, or, as he put it, what the "courts enforce." He had said it rather softly, and it had not attracted much attention, but he thought the concept had potential for growth.

Holmes steered clear of using the word "pragmatism"; systematizing his ideas could only lead to rigidity. But elements of the new philosophy are tacit in much of Holmes's writing and in 1872, Holmes used his own review of an article by the well-known English legal scholar, Frederick Pollock, as a port of embarkation for what he wanted to say about a pragmatic aspect of the law. In essence, he said that the law was what the traffic would bear, what worked in a given place at a given time:

What more . . . is law, than that we believe that the motive which we think that it offers to the judges will prevail, and will induce them to decide a certain case in a certain way, and so shape our conduct on that anticipation? A precedent may not be followed; a statute may be emptied of its contents by construction, or may be repealed without a saving clause after we have acted on it; but we expect the reverse, and if our expectations come true, we say that we have been subject to law in the matter in hand. . . . The only question for lawyers is, how will the judges act?

Or, as he had said in "Codes, and the Arrangement of the Law," law was what the courts enforced. His theme required explication, refining, but he thought he had struck gold.

The first years of the 1870s had been glorious, difficult and enervating, but glorious—like the war. He had moved quietly but determinedly from earthwork to earthwork, assaulting each in its turn, and the thrill of his small victories had left a pleasant taste in his mouth. When he talked about faith, "trusting to courage and to time" was what he meant.

Not that there hadn't been disappointments. His hunger to influence the course of the law required that he get his material before the influential men of his profession, and he sent proofs of "The Theory of Torts" to Justice Charles Doe of the New Hampshire Supreme Court, only to be disappointed when the judge failed to acknowledge Holmes as the author of an idea that surfaced in one of Doe's opinions (*Stewart* v. *Emerson*) for his court. But he had also won a medal or two. A dissent by U.S. Supreme Court Justice Stephen J. Field (*Hepburn* v. *Griswold*) followed a legal argument Holmes had put forward in an article he had written for the *American Law Review*.

Overall, the satisfactions had outweighed the disappointments. He had enjoyed provoking the young men in his Harvard classes to intellectual endeavor. Seeing his work in print was thrilling. Intellectually it had been a heady time. But if he was going to support a wife, he had better get his law practice in order.

CHAPTER *11*

Marriage

BEGINNING IN JANUARY 1872, when exploration of the jungles of legal scholarship was crowding nearly everything else out of Wendell Holmes's life, Dr. Holmes's "The Poet at the Breakfast-Table" was running in the *Atlantic Monthly*. A major character was called the Young Astronomer. He was so like the doctor's thirty-one-year-old son in temperament and intellect that no one who knew Wendell could have failed to recognize the subject of the portrait. Apparent in every line is the doctor's paternal concern for this solitary young man, this "watcher of stars" who lived in a "world beyond the imagination of poets"; the "daily home" of his thought resided in "illimitable space, hovering between the two eternities." Sometimes, said the doctor, his voice mournful, this "strange unearthly being" emerged from his long night's watching "so pale and worn, that one would think the cold moonlight had stricken him with some malign effluence. . . . At such times he seems more like one who has come from a planet farther away from the sun than our earth. . . ." He was lonely, to be sure, "dwelling far apart from the thoughts and cares of the planet on which he lives,—an enthusiast who gives his life to knowledge; a student of antiquity." He needed to understand so desperately how his universe had come to be.

Dr. Holmes could but weep for Scheherazade, the vivacious young girl he had created especially to divert his pale student who was "burning away, like his own midnight lamp, with only dead men's hands to hold. . . ." Her own "soft, warm, living hands . . . would ask nothing better than to bring the blood back into those cold thin fingers." But, alas, his heart was "unawakened," and he seemed "farther away from life than any student whose head bent downwards over his books. His

eyes are turned away from all human things." The father in the poet-
doctor could only grieve for the son in whom life as the world knew it
appeared to throb no longer. "How cold," he said in eulogy, "the moonlight is that falls upon his forehead, and how white he looks in it!"

The son, however, though he could not entirely bank those intellectual fires, now blazing out of control, did at last come down from his
private Olympus and fall flat out in love. He did finally take notice of
Scheherazade, did finally "feel the breath of a young girl against his
cheek as she looks over his shoulder," and one bonny day in June of
1872, he married Fanny Bowditch Dixwell, who had been his "most
intimate friend for many years."

The private personal currents of electricity that drew these two together cannot entirely be accounted for. That they had characteristics
in common—wit, intelligence and respect for learning, an interest in
art, similar Brahmin backgrounds, a distrust of "come-outers," a sense
of fun and the ridiculous, a strong sense of privacy—is apparent. That
they were in other respects complementary is equally apparent. His ad-
venturousness was counterweight to her more earthbound inclinations.
His sociability balanced her inclination to solitude, his penchant for
flirtation balanced her utter devotion to him. What for Wendell set
Fanny apart from Cora Crowninshield, Clover Hooper, or Minny Temple, what for Fanny set Wendell apart from William James, can only be
attributed to the ever mysterious causes of sexual attraction, not amenable to analysis and understood perhaps only by the lovers themselves.

Fanny's pedigree was quite as distinguished as Wendell's. Her father, Epes Sargent Dixwell, was descended from the Puritan John Dixwell of Folkston, who had been a member of Parliament, then had sat
on the English High Court of Justice that tried and condemned to death
Charles I. At the restoration, he had fled to the New World where he
had planted the American branch of the Dixwells, who took their proper
places among the traders and professional men of Boston.

She was the daughter of Mary Ingersoll Bowditch Dixwell and
granddaughter of Nathaniel Bowditch, astronomer, mathematician, and
student of the navigational sciences; author of *The Practical Navigator*
(first edition, London, 1772); trustee of the Athenaeum, Harvard Overseer, and first actuary at Massachusetts Hospital Life Insurance Company. With an annual salary of $6,000 during the 1820s, he was one of
the highest-paid business executives in America.

The best blood of Boston—Boardman, Bowditch, Sargent, Ingersoll,
Pickering—mixed in Dixwell veins. In the highly structured and closed
society in which Fanny and Wendell had been brought up, marriage

outside their class would have been difficult if not impossible. Much later Wendell referred in passing to good times shared with young women who worked in the local textile mills, but they remain shadowy figures, anonymous; the young women's names that appear in his diaries were limited to members of Boston's inner circle.

Neither rich nor poor in material things, Dixwells, like Holmeses, stepped naturally into the places reserved for them in the local intellectual aristocracy that flourished apart from the mercantile aristocracy. The proprietor of the private school where Wendell Holmes and other boys from prominent Boston families prepared for Harvard College, a lifelong student of the classics, and a moderately talented player of the flute, Epes Dixwell chose his companions from among the learned men of the Harvard faculty and spent his leisure hours talking shop with fellow members of Asa Gray's Scientific Club.

Fanny Dixwell, the oldest of the six Dixwell children, was born December 11, 1840, three months before Wendell. Virtually nothing is known about her girlhood. Whether her formal education extended beyond the obligatory singing and dancing lessons and a few terms at a local academy where embroidery was the focal point of the curriculum can only be conjectured. Her sister, Susan, five years Fanny's junior, attended Miss Bowen's Sewing School where she acquired a certain expertise, and it is apparent that Fanny also had some serious training in the decorative arts. Higher education, in mid-nineteenth century, however, was believed to damage the female reproductive system, and it remained predominantly a male preserve until establishment of the women's colleges a quarter century or so later. If Fanny felt the stirrings her mother-in-law-to-be had felt as a young woman, she left no record of it.

Fanny's adult reading ranged from scholarly biography to the humor of Don Marquis and Stephen Leacock. Much of the poetry in the Holmes library—Milton, the Rossettis, Lady Gregory, Tennyson, Elizabethan songs—contains her bookplate. A whimsical woman with a keen sense of humor herself and an equally keen appreciation of it in others, she also owned a number of children's books, some of which she acquired as an adult. Her literary tastes, while eclectic, reveal a trained and inquisitive mind, but whether it was self- or academy-trained remains one more elusive detail of her life.

She had a charming public persona. She could also be quiet and unassuming. A friend once commented that "the great thing about [her] was that no one knew what went on in her mind." She was essentially a shy and private woman so stand-offish that her mother-in-law "never trust[ed]" herself to select a Christmas present for her and was reduced to giving her "a little additional sum . . . hoping you will find something that you want." It was said by some who knew her that she had no close friends and "hated" most of her sisters, who had married younger and fulfilled their destinies as mothers early. As she grew older, her inclination to solitude became more pronounced, and in time she became a virtual recluse and a symbol of unsociability for other Bostonians.

"I'm getting to be worse than Mrs. Holmes," complained Clover Adams, nee Hooper, of her own life.

Wendell never forgot the day of their engagement. He had once again taken Thomas Hobbes's *Leviathan* out of the Athenaeum library and started down Beacon Street with it—almost an exact replay of the scene of the decade before when news of his army commission reached him at the same spot. "But on the way home," he reminisced in the stiff Victorian manner that characterized speech on personal relations in his time and place,

I called on Miss Fanny Dixwell and she did me the honor to accept my proposal of marriage. So I took it back again.

Fanny later gave him a first edition.

He wrote his good news immediately and "with a sort of trembling . . . after such an interval" to Mrs. Kennedy in Hagerstown, Maryland, who had cared for him following the Battle of Antietam.

Cambridge society was surprised that so shy and retiring a woman as Fanny Dixwell had caught so popular a young man. The elder Holmeses could hardly have been more pleased with their son's choice. At thirty-one, in the society in which they lived, neither Fanny nor Wendell was considered young, and there may have been some concern for the future of their oldest offspring. Two of Fanny's sisters, both younger, had already married, and the two youngest Holmeses were, after all, married and settled into their prescribed roles.

Upon announcement of Wendell's engagement in March 1872, Dr. Holmes described Fanny as a "very superior and a very charming woman" who would "make friends of all who need her." The "attachment," he added, was a "very long and faithful one . . . dating almost from childhood." The Holmeses knew Fanny "thoroughly" and "value[d] and love[d] her very much."

At the same time his wife revealed none of the mother's natural reluctance to share a son with whom she had enjoyed a special relationship, but spoke only of her delight in his approaching marriage. "We love Fanny very dearly," she told Mary Dixwell, Fanny's mother and Wendell's "almost second mother." ". . . And they have so grown up together, and loved each other so long, that we surely have reason to trust that their married life will be all we could ask for them—The love of a good woman is the greatest blessing a man can have—And I am very grateful that I have such a daughter-in-law."

Fanny Dixwell and Wendell Holmes were married on Monday, June 17, 1872, the ninety-seventh anniversary of the Battle of Bunker Hill which Boston was celebrating with parades and fireworks. Wendell sandwiched the ceremony between his editorial duties at the *American Law Review* and his reading of Johann Gottlieb Heineccius's *Recitationes in elementa juris civilis,* followed shortly by Immanuel Kant's *Eléments metaphysiques de la Doctrine du Droit* (in translation).

Although the families of the bride and bridegroom were nominal Unitarians, "for reasons of their own" they were married in Christ Episcopal Church, Cambridge, by the young Episcopalian newcomer Phillips Brooks, whom they had imported for the occasion from his own Trinity Church in Boston. The reasons for the change of venue are not entirely clear; the First (Unitarian) Parish had no minister at the time, so Christ Church offered a viable alternative. The minister there, however, Nicholas Hoppin, was old and his parishioners were beginning to realize he had outlived his usefulness as a pastor. Phillips Brooks's theological insights, on the other hand, which he delivered with unusual passion and power, had been packing in even the Unitarians to hear his Sunday morning sermons at Trinity almost since he had arrived in Boston three years before. Perhaps most important in the choosing of a minister, at least to Wendell, was the stirring performance Brooks, then a comparative unknown, had given at Harvard's Commemoration Day in 1865.

No description of the wedding survives. Whether it was large or small, formal or informal, early or late, is not known. William James came, as did his father, but beyond that the record is silent. Wendell noted it on his list of books he was reading:

June 17   *Married   sole editor of Law Rev.*

The couple was unable to take a wedding trip right away. Fanny fell ill with rheumatic fever, which confined her for several months to their little rooms at Dr. Holmes's, where they planned to live temporarily.

Their finances were severely limited. Following the fire engines to local conflagrations was a staple of their entertainment. Luxuries, including the theater which Wendell loved, were out of reach. He would gaze with longing at the playbills on his way home from the office, then buy a pint of ice cream to share with Fanny while they jeered at the "nobs."

"Well," he later confessed, "it was as good as a comedy, the fun we had."

By 1872, when Fanny and Wendell were married, Massachusetts, like many American states, had passed various measures liberating women from legal disabilities imposed by the Old and New Testaments and the English common law which traditionally considered a married couple one person—the husband. This revolution in married women's legal status had been quietly accomplished during the first half of the nineteenth century, partly because it was less a revolution than a simple legalization of what had been going on extralegally for some years and partly because male relatives of women were tired of watching fortune hunters and debt-ridden husbands dissipate women's dowries and inheritances. Although Fanny couldn't vote or serve on a jury, she now could own property, enter into contracts, "perform any labor or service on her sole and separate account"; she could make a will, sue and be sued, and had substantially more control over her life than had her mother and grandmother.

Old attitudes die hard, however, and not even the combination of the Revolution's egalitarian mood, the emancipation of slaves less than a century later, and the enactments of the married women's property acts by the state legislatures could lighten the burdens of women's psychological heritage. Legally, Fanny was emancipated; psychologically, she remained in thrall.

Fanny had been born into a man's world where for the most part women remained adjuncts of men, passing from dependence upon parents to dependence upon husbands, their only significance the reflected glory of brothers, fathers, or husbands. She was born into a world in which men encouraged women's meekness, their helplessness, their reluctance to have opinions, then went off to their clubs when life at home became too dull.

The Industrial Revolution that was enriching mankind materially was impoverishing women like Fanny psychologically by putting them out of their traditional homemaking roles, idling minds and bodies both.

Work for women was becoming a disgrace, and a man's ability to keep the women in his family unemployed was becoming a point of pride, a measurement of his wealth and importance.

A few exceptions were defying social conventions, redefining themselves, and at last entering the legal and medical professions, but it was still a very few, and, like Dr. Prance in Henry James's *The Bostonians,* described as "dry, hard, without a curve, an inflection or a grace," they were often ridiculed by the community. Those Boston women who worked outside the home in the nearby textile mills and shoe factories were not of Fanny's social class.

Like her mother and mother-in-law before her, Fanny seemed content to comply with contemporary convention and to occupy the position God, Nature, her forebears, and nineteenth-century society had assigned her. She was to find her destiny in marriage. At the same time, she and Wendell appear to have worked out within the acceptable limitations a partnership that provided adventure and security to both partners. Their interests in external matters were largely exclusive; their interest in each other, mutual, at least for the foreseeable future.

The philanthropic social service organizations and women's clubs that were springing up in the second half of the nineteenth century to find work for women's newly idle hands did not seem to interest Fanny, and her name does not appear on the rolls of local associations. Her contempt for "come-outers" would have prevented her joining any. Whatever nondomestic instincts she had, she channeled into her needlework—socially approved, even encouraged—which she transformed from the usual sampler into what was really high art—from prose to poetry in thread. While Wendell worked with his head, she worked with her hands. The energies and intensity that Wendell devoted to scholarship and making a reputation during the first ten years of their marriage, Fanny put into her landscapes and seascapes: explosions of color and light that bewitched all who saw them. But she appears to have nurtured no ambitions and sought no public recognition— indeed she would have recoiled from it. She appears to have been content to bask in her beloved Wendell's shadow, to fulfill herself in him. He was her polestar. Intuitively, she seemed to grasp the intensity of her husband's ambition and to make realization of his potential her responsibility, although she probably was not conversant with the complexities of his professional concerns or with the tortuous twistings and turnings of the ideas that swirled through his abstraction-oriented intellect. In her relationship with her husband, Fanny replicated that between her father- and mother-in-law, about whom a friend once observed: "[H]is wife absorbed her life in his, and mounted guard to make sure that interruption was impossible."

Marian Denman Frankfurter once asked her husband, Felix, about their friends the Holmeses' mutual emotional dependency:

> Why are some people pillows and bosoms and some people the needers of pillows?

To which he replied:

> As to bosoms and pillows—it's all a more or less, is't not, tho in the concrete instance it looks as if the Fanny Holmeses . . . are all pillows for their Lords' needs.

Which does not mean that Fanny, though barely five feet tall and of frail build, was passive or compliant. She harbored, after all, the genes of a regicide within. She was not subordinate. On the contrary. Despite a soft heart that turned to mush when she encountered even fictionalized accounts of cruelty to children, she was assertive, strong, and resilient at the same time she offered loving companionship. She was also a keen and critical observer of human nature and did not spare the acid of her tongue when she confronted its absurdities. Bostonians and later Washingtonians, right up to the president himself, were well acquainted with her sting. She damned, however, the peccadillo, not the situation that had produced it, and if she sometimes found the Boston ambience unpalatable, she remained intensely and stubbornly loyal. She understood her husband, his bouts with despair, his ambition, his hopes and yearnings, and she knew how to deal with each.

In private, she was not above bursting Wendell's balloons, though she did it in a playful, affectionate way that punctured his pomposities without damaging his ego—a feat that must have required no little dexterity. She had the knack, too, of timing her pranks and caustic observations, her raids into male territory, so that they distracted him, dragged him out of his intellectual isolation, and made him laugh with all the abandon of any ordinary mortal. He sometimes referred to her affectionately as that "she-devil," at other times as "Dicky," perhaps because her movements were canarylike, more likely because as a schoolboy, Wendell had referred to her father by that name.

She loved him with all the fervor of youth as long as she lived. She had wanted "to throw [herself] away" when her "dearest, dearest, Dearest" Wendell disappeared from view aboard the Europe-bound *Sax-*

onia in June of 1907. She would spend the summer "left here to love and long for" him. She smoothed away irritations, calmed his fears, gave him strength when he needed it. She fed his vanity, teased his pomposities, diverted him when he wandered too far into the nether regions of thought, tolerated his flirtations, and admired him enormously—all of which such an ambitious and self-centered man required. She had, he once said, "devoted her powers to surrounding [him] with enchantment."

And he loved her back in his fashion, although he was not at bottom a giving person. His flirtations with other women, mild though most of them were, must have hurt her deeply. Beyond an occasional caustic comment, however, no record of Fanny's feelings regarding Wendell's wanderlust has survived. He probably loved Fanny more than anyone in his life except possibly his mother, with whom, his wartime letters make clear, he shared a special bond, and Lady Clare Castletown of Doneraile, County Cork, Ireland, his "Beloved Hibernia," with whom he was later to enjoy a very different sort of loving relationship.

His attitude toward women in general was complex. On meeting a woman for the first time, he claimed to see her not as a woman but as a "human being—one is curious as to the new personality—one wants to know its feelings and views and to lay one's cards on the table and submit them to the acceptance or rejection of the other. It is human being, not man or woman." He could in good conscience swear he took "thoughts and opinions simply as such without regard to where they came from and [did his] best to weigh them." On the other hand, feelings were substantially modified by differences in sex, and he guessed "a woman hardly would wish them not to be." There was, he added, "a sight of difference between thoughts that come accompanied by the ever poignant personal interest that women inspire in a man, and vice versa, and those that come from a potential enemy in a dress coat."

In Fanny's case, the two fundamental attitudes converged, merged, and may not have been entirely consistent. Taking her as a human being, he encouraged her art, although he may have been Victorian enough to be grateful she did not dress up in tailored clothes and practice law or medicine. He cherished her companionship, though for serious intellectual talk he always had male friends and, in the early years of his marriage, male clubs. He relished her wit, admired her strong will, and deferred to her domestic judgment, which she had developed and honed during years of helping to care for five siblings.

Wendell never ceased to marvel at Fanny's ability to transform wherever they were living into a warm and welcoming home. Even the drab little rooms above a Beacon Street drugstore which they rented after living briefly with the elder Holmeses after their marriage, Fanny turned into a charming apartment with attractions aside from the sense of freedom and adventure combined with the sheer joy of being together alone that accompanies the first independence and enchantment of the early years of marriage. She had, Wendell said, made "roses bloom on a broomstick." Later, in their Washington home, it was Fanny who was responsible for installing the few modern conveniences Wendell would tolerate—electricity, elevator, telephone, and vacuum cleaner.

Taking Fanny as a member of the opposite sex, he savored her single-minded devotion, no doubt found it satisfied some need that lay deep within. She was his "pillow," his warmth, his comfort, the security that allowed his intellect to adventure outside the charted roads. But it may have been too difficult for so aggressively ambitious and intellectual a man to reciprocate in kind.

The marriage was, of course, childless. On the delicate subject of sexual relations, one can only speculate. Their childlessness, however, is not surprising.

Despite Victorian America's reputation for prudishness, sexual relations by mid-nineteenth century were becoming less and less associated with reproduction and increasingly associated with physical and emotional satisfaction, at the same time that birth control methods were improving. Hands to work the farms were no longer needed, and reproduction was no longer a requirement; married love for its own sake was permissible and possible.

Fanny, it was said by those who knew her, would have loved children. But she was thirty-two when she married, and the risks of childbearing at her advanced age in uncertain medical times may have inhibited her. It is also possible that she was infertile, a common ailment among women who married later in life. She partially compensated by filling the house with small animals—mice, birds, cats—and enjoying the children of friends and relatives. She had been known to collect as many as fifteen small neighborhood children and whisk them off to the circus—"unlimited peanuts and a great lark" was standard fare for the adventure.

Wendell liked children, too. He doted on a young cousin who lived with them briefly later in Washington, and wrote whimsical letters to the child of one of Fanny's sisters; they rivaled in imaginative quality Goliath Tittle's letters to the Holmes children those many years ago. As an uncle figure, Wendell was perfect: tall, handsome, and, most important, indulgent, a reincarnation of Uncle John. But a benign and indulgent uncle could maintain his remoteness. He need not give of himself the way a father was often required to do in a relationship he could not always control. Wendell undoubtedly preferred the role of uncle to that of father.

Too, he may have feared a rivalry for Fanny's attention. Perhaps he also feared duplicating his own ambiguous relationship with his father. Possibly he feared distraction from the goals laid out by his high ambition, or some Malthusian instinct, never far below the surface, may have deterred him. In any case, he did not yearn for fatherhood. He preferred to leave as his legacy his mark on the law. He preferred to shape the cold body of the law rather than to mold a warm and living human being.

"I am so far abnormal," he confided to a friend as he neared ninety, "that I am glad I have none." He added: "It might be said that to have them is part of the manifest destiny of man as of other creatures but the latter he can't help—and part of his destiny is to choose." He might say some "sad things," he continued, but he wouldn't, although it was obviously a subject about which he had thought a good deal. "Of course," he added, resuming the detachment he adopted when intimate personal matters arose, "if I should break down before dying it would be awkward, as there is no one to look after me as a child would. But," he concluded airily, "I daresay my nephew and my friends would cook up something."

On an earlier occasion, Judge Learned Hand had asked Holmes whether or not he regretted his childlessness. The depth of Holmes's emotion was apparent. He did not answer right away but averted his eyes. Finally, according to Hand, Holmes said, "very quietly (still not looking at me): 'This is not the kind of world I want to bring anyone else into.' "

Johnny Morse said Holmes was sexually impotent*—a vague term covering a multitude of sexual inadequacies common to many men in different degrees at different times with different sexual partners. The specific causes are often elusive. For Holmes, a diagnosis of impotence is not impossible, however. His medical history, for example, allows, although it does not require, room for that condition. It is possible that the bullet that lodged in his neck at Antietam and that he later said

*An unsigned memorandum dated April 5, 1961, written on Harvard Law School stationery and in the hand of Mark DeWolfe Howe, was discovered among the Holmes papers at Harvard Law School: "Lunching with Sam[uel Eliot] Morison and Lewis Einstein at Somerset Club S.M. noted that in that very dining room John T. Morse, Jr., had told him in all seriousness that OWH was sexually impotent. Neither Morison nor Einstein seemed to take any stock in Morse's announcement."

gave him an occasional attack of what was then known as neuralgia had damaged a nerve connected to his lower anatomy. He also complained frequently of pain in his lower back, of what nineteenth-century physicians lumped under the term lumbago. Physicians today recognize connections between back ailments and sexual impotence.

Holmes's psychosocial profile also does not rule out such a condition, although the record is silent. Johnny Morse's allegation notwithstanding—and the evidence he offered in support, if any, is not known—sexual impotence was not the sort of matter that found its way into the journals and memoirs of nineteenth-century Bostonians.

It is possible, though, that his own and Fanny's fears of the results of sexual intimacy, singly or in combination, may well have contributed to a state of sexual helplessness in Wendell and also perhaps to Fanny's ability to respond, inhibiting the free expression of sexual feelings in both. Add to this the prudish social conventions of Victorian Boston, in which even piano legs were modestly hidden and marriage manuals discussed sex as a necessary evil, distasteful and dangerous to health. Consider the proximity of parental authority during the early time of their marriage. Although it was common practice in nineteenth-century America for a man to bring his bride to live in his parents' home for a time, such a move on Wendell's part—aged thirty-one and still "swallow[ing] and digest[ing]" his famous father—was not likely to enhance either his sense of his masculinity or his ability to distance himself from the autocrat of the breakfast table.

Wendell's not being by nature a giving person perhaps inhibited his ability to truly love another human being, to give of himself, and may have added still another burden to his sexual prowess. It is possible that outwardly he disguised this psychic lameness with his well-known tendency to indulge in casual—and unconsummated—flirtations with women to whom he need not give a great deal beyond an afternoon's or an evening's charming conversation or periodic exchanges of sexually inspired banter by mail.

He does not appear to have suffered unduly from feelings of professional inadequacy, a common source of sexual impotence, though he hungered for the approval of his colleagues and privately grieved when it was not forthcoming. It is possible, though, that his intense ambition, which sometimes accompanies impotence, contributed to it on the one hand and disguised it on the other.

Whether or not Fanny Dixwell and Wendell Holmes were sexually companionable, they seem to have been psychologically companionable: two Boston Brahmins, the one a lover, the other a beloved; the one a giver, the other a taker; the one a "pillow," the other a "needer of pillows." The marriage endured for nearly sixty years, until Fanny died in 1929. Wendell once counselled a friend:

> I believe you will find as I think you know I have found, that marriage develops, confirms, and sustains all that is best in us.

But work remained "two-thirds" of his life, and professionally, he remained the Young Astronomer, detached, dedicated, and determined in his search for a route to the stars.

CHAPTER *12*

Scholar/Lawyer

ON MARCH 3, 1873, five days before his thirty-second birthday, Wendell Holmes joined the law firm George Shattuck had established with William Adams Munroe three years before. The new addition made it Shattuck, Holmes, and Munroe. The editing of Kent's *Commentaries* was finally done, and Fanny was helping him to read proof; the volumes would be in print before the year was out. In July, his last major article for three years, "The Theory of Torts," appeared in the *American Law Review*. That same month Holmes turned over the editorship of the journal to Moorfield Storey, a politically active young attorney and fellow member of the unnamed social club to which Holmes belonged, and Samuel Hoar, Judge Hoar's son and, later, a contender for both court seats to which Holmes was appointed. Holmes did not return to his lectureship at Harvard after the spring 1873 term, and he leavened his reading of legal and philosophic tomes with Thomas Hardy, William Morris, Robert Browning, and Herbert Spencer, whose *Study of Sociology* Dr. Holmes was reviewing for the December 11 issue of the *Boston Medical and Surgical Journal*. If Holmes seemed to have abandoned his scholarly pursuits, actually he had only suspended them while he settled down to the full-time practice of his profession. He had not reconciled himself to the ambience of the business world, or, undoubtedly, to the emotional demands of a law practice in which personal contact with clients and their problems was an integral part, and he wished profoundly that "the necessity of making a living" had not limited his choices. Given, however, "that the above necessity exist[ed]," he was "thankful" for the situation in which he found himself.

When he joined Shattuck's law firm, he had been able to exact the condition that he would not be expected to work at night. Then a summer vacation at Milton "quite made [him] over." His relations with his senior partner were so friendly that in the fall of 1873 the young Holmeses, despite their poverty, bought a summer house near Shattuck's place in Mattapoisett on the South shore. The two men drove together, sailed together, and dined together. The usual summer-house luxuries, however, still eluded Wendell and Fanny, and they had to consider carefully the purchase of so insignificant an item as a wheelbarrow to replace the old shutter on which they had been accustomed to transporting manure from flower bed to flower bed. William James found his friend Wendell, with whom he spent three "very pleasant" days at Mattapoisett in 1876, looking quite different from the pallid companion whose imperturbable logic had so often tested his own intellectual mettle.

> . . . I fell quite in love with she [James told his brother Henry in London] and he exemplified in the most ridiculous way Michelet's "marriage de l'homme et de la terre." I told him that he looked like Millet's peasant figures as he stooped over his little plants in his flannel shirt and trousers.

But no change of clothing could disguise the essential Holmes.

> He is a powerful battery [James added], formed like a planing machine to gouge a deep self-beneficial groove through life; and his virtues and faults were thrown into singular relief by the lonesomeness of the shore, which makes every object, rock or shrub, stand out so vividly, seemed also to put him and his wife under a sort of lens.

In the summer of 1874, Mr. and Mrs. Oliver Wendell Holmes, Jr., after a two-year delay, finally took their wedding trip. They sailed for England and a tour of the Continent. It was Fanny's first trip abroad, and Wendell had the fun of showing her the sights and introducing her to his friends. Dr. Holmes's reputation dogged his son in England, too, where his work was widely read. Prominent Englishmen broke the ice at social gatherings by asking whether Wendell was the son of Oliver Wendell Holmes. To which Wendell invariably replied: "No, he was [sic] my father." These little slights, however, did not lessen Wendell's appreciation of things English, and he always felt twice the man I was, after I visit London [where] society is hard to get into . . . there are too many interesting people in London. You must interest, and must interest people who, being in the center of the world, have seen all kinds of superlatives.

That summer the young Holmeses dined with Robert Browning and Anthony Trollope, took tea with Thomas Carlyle, and breakfasted with Sir Henry Maine, whose work in legal history Holmes admired, spent country weekends with the titled, and renewed acquaintances with Leslie Stephen, James Bryce, Albert Dicey, and other representatives of the British legal and political illuminati.

It was on this trip that Holmes met the English legal scholar Frederick Pollock (later Sir Frederick),* with whom he maintained a transatlantic friendship for more than half a century. Pollock's son John speculated that their mutual friend Leslie Stephen introduced them; on the other hand, the younger Pollock thought it possible his grandparents, whom he believed were acquainted with Dr. Holmes, could have engineered the meeting. Holmes once commented that Pollock had "made a dinner that I might meet him."

Holmes already knew Pollock by reputation. He had commented on Pollock's writing for the *American Law Review*'s "Book Notices," and when the two men, whose scholarly hearts beat almost as one, finally met, Pollock remarked, "there was no stage of acquaintance ripening into friendship; we understood one another and were friends without more ado." Already, he explained, "we were pursuing the same ideal; insofar as our methods were not identical, the diversity was of the kind that makes not for indifference but for harmony; we hardly ever disagreed on a matter of principle, not often in our results, and when we did it was on outlying details or on some minor problem of purely speculative interest." For nearly six decades "My dear Holmes" and "My beloved Frederick" entrusted their private thoughts on philosophy, history, literature, and, above all, law, to each other. Their contacts with life were largely intellectual and philosophical—events of their personal lives are almost entirely absent from the correspondence. The relationship was so dispassionate that even the detached Holmes complained he "never got inside" Pollock's "external indifference."

---

*On March 8, 1941, the hundredth anniversary of Holmes's birth, the Harvard University Press published the *Holmes-Pollock Letters The Correspondence of Mr. Justice Holmes and Sir Frederick Pollock 1874–1932*, edited by Mark DeWolfe Howe.

If the correspondence had a flaw, it was Holmes's handwriting, aptly described by John Pollock:

At first blush you would take Holmes's script for a fine piece of calligraphy; it had a certain beauty of its own. But in the same second you became aware that something was surely amiss with your eyesight. What had seemed, from their general shape and spacing to be words, dissolved into hieroglyphics. The longer they were studied, the more obscure they became, until you wondered whether any message at all lay hid therein. It was as if a demented fly had followed the writer's pen across the page.

Holmes "grieve[d] that heathens rage[d] against [his] handwriting," but he had become "accustomed to it."

Pollock's store of general knowledge—his allusions "to more things I don't know on a sheet of paper than I can find in the Bible"—sometimes baffled Holmes, although Holmes more than made up in vitality for his own shortcoming. What emerges from this correspondence is a portrait of two men, cultured, educated, thoughtful, and, above all, eminently civilized.

A ball at Devonshire House reminded Fanny of her English origins. As she ascended the circular marble staircase, "the blood of the Dixwells rose from a long sleep and was at home again." The middle-aged women there she described as "fat and comfortable." Fanny caricatured in her diary most of the people she was meeting abroad, British and American both. One of her hosts she described as a "twinkling hippopotamas" and an American family as a "portable trunk of nuisances."

Fanny was not yet the recluse she became in later years, and she seemed to enjoy the trip, according to her comments on the dinners and garden parties she attended. Daytime London was segregated by gender, and Fanny was expected to entertain herself in the shops or taking tea with her women friends, while Wendell visited the courts and otherwise communed with men of similar professional and intellectual interests.

What Fanny did not enjoy, however, was Wendell's bringing along his familiar predilection for the company of other women. He was utterly charmed by the women he was seated next to at dinner, as they usually were by him. The loan of a book was a sure way to catch his attention and he would, of course, be required to return it. Said Fanny in disgust on one such occasion: "Wendell to see his charmer and return the book. Brought the book back with him."

His talk charmed men as well as women. John Pollock described it many years later:

> Holmes talked a great deal and as the natural centre of the company in which he found himself. His pleasant high pitched voice with its slight burr lent an almost impish charm to the fluency with which he would catch a subject, toss it into the air, make it dance and play a hundred tricks, and bring it to solid earth again. There was no trace of flippancy, but a spice of enjoyment even in the serious treatment of a serious subject. Nor is "impish" altogether the right word. If there was often a good touch of Puck in Holmes's talk, it was rather perhaps in the end Prospero who came to mind, for it was rare that he talked without an elevating and ennobling subject. As he talked he drew inspiration from his company; he challenged and desired response, contradiction, and development. He liked to have the ball caught and tossed back to him, so that he could send it spinning away again with a fresh twist. Talk was a means of clarifying ideas, of moving towards the truth; but it was a great game, too.

Holmes admitted that if he lost both arms and both legs and had to be carried every day into the marketplace and allowed to talk, he "would have all that [he] wanted of life."

On July 11, Fanny and Wendell left London for France where, as Wendell had in the summer of 1866, they became ordinary tourists. They had no contacts on the Continent, no acquaintances to renew, no friends among the illuminati. Together they saw the conventional sights in Paris and Geneva, Venice, and Milan. Among the souvenirs they acquired from the famous glassblowers of Venice was a pretty little perfume bottle, which Fanny kept on her dressing table until her death.

In early August they returned to England, then sailed at the end of the month aboard the *Athens* for Boston. For Fanny, the journey across the Atlantic was unpleasant, and she moaned to her diary of the "pitching rolling tossing tossing rolling pitching." At the end she vowed "never, never, never to put myself in such a fix again."

They landed on Tuesday, September 8, with sixty cents in their pockets. To Fanny, the Common never looked more "beautiful."

Wendell returned to work at Shattuck, Holmes, and Munroe. Regard for the firm within corporate Boston ranged out of proportion to its youth and small size. The senior partner, forty-four-year-old Shattuck, whose full beard gave him a look of maturity as well as distinction, was practicing law while Wendell was still at Mr. Dixwell's school and was in 1873 a leader of the Boston bar. Wendell never knew his mentor's equal "in all-round capacity to have his way in a case, taking into account all the honorable things that sooner or later may have to be done before success is reached. He was vehement in attack and stubborn in defence. He was fertile in resource and very quick in seeing all the bearings of a fact or a piece of testimony, a matter in which most men of weighty ability are slow. He was a great cross-examiner. He was a speaker who brought himself home to juries, and who was a master in the argument of questions of law."

William Munroe was two years Holmes's junior and too young to have made a name for himself at the bar. Although Harvard- and Harvard Law School—educated and a Republican, as a Baptist he did not quite fit into the social world of Brahmin Boston where the standards were set by Episcopalians, Unitarians, and those Calvinists who had survived the strong currents of theological liberalization. He was not a member of the prestigious Saturday Club or St. Botolph's or the Union Club. He belonged rather to the unchic Boston Baptist Social Union and was a trustee of the Newton Theological Institution. He spent much of the time he was not in the law office quietly getting elected to minor political positions in Cambridge, of which he was a native.

The firm had no typewriters or stenographers. It had, instead, the quiet and steady managerial talents of Gustave Magnitzky. A recent immigrant from Polish Prussia when the Civil War broke out, Magnitzky had joined the Union forces and served as Holmes's first sergeant in Company G of the Massachusetts Twentieth. His gallantry had earned him a captaincy. As the efficient manager of Shattuck, Holmes, and Munroe and its successors for nearly forty years, he became one of the best-known figures in legal Boston.

Shattuck, Holmes, and Munroe accepted the social milieu as they found it and practiced entirely within it. Shattuck's social conscience, in the noblesse oblige fashion of the time and place, required him to give generously to local charities, institutions, and literary enterprises, and he served for many years as trustee of the State Library and the Boston Public Library as well as an Overseer of Harvard University. Shattuck's social conscience did not, however, require that he donate legal services to the poor. *Pro bono* work by American law firms was still a phenomenon of the future. Organized legal aid work, the first of its kind, began in New York only in 1876. The Boston Legal Aid Society, which became a model for those of other cities, did not open until

1900. Federal judges were not authorized to assign attorneys to the poor until 1892, and the mind-set of the legal profession during the second half of the nineteenth century was as laissez-faire as that of the most aggressive railroad magnate. Boston's less fortunate—criminal defendants, the poor victims of labor exploitation and slumlords and streetcar accidents, widows, orphans, and Irish immigrants—did not take their legal problems to Shattuck, Holmes, and Munroe. George Shattuck was known as one of the best corporation lawyers of his time, and his firm lived off the power elite, representing the community's captains of commerce and industry and those individual clients who could pay. Litigation of social and political issues was left to men like Richard Henry Dana, who had become a lawyer following the sea voyage that resulted in *Two Years Before the Mast* and who had defended runaway slaves before the war; men like Moorfield Storey, a puritanical politician as a young man who later mingled representation of blacks and American Indians with his work for Jordan Marsh and Company; and men like Louis Brandeis, who accommodated social advocacy to the practice of corporation law. But the legal problems of the poor did not attract the Boston bar, of whose social conscience Holmes's cousin and childhood friend Johnny Morse was perhaps representative.

As well as a Brahmin heritage and a Harvard education, Johnny Morse shared with his cousin Wendell Holmes a distinguished grandfather—Judge Charles Jackson. Although he was aware that his own abilities were above average, he did not, however, have the same fire in his belly that his cousin and his grandfather had. Nor could he tolerate as well as Holmes could the post–Civil War challenges to traditional Brahmin values being made by fast-growing labor unions, the democratic social and political forces unleashed by the heavy immigration, and all the other side effects of the new industrial capitalism. Along with other class-conscious conservatives in late-nineteenth-century Boston—Henry and Brooks Adams, Charles Eliot Norton, William Sturgis Bigelow, and others of that ilk—Morse refused to face so precarious a future and retreated from it. As he plodded through his thirties alongside his ambitious and intellectually adventurous cousin, he was winding down his brief legal career, which he had always "hated" anyway, and devoting his energies more and more to the writing of undistinguished biography, to his horses, his goats, and his clubs. He described himself as a man who "stands aside and makes no effort."

Not so Holmes. His study of legal history and the very constancy of change in human society through the centuries perhaps afforded him a different perspective on the events of the late nineteenth century, and he did not retreat. Some positive aspects of his law practice no doubt helped him face the day-to-day routine at the office.

Although a career in commerce had always repelled him and he by far preferred the currency of ideas to that of the countinghouse, Holmes could not suppress a certain admiration for successful businessmen, including those he met at the office. They often seemed Jim Hills in miniature. Hill and the other entrepreneurs Holmes was in fact imitating in another medium, whether he realized it or not, he believed represented

> one of the greatest forms of human power—an immense mastery of economic details—and equal grasp of the principles—and ability and courage to put their conclusions into practice with brilliant success.

Change the word "economic" to "legal," be patient with "brilliant success," and you have Wendell Holmes in his mid-thirties.

Holmes's attention was also drawn to the little cases that came to the firm, the staples of daily law practice that, born out of the forces that were remolding contemporary American society, contained the raw materials of future universal legal institutions. They did not "deal with the Constitution or a telephone company"; yet they had within them "the germ of some wider theory, and therefore of some profound interstitial change in the very tissue of law."

Perhaps out of the case of the *Becherdass Ambaidass,* in which Holmes and Shattuck successfully defended a British shipowner against his sailors' wage claims, a rule would in time evolve establishing whether disputes between foreign ships and seamen anchored in American ports fell under the jurisdiction of American courts or whether they should be "left to settle their differences before their own tribunals." At the time Holmes and Shattuck argued their case, jurisdiction was left to judicial discretion. Signposts to future negligence principles were not obvious when Holmes and Shattuck defended the Winnisimmet Company against the suit brought by George Joy* after he had fallen off its ferry into Boston harbor, but then legal principles had been fashioned out of lesser cases.

Every once in a while Holmes had a chance to try something a little different. The fun came with cases like *Temple* v. *Turner,* for which he could adapt his historical discoveries to the day-to-day demands of his

---

* *Joy* v. *Winnisimmet Co.* 114 Mass. 63 (1873).

legal practice; at the same time he could lead the Massachusetts Supreme Judicial Court, the state's highest, on a short excursion into antiquity to show how legal archaeology brought understanding of modern principles out of their origins in the ruins.

Another dispute over wages, *Temple* v. *Turner* involved the suit by a sailor (Temple) for breach of contract by his ship's captain (Turner) who had hired him for a specified sum, then failed to pay up. Representing Captain Turner, Holmes had won in the lower court where the judge had held that Holmes's client, not being the owner of the ship, was not liable for wages still unpaid at the end of the voyage. Temple appealed to the Massachusetts Supreme Judicial Court. Holmes once again trekked back into Roman law and tried to show the court how the ancient rule that would at one time have made the captain liable for the sailor's unpaid wages had been modified, first by the Romans themselves, then by medieval judges, and finally by the modern field of law called agency which outlined the extent of a man's responsibilities as the agent of another. By the late nineteenth century, said Holmes, the captain might be "a mere conduit pipe" to carry out the errands of the owner.

Chief Justice Horace Gray made short work of Holmes's living history. His own authority recognized the "established rule, so ancient that [he] knew not its origin, that seamen may recover their wages against the master," or captain. Holmes's eloquence notwithstanding, Gray reversed the lower court and ruled against him.

It was, perhaps, Holmes's familiarity with and mastery of the traditions of maritime law and the straightforward way in which he was capable of presenting it that made his reputation in this field. In any case, he found his expertise in demand.

In August of 1877, Holmes and Shattuck appeared in the Circuit Court for the District of Massachusetts, presided over at the time by Justice Nathan Clifford of the U.S. Supreme Court. They represented Joseph Nickerson of Boston and his shipowning partners, mostly relatives, whose vessel, *Concordia,* had deviated from her course while carrying a load of cotton from New Orleans to Liverpool, in order to repair a boiler leak and take on coal at Nova Scotia, and had run aground there. The ship was wrecked and the cargo lost. The New Orleans Mutual Insurance Company, having paid off the shippers, was suing the Nickersons,* charging that the *Concordia* had not been seaworthy

---

* *New Orleans Mutual Insurance Co.* v. *Nickerson.* Case no. 778, 779, 780, U.S. Circuit Court for the District of Mass. (1877).

when she left New Orleans and that the ship's officers knew it; further, that the captain had intended all along to put in at Nova Scotia where, they had persuaded Judge John Lowell, a defect in the construction of the ship had caused a leak in the boilers and the diversion to Nova Scotia had been unavoidable. The insurance company, represented by Richard Henry Dana, appealed.

The case was not particularly complex. The ship either was or was not seaworthy on leaving New Orleans; it either held or did not hold sufficient fuel to take her to Liverpool; the captain either did or did not intend to make an intermediate stop in Nova Scotia for the purpose of getting a bargain on fuel. Everything depended on the credibility of the witnesses.

Holmes's witnesses—the ship's captain, the chief engineer, second mate, government safety inspectors among them—testified that on leaving New Orleans, there was every expectation that the *Concordia* would reach Liverpool approximately twenty-eight days later, although as a precaution, she carried coal enough for at least thirty days. Dana's witnesses refuted all Holmes's witnesses said. The first assistant engineer testified that the *Concordia* had not in fact held enough coal to make Liverpool and that she was not in fact seaworthy, her boilers and machinery being defective on sailing. A merchant who sold coal to the captain testified that the captain told him coal was too dear in New Orleans and he thought he would stop elsewhere to take on his full supply. A marine inspector said he had heard the captain state in casual conversation that he intended to put in at some other port for fuel.

Whom could Judge Clifford believe?

"[A]fter diligent study of the whole record," he was persuaded by Holmes's witnesses. The first engineer's testimony that the *Concordia* had not been seaworthy on sailing, he concluded, was "disproved by the evidence." There was, furthermore, "no direct proof" that the *Concordia*'s captain had intended to shop for fuel in Nova Scotia. As for the casual comments by the captain regarding those intentions, these could hardly carry much evidentiary weight. And he affirmed Judge Lowell's earlier decision.

No major principles of maritime law emerged during Holmes's defense of the Nickersons. The case, which generated not a little acerbity on both sides, did demonstrate, however, that Holmes could when required suppress his natural and persistent intellectuality and perform as scrappily as any other man at the bar. Dana's son, who assisted in the case, described Holmes's demeanor during the proceedings:

He made a decided attempt at oratory. He never spoke in a conversational tone. His sentences were well ballanced [*sic*], finished and telling. . . . The best example of rhetoric was calling our witnesses "wreckers," while the only testimony in which the word was used was that some wreckers had stolen some cotton lying on the beach. The witnesses he referred to were, in fact, a retired Cunard captain and the present Port Warden of Halifax, the telegraph operator, the justice of peace of the place. . . . We trust much to the Judge's careful study of the case . . . as the evidence was so roughly handled by the other side.

In 1878, Holmes's performance in admiralty law brought him within a coat of paint of a federal judgeship. Following the death of federal Circuit Court Judge George F. Shepley that year, it was generally expected that Judge John Lowell of the federal district court would be promoted to circuit judge, leaving a vacancy in the lower federal court where a rush of admiralty cases was expected. Members of the Boston bar immediately began writing their contacts among the members of President Rutherford B. Hayes's (Harvard Law School, 1845) administration in behalf of their fellow lawyer, Oliver Wendell Holmes, Jr. A group of attorneys co-signed a letter to Attorney General Charles Devens of Massachusetts, who was later to sit with Holmes on the Massachusetts Supreme Judicial Court, describing Holmes as the "fittest occupant of the position both for his general and special qualifications." J. P. Putnam wrote William Maxwell Evarts, secretary of state, that "no man, among all those whom I have heard named for the office, is . . . better qualified for the position"; Putnam had no doubt Holmes's appointment would be "entirely satisfactory" to the Massachusetts bar. Godfrey Morse of the Boston bar told President Hayes that in his opinion Holmes was an "able, learned, upright and good man and lawyer" who would bring honor to the bench. Chief Justice Gray joined the movement for Holmes's appointment, working behind the scenes. Gray's half brother and longtime friend of Holmes, John Gray, wrote Charles Cotesworth Beaman in the state department, who happened to be married to Secretary Evarts's daughter as well as a Harvard classmate of Holmes's, that Holmes had been "solicited" by several members of the bar, "not his personal friends," and had "consented to accept" the judgeship, should it be offered. Holmes did not, however, want to "take any personal steps himself." Gray added that Holmes's knowledge of admiralty law was "singularly exact and profound."

The subject of all the solicitation was "in a mild excitement." The judgeship would, he confided precipitately to Frederick Pollock, enable him "to work in the way I want to and so I should like it—although it would cost me a pang to leave my partners," and if he was appointed, he "should hardly know whether to be glad or sorry." In the meantime, he could not, typically, "help feeling nervous about the result until the thing is settled."

The scenario plotted by the Bostonians was never staged. The president had other plans. At first he considered leaving Judge Lowell where he was and subsequently offered the vacancy on the circuit court to several prominent Massachusetts lawyers including Senator George F. Hoar and Attorney General Devens himself. Holmes's partner George Shattuck was also considered, but was said to be in failing health and his name was dropped. When all the men the president approached declined, he finally promoted Lowell to the circuit court and then began to look for a replacement for Lowell's district court seat. The president was aware of the strong support for Holmes, who happened to be a Republican, and discussed him with Devens and Hoar.

"I rather think Holmes is the man," Hayes told them.

But Hoar, who also was to object to Holmes's appointment to the U.S. Supreme Court a quarter-century later, countered with the name of one of his own friends, Thomas W. Nelson of Worcester, and at once outlined Nelson's superior qualities.

The president turned to Devens. "Do you agree, Mr. Attorney General?" he asked.

"I do," Devens replied.

"Then Nelson be it," the president concluded. Nelson accepted the appointment, and the door closed on one of the might-have-beens of history. Had Hayes gone ahead and appointed Holmes to the federal court in 1878, it is far from certain that Holmes would have written *The Common Law* or that he would have been appointed to the Massachusetts Supreme Judicial Court from which he sprang to the U.S. Supreme Court. He might well have lived out his years as a minor federal judge. But luck was with him, though he could not have known it at the time.

Undoubtedly at the time he was disappointed. He had come so close, so near to achieving a position from which he might really influence the development of law, might give his ideas a life they could not have while he remained only a practitioner. He could almost see those "men who never heard of him . . . moving to the measure of his thought." But that would have to wait.

* * *

WENDELL HOLMES SAW the United States Supreme Court in action for the first time in early 1879, when he represented a client there for the only time in his legal career. As he looked around the old Senate chamber on the main floor of the Capitol where the Court met at the time, as he absorbed the grandeur of the marble columns and the busts of dead justices overseeing the proceedings, he decided the scene needed "only a black boy with gold bangles, holding a leash of gray-hounds at one end of the bench, to be a living picture by Paul Veronese. . . ." Like many lawyers who arrive at the Supreme Court from remote sections of the country to argue there, Holmes probably was admitted to the Supreme Court bar especially for the occasion—January 16, 1879.

The case, *United States* v. *Ames,* made up in complexity what it lacked in historical significance or human drama. It involved a suit by the federal government against the estate of the late Oakes Ames, five-term congressman from Massachusetts whose bent for financial specu-lation had brought him a fortune as manager of the infamous Credit Mobilier Company as well as a reputation for political corruption. The ensuing disgrace, added to financial anxieties, may have been responsi-ble for his death in 1873.

The case that brought Holmes and Shattuck to Washington involved Ames's part ownership of 1,120 bales of cotton that had been seized as enemy property by Union forces in New Orleans in 1865. A series of proceedings in the federal courts in Louisiana had found the owners of the cargo heavily in debt to the government, and the government was trying to collect the money. Holmes and Shattuck had been engaged by the executors of Ames's estate to prevent it from doing so.

Whether Holmes or Shattuck wrote the brief for the defense is not clear. Only printed copies survive: those in the records of the U.S. Supreme Court and Holmes's own, heavily annotated, among the books he left to the Library of Congress. It is, however, a highly technical argument involving jurisdictional and procedural matters in courts of equity, admiralty, and common law, and reveals no characteristic thread of thought of either partner. Nor does the record reveal which of the partners actually presented the case to the justices.

The Bostonians were successful. In a 7 to 1 decision (Justice Ward Hunt took no part in the case, Justice Joseph P. Bradley dissented), Justice Clifford, whom Holmes two years before had persuaded of the rightness of his cause in *New Orleans Mutual Insurance Co.* v. *Nickerson,* concluded that "the claim of the United States [was] not well founded."

In addition to arguing *United States* v. *Ames* in the U.S. Supreme Court, Holmes argued thirty-two cases before the Massachusetts Supreme Judicial Court, the state's highest, during his life as a practitioner, 1867–81, winning fourteen and losing eighteen. These cases were not particularly dramatic; they did not involve, for the most part, great principles of law, large sums of money, or important aspects of public policy. They were, nevertheless, valuable for the advancement of Holmes's career.

He observed the methods of his colleagues, and he himself became a familiar and respected figure in the Boston legal community, not brilliant like Sidney Bartlett, perhaps, but a lawyer to be reckoned with. At the same time, he represented no radical interests and seemed, if the interests of his clients might be admitted as evidence, to be quite safe politically.

He learned a lot from these cases, too. The practicalities of the courtroom at first hand, for example, and how to appraise and predict judicial reaction. He had enunciated his "prediction theory" of law when he wrote in the *American Law Review* in 1872: "The only question for lawyers is, how will the judges act?" He was learning that Judge Lowell's jurisprudence hinged on his sense of justice and Judge Gray's on his respect for tradition. Indeed Judge Gray carried it further than most judges and went so far as to communicate his displeasure when Holmes one day appeared in Gray's courtroom informally dressed.

Holmes learned, once again, to survive under fire—a different sort of fire than the one that gave him his first lessons, perhaps, but nonetheless real. And he learned, as Dr. Holmes had learned when he undertook to make a medical case via the essay, to master the complex facts of an issue, to organize them in an orderly fashion, and to present them effectively.

Perhaps most important of all, he learned from firsthand experience how contemporary legal issues inevitably reflected contemporary social and political concerns. When he defended John Spaulding against Manuel Arvilla's suit to recover damages for the latter's injuries sustained in Spaulding's sugar refinery, he saw for himself a common occurrence in newly industrialized New England.* Such matters as failures to deliver manufactured goods, and the complexities of partnership, intro-

---

* *Arvilla* v. *Spaulding.* 121 Mass. 505 (1877).

duced him to the intricacies of contemporary economics. The rapid urbanization that was increasing the price of and diminishing the availability of land brought him cases involving such matters as disputes over property values, tenement ownership—an increasingly profitable enterprise in growing Boston—land development, and tax assessments.*

Holmes's success and the growth of his reputation as a lawyer notwithstanding, he still was not satisfied with private practice as a way of life. Again he yearned for the adventures of the mind he seemed to have all but abandoned, and it became his custom on arrival at the office in the morning to approach one of the firm's young associates, Glendower Evans, with the challenge:

Mr. Evans, I am ready to contradict any statement you will make.

Whereupon the two would sit down together and talk, sometimes all day.

By 1876, the number of cases in which Holmes was involved began to taper off, and in 1876, his work began again to appear in the *American Law Review*. He had just turned thirty-five. If his life was to proceed on schedule, if he was to impose himself on the world within the time frame he had created, he had but five years left to do it, to discover whether or not there were, as he believed there must be, unifying concepts threading through that massive body of material called the law. The approach of the self-imposed deadline gave his studies a new urgency:

It often is said, and with a good deal of truth, that men reach their highest mark between thirty and forty. Perhaps the statement seems more significant than it really is, because men generally have settled down to their permanent occupation by thirty, and in the course of the next ten years are likely to have found such leading and dominant conceptions as they are going to find; the rest of life is working out details.

---

* See *West* v. *Platt*. 120 Mass. 421 (1876). *Whitcomb* v. *Convers*. 119 Mass. 38 (1873). *Burt* v. *Merchants' Insurance Co*. 115 Mass. 1 (1874). *Woodward* v. *Boston*. 115 Mass. 81 (1874). *Hyannis Savings Bank* v. *Moors*. 120 Mass. 459 (1876). *Treadwell* v. *Boston*. 123 Mass. 23 (1877).

CHAPTER 13

The Common Law

DURING THE HALF-DECADE between the appearance in 1876 of "Primitive Notions in Modern Law" in the *American Law Review* and publication of *The Common Law* in 1881, just five days before his fortieth birthday, Holmes put aside nearly all his other interests to devote himself to the laborious digging out of the legal principles on which he hoped to construct a theory of law. These were the "black years," as hellish in their own way as anything Holmes had endured in the war. His intellectual life was at stake, and these years demanded qualities as heroic in their own way as those Little Abbott had demonstrated on the battlefield. Emerson had shown the way when he wrote: "Always do what you are afraid to do."

Making a living required Holmes to practice his profession by day, but he devoted his evenings almost entirely to scholarly pursuits, sitting hunched over his books in the Social Law Library until it closed at nine, unwinding on an hour's walk around the Common with a fellow scholar. Elected a member of Harvard's Board of Overseers in 1876 and in that capacity appointed to the Committee to Visit the Law School, of which Shattuck was already a member and which Johnny Morse would join a few years later, he kept in touch with events there. Other than that, however, he confined himself almost exclusively to his studies. He would never again work so hard, extend himself so far.

He seems during this time to have cut himself off from the social life men of his age and station enjoyed, although he made exceptions for events it might be politically prudent to attend if he wanted to get on— he had decided he wanted to be chief justice of the Massachusetts Supreme Judicial Court and after that a justice of the United States Supreme Court and already had announced his aims on one of his evening walks around the Common. He was listed, for example, along with Chief Justice Horace Gray of the Massachusetts Supreme Judicial Court, and Henry Cabot Lodge, Holmes's former student who was beginning to make a name for himself in Republican politics, among the guests at a dinner Charles Francis Adams, Jr., gave for the prominent Boston lawyer Richard Henry Dana in July 1879. He entertained visiting Englishmen and was willing to open a bottle of wine when old Harvard friend John Fiske and his wife came to call. But he appears to have had little use for conventional small talk and to have been more inclined to base social intercourse on serious discussion regarding his own intellectual interests.

His relationship with William James seems to have cooled; they saw each other less and less. James had detected an intellectual hardness that he did not admire in his old friend; at the same time Holmes found James's intellect, formerly as hard as his own, he thought, inclining now too far toward the mystical, ceding reason to faith. Or as Holmes put it:

> His reason made him sceptical and his wishes led him to turn down the lights so as to give miracle a chance.

They did not meet with the same sympathetic understanding that had once existed between them. They had found the selves for which they then had been searching together, Holmes's in the law, James's in the new science of psychology, and their interests as well as their attitudes had diverged. Their old friend the Cosmos would have to await the next generation of explorers.

For Holmes, John Gray, a proper Bostonian with a scholarly interest in the law, took up where James had left off, although the extravagant effusions of youthful affection were missing from this more mature relationship. In Holmes's friendships now, it was common professional concerns that mattered, that promoted intimacy.

During this time, a bright new face appeared among the members of the local bar. Young Louis Brandeis of Louisville, Kentucky, 1878 graduate of Harvard Law School which he had entered at age eighteen and where he had compiled an academic record unequaled for at least a half-century, returned to Boston to practice law. He and Samuel D. Warren, whose family's roots ran deep in the New England soil and who briefly had been an associate at Shattuck, Holmes, and Munroe, established a little law firm on Devonshire Street where Holmes drank champagne to celebrate opening day. Boston was too busy fending off the Irish to worry about this single bright and personable young Jew who had dropped into their midst, and its first families welcomed him, took him into the best homes and clubs. He had been friendly with several of Boston's first families during his law school days. Now he expanded his circle, often through his law partner. He dined at the Exchange and Union clubs, was secretary of the Boston Art Club, and, a rider of some ability, he organized the Dedham Polo Club.

Holmes was immediately attracted to Brandeis, the first of several outlanders with whom he became friends, and invited him to spend a weekend at Mattapoisett. Already their views on the law were as different as their ethnic backgrounds. While Holmes inclined to the scholarly, the abstract, Brandeis did not mind dirtying his hands in the day-to-day application of the law. Still, Holmes admired Brandeis's incisive mind and delighted in his informed conversation, which always tended toward the serious, or, as Holmes put it, rarely "descended to the vernacular." The two began to spend occasional intellectual evenings together, discussing the finer points of law and commenting on each other's articles.

At the same time Holmes was forming a friendship with Brandeis, his dedication to his work was isolating him psychically from Boston, beginning to pull him away from the milieu into which he had been born. Not all Bostonians understood the self-imposed isolation, the scholarly work, or his single-minded devotion to it. They might have better understood it if he had spent his efforts and splendid energies on getting ahead as a practicing lawyer—that sort of success was of good, old-fashioned value in Brahmin Boston. But removing himself from the social stream for such a nebulous undertaking as scholarship at his age seemed to puzzle them.

His unfamiliarity with contemporary events perhaps symbolized an inward sense of alienation. He felt so out of touch with what was going on that he asked a friend to send him articles on "politico-legal subjects which are from time to time before the public." He knew "nothing about politics and live questions, as of necessity [he was] wholly buried in dead ones for some time to come."

The isolation was as terrible as any Holmes had ever known, even in the war—this work he was embarked on required in fact the same kind of courage and endurance the war had. He was living in a "black gulf of solitude, more isolation than that which surrounds a dying man," a "black frozen night in which there were no flowers, no spring, no easy joys." He had no charts to guide him, and voices of authority warned "that in the crush of that ice any craft might sink." How many times was he tempted to turn back? The "fogs of doubt so thick that one can't always see the compass" made the journey almost unbearable. Yet, combined with his intense ambition, his capacity to survive and produce under such conditions—fine-honed in the crucible of war—gave him the strength and courage to reject tradition, legal and other, and to withstand both internal and external pressures.

Holmes knew, without charts, as the early explorers of earth about whom he liked to read and later explorers of space knew, that what he sought was there. It waited only to be unearthed from its grave in the remote human past. He needed, like the explorers early and late, only the intelligence, the stamina, and the will to find it. Especially the will. His advice to others, after the "black frozen night" had ended, always focused on the will, the "fire in your belly that keeps your heart and aim warm through dull and hopeless months."

Never forgetting that "the meanest seeming details are organic parts of a mighty whole—that every fact in the universe—has the universe behind it and belongs to the science of life," he gathered together all those "facts which before lay scattered in an organic mess" and shot them "through the magnetic current of his thought," so that they would "leap into an organic order, and live and bear fruit."

American legal scholarship in the 1870s was ripe for the kind of corrective surgery Holmes was about to perform. The traditions of the natural law—the law of nature transmitted by divine will—as explicated by Blackstone and Kent, its roots running deep into the soil of ancient Greece and Rome, had outlived its usefulness. Its immutable principles comforted. Its abstract and logical nature satisfied. Its simplicity, certainty, and reasonableness continued to be appealing. But its inertia kept it from dealing with the disorder and changefulness and all the other complexities of nineteenth-century life. The traditionalists "discovered" law which was deduced from the unchanging nature of things— Chief Justice Gray's "established rule, so ancient that [he] knew not its origin, that seamen may recover their wages against the master" was a good example. That the law's development might have been progressive was not generally recognized. Even the early historicists like Friedrich von Savigny in Germany and Henry Maine, whom Holmes admired for their innovative perspective on law as history, had not seen law as evolutionary, responsive to the social and political environment. The historicists had only changed the milieu, and "discovered" their law in history instead of nature, but it remained static and mechanical and created the fiction that judges did not make law but only applied the proper established principles in deciding their cases.

Holmes's investigations were telling him otherwise. His expanded reading, which now included such anthropological works as G. W. Dasent's *The Story of Burnt Njal; or, Life in Iceland at the End of the Tenth Century* and Hans Staden's memoir of his *Captivity . . . Among the Wild Tribes of Eastern Brazil* in mid-16th century, texts dealing with earliest Greek, Roman, Hebrew, French, and Anglo-Saxon institutions, as well as various books on ancient religions, along with the law reports, had persuaded Holmes he was seeing "reflected . . . the lives of all men that have been!" He not only was finding intimations of familiar legal concepts in the alarms and excursions of earliest men but could watch them unfold over the centuries, reworked and reinterpreted in each generation as social and political necessity demanded; many were virtually unrecognizable now. But what he saw convinced him that law was one of the most articulate expressions of the underlying forces in human history, and he set off on the last leg of his journey of exploration and discovery, which was carrying him far beyond Rome in both time and space.

He had long envisioned a work on the common law that would "supplant Blackstone and Kent's Commentaries." He couldn't "answer for unconscious elements," but he was sure

> the movement came from within—from the passionate demand that what sounded so arbitrary in Blackstone, for instance, should give some reasonable meaning—that the law should be proved, if it could be, to be worthy of the interest of an intelligent man—(that was the form the question took then).

The need for such a volume underlies much of his writing in the *American Law Review*. As early as January 1871, reviewing C. G. Addison's *The Law of Torts,* he had longed "for the day when we may see these subjects treated by a writer capable of dealing with them philosophically and self-sacrificing enough to write a treatise as if it were an integral part of a commentary on the entire body of the law." Some months later, in October, in his review of Ram's *Science of Legal Judgment,* he was hoping someone would produce a balanced treatise on the "sources of the law which . . . will form a chapter of jurisprudence which is not yet written, and which it is worthy of an aspiring mind to write." In that same issue, Holmes himself in his "Misunderstandings of the Civil Law" had begun to probe some obscurities that had found their way into modern jurisprudence.

He originally thought of writing a "New First Book of the law" in which he would construct a "new Jurisprudence." But he did not immediately put his material into book form. The results of his research first appeared as a series of articles in the *American Law Review*: dry, technical analyses of particular areas of the law: possession (1878), common carriers (1879), trespass and negligence (1880), all introduced by the two-part essay on "Primitive Notions in Modern Law" (1876–77). But their aridness could not conceal their originality, nor their jungles of detail the connections he was making with the centuries. He was sure he had caught on to something valuable.

In the euphoria of discovery, he sent a copy of the first article, "Primitive Notions in Modern Law," to the aging Emerson, along with a note:

> If the clothing of detail does not stand in the way I hope the ideas may not be uninteresting to you. It seems to me that I have learned, after a laborious and somewhat painful period of probation that the law opens a way to philosophy as well as anything else, if pursued far enough, and I hope to prove it before I die. Accept this little piece as written in that faith, and as a slight mark of gratitude and respect I feel for you who more than anyone else first started the philosophical ferment in my mind.

Holmes shot off a copy of "Possession" to Sir Henry Maine, who was "much interested," but was prevented by the press of his duties as a member of the Indian Council, professor of jurisprudence at Oxford, and Master of Trinity Hall, Cambridge, from writing a critique of it. Holmes favored Pollock with copies of all the articles. He, too, believed his scholarly American friend was on to something. He thought Holmes's "position seem[ed] well made out by evidence and analogy" and his work "important for the scientific understanding of the law," but he was not sure "whether it would be at all possible, until much more has been done in this way, to produce a really good institutional book." "Common Carriers and the Common Law" Holmes also sent to Arthur Sedgwick, his former co-editor at the *American Law Review* and in 1879 an editor of the *Nation*, "without," Holmes said coyly,

> any thought of getting you to take trouble with regard to it but of course I am not so super human as to deny that it would be a great pleasure to me if it were mentioned in the *Nation*.

Sedgwick complied, and a five-hundred-word flattering notice of Holmes's essay appeared in the *Nation,* which, said Holmes, "pleased me very much."

Later in 1879, a twenty-three-year-old Harvard Law School student named Abbott Lawrence Lowell suggested to his father, Augustus, the Lowell family's obligatory representative on the prestigious Lowell Institute's board of trustees and selector of speakers for its popular lecture series, that he invite Holmes to give a series on the law. Holmes could not have been more gratified. The beneficiary of a fund established in 1836 by industrialist John Lowell, Jr., the Lowell Institute, with links to Athenaeum, banking, Unitarian, and Beacon Hill Boston, had quickly become a leading New England dispenser of culture. An invitation to lecture there was coveted by every scholar in town.

But could he do it? Had he the stamina left? Was he ready? Would anyone be interested? Was he prepared to challenge the old "guv'nor"? Dr. Holmes had lectured to standing-room-only audiences when Wendell was a boy, but the subject had been the English poets, a subject within the experience of every literate Bostonian. The common law was alien territory to most Bostonians, and legal history was unfamiliar even to many lawyers.

By the "weight of a hair" he decided to accept Lowell's invitation, and thus "changed the whole course of [his] life."

Wendell immediately—January 1, 1880—went to work rewriting, rearranging, and enlarging on the material he had gathered for his *American Law Review* articles, rehabilitating it for adaptation to the lecture series. If he was pleased by the invitation to speak at the Institute, he was also "very hard driven with work, day and night." His law practice still occupied his days, but his nights were devoted to preparing the lectures. One made progress "but slowly when his only chance is to sit down after dinner and after a day of more or less hard work. The frame of mind needful for successful speculation is so different from that into which business puts one."

The lectures began on November 23, 1880. Huntington Hall on Tremont Street was nearly full, with young men reported to outnumber older, although the latter were also liberally represented. Brooks Adams was there in company with Louis Brandeis. Chief Justice Gray and a sprinkling of state legislators were also noticed in the audience.

Holmes delivered his lecture without referring to his manuscript, as if, a member of the audience later recalled, "he were narrating offhand some interesting story, or telling of the happening of some event of absorbing interest." Holmes claimed to have simplified the material; it was doubtful, however, the writer continued, that many in the audience understood the "abstruse reasoning of the lectures." Nevertheless, Holmes held their interest "to the end."

> The manner of delivery . . . seemed then, as it does now, a marvelous intellectual performance, for the delivery of them was not a matter of memory so much as a process of reasoning at the moment, by a mind thoroughly imbued with the subject.

The lectures continued—without interruption even for Christmas Eve, although the audience was smaller that night—on Tuesday and Friday nights, ending the night of Friday, December 31 with a summary of the first eleven lectures. The *Boston Daily Advertiser,* in which the entire series had been covered in some detail, reported that "no other course in the institute in recent years has been attended by so large a proportion of young men—an evidence both of the interest they have in the law and of the power of Mr. Holmes to interest them."

The invitation to deliver the Lowell Lectures had two immediate effects on Holmes's professional progress. He achieved a local prominence no article in the arcane pages of the *American Law Review* could have achieved for him. And it encouraged him "to do what was in my power to accomplish my wish": to organize and publish in book form his major findings regarding the development of legal institutions. The necessity of preparing the lectures, he explained, "made it easier to go farther, and to prepare for printing, and accordingly I did so."

The result of his efforts, his book, *The Common Law,* was published by the local leader in legal publishing at the time, Little, Brown & Company, on March 3, 1881, and was duly celebrated with a bottle of champagne, the cork to which Holmes put away in his desk drawer for safekeeping. There was some suggestion the book fell into the "ordinary literary" category of work, for which the royalty was 15 percent, but Holmes held out for the 20 percent customarily paid to authors of law books "on account of the superior amount of intellect required (we keep our smiles to ourselves)." The first edition sold for $4. Little, Brown, which also published, among other best-sellers at the time, John Bartlett's *Familiar Quotations* and Louisa May Alcott's *Little Women,* would not get rich on Holmes, but his sales were respectable for a book of its kind: 245 copies its first month, 500 its first year, 1,041 its first five years. It was still selling a hundred or so copies a year in the late 1890s.

The Common Law was not a book for those Holmes liked to call "squirts." As in his articles for the *American Law Review,* the prose is dry and turgid with only occasional flashes of the stylistic elegance for which Holmes later was recognized. The reader plods through, his or her task only infrequently lightened with an epigram or a felicitous phrase. He assumed the reader's familiarity with ancient Greek and Roman legal institutions, the English kings and the dates of their reigns—information a cultured nineteenth-century gentleman would have at his fingertips, of course—and with the work of earlier legal commentators and judges. He assumed a working knowledge of Latin, Greek, and French, as well as legal phraseology, obsolete as well as contemporary. The cases with which he illustrated his points and the commentaries he cited often lack any reference to the time in which they were decided; foreign phrases are untranslated.

Nevertheless, *The Common Law* was a distinguished and original contribution to legal scholarship. Having learned at Harvard Law School what the law was and discussed in the *American Law Review* what others thought it was, it was Holmes's turn to present his views on what *he* thought it was. He "made the thread, wove the cloth and cut the pattern."

He had tried to look at the law as an "organic whole" and to understand the relationship between "tradition on the one side and the changing desires and needs of a community on the other." The path he followed was not well traveled. The spirit of Emerson's ideal American Scholar, independent and original, was reincarnated in the pages of *The Common Law*. The bold, challenging spirit of "Books," Holmes's own publishing debut at seventeen, rippled through it. He looked beyond the canons of conventional contemporary legal scholarship and sought his material in history.

History was in his genes. Grandfather Abiel Holmes, whose masterpiece also had required ten years of devoted scholarship while he plied his profession, had been historian almost as much as clergyman. At seventeen, Wendell himself had written that history "should be the finest, in fact, the all-comprehending study."

He cultivated "association with the past." He considered "among the foundations of [his] soul" the granite rocks and barberry bushes of Boston's North Shore that Olivers, Wendells, Holmeses, perhaps even Norsemen, before him had known. He found the steps leading down from Montgomery Place where he had been born to Province Street "the most venerable monument that the past can show."

He loved "every brick and shingle of the old Massachusetts towns" where once his Puritan ancestors "worked and prayed," and he thought it "a noble and pious thing to do whatever we may by written word and moulded bronze and sculptured stone to keep our memories, our reverence and our love alive and to hand them on to new generations all too ready to forget."

He took special pleasure in the fact that President George Washington had taken tea at the house of Great-Grandfather Jackson. He treasured, too, the tomahawk Great-Grandfather David Holmes had brought back from the French and Indian Wars.

Occasional visits to Salem's House of Seven Gables, with its secret staircase, reminded him pleasurably of the Indians, witches, and smugglers who inhabited Boston's past. He liked in summer to poke around the old burying ground at Marblehead, reached by zigzagging to the top of the hill where the first settlers were buried—a spot "pretty near heaven," as he described it—from which one could look far out to sea. He liked to visit the gravestones of the early settlers, sea captains, sailors, and Revolutionary War heroes. The dedication at Gloucester of a memorial to local sailors lost at sea moved him to tears. He owned a mirror that once had hung in a Boston house requisitioned by the British during the Revolution.

"Sometimes I look in it," he would muse, "and think I see Lord Howe's bewigged face. Do you see it?" he would ask excitedly, "do you see it?"

The personal satisfaction he found in his family's historical past he translated into the intellectual satisfaction he found in the continuity of the law's historical path.

He recognized no single book as *the* source of his conclusions. He simply had "rooted around and made notes until the theory gradually emerged." Austin was there, as were Maine and Darwin, all overlaid with readings in anthropology, decidedly a newcomer to legal scholarship. Old friend, Harvard medievalist, and fellow student of social institutions, Henry Adams, sent Holmes his own books on German legal history which he hoped would "prove useful in your investigations." Even before Adams did that, however, he had published in 1876, with Henry Cabot Lodge and other bright young men, *Essays in Anglo-Saxon Law,* in which the authors had renounced the traditional Roman sources of contemporary law and looked for illumination in the forests of Teutonic Europe. There they had found surprising examples of democratic principles in action, principles that readily migrated to Anglo-Saxon England. Holmes reviewed the volume with enthusiasm in the *American Law Review,* although he seemed to think Adams and his colleagues may on occasion have stretched the facts to fit their thesis.

Holmes was prodded into following his friends' adventures along similar unorthodox paths. Holmes, however, traveled farther than Adams. He searched for models among the aborigines of Brazilian rain forests, among the tiger-hunting Kukis of southern Asia, and in tenth-century Icelandic criminal courts. Jewish, Greek, Teutonic, Anglo-Saxon, and Roman legal traditions had come under his microscope. Trends in history, economics, and philosophy had been canvassed. And he had advanced the historical heresy that the way those ancient and primitive tribesmen, especially German as transmitted by Anglo-Saxons, had dealt with cattle-thieves was the source of much of what went on in nineteenth-century English and American courtrooms. The praetors of ancient Rome were less involved than had been thought.

In his search for "the rationale of the cardinal doctrines" of the common law, Holmes had watched in his journeys to remote areas of the world the antecedents of contemporary law emerging from the archaic customs of primitive societies and responding over centuries to the demands and concerns of subsequent generations. He had been able to trace, for example, the origins of modern concepts of legal liability in the ancient thirst for vengeance and the working out of blood feuds. He saw how earliest men began to regulate private vengeance by setting limits on the amount of retaliation permitted. He saw how early Saxon law substituted the payment of a fixed amount of money to end a feud, a custom which in turn gave way to establishment of the king's courts and expression to royal greed by making offenses crimes against the state and fines payable to the royal coffers.

He discovered that contemporary ideas connected with guilt originated in the superstitious primitive mind, which assigned motive to malevolence on the part of the offender, even an inanimate one; Kukis of southern Asia avenging the death of a tribesman who has fallen from a tree by cutting down the tree and scattering the chips; Greeks exiling an axe that had caused a death. Out of such customs psychological and subjective—"internal"—criteria for judging offenses emerged; they came in time to encompass moral standards, necessarily imprecise and unpredictable. Holmes argued in *The Common Law* that standards of guilt, if they are to be precise and predictable—to offer scientific certainty— must be external, objective, and embrace the standards of conduct shared by the community. If legal concepts were formulated on the basis of experience—what the law is—and Holmes felt sure they were, then morality—what the law ought to be—didn't matter.

All societies, ancient and modern, primitive and sophisticated, he discovered—and this discovery was to become a linchpin of his constitutional jurisprudence—traditionally sacrificed the individual's interests to those of the larger group. When conscripts were required, they were seized and marched off, "with bayonets in the rear to their death."

Holmes reinforced his conviction that laws devised for specific purposes often survived for centuries after their original purpose had been served and their rationale had been forgotten, adapting time after time to new environments. And he confirmed his theory that the element of force was the cornerstone of all law, whether the king's will, the judge's decision, the legislator's enactment, or the simple thrusting off of an extra person from a lifeboat.

His principal discovery, the one that set his book apart from the others and the one that later was to set Holmes apart from judges of his time—men who looked to logic, tradition, to God for their jurisprudence—was the concept that law, not unlike the structure of the elephant, was not an abstraction, was not at all static, but was evolutionary and responded to the social and economic environment of which it was a part and was "forever adopting new principles from life at one end and it retains old ones from history at the other." Natural selection was at work in the law, too. He stated his famous conclusion in the first paragraph of his book. It is one of the most quoted passages in legal history:

> The life of the law has not been logic: it has been experience. The felt necessities of the time, the prevalent moral and political theories, intuitions of public policy, avowed or unconscious, even the prejudices which judges share with their fellow-men, have had a good deal more to do than the syllogism in determining the rules by which men should be governed. The law embodies the story of a nation's development through many centuries, and it cannot be dealt with as if it contained only the axioms and corollaries of a book of mathematics. In order to know what it is, we must know what it has been, and what it tends to become. We must alternately consult history and existing theories of legislation. But the most difficult labor will be to understand the combination of the two into new products at every stage.

In 1881, it shook the little world of lawyers and judges who had been raised on Blackstone's theory that the law, given by God Himself, was immutable and eternal and judges had only to discover its contents. It took some years for them to come around to the view that the law was flexible, responsive to changing social and economic climates, and amenable to empirical methods of analysis.

But Holmes had succeeded. He had applied to the law the tools of science. He had found there were in fact unifying concepts woven through the law. And he had broken new intellectual trails, using history to guide him. He had given the law a vitality it never before had possessed. He had wrested legal history from the aridity of syllogism and abstraction and placed it in the context of human experience, demonstrating that the corpus of the law was neither ukase from God nor derived from Nature, but, like the little toe and the structure of the horse, was a constantly evolving thing, a response to the continually developing social and economic environment. The finished product had been worth the unbearable discouragements, the isolation, the "black gulf of solitude," frustrations and fears, all behind him now. Was it for this he had survived the war?

In an exultant mood, he wrote Louis Brandeis the day after his fortieth birthday that he was "now a man of leisure in the evenings" and would be glad to see him. But leisure did not suit Holmes. Postpartum depression struck shortly after publication. His gums began to bleed, and he thought "the end was coming" until his dentist assured him he had a common ailment caused by the vigorous use of the toothbrush. While he waited anxiously for reviews of his book, he settled down with ten volumes of Casanova's memoirs which "put a wiggle" into him, and ever after he reserved Casanova, which he considered "one of the great books of the world," for times when his mental state needed uplift.

The reviews were not long coming. In May 1881, the *American Law Review,* in whose pages so much of *The Common Law* had originated, devoted an unusual seven pages to its praise, calling the author's research "extraordinary," his text "ingenious," and his insights "brilliant." The former *American Law Review* editor, the reviewer continued,

> undoes the present, turns familiar thoughts wrong side out, puts himself in the midst of the old order of things, and then makes those unexpected and apparently haphazard connections which establish the continuity, and prove, as it were, the intangible apostolic succession. . . .
>
> One of the most instructive things in the book is the clear way in which it sets out the complicated influences which work the law into shape, and its practical common-sense recognition of the fact that, however conservative and continuous our system has been, it has yet felt at every stage the living power of man interfering to make things as he wants them.

At about the same time, a reviewer for the *Albany Law Journal* predicted *The Common Law* would be "welcomed by every student of the law who reads with other motives than the desire of better fitting himself to win a case." Despite his achievement, Holmes, even now, could not escape his father's shadow; the reviewer referred prominently to his famous parent. A later, longer review in the same journal was equally complimentary, describing Holmes as "master of his subject" and his book as an "indispensable auxiliary" to "every person who desires to be informed of the progress of the jurisprudence of the common law, and of what our scientific jurists are contributing to this progress."

The *Nation,* of which Holmes's friend Arthur Sedgwick was still editor, considered *The Common Law* a significant if overwritten contribution to the literature of legal history, containing

> much that is novel and brilliant, and show[ing] calm consideration and
> unusually profound legal study . . . yet we must admit that it is injured by
> long and philosophical discussion of intent and the like, which, if they
> were worth preserving anywhere, would only be so in a condensed form,
> as a part of a complete philosophical treatment of the subject. . . . Printed
> here, they give a tediously discursive and aimless air to the book and hide
> its real historical value.

Holmes was "exceedingly gratified and obliged" that Fred Pollock had resolved his original doubts about the viability of a book constructed out of Holmes's *American Law Review* articles and reviewed his book favorably for *The Saturday Review of Politics, Literature, Science, and the Arts* (London), calling it

> a searching historical and analytical criticism of several of the leading no-
> tions of English law; not an antiquarian discussion first and a theoretical
> discussion afterwards but a continuous study in the joint light of policy and
> history. . . .

A scholar himself, Pollock knew enough about Holmes's data to dispute some of the minor details; "altogether," he thought, however,

> Mr. Holmes's book will be a most valuable—we should almost say an indis-
> pensable—companion to the scientific student of legal history.

Although Holmes's work was virtually unknown outside the northeastern United States, for he was an American and a lawyer rather than an academic, the London *Spectator* described *The Common Law* as "the most original work of legal speculation which has appeared in English since the publication of Sir Henry Maine's *Ancient Law*" and complimented the author on his ability to combine with a fine sense of balance the methods of Maine with those of Austin, to put together a completely novel work.

Rufus Waples paid Holmes the ultimate compliment when he incorporated some of Holmes's ideas into his *Proceedings in Rem,* published in 1882; Waples, however, wrote without acknowledgment, and the ambitious young Holmes, anxious to leave his own imprint on legal scholarship, was miffed. He protested to Thomas M. Cooley, a well-known constitutional scholar who had written the introduction to Waples's book and with whom Holmes was on correspondent's terms:

> It is not merely that he takes for his starting point ideas which I have no reason to doubt were original with me and which I spent much time and labor in stating and proving, but that the citations which I gathered from various sources occur in such wise as to earmark the indebtedness to my mind.

Holmes was pleased that his work was helpful to other scholars, he added, but he believed such assistance ought to be acknowledged.

Cooley sent Holmes's letter on to Waples. Waples replied indignantly: "I am surprised that he should claim any ideas of my treatise." Waples had written his article before he had "even known" of Holmes's "Primitive Notions in Modern Law," the *American Law Review* article which had been the foundation for Chapter 1 of *The Common Law.* Waples added:

> I have never seen his book. I cited some five or six authorities (illustrative of ideas expressed in my first chapter before reading the article) which had been previously cited by him and I made references to the original sources. They made no change in the idea and plan of the work.

If Holmes had expected an apology, perhaps even some public acknowledgment of intellectual debt, he was disappointed. Larger events, however, were crowding in on him and making slights like Waples's seem trivial at most.

IN THE SPRING of 1881, shortly after *The Common Law* was published, Fanny overcame her natural distaste for public notice and loaned fourteen panels of her needlework to the Boston Museum of Fine Arts and later to the Ladies' Decorative Art Society in New York City.

Her work was every bit as precedent-shattering as Wendell's, and her reviews every bit as favorable. Her subjects—a sea lit by moonlight, an apple orchard in bloom, a field of daisies framed by evergreens, a winter twilight, a storm of wind and snow for which she was said to have used white human hairs when she could not obtain fine enough cotton—were unconventional. Her style was described as "delicately poetic." The *Nation*'s art critic compared Fanny's needlework to watercolor. Mariana G. Van Rensselaer, scholarly author and art critic for the *American Architect and Building News,* concluded that "Mrs. Holmes's work ought to make a reputation for her that will not be confined to this country alone. Every one here has admired it, although it has gone counter to so many preconceived ideas and to so much popular practice." She urged women to "imitate" not Mrs. Holmes, but Mrs. Holmes's "efforts to do something individual."

The decade of the 1870s, although the younger Holmeses had isolated themselves from the society which they had been expected to join and to which they had been expected to contribute, had nevertheless been fruitful and productive for them both. Each had realized an inner potential he and she had long desired. In Fanny's case, however, the path to high art inexplicably now came to a dead end. This first public display of her work was the last; for reasons known only to herself, she destroyed it prior to moving to Washington in 1902. It was in fact the last time Fanny Holmes was mentioned in the public press until her obituary in 1929.

For Wendell, of course, it was quite another matter. He had only just begun. The best was yet to come.

IN 1882, PRESIDENT Charles William Eliot was still engaged in transforming Harvard from the provincial, tradition-bound, socially elitist institution Wendell Holmes had attended as an undergraduate and law student into a first-class university in which education was held superior to training. Not all of Brahmin Boston found Eliot's innovations acceptable, and, Samuel Eliot Morison commented, outsiders overhearing "the conversation of Boston clubs in those days might have concluded that President Eliot was 'Public Enemy No. 1.'" Nevertheless he pressed on.

Eliot's statement in his 1879–80 *Annual Report* that the rapidly growing Harvard Law School had "urgent need of a new building" attracted within a few weeks a contribution of $100,000 for that purpose from the aging Edward Austin of Boston, and H. H. Richardson's Romanesque lecture hall shortly began to rise near the old "gambrel-roofed" house—Dr. Holmes had sold the family estate in 1871 to the university for $55,000 with the proviso that his brother John could stay on for five years. In his 1880–81 *Annual Report,* Eliot solicited funds for a new professorship of law, and, believing the funds were forthcoming, in the fall of 1881 opened negotiations designed to engage the scholarly Oliver Wendell Holmes, Jr., as that new professor.

Holmes had not yet buttoned down his future, thinking perhaps that his growing prominence in the legal community ought to bring certain rewards—something more professionally elevating than election to the Saturday Club or an invitation to speak at Harvard's commencement. By the time the Harvard Class of 1861 sat down at the banquet table in the Hotel Brunswick for its twentieth reunion in June of 1881, Holmes, by virtue of his articles in the influential *American Law Review* and his book's having been published, was probably one of the most professionally successful members of his class. But these relatively minor rewards were not enough for so ambitious a man. He was not unaware that his name had been advanced when in recent years vacancies on various local courts had occurred. He would, no doubt, have preferred a judgeship to a professorship, and he had not changed his mind about Langdell over the past decade. But he was interested in Eliot's proposal and, as he said, he was "not inclined to wait for contingencies the arising of which might not affect my determination."

He was interested, however, only under certain conditions.

He wanted the professorship to be entitled Jurisprudence, the title to convey the understanding that he was expected to devote "a reasonable proportion" of his time to "such investigations as are embodied in my book on the Common Law or other studies touching the history and philosophy of law." He was not unwilling to teach "any particular branches of the law like the other professors." He only wanted it understood that what he regarded as his specialty be regarded by the university "as an important part of my functions."

The beginning salary of $4,500 would do, but as "the taking of this place will invoke a pecuniary sacrifice," he asked that when any law professor's salary was raised, his own also would be raised. "I have to be particular on the money question," he explained, "as I must live on my salary."

He saved what turned out to be the most important condition for last. "If a judgeship should be offered me," he declared, "I should not wish to feel bound in honor not to consider it, although I do not know that I should take it and although my present acceptance will diminish the chance of such an offer and is for that reason against the advice of many of my friends."

Eliot replied that the title of the professorship presented "no difficulty." The salary, however, was a different matter. Known for his efforts to keep salaries at a minimum, Eliot was not above provoking tears with his recitations on Harvard's poverty. Holmes would have to make do with $4,500; Eliot could guarantee neither a specific increase, nor even against reduction. "The stability of University salaries," he explained, "rests entirely upon custom and the development of the resources of the University." As to Holmes's final condition, Eliot did not intend to bind Holmes to the professorship. "In accepting a professorship here," he said, "you do not pledge yourself to remain any definite time, & you remain free to accept a better position or more congenial employment elsewhere." Except, he added: "your return to the practice of your profession simply within any period less than five years would be acceptable to the Corporation and Faculty only in the improbable case that you had not succeeded as a teacher of law." And he promised to "set about getting an endowment at once, hoping to secure it in a few days."

When Holmes realized Eliot had not yet obtained the funds for the proferred professorship, he withdrew his acceptance of it. He was, he explained, "unwilling that a subscription should be raised on the understanding that I am pledged to fill the place and (by implication) desire it." Such an understanding "would impose on me a greater honorary obligation than I assumed in my letter of acceptance, and the contributions would certainly take the form in the mind of some of the contributors, of a favor to me." He wished, however, to keep his options open, and, should funds materialize independent of his own position in the matter, he would be interested in reconsidering Eliot's offer.

Enter Professor James B. Thayer for whom Holmes had done donkey work at Chandler, Shattuck, and Thayer during his first months at the bar, with whom he had worked on Kent's *Commentaries,* and who already was a member of the Harvard Law School faculty. Thayer suppressed his chagrin at Holmes's theft of the limelight following publication of the Kent, called on Holmes, and found, as he had suspected, that Holmes was still willing to accept a professorship; he was only unwilling to have his friends solicited. Thayer offered to raise the money; Eliot was "much relieved and said he would resume matters, without seeing H."

Then Horace Gray, still chief justice of the Massachusetts Supreme Judicial Court, was appointed to the United States Supreme Court, and the question of a vacancy on the state court further postponed the matter of Holmes's professorship since he could conceivably be appointed to it. Instead, however, Governor John Davis Long promoted Judge Marcus Morton to the chief justiceship and named Charles Allen to the vacancy created by Morton's elevation.

On January 10, 1882, at the regular law school faculty meeting, Eliot surveyed those present—Thayer, Langdell, and James Barr Ames—regarding the possibilities of obtaining an endowment for another professorship. Langdell and Ames were pessimistic. Thayer said he would like to try, and on the following Saturday, January 14, called on Eliot to discuss the matter further. Eliot consented, and Thayer "began to move about that day." He talked first to George Shattuck, then to some others. Louis Brandeis had dined with Thayer recently and had put forward the names of men he thought would be able and willing to help. The list soon narrowed to William F. Weld, a recent student who had expressed fond feelings for the institution, although he had failed to take his degree. He had inherited $3 million from his grandfather. With the assistance of Brandeis, Thayer persuaded Weld to contribute $70,000 to $80,000 (later raised to $90,000) in 6 percent and 5 percent bonds. Weld agreed to see the treasurer in the morning and arrange matters. Thayer further suggested Weld request the appointment of Holmes— "thus having the satisfaction not only of giving his name to the endowment but of connecting with the matter the beginning of H.'s career as professor." Weld agreed immediately.

Thayer stopped by Holmes's law office and told him "it was all arranged and he had better make ready to come out." He then called on Eliot to tell him the mission was accomplished.

On January 23, 1882, the president and fellows of Harvard University elected Oliver Wendell Holmes, Jr., professor of law. On March 30, Holmes resigned from the Board of Overseers, pleading "considerations of expediency, if not the spirit of the law concerning eligibility to the office of Overseer, mak[ing] it undesirable that a Professor should act as a member. . . ." And the annual catalogue included among the law school faculty "Professor Holmes" alongside his good friend Professor Gray; Professors Langdell, Ames, and Thayer; and his friends Brooks Adams, instructor in constitutional law, and Louis Brandeis, instructor in evidence.

It had been a year since *The Common Law* had been published, but Holmes still looked "weary," and on May 20, he and Fanny sailed aboard the *Parthia* for England where proper Bostonians were accustomed to

going for rest, rehabilitation, and reinforcement of their aristocratic inclinations against the increasingly frequent incursions of democracy.

The same names—Bryce, Kennaway, Dicey, Maine, Pollock, Stephen—the same places—Athenaeum, Oxford, Orleans House—grace the
pages of Holmes's diary for that summer of 1882 that filled his diary in
1866 and 1874. A trip to the Continent—ten days in Paris, then the
cities of Switzerland followed by Germany for the first time—where, as
previously, the Holmeses were tourists rather than honored guests—
back to London on August 15, and home in time for the opening of the
law school term on September 28 completed the itinerary.

Holmes's academic schedule—Torts, Agency and Carriers, Surety
and Mortgages, Jurisprudence, and Admiralty—combined the independent research he had done for the *American Law Review,* the editing of
Kent's *Commentaries,* the Lowell Lectures, and *The Common Law* with
work he had done in his private practice. He had only once again to
rearrange the material.

Interestingly, as Wendell embarked on his new career at Harvard
Law School, Dr. Holmes was ending thirty-six years on the faculty of
Harvard Medical School. Citing the pressures of publishing, he sent in
his resignation on September 9 and on November 28 delivered his last
lecture as Parkman Professor of Anatomy and Physiology to a standing-
room-only audience. Students from all the classes mingled with gray-
haired practitioners assembled to hear their old teacher. The thunder-
ous applause and presentation of a loving cup inscribed with a quotation
from one of his own poems unnerved him, and he recovered his poise
only with effort.

The younger Holmes did not even complete the first term. On December 8, 1882, the contingency against which he had explicitly protected himself in his negotiations with President Eliot occurred. Governor Long offered him the vacancy on the Massachusetts Supreme
Judicial Court created by the resignation of Judge Otis P. Lord.

Judge Lord had sent the governor his resignation on December 1.
During the week-long interim between Lord's resignation and Holmes's
appointment, Boston gossiped, the question on every lawyer's lips, "Who?"
Some expressed their wishes directly to the governor. Solomon Lincoln,
a prominent member of the Boston bar, was on the governor's short list.
W. G. Russell, chairman of the Harvard Overseers Visiting Committee,
recommended Holmes as "one versed in the modern methods of the
study of the science and practice of the law." Senator Hoar, with whom
Governor Long had competed unsuccessfully for a senatorial nomination

in 1876, would have liked to see his nephew Samuel Hoar appointed. Robert R. Bishop of the Superior Court was also prominently mentioned. George Shattuck, although he was Holmes's good friend and former law partner, in fact went so far as to write the governor in behalf of Bishop whose "learning," "intelligence," and "judgment" he particularly admired. As an afterthought Shattuck added: "As the name of Prof. OW Holmes Jr has been mentioned in connection with the vacancy on the Supreme Court, I do not wish to be considered as in any way opposing his appointment."

Holmes's name was not unknown to the governor. James Bradley Thayer himself had advanced it for consideration when Judge Seth Ames had resigned from the Supreme Judicial Court in early 1881, before the matter of appointment to the law school faculty had arisen. Holmes himself had not been idle, having invited the governor to a Law Club dinner he was giving in 1880 at his father's house.

The week sped by with no word from the governor, who recently had been elected to represent Massachusetts in the U.S. Congress and whose days in the executive office were numbered. John Davis Long, a Republican, had one foot in the past and the other in the present. He was a social and economic conservative whose Christian conscience had sensitized him to misfortune and injustice, an ambitious man who recognized party regularity as a key to success, but whose progressive instincts had on occasion steered him into reform politics.

He was the descendant of seventeenth-century settlers, and, although born in "moderate circumstances," remained loyal to his background. In late-nineteenth-century Boston, party affiliation may have carried less significance than family background. It was important for frock-coated Brahmins, snug in their mansions on Beacon Hill, to stick together in matters of local government, although the battle was for all practical purposes already lost. Irish Democratic votes had recently elected Benjamin F. Butler governor of Massachusetts, and in two years would elect Hugh O'Brien mayor of Boston; Irishmen sat on the Common Council and the Board of Aldermen. Their little ward organizations, although still badly organized, were increasing in numbers, efficiency, and power. Bastions of Brahmin influence were falling to Irish Democratic pressures. The judiciary must remain pure: patrician, Protestant, and impenetrable.

In the end, Long settled for a man as double-visioned as he himself: a Brahmin, Republican, Civil War veteran (still a political asset in 1882), and prominent scholar whose approach to jurisprudence might turn out to be more modern than anyone realized at the time. Wendell Holmes, son of Brahmin Boston's most popular publicist, would be a safe appointment. His reputation for scholarship, particularly the new fame he had won with *The Common Law,* should make it a distinguished one.

On Friday, December 8, Long sent for George Shattuck and told him the appointment was Holmes's if Holmes wanted it. Long, however, had to have his answer by 3 P.M. Shattuck immediately called a carriage, collected Fanny, and sped to the law school where he found the nominee lunching with a colleague. The trio returned to Boston, dropping Wendell at the governor's office.

Was there ever any doubt what Holmes would do? The governor's invitation was Holmes's command: the next earthwork to be taken. Without discussing the matter with anyone at Harvard, Wendell accepted the appointment. The Governor's Council, a colonial body elected from Massachusetts's eight districts whose function was—and is—to pass on gubernatorial appointments, approved, and, in essence, Holmes's life for the next half-century was sealed. Long noted the appointment in his journal, adding with obvious pride, "every member of that Court, seven in all, will, when Holmes is commissioned by me, hold his appointment from my hands."

A surprised Harvard read about it next day in the *Boston Daily Advertiser.* Holmes did call on President Eliot on the Saturday, but, unable to find him, left his card and a request to see him the following Monday. For unspecified reasons, Holmes and Eliot did not meet until Tuesday night, when Holmes appeared late at the faculty meeting. The atmosphere was tense. Holmes "made a long, excited and wholly ineffective attempt to account for his going . . . but no person said a word, *not* one, except E. himself now and then, 'it did not seem kind,' [Eliot] said, 'to leave him talking all alone.' " Otherwise Holmes discussed the matter with no one except John Gray, and when others broached the subject, "he seemed to have no sense of any impropriety in what he has done," but only alluded to his reserving, in his original negotiations with Eliot, the right to take a judgeship. Thayer never forgave him.

Holmes, of course [Thayer wrote], is entitled to the excuse which this may furnish! And it cannot be denied that he is within the line of his legal right. But what shall be said of his sense of what is morally admissible,— of his sense of honor, of justice, of consideration for the rights of others and of their sensibilities, when he could do what he did; of his personal self-respect, indeed.

The only symptom of sensibility that he shows . . . is that he says (at the faculty meeting) that he does see that he ought not to have been required to answer so soon. To be sure! Long had had Lord's resignation for a week. There were three weeks and more before Long's reign is over. If his council was not regularly to meet again for some days, yet could it not be called together in extra session? What was he going to do if H. *didn't* accept? The nomination must lie over for a week. Could he not have intimated that he *probably* would accept and had the name go in and the news not published, and so have secured a chance to sleep over it and to confer with those who had a right to be consulted? But he took it at once and seems never to have thought and not to know now that it was an unhandsome, and indecent action.

He lost his head perhaps? But my experience with him in editing Kent, which I had been willing to forget, comes all back again and assures me that this conduct is characteristic,—that he is, with all his attractive qualities and his solid merits, wanting sadly in the noblest region of human character,—selfish, vain, thoughtless of others.

All Holmes's charm, wit, and apparent concern for his friends had not hidden from William James the fact that personally he was a "powerful battery, formed like a planing machine to gouge a deep self-beneficial groove through life," and all his intellectual brilliance and scholarly stamina that had justly earned the judicial appointment could not hide from Thayer his professional aggressiveness.

Regarding his legal and/or moral responsibility to return any of the salary he had received, Holmes solicited the advice of Francis W. Parker, prominent local lawyer and member of the Board of Overseers whom Holmes described as "the most squaretoed seeming of anglicised yankees—who had a green baize door to his office with 'Mr. Parker' on it— . . . but who had an inner fire that he didn't show often." Parker, who discussed the matter with the Harvard treasurer after he reviewed the Eliot-Holmes correspondence, decided Holmes had no such responsibility, that his contract with the university "was expressly terminable upon Mr Holmes appointment as a Judge." The university had taken "the risk of the time when it would be so terminated." Financially, it was Holmes, who had sacrificed his legal practice to prepare academic lectures, who was the loser; the university, after all, still had Weld's $90,000.

Furthermore, it was doubtful Holmes could have turned down the appointment, which brought with it "the same obligation (considering the position of the Court,) that a military appointment would bring to a soldier. It also entails a sacrifice of comfort, taste, and natural vocation, with no advantage in pecuniary compensation, when the increase of expense is considered." It remained to be considered, said Parker in his covering letter, "whether you prefer to deal with the College, as a Charity, as one sometimes deals with a woman, or a poor person,—that is give him, or her, both ends of the bargain. When one can afford it, this is sometimes one of the greatest of luxuries, & the most comfortable of recollections."

There is no indication that Holmes returned any of his salary. He did in 1882 contribute $1,000 to the law school. In time, Holmes's relations with Harvard were patched up, and in 1895 he received an honorary degree, a gesture Holmes interpreted as a sign Eliot had "buried the hatchet and no longer bears me malice for giving up my professorship for a judgeship—which I expressly and in writing reserved the right to do . . . but which he was inclined to let people understand was not fair."

Boston was sanguine about his appointment to the state's highest court. The *Boston Globe* predicted Holmes would "fill the position with dignity and ability." The *Boston Daily Advertiser* described him as both "learned in the history and philosophy of the law" as well as "familiar with practice and the busy affairs of men." If he seemed a "young man for so lofty a station," he possessed "qualifications far in advance of his years."

It was what Holmes had been practicing for all his life. All those threads that often had seemed irrelevant to the pattern of his life were coming together. Family, old and established, had given him a liberating sense of security that allowed him to challenge tradition. Soldiering had taught him about determination and showed him what courage meant at the same time it had demanded both from him. As a student at Harvard Law School he had mastered the "ragbag of details" that made up the law in mid-nineteenth century. As a young lawyer he had experienced the law office and the courtroom, then reinterpreted what the masters said about the law. As a slightly older lawyer, he had had the audacity to advance his original ideas about the law. It remained only for him to decide the law.

The judgeship would take him out of the academic "cloister," where the purpose was to "find out how God thinks," and put him once again on the firing line, a participant in the "action and passion" of his time. It was an opportunity to influence the law as he never could have as a practicing lawyer or scholar or academic. It was power, fame, ambition fulfilled, the burdens of duty shouldered once more—Holmes would have found it as impossible to turn down the governor as to disobey an order of General Sedgwick's. He expected it would offer the kind of challenge he sought:

My motives so far as I could disentangle them in half an hour which is all the time I had to decide the momentous question—were in a word that I thought the chance to gain an all round experience of the law not to be neglected and especially that I did not think one could without moral loss decline any share in the practical struggle of life which naturally offered itself and for which he believed himself fitted. I had already realized at Cambridge that the field for generalization inside the body of the law was small that the day would soon come when I felt that the only remaining problems were of detail and that as a philosopher he must go over into other fields—whether of ethics—theory of legislation—political economy or an-thropology—history etc. depending on the individual, but that somehow he must extend his range. I was however as happy as a man could desire but I felt that if I declined the struggle offered me I should never be so happy again—I should feel that I had chosen the less manly course.

Holmes took his seat among the other six august judges, all of whom were older than he, on January 3, 1883. George Shattuck reported to Fanny that her husband "appeared to immense advantage this morning. He was dignified and serious and had on his face the marks of mind—force of intellect. . . ." He was immediately consumed by the work and found he was neglecting correspondence and "everything but business." He liked it "far better than [he] dreamed beforehand. The experience is most varied—very different from that one gets at the bar—and [he was] satisfied most valuable for an all round view of the law."

Part VI

JUDGE IN MASSACHUSETTS

I can see what the law is like. It's like a single-bed blanket on a double-bed, and three folks in the bed and a cold night. There ain't ever enough blanket to cover the case, no matter how much pulling and hauling, and somebody is always going to nigh catch pneumonia. Hell, the law is like the pants you bought last year for a growing boy, but it is always this year and the seams are popped and the shankbones to the breeze. The law is always too short and too tight for growing humankind. The best you can do is do something and then make up some law to fit and by the time that law gets on the books you would have done something different.

—Robert Penn Warren, *All the King's Men*

CHAPTER 14

The Fallow Years

AMERICANS SHARE THE feeling that a judge is in some indefinable way possessed of superior wisdom. Even an unimpressive practicing lawyer suddenly commands respect when he is elevated to the bench. Dr. Holmes, who had not been one to exaggerate his son's legal talents before, put Wendell's appointment into the familiar perspective after:

> To think of it,—my little boy a Judge, and able to send me to jail if I don't behave myself.

Young lawyers who argued cases before Holmes were as impressed with the newcomer to the Massachusetts Supreme Judicial Court as George Shattuck had been. He looked as well as acted the part. His bearing, his robust good health, and his authoritative manner made him appear to have been born to it. Some found his mental agility intimidating. His native courtesy never failed him, but

> his mind was so extraordinarily quick and incisive, he was such an alert and sharply attentive listener, his questions went so to the root of the case, that it was rather an ordeal to appear before him. In arguing a case you felt that when your sentence was half done he had seen the end of it, and before the argument was a third finished that he had seen the whole course of reasoning and was wondering whether it was sound.

He didn't like young lawyers who came before him with great piles of legal tomes under their arms, all marked with the relevant citations to be discussed during the argument. He was apt to remind any such sinners that

One citation will be enough, *if it is in point.*

On the other hand, he would go out of his way to compliment a young lawyer whose argument he admired. He might have it printed in the *Massachusetts Reports,* a rare privilege, or seek out the fellow in the law library:

I want to compliment you on your argument yesterday before the Court. It was a good argument. I am not going to say you are going to win, but I liked it.

On January 22, 1883, less than three weeks after he had taken his seat, Holmes handed down the first of 1,290 opinions he wrote for the court majority over the next twenty years; only one was reversed by the U.S. Supreme Court.* Like most first opinions, *Weber* v. *Couch* was unanimous, unadventurous, and unobjectionable. It was also brief, a harbinger of the thousands of opinions he wrote during his fifty-year judicial career. He detested judicial prolixity as much as if not more than lawyer's prolixity, and having caught in the first two or three minutes of a lawyer's presentation the point of the argument, Holmes was apt to write personal letters during the rest, all the while presenting an "attentive manner calculated to make counsel think you are taking notes." He once suggested to a lawyer that he read risqué novels to learn the art of innuendo. Holmes used these two decades on the Massachusetts court to perfect his powers of expression. His opinions lacked the epigrammatic pungency of his later work. He wrote detailed factual analyses, to which he often added theory and history, and he assumed intelligence and a minimum of general knowledge on the part of his readers. He derided one of his fellow jurists who "always took two pages to explain the machinery" in accident cases.

I have written a great many accident cases, and I thank God I never understood the machinery. Writing an opinion is just like making an etching, or painting a picture. The point of contact is the important thing. You have got two wheels and a squeezed finger, and there you are.

* *Heard* v. *Sturgis.* 146 Mass. 545 (1888); reversed by *Williams* v. *Heard.* 140 U.S. 529 (1891).

Justice Oliver Wendell Holmes, still a distinguished figure at 89. Tributes from world leaders and an adulatory radio broadcast marked his 90th birthday the following year. *Library of Congress Collections*

Holmes and friend, the crossing-tender at Beverly Farms with whom Holmes visited daily during his walks around the little North Shore village where he summered. *Harvard Law Art Collection*

The gambrel-roofed house, Cambridge, home of Abiel Holmes and birthplace of Dr. Holmes. Legend peopled it with Continental militiamen who dented the floor with their firelocks while they planned the Battle of Bunker Hill. In this picture, Austin Hall, part of Harvard Law School, rises in the background at left. The house was later razed, but the area behind it continued to be known as Holmes Field. *Library of Congress Collections*

The Autocrat of the Breakfast Table: Dr. Holmes (1809–1894) in his study at 296 Beacon Street, Boston. *Library of Congress Collections*

Reverend Abiel Holmes, early historian of some stature, controversial Calvinist, father of Dr. Oliver Wendell Holmes, and grandfather of Justice Holmes. *Harvard Law Art Collection*

Dr. Holmes reading his essay on childbed fever to the Boston Society for Medical Improvement in 1843. His conclusion that childbed fever was contagious, passed from patient to patient by nurses, midwives, and physicians, challenged the conventional medical wisdom of the time. He was vindicated during his lifetime in the new science of bacteriology. *Painting by Dean Cornwell reproduced with the permission of Wyeth-Ayerst Laboratories*

Amelia Lee Holmes, née Jackson, Justice Holmes's mother. She sometimes wished she had been born poor "to have the pleasure of exerting [herself]." *Harvard Law Art Collection*

"My dear! not marry Mr. Jackson!" replied Justice Holmes's grandmother, herself a Cabot, to her daughter-in-law's question of why she had. The father of Amelia Lee Jackson Holmes, Charles Jackson was prosperous and prominent in Boston society. In 1813 he gave up his thriving law practice to serve on the Massachusetts Supreme Judicial Court. *Library of Congress Collections*

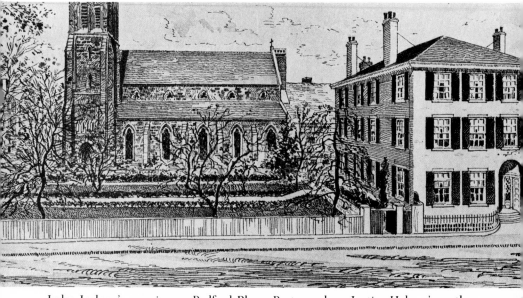

Judge Jackson's mansion on Bedford Place, Boston, where Justice Holmes's mother grew up. The street could as well have been called Jackson Place. Jacksons lived in five of its seve[n] houses. *Library of Congress Collections*

John T. ("Fatty") Morse, Jr., cousin and boyhood companion to Wendell Holmes. He taught Wendell "all the evil [he] knew as a boy." *National Cyclopedia of American Biography*

Edward Jackson Holmes inherited hi[s] father's asthma along with his father'[s] wit. Though he did everything righ[t] even to marrying a Wigglesworth, poo[r] health forced him to give up his law practice early, and he spent much o[f] his life searching for a climate in which he could breathe. He died in 1884 a[t] the age of 38. *Harvard Law Art Collection*

Epes Sargent Dixwell, "Dicky," schoolmaster and boyhood hero to young Wendell Holmes. Later he became Wendell's father-in-law. *Harvard Law Art Collection*

Amelia Holmes inherited her father's gregariousness and vivacity, but not his robust constitution. She died in 1889 at the comparatively young age of 46. *Harvard Law Art Collection*

Sprigs: The young Holmeses. Left to right, Edward Jackson, 9; Amelia, 11½; Oliver Wendell, Jr., 14. *Harvard Law Art Collection*

Ralph Waldo Emerson, the "firebrand" of Wendell's youth, the "spark that started a flame" in him. *Library of Congress Collections*

Captain Oliver Wendell Holmes, Jr. Fanny, his wife, always said that if it hadn't been for his Civil War experiences, Wendell would have been a "coxcomb." *Harvard Law Art Collection*

Henry L. ("Little") Abbott. The memory of Abbott the Copperhead, who died for goals in which he didn't believe, haunted Holmes, the accidental survivor, for years. *Harvard Law Art Collection*

Norwood Penrose ("Pen" Hallowell, described by hi friend Wendell Holmes as "savage abolitionist, a fighting Quaker who blushed a his own militancy." A Twentieth Massachusett infantrymen, the two share their meager mess, wearyin marches, and blood-staine blankets. *Harvard Law Col lection*

Battle of Ball's Bluff, Virginia, a struggle marked by mismanagement and confusion durin which Holmes was badly wounded. This picture shows the early hours of the battle. Later Union troops and cannon were forced back over the 150-foot-high bluff (at right) into th Potomac River below; its icy waters and strong currents, along with Confederate guns, mad short work of them. *Library of Congress Collections*

The bodies of Confederate soldiers strewn along the Hagerstown Pike following the Battle of Antietam (Maryland). Holmes received his second wound during this carnage. Afterwards every barn, house, and haystack formed the nucleus of a hospital. *Library of Congress Collections*

Holmes was wounded in the heel near Fredericksburg on the way to Chancellorsville (Virginia). Many years later he confessed he had prayed he might lose the foot so he would not have to return to the front. The wound did, however, keep him out of Gettysburg, where the Twentieth Massachusetts lost half its enlisted men and 10 out of 13 of its officers. He was to have his "opportunity." *Library of Congress Collections*

Fanny Bowditch Dixwell, granddaughter of Nathaniel Bowditch (*The Practical Navigator*) and daughter of schoolmaster Epes Dixwell, married Wendell Holmes in 1872, about the time he was embarking on the intense scholarship that would result in *The Common Law*. The marriage was not without difficulties. Still, she taught him "how many poems and pictures are to be seen all about one, if one looks." *Harvard Law Art Collection*

While Wendell worked with his head, Fanny worked with her hands. Here, one of her embroidery panels which art critics described as "delicately poetic." *Harvard Law Art Collection*

A page of Holmes's notes for his book *The Common Law* (1881). He half filled a large black notebook with his scholarly jottings, calling it, appropriately, his "Black Book." When he was finished, he filled the other half with lists of the books he had read. *Reproduced from the "Black Book" in the possession of H. Chapman Rose*

Holmes at 42, not long after he finished *The Common Law*. William James had described him during the time he labored on his book as "a powerful battery formed like a planing machine to gouge a deep self-beneficial groove through life. . . ." *Harvard Law Art Collection*

William James, with whom Holmes twisted the tail of the cosmos over glasses of whiskey as a young lawyer and scholar in Boston. Later, their divergent views of the cosmos took them along different paths, and their once warm friendship waned. *Library of Congress Collections*

Governor John Davis Long of Massachusetts appointed Professor Oliver Wendell Holmes of the Harvard Law School to the Massachusetts Supreme Judicial Court in 1882. Holmes was Long's last appointment to the court. He had already been elected to the United States Congress; later he served as William McKinley's Secretary of the Navy. *Library of Congress Collections*

Lady Clare Castletown, Holmes's "Beloved Hibernia." Holmes's relationship with her was as emotionally charged as any he ever experienced. *Harvard Law Art Collection*

Henry James, friend—with his brother, William—of Holmes's youth. In time, intellectual and emotional differences cooled their relationship. Nevertheless, Holmes ritually visited James in his more or less regular trips to England in the 1890s and early 1900s. *Library of Congress Collections*

Theodore Roosevelt on the veranda of his home in Oyster Bay, Long Island. He appointed Holmes to the United States Supreme Court in 1902. *Library of Congress Collections*

1720 I Street NW, the Holmeses' home in Washington from 1903 to 1935. *United States Supreme Court Collection*

Theodore Roosevelt goes to the mat (1904) to wrest control of northwestern railroads from the financially powerful Northern Securities Company. To his chagrin, his recent appointee, Oliver Wendell Holmes, dissented from the Supreme Court's opinion, bringing the Sherman Anti-Trust Act to bear on the giant corporation. *Library of Congress Collections*

The living rooms at 1720 I Street. Callers said it was the only house in Washington that had the aura of Beacon Hill in Boston, with its Victorian horsehair furniture and smell of butcher's wax. *Library of Congress Collections*

Holmes's study at 1720 I Street. The big leather chair at the right had an adjustable mechanical footrest. Holmes often dozed there in later years. *United States Supreme Court Collection*

The United States Supreme Court ascending the bench, 1906: left to right, William H. Moody, Holmes, William R. Day, Joseph McKenna, Rufus W. Peckham, Edward D. White, David J. Brewer, John Marshall Harlan, Chief Justice Melville W. Fuller. *Library of Congress Collections*

m Crow. Like the Supreme Court's, Holmes's record in
vil rights cases was mixed during the thirty years he sat
n the court. *Plessy* v. *Ferguson* (1896), out of which came
ne separate-but-equal formula that governed race rela-
ons for more than half a century, remained *the* prece-
ent as long as Holmes sat on the court. *Library of Congress
ollections*

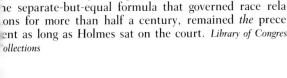

ustice Oliver Wendell Holmes in 1913, at the age of 72,
his usual attire. Only at Beverly Farms did he relax in
oft shirts and collars. *Library of Congress Collections*

he United States Supreme Court, 1914: left to right, William R. Day, Mahlon Pitney,
oseph McKenna, Willis Van Devanter, Chief Justice Edward D. White, Joseph R. Lamar,
Iolmes, James C. McReynolds, Charles Evans Hughes. *Library of Congress Collections*

Professor Felix Frankfurter of the Harvard Law School. He was the nucleus of a group of young men who clustered around Holmes about the time Holmes began to realize he was growing old while his contemporaries were dying. These youngsters seemed to give the older man some sense of security. *Library of Congress Collections*

Eugene V. Debs, Socialist candidate for president *(right)*, was sentenced to prison under the wartime Sedition Act which punished political speech. Holmes in 1919 wrote the Supreme Court opinion affirming Debs's conviction. *Library of Congress Collections*

The breaker boys. Their lungs already congested, children pick slate from coal in a Pennsylvania mine. In 1918, Holmes dissented with rare passion from the Supreme Court's opinion striking down the Keating-Owen child labor bill. *Library of Congress Collections*

Holmes, left, and Chief Justice William Howard Taft, March 8, 1926, Holmes's 85th birthday. Taft's jollity made him "just natchally" loved by everyone. It masked, however, an unbendable will. *Library of Congress Collections*

Supreme Court justices visit the White House, October 8, 1929: left to right, Willis Van Devanter, Harlan Fiske Stone, George Sutherland, Chief Justice William Howard Taft, Pierce Butler, Holmes, and Louis Dembitz Brandeis. *United States Supreme Court Collection*

Sacco and Vanzetti, front center, handcuffed together, 1927. Felix Frankfurter risked his professional reputation in trying to win a new trial for the two men. His close friends Justices Holmes and Brandeis refused to stay their execution. *Library of Congress Collections*

Rosika Schwimmer, Hungarian-born author, feminist, and pacifist, was denied American citizenship because she refused to swear to "take up arms" in defense of her adopted country. In 1929, the Supreme Court concluded Schwimmer and her ideas were indeed unwelcome in the United States. Holmes dissented vigorously. The Constitution, he declared, protected "not free thought for those who agree with us but freedom for the thought that we hate." *Library of Congress Collections*

The United States Supreme Court, 1932: left to righ James C. McReynolds, Harlan Fiske Stone, Holmes, Georg Sutherland, Chief Justice Charles Evans Hughes, Pierce Bu ler, Willis Van Devanter, Owen Roberts, Louis Dembitz Bran deis. *Library of Congress Collections*

Holmes and Brandeis, the yin and the yang. Holmes the *May flower* aristocrat and Brandeis the son of immigrant Jews, Holm the dispassionate and Brandeis the advocate, Holmes the styli and Brandeis the technician found common ground in the concept of constitutional law as fluid and constantly develo ing. *United States Supreme Court Historical Society Collections*

"Soldiers don't mind the rain." Taps for Justice Holmes at Arlington National Cemetery, March 8, 1935. *United States Supreme Court Historical Society Collections*

He rejoiced whenever in his opinions he could reduce a page to a paragraph, a paragraph to a phrase, a phrase to a single word. This first opinion occupied a single page and a half in the *Massachusetts Reports.*

The outcome in *Weber* v. *Couch,* a private dispute over the payment of a debt, mattered only to the plaintiff and defendant. And it was a dull case. Holmes had no opportunity to call on the Massachusetts constitution or to cite a lot of landmark precedents. It was hardly a challenge to the lively intellect of a former Harvard Law School professor and the eminent author of *The Common Law.* If *Weber* v. *Couch* was typical of the cases that came to the state's highest court, Holmes would have little chance to plumb the nether regions of the legal universe as he so longed to do. Cases requiring such limited exploration and having such limited application would hardly allow him "to confirm some theories" of his book or to translate his understanding of the law into principles governing "the practical struggle of life"—the tasks for which he believed himself fitted and for which he had accepted appointment to the bench.

For the most part, the cases that came to the Massachusetts Supreme Judicial Court during Holmes's two decades there *were* dull and of interest largely to the parties to the suits—cases much like the ones he had argued as a lawyer before this same court. Many were private disputes involving mortgages, bankruptcy, inheritances, insurance claims, and marital arguments—interesting exercises, but hardly calculated to bring Holmes the rewards and recognition for which he hungered.

However, like court dockets generally, that of Massachusetts's highest court in the final quarter of the nineteenth century was not entirely limited to private matters but also on occasion reflected the economic and social developments that were altering the state's psyche, and a number of public questions did in fact relieve the monotony of the private disputes between Citizen A and Citizen B over damages to be awarded for injuries sustained when A fell into B's coal-hole.

Conflict was inevitable as Massachusetts became increasingly urbanized and industrialized, the smokestacks of the textile mills at Lawrence and Lowell spewing the money that lured farmers off their farms and hordes of European immigrants to the Northeast. These developments affecting the social and economic ecology were illuminated by the new kinds of issues that appeared on the docket of the state's highest court: employer liability for industrial accidents, municipal liability for accidents occurring on public property, the state's power to regulate public utilities, public education and public health, questions involving the right of municipalities to take land for public purposes—"public" was the operative word; it was a time of redefining the public purpose and government's relationship to the governed. At the same time, businessmen and industrialists were searching for legal devices that would nullify, or at least modify, government restrictions, allowing the burgeoning corporations to develop freely.

Courts found themselves with the unenviable responsibility for settling disputes between capital and labor, which were becoming increasingly violent as the labor movement grew in strength—membership in the Knights of Labor peaked at more than 700,000 in 1886; the American Federation of Labor, a national craft union formed to agitate for shorter hours and higher wages, was born the same year; other unions, some affiliated with Marxist and socialist organizations, followed.

The rapid advances of newly industrialized society, prologue to the economic and social dramas of the twentieth century, when Holmes's theater of operations was moved to the national scene, required new judicial approaches; precedent did not always adequately answer the questions that arose; tradition was useless in late-nineteenth-century America. Coming to the bench fresh from his study of legal history and convinced of the evolutionary nature of the law, Holmes understood the power of social and economic forces to modify the rules men lived by and recognized the necessity for judges to adapt. Not all of the brethren were so flexible, and even Holmes was not able to release his grip on the past 100 percent of the time.

Holmes's route to the Massachusetts Supreme Judicial Court—via scholarship—was unusual, and he had little in common with his brethren professionally. The other six men with whom he began his judicial life had taken more conventional—political—routes. He could talk to Charles Devens about Ball's Bluff where both had been wounded, but after than, their interests diverged. Devens had been U.S. attorney general in Rutherford B. Hayes's administration. Holmes could discuss the work of the Committee to Visit the Law Schools with fellow Harvard Overseer and senior associate justice, Walbridge A. Field, but Field's prior experience had been in the Justice Department—as assistant attorney general in Ulysses S. Grant's administration—and in Congress. Charles Allen had been state attorney general; Chief Justice Marcus Morton had been a member of the state legislature as had Waldo Coburn. The chief justice also had been a judge of the superior court. All had had private law practices at one time or another, but five of the six had come from outside increasingly urbanized Boston, and the problems were not yet quite the same. There was no one with whom Holmes could establish a close friendship, even though their social perspectives were similar.

Patricians all, they reflected the prevailing local social and economic orders to which their political sponsor, Governor Long, belonged. Those who had not gone to Harvard had matriculated at equally acceptable New England institutions—Amherst, Yale, Dartmouth, Brown, Bowdoin. Five of the seven had gone to Harvard Law School at a time when most lawyers learned their law as apprentices to some older, experienced man. All were Republicans, Protestants, and, like the court on which they sat, traced their roots to seventeenth-century New England settlers.

It was clear that no Irish need apply, although they had by the 1880s infiltrated the Boston police and fire departments, City Hall, and the State House, and in 1884 elected Democrat Hugh O'Brien mayor. The judiciary remained out of reach, as did much of the legal community, as the immigrants changed the face of Dr. Holmes's Boston and would before the century was over outnumber Yankees by about three to one. Feeling crowded, the traditional Brahmin keepers of the public trust could only withdraw into themselves and grumble peevishly about the intruders. As Thomas Apley told his son, George:

[A]ffairs will always be controlled by a small group. I, and my group, have controlled them. . . . It is not a pleasant thing for me to feel that the Irish are going to run the affairs of this city. . . . This talk about the common good is arrant Socialism and nonsense. You and I do not stand for the common good. We stand for a small class. When control is gone, and it is slipping fast, Boston will become moribund, atrophied.

If the old Calvinist concept of an "elect" had been extracted from the New England theology, it had remained an integral part of the social landscape, and, the local sense of family reinforced by the threat from below, Bostonians stood firm against the newly arrived outsiders, united by common bonds of ancestry, background, and prejudices.

An occasional Shea, Dooley, Burke, or Riley slipped into the courthouse to argue a case, but the vast majority of lawyers who appeared before Holmes still came from local establishment families: Appletons, Wares, Wentworths, Peabodys, Perkinses, and Wigglesworths. Those Irish who frequented the courthouse with any regularity were largely gamblers, saloonkeepers accused of wrongfully plying their trade, plumbers suing for their fees, or the unfortunate victims of open sewers.

Holmes's appointment to the Massachusetts Supreme Judicial Court made a marked change in his professional way of life. Until then he had been independent, often a loner, particularly when he was engaged in his scholarly enterprises. Now, for the first time, he was not a free agent. He was writing for up to six other judges in addition to himself; as Felix Frankfurter put it much later, an opinion for the court is a symphony, not a solo. His analyses as well as the results in the cases were subjected to the others' close scrutiny. There would be no more solo flights of fancy into the ancient world of the blood feud. There was no time for it. The docket was always crowded, and the court could not afford the intellectual creativity to which Holmes had been accustomed. If he wanted to do more than just decide cases, if he hoped to shape the law in Massachusetts, if he expected a century later that his thoughts should "become a force and men who never heard of him begin to move according to his command," he would have to get all those other judges to agree, and he would have to do it fast.

All issues were hammered out in "long consultation[s] in which every man's hand is more or less against everyone else." Holmes tended to think of the discussion as "hogwash." When the brethren "went for" his opinions, however, he was "ready to maintain that every word is better than any part of the Ten Commandments."

It was a collegiality to which he had not been accustomed and to which he had difficulty in adapting. It was one of the least attractive aspects of his court work, and he complained to friends that in his writing he had been forced to "cut down the discussion in which I aired some of my views." Sixteen years after joining the state court, he still was apt to make "sharp comments" on his brethren's work, particularly if he felt "nervous and irritable." He still had difficulty affecting "the continuous adjustment to the point of view of others" when he himself held "strong and clear convictions."

Nevertheless, his dissents, while forceful, were rare—he wrote only twelve during the two decades he sat on the state court and voted in dissent in only eleven others. It was his "almost invariable practice" to "defer" to his brethren "in silence."

During the early years, the novelty of judging absorbed Holmes; he found the experience "most varied" and the contact with the vagaries of human nature interesting. Although he complained that

> we are very hard worked and some of the older judges affirm that no one can do all the work without breaking down,

at the same time he often asked the chief justice "to assign as many cases as he wd., to me"; he liked "to write as many of our decisions as I can" and to boast he was "as busy as a witch in a gale of wind." But he found little time for the scholarship he so loved, and at midpoint in his years on the Massachusetts court, he grumbled to Frederick Pollock who as professor of jurisprudence at Oxford, editor of the *Law Quarterly Review*—which Pollock had founded—and author of numerous books and essays on legal subjects was almost totally engrossed in scholarly pursuits, that he himself was

> so absorbed in the actualities and immediacies that I can only envy your learned explorations.

The court's routine was as demanding as anything Holmes had experienced as a practicing lawyer. The judges worked a five-and-a-half-day week—til noon on Saturdays. They were provided with neither law clerks nor offices, and did their writing at home or their law offices if they had one. Vacations were irregular and depended upon the individual judge's caseload. Early each September, the full court met in Boston, where it occupied two courtrooms in what became known as the Old Courthouse in Pemberton Square. Five of the seven then fanned out to hold court in the far-flung counties of the state, generally returning to Boston for Sunday and occasionally, depending on the fullness of the docket, for one or two more days each week. Inside the back cover of each volume of *Massachusetts Reports*, Holmes kept a running count of the opinions he had written during the period the volume covered. For all its demands, however, Holmes's new job afforded him for the first time a regular workday schedule, leaving his evenings free. He continued to read after dinner, but not with the same urgency as previously.

For nearly nineteen of the twenty years Holmes sat on the Massachusetts Supreme Judicial Court, the judges did not wear robes. For a brief time after the Revolution, they had followed the English tradition and worn both wigs and robes. Then they discarded both after a dispute between Chief Justice Francis Dana and one of the associate justices regarding court dress. When Holmes joined the court, street clothes were still the court fashion.

The Massachusetts Supreme Judicial Court was one of America's oldest in continuous existence. It was a direct descendant of the Massachusetts Superior Court of Judicature to which, in 1693, the witchcraft cases were presented. Several decades later, in 1761, James Otis made his impassioned arguments against the writs of assistance in the same court and laid the foundation for the Fourth Amendment to the United States Constitution. The judges sitting at the end of the nineteenth century—the latest members of the apostolic succession—were heirs to two centuries of legal tradition.

Along with Jackson genes, Holmes as judge had inherited the legal traditions of Grandfather Jackson's early-nineteenth-century court. Although Charles Jackson, who had learned his law in the Newburyport office of the great Massachusetts chief justice Theophilus Parsons and been friend to Joseph Story, had died in 1855, when Holmes was only a boy of fourteen, the memories of that long-ago bench were as much a part of the younger man's judicial baggage as were the heavy leather-bound volumes that had belonged to his grandfather and would fill several shelves of his own library.

Charles Jackson's court reflected the mainstream of New England thinking during the early decades of the nineteenth century. It was liberal in religious matters and conservative in economic and political matters. It is best remembered for its contributions to the cause of religious freedom in Massachusetts and its opposition to the War of 1812.

This theological liberalism coincided with popular theological trends—the number of Calvinists was dwindling, the number of Unitarians, increasing and challenging the religious content of secular Massachusetts law, which had been established early by local Calvinist majorities and written into the Constitution of 1780. Charles Jackson and his brethren were willing to break new paths and remove some of the Calvinists' principles and prerogatives, including control of church property by an orthodox minority* and tax support of orthodox clergy that discriminated against the unorthodox.† Charles Jackson, although personally a subscriber to the new theology with which the court opinions coincided, which they indeed encouraged, did not write any of these liberating opinions; he did, however, concur in them, and among his papers was later found a note indicating he would go so far as to prohibit compulsory church attendance.

In other matters, however, Jackson's court was substantially more conservative. Politically, the justices tended to treat Massachusetts as an independent nation only incidentally affiliated with the United States—particularly when national policy conflicted with what were considered the best interests of Massachusetts. It was a time of formulating rela-

* *Baker* v. *Fales*. 16 Mass. 488 (1820).
† *Adams* v. *Howe*. 14 Mass. 340 (1817).

tionships between the nation and the states, both partners to the alliance being still rather inexperienced in the complex ways of federalism, and the attitude expressed by the Massachusetts judges was not uncommon. Judge Jackson himself, whose heart was with the Essex Junto to which his father and uncle had belonged and which, had it had its way, would have taken New England out of the Union, actually defied a decision of the United States Supreme Court* when in 1816 he upheld the validity of a contract to buy a British license—a kind of safe-conduct pass on the high seas—for an American freighter during the War of 1812.† The ostensible rationale was a legal one. But the political factor can hardly be ignored. Uninterrupted trade for New England ranked among the local establishment far ahead of the national interest, especially during the War of 1812.

In economic and social matters also, that early court was conservative, though not entirely opposed to change and apt to allow the legislature some leeway:

> [O]ur duty is to give effect to such acts of the legislature as they have the constitutional authority to make, without regarding their evil tendency or inexpediency. Subsequent legislatures may correct the proceedings of their predecessors which may be found to have been improvident or pernicious. And if a law, however complained of, is suffered to remain unrepealed, the only presumption is, that it is the will of the community that such should be the law. (*Adams* v. *Howe*, 14 Mass. 340, 344, 1817)

In most economic matters, Judge Jackson, who had a substantial financial interest in the family textile mills, and his brethren, despite their willingness to defer to legislative authority, did their judicial best to protect contract and property rights, and strongly supported a virile laissez-faire competition, the less interference with business on the part of government the better. It was every man for himself, and if a man accidentally destroyed the foundations of his neighbor's house with his digging, well, that was the neighbor's problem; he ought to understand the risks of living close to another.‡ Jackson himself was so conservative that John Quincy Adams claimed

he cares not a peppercorn for the interest of the whole people.

* *The Hiram*. 8 Cranch 444 (1814).
† *Coolidge* v. *Inglee*. 13 Mass. 26 (1816).
‡ *Thurston* v. *Hancock*. 12 Mass. 220 (1815).

Although not explicit, there was an undercurrent in the court's opinions that it would be untrammeled individual initiative and enterprise, not government protection—except in tariff matters, of course—that would build Massachusetts, New England, and the new United States. This way of thinking had changed very little sixty years later, when Charles Jackson's grandson and judicial heir took his seat on the same court. Trained to tradition, the Massachusetts judges had no wish to challenge the conventional order of affairs.

By the concluding decades of the nineteenth century, the Massachusetts judges were more or less willing to concede certain minor police powers to municipal and state governments. They would allow, for example, certain public health and safety ordinances such as regulation of the keeping of swine* or of blasting out rock within the city limits,† although they declared "unauthorized by statute" a city ordinance prohibiting the riding or driving of a horse in its streets "at an immoderate gait, so as to endanger or expose to injury any person."‡ They upheld some moderately progressive measures such as a Holyoke ordinance requiring public accountability of the superintendent of sewers,§ the allocation of public money for a sewage system,‖ and authorization of the state to take land for the improvement of Boston harbor.# Holmes joined the majority in all of these.

Other measures they did not allow. Between 1813 and 1891, the judges of the Massachusetts Supreme Judicial Court declared thirty-five acts of the state legislature unconstitutional. During Holmes's first decade on the court, they demonstrated their hostility to social and economic change by nullifying between 1882 and 1891 six statutes, nearly 20 percent of the total for seventy-eight years. These involved such controversial contemporary urban issues as public regulation of railroad rates, labor relations, and assessment of private citizens for street construction.

If the other judges on the high court feared that Holmes's scholarly or youthful vision of jurisprudence might not coincide with theirs or regarded him with uncertainty, they needn't have, at least not for the first decade. Jurisprudentially, he was quite docile those ten years. He disagreed with the majority strongly enough to write only three dis-

* *Quincy* v. *Kenhard*. 151 Mass. 563 (1890).
† *Commonwealth* v. *Parks*. 155 Mass. 531 (1892).
‡ *Commonwealth* v. *Roy*. 140 Mass. 432 (1896).
§ *Colkins* v. *Holyoke*. 146 Mass. 298 (1888).
‖ *Kingman* v. *Pittner*. 153 Mass. 566 (1891).
Moore v. *Sandford*. 151 Mass. 286 (1890).

sents* during that time. Partly, it does not do for an inexperienced newcomer to overassert himself; although Holmes as lawyer had argued a number of times before the Massachusetts Supreme Judicial Court, it is unlikely he was on familiar terms with its judges. They had all had private law practices at one time or another before entering public life, but only Field had practiced in Boston proper; the other five had come from as far west as Greenfield as well as nearby towns. Establishing a professional rapport with six men who were practically strangers, as well as older and more experienced, required time. Partly, too, the consuming work of the previous decade must have depleted Holmes's resources. Personal as well as professional matters were marked by a spirit of lassitude. A farmer might have said this was a fallow period, when the land was let lie idle and untilled in order to increase its future fertility and productivity.

If he was quiet during these years, he was not, however, asleep. He was learning his craft, to express himself; working out a jurisprudence, establishing a professional rapport with his brethren, discovering "high ambition and ideal in this externally dull routine and much of the passion of life."

He played, as had his father before him, the quintessential Bostonian: a little aloof as befitted a judge, a little self-conscious, a little provincial, a little straightlaced. He was well cast in the part: tall and erect, "lean as a race horse," his still thick hair just beginning to gray, his mustaches fierce as a cavalryman's.

He had his books, his clubs, his friends, his flirtations, and his work. His reading now was of a "desultory" sort, amounting at times to no more than reading a little poetry out loud and French novels to himself. He made it a point to call on the John Grays on Tuesdays. Owen Wister, a young Harvard Law School student and representative of the Philadelphia gentry, called regularly on the Holmeses, offering witty conversation and a taste for zestful living. To satisfy an increasing craving for the energizing company of the young, a result perhaps of his childlessness, he periodically went out to Cambridge to dine with Wister and the other Harvard Law School students who lived together in a group house on the Appian Way. But he did not venture outside the confines of his class for companionship. Friday nights at the theater became a comfortable habit. Occasional meals with the all-male Saturday Club to which he had been elected in 1880 and which he described

* *New England Trust* v. *Eaton.* 140 Mass. 532 (1886); *Merrill* v. *Peaslee.* 146 Mass. 460 (1886); *Commonwealth* v. *Perry.* 155 Mass. 117 (1891).

as consisting "of great swells, and is sometimes pleasant and not infrequently dull."

On becoming a judge, a man became subject to a number of constraints, and Holmes observed them meticulously. For the first five years, he absented himself from the bench whenever George Shattuck, his former law partner, argued before his court. He declined to join the Boston Memorial Association, although he said he sympathized with its "objects," and he refused to go ashore when Shattuck's boat landed on Martha's Vineyard because a "no trespassing" sign forbade it; he "thought it unbecoming that a Judge of the Sup. Jud. Court should be had up before a Justice of the Peace." He hesitated to drink with Owen Wister at the Parker House, although in recent years he had been accustomed to dining out and drinking champagne in Cambridge with Wister and his friends.

"Come up to my house," Holmes now urged the young man, explaining in his half-embarrassed way that "before I went on the Bench, I didn't mind—but—you understand I think—I don't somehow cotton to the notion of our Judges hobnobbing in hotel bars and saloons. The Bench should stand aloof from indiscriminate familiarities."

In the early summer of 1883, the first summer of the judgeship, Fanny, cheered by Holmes's new $6,000 salary, went househunting. The next word the new judge heard on the subject was an invitation to dine one night at 9 Chestnut Street. He accepted. Thirty-nine years later, at the age of eighty-one, Holmes recalled that Fanny then packed him off to Europe for the rest of the summer while she whipped the house into shape. There is no indication that Holmes was in Europe in 1883; he and Fanny had been there together in 1882, and it is unlikely he would have returned so soon. He was probably right, though, that it was Fanny who whipped the house into liveable shape.

At last they were able to leave the little second-floor apartment with its solitary gas ring for a kitchen where they had lived for nearly a decade, and move into a real house. It stood in a quiet, pleasant, typically Bostonian neighborhood of substantial houses and horse chestnut trees about ten blocks from Dr. Holmes's Beacon Street brownstone and within walking distance of the courthouse.

Before Holmes was appointed to the court, he and Fanny annually spent the last two weeks in August and the first two in September at their summer place in Mattapoisett on Buzzard's Bay, a place Holmes always referred to as a "center of romantic delight." Despite the court's heavy docket, they still managed to spend at least part of the summer there. There they gardened with an unaccustomed gusto and entertained at informal suppers featuring homemade red wine punch and lively conversation in the Holmes tradition:

> His talk would always bubble and sparkle from him, a stream of seriousness and laughter, imagination and philosophy, in which enthusiasm was undying; and the style of a master in English marked his improvisations.

It was a comfortable and agreeable routine, if not particularly exciting. Life was for the time being an "artichoke": "each day, week, month, year gives you one little bit which you nibble off—but precious little to what you throw away." Holmes was, however, enjoying it, he admitted, "as keenly as most people." And although the Puritan in him rarely allowed such indulgence, he did "despise making the most of one's time. Half the pleasure of life consists of the opportunities one has neglected."

Shortly after Holmes took his seat on the state court, his name was mentioned as a Republican candidate for the Massachusetts gubernatorial nomination. His friend and former student, Henry Cabot Lodge, who had abandoned the study of early law for American history and politics, and had been chosen chairman of the Massachusetts Republican State Central Committee, urged Holmes to accept, adding that the governorship would lead inevitably in time to a nomination for United States senator.

Holmes was not a true democrat. He was an elitist. The mixing with the multitudes that political office required held no appeal for him. The judiciary allowed him to have it both ways. He could deal with democratic issues while he sat above the mobs, and he replied to Lodge, "I don't give a damn about being Senator."

At the invitation of the John H. Sedgwick Post No. 4, Grand Army of the Republic, Holmes and Fanny journeyed to the little village of Keene, New Hampshire, on Memorial Day, 1884. There a flag-waving crowd heard him tell, in the poignant prose he reserved for just that purpose, what his war had meant to him. For Holmes, it was a rare personal and passionate statement, and it undoubtedly recalled for those old soldiers in the audience—many of them clad in Union blue—the days of their youth when

> through our great good fortune . . . our hearts were touched with fire.

Two decades after he was mustered out, Holmes had not forgotten a shot, a battleground, or a comrade. He talked of the courage he had witnessed, the comradeship he had experienced, the "snowy heights of honor" the soldiers of his war had scaled.* Of his fallen friends he spoke most poignantly, recalling the particular heroism and selflessness of each as if by describing them and their deeds, he could confer upon them new life and purpose. He seemed to feel it was the survivor's responsibility—his solemn duty—to keep their names and deeds alive, to ensure that they had not died in vain.

Under the heading "Dead Yet Living," the full text of the speech was reprinted the next day in the *Boston Daily Advertiser* for all of Boston to read. It is one of Holmes's most frequently cited works.

The deep feeling he showed and the richness of the prose he spoke in "Dead Yet Living" may well have been the reason he was asked, shortly afterwards, to respond to the toast "Harvard College in the War" at the annual Harvard alumni dinner. The fete was held on June 25 in Memorial Hall, Harvard's monument to its own Civil War dead. Although Harvard's having so far failed to award him an honorary degree rankled, Holmes spoke eloquently to the occasion, praising his alma mater for helping "men of lofty natures to make good their faculties," for establishing Memorial Hall as a "symbol of man's destiny and power for duty, but a symbol also of that something more by which duty is swallowed up in generosity, that something more which led men . . . to toss life and hope like a flower at the feet of their country and their cause."

A month later, on July 28, the first in a series of deaths in Holmes's immediate family occurred. His younger brother, Ned, who had done everything right, even to marrying a Wigglesworth, died at his summer home in Milton. Ned had inherited his father's asthma along with his father's wit; the former, combined with malaria he was supposed to have picked up in Washington during the year he spent there working for Senator Sumner and the Senate Foreign Relations Committee, had forced him to give up the law as a profession some years before, and he had become known as a connoisseur of antique bronzes. He had spent considerable time fighting his affliction on trips abroad and in the mild, clear air of Lakewood, New Jersey, and had been optimistic enough about his condition to purchase, shortly before his death, a house on Beacon Street, Boston, opposite the Public Garden. But all the efforts of nature and modern medicine had failed him, and he died of heart disease at the comparatively young age of thirty-eight, leaving, in addi-

---

*He who yearned for immortality achieved perhaps an unsought honor when the words he spoke on that balmy spring day in 1884—"it is the moment . . . to recall what our country had done for each of us, and to ask ourselves what we can do for our country in return"—were paraphrased by the new American President on a cold snowy day in Washington nearly seventy-seven years later: "ask not what your country can do for you: Ask what you can do for your country."

tion to his wife, an eleven-year-old son, also called Edward Jackson Holmes, and his older brother to carry on the Holmes name.

As 1884 was drawing to a close, a case came to the Massachusetts Supreme Judicial Court that offered Holmes a rare opportunity to study it "to the bottom," to draw on his knowledge of the English common law, to overturn a precedent he felt might have been misunderstood during the intervening seventy-five years, and to "confirm some theories" of his book. The case* was an appeal from a conviction for malpractice.

A Dr. Franklin Pierce, attending one Mary A. Bemis of West Boylston, prescribed poultices of kerosene to be applied to her body, arms, and legs, as treatment for some unnamed illness. The poultices were to be renewed every three hours. Within the first two hours, however, Mrs. Bemis was experiencing great "pain and distress," and the physician was called back. He examined his patient and concluded that the treatment was "doing just what he wanted, like a poultice on a boil, drawing it out; that it was her only salvation." On the advice of the doctor, who claimed he had used the treatment successfully in the past, it was continued for three days. Mrs. Bemis's body blistered and burned; the skin came off, sores appeared. Dr. Pierce was discharged, and other physicians were called in. They pronounced the patient, however, "past recovery," and she died within a few days.

Dr. Pierce was indicted on five counts of manslaughter, tried, and convicted. He appealed on the grounds that the judge in a similar case, *Commonwealth* v. *Thompson* (1809), had instructed the jury, and the jury had agreed, that "to constitute manslaughter, the killing must have been a consequence of some unlawful act. Now, there is no law which prohibits any man from prescribing for a sick person with his consent, if he honestly intends to cure him by his prescription."

Holmes suspected that the court reporter of *Commonwealth* v. *Thompson,* who had missed the trial and obtained the details of it secondhand, might have transcribed the case inaccurately, or that perhaps the English precedent on which the American court had relied in 1809 had been misunderstood. He doubted physicians were meant to be given such a wide latitude, and he himself would not grant it.

That a verdict of guilty required a killing to be the consequence of an independently unlawful act might once have been the law, Holmes added, but his own reading of early English precedents as well as contemporary cases indicated that the law since then had come to recognize

* *Commonwealth* v. *Pierce.* 138 Mass. 165 (1884).

equally "that a man may commit murder or manslaughter by doing otherwise lawful acts recklessly, as that he may by doing acts unlawful for independent reasons, from which death accidently ensues."

The purpose of the criminal law, Holmes had written in *The Common Law,* was "only to induce external conformity to rule"; it was not for atonement of sin. Standards of legal liability, if they were to be precise, predictable, and applied equally to all—that is, if they were to develop beyond the notion of vengeance and speak for a civilized community—must be external, objective, and coincide with the standards shared by the community. In *Commonwealth* v. *Pierce,* writing for a unanimous court, he demonstrated what he meant.

His court's task was to decide whether Dr. Pierce's good intentions had justified his behavior, which is what had gotten Dr. Thompson's acquittal in 1809, or whether he was guilty of a crime. The court, Holmes concluded, could not recognize a privilege to do acts manifestly endangering human life on the ground of good intentions alone. When external, objective standards were applied to Dr. Pierce's case, and the court considered not his intention to save Mrs. Bemis's life but only the consequences of his application of kerosene poultices—her death—his behavior was criminal.

If he was guilty of a crime, was it murder or manslaughter? It all depended. In *The Common Law,* he had used one of Blackstone's examples to explain the differences:

> When a workman flings down a stone or piece of timber into the street, and kills a man; this may be either misadventure, manslaughter, or murder, according to the circumstances under which the original act was done: if it were in a country village, where few passengers are, and he calls out to all people to have a care, it is misadventure only; but if it were in London . . . where people are continually passing, it is manslaughter, though he gives loud warning; and murder, if he knows of their passing, and gives no warning at all.

If an ordinarily prudent man foresaw death as the consequence of his behavior, like the workman in the last example, his behavior involved malice and the crime was murder. If the same man foresaw some lesser but still considerable danger, and death resulted instead, like the workman in the second example, the crime was manslaughter. Dr. Pierce had seen Mrs. Bemis's "pain and distress," but was clearly ignorant of the mortal danger his ordering of kerosene poultices involved, and he was judged negligent and guilty of manslaughter.

Commonwealth v. *Pierce* was not the kind of case that caught the public eye and stirred up emotions, but it was the kind of case he liked to write. It required some scholarship, some skillful analysis, offered an opportunity to call on some theories he had advanced in *The Common Law,* and he described it to his friend Pollock with some considerable pride.

Holmes's commitment to the external standard, the objective criterion, in these legal liability cases that came to the court allowed him to indulge a personal tendency to detachment from human affairs—which undoubtedly was not without its attractiveness for him. Applied in cases involving emotionally charged issues, Holmes himself need never shed an irrelevant tear. Committed to objectivity, he need never factor either the human mind or heart into a judicial decision.

Which did not mean that judges could reduce cases to mathematical formulas. Just cause exonerated—self-defense justified murder. So did certain policy considerations: since society valued free enterprise over the individual's financial security, a merchant had a perfect right to ruin a competitor. He was, in the language of the law, privileged, which was only another way of saying that the law evolved out of the conflicts in changing social and economic values. It was up to the judge to balance the privilege against the harm done.

Many judges disagreed. They contended that the law could not ignore intent as a criterion for assigning legal responsibility, that application of the external standard tended to minimize the factor of personal accountability, and so contributed to the dissolution of intellectual integrity, to the commission of wrongful acts. Holmes was never persuaded. More than forty years later he commented to a friend:

As to your doctors and judges on uncontrollable impulses I think the short answer is that the law establishes certain minima of social conduct that a man must conform to at his peril. . . . I am entirely impatient of any but broad distinctions. Otherwise we are lost in a maze of determinism. If I were having a philosophical talk with a man I was going to have hanged (or electrocuted) I should say, I don't doubt that your act was inevitable for you but to make it avoidable by others we propose to sacrifice you to the common good. You may regard yourself as a soldier dying for your country if you like. But the law must keep its promises.

During the decade of the eighties, Holmes established a reputation as an after-dinner speaker. His prose was livelier than most, his talks were briefer, and his themes, conventional.* He emphasized the nobility of his calling, its involvement in the "stream of life" with all life's "passions, its battles, its despair, its triumphs." These early talks were paeans of praise for the law.

For Holmes's first such address—to the Suffolk (Boston) Bar Association in February 1885—

> the only thought that could come into my mind, the only words that could spring to my lips were a hymn to her in whose name we are met here tonight—to our mistress, the Law.

He spoke of the law not like a lawyer who saw it only as a means of making a living, but more like a painter discussing his art. Although he had found it an unappetizing "ragbag of details" during his early months at Harvard Law School, and although the cases he had been assigned to write during the months immediately preceding this address—disputes involving mortgages, disorderly conduct, contracts, libel, the everyday fare of the court's docket—had not been particularly exciting or challenging, Holmes presented a dazzling and noble vision of his "mistress" and dressed her in elegant metaphor. When he thought of the law, he told the lawyers assembled in the dining room of the Hotel Vendome that night, he saw

> A princess mightier than she who once wrought at Bayeux, eternally weaving into her web figures of the ever-lengthening past—figures too dim to be noticed by the idle, too symbolic to be interpreted by her pupils, but to the discerning eye disclosing every painful step and every world-shaking contest by which mankind has worked and fought its way from isolation to organic social life.

With obvious pride, Holmes dispatched the next day a copy of the speech to Pollock, and the editors of the *Albany Law Journal,* who had been present at the dinner, reprinted the text in their May 23, 1885, issue.

In 1886, Holmes was forty-five years old and apparently in good health. His only complaint was that he "started eye glasses" that year. He began the year with a sentimental journey to First Church, Cambridge, where Grandfather Abiel Holmes had been preacher and which was celebrating its 250th anniversary in 1886. For the first time since

---

* *The Occasional Speeches of Justice Oliver Wendell Holmes,* compiled by Mark DeWolfe Howe, was published by Harvard University Press, Cambridge, Massachusetts, in 1962.

the parish split in 1829, members of both churches came together. They sang hymns written by the controversial pastor and his son the verse writer, and they heard Judge Holmes, representing the third generation of Holmeses, remind them of the richness of their Puritan heritage.

It was reported that his speeches sounded spontaneous, although they actually were well rehearsed, usually for the critical Fanny. He injected just enough of his personal feelings about a subject to involve his audience in it intimately.

Five days after he spoke at First Church, he opened a series of lectures on the various professions to Harvard undergraduates about to choose theirs.

> Of course the law is not the place for the artist or the poet. The law is the calling of thinkers . . . and I say no longer with any doubt—that a man may live greatly in the law as well as elsewhere; that there as well as elsewhere his thought may find its unity in an infinite perspective; that there as well as elsewhere he may wreak himself upon life, may drink the bitter cup of heroism, may wear his heart out after the unattainable.

On June 30, 1886, Holmes received an LL.D. from Yale. On the same day his father received a similar honor from Oxford University—his third that year, having already received degrees from Cambridge and the University of Edinburgh. The newspapers, Holmes told a friend, were saying "our family was becoming famous by degrees." The judge was flattered enough to miss the twenty-fifth anniversary of his Harvard class the night before the ceremony in order to travel to New Haven. (Fanny's sense of duty prevented her from accompanying Holmes to New Haven; Dr. Holmes and his daughter being abroad, she stayed at the elder Holmes's Beverly Farms place to care for her mother-in-law, whose health had begun to fail.) Holmes accepted the degree with proper gratitude, the usual compliments to the awarding institution, and in the romantic military metaphor that audiences had begun to expect from him: "like the little blow upon the shoulder from the sword of a master of war which in ancient days adjudged that a soldier had won his spurs and pledged his life to decline no combat in the future." Continuing what had become a habit with the media, the *New Haven Palladium* identified the forty-five-year-old appellate judge as the son of the "autocrat" and "less well known" than the other degree recipients.

The Harvard *Daily Crimson* reported the applause was "deafening" on the afternoon of November 5, 1886, when Holmes rose to give the principal oration at the meeting of the new Harvard Law School Association, which had been established largely through the efforts of his friend Louis Brandeis. Holmes told the four hundred alumni and dignitaries gathered in Sanders Theater exactly what they wanted to hear: how the law school had, almost since its inception, taught law "in the grand manner," its professors in the forefront of the significant developments in legal scholarship, its graduates consistently found among the leaders of the bar and other professions.

Probably at about this time—although the only existing copy of his speech is not dated—Holmes, whose intense desire to shape the law— to matter—was perhaps enhanced by his childlessness, the implications of which became clearer with age, as well as frustrated by the sort of work he was assigned on the Supreme Judicial Court, sought to persuade members of the Essex bar of their immortality. It was almost as if he was trying to convince himself of his own significance, and if the word "decide" were substituted for the word "argue," the paragraph could well be a self-portrait:

> You argue a case in Essex. And what has the world outside to do with that, you say. Yet you have confirmed or modified or perhaps have suggested for the first time a principle which will find its way into the reports and from the reports into the textbooks and so into the thought of the common law, and so into its share in governing the conduct of civilized men. Our every act rings through the world of being.

With possibly similar intent, though in different words, he told alumni of Boston University Law School a few years later that they were "shaping the future."

At about this time, a particularly grisly episode occurred involving one of Holmes's young friends, John Jay Chapman, grandson of the abolitionist Maria Weston Chapman, later American man of letters, and in 1887 a student at Harvard Law School—one of Owen Wister's group with whom Holmes occasionally took meals. On the surface, Chapman was genial and witty; in love, he became a madman.

In 1887, he was in love with Minna Timmins and she with him. When Percival Lowell, whom Chapman mistakenly thought was a rival, appeared at a party in Brookline, Chapman took him out in the garden and beat him, then in expiation deliberately burned his own hand in a coal fire. The hand had to be amputated.

During Chapman's hospital stay, Holmes visited him regularly, trying to persuade the young man to talk out his jealous rages. He also acted as intermediary between Chapman and Minna, whom hospital authorities refused to admit to Chapman's room. Chapman, however, mistook Holmes's fatherly friendliness to Minna, who was half his age, for sexual attraction, and in his later letters to Minna, as well as in his memoirs, he heaped abuse on the older man. Holmes was "polluted in his body and soul." He had the "interests of a parasite and jackall." He sat by Chapman's bedside and "breathed [illegible] him like a cat." Chapman hated him, who "always touched the thing [the stump?] with a touch that was cold and had sex in it." Minna had shown Holmes "a letter of mine and spoken about me—and when I accused her—had said he was the father of her inmost"—a phrase that particularly infuriated Chapman—and she "always confided in him." Although the Holmeses housed Chapman until he was able to take care of himself after he left the hospital, Chapman refused to have anything more to do with Holmes in the future, and went so far as to contemplate Holmes's murder.

In the summer of 1886, Dr. Holmes and his widowed daughter, Amelia Sargent, had had to accelerate their return from abroad because the elder Mrs. Holmes, who had been complaining of declining strength for some time, suffered a breakdown. Her "mental condition unfits her for the duties and sensibilities of the office which she has long and faithfully discharged," and Dr. Holmes enlisted the help of a friend in finding a housekeeper—he wanted a *"lady"* who would be a "fitting companion" for his wife and could at the same time manage his own "domestic affairs." Mrs. Holmes's "bodily health" remained good for a time, but her mental health gradually but steadily deteriorated until she became childlike. She lingered a winter and a summer, but a second winter proved too much, and in February 1888, at the age of seventy, she died, giving the younger Holmes "a tug that goes far down to the roots."

Beyond her son's intimate expressions of affection in his letters home from the front—"good night my loveliest and sweetest," "Dear Mammy"—little evidence of Amelia Holmes's time on earth remains. Like all her family, she was a private person and left no journals or letters. She was not a "come-outer" and except for her brief but effective management of the local branch of the U.S. Sanitary Commission during the Civil War, she seems to have devoted herself entirely to her family, shielding her husband from the liabilities of fame and lavishing on her children the gentle love of which a sense of security is born—the sort of security with which all things are possible and without which nothing is possible.

Shortly after her death, Fanny's and Wendell's house at Mattapoisett burned down. Their spirits inevitably depressed, they did not settle on another vacation place but spent most of May and part of June 1888 touring America by railroad. They set out for California on May 5, stopped briefly in Chicago where Holmes was presented to Melville W. Fuller, chief justice of the United States, and continued on to San Diego, then turned up the Pacific coast to Washington state and British Columbia. On June 8, they were back in Boston—"9,000 miles in one car!" They checked in with Dr. Holmes at Beverly Farms—where he had been vacationing summers for several years—then left again for nearly two months at Niagara Falls and serious recuperation.

Following her mother's death, the widowed Amelia Sargent moved into her father's Beacon Street house to take charge. She, however, had had a heart attack the previous winter and was none too robust herself. Just over a year later, Amelia, too, fell seriously ill, and in April 1889, just forty-six years old, she died.

The immediate practical result of the series of deaths in Holmes's family was his moving back into his father's house after nearly a decade and a half of independence. Cousin Johnny Morse thought the move boded ill; Wendell was definitely not a "filial" type, and Morse had a "shrewd suspicion" that Fanny was "not passionately fond of her father-in-law." Duty, however, outweighed desire, and Fanny and Wendell gave up their cherished Chestnut Street house and went to live on Beacon Street with the seventy-nine-year-old doctor, for whom the loss of his wife and daughter was worsened by the diminishing of his sight and general decline in health.

Whatever irritations surfaced during the five years left to Dr. Holmes, Fanny suppressed in her gentle, quiet way, at the same time she ran the house and made him comfortable. If, as Johnny Morse had intimated, she resented her father-in-law's antics, she kept it to herself. The old man called her "Mrs. Judge" and described her as a "helpful, hopeful, powerful as well as brilliant woman."

The emotional toll of the three deaths, combined with the prospect of moving back to his father's house and perhaps some aftertaste of the Chapman episode, plus the loss of the Mattapoisett house, all within the space of a few years, seems to have been substantial. Holmes could not stop to mourn any more than he could have interrupted his war to mourn his fallen comrades. Grief, after all, distracted from the business at hand, and the business at hand distracted from grief. He missed no court arguments and was in fact present on the bench the day his sister died. But his demeanor was joyless and often melancholy.

It is possible these personal losses softened him sufficiently for professional frustrations to depress him more than usual. Undoubtedly it irked him to operate at less than full capacity, however necessary it had been during this decade to rearrange his professional life and refuel intellectually. Marriage, a pleasant home, prominence in the community, an interesting job, all the usual things men strive for, did not satisfy him. His comfortable existence was bringing only ennui. He believed himself destined for larger things. It was not for this he had survived a war.

Perhaps he foresaw—and feared—the power of complacency as he looked around at the stolid lives of Boston's ruling class. In fact he had recently told a group of Harvard undergraduates that he feared for a world in which "the ideal will be content and dignified acceptance of life, rather than aspiration and the passion for achievement." He hoped with all his adventurous heart that their generation retained "the barbaric thirst for conquest, and there is still something left to conquer."

During the decade before appointment to the bench, Holmes had lived alone in his books, alone and free in his private laboratory of thought. On his return to earth, he seemed not to feel entirely attuned to its rhythms, and he confessed he had had himself in mind when he described one of his brethren as "lonely . . . walking apart in meditative silence, and dreaming . . . the dream of spiritual reign."

In any case, his joylessness, even frustration and alienation, showed to those who observed him at close range. Owen Wister detected a "melancholy" in Holmes's spirit and Holmes himself admitted his "spirit [was] somewhat collapsed and flat for the moment." He could not explain it fully. But, ignoring the devastating personal tragedies with which he had had to cope during the eighties, he suggested that in part he might be "a little happier if I believed more implicitly in the things I would die for," and in part, he added, he was egocentric enough to require appreciation of his work, an appreciation that had not been forthcoming. Since, however, such thoughts were not productive, he submerged them in his work, which he thought deserved a better reception.

Fanny's antidote to depression was to pack him off to England for the summer. A trip abroad always restored his spirits, although she suggested it on the pretext that it would "make the first summer easier for my father." Wendell eventually agreed to go even though he had to go alone—there was not enough money for two to go, and in any event, Fanny was needed on Beacon Street.

Although Holmes's *The Common Law* was not unknown in England and he had been a judge of Massachusetts's highest court for six years, Dr. Holmes's need to be needed seems not to have diminished, and he was still writing letters of introduction for his son; whether out of a father's pride or a shrewd perception of British biases, the doctor still emphasized in these letters his son's military service and rank during the Civil War.

Henry James, who by 1889 had settled permanently in England, reported from London that Holmes's visit to the British capital was "a most brilliant success," that Wendell, at forty-eight, was "as pleasant as possible, young-looking [*sic*] and handsomer than ever. Flirting as desperately too. I suppose," the novelist's sister, Alice, observed, "that his idea of 'heaven is still flirting with pretty girls,' as he used to say."

The trip was only partially successful. The winter after his return still was not "sprightly, what with not feeling very well, and the adjustment to a new situation—living in my father's house instead of my own, etc."

The move to Beacon Street did not seem to diminish Holmes's leisure-time reading—the intense all-night sessions of scholarly investigation had ended with publication of *The Common Law*—and his lists for 1889 and 1890 hold the usual mix of philosophy (Schopenhauer, Hegel, Lotze), history both political (McMaster's *History of the People of the United States*) and legal (Maine's *Early Law and Custom*), biography (Carlyle's *Frederick the Great*) and autobiography (Benjamin Franklin), fiction (Dickens, Dostoevski, Hardy, Mark Twain) and poetry (Spenser, Wordsworth, Ovid). Several books, including Spenser's *Faerie Queene* and Homer's *Iliad,* were read aloud, probably by Fanny while Holmes played solitaire in the evening. William James's *Principles of Psychology* was published in 1890. Naturally the author sent a copy to his old friend, who read "every word of it—with delight and admiration" and pronounced it a "noble work" that would make James's reputation, although he could not resist taking issue on some of James's points.

The two men did not seek each other out now. They rarely met except casually at their clubs. Their paths had diverged sharply. The bonds that had united them had loosened and the companionable evenings when they twisted the tail of the cosmos and shared the intensity of youth were but memories now.

TOWARD THE END of Holmes's first decade on the Massachusetts Supreme Judicial Court, a series of cases before him offered a rare opportunity to explore a problem of liability in tort law that had long interested him. They did not involve burning issues and did not cause a stir among either Holmes's brethren or the general public. The first, *Clifford* v. *Atlantic Mills,* in 1888, involved a suit for personal injuries sustained when snow falling from a building hit the plaintiff. The second, *Elmer* v. *Fessenden,* in 1890, was a case of slander. The third, *Tasker* v. *Stanley,* in 1891, was an alienation of affections case. All three involved determining the legal liability of an innocent third person in actions for damages.

If the tendency of a wrongful act to cause damages is the test of the actor's legal responsibility, as the application of kerosene poultices to a human body had a tendency to cause death in *Commonwealth* v. *Pierce,* what, Holmes liked to ask, was the legal responsibility of a seller of firearms when one of his customers shot someone? He was not satisfied with the conventional legal thinking that the law stopped with the final wrongdoer. Why did it? he wondered. Conventional legal wisdom held it was because the last actor was responsible for the consequences. But, Holmes argued, an innocent third person might enter the picture later, one who repeated a slander, for example. Then what?

The true standard for determining legal liability, Holmes concluded, involved a test of reasonableness. A man was reasonably *"presumed not to contemplate illegal conduct of others"* and was not legally liable "unless it is shown that he actually did contemplate it." A firearms merchant reasonably could expect his customers to shoot squirrels and rabbits, not their neighbors or their wives' lovers, and he was not liable when they used his products for the latter.

His perfect hypothetical case involving a seller of firearms never came before Holmes, but others involving the same principle did. In the personal injuries case, Holmes, for a unanimous court, held the owner of the building—the innocent third person, analogous to the firearms merchant—not responsible for the damage done, since his tenant might reasonably have been expected to prevent the accident. In the slander case, a physician had circulated, though he had not originated, a false story that a local textile manufacturer was supplying his workers with thread containing arsenic, and the workers had left the manufacturer's employ. Holmes, again for a unanimous court, held the defendant, who had only repeated someone else's story, not liable for the damages asked.

In *Tasker* v. *Stanley,* a husband was suing a friend of his wife's for persuading her to leave him. Holmes, for still another unanimous court, held the friend, the innocent third person, not legally liable. First of all, he said, it was not a "great crime" for a woman to leave her husband, and even if it were, one could reasonably expect that a "married woman must be supposed to be capable of receiving advice to separate from her husband without losing her reason or responsibility." In his early drafts of the opinion, Holmes had elaborated on the logic that had led him to his conclusion, but his brethren had objected, and he was persuaded to "cut down the discussion." Taking the three cases together, however, he felt he had established a principle of legal liability. He had wanted, he said, to get it all "on the footing of the reasonably-to-be-contemplated," which was another way of describing the standards, or the will, of the community.

Writing opinions like these, ferreting out the principle that bound them together, why, it was almost as much fun as putting together *The Common Law* had been. Undoubtedly it was what he had thought judging would be all about. But opportunities like these were all too infrequent. One of the Holmes legends has it that he used to suggest that his brethren shorten their opinions and put the clutter in a letter to a friend. Taking his own advice, Holmes sent the opinions to Pollock along with the views he had wanted to air in them.

In the same year he wrote *Tasker,* he also wrote his first dissent in a labor relations case—only his third dissent during the entire decade. *Commonwealth* v. *Perry* came to the court at a time when Holmes's thoughts on the function of law in a complex urban industrial society were maturing and when perhaps he was feeling a little freer to express them.

In 1891, a somewhat progressive state legislature, which in 1874 had passed a ten-hour act for women and children working in factories, had passed a law prohibiting employers from fining or withholding wages from weavers in the local textile mills whose work was less than perfect. The test case was becoming an accepted stage in the legislative life cycle, and textile manufacturer Josiah Perry immediately fined one of his weavers forty cents "for imperfections that had arisen during the process of weaving in the cloth and material." A jury had found Perry guilty.

Judges at the time did not fully trust the legislatures, which were enacting all sorts of regulatory measures in response to voters' demands. It was becoming harder and harder to find authority for the lawmakers' behavior. Reflecting the views of the late-nineteenth-century American establishment, the Massachusetts Supreme Judicial Court reversed the lower court in *Commonwealth* v. *Perry.* That particular statute violated, declared Marcus P. Knowlton, who had been appointed to the court in 1887, that liberty of contract guaranteed by the state and federal constitutions to both employer and employee in an important industry "essential to the welfare of the community."

Holmes's dissent was then, as it often was later, reluctant. Many times he simply noted his disagreement, because he felt written dissents

detracted from the authority of the majority opinion. Only the importance of the question in *Perry* persuaded him to write. At stake were
two desirable goals. It was to the state's advantage to protect both the
employer from shoddy work and the employee from exploitation. As he
often would during his judicial life, Holmes, who had declared in *The
Common Law* that the "first requirement of a sound body of law is, that
it should correspond with the actual feelings and demands of the community," deferred to the judgment of the legislature—which represented those feelings and demands and had decided to protect the employee when it passed the law at issue in this case. It may very well be,
Holmes declared, that a political economist might describe the measure
in question as unreasonable; still, he argued, he "should not be willing
or think myself authorized to overturn legislation on that ground." The
concept became a linchpin of his jurisprudence on which he would rely
in 1921 and 1931 as well as in 1891.

He did not necessarily approve of the legislation he upheld; most of
it in fact disturbed him. He did not "respect the passion for equality"
and had no interest in men's efforts to "regenerate society via property."
Privately, he shared many of the biases his brethren held. He had no
love for labor and little acquaintance with conditions of the industrial
world in which cases like *Perry* originated. But his personal prejudices
also did not constitute grounds for striking down legislation.

Of all the labor relations cases, the most numerous were those involving industrial accidents, which, in those early days of unpoliced and
unregulated factory conditions and inexperienced operators of newly devised and complicated machinery, were plentiful, and the legal questions surrounding them crowded court dockets not only in Massachusetts but wherever factory smokestacks striped the skyline.

In 1887, the state legislature had passed an Employers' Liability
Act. While it limited recovery claims to $4,000 in cases of injury and
$5,000 in cases of death, it had been intended to create a legal remedy
for the conscientious and careful workman in the event of an accident.
The Supreme Judicial Court did not nullify the act, but found ways
around it. As construed by that court, the act in the end did little to
expand the liability of the employer. Underlying the Massachusetts cases
and explicit in most was the assumption of the common law that an
employee knew the risks when he accepted a job and should exercise
due care—that the operator of a circular saw understood the dangers in
its use,* that the cook on a steam tug was familiar with bow lines and

---

* *Wheeler* v. *Watson*. 135 Mass. 294 (1883).

realized the potential for injury if he entangled himself in one,* that an experienced and properly cautious carpenter does not fall through the open spaces in the floors of an uncompleted building in which he is working.† Employers during these years were rarely held liable for the deaths and injuries that occurred in the workplace by the Massachusetts Supreme Judicial Court, including Holmes, who dissented from none and wrote for the majority in 1890, in a case involving the death of a railroad switchman, that there could be no doubt that the employee had assumed certain risks when he was hired, and that even if his conduct was not negligent, his work involved dangers "manifest" to him, and he "could not complain of the consequences."‡

Holmes had reason to be optimistic during these middle years on the Massachusetts Supreme Judicial Court. He had passed the milestone of fifty. He had written—to his apparent satisfaction—a seminal work on the development of the law by the time he was forty. As a judge of the state's highest court, he was a respected member of the community, what a later generation called a VIP. On October 21, 1891, the thirtieth anniversary of the Battle of Ball's Bluff, Little, Brown & Company, which had published *The Common Law* ten years before, brought out the first of several editions of Holmes's speeches, an unusual compliment to a state judge. (Bothered by a chronic cough, which was later diagnosed as asthma, he made the first of several unsuccessful attempts to break his smoking habit the same year.) But his melancholy of the recent past seems to have persisted:

> I am dying, Egypt, dying . . . every man of 50 is

and may have been exacerbated by a pervasive sense of resignation. As his first decade on the Massachusetts court drew to a close, Holmes seemed resigned to living with his father, resigned to churning out the court's work—over which he had stopped rhapsodizing to Pollock the way he had in the first two months—resigned to the settled quality of his life—his marriage, his profession, his friends—resigned to the infrequency of new challenges and interests appearing on his horizon. He had been waiting and waiting to be a judge, to begin his real life for which he had been preparing for so long. Now that he was a judge, he seemed to be asking, "Is that all?"

Williams v. *Churchill*. 137 Mass. 243 (1884).
† *Murphy* v. *Greeley*. 146 Mass. 196 (1890).
‡ *Boyle* v. *New York & New England Railroad Co.* 151 Mass. 102 (1890).

CHAPTER 15

Practice Flights

INDEED IT WAS not all.

In ten years on the Massachusetts Supreme Judicial Court, Holmes had developed a facility for interpreting state law. During the past decade he had become so familiar with precedent and had built up such an inventory of legal principles that he no longer required lengthy consideration of cases, but immediately discerned the points at issue and recalled the appropriate antecedents from the casebook of his mind. A younger justice could only gape in admiration when one summer day he brought to Beverly Farms a question that had come up in court during Holmes's absence. Holmes casually leafed through the material, took out a sheet of paper, and in ten or so lines, scribbled an answer acceptable to the court without change.

Over the years on the Massachusetts court, Holmes also had developed a virile style of opinion writing that sometimes bordered on the epigrammatic, a sense of judicial construction, and a manner of judicial thinking. He had begun to work random conclusions into viable judicial principles, and threads that could be followed from case to case were beginning to emerge. Indeed, these years on the Massachusetts court clearly foreshadowed his later years on the United States Supreme Court, where it was often noted that he used common law formulas developed on the Massachusetts court to solve constitutional problems and where his state court–learned tolerance of legislative experimentation attracted considerable attention and was ultimately even given a name—judicial restraint.

By the second decade of Holmes's state judgeship, four of the justices who had sat on the court when Holmes was appointed had either died or resigned. Walbridge Abner Field had succeeded to the chief justiceship, and Holmes had moved up the escalator to third in seniority. Their successors, however, had wrought no change in the WASPish character of the court; it was still dominated by justices who held a firm faith in the established order of public affairs.

Holmes, though, was developing a sense of contemporary industrial America, a fluid society that could not be contained in the traditional social and economic straitjackets. His skepticism of arid legal principles was reinforced, and a new self-confidence allowed him to speak his judicial mind. During this second decade on the state court, he wrote nine of his twelve dissenting opinions and cast all eleven of his separate dissenting votes. For many men their fifties mean being, relying on settled principles of life; for Holmes his fifties meant still becoming.

Early in this period, Holmes was assigned the writing of his first court opinion involving freedom of speech.* At the time, the issue was not so explosive as it became three decades later, and this early excursion into the area is notable largely for comparison purposes. John J. McAuliffe had been dismissed from the New Bedford police force for engaging in political activities forbidden by municipal regulation. The officer took his case to court on grounds that his constitutional right to freedom of speech had been abridged. Holmes for a unanimous court denied McAuliffe's contention without even addressing the freedom-of-speech question. The officer, he declared, "may have a constitutional right to talk politics, but he has no constitutional right to be a policeman." Whatever applause he may have won from what he called the "respectable classes" for his decision in McAuliffe, however, Holmes lost later that same year for a dissent that contributed to his future reputation as a "dangerous radical."

The Massachusetts constitution authorized the governor, his council, and the state legislature to ask the advice of the Supreme Judicial Court on important questions of law, a privilege of which the legislators frequently took advantage. In the spring of 1892, they asked the judges to decide the constitutionality of pending legislation that directed the cities and towns of the state to buy wood and coal for sale to residents as fuel—"a step towards Communism," as Holmes wryly put it to Pollock. Indeed, it was a time when many Americans were highly sensitive to the threat of collectivism infecting private enterprise, and they seemed to feel that municipal ownership of so much as a hairpin portended a dangerous spreading of the disease.

---

* McAuliffe v. New Bedford. 155 Mass. 216 (1892).

As the justices prepared to take up the case, the outcome was uncertain. Holmes predicted he would be in the minority when he proposed that the lawmakers were acting within the limits of their authority. On the other hand, he admitted, he might "well come out on the other side," or the others might even agree with him.

The local establishment gave a perceptible collective sigh of relief when the court majority answered the legislature in a firm negative; the judges could see no reason why the communities of Massachusetts should get involved in the fuel business any more than other businesses traditionally operated by private enterprise. Whenever bars came down, limits became harder to fix. Given an inch, government would take a yard, and where would it all end, except in government involvement in every aspect of life?

After considering the question at some length, Holmes, as he originally predicted, found himself in the minority. In a dissent of fewer than 150 words, he told his brethren what he thought. He was not then, had never been, and never was afterward a socialist—he dared "some follower of [Edward] Bellamy," author of *Looking Backward,* to write him "on the footing of my supposed sympathy that I might tell him what a donkey I consider his lord and master to be." But he failed to see the distinction between the offering for sale of wood and coal by a public body and the offering for sale by that same body of other necessities of life. The majority had admitted that municipalities for years had supplied residents with water and even longer with education; only two years before, answering a similar question put to the court by the legislature, the judges had approved the manufacture, distribution, and sale of gas and electricity to local citizens. In Holmes's view, the purpose was "no less public" when the item was wood or coal than when it was one of the others, "to say nothing of cases like the support of paupers or the taking of land for railroads or public markets."

Whether the pending legislation was necessary or expedient did not concern Holmes or the court. He saw, however, no basis "for denying the power of the Legislature to enact the laws mentioned in the questions proposed."

Perhaps he took some pleasure in assuming the role of the Brahmins' bad boy—a role he had enjoyed first as a Harvard undergraduate. Three days after the court handed down its decision, he proudly told a friend the newspapers were calling him a "blooming communist." In fact, however, the newspapers did not call him a "blooming communist." Most of the local papers wrote the story straight, and an editorial in the *Boston Post* congratulated Holmes on his dissent, called him "squarely in line with the progressive movement of the people," and hoped "the rest [would] catch up with him in the course of time."

Politics and personal eccentricities aside, contrasting the majority's opinion with Holmes's dissent in the municipal coal and wood sales case points up a principle which marked his jurisprudence for the rest of his judicial life whenever constitutional questions arose. Many judges, including those on the Massachusetts Supreme Judicial Court, searched their constitutions for a positive grant of authority for specific legislation. As the court stated regarding municipal sales of coal and wood, "We know of nothing in the history of the adoption of the Constitution that gives any countenance to the theory that the buying and selling of such articles as wood and coal for the use of the inhabitants was regarded at that time as one of the ordinary functions of the government which was to be established. There are nowhere in the Constitution any provisions which tend to show that the government was established for the purpose of carrying on the buying and selling of such merchandise. . . ." It was a specificity that made a constitution rigid and narrow in its application, entirely unequipped to absorb the shocks of social and economic change.

Holmes's view of constitutional jurisprudence was more flexible and expansive, allowing for the inevitable bouncing about of civilization. He searched his constitution not for the positive grant of authority but for its prohibition:

> Every presumption is in favor of the validity of a legislative act. It is for the petitioner to show that its rights are invaded by this legislative act. . . . (*Northampton* v. *County Commissioners.* 145 Mass. 108, 1887)

The legislature, he believed, although he knew his principle did not "command his brethren's assent," had absolute power, "except so far as expressly or by implication it is prohibited by the Constitution—that the question always is where do you find the prohibition—not where do you find the power." It became Holmes's habit not to find statutes constitutional but to find them not unconstitutional—a legal litotes that made a substantial difference in constitutional interpretation.

The following year, 1893, the court, unable to discover a constitutional grant of power to the legislators to act as they had, declared unconstitutional a statute allowing the transfer of a city-owned cemetery to a private corporation.* Holmes wrote a dissent, but did not deliver it

---

* *Mount Hope Cemetery* v. *Boston.* 158 Mass. 509 (1893).

and regretted his failure for the rest of his life. "I don't know," he reminisced twenty-eight years later, no detail of the case forgotten, "as the dissent probably would have been inadequate but my doubts have remained, with the consciousness that I haven't studied the question to the bottom."

As the usual cold and snow ushered in the winter of 1893–94, and Holmes fought his annual bout with the *grippe,* the Massachusetts legislators submitted another explosive issue to the Supreme Judicial Court: women's suffrage by referendum. Was it constitutional, the lawmakers asked, to submit an act granting women the right to vote in town and city elections to voters in a statewide election? Or, alternatively, should the act be submitted to local option?

The judges were less disturbed by the possibility that women might vote than by the idea of government by referendum, which was a favorite political device of Populists. Once established, such a device held infinite possibilities, all of them dangerous to traditional values. Happily for the judges, they could discover no such grant of power to the legislature. Historically, they argued, government in Massachusetts had been by legislative act—representative rather than democratic—and the powers of the people were thereby limited. The proposed legislation was not constitutional.

Once again Holmes separated himself from his brethren and from the local ruling class. He agreed that the state constitution established a representative system of government, not a pure democracy, and a legislature as the law-making body. He thought, however, that "in construing the Constitution, we should remember that it is a frame of government for men of opposite opinions and for the future, and therefore not hastily import into it our own views, or unexpressed limitations derived merely from the practice of the past." He searched the Massachusetts constitution in vain for evidence that the question of the referendum even had occurred to the authors, much less had they forbidden it. The proposed legislation was clearly not unconstitutional.

Once again, he played the bad boy of the bench. "[A]mong the respectable," he boasted to Pollock, "there are some who regard me as a dangerous radical! If I had seen fit to clothe my views in different language I dare say I could have been a pet of the proletariat—whereas they care nothing for me and some of the others distrust me. The issues might become very grave, but in actual fact I don't expect anything particular will happen to any of us on that score."

Bostonians thought of Holmes as a "queer and witty fish," but his

opinions were beginning to be noticed by legal scholars in other parts of
the country, and in late spring 1894, he received an invitation to speak
at the American Bar Association's annual meeting at Saratoga, New
York, in August. Surprisingly, he declined. Possibly he didn't want to
leave his father, who at eighty-five was weakening rapidly. Perhaps
Holmes himself required the whole summer to recuperate from the hard
work of the recent court terms. Perhaps he had other commitments; the
Pollocks were coming that summer, and he didn't want to miss them.
In any case, he did not speak to the national bar the first time he was
asked.

HARVARD'S CLASS OF '29 held its last several meetings at Dr.
Holmes's Beacon Street home. The class poet had written his last ode
for the diminishing group, and the final get-togethers were "quiet, social, *talking* meetings, the Doctor of course doing the *live* talking," those
few present having to shout so that S. F. Smith could hear what was
said. Dr. Holmes was nearly the last leaf on '29's tree—only Smith and
Samuel May survived him,

> And the names he loved to hear
> Have been carved for many a year
> On the tomb.

The old Saturday Club, Hawthorne, Longfellow, Melville, Emerson:
they, too, were dead. Frail little Ned, the two Amelias, wife-mother
and daughter. Only Wendell was left.

Wendell still took him for walks, gave the doctor his arm to lean on,
and when the old man breathed the fresh crisp air, he could for a few
minutes forget his age and step along, although he no longer could match
his tall son's strides. He could still be found nodding off in his gallery
pew at King's Chapel on Sundays, less often at Symphony rehearsals,
which it had been his habit to attend, and hardly ever nowadays at the
local public gatherings where he had so often been one of the most
popular parts of the entertainment.

Age had diminished his effervescence, and by 1893 his body had
grown substantially feebler. The summer of 1894 he rented as usual
the large (eight bedrooms) but unpretentious Victorian house overlooking the sea at Beverly Farms, a forty-five-minute train ride from Boston.
Since their own house at Mattapoisett had burned down, Wendell and

Fanny had been keeping him company there summers, all three restoring their bodies and minds, preparing for the long dark New England winter ahead. This year, on his return to Boston in late September, Dr. Holmes's asthma worsened. His physician was summoned, and the asthma conquered, but the attack left him so weak he never rallied, never left his bed again. Each day he grew gradually weaker.

Just before noon on Sunday, October 7, 1894, the total exhaustion of old age overcame him, and before stimulants could be administered, he slipped quietly into unconsciousness. His doctor arrived a quarter of an hour later, in time to see him close his eyes in death, his family gathered at his bedside. He was eighty-five years old.

A funeral service, simple but well attended by the local illustrious, was held on the Wednesday following at King's Chapel, which had been wreathed in flowers for the occasion. A handful of family members and close friends joined the cortege as it wound along Boston's narrow cobbled streets and across the Charles under gloomy, rain-laden skies to Mount Auburn Cemetery, Cambridge, burying ground of Brahmins, where he disappeared into the grave next to his wife in the Jackson plot.

The younger Holmes faced "rather solemnity than sadness." He felt his father "had had all that he could have from life and he quietly ceased breathing" as Fanny and Wendell "stood by his side, after a serene and happy summer," and just as Wendell was "apprehending that the future had only suffering in store for him."

Holmes the elder and Holmes the younger never seemed to have developed a genuine empathy, to have reached the point where they truly liked—as opposed to loved—each other, understood each other's faults and respected each other's strengths. They exhilarated and exasperated each other, but real intimacy seems to have eluded them, and although at the age of fifty-three, the younger could drop the "Jr." from his name, literally and figuratively, he had not yet entirely "swallow[ed] and digest[ed]" the elder. He seemed still to strive against the elder's accomplishments, however impressive his own.

After Dr. Holmes's death, the younger Holmeses, Fanny and Wendell, stayed on in the Beacon Street house, which Wendell had inherited along with some $68,000 in cash, stocks, bonds, real estate investments, the royalties from Dr. Holmes's books, the family silver and portraits, his large library, and other personal possessions. As custom dictated, he inherited Dr. Holmes's share in the Athenaeum, which Wendell may not have known had been purchased with books from the doctor's library a half-century before when money was not so plentiful.

Wendell was not particularly fond of the doctor's house, but it meant something to him that his parents had built it and died in it, and his brother and sister had been buried from it. Reminders of its former occupants were not entirely removed. The portrait of Grandfather Abiel Holmes still hung over the staircase in the front hall, and the mirror which the diminutive Dr. Holmes had placed low on a closet wall so he could more easily brush his hair still hung there years later. But Fanny made some changes, too. Several pieces of furniture and various pictures went into storage; others came out; still others were newly purchased. Fresh paint and new fixtures appeared, and shortly the house began to look less like an extension of the doctor and more as if it belonged to its new owners.

IN 1895, ANOTHER case involving free speech issues came to the Massachusetts Supreme Judicial Court, and Holmes was assigned to write it. In this one, William F. Davis contended his right to free speech had been violated when he was convicted for making a speech on Boston Common without a permit.* Relying on a previous case in which the West Roxbury Park Commission had been allowed by the court to limit the use of local parks,† Holmes declared that the legislature had the power to control the use of such public places:

> For the legislature . . . to forbid public speaking in a highway or public park is no more an infringement of the rights of a member of the public than for the owner of a private house to forbid it in his house.‡

Civil liberties questions did not particularly interest Holmes. He didn't believe much in rights. He was much more attentive to the complexities of the tort cases that came to the court in significantly larger numbers, and the case for freedom of speech, no burning theme in the 1890s, had made virtually no headway since Holmes, for the court, had upheld the dismissal from the force of the New Bedford policeman in 1892.

Ever ready to abandon the persona of Holmes the judge for that of Holmes the Civil War veteran, he shocked much of Boston when on Memorial Day, 1895, at a meeting of Harvard seniors, he declared "combat and pain . . . the portion of man" and rated the credo of the military

---

* *Commonwealth* v. *Davis.* 162 Mass. 510 (1895).
† *Commonwealth* v. *Abrahams.* 156 Mass. 57 (1892).
‡ Davis took his case to the United States Supreme Court, which unanimously affirmed Holmes's decision (*Davis* v. *Massachusetts.* 167 U.S. 43, 1897).

man—honor, duty, obedience—above what he considered the crass pursuit of money and easy living that he believed had come to dominate American society. The new heroes were the captains of industry—Hill, Fisk, Morgan, Vanderbilt. Holmes, who had grown to adulthood among the local literati during New England's Augustan Age, admired their initiative and originality in putting America's resources to work, but detested the single-minded accumulation of wealth. His own heroes remained the Little Abbotts, the John Sedgwicks, the Pen Hallowells, and all the others of that ilk at whose side he had fought.

At the time Holmes gave this speech, which was called "The Soldier's Faith," relations between the United States and Great Britain were strained over the boundary between British Guiana and Venezuela. The *Harvard Graduates' Magazine* had contracted with Holmes to publish it in the September issue, but despite Holmes's impatience, publication was delayed. By the time the speech came out in the December issue, which is probably where Wendell Phillips Garrison, Holmes's former classmate at Harvard, read it, the border dispute in South America had worsened, and President Grover Cleveland was threatening to intervene and fix the boundary himself under the authority of the Monroe Doctrine. Garrison, in 1895, was editor of the New York–based magazine the *Nation,* and he accused Holmes in his editorial pages of talking "sentimental Jingoism" and exacerbating international tensions. Garrison reminded Holmes that the Fourth of July festival had done "enough to perpetuate hostile feeling between England and America, and to make the flag a symbol above all else to the youth of the land." Holmes in his speech had abused the Memorial Day exercises.

Holmes could only scoff at Garrison's words. It was plain to him the man had listened with only one ear, as had all the other critics who had called him a warmonger, even a fascist. Garrison had heard Holmes say that "the struggle for life is the order of the world," that man's "destiny is battle," that the "ideals of the past for men have been drawn from war"; he had caught the sharpness in Holmes's tone when Holmes belittled "this snug over-safe corner of the world."

But clearly Garrison had missed Holmes's pronouncement that "War, when you are at it, is horrible and dull." He seems not to have heard Holmes's recollections of seeing and hearing the "shrieking fragments go tearing through your company," and knowing that the "next or the next shot carries your fate." Garrison seems not to have paid attention when Holmes described a picket-line "at night in a black and unknown wood . . . hearing the spat of bullets upon the trees," feeling your foot "slip upon a dead man's body." Garrison had ignored the acid in Holmes's voice when Holmes attacked the materialism he was finding so prevalent in contemporary society:

> I once heard a man say, "Where Vanderbilt sits, there is the head of the table. I teach my son to be rich." He said what many think . . . the man who commands the attention of his fellows is the man of wealth. Commerce is the great power. The aspirations of the world are those of commerce. . . .

And Garrison entirely missed the main point of "The Soldier's Faith." It was "not intended," Holmes said, "as it was stupidly taken by man, to advise young men to wade in gore, but to illustrate the theme of how we all honor a man who dies in a cause he little understands, and romantically transcends his more common self." It was not war itself, but the qualities that war—or dueling or polo or any "high and dangerous action"—demanded of men that the materialistic world of the late nineteenth century ought to reinstate, qualities of selflessness, honor, and, perhaps most important, "that unspeakable somewhat which makes [man] capable of miracle, able to lift himself by the might of his own soul, unaided, able to face annihilation for a blind belief." Such qualities did not emerge in the single-minded pursuit of money.

Perhaps Holmes *had* overdone the references to war. He had only intended to illustrate, in the most dramatic way he knew—calling on the profoundest experience he had ever had and describing it in the bluntest terms he could—the contrast between the heroism of the soldier, as he faced the ultimate testing, and the materialists he saw all around him, at his clubs, in State Street, in the cases that came to his court.

Holmes's old friend, Henry James, by 1895 a famous author and expatriate from his own country and from the very qualities Holmes was complaining of, caught Holmes's meaning, although his praise was qualified. Undoubtedly anticipating sympathy with his thesis, Holmes had sent James a copy of the speech. James described it to his brother William as "rarely beautiful" and "ever so fine to read, but with the always strange something unreal or meagre his things have for me—unreal in their connection with his own remainder, as it were, and not *wholly* artful in expression." But he promised to write Holmes "in a high key," which shortly afterwards he did, thanking Holmes for offering him "the great emotion, for me, of the season," and envying Holmes "the right

. . . to so gallant a thesis; so few & far between are the men that have it—among the men who can use it."

And in New York City, the police commissioner and soon-to-be governor of the state, Theodore Roosevelt, who could always find room in his heart for a little jingoism, wrote his friend and political alter ego, Henry Cabot Lodge, then vacationing in Nahant, Massachusetts, the first of a series of favorable comments on Holmes's work: "By Jove," he exclaimed, "that speech of Holmes's was fine."

Less than a month later, Holmes, along with two of his scholarly friends, John Chipman Gray and Frederick Pollock, sat on the platform at the Harvard commencement to receive an honorary degree from President Eliot. For Holmes, the honor came too late for him to appreciate it properly. He took it as a sign that Eliot had at last "buried the hatchet" and no longer bore him "malice" for abandoning his professorship at Harvard and accepting the judgeship. A period was at last put to one sentence of his life.

A healthy part of the summer of 1895 Holmes spent learning to ride a bicycle. He had been feeling confined and not a little bored by the old familiar reading, driving, and napping routine during the long summer days at the Beverly Farms house, which he continued to rent after Dr. Holmes's death, and finally bought in 1909, and he bought for himself one of the new vehicles, the craze for which, since they had been introduced in 1876 at the Centennial exhibition, was sweeping the country. Robert Grant of the Suffolk County Probate Court had one. So did Brooks Adams. Holmes's was an American Humber, but one could buy a cheaper, less streamlined model at almost any sewing machine factory.

After his first lesson, he was stiff and felt he "never should learn. Violent exercise," he explained, "upsets an old sportsman who has done nothing more vigorous than a quick toddle for years." Twisted body parts and numerous black and blue marks characterized the early days of his riding, but it pleased him mightily to know he could at his age "tumble off and not break." In no time he was "powder[ing] ahead at a comfortable judicial speed" and deriving much pleasure from it.

Both hands were required on the handlebars that first summer, however, and there was no fancy stuff. Judge Grant encountered Holmes one day on a narrow wooden bridge. He was "grasping the handles of his machine as if it were a demon." Grant waved. Holmes hung on to the bicycle and seemed not to notice. A few days later, Grant overheard him saying

Bob Grant waved at me from his bicycle, d— him. The next chance I get, I'll overrule him.

The bicycle nevertheless expanded Holmes's horizons, physically and socially. He no longer envied the free-roving yachts he could see from his window. He had his own means to freedom, five miles a day that first summer. Young women noticed him, and he flirted back. He also found his vehicle a "great democratic bond" that linked him with "laboring men who also are learning on most brotherly terms." Some years later, Holmes challenged Harold Laski with the proposition that whoever had invented the bicycle "did more for human happiness . . . than a dozen Bismarcks or Cavours."

IN THE SPRING of 1896, Fanny Holmes was fifty-five years old, almost fifty-six. She had periodic trouble with her eyes. She may have been postmenopausal, usually not the most creative period of a woman's life. Whether by design or accident, she was childless, considered a failing in a society that defined a woman's worth by motherhood.

When at her marriage she moved, in the time-honored fashion, from the security of her childhood home in Cambridge, where she had been surrounded by family and friends, to her husband's home in Boston, a city noted more for its iciness than for its cordiality, she became for the first time in her life a stranger, which could only have exacerbated the effect of the natural shyness and reticence she was said to have inherited from the Dixwells. "Things hurt her that I didn't mind," Wendell once said. His dalliances could not have done anything for her self-esteem. Boston matrons gossiped about him in their drawing rooms. One young husband threatened to divorce his wife if she spent another evening with Wendell Holmes. A female acquaintance visited a mutual friend regularly, and a room of the house was always reserved for Wendell's afternoon call.

His flirtations to date apparently had been harmless adventures in which he seems to have done nothing more compromising than quote poetry and offer amusing conversation—in the end, he would rather kiss a woman's hand than kiss a woman. But to a woman as sensitive and devoted as Fanny, his rovings had to have been damaging. It was said she feared even to open his letters from Europe lest she discover a hint of some philandering to distress her, and she kept the shades drawn at home, excluding, at least metaphorically, all the unwanted intrusions, including Wendell's flirtations. The sexual competition that much later brought Eleanor Roosevelt out of herself and caused her to channel her abundant energies into public affairs seems to have had the opposite effect on Fanny Holmes. Her despair only activated those dangerous centripetal forces that came to dominate her.

To add to her troubles, in the spring of 1896, she suffered another attack of rheumatic fever that permanently affected her health and appearance. She had been pretty as a young woman. Now she lost weight, her hair fell out, and the old vivaciousness seemed to have been washed out of her. The illness apparently completed the job nature and psychological pressures had left partially undone. She retreated into solitude, became a recluse, and took pains to hide the inner woman. She wrote few letters and ventured out of her home only rarely.

The effect of this aspect of Fanny's personality on Wendell is difficult to measure. Being a very private person himself, he undoubtedly understood and sympathized with most of her impulses, although it is unlikely he was aware of her jealousies. Remembering—another time, another place, another girl—could not but have caused him pain.

He himself, however, did not accompany her on her withdrawal from the outside world. On the contrary. More gregarious to begin with and in the mid-nineties experiencing a period of creativity and expansiveness, Wendell was enlarging his circle of friends. He was not above chatting with a stranger in a restaurant, then inviting him home for a cigar and a jaw. A well-known public figure himself now, Holmes also formed friendships with the prominent. He had the Sidney Webbs to lunch and the governor to dinner. Distinguished academicians and lawyers he had met on his trips abroad looked him up when they came to America. At the same time, he continued to participate in Boston's social life alone, the extra man at dinner parties, a fresh face at the tea table. So it perhaps seemed only natural that in the summer of 1896, Fanny, exhausted by her illness, should send him off to Europe alone—and inadvertently into the most emotionally charged affair he would ever know.

He had hated to go and leave Fanny who, although "much better," still seemed "weak." He went, however. He believed it "rub[bed] off one's rust to get among a new lot of people with different modes of thought."

He arrived in London on Saturday, June 27, at 3 A.M. Jet lag being a phenomenon of the future, he began later that same day the round of luncheons, teas, and dinners where the "new lot of people" would rub off his accumulated rust. Names of titled hosts and hostesses dominate his diary entries. John Stuart Mill and others he had met on his first trip abroad in 1866 had died in the interim, but Holmes still had a number of old friends to catch up with, including the usual contingent of women friends plus the British politician and diplomat James Bryce, jurist and legal scholar Albert Venn Dicey, Leslie Stephen, and, of course, Fred Pollock. The pace was "tremendous," but also "very fatiguing." He replenished his wardrobe in Old Bond Street and Piccadilly—several shirts, two pairs of calf boots, silk-lined black frock coat, several pairs of trousers, "knicker breeches," vests, a morning jacket, and an opera hat. Henry James came up to London from Surrey, where he had been living, to dine with Holmes on August 15. They had tea together the next day, and James saw his old friend off to Ireland, an unscheduled side trip that changed the tenor of Holmes's life for a period.

In early July, Holmes had begun to lunch and dine irregularly but often with a Lady Castletown at her fashionable Eaton Place townhouse. They apparently had met casually before, perhaps at some mutual friend's during one of Holmes's previous trips abroad, and in 1892, he had sent her the recently published first edition of his speeches. In mid-August, Holmes left London for Doneraile Court in Doneraile, County Cork, Ireland, Lady Castletown's ancestral home, where he stayed nearly a week—"an enchanting finish to a generally rejuvenating experience." Their correspondence began when Holmes left for Boston.

"It is the stopping so sudden that hurts," he cried out from the deck of the *Etruria,* which was relentlessly carrying him back to Boston. "I can only cling to your hand for a moment until the earth puts its shoulder between us—which is more than the world can do I hope in twenty years . . . my heart aches to think how long it may be."

He cried out again next day: "I sent you a line of farewell last night and now am well out to sea. But still I can't break off. There are so many things I should have said but only thought of too late."

He had a smoke with an old priest who had come aboard with him at Queenstown and "he seemed to keep me a little nearer to Hibernia. It is a gray morning with a leaden sea and I too am somewhat leaden— not from the sea."

Three days out he wrote: "The farther I get away the harder does it seem."

Whether he was postponing his return to domestic realities, or whether fatigue delayed him—the former seems more probable, although he blamed the latter—Holmes did not go directly to Beverly Farms and Fanny on his arrival in Boston but stayed in town for the night. His devoted Fanny, however, could not wait. "[A]lthough far from well," she hired a driver and horses and raced the thirty or forty miles from the North Shore to Boston, arriving at half past one in the morning. Rather lamely, he explained he had been torn between "joy" at seeing her and "shame to have her make the effort rather than myself—although I knew I ought not to do it on the infernal consideration of health which I have to remember all the time."

Over the next two years, Lady Castletown and Holmes corresponded regularly and, at least on Holmes's part, passionately, Holmes's heart giving a "jump" when he spotted her handwriting in his mailbox and feeling "bereaved" when "any long time elapses without my hearing from you." He lived from one expression of "tender feeling" to the next. He read and reread her letters, faithfully wore a keepsake she had sent him, and carried in his pocket a handkerchief "with a little infinitesimal dark smear upon it—with it I once rubbed away a—Do you remember?" Holmes in love was by turns abject, affectionate, anxious and depressed, emotional, exalted, confiding—as he was to no other—jealous, and whimsical.

Clare Castletown—the former Emily Ursula Clare St. Leger—was the only child of the fourth Viscount of Doneraile, whose earliest known ancestors had crossed the Channel with William the Conqueror. She was the wife of Bernard Edward Barnaby Fitzpatrick, K.P., P.C., C.M.G., second Baron Castletown of Upper Ossory, descendant of Irish chieftains, Eton- and Oxford-educated, officer in the First Life Guards, former sheriff of Queen's County and M.P. (conservative) for Portarlington; outdoorsman, big game hunter, and intrepid traveler to the world's out-of-the-way places.

Whether the long-suffering Fanny knew of her husband's involvement with Clare Castletown is uncertain. Holmes tried to keep it secret, urging Clare to "address always Court House, Boston." Holmes burned her letters to him and reminded her regularly to do the same with his.* But some friends were certain Fanny knew. What it cost her to tolerate it, however, probably never will be known. Had Fanny fussed, she would have been cast as the shrewish wife. Although she risked encouraging the relationship between Clare and Wendell, paying out the rope undoubtedly was safest, inflicted the least damage on her own marriage.

The relationship between Clare and Holmes differed from that between Fanny and Holmes. The electric current between Fanny and Wendell was strong and constant and did not require daily speeches.

---

*Fortunately for the claims of history, Clare Castletown did not do as Holmes directed. His letters to her were preserved by a cousin and ultimately turned over to the Harvard Law School, where they were incorporated into the body of Holmes's papers.

The geographical distance between Clare and Holmes increased uncertainties, necessitated frequent reassurances. Fanny brought the happiness of security; her devotion was unequivocal. Clare, a member of a continental society that did not disapprove of extramarital relationships, and free to indulge in others, seems to have diluted what happiness she offered Holmes with pain and anxiety, elements that had not previously marred the friendships Holmes had maintained with women, who seemed to succumb readily to his charm.

Clare Castletown, whom Holmes addressed affectionately as his "Beloved Hibernia," was a perfect romantic interlude for him as he entered the dangerously restless years of middle age. A few years before, he had mourned that he was "dying, Egypt, dying. . . ." She was, first of all, perfectly safe—living three thousand miles away, she was not likely to create a scandal. She was twelve years younger than he. The old armor, polished wainscoting, and family portraits at Doneraile Court appealed to the Brahmin in him, and she appears to have been everything that Fanny was not. Fanny was like Boston; Clare was more like Paris. She shared with Fanny the quick intelligence and keen wit that Holmes so appreciated, but while Fanny at this stage of her life was hiding from life behind drawn shades, Clare was riding out to meet it. He perhaps missed that in Fanny now. From all accounts, Clare loved life in all its brilliant and challenging manifestations. She was remembered as a daring horsewoman, a fine musician, gracious hostess, entertaining conversationalist, and accomplished linguist.

As she was to him, he was to her. The handsome and urbane American judge who talked literature and philosophy so amusingly undoubtedly offered a kind of relief from the locker-room world of shooting and soldiering that was her husband's. She had stalked reindeer with him in Norwegian mountains, climbed cliffs above the Irish coast, fished in the bays, fled Utes in Colorado, and explored less traveled areas of Egypt and Morocco. She may have been ready for a different sort of relationship, something less vigorously masculine, more attuned to the gentler, feminine, and aesthetic side of her nature.

Wendell Holmes in love was an emotional wreck. He spent blocks of time imagining her in the places where they had spent their too few and too brief hours together, remembering the kiss that "missed the lips and fell upon the tip of the nose." He recalled her "rose-scented hair," revived the memory of their last walk together whenever he came upon his boots still "stiff from the wetting of that day and dull from the oiling they got after wards." He sometimes departed at dinner from his usual teetotalism and drank Irish whiskey "in honor of Doneraile."

He teased her about her British roots, reminded her of them near the anniversary date of the Battle of Bunker Hill, the monument to which he could see from his drawing-room window. (That June 17 was also his wedding anniversary he tactfully did not report.)

Back on the bench, he had difficulty concentrating on the lawyers before him, for "thinking of an Irish conservatory" in which he still could hear the splash of the fountain. While the judges discussed and decided cases, Holmes wrote to Clare of life and love and law and all the things that mattered. He let his pen "follow its own course to you not knowing beforehand where it will come out." He pretended the inkstand in his chambers was Clare; he begged for her photograph and kissed her hands on every page.

He longed for a "magic carpet" to carry him off "to that conservatory for an hour when you were there." In his fantasies, he swept her off to a chateau in Savoy.

It appears that Lady Castletown was not quite so deeply involved as Holmes was. He complained of feeling "a little cool breath of transitoriness," and inwardly writhed at her hints "of all manner of new men." He noticed "that for a long time I have heard no more of the substantial *other*—the same I suppose who wanted to kill me etc. Will you kindly advert to him. Is he still in statu quo? Whatever that may have been? Has his importance grown? or how otherwise? Or has he happily demised?" Holmes "hated the thought" that anyone except himself should "know anything about [her] real feelings," although "some of [her] hints" made him wonder whether he really knew anything about her. He wanted to know "every minutest movement of [her] mind—every thought and whim—and eat them." He wanted to know every detail of her health, her doings, her thoughts, her feelings. He wished she "would just pulsate onto the page and record the whole of [her] self." He was exasperated when she hinted "at a long letter laying bare [her] inmost soul," then reneged.

He constantly sought reassurance, thought until they had "got accustomed to each other and perhaps always," he needed to be told "there has been no change, that one is still as dear as ever or a little more so (you are). . . ." He longed to see her; should they, he pleaded, "ever have that divine solitude of Doneraile together again?" The time, however, had not yet come. He would have to make do long distance.

BEFORE HOLMES LEFT for England in the summer of 1896, he had heard lawyers for Frederick O. Vegelahn, a local furniture manu-

facturer, argue the case for use of the injunction against striking upholsterers, members of the new trade unions that were forcing employers to ameliorate working conditions. *Vegelahn* v. *Guntner* was an important
case, and the court, which saw itself as the guardian of threatened
traditions, was cautious. The case was still on the docket when Holmes
returned for the fall term.

Like freedom of speech, the cause of labor was not making much
headway in the Boston of the 1890s. Many working men were immigrants, and xenophobia was prevalent among the respectable people; their
representative in the U.S. Senate, Republican Henry Cabot Lodge, elected
in 1893 to the seat that was once Daniel Webster's, was trying in 1896
to push a bill limiting the number of immigrants through the Senate.
Memories of labor violence were still fresh in local minds. Bostonians—
along with other Americans—well remembered the 1886 bombing of
Chicago's Haymarket Square. They recalled all too vividly the 1892 violence in Henry Clay Frick's Carnegie Steel Company in Homestead,
Pennsylvania, and they talked over brandy at the Tavern Club about
the 1894 Pullman Strike in Chicago when President Grover Cleveland
sent federal troops to move the mails, and a little-known federal judge
in Cincinnati, Ohio, William Howard Taft, wrote to his wife:

> Word comes that 30 men have been killed by the federal troops. Though it
> is bloody business, everybody hopes that it is true.

The issues in *Vegelahn* v. *Guntner* (George M. Guntner, agent for
the union) were typical. Unionized upholsterers, employed at Vegelahn's factory, had submitted a request for a nine-hour working day and
a pay increase. When Vegelahn refused, the upholsterers called a strike
and assigned pickets to patrol the streets in front of the factory to prevent Vegelahn from hiring outsiders. Vegelahn went to the courts for
an injunction prohibiting the pickets. Sitting in equity session, Holmes
granted one temporarily, until the full Supreme Judicial Court could
consider the questions the case raised.

It could hardly have been surprising when in November 1896, the
judges of the Massachusetts Supreme Judicial Court, speaking in traditional terms of the upholsterers' liability for damage to Vegelahn's
business, decided, six to one, that the picketing in question was an
"unlawful interference" with the constitutionally secured right of an
employer to "engage all persons willing to work for him" and his employees' "corresponding right to enter into or remain in the employment

of any person or corporation willing to employ them." The injunction must stand. A decade later, Holmes would encounter the same reasoning in the federal arena. Then it would be called "freedom of contract" guaranteed under the Fourteenth Amendment to the federal Constitution.

Holmes's "almost invariable practice" when he was unable to "bring [his] brethren to share [his] convictions" was to "defer to them in silence." In the Vegelahn case, however, he believed the "less popular view of the law" ought to be stated. As the sole dissenter, he could afford the luxury of presenting the radical side of the issue; the court had kept Massachusetts safe from further inroads by labor. Had he been the deciding vote in the court consultation, however, what would he have done?

During his first decade on the Supreme Judicial Court, in 1888, Holmes had joined the majority in issuing an injunction against striking employees in a similar case, *Sherry v. Perkins.* In that case, however, an undercurrent of violence colored the questions presented to the court. In *Vegelahn,* the factor of violence was entirely absent, which made Holmes's dissent a good deal easier. Over the intervening years, in an effort to understand labor's aims, he had become acquainted with one of the local labor leaders, and the two men had discussed the state of labor's world "with some little profit." Holmes had reconsidered some principles of public policy involved in the changing relations between labor and capital and had come to the conclusion—had published it in the *Harvard Law Review* two years before—that courts, which consistently upheld the right of businesses to combine against their competitors and struck down labor's attempts to accomplish the same ends, might well be "flying in the face of the organization of the world which is taking place so fast, and of its inevitable consequences."

Vegelahn required a judge to decide between two established principles of public policy that had come into conflict: combination and conspiracy to injure another's business was a cause for action; on the other hand, ruining another's business was what competition was all about, and hadn't society generally accepted the idea that free competition was "worth more than it costs"? On that ground, the infliction of damage was, as lawyers said, "privileged," or in other words, public policy considerations outweighed strict measurements of liability. Combination and conspiracy could be justified if public policy and "social advantage" made them desirable. Holmes assumed his brethren would agree that the conflict between labor and capital was competition in the usual sense. If they preferred, he would substitute "free struggle for life," the Darwinian concept he had developed twenty years before in his article on the London gas-strokers' strike. He concluded:

> One of the eternal conflicts out of which life is made up is that between the effort of every man to get the most he can for his services, and that of society, disguised under the name of capital, to get his services for the least possible return. Combination on the one side is patent and powerful. Combination on the other is the necessary and desirable counterpart, if the battle is to be carried on in a fair and equal way.

Dissenting in *Vegelahn* had been "painful," but he had "to face the music once in a while." He boasted that "men of weight in this community" had for some years considered him a "very dangerous man"; he dismissed the characterization as a misunderstanding of judicial impartiality—too often thought to be "impartiality within the limits of the prejudices of the judge's class—not more." Shortly after the decision was handed down, a local labor leader approached Holmes to compliment him on his dissent. Holmes, who prided himself on his own impartiality, replied: "You wait—you'll hate me like Hell the next time."

Three months later, in January 1897, Holmes delivered one of his best-known speeches, "The Path of the Law," at the dedication of a new hall at Boston University School of Law; it was reprinted in the *Harvard Law Review* for March 25, 1897. During the decade of the eighties, he had stressed in his speeches the nobility of the law as a calling, trying to make lawyers aware that they were engaged in more than a trade, that they were involved in the subtle process of shaping the law. During the decade of the nineties, he advanced his ideas of the architecture of the law.

In his book, *The Common Law,* he had developed a number of general legal principles that had evolved over hundreds of years out of the changing needs and desires of society. In "The Path of the Law," sixteen years later, after debunking the prevalent twin fallacies of legal evolution out of ethical systems and theoretical logic, he tried to demonstrate the importance of the law's keeping pace with social and economic change.

He declared it "revolting to have no better reason for a rule of law than that so it was laid down in the time of Henry IV." It was "still more revolting if the ground upon which it was laid down have vanished long since, and the rule simply persists from blind imitation of the past."

Perhaps recalling his recent encounters with his brethren as they thrashed out the Vegelahn case, he criticized judges for failing "adequately to recognize their duty of weighing considerations of social advantage." Socialism, for example, had scared "the comfortable classes of the community," and Holmes suspected that the fear that some socialist principle lurked in every piece of progressive legislation and behind every working man's complaint had "influenced judicial action." He was really rather weary of watching judges reach outside their constitutions for ways to save "economic principles which prevailed about fifty years ago."

That winter and spring of 1897, Holmes did little outside of his courtwork. Every time he "fired off" the opinions he had been assigned, a new pile appeared. But at the moment he liked what he was doing, and had found that "the main excitement of life" for him was the "gradual weaving of his contribution into the practical system of law." He had found that the end was "unattainable," but the pursuit was "satisfying."

George Shattuck, who had been a kind of professional father to Holmes, died that spring. They had been friends for three decades. Holmes believed he owed the older man more than he ever had owed "anyone else in the world, outside [his] immediate family." Holmes would not soon forget the "benevolent beaming in his face and heart," and his passing meant still another vacancy in the life of a man who had within little more than a decade lost all his immediate family.

Not everyone thought of Holmes as a dangerous man. There were others who were talking about him as a potential appointment to the United States Supreme Court. He tried not to listen, realizing that New England's quota was one justice (Horace Gray in 1897) and that "politics count for much." But he confessed he would like to know that *his* word "was always the last."

Brown University invited Holmes to speak at its annual alumni dinner held the night before commencement in June. Holmes thought he was to receive an honorary degree, but realized shortly before he left for Providence that he was to have his "trouble for nothing." He and Fanny had been reading aloud from Fridtjof Nansen's recently published *Farthest North*—"as beautiful as a Greek statue"—and *The First Crossing of Greenland,* and Holmes delivered to those young men standing nervously at the brink of life an address crammed with the imagery of arctic exploration as a metaphor for individual struggle and calculated to inspire them to "start for the pole."

Ned's son, Edward Jackson Holmes, also called "Ned," was married that summer. Fanny emerged from her solitude long enough to accompany Wendell in a hired horse and buggy to the wedding in Windsor,

Vermont. The enchantment of the drive through the Connecticut Valley, the music of bobolinks, the beauty of the New England hills, all combined to rejuvenate, at least temporarily, Fanny who was "wonderful in her sources of imaginative humor and forethought and seemed to awaken to a life and joy which she has not known for a good while." He hoped in vain, however, that the trip marked a new beginning.

At Beverly Farms that summer, the bicycle was still one of Holmes's favorite occupations. All decked out in pink silk shirt, worn felt hat, and white cotton breeches, he and Brooks Adams would pedal fifteen or twenty miles a day over the unfinished roads along the North Shore, talking "on all subjects of earth and heaven." They divided sharply, for example, on the viability of Holmes's beloved "external standard" of measuring legal liability, Holmes arguing that a man's mental state was irrelevant to his behavior, Adams answering that the law could not ignore the mind's role in a man's behavior; solely objective criteria would in the end destroy a man's sense of social responsibility.

By August of 1897, a year had passed since Holmes had been at Doneraile with Lady Castletown, but he thought he and she were "closer to each other today than ever." He imagined himself with her in the conservatory—"and the things I say are true and you like them no less." Time had made their "intimacy more settled and more certain," though he still fretted he might misunderstand her "hints that may mean much or nothing." He took them "to mean much."

By the winter of 1897, Holmes was making plans to return to his "Beloved Hibernia" the following summer. In December, he told her it was still too soon to decide whether "this year is to be made happier to me by seeing you again." Fanny suggested he go, but he knew "very well that if I do her summer will be duller than if I remain." In addition, Fanny still had not fully recovered from the rheumatic fever of the year before and he couldn't "bear" to leave her "until she seems better than she does now." He was, he told Clare, "rather balled up."

A month later, in January 1898, Lady Castletown was clearly tempting him. "When you take your tone of bonhommie," he wrote her, "sunlight returns and when you show a touch of deeper feeling I pay for it at this end in joy. For the last weeks you have been adorable— and I keep saying to myself Oh if I *should* see her this summer—my wife rather eggs me to go. It is pure generosity on her part because she thinks I shall enjoy it etc."

A week later, he was less certain, although still eager. "For some reason," he told her, "I know not what you seem particularly near in these later days—perhaps because I am thinking so much as to my chances of seeing you this summer." He had not, however, been "quite as well as usual" in recent months, and he thought he would talk with his doctor before committing himself to the trip—"though," he added, "this doesn't mean that I shall come if he says yes."

She would have to make the trip worth it. "Do you swear," he demanded, "that I should see a great deal of you if I come? or would it depend on chances which I will not seek to analyze more precisely?"

Ten days later Holmes approached the chief justice about his summer plans. If he decided to go to Europe, he asked, could the final conference of the court be moved from June 21 back to June 14? The chief justice "hummed and hawed and didn't commit himself—but I *guess* (as we say) I can make them do what I want when the time comes, if I go."

In the meantime, Holmes brought Clare closer by rereading some of her letters before "committing them to the flames." He found them more charming than ever, and "less hard-hearted than [he] had imagined when [he] first read them." He supposed his "first impression was because [he] wanted so much." The letters made him "quite wild" to see her.

By mid-February, he had "very little doubt" that he would "come over this summer unless something goes wrong unexpectedly." He imagined "all sorts of adorable romantic visits or excursions, such as England is full of— . . . even a hansom in London is an enchanted solitude. But indeed there will be enchantment wherever I see you and when I think of it with any realizing feeling my heart stands still."

Lady Castletown had provided him with a list of places to stay, but he rather favored Mackellar's in Dover Street where he had stayed before and where he had had a room and a little parlor on the ground floor. "I have even known," he wrote temptingly, "a lady to venture in on occasion, when we were going somewhere together. . . . I long to see you."

Traveling at the time with her husband in Morocco, Lady Castletown appears to have been unable or unwilling to commit herself to the romantic adventures Holmes offered her, and he wrote in mid-March, disappointment spilling over into indignation, "I shall wait anxiously for an answer to my enquiries whether your last letter meant that there was any, the slightest doubt of my seeing you *somewhere*. I have assumed that you would make an effort if one were necessary. I need not say that I would. The spring is in the air and you are in my heart."

In the meantime, the U.S.S. *Maine* had been blown up in Havana harbor, and the usual contingent of jingoists was marching. Added to Lady Castletown's uncertainty of their meeting, the possibility of war with Spain cut sharply into Holmes's expectations for a trip abroad that summer. Everything was shaky, he told her, except his affection. Nevertheless, he continued to hope, and was "working like a fiend" to set his affairs in order—just in case.

By the end of May, John Hay's "splendid little war" had begun in earnest, and Holmes's hopes for his trip abroad grew dimmer still; he worried, along with many other people situated near the East Coast, lest a new Spanish armada arrive to bomb them into submission.

Then, on the first of May, Admiral John Dewey and his Pacific fleet steamed into Manila Bay and entirely destroyed its Spanish counterpart which, for all its size, was ill trained and ill armed. With the fall of the Philippines, the war was for all intents and purposes over. It remained only for Theodore Roosevelt and his Rough Riders, along with the U.S. Army, to subdue the Spanish forces in Cuba, and America's Atlantic naval squadrons to dispatch the Cuban remnant of the Spanish fleet to the bottom of the sea.

"Dewey's success gives me wild hopes," Holmes wrote his dearest Hibernia on May 3, although his uncertainty had not ended. He had, he said, "learned caution by experience."

By early June, Holmes was all but committed. "Today," he reported on June 7, "it looks more as if I should come. The vicissitudes I go through with regard to the chances of seeing you . . . are really very wearing. I will try to avoid talking about it until I am more certain." Two days later he was "nigh insane with the question of coming to England." He had just about decided to postpone it, when Fanny stepped in, urged him to go, and threatened "horrid results if I do not. I fear," he added, "I shall be a selfish pig if I do, and I don't know." As he wrote, his mind was running ahead of his pen, and he "almost decided not to come. I will not go into the reasons which really amount to a delicate balancing of what is the fair thing etc. under existing circumstances—but I do entreat you neither to scold nor to turn away in vexation." He was more disappointed than he could describe, and desperately implored her: "If I have entered into your life hold fast to me even though it has to be with a hand (I kiss it) stretched across the Atlantic."

And then he changed his mind again. By mid-June he was asking the Pollocks to reserve for him a bedroom and sitting-room parlor at Mackellars. To another friend he explained: "Mrs. Holmes made up her mind that I needed the change, and I deferred, if I did not come round, to her way of thinking. Naturally I am skipping about a bit to get ready and get off."

At last, on June 25, he sailed aboard the *Umbria*. He wrote proudly in his diary the first night out that he had sat on the captain's right at dinner.

He landed at Queenstown on Saturday, July 2, and by Sunday midday he was lunching in London with the Pollocks, the beginning that summer of rubbing off the rust. The usual round of luncheons, calls, teas, and dinners with the titled and otherwise prominent followed at the usual steady pace. He was one of Henry James's first guests at Lamb House, James's new place in Sussex.

So far he did not mention what seemed to have been the main purpose of his journey. His diary holds no references to lunches or dinners in Eaton Place, although he later spoke of wonderful experiences in a hansom cab he wouldn't mind repeating. On Friday, July 29, he left for Ireland where he spent almost a week at Granston Manor in Abbeyleix, in Upper Ossory, a wedding present to the young Castletowns from Lord Castletown's father. Even then he did not mention Clare's name, although he did Lord Castletown's and listed him as a good friend whom he had acquired on this trip.

On Friday, August 5, he started back to London, where, according to his diary, he began a second round of social events, but, according to the sparsity of entries in his diary, at a somewhat reduced pace.

Toward the end of August, he returned to Ireland, arriving at Doneraile on August 22, whereupon he scribbled in his diary an unintelligible note about the conservatory. Alas, three days later, he suffered a painful attack of shingles, the "visible signs of which [he] was ashamed," which tormented him for several weeks and whose soreness did not leave him for several months. Although he was in misery, he stayed on until August 27 when he boarded the *Etruria* and started for home. The Nantucket Light Ship was spotted on Friday, September 2; the *Etruria* docked in New York at 9:30 A.M. on the following day, and Holmes, exhausted and ill, caught a train for Boston immediately.

It is apparent from Holmes's subsequent letters to his "curly headed Norman angel" that the emotional content of their relationship had deepened that summer:

I am here in the kind of collapse that comes after nervous tension. . . . I hope my voyage letter caught the return steamer so that you will get it by

the end of the week. I think you will see from it how I yearn and long for
you. Your telegram met me and gave me a joy which I can't express. . . .
I loved your "tender" and hugged it to my heart. And now do you think
that you can meet time and distractions and still care for me as much? I
believe you will. I firmly believe that time will make no difference to me.
O my dear what joy it is to feel the inner chambers of one's soul open for
the other to walk in and out of at will. It was just beginning with you. Do
not cut it off because of a little salt water.

He hinted that she was his "dark lady," and talked of the case of another man who wanted "to make many a mother if his existing encum-
brances only might be gathered away, as he had a lawful lady." It was
Holmes's first hint that were he not married, things might have been
different. Previously he had told her somewhat sternly: "My life is my
wife and my work," then softened the harshness of his tone with: "but
as you see that does not prevent a romantic feeling which it would cut
me to the heart to have you repudiate."

Three days later, he was going to try, "by aid of a bike," to forget
her for an hour or two a day, but had little hope of success. He would
be biking alone, an activity "conducive to reverie," and he was more
likely to break his nose "from forgetting to watch the road than to succeed in [his] attempt." He relived their time together: "Oh my dear I
go with you to all the places where you remember me. Each has its own
particular charm. Only it seems that if I might be with you in each
once more I should be would be must be nicer than the last time and
make sure that every memory should be of unmixed charm. . . . Do
assure me that the pain of separation does not outweigh the joy of confidence and belief in the abiding. . . . I kiss your hands—your feet if
you like and send my love."

He "devoutly" believed their love could defy time and distance, and
he longed to hear her "repeat again and again" that she believed it equally
devoutly—that it would not be different when she had become "accustomed to separation and when all the distracting influences begin to
work once more." He longed, in fact, "to know a lot of things more
definitely." He wondered if she revisited the conservatory. Before he
went abroad in June, he had prayed he might keep his health until he
had seen her once more. Now, in September, he renewed his prayer
that he might see her still another time. "Surely," he reminded her of
their intimacy, "you will never again find it hard to talk from your
heart. I feel as if we should begin where we left off, no matter what
time had elapsed. Meantime let us talk straight in our letters as you do

so adorably in the one which I have received and which I hug to my bosom." He skipped a local garden party, partly because shingles still kept him feeling "rather seedy," but more because he "did not want to see the gay world if [Clare] were not there."

The old doubts began to creep in again. He began to wonder about other men in her life. He was resigned to worrying a good deal "before reaching the equilibrium of perfect knowledge." Faith was all he had, but he had an abundance of it. "I believe in you," he told her, "and trust you and love you dearly. I long long long for you and think think about you."

A few more letters of this ilk followed, and then suddenly the correspondence as well as Holmes's expressions of ardor tapered off. Whatever subtle deepening of their relationship had occurred during that last summer may have made Clare realize that Holmes was serious, something she perhaps had not counted on. Their expectations for such affairs were quite different. For Holmes, the relationship was unique, the commitment strong and enduring. For Clare, the handsome Yankee was undoubtedly a casual playmate whom she enjoyed for a time but in the European way was ready to discard as nonchalantly as a dancing partner. Perhaps she had already found another playmate who talked as prettily and was more accessible. She was obviously not Holmes's alone even during the best times of their relationship, and it was said she had been another's mistress. She suggested to Holmes that time and distance made it "impossible to really keep in touch."

The suggestion hurt him and she made his "heart bleed." He clung fiercely to the expectation that it was "possible to be unchanged after 20 years." A year's separation had not changed his feeling for her; he "care[d] for" her "just as much as when [they] were together," and every year "new little roots grow out and bind you tighter." He urged her to write, his desperation apparent in his prose, and say she was not "taking back anything [she] said when [he] was there." He pleaded with her to confirm that she loved him "still the same." Despite his anguish, time, distance, prior commitments, differing ways of life, all combined to defeat them.

Most of the later letters that have survived are less passionate, less personal, and more general. Holmes returned to England and Ireland, even to Doneraile, several times after 1898, but it was never again the island of enchantment it once had been.

Were Holmes and Clare Castletown lovers? There is no solid evidence either way, but probably not. On Holmes's part, there is the question of sexual impotence to consider. If it was true—and again, there is no solid evidence either way—and if the cause was physiological, the question need not even be asked. If it was true, and if the cause was psychological, it is entirely possible that he could be impotent in Boston but not necessarily so in Ireland, where he may have felt freed of the usual constraints and where a singularly attractive and experienced woman of the world had transformed him from a straitlaced judge to a passionate suitor years younger in spirit if not in chronological age.

The evidence, however, although circumstantial, points to a highly charged emotional, but not a physical relationship. Europe may have been permissive, but the circles in which Holmes moved in Boston were not, and however freer he might have felt away from home, he undoubtedly was always conscious of his position and not one to defy fundamental social protocols. His letters, passionate though they were, were not the letters of sexual intimacy. Contrast them, for example, with the letters of Edith Wharton and W. Morton Fullerton, who *were* lovers. While Mrs. Wharton recalls their secret rendezvous in a London hotel, Holmes can only refer enigmatically to what happened in the conservatory at Doneraile, as if that was the setting for their most ardent romancing—undoubtedly a place with severe limitations on activities amounting to more than a few furtive kisses. There is, too, a sense of completedness about the Wharton-Fullerton correspondence that the Holmes-Castletown letters lack.

Their involvement was probably not physical but emotional, which is not to say it was lesser in degree. The emotional engagement was deep, the commitment, at least on Holmes's part, serious. A physical relationship, while it undoubtedly would have enhanced the association, does not seem to have been necessary for deepening it.

HOLMES HAD BEEN back from abroad less than a month when a case came to the court that allowed him to unwrite one of those "revolting" rules that had been laid down hundreds of years ago, the grounds for which had "vanished long since" and the rule simply "persist[ed] from blind imitation of the past." The case, *Commonwealth* v. *Cleary,* was an appeal from a conviction for rape.

Shortly after 10:30 in the evening, a fourteen-year-old-girl, crying, excited, and frightened, had run to a friend's house. At midnight, the friend took her home, still frightened and trembling. Her mother put her to bed. The following morning, the youngster told her mother she had been raped the night before. Although an old rule of evidence required that the victim's complaint must be "fresh"—made immediately following the crime—the trial judge had admitted the victim's statement, and the alleged rapist had been convicted. He had appealed on the ground that the victim's statement had been "too remote in point of time to be admissible."

Holmes, for a unanimous court, affirmed the conviction. He ventured that the child had not been in a condition to speak until she had rested. The old rule was based on a "natural presumption that a virtuous woman would disclose it at the first suitable opportunity." Holmes disagreed. He thought rape was "about the last crime" in which such a presumption could be made. He could easily conceive of a pickpocket's victim talking about it, but what "sensitive woman" would be willing immediately to "disclose such a horror"?

Looking into the history of the rule, Holmes discovered the reason for it. The victim of a rape in those ancient days had been required to raise hue and cry immediately so the offender could be pursued. Nineteenth-century New Englanders, however, had developed more sophisticated methods of pursuit and systems of evidence. The rule had long outlived its usefulness. Holmes called it a "perverted survival" of an "ancient requirement." The youngster's statement was admissible; the old rule was dead in Massachusetts.

Shortly after the decision in *Commonwealth* v. *Cleary* was handed down, Holmes used that case and several others in which he had participated or with which he was otherwise familiar to elaborate on what he had written. The occasion was a major address on January 17, 1899, to the New York State Bar Association. Called "Law in Science and Science in Law," it was reprinted in the *Harvard Law Review* for February 25, 1899.

It was a long and scholarly disquisition, with excursions into property transfer practices among fifth-century Germanic tribes, and the ancient origins of surety as well as the early legal requirements in cases of rape, and it would have required the undivided attention of the assembled lawyers to pursue Holmes as he twisted and turned through his collection of legal antiquities. In *The Common Law,* he had demonstrated the development of contemporary legal concepts from primitive practices. In "The Path of the Law," he illustrated how overreliance on tradition impeded the natural development of the law. In "Law in Science and Science in Law," he dealt with theoretical aspects of legal history and described the processes of legal evolution: how an early legal practice might die a natural death, how another might adapt to a purpose other than its original one, how still another could survive intact for centuries, although it no longer expressed the desires of the community and had lost its vitality along with its utility.

After nearly two decades on Massachusetts's highest court, he was no longer surprised at the slow pace of legal evolution. "Judges," he explained, returning to a theme of "The Path of the Law," "are commonly elderly men, and are more likely to hate at sight any analysis to which they are not accustomed, and which disturbs repose of mind, than to fall in love with novelties." His object, he said, was "not so much to point out what seem . . . to be fallacies in particular cases as to enforce by various examples and in various applications the need of scrutinizing the reasons for the rules which we follow, and of not being contented with hollow forms of words merely because they have been used very often and have been repeated from one end of the union to the other."

History was useful to explain the past, but too many people used it to straitjacket the present. In advising men who aspired to careers in the law, he recommended not Blackstone or Coke on Littleton, the bibles of his generation of law students, but—as a "labor-saving" device— "books nearest to everyday life and common modes of thought." Law, he said, was a "practical thing. The first thing you want to aim at is to make it a practical weapon in your hands."

In the summer of 1899, Holmes achieved one of the two goals he had set for himself in his youth. On the death after a long illness of Chief Justice Field in July, Holmes, fifty-eight years old and sole survivor of the court he had joined in 1882, succeeded smoothly as if by foregone conclusion to the chief justiceship of Massachusetts. He presided for the first time on September 12, 1899, at the court's session in Pittsfield. The court clerk read his and William C. Loring's commissions in open court. Loring was the new associate justice appointed to fill out the court when Holmes moved up. A veteran of fifty-two years at the Berkshire County bar, Marshall Wilcox of Pittsfield welcomed Holmes to the county by recalling the chief justice's "early residence" there.

The succession held no terrors for Holmes; as senior associate justice he had been "bossing the show" ever since Chief Justice Field had fallen on his way from the courthouse to the Union Club in Boston six months before. At last, though, Holmes was able to write all the opinions he could handle—he need no longer plead with the chief justice for more work—and in fact during these last years on the state court, he did increase his annual output by thirty-five or so opinions. A year later he gleefully told Henry James he was firing away at high pressure with breech loading speed. . . . All there is is a nervous spasm and it pays better in the long run to take it in the form of intellectual explosions than in women or wine.

Unfortunately, the joy of promotion to higher office was mixed with personal sorrow. Toward the end of the year, both Uncle John Holmes, who had given pleasure to so many of the lives he touched, and Epes Dixwell, who had given Fanny life, Wendell learning, and both of them love, died, Uncle John at the age of eighty-seven, Epes Dixwell at the age of ninety-two.

In September 1899, shortly after Holmes succeeded to the chief justiceship, another divisive labor question reached the Massachusetts Supreme Judicial Court—that of the closed shop. *Plant* v. *Wood* involved a two-year-old contest for supremacy between two unions of painters and decorators for control of the business in the Springfield area, with one of the unions threatening strikes and boycotts unless it alone was recognized by employers. There had been no violence, and no property had been damaged; the aggressors had in fact been "courteous in manner," their language had been "mild" and "suave." The rival organization, however, resisted the overtures and sought to enjoin the conspirators from attempting to interfere with employment. The Superior Court granted the injunction.

It required the judges a year to make their decision, but ultimately the Massachusetts Supreme Judicial Court upheld the lower court. Once again, Holmes was the sole dissenter.

The majority reiterated much that it had said in the Vegelahn case four years before. Every man had a traditional right to "dispose of his labor with full freedom." It was a long-recognized legal right and was "entitled to legal protection" from obstruction. Physical violence or injury need not be present; it was "not necessary that the liberty of the body should be restrained. Restraint of the mind" was sufficient to bring the law into play.

Hoping perhaps to hoist Holmes by his own petard, the majority went on to adopt the reasoning of his dissent in *Vegelahn*. The behavior of the aggressors had been calculated to cause financial damage and had done so. Unless, then, there was justifiable cause, unless public policy countenanced it, unless the conduct was privileged, the acts were malicious and unlawful.

Holmes was pleased to note that his brethren adopted his own legal rationale, and he went along with their opinion to that point. He was not, however, entirely persuaded, and he felt compelled to dissent.

The majority had not been able to find the justification; the judges saw no necessity for the plaintiffs to join the rival union. They saw only the right of the plaintiffs "to be free from molestation," and they found the conduct of the aggressors "intolerable, and inconsistent with the spirit of our laws." The injunction must stand.

Holmes seems to have been amused by, even to have enjoyed his early reputation as a radical—Dr. Holmes's innovative work on childbed fever had earned him a similar reputation among the medical profession's old guard. But by 1900, he may have wearied of it, realizing it was conferred not for the legal substance of his opinions but because the public thought he was advocating labor's cause. In *Plant* v. *Wood*, he carefully distanced himself from the political undercurrents and declared his complete neutrality. He cherished, after all, "no illusions as to the meaning and effect of strikes." He recognized the strike only as a "lawful instrument in the universal struggle of life," and may the best man win.

He did not have to look very far to find justification for the conduct of the aggressive union. He assumed his brethren would have found lawful the threat of a boycott or strike intended to raise wages directly. This case was only "one degree more remote." The purpose of the conduct in question had been to strengthen one union "as a preliminary and means to enable it to make a better fight on questions of wages or other matters of clashing interests." Unity of organization, he believed, was "necessary to make the contest of labor effectual"—"if the battle is to be carried on in a fair and equal way," as he had said in *Vegelahn*—and he believed it lawful for a body of workmen to try by combination to get more than they had been getting, "even at the expense of their fellows."

THE LAST MASSACHUSETTS Supreme Judicial Court judge to have his portrait painted wearing his robe had been Increase Sumner, who had resigned in 1797 to become governor. The justices had been sitting robeless for more than a century when in March 1901, in response to a petition from thirty or forty leading members of the local bar, they again appeared in the courtroom wearing black silk robes. They had kept their preparations secret for some time and planned to "astonish" the bar when they appeared. When the great day came, however, a visiting clergyman, invited to open the court session, found on arrival "a roomful of dignified gentlemen wandering about in a bewildered fashion, some of them with their gowns still in their hands, one or two with their gowns put on askew." Holmes welcomed him heartily.

"Ah, an expert," he said, as the visitor showed him and his brethren how to carry the ribbons across their chests and tie them behind so they could march into court with the dignity the occasion required. As word got out that the justices had changed their clothes, the courtroom filled with the curious.

Holmes thought the new robes would "add to the dignity of the judicial proceedings." Then, with the same detachment with which he allowed an enactment of the legislature to stand, he added that the new fashion "would inconvenience no one except the justices themselves and followed the wishes of the bar."

Two full summers had passed since Holmes last visited the mother country, and in the summer of 1901, undoubtedly feeling the need for spiritual refreshment, he sailed for England aboard the *Umbria*. The customary social whirl awaited him, punctuated by meetings with "Ly C." and capped with a visit to Ireland, although the reunion did not seem to affect him so deeply as that in 1898 had, and he seems to have retained his emotional equilibrium. He stayed once again at Mackellar's Hotel in Dover Street and saw all his old friends, who were "properly effusive—perhaps a trifle more gray hair . . . than once—but the tremulo is not quite banished."

He had kept in touch with Henry James. During the winter before Holmes sailed, he and Fanny had been reading aloud from James's *A Little Tour in France* (1885). He sometimes grieved that while he and James "retain[ed] the old affection there [was] no communication between [them] on [their] respective activities and interests." But he thought it would be "all right" when they met; old friends, they would take up where they had left off. James "rejoice[d]" at the prospect of their reunion even though Holmes on his visits to England was in the habit of baiting James because the latter had chosen to escape abroad rather than face the pressures of American life. If so, James apparently took it well. His attitude remained affectionate toward his old friend, although his expressions of friendship may well have been less for Holmes himself than for a cherished time and place that had long ago ceased to exist for Henry James.

After several weeks of "luncheon and dinners every day" Holmes had had *"all"* he wanted, and on August 25, he sailed aboard the *Campania* for Boston, which he would be "overjoyed to reach." He adored English society. It was "difficult of access and yet the most democratic in the world." If you had something to contribute, "you are passed around pretty quickly." But at the end of the summer he was tired and ready to resume the old comfortable routine. A little time at Beverly Farms with Fanny and among people he had lived amid for years ought to prepare him for almost anything a chief justice of Massachusetts should have to face.

As he approached the two-decade point of his judgeship, Holmes stopped momentarily to take stock. The bar thought he "talk[ed] too much," didn't "give 'em a chance enough to develop their ideas," and he vowed to be a "monument hereafter" even though he thought it "uncivilized to have to listen to speechifying instead of telling at once where my trouble is when I am the man they want to convince."

There were times during the last two decades when he had thought that "every man's hand was against [him]," and he grieved that

we judges . . . are taken rather adversely—every decision is disagreeable to one side and the traditional compensation is to blackguard the judge.

He was frankly disappointed that he had not been able to influence the law of Massachusetts in the ways he had hoped. When he looked into his docket book, he found about a thousand cases:

A thousand cases, many of them upon trifling or transitory matters, to represent half a lifetime! A thousand cases, when one would have liked to study to the bottom and to say his say on every question which the law ever has presented, and then to go on and invent new problems which should be the test of doctrine, and then to generalize it all and write it in continuous, logical philosophic exposition, setting forth the whole corpus with its roots in history and its justification of expedience real or supposed!

Despite the flood of cases and the constant pressures to churn out opinions in such a wide variety of cases, Holmes had tried to bring some perspective to his work, "to see the law as an organic whole . . . as a reaction between tradition on the one side and the changing desires and needs of a community on the other." As he considered the options available to resolve constitutional conflicts, to work out formulas for fixing legal responsibility in tort cases, or to settle contract disputes, he had tried to realize that society's "different portions want[ed] different things and that [his] business was to express not [his] personal wish, but the resultant, as nearly as [he] could guess, of the pressure of the past and the conflicting wills of the present."

All people remembered afterward, however, was that he had spoken out for the rights of organized labor in *Vegelahn* v. *Guntner* and *Plant* v. *Wood*. Nobody remembered that he had tried to dissociate himself personally from labor's cause, noting that he cherished "no illusions as to the meaning and effect of strikes." People only remembered that he had said the strike was "a lawful instrument in the universal struggle of life."

He had defied the code of the Boston gentlemen and the gentlemen did not soon forget it. And when not long afterward he was nominated for the United States Supreme Court, what opposition emerged originated among the Boston gentlemen. It was, however, precisely Holmes's judicial position regarding labor relations that contributed significantly to Theodore Roosevelt's interest in Holmes's appointment to the United States Supreme Court—that and perhaps a vague recollection that a few years before, Holmes's "Soldier's Faith" had seemed to strike the proper militaristic tone. Roosevelt, who had been kicked upstairs to the relative ineffectiveness of the vice presidency, who now in 1902, thanks to an assassin's bullet, was president of the United States, and whose reform programs included a place for labor in his "square deal," no doubt discerned in Holmes a judge who looked at social and economic problems from a modern perspective. The author of the dissent in the Vegelahn case could be an invaluable asset to the federal judiciary and to a progressive president whose own party was dominated by conservatives. It would make a substantial difference, Roosevelt said, "whether a Judge of the Supreme Court came down heads or tails."

Part *VII*

THE WASHINGTON YEARS

Whenever a law that the judge holds to be unconstitutional
is invoked in a tribunal of the United States, he may refuse
to admit it as a rule; this power is the only one peculiar to
the American magistrate, but it gives rise to immense
political influence. In truth, few laws can escape the
searching analysis of the judicial for any length of time, for
there are few that are not prejudicial to some private
interest or other, and none that may not be brought before a
court of justice by the choice of parties or by the necessity of
the case.

—Alexis de Tocqueville, *Democracy in America*

CHAPTER *16*

Appointment

BOTH ACCIDENTS OF history responsible for Holmes's appointment to the United States Supreme Court might have been prevented. William McKinley might have been more cautious in his public appearances, thus reducing the chances of an assassin's success, and Holmes might have followed Boston's example and snubbed his old friend Henry Cabot Lodge during a political crisis in the latter's life. But neither of these iffy events occurred, and just after the twentieth century dawned, Holmes stood at the brink of fulfilling an ambition he had cherished for many years.

Horace Gray of Massachusetts, associate justice of the United States Supreme Court, was seventy-three years old in 1901 when William McKinley was inaugurated for the second time, and the question of Gray's successor was already on the president's mind. Tradition suggested but did not require that Gray's replacement come from Massachusetts, or at least New England. McKinley opted to follow tradition and went for recommendations to his secretary of the Navy, John Davis Long, former governor of Massachusetts and sponsor of Oliver Wendell Holmes on the state supreme court. Long recommended not Holmes this time, but Alfred Hemenway, his own former law partner and a prominent member of the Boston bar. Hemenway was sounded out, found willing to accept the nomination, and the matter seemed settled; Justice Gray had only to resign.

In late April, McKinley left Washington on a transcontinental train trip. He did not return. On September 6, in Buffalo, New York, he was shot while shaking hands with the crowds that had come there to see the Pan American Exposition. He hovered between life and death for eight days. He died on September 14, and "that damned cowboy" became president of the United States.

In February of 1902, the aging Justice Gray suffered a stroke. Although he did not resign immediately, speculation regarding his successor immediately began. First it was reported that Chief Justice Oliver Wendell Holmes of Massachusetts was to be appointed; then it was reported he was not. Roosevelt in any case did not feel bound by the informal arrangement his predecessor had made with Hemenway.

For some months Gray had hoped to return to the court, but the deterioration of his health accelerated. Both his family and physician urged him to resign, and rumor soon accomplished what the importunings of those close to him had failed to do. Henry Cabot Lodge, junior senator from Massachusetts, quickly got in touch with his close political and personal friend, Theodore Roosevelt:

> I hear that Judge Gray is so much more weak that he has resigned. I do not know whether it is true but if it is I want of course to talk with you before you decide.

There was no telling what maverick the president might discover among the assortment of unorthodox people with whom he socialized. He was capable of acting precipitately and impulsively. Lodge wanted to be certain he put one of their crowd on the U.S. Supreme Court. Although Senator George F. Hoar outranked Lodge in the Senate and was dispensing Massachusetts patronage when Lodge was nothing but a young history teacher, and Hoar's wishes would have to be considered in regard to the court appointment, Lodge was the man to whom Roosevelt listened.

The eighteen-year-old friendship between Lodge and Roosevelt had been forged at the Republican Convention of 1884, to which they had been delegates from their respective states, Massachusetts and New York. Together they had opposed the presidential nomination of James G. Blaine of Maine whose cavalier attitude toward reform and scandalous carryings on as congressman, speaker of the house, and secretary of state sickened them, and had offended the Republican party leadership by putting forth a candidate of their own, Senator George F. Edmunds of Vermont, not a particularly creative senator, but a pillar of morality. Although Lodge "dislike[d] and distrust[ed]" Blaine "thoroughly," Lodge— unlike many of his associates including his new friend, Theodore Roosevelt—supported the party's choice, explaining via the usual political euphemism that he could do more for reform within than without the party, and he dutifully campaigned for the national Republican ticket in Massachusetts, even ran himself for Congress. Like Blaine, Lodge was defeated in the general election in November, but his party loyalty earned him another nomination in 1886, and he was elected; he served six years in the House of Representatives before he was finally elected to the Senate, where he remained until his death in 1924.

If any positive gain for Lodge came out of the political campaigns of 1884, it was the cementing of his friendship with Theodore Roosevelt; they remained close both politically and personally. For the rest of their lives, they were "Cabot" and "Theodore," whatever high offices they achieved.

They were an unlikely pair. Although he attained high political office, Henry Cabot Lodge, of the socially prominent Boston Cabots and Lodges, was not a natural political animal. He was an observer, an intellectual, a writer of history books and a former history instructor at Harvard whose classes had been avoided by Roosevelt as a student because Lodge had a reputation for demanding too much and grading papers too severely. He had to force his smile when the shoemakers and farmers and tailors of Massachusetts lined up to shake his hand. Roosevelt, on the other hand, a scion of the New York Roosevelts and no less an aristocrat than his friend, was a doer and a beaming presence; he could make each farmer, each tailor, each shoemaker believe he was shaking hands with a long-lost friend. What bound these two opposites together were their shared views on the significant national issues of the day, their strong Republicanism, and their kinship, social as well as political, to the men with money and manners, the traditional American ruling class who shared similar backgrounds and experiences, friends, schools, and clubs; they intermarried—Roosevelt's first wife had been a Lee, of the Boston Lees, to whom Holmes's mother was close kin—and reproduced themselves, and with only a few exceptions, it was the men of this class who had been the judges, senators, and presidents since the earliest days of American nationhood.

Holmes's Civil War record, his Brahminness, his Republican party loyalty, his contributions to legal history, his authorship of *The Common Law,* even his record as a judge in Massachusetts might have gone unnoticed, and he might have lived out the remainder of his judicial life as chief justice of the Massachusetts Supreme Judicial Court, had he not been an old and loyal friend of Henry Cabot Lodge.

Holmes had known Lodge long before Lodge had become a U.S. senator, although Holmes later said, "I saw him little and rarely got talk that hit me where I lived." Lodge was nine years younger than Holmes, but they had been "thrown together from time to time," and had shared a number of experiences: a Boston Brahmin's upbringing, friendships with fellow members of the establishment, Mr. Sullivan's grammar school, Mr. Dixwell's Latin School, Harvard College where Lodge had been one of Holmes's students in constitutional law, the burlesques of Hasty Pudding, Harvard Law School, and summering on the North Shore. Holmes had in fact been present at Lodge's summer place in Nahant and had shared the general family joy the day Cabot passed the entrance examinations for Harvard College. In 1867, the two young men had gone on a hunting trip to Illinois where they had shot prairie chickens together.

Two explanations for Lodge's strong advocacy of Holmes for the U.S. Supreme Court have been advanced. It was rumored at the time that a nonpartisan, anti-Lodge faction in Massachusetts was planning to nominate Holmes for the Senate next time, and Lodge was heading them off. This is patently false. Holmes never would have run for the Senate, and Lodge, who had discussed elective office with him previously, knew it. The second explanation is more likely: a fellow Brahmin's loyalty and sense of obligation to an old friend.

The incident which forever bound Lodge to Holmes—Lodge never forgave an enemy, but he also never forgot a friend—occurred in the summer of 1884, following the Republican National Convention that had been so disastrous for Lodge and Roosevelt. Lodge's loyalty to Blaine, which had earned his party's appreciation, had cost him dearly among his friends, who, believing he had put political ambition ahead of integrity, cut him dead; he was practically an outcast in Boston. Critical letters poured in. "Only God and his mother know what that poor boy suffers," his mother told a close friend, tears streaming down her face.

Judge Wendell Holmes, however, was one of the few who had stood by Lodge, made a point in fact of crossing the street to speak to him, to shake his hand publicly, and to assure him he had been right to support the Republican ticket. "In his position on the Republican Committee," Holmes believed that "as a gentleman," Lodge could not have done otherwise. Lodge never forgot Holmes's kindness, and when in the spring of 1902, it became clear that Horace Gray was too sick to return to his seat on the U.S. Supreme Court, Lodge opened his campaign to put his loyal friend, Wendell Holmes, in Gray's place.* He called on Gray at

---

*Holmes was not the only beneficiary of Lodge's largesse. "For all people who stood by me then I have felt a gratitude ever since which nothing can efface," Lodge wrote in 1908. He helped George H. Lyman, who also supported him, become a collector of the Port of Boston, and William Wharton, another loyal friend, become an assistant secretary of state.

Nahant, to which he had scurried following the adjournment of Congress. They discussed Gray's successor, and Gray agreed that if Roosevelt did not want to appoint his secretary of the Navy, forty-nine-year-old William H. Moody, because of Moody's comparative youth, Holmes was next best.

Not everyone in Massachusetts was so agreeable to the appointment of Holmes as were Lodge and Gray. Eben S. Draper, a local textile manufacturer, opened his own campaign to stop Holmes's appointment and suggested a noncontroversial U.S. Circuit Court judge, Francis Cabot Lowell III, to replace Gray. Lowell, Draper said, was "most eminently judicial in his mind . . . absolutely honest . . . and of very much more than ordinary ability." "Some of the state's most eminent lawyers" would consider Lowell's appointment "a most excellent one." They also thought the appointment of "our present Chief Justice" would be a "very serious mistake." Lodge replied that he himself favored Chief Justice Holmes. Draper persisted:

> There is no man that has a higher respect for the personality of the gentleman referred to than I do, but I think it would be a very grave and serious mistake if he should be appointed to the Supreme Bench of the United States. While it would naturally be difficult to get lawyers to express this opinion under all the circumstances, I know that there are many prominent lawyers in Massachusetts who have this feeling very strongly. They think he is erratic, and that he is not a safe man for such an important position.

When Lowell's name did not appear in the speculations, Draper wrote again. He had heard that Samuel Hoar, Senator Hoar's nephew, was in the running. He felt

> perfectly certain that the appointment of Mr. Hoar would give a great deal better satisfaction to all the business interests of the state than would the appointment of Judge Holmes, and I also believe the legal profession would be better pleased.
>
> [S]peaking politically . . . I think the appointment would be a great deal better. Mr. Hoar has always been a staunch Republican, and has taken an interest in the work of the party always, and has a great deal of influence. He is an honest, able, and fearless man, and his relationship to Senator Hoar would at the present time make it an extremely graceful thing for the President to appoint him. I think it would help the President very much with the entire party in the state. . . .

Draper left it unsaid, but Lodge knew he was referring to Holmes's dissents in the Perry, Vegelahn, and Wood cases, and that Holmes had flirted with socialistic concepts in his dissent to that advisory opinion on municipal coal and wood sales. Roosevelt seriously considered Draper's candidate, Judge Lowell, but rejected him.

Knowing Gray would resign shortly, Lodge presented his candidate to the president, hoping perhaps that his personal influence with Roosevelt would outweigh local opposition. Holmes, Lodge reminded Roosevelt, was chief justice of Massachusetts.

It would be hard to pass him by—hard on him. He is as Judge Gray says profoundly learned and of brilliant mind.

Although Lodge expected Holmes's appointment would prove a popular one, it would not, of course, be without opposition. Hoar and others would object on the grounds of Holmes's labor opinions. Lodge had talked, he told Roosevelt, with members of the local bar and had concluded that "these decisions are the basis of all the opposition"; at least one lawyer described Holmes as positively "dangerous" on labor matters. Lodge dismissed the comment as "of no importance, really," and reiterated how disappointed he would be if the president passed over his friend Wendell. "I know how he would feel it," Lodge said, "and I am very fond of him and he is in the line of promotion." (Horace Gray had been appointed when he was chief justice of Massachusetts.)

Roosevelt reacted about the way John Adams might have reacted if Cabot Lodge had recommended John Marshall for appointment to the U.S. Supreme Court. He wanted to be certain Holmes was "in entire sympathy with our views."

When the news of McKinley's being shot reached J. P. Morgan, the financier was said to have first cursed, then staggered to his desk while his face alternately reddened and paled. Charles M. Schwab of the United States Steel Corporation was quoted as saying that if McKinley died, "business would surely suffer." The specter of a White House inhabited by Theodore Roosevelt, with his reputation as a reform-minded New York State assemblyman and president of the New York City Board of Police Commissioners, was not a pleasant one for businessmen to contemplate.

Brimming with self-confidence and energy, ebullient, impulsive, and essentially conservative underneath his widely publicized cloak of progressivism—the creature of his upper-class background—Roosevelt was the first president since Lincoln to fully understand the nature of presidential power, and he did not hesitate to use it in trying to ease the transition from the individualistic agricultural society of an earlier America to the interdependent, cooperative society which the new industrialism had created in the second half of the nineteenth century. Like many men of his class, he thought it "incumbent upon the man with whom things have prospered to be in a certain sense the keeper of his brother with whom life has gone hard." Physiologically so nearsighted that he once mistook a statue of Apollo for one of Diana, he was politically so farsighted that, like his cousin Franklin later in the century, he wanted to apply stringent measures to a floundering economy not in order to destroy it—although both Roosevelts were accused of betraying their class—but in order to preserve it.

He was to call his program the "Square Deal." No revolutionary impulses reverberated through his being, and he aimed his shafts at the extremes of both right and left, although he was balked at every step by conservative Republicans in Congress. He intended only, through moderate government regulation—never government ownership—of finance, business, industry, and transportation, to ameliorate the widespread poverty that had resulted from the amassing of great wealth in the hands of a few. He stood, however, far from sponsoring anything like wholesale democracy. He would curb the abuses of his own crowd because he feared revolution if he didn't. "They had better accept me," he said, "I am on their side. I believe in wealth. I belong to their class. They had much better accept me, instead of some [William Jennings] Bryan who'll come along and ride over them roughshod."

Holmes's labor opinions interested the president. At the time Lodge was pleading Holmes's case, Roosevelt was preoccupied with a coal strike—"as difficult as it well could be"—that threatened not only national economic disaster but also the defeat of the Republican party in the approaching congressional elections unless the administration could somehow persuade labor and management to work out their differences. Part of Roosevelt's reputation as a Progressive was based on his support as a New York State assemblyman of a bill to prohibit the manufacture of cigars in the tenement houses of New York City. He was one of the few from his social class who sensed that "More and more the labor movement in this country will become a factor of vital importance, not merely in our social but in our political development." Unless his crowd not only did justice, but also could "show the wage-workers that [they were] doing justice," Roosevelt predicted the country would "someday go down before a radical and extreme democracy with a crash which will be disastrous to the nation."

Roosevelt thought Holmes's labor opinions a "strong point" in Holmes's favor. "The ablest lawyers and greatest judges," he added, were "men whose past has naturally brought them into close relationship with the wealthiest and most powerful clients, and I am glad to find a judge who has been able to preserve his aloofness of mind so as to keep his broad humanity of feeling and his sympathy for the class from which he has not drawn his clients." Holmes's reputation, in other words, could only help the administration in its dealings with organized labor.

Recalling perhaps Holmes's "The Soldier's Faith," which he had given on Memorial Day, 1895, and about which Roosevelt had been so enthusiastic—although in 1902 he referred to it mistakenly as Holmes's "Phi Beta Kappa speech"—the president expected he could rely on Holmes "to be in favor of those principles in which I so earnestly believe." Given the popular interpretation of "The Soldier's Faith," and Roosevelt's taste for American imperialism, the "principles" in which he "so earnestly" believed may well have been a veiled reference to what were known as the "insular cases," which had split the Supreme Court only a few months before.

These cases dealt with relations between the United States and its newly acquired overseas possessions, Puerto Rico, Hawaii, Guam, and the Philippines. They posed the question whether these territories were an integral part of the United States, like New Jersey—in the popular idiom of the time, whether the Constitution followed the flag—or whether new territories should be treated as subject nations. Many people in the United States agreed with Senator Francis G. Newlands of Nevada that the "ignorance and inferiority" of the native populations made constitutional government in the territories neither practical nor desirable. The real issue, however, was economic. If the territories enjoyed the same status as New Jersey, their exports to the United States came in duty-free, and their manufacturers were on the same footing as American industrialists, clearly an unwelcome competition. When two cases involving tariffs on Puerto Rican imports came to the U.S. Supreme Court in 1901, the justices, 5 to 4 with Horace Gray in the majority, arrived at a complicated compromise that treated Puerto Rico as neither a state nor a subject nation, but left its status up to Congress.* If and when Congress decided to incorporate a territory, the Constitution would then apply; until then, however, the territories were constitutionally all but defenseless, and the tariffs were safe. Or, as Mr. Dooley put it, "the Constitution follows the flag on Mondays, Wednesdays, and Fri-

* *DeLima* v. *Bidwell.* 182 U.S. 1 (1901) and *Downes* v. *Bidwell.* 182 U.S. 244 (1901).

days." The compromise satisfied the Republicans, but the Supreme Court
majority was slim. A vociferous minority which "stood for reactionary
folly" posed a constant threat. How, the president wanted to know,
would Holmes react in future insular cases?

Roosevelt recognized Holmes's "high character" and "high reputation"; in addition, "his father's name entitle[d] the son to honor." The
chief justiceship of Massachusetts guaranteed "the highest professional
standing." Still, there was something more about Holmes that vexed the
president. Hadn't he sounded awfully soft on judicial power in that
speech he gave a year or so ago on the centennial of John Marshall's
ascension to the chief justiceship of the United States? The address,
Roosevelt told Lodge, had been "unworthy of the subject," and Holmes
had shown a "total incapacity to grasp what Marshall did."

Holmes's address on John Marshall was not in fact as forceful as
Lodge's had been on the same anniversary. Lodge had thundered:

> At one stroke . . . Marshall asserted the supremacy of the Constitution
> and the power of the court in relation to the other branches of the National
> Government. . . . He made men understand that a tribunal existed before
> which States could be forced to plead, by which State laws could be an-
> nulled, and which was created by the Constitution. He took the dry clauses
> of the Constitution and breathed into them the breath of life.

Had Roosevelt been familiar with the reasoning of those state court
opinions of Holmes in which the Massachusetts judge had deferred emphatically to legislative power—Holmes's dissent in *Commonwealth* v.
Perry, for example, or his dissent in the advisory opinion involving municipal sales of wood and coal—the president would have known then
that Holmes was no John Marshall, that however warm the personal
relationship between Cabot and his Massachusetts friend, Holmes could
never have made the speech Lodge had made, that his noncommittal

> if American law were to be represented by a single figure skeptic and wor-
> shipper alike would agree without dispute that the figure could be but one
> alone . . . John Marshall.

was as far as Holmes could go. What, Roosevelt wanted to know, did
Cabot think?

While Roosevelt was composing this very letter to Lodge, Justice
Gray's resignation arrived—it was to take effect either on the appointment of a successor, or as Roosevelt otherwise desired. Speed now be-

came imperative. Perhaps, the president suggested, Lodge might further sound out Holmes, and if he still appeared to be dependable, Holmes might visit Roosevelt at the summer White House in Oyster Bay, Long Island, during which Roosevelt could discover for himself Holmes's views. If Holmes then passed this final test, his appointment could be announced immediately.

Lodge agreed "most profoundly" with the president's comments and promised to talk to Holmes "with absolute frankness," for the senator would not consider his "best beloved" for the Supreme Court "unless he held the position you describe." Lodge promised to elicit Holmes's views; if—and only if—Holmes was "absolutely and wholly allright— entirely with us"—Lodge would send him to Roosevelt at Oyster Bay.

Lodge immediately scheduled a date to meet Holmes; their discussion served only to reinforce Lodge's enthusiasm for his old friend's appointment. Holmes was, the senator concluded, "our kind right through," and he passed him up to the president.

Holmes's friend Richard Olney, a former attorney general and secretary of state, had been keeping him up to date on events in the nation's capital, and Holmes himself was neither unaware that his name was under consideration for the Supreme Court vacancy nor uninterested in the outcome of the talks. Gossip and the newspapers kept the subject alive all that summer, while the subject of the discussions, when he wasn't presiding in the state court, tried to relax at the summer house in Beverly Farms where he and Fanny had established a comfortable vacation routine of reading and driving about the rugged North Shore countryside.

Horace Gray himself wrote Holmes in a shaky hand that his health had not improved as rapidly as he would have liked, that he did not think in his condition he could resume the work of the Supreme Court, and that he had sent in his resignation to the president. Gray undoubtedly meant to reassure Holmes, but suspense generally made Holmes nervous, and the letter may well have added to the tension. Perhaps recalling his disappointment in the outcome when he had last (1878) been considered for a federal judgeship and had broadcast his interest in it precipitately, he did not even tell his friend Pollock that his name had been suggested for the Supreme Court.

He rode his bicycle for recreation and exercise, worried about getting fat—his clothes had become "instruments of torture"—and dabbled in negotiations between author (his friend Owen Wister) and publisher (Houghton Mifflin) for a biography of his father. (The book never materialized.) He journeyed to Ipswich to speak at the unveiling of memorial tablets to two of his earliest American ancestors, Governor Thomas Dudley of Massachusetts and his daughter, Ann Bradstreet, New England's first published poet. And he drowned his anxieties in books, going "agreeably down hill" from philosophy (Josiah Royce's *The World and the Individual* and William James's *The Varieties of Religious Experience*) to Flaubert (*L'Education Sentimentale*) and finally to a "book which I put in my pocket if I see a lady coming."

He arrived in Oyster Bay on July 24. The president, however, was off for the day in his yacht, and his return was delayed by fog. Holmes dined that night with the Roosevelt children, who quizzed him about his participation in the Civil War. It was still one of his favorite subjects, and undoubtedly he enjoyed indulging the youngsters' interest in it; although the memories were forty years old now, they were still vivid.

The discussion between the American president and the Massachusetts judge, when it finally took place the following morning, pleased both men. Roosevelt was "entirely satisfied" with Holmes's views. The president knew exactly how to appeal to Holmes, who suffered from feelings that his work was not fully appreciated: He offered the nomination in a way that Holmes could "regard [it] as a triumph . . . a reward for much hard work." Holmes was given to understand that the Supreme Court nomination was his, although he was to tell no one but Lodge for the time being, so he scribbled into his reading list for 1902:

July 25. Presdt offered me Judgeship

Roosevelt was not ready to announce his decision publicly. Senatorial courtesy required that Senator Hoar, not only the senior senator from Massachusetts but also chairman of the Senate Judiciary Committee, be placated. Hoar had successfully opposed Holmes's appointment to the federal bench in 1878 and unsuccessfully to the Massachusetts bench in 1882. As Holmes was to put it later, "I think [Hoar] doesn't lie awake nights loving me."

When Roosevelt assumed the presidency in 1901, Hoar expressed "great satisfaction" that his colleague from Massachusetts, Henry Cabot Lodge, and the new chief executive enjoyed such a close relationship. Although Hoar and Lodge represented different generations in politics— Hoar had been a senator since 1877, when Lodge was in his first year of teaching at Harvard and a virtual neophyte in politics—they saw eye to eye on many matters. Both men, alumni of Harvard College and Harvard Law School, had worked for the defeat of Benjamin F. Butler in his various campaigns for congressman and governor of Massachusetts.

Party loyalty was high on the list of priorities of both men, and both men had supported Blaine in 1884—at some personal cost. The nomination of Oliver Wendell Holmes to the U.S. Supreme Court, however, nearly ruined their amiable political partnership.

Hoar was furious, more perhaps because Lodge had gone behind his, the senior senator's, back than because he was still trying to get his nephew, Samuel Hoar, made a judge or because he had serious reservations about Holmes's ability. He wrapped his anger, however, in criticism of Roosevelt's arrogance toward the public.

There was no doubt, Hoar told Roosevelt when he was informed of the president's intentions in late July, that the chief executive had an "absolute right" to make appointments with or without his or anyone else's advice. The traditional method, however, Hoar reminded Roosevelt, had been to let the public know of the vacancy, allow a reasonable time for those interested—especially the legal profession—to publicize their views, and to make the appointment while the Senate was in session. Roosevelt had ignored the rules. While Hoar's letter was in transit, Roosevelt reiterated his confidence in Holmes. "I hope Hoar will be reasonable," he told Lodge, "but I shall send in Holmes's appointment anyway."

Hoar, however, was not inclined to be reasonable. He could hardly oppose the chief justice of his state publicly with impunity, especially when his own nephew was in the running for the appointment, so he protested confidentially to Lodge. He admitted Holmes was an accomplished man, but

> his accomplishments are literary and social, and as an investigator of the history of jurisprudence, and not judicial. He lacks strength.

His opinions, Hoar complained, as Draper had previously, had no respect among members of the legal profession, and when he succeeded to the chief justiceship of the Massachusetts high court,

> all the strong men of the profession thought his appointment a distinct lowering of the standards of our Supreme Court. . . . In his opinions he runs to subtleties and refinements, and no decision of his makes a great landmark in jurisprudence or serves as a guide for the courts in after cases.

Hoar supposed the press and the public, "who know little, except that Judge Holmes is an accomplished and agreeable gentleman, with a charming literary style, will think it is all right." Among the lawyers he made a practice of talking to wherever he met them in his journeys about the state, he "never heard anybody speak of Judge Holmes as an able judge."

The president had enough trouble in the Congress; he wanted none with Hoar and tried to make amends, explaining that he had not discussed the matter with Hoar sooner partly because he had not known when Justice Gray would resign and partly because he had assumed a prominent Massachusetts man would be entirely satisfactory to the state's senior senator. If Hoar had evidence of Holmes's unfitness, he should submit it, but quickly; Roosevelt was not one to tarry when his mind was made up.

Even after Roosevelt announced Holmes's appointment, Hoar continued to berate Holmes, although he promised "everything [he] can do and say will be toward making the best of it," and he "would be sorry to have [Lodge] or the President think that [he was] petulant, or unreasonable, or governed by any desire except to have one of the greatest acts of his administration performed in a great way." Nevertheless, Hoar told Lodge, a bright young Worcester lawyer recently had told Hoar that he and his law partners had agreed that a new chief justice in Massachusetts would be "a great improvement." Another had ventured the opinion that perhaps on the Supreme Court of the United States, working among such strong men, Holmes "would get rid of his crankiness," but his partner had replied he didn't think "that was possible."

Hoar, however, capitulated. "I dare say," he told Lodge, "the matter of the Associate Justice would have turned out pretty much in the same way if the President had taken six months to consider it, and had consulted everybody. So I do not mean to worry about it any more."

Roosevelt finally announced Holmes's nomination on August 11 and predicted unanimous confirmation by the Senate. Holmes reacted to it by going bicycling with Brooks Adams, who fancied himself an informal advisor to Roosevelt—he called himself the Roosevelt administration's "unofficial philosopher"—and who also had recommended Holmes's nomination to the court. When the newspaper reporters swarmed at Beverly Farms and interrupted Holmes's dinner, he feigned surprise, as was—and is—traditional. If the report of his nomination was true, he told them, he would "certainly accept. Personally I know nothing of the matter beyond what you tell me, my first intimation that I had been, or was going to be, chosen coming from the press."

"When will you resign your present position?" a reporter asked.

"Hardly before the Senate approves the President's nomination," replied Holmes, who was not unaware of the vagaries of politics or that the "money powers" considered him "dangerous." Except to add that he was appreciative of the nomination and "the honor it conveys," he refused to make any further comment. He did not, he said, "like to be interviewed."

Holmes's nomination was received with varying degrees of enthusiasm and intelligence. He himself was not so sure how to respond to it, and his emotions were mixed, though it was unlikely he would not obey his commander-in-chief's order to charge the next earthworks. While the appointment had been hanging fire, he had written to William James a cool and formal acknowledgment of James's gift of *The Varieties of Religious Experience*. The tone was as if they had never met, had never as young men twisted the tail of the cosmos over whiskey in Holmes's little room on Beacon Street. Four days after the appointment was announced, a more relaxed Holmes, overcome perhaps by the nostalgia accompanying anticipation of the dramatic changes about to occur in his life, wrote James with considerable more warmth:

> Some day, here, in Heaven, or in the world outside of time and space . . . we shall talk together again with that intimacy of understanding and mutual stimulus which we have known and I never forget.

Leaving Boston, home for sixty-one years, would not be easy, and he talked of the "sadness of heart that goes along with much joy." He was "Well," but didn't know whether he was "happy or not":

> There is much that is oppressive in the moment—and I find that I usually put out a good deal of emotion before I discover what I am feeling.

People who knew Holmes disagreed about whether he actually was so eager for the Supreme Court appointment as generally has been assumed. Francis Biddle, one of Holmes's secretaries (1911–12) and author of an early biography of Holmes, wrote that the judge wavered, that he had not been eager to leave the chief justiceship of Massachusetts to become what he called a "side-judge" and only Fanny's importunings had persuaded him to accept. Thomas G. Corcoran, another secretary (1926–27), wrote a similar account. Felix Frankfurter, long a close friend of Holmes's, dissented. He took issue with Biddle directly: "I do not believe Holmes and Mrs. Holmes talked in the way in which you indicate when he was asked to come down here. He certainly did not lack self-confidence and he was eager to come. The real question was whether she was ready to come out of the retirement which she had created for herself in Boston."

Fanny in fact, whatever she told Biddle long after the fact, indicated at the time of Wendell's nomination that she might indeed not have been ready. She was trying not to think about Washington, and when she did, she remembered a friend who had thought he was going to be made ambassador to the Court of Saint James, and then another was sent in his place. She kept on wearing her "plain brown dress" and was making "no new plans." Her one concession to the future was in deciding not to put down the thick carpets as she usually did on the first of September. Almost wistfully, after the nomination was announced, she would remind friends that "perhaps the Senate will not confirm the nomination"; she could not think of anything Washington offered to compensate for what she was leaving behind.

It was whispered within the legal establishment that certain lawyers were not sorry to be losing the chief justice. They complained he was too much of a scholar, dogmatically logical, and too quick to take an all-round view of a case.

Inclined to take stock of his past achievement on momentous occasions, Holmes would not have been satisfied if he gave credence to what the newspapers were saying. Most of the editorials focused on his labor opinions. The *Literary Digest* pronounced the nomination "more interesting than momentous" and the nominee "friendly to the labor unions." The *Independent* declared that "workingmen generally will welcome Justice Holmes's accession to the Supreme Court bench, as he has long been the consistent friend of organized labor wherever he has found it acting within its rights." The *World* agreed: "The quality of a radical is perhaps strikingly shown in his stand on industrial questions, of which he is a student. His legal opinions have almost always leaned to the side of the laborer." The *Boston Evening Transcript* added: "Justice Holmes has not been a great judge. He has been more of a literary feller than one often finds on the bench, and he has a strong tendency to be brilliant rather than sound. . . . The new justice embodies new views of new questions . . . those which involve the rights of capital and labor under the novel conditions bred of modern tendencies toward the consolidation of wealth and organization of labor. We must consider it, on the whole, a fortunate circumstance that Justice Holmes has made a record in Massachusetts as a defender of the right of laboring men to organize and to seek the ends of such organization."

Those periodicals that did not concentrate on Holmes's labor opinions worried what he would do in future insular cases. Conceding that

Holmes's nomination would be "extremely popular," the *New York Times* rated his work below that of "the country's jurists of the first rank" and frankly wondered whether Holmes would unite with the dissenters in the insular cases to reverse them. The editors thought this contingency possible but "improbable."

Holmes deplored these political assessments of his judicial career. They made him look like a dispenser of favors when in fact he had tried to maintain strict neutrality. A reputation as a dispenser of favors to organized labor, in addition to his own distaste for it, could mean death to a Supreme Court nomination in the Senate. He had hoped his contributions to the development of the law over the past twenty years, perhaps even his book, might have been mentioned. Editorials identifying him as the son of the Autocrat of the Breakfast-Table particularly jarred him; the younger Holmes had hoped he had made his own place by this time. He complained that "they don't know much more than that I took the labor side in *Vegelahn* v *Guntner.*" It made him "sick" that he had "broken his heart in trying to make every word living and real" to watch "duffers" discuss in print matters about which they knew nothing. The "moment of ostensible triumph" had been virtually ruined. If he hadn't done his "share in the way of putting in new and remodeling old thought for the last 20 years," he had "deluded" himself. "[I]n the main damn the lot of them."

A few days after Holmes's nomination was announced, he sat talking to a *World* reporter on the veranda of his home at Beverly Farms. Outwardly he seemed relaxed in a "roomy" sack coat and moccasins until an unaccustomed bitterness crept into his tone. Editors, he said, seemed "to labor under the impression that I am a self-appointed leader of a new school of socialism." Propriety prohibited him from commenting on his Massachusetts court opinions, of course, but he suggested that the "critics and commentators read them first and write afterward."

Ranking Holmes "in natural succession to Mr. Justice [Joseph] Story, Mr. Justice [Benjamin R.] Curtis, and Mr. Justice Gray," the chief justice of the United States, Melville Weston Fuller, whom Holmes had met in Chicago during his transcontinental trip in 1888, sent Holmes a message of "warmest welcome" from the Court. Justice John Marshall Harlan, the liberal senior associate justice, seeing perhaps a potential ally in the new appointee, predicted that "Holmes will, undoubtedly be a valuable accession to our Court, though this opinion is based upon his reputation rather than upon any personal knowledge I have of his ability. It is gratifying to observe that the appointment is favorably regarded by the country."

Because the U.S. Senate, which the Constitution requires to confirm all federal judicial appointments, was not in session when Holmes was nominated in 1902, and was not expected to be until after the Court term opened in early October, the question of a recess appointment arose. Holmes wanted no part of an appointment that subjected the nominee to the uncertainties of politics and held him hostage in the performance of his official duties. He wanted to continue on the Massachusetts court until the Senate confirmed him. Both Lodge and Roosevelt agreed this was the proper course. They had no reason to worry. Between 1795, when the Senate rejected John Rutledge for chief justice, and 1902, the Senate had rejected outright only seven other nominations to the U.S. Supreme Court. No difficulties in the confirmation of Holmes, who appeared to have broad national support, were expected.

Holmes spent the intervening months, in addition to presiding as usual in court, "burning papers, clearing up—horrid hob," at the same time "not yet assum[ing] that the change [was] to be." He tried to keep his "mind in the present" until the Senate confirmed him, and yet he had "to bother about arrangements and [was] interrupted and upset even more than if it was all certain." Recognizing his family's, especially Dr. Holmes's, ties to the Pittsfield area, he had unloaded a thousand of the doctor's books at the Berkshire Athenaeum some years before. He had mixed emotions about this current housecleaning. Getting rid of the accumulation of so many years made him feel better; on the other hand, he hated to see so much of the past disappear. His home "purged" of "everything that is not vital" made him feel "like a cut flower."

Marcus P. Knowlton, senior judge on the Massachusetts Supreme Judicial Court, who expected to succeed Holmes as chief justice, added to Holmes's anxieties. He was like "a fish out of water" waiting for Holmes to leave, even suggested that Holmes's remaining as chief justice would be interpreted as lack of interest in his federal appointment. Lodge reassured Holmes that he was taking the proper course, not to worry. Chief Justice Fuller injected another intimation of reality when he asked Holmes to be ready to take the oath and his seat on December 8—to which Holmes readily agreed, assuming that the Senate had confirmed his appointment.

In late October, a trip to Chicago to speak at the dedication of Northwestern University's new law school building temporarily diverted him. But he need not have worried. Events spun out smoothly, according to the president's script. Senator Hoar yielded with grace, and his judiciary committee reported favorably on the nomination. On December 4, the full Senate voted unanimously and without debate to confirm it. Senator Hoar himself informed Holmes by telegram that very day.

The night before, at Young's in Boston, two hundred lawyers of the Middlesex Bar Association listened to him say an emotional farewell. As was his custom, he spoke in the metaphor of the military.

> To have the chance to do one's share in shaping the laws of the whole country spreads over one the hush that one used to feel when one was awaiting the beginning of a battle. One does not forget the danger, but if victory should come! Victory shall come—with that the personal apprehension grows dim. The forces of one's soul rally and gather to a point. One looks down the line and catches the eye of friends—he waves his sword—it may be the last time for him or them—but the advance is about to begin. The troops are deployed. They will follow their leader. We will not falter, we will not fail. We will reach the earthworks if we live, and if we fail we will leave our spirit in those who follow, and they will not turn back. All is ready. Bugler, blow the charge.

There were a few snickers, and young Dixon Weston chuckled to his Uncle Melville (Chief Justice Fuller): "There is about to be a charge on your court."

Three days later, on December 6, Holmes arrived in Washington, where he was met at Union Station by an elderly black man who told him he had been Justice Gray's messenger and intended to continue on in that position with the new justice.

CHAPTER *17*

Settling In

On DECEMBER 8, 1902, the most recent appointee to the Supreme Court of the United States—and the first justice appointed in the twentieth century—Oliver Wendell Holmes of Massachusetts, was escorted by his new brethren into the crowded courtroom in the United States Capitol. Hardly anyone noticed that he paused briefly to hand the court reporter a telegram he wanted sent to the governor of Massachusetts. It was his resignation as chief justice of that state. Only now, seconds before he was to take the oath of his new office, could he believe in his appointment, acknowledge it officially.

Tall and slender, his silver mustaches and unruly eyebrows adding to a sense of aristocratic origins, his angular features recalling the craggy shoreline of his native New England, Holmes looked the picture of judicial dignity. In a ceremony that required less than three minutes, he repeated the oath of office in his halting, methodical speech and claimed his seat next to Justice Rufus Wheeler Peckham of New York—the seat to the extreme left of the chief justice, the traditional place of the most junior member of the Court. He shook hands with Peckham, the others bowed to him, and the Court went about its customary business of handing down decisions.

Holmes was the fifth justice in the court's history to come from Massachusetts, which had been represented on it for eighty-one of the institution's 113 years—by William Cushing, Joseph Story, Benjamin Curtis, and Holmes's immediate predecessor, Horace Gray. Holmes himself was to serve nearly thirty years under four chief justices (Fuller, White, Taft, Hughes) and six presidents (Roosevelt, Taft, Woodrow

Wilson, Warren G. Harding, Calvin Coolidge, Herbert Hoover—from Roosevelt to Roosevelt).

He had his admirers. His colleagues respected him and Brandeis had always said he was "the best intellectual machine." But he was not a national figure in 1902, only a state judge little known outside Massachusetts. Twenty years before he had written a scholarly book but it was of interest largely to other scholars, and the name Holmes still conjured up in the public mind sentimental couplets from the best loved of his father's verse. Still, it had been his good fortune to be placed among the most influential group of men in the United States. Only the presidency was more vigorously sought than a seat on the U.S. Supreme Court. Cabinet officers and senators willingly abandoned their political careers when called to the Court, whose impact on American history was second to no other branch of government.

There they sat, august and isolated, removed from the rough-and-tumble of the world around them, as if they looked with Olympian detachment on events that threatened to disrupt the operations of the planet. The pomp and dignity made it easier for them to pronounce judgment. A world of education and manners, emphasized by rich velvet drapes, thick carpets, leather chairs, and fine old wood, separated them from the lantern-lit railroad yards of New York and the mine-scarred hills of Arkansas—and all the other places where the cases they heard originated. Very little of that world intruded here. They were not, however, automatons or abstractions, living in a legalistic vacuum. Donning the black robes did not make eunuchs of them. As Holmes himself had noted in the opening lines of *The Common Law*, they were men, like other men, affected by their environment and their genes. Social class, geography, and personal economics colored their outlooks. They shared prejudices and passions, personal drives and professional ambitions. They had political preferences and religious allegiances—all of which had had "more to do than the syllogism in determining the rules by which men should be governed."

In 1902, the U.S. Supreme Court was not exactly a melting pot, but it was not so homogeneous as the Massachusetts Supreme Judicial Court had been, either. Holmes would have to adjust to dealing with men not from the several regions of the same state, but from the various regions of a vast continent. They ranged in age from fifty-seven to seventy; Joseph McKenna of California, a frail-looking, birdlike little man who wore rubber boots, a scarf, and an overcoat all the year round, was the youngest; John Marshall Harlan of Kentucky, a bald-domed, ruddy-complexioned giant of a man known as the last of the tobacco-spitting justices, was the oldest; on the bench he had developed a habit of pacing up and down behind his colleagues when he was bored, stopping in front of the spittoons placed at each end. They were Republicans, Democrats, Episcopalians, Congregationalists, Methodists, and Roman Catholics. Three—Holmes, Harlan, and Edward Douglass White of Louisiana—were Civil War veterans. One—Henry Billings Brown of Michigan—had hired a substitute to do his part in the war.

Significant commonalities, however, also marked this group of judges. Holmes would hardly have to adjust to the fact that nearly all his brethren came from the upper echelons of American society,* as had his Massachusetts colleagues. There were no railroad switch operators among the relatives of his eight new ones.

Old families of some distinction were also part of the judicial cachet in 1902. Chief Justice Fuller had had an ancestor on the *Mayflower,* a grandfather on the Maine Supreme Court, and several relatives prominent in the nineteenth-century New England bar. John Marshall Harlan's earliest known American ancestor was an English Quaker, George Harlan, who settled in New Castle, Delaware, in 1687. Henry Billings Brown had been born in South Lee, Massachusetts, to a New England Puritan family in which, he was fond of boasting, "there has been no admixture of blood for 250 years." Of the nine Supreme Court justices in 1902, only Joseph McKenna was not a Brahmin; his parents were poor Irish immigrants, his father a neighborhood baker.

Nearly all had had at least a smattering of formal law school education—Harvard, Yale, Albany, University of Louisiana—although at the time these men were learning their law, it was more usual to get a legal education by reading in an experienced and established attorney's office. McKenna, the exception, read law books to acquire the knowledge he needed to pass the California bar. He never felt quite sure of himself among his university-educated brethren, and just before he took his seat on the U.S. Supreme Court in 1898, he spent a period studying law at Columbia University Law School. This did not satisfy him, and during his early days on the Court, he was "frequently irritable, nervous, and rather unhappy because he was not familiar with the law nor able to construct an opinion that would express adequately the convictions of his colleagues." As a result he wrote interminable opinions filled

---

* Upper-class origins was a characteristic not only of the Fuller Court but of all the courts prior to the twentieth century. Of the fifty-six justices appointed during the eighteenth and nineteenth centuries, twenty-nine came from upper-class families (owners of large plantations, industrialists, bankers, merchants), twenty-one from middle-class families (lawyers, doctors, academics, clergymen), and six from lower-class families (subsistence farmers, pioneers, owners of small businesses).

with precedents, as if he was trying to convince not only his brethren but also himself that his judicial reasoning was sound. Envious perhaps of Holmes's large and handsome physical appearance and his even larger intellect, his Brahmin origins and elitist education, McKenna developed a sense of rivalry with the learned judge from Massachusetts. Their relations always remained cordial on the surface, but McKenna, sometimes to Holmes's annoyance, became Holmes's severest critic when opinions were circulated for the brethren's comments.

Holmes could feel comfortable in a professional way among his new colleagues. They shared earlier professional lives on local or state benches (except for Chief Justice Fuller) and at the bar, representing railroads, banks, and merchants. They knew their way around and understood the legal complexities of corporate America. But they were more politically oriented, less familiar with the paths and byways of John Austin's or Henry Maine's work, and there were no scholars among them with whom Holmes could share his philosophical speculations.

Like Holmes, all of them owed their present positions to a significant relationship with a powerful political figure. To win a seat on the Supreme Court, one does not take an examination in constitutional law; one need not even know anything about the subject. To win a seat on the Supreme Court, one knows the right people and holds the right views. In the matter of Supreme Court appointments, the cream does not necessarily rise to the top.

Chief Justice Fuller owed the twenty-two terms he sat on the Supreme Court to his deep devotion to the Democratic Party and his personal friendship with President Grover Cleveland. He had attended faithfully as a delegate every Democratic National Convention between 1864 and 1880; in 1884, while young Henry Cabot Lodge was working for Blaine, Fuller was working for Cleveland, the winner against Blaine. In return, Cleveland had nominated Fuller to succeed Chief Justice Morrison R. Waite on the death of the latter in March 1888. The press described Fuller as "the most obscure man ever appointed Chief Justice."

Although John Harlan had come to the party of Lincoln in mid-career—he had voted for General George B. McClellan in 1864, had opposed the Thirteenth Amendment to the Constitution as well as the Emancipation Proclamation—he owed his Supreme Court seat to a grateful Republican president, Rutherford B. Hayes. As head of the Kentucky delegation to the Republican National Convention in 1876, Harlan had been instrumental in securing the nomination for Hayes by switching Kentucky's votes from another candidate at a crucial moment.

It was rumored later that at a secret caucus prior to the balloting, Harlan had been promised a Supreme Court appointment in return for his loyalty to Hayes.

The very conservative Republican David Josiah Brewer, next in seniority to Harlan, owed his appointment to the patronage of Benjamin Harrison's general factotum in the Senate, Preston B. Plumb, whose henchman Brewer had once been back in Kansas.

The specific reasons for Edward Douglass White's appointment to the U.S. Supreme Court in 1894 remain clouded, although all suppositions originate in the political. It is unclear whether his nomination was a reward for Senator White's donkey work in the Senate in behalf of a number of the Cleveland administration's programs; whether he was kicked upstairs in order to get him out of the Senate, where, at the time of his appointment, he was uncustomarily *opposing* an important administration bill; or whether Cleveland, whose previous attempts to replace Justice Samuel Blatchford had been defeated in the Senate, believed the senators would not reject a fellow senator.

The decisions of these men, known as the Fuller Court in 1902, mattered to millions of ordinary Americans, however wrapped in abstraction their writing was. Questions of whether an employer was liable in the case of a railroad car's brake failure; whether the city of Chicago should be prohibited from dumping its sewage into the Mississippi River and contaminating towns and farmlands downstream; whether the owner of a bakery might work his employees as many hours as it suited him: This was the human stuff out of which the justices fashioned public policy.

When Holmes took his seat in 1902, the justices heard these cases in a courtroom that was the last in a series of quarters assigned them since that first "uncommonly crowded" organization session held at the Royal Exchange building in lower Manhattan on February 1, 1790. All of these assignments had been leftovers, spaces unwanted or unneeded by the other branches of government. The judiciary, possessing neither the purse of the legislative nor the sword of the executive, was at first the stepchild of the other two, its status clearly illustrated in the assignment of its meeting places.

After two sessions in the Royal Exchange, during which the Court decided no cases, the justices moved, with the rest of the government, to the new federal capital at Philadelphia. They spent two days—the entire February 1791 term—at Independence Hall, then reconvened for the August term at City Hall, where they settled down for ten uneventful years. When the government moved to Washington in 1800, the justices tagged along, almost an afterthought, for no arrangements had been made to house them. Not until late January 1801, two weeks before the February term was scheduled to open, were steps taken to provide a meeting place for the nation's highest court. Finally it was allotted a small—twenty-four by thirty feet—not particularly dignified room, what amounted to a clerk's office, really, in the north wing of the unfinished Capitol, one of several it inhabited over the next century. Here in 1803, Chief Justice John Marshall's court decided the landmark case of *Marbury* v. *Madison,* recognized by every student of American history as the precedent establishing the Supreme Court's authority to decide the constitutionality of acts of Congress—in effect, the Court's supremacy as the final arbiter of the Constitution. From that moment forward, the Court's power and authority increased until ultimately it took its rightful place as a coequal branch of government.

In 1819, the bench was shifted to a basement room underneath the Senate chamber, where it remained for forty years. "What a potato hole of a place, this!" a Western lawyer complained in 1859. Nonetheless, it was in this dark and airless chamber that all the early significant constitutional cases were argued and decisions delivered.

In 1860, the Senate was forced into larger quarters by the growing number of members from new states admitted to the Union, and the Supreme Court moved into the old Senate chamber, a semicircular room on the main floor of the Capitol between the Senate and the House. It had a vaulted ceiling, gray walls, columns of gray Potomac marble, and white busts of dead justices overseeing the proceedings; it was the most imposing room the Court had occupied to date. The Court remained there through Holmes's time, until 1935 in fact, when it moved into its own building across the street. After 1935, the justices were provided, for the first time, with offices. During Holmes's years, they worked at home and circulated their opinions by messenger, meeting only on court and conference days.

In the early days of a resident Supreme Court bar, congressmen deserted their own chambers to listen to Daniel Webster, Luther Martin, his golden tongue further loosened by brandy, Henry Clay, Rufus Choate, and Francis Scott Key present the cases for their clients. It was the best show in town, frequented by Washington society as well as senators and representatives. The cases were few in number, the pace of the Court leisurely. Arguments were not measured in minutes or even hours, as they later were, but in days, and there was time for oratory. The Court had been known to pause while Luther Martin sobered up; it had been known to start over because a woman in the audience had missed the opening minutes. As transportation to and from Washington improved, the resident Supreme Court bar disappeared, and lawyers from all over the nation came to the capital to argue their own cases. During Holmes's years on the Court, a conservative estimate of the Supreme Court bar nationally stood at thirty thousand.

Backwoodsmen and city slickers, young, old, suave, forceful, stumbling, inexperienced, well prepared, ill prepared: Holmes rated them as "kitchen-knives, razors and stings"; average but undistinguished performers were the kitchen-knives; slightly sharper ones were razors; and those with obvious legal talent, stings. Some caught the justices' attention; others did not, and the sight of a justice or two sleeping through an argument was not uncommon. Holmes on one occasion, suddenly awaking from a nap and finding a kitchen-knife droning on at the dais, was heard as far as the back row of the courtroom to splutter "Jesus Christ!," then drop back to sleep.

As he had been in Massachusetts, Holmes was in fact bored by oral argument. He could still assimilate the point of a case in the first sentences the lawyer spoke, and he would lean back in his chair and close his eyes—"my only chance to follow my own thoughts."

Eloquence, or the lack of it, neither won nor lost cases; nevertheless, oral argument remained at the heart of the appellate process—an opportunity for the justices, through a question-and-answer format, to test the hypotheses put forward in the lawyers' briefs and for the lawyers to correct any misunderstandings that might have arisen. It could be grueling for a lawyer. Prepared texts were frowned on—the justices had, after all, read the prepared texts, the briefs—and it was impossible to anticipate every question the justices put. Some years after Holmes's death, Robert Jackson, when he was solicitor general, the man who argues the federal government's cases in the Supreme Court, used to say he made three arguments in every case he presented: "First," he explained, "came the case that I planned—as I thought, logical, coherent, complete. Second was the one actually presented—interrupted, incoherent, disjointed, disappointing. The third was the utterly devastating argument that I thought of after going to bed that night."

For generations, Monday was the day for delivering opinions. Traditionally, cases were argued Tuesday through Friday. Saturday was conference day. On the floor below the courtroom was the conference room where the justices met to discuss, deliberate, and vote on the cases they had heard argued during the week. The vote, of course, was not always final. Justices lobbied other justices and minds changed; circulated dissents persuaded and a minority became a majority; a decision was tentative until announced from the bench, and Felix Frankfurter recalled during his own time as a justice at least one important case "held up for decision as we marched to our seats on the bench because shortly before there was a change in the voting." Until 1909, when a leak was rumored, page boys sat on a nearby leather sofa ready to run the justices' errands during the deliberations; after that, the pages were excluded from the conference room, and the proceedings once again became the capital's best-kept secret—so secret that opinions were printed not by the Government Printing Office but by a small private firm; so secret that opinions were split up among several compositors so that no series of paragraphs could disclose the court's holding, and only one man—the trusted head of the firm—handled the opening and closing sections. Leaks still occurred occasionally, but not often.

Supreme Court tradition has it that John Marshall's Court kept a supply of Madeira handy, to be drunk on rainy conference days. Since it did not rain in Washington on every conference day, the chief justice was supposed to have decided the brethren might legitimately imbibe anyway, since it must be raining somewhere within their jurisdiction. The story made the rounds of Washington administration after administration. Then one day, Charles Butler, the Court's reporter, asked Justice Brewer whether it had any basis in fact.

"Why, Mr. Reporter," Brewer replied, "the story is not only true, but you ought to know that the Court sustained the constitutionality of the acquisition of the Philippines so as to be sure of having plenty of rainy seasons."

A natural loner, Holmes had required a substantial period of adjustment before he could tolerate the collegiality of the Massachusetts Supreme Judicial Court; the U.S. Supreme Court's similar system was to require another such period, as he settled down to work with new colleagues whose eccentricities he would have to learn. He was frequently "bored" by the conference proceedings during which he had to listen to the repetition of "arguments that already have bored me once." Perhaps only half in jest, he told the Court reporter one evening as they strolled home together after a dinner party: "Butler, you don't know how tiresome it is to have to discuss legal problems with eight other men, none of whom know any law."

Majorities and minorities were staked out during the weekly conferences. Beneath the veneer of decorum that marked the justices' relations with each other—they addressed each other as "Judge," never "Wendell" or "John" or "Rufus"; Fuller was "Chief Justice," never "Chief"—there lurked a reservoir of irascibility. There were justices who regarded differences of opinion as a "cockfight," others who enlivened the proceedings with their good humor. The good humor of Chief Justice Fuller, who presided with quiet authority and mellow firmness, as well as tact and humor, saved many a discussion from becoming a cockfight. Holmes, who called on the chief justice regularly on Sundays, ostensibly to discuss Court work but also to try to alleviate Fuller's loneliness after his wife's death, described the chief justice as having the "business of the court at his fingers' ends"; he was, in his conference manner, "perfectly courteous, prompt, decided. He turned off the matters that daily call for action easily, swiftly, with the least possible friction, with imperturbable good humor, and with humor that relieved any tension with a laugh."

The task of the chief justice was to keep the Court's business moving apace, to keep the cockfights from dominating the proceedings, to settle the differences, to unite the Court as nearly as possible, and to assign, when he was in the majority, the writing of the Court's opinions. The chief justice's most important function, the choice of the Court's spokesman, required a high degree of judiciousness and tact. A given was that the work of the Court be distributed evenly and fairly. But that was only the starting point. Should a particular opinion be assigned to a justice who was an expert in the area of the law at issue? Or should it be assigned to one who would write it narrowly—one who had dissented in a similar case previously, for example? Perhaps another justice would use the opportunity to plant the seeds of future judicial direction; care had to be taken not to "embarrass the future too much." Who should write the opinion certain to arouse controversy? Often the chief justice himself assumed that responsibility. Political considerations mattered a good deal. Some chief justices made the choices easily; others agonized over them, and some have chosen more wisely than others.

Following the assignment of opinions, each justice wrote his, then circulated it to the others for comments, a practice Holmes tolerated but never really adjusted to. Nearly two decades after he joined the Court he complained that one of his opinions as originally written "had a tiny pair of testicles—but the scruples of my brethren have caused their removal and it sings in a very soft voice now."

Many of the same kinds of questions were plaguing the nation in 1902 that had plagued Massachusetts when Holmes sat on the court there, only the scale was considerably larger when viewed from Washington. By the time Holmes joined the U.S. Supreme Court, the Reconstruction period had long since passed, and the physical conquest of the continent was about complete. Now, manifest destiny had caught the imagination of corporate America, and the economic subjugation of the continent was in progress. Railroads connected the Atlantic and Pacific, and the heretofore unparalleled rapid development of mass-production technology, offspring of scientific discovery, during the second half of the nineteenth century had resulted in a period of unparalleled inter-state economic and industrial expansion. High-speed transportation and distribution of goods followed naturally.

This rapid and uncontrolled development of industry resulted in the erection of giant corporations and consolidation of the nation's wealth. Money accumulated in the hands of a few ruthlessly daring individu-als—Rockefeller, Morgan, Hill, Fisk, Vanderbilt, and other magnates who became known collectively as the robber barons and whose amass-ing of wealth was matched only by their amassing of political power, as they bought their way into banking commissions, law enforcement or-ganizations, railroad commissions, and the councils of local government. The distinguishing characteristic of this period—which occupied the last quarter of the nineteenth century and the early decades of the twentieth—was the uncontrolled and seemingly uncontrollable advance of laissez-faire capitalism.

All this technological and industrial progress, however, was taking a large toll in America's human resources, as it had in Massachusetts's human resources. For the farmer, forced to pay exorbitant freight rates to ship his produce, it often meant bankruptcy. For the railroad worker, who worked at the whim of Jim Hill and on Jim Hill's terms, it meant low wages, long hours, dangerous machinery, and no recourse when legs or lives were lost. For countless thousands of bakers, laundry em-ployees, textile workers, miners, tobacco rollers, steelworkers, it meant living in sunless, airless tenements, working in sunless, airless facto-ries, back-breaking hours, wage slavery, disease, dirt, and, often, pre-mature death.

The reaction to this concentration of wealth and influence in the hands of a few was the birth of the Progressive movement. It was spear-headed by journalists like Lincoln Steffens, Ida M. Tarbell, Upton Sin-clair, and Jacob Riis who attacked in their writings the corruption in industry and government as well as the social conditions in which so many Americans lived. It was led by politicians like Robert M. La-Follette who as governor of Wisconsin initiated such reforms as rate-fixing commissions to oversee the railroads, a state civil service, banking regulation, minimum wage laws, and various conservation statutes. And it was carried on by lawyers like Charles Evans Hughes in New York who exposed, first, the corruption in the local utilities industry, then the scandalous machinations of the insurance industry; he was aided in the latter enterprise by Louis Brandeis of Boston, who went on to fight in the courts for social reforms.

On the national level, the Congress, attempting to cope with the new economic and social realities, went on a spree of legislative reform, beginning in 1887 with establishment of the first federal administrative agency, the Interstate Commerce Commission (ICC), designed to enforce regulation of the railroads. The lawmakers followed this in 1890 with the Sherman Anti-Trust Act, meant to control the trusts. The Elkins Act (1903), aimed at further railroad regulation; the Federal Employers' Liability Act (1906), intended to fix employers' responsibility for managerial negligence and defective equipment; the Hepburn Act (also 1906), a broadening of the jurisdiction of the ICC; the Meat Inspection Act (1906), providing for federal supervision of the meat-packing industry; and the Pure Food and Drug Act (1906), prohibiting shipment of adulterated food and drugs in interstate commerce, were all meant to bring some semblance of control to the out-of-control industrial and financial empires and to alleviate some of the poverty and other difficulties of the laundresses, farmers, railroad brakemen, and miners—all those ordinary Americans who kept the legislators in office.

It fell to the judiciary to arbitrate between the two Americas, social and corporate, between the rights of the individual and the rights of society. The Fuller Court was, typically, a court of older men, at least a generation behind the ordinary Americans who were most feeling the pressures of the new economic and social forces. Overall it was a conservative court, the product and reflection both of political conservatism. Largely unwilling to restrain the absolute freedom of the new capitalists and industrialists to operate as they chose, the justices of the early twentieth century tended to fall back on the shibboleths of the past and to attempt to prolong the existence of a world that was disappearing rapidly, a world that considered the imposition of a 2 percent income tax communistic and social welfare measures legislative quackery. It was sorely in need of a Holmes whose felicitous amalgamation of vast legal learning, exuberant skepticism, and willingness to break with legal tradition, to tolerate social and economic disruption of his own world if that was what people wanted, seemed to have been fashioned for this particular time in history.

*   *   *

THE BREAK WITH Boston was wrenching, easier perhaps for Wendell, who had his work, than for Fanny, who could not be solaced even by snow on the ground and sleigh rides—she could not think of the Washington winter as "real." They intended to continue summering at Beverly Farms, and they had rented, not sold, the Beacon Street house to which they thought they might want to return at "the end of life." They had not been in town much more than two months when Fanny was counting the years until she could "sit in the Bow Window in Boston again." She had "fixed 10 years in [her] own mind for [their] stay" in Washington—the period coinciding with the time Holmes would have to serve on the Supreme Court to be eligible for retirement at full pay—and she found herself thinking constantly "of the place from which we fled that strange December night."

The place where Olivers, Wendells, and Holmeses had trod the familiar narrow streets and watched for returning merchantmen from familiar wooden wharves, or waited for spring on Boston Common; where family names endured for centuries, faces disappeared only at death, and people knew who lived in every house; the place where even safe-deposit boxes were handed down from father to son and relinquishing at last Dr. Holmes's had had a "touch of the irrevocable in it" that made Wendell "shudder." They were exchanging this womblike warmth and security for the cold uncertainties of Washington's amorphous and transient world where the shifting sands of politics required that faces change with every administration and foreign monarchs moved their representatives about like pieces on a chess board: "a place of continuous farewells" someone called it.

The men and women the Holmeses met in Washington were Texans or Californians or Kentuckians—even Germans, Swedes, or Italians—first, Washingtonians second. In the nation's capital, family names meant little, traditions less. Neighbors moved away, and faces disappeared with monotonous regularity.

Despite their intention to return to Beacon Street one day, the Holmeses made the move to Washington with some sense of finality. Fanny had destroyed all but a few of her embroideries; Wendell had burned his papers; the work on the Massachusetts court became a "closed volume locked up in a distant safe." The train could carry the Holmeses from Boston to Washington, but there was no vehicle in the world which could carry them emotionally away from the place where their roots had been so deeply planted. The man who could kick legal tradition in the teeth intellectually could not tear himself emotionally from the genteel social tradition into which he had been born. From his high stiff collars to the toes of his polished black boots, he remained a Boston Brahmin.

When Holmes arrived in Washington, he was so green he didn't even know how to address Chief Justice Fuller; should it be "Chief Justice" or "Mr. Chief Justice"? Although he had argued in the United States Supreme Court as a young lawyer, the mud of Civil War Washington was the picture of the city he carried in his head.

Actually, by the time the Holmeses arrived in 1902, Washington had become a stately city of broad tree-lined streets, impressive buildings, strategically placed statues of patriots, and colorfully planted parks and traffic circles; it was undergoing at that very time a beauty treatment. The previous January, a specially appointed Park Commission had published a grandiose multi-million-dollar beautification plan calling for new parks and boulevards, museums and galleries lining the Mall, a memorial to Abraham Lincoln at the far end of the Mall, a bridge across the Potomac connecting the new Memorial with the Arlington National Cemetery, a sunken garden, fountains, a reflecting pool at the foot of the Washington Monument, the draining of the Anacostia malarial swamps, and a number of recreation areas including facilities for boating and swimming in the Tidal Basin. Congress idled for the requisite period of time, appropriating money for new office buildings for senators and representatives rather than improvement of the city. Ultimately, however, over the next two decades, many of the Park Commission's proposals were implemented, and Washington became, superficially at least, "The City Beautiful."

Churchmen and charity organizations had unsuccessfully urged the Park Commission to include in its master plan suggestions for improving the poor neighborhoods of the city. During the first decade of the twentieth century, Washington held the largest black population of any city in the world, much of it living in sheds, shanties, and tenements with leaking roofs and open privies within easy walking distance of the Capitol itself.

Official Washington as well as society Washington, drawn from the political ruling classes of America and the cultured capitals of the world, ignored its black slums, rarely acknowledging their existence behind the gleaming marble facades of its public buildings and the handsome Federalist-style homes that lined its green squares. Until 1954, Washington was a Southern city, segregated and acutely race conscious. Southerners could not forgive Theodore Roosevelt for inviting Dr. Booker T. Washington of the Tuskegee Institute to dine at the White House a little over a year before the Holmeses arrived. Not long after Holmes arrived, he himself described with some astonishment a White House reception from which a group of Southerners, including one of his own "pal[s]," bolted because there was a black present. It was not until 1947 that a black correspondent was admitted to the Senate Press Gallery.

The city's beauty, if pockmarked by slums, at least was not spoiled by industrial smokestacks spewing black clouds into its clean skies. Washington was from the beginning—and remains now—a company town, and its industry is government. Henry Adams might have invented the culturally raw and morally insensitive city into which the Holmeses were settling in 1902. It had a power-oriented code of its own, and it required some time for Holmes to become accustomed to being pumped regarding Court matters and to the blatantly self-serving and sometimes scandalous behavior of the political figures he was meeting. He had to learn always to "suspect ulterior motives—and to ask 'why did he say that.' " Every Mark Hanna, the late President McKinley's political alter ego whom Holmes genuinely liked, had his counterpart in a crude political manipulator who intimidated dinner tables with profanity and inappropriate personal remarks. Every woman as "delightful" as Edith Roosevelt had her counterpart in the "Gracious Lady . . . generally large but needn't be . . . imperfectly educated—more or less rich" who "plays at demi-princess." Life in Washington, Holmes was sorry to say, tended "to make one rather more cynical." Since his arrival he had begun to "doubt the disinterested devotion of most." The impermanence of the political structure never failed to strike him:

> the way that mighty men appear here, have their day and are forgotten. . . . Each cabinet thinks itself a halo and in a puff the sunlight vanishes and they are but obscure moths. . . . And no one cares.

First-class restaurants, good theater, and music, which the Holmeses had left behind in Boston, were scarce in Washington at the turn of the century, and Washingtonians occupied themselves with frequent receptions, dinners, and the weekly "at homes" that had to be given by all officialdom. Politics and diplomacy dominated social as well as professional Washington, dictated the nuances of protocol, supplied the substance of conversations in streets and salons.

Holmes enjoyed "seeing men of might engaged in laughing and making laugh" at the dinner tables where congressmen from the Great Plains, the New England coast, and the bayou country relaxed together with diplomats of all races and tongues, and discussed business informally, uninhibited by rules of procedure and without fear of publication. He enjoyed the social season as a whole; it was a "relief, because it turns off from law," at least at the beginning; as it droned on through the winter, it became "almost another task." Fanny, who seemed to have been born again and in the early Washington years lived a social life considered normal for upper-echelon Washingtonians, feared that she was "bumbling along from one social mistake to another."

Her fears were groundless. The Holmeses were among the most popular couples in Washington, constantly in demand for dinner parties. They dined out nearly every night, except when they invited people in, which they did with some regularity. Generals, congressmen, judges, cabinet members, papal envoys, and ambassadors came to their table, which seated twenty-two. Holmes preferred his social life at home, "perhaps because I don't know anything about it till it happens."

Social Washington attended the traditional—for the judiciary—"at homes" on Monday afternoons; the Holmeses gave their first one on the first Monday in January 1903, only weeks after their arrival. Close friends enjoyed their small, intimate dinners at which the quality of the talk outshone what Holmes liked to refer to as the "Victuals." It became the Holmeses' custom, too, to set two extra places for every meal so no one would feel embarrassed at dropping in at mealtime.

Hostesses and guests both remembered their bon mots long after the champagne had stopped bubbling. He was gregarious, his talk racy, witty, and urbane, his manners "so perfect one forgot all about manners." He charmed with his ability to listen, dazzled with his brilliance, touched all with his gaiety and humor. Fanny was no less attractive. Her tongue was as vivacious as Wendell's, and she became known for her caustic comments.

Perhaps it was the transitory quality of Washington life which covered up a subconscious desire for order that started the local custom. But all social life in the capital proceeded along strict rules of protocol and was full of pitfalls for the ignorant and unwary. A dinner party was a "terror" to the host. Whether a Supreme Court justice ate his roast beef to the right or left of an ambassador, whether a cabinet member called on a senator's wife or vice versa, were questions of paramount importance in Washington. The smallest error made men and women sulk. Some justices would leave the table if improperly placed. Observed Holmes shortly after his arrival:

One's first impression is that this is not a place to make you proud of your country.

Despite her homesickness, Fanny did her best to make the move a success for Wendell; she suppressed her instincts for reclusiveness and conformed to the social rules, made her required calls, even boasted that she was "getting on well" with them. The system seemed to amuse more than irritate her. Holmes himself referred to it as a "ridiculous bore" and prided himself on not following protocol as strictly as his predecessor had. When, however, the judiciary and the diplomatic corps feuded over a matter of seating precedence, he told Chief Justice Fuller that "in future if I am placed wrong in that regard I shall go to the White House no more. I can stop dining out without regret if it means that."

The Holmeses settled into their adopted city with a minimum of fuss. For the first few months they rented a house at 10 Lafayette Square across from the White House, which was "comfortable enough," but they couldn't stay on long because the owner was returning. After deciding he could not afford his predecessor's home, Holmes sold "odds and ends" of stock in the Pennsylvania Railroad, American Telephone and Telegraph Company, and the Puget Sound Improvement Company, and bought for $30,000 the dignified red-brick house at 1720 I Street where he and Fanny, Fanny's time limit notwithstanding, lived the rest of their days in Washington.

The house required considerable renovation, and Fanny struggled daily with plumbers and painters after Wendell went off to court. She had "every kind of obstacle from a hitch in the title that delayed us six weeks at the beginning to the detailed incompetency and general slackness of most people in this town."

The four stories of the house held upwards of eighteen rooms, including, in addition to seven bedrooms, a library, and the usual living chambers, a sitting room for the help, and a "colored man's room." Still, it was small enough that Holmes had to take men to his library upstairs for their after-dinner cigars. The Holmeses, essentially Victorian in their tastes, furnished it with family heirlooms and other antiques, Sheraton and Duncan Phyfe tables, Chippendale and Hepplewhite chairs, fringed Tiffany glass lampshades, oriental rugs, and lacquered Japanese pieces. Callers said it was the only house in Washington that smelled like Beacon Hill in Boston, with its horsehair furniture and butcher's wax.

Holmes was thrilled with his purchase and expected to feel "more at home there than I ever did in Beacon Street. . . . That was my father's—not mine," he added, the old rivalry surfacing once more, although he was sixty-one years old, a Supreme Court justice, and his father had been dead nearly a decade.

He was especially thrilled with his library, which was lined with white bookshelves. He fairly pulsated with joy the day—10 A.M. to 7 P.M.—on which he arranged his books on the shelves, pronouncing his collection *"fecundissimus."* The overstuffed leather chairs and the presence of his accumulated treasures—including the cork from the bottle of champagne Holmes and George Shattuck had shared when *The Common Law* was published, his will, his Civil War sword, Grandfather Jackson's writing desk, and various other things "that belonged to forgotten great-granddaddies"—made it a perfect place for Holmes to write his opinions for the Court. Sunlight streamed in the windows, which overlooked a small garden, and in the distance he glimpsed over the intervening roofs the Washington Monument with its "Eternal wonder of changing light upon it." The accoutrements of a modern office never seduced him. Only Fanny's persistence convinced him in later years to install a telephone, and a typewriter would have had to have been brought in "over his dead body." Although basically a male preserve, the library was not entirely denied the playful presence of Fanny, who was apt to interrupt the serious work while she hunted for her scissors or to usher in visitors with some remark like "You will find him there, reading one of those naughty French novels."

Evenings when social duties did not require the Holmeses' presence, it was their custom to read together after dinner, Fanny reading aloud while Wendell played solitaire. Summers were given over almost entirely to reading, except for meals, daily drives, and the hours necessarily devoted to studying the petitions for certiorari—requests for the Court's consideration of cases—which followed the justices to their summer places.

Reading was an important part of Holmes's life, whether the subject was "naughty French novels," Salic law, or the latest writings of the friend of his youth, Henry James, whose work Holmes once described as "50 years of polite conversation and nothing doing." That since childhood Wendell should have devoted a good deal of time to reading and derived a good deal of pleasure from it was perhaps only natural in the home of Dr. Holmes, who believed that a Brahmin was partly defined by the books he owned and who undoubtedly had seen to it that his elder son would be "at home wherever he smell[ed] the invigorating fragrance of Russian leather." What was not available on the bookshelves at home could often be borrowed from the Boston Athenaeum.

At the end of his life, this elder son owned some fourteen thousand volumes. Upwards of ten thousand of them were housed in his second-floor library; another two thousand or so were shelved in various bed-rooms, the living room, and a third-floor storage facility; the rest, many of them comparatively light reading, were at Beverly Farms. The bulk of them Holmes had bought at home or abroad. As his fame spread, authors and publishers sent him review copies: among them, Milt Gross gave him an autographed copy of *He Done Her Wrong*, Ramsay Macdonald inscribed his *American Speeches* "in memory of his very delightful visit," and Herbert Hoover contributed *The Challenge of Liberty*. Friends— Frederick Pollock, John Gray, Henry and Brooks Adams, William and Henry James—laid their offerings at Holmes's feet. He also inherited a substantial number from his father and grandfathers, some of which they had written, and shortly after Holmes moved into the I Street house, he erected a "family shrine over one of the fireplaces in the two rooms which make my library where I have put all the works of my two grandfathers and my father and myself and presentation copies of the local illustrious, Emerson, Hawthorne, Longfellow, *et alteri*."

The books were more or less systematically arranged by author and subject on the shelves. Law made up the largest sections: *United States Reports, Massachusetts Reports*—he especially liked to have the "yard of product" at hand, the eight separately bound volumes of his own opin-ions—German legal tomes, the rich-smelling calf-bound volumes on En-glish, French, and American law that had belonged to Grandfather Jackson, old English court reports. He loved the old. He liked "to have books in [his] library that were on shelves before America was discov-ered." He owned none so old, but he did have some rare volumes printed in the sixteenth and seventeenth centuries. Yards and yards of Massa-chusetts Historical Society *Proceedings* and other of the institution's publications shared space with the books of his own childhood which he had preserved: *Little Red Riding Hood, King Lucky's Boys, Cinderella*, and several others.

Holmes's collection was heterogeneous, and he was an eclectic reader. Books of travel, racy and not-so-racy French novels, mystery stories, American best-sellers, and humor spiced the collection of law, philoso-phy, history, anthropology, psychology, art, poetry, even demonology. Exploration thrilled him. He owned books in French, books in German, the writings of the ancients in the original Greek and Latin, books in Spanish, Dante in Italian, Dante in English. Shakespeare in several editions. His correspondence is filled with his literary adventures.

"Lord," he groaned, "what big books I have read simply to make sure that they had nothing to say (to me)."

He read only partly for pleasure or information. He had a Puritan sense of compulsion to work his way through the world's great literature, to familiarize himself with those works with which a gentleman of his time and place ought to be acquainted, and he said, perhaps only half joking, that he believed somewhere in heaven a great book of records was being kept where he got credit for dull but worthy books read. In the meantime, he kept his own record, inscribing in his Black Book the authors and titles of every book he finished.

He finished nearly all he started, like the good Puritan he sometimes could not help being. He knew people who "rip[ped] out [a book's] guts and pass[ed] on." He himself couldn't do it. He trudged on through, word by word, line by line. He began at the "once upon a time" and went on "scrupulously" to the end, then "put it down in [his] list like a good little boy." D. H. Lawrence's *Lady Chatterley's Lover* was one of the few exceptions, the book he never finished: "Not enough lubricity," he concluded, "to relieve it from being dull. I am surprised that reviewers found him worth talking about." William Wordsworth's romantic poetry tried him sorely, but each time he was about to give up, "the old boy would give a wiggle that connected you with the eternal," and Holmes forged on. He tried to treat a "great author like a friend": to let the man "bore" him for a while "with things that don't seem important." Love inevitably followed, and he began to "see their importance—probably just because they are important to him" and he had, after all, become a friend. The author "gets into your blood and there is nothing like him."

Since he had first expected as an undergraduate to discover the secrets of the universe revealed in Plato's writings, Holmes seemed to have read with that goal in mind; he seemed always to be searching for some Truth that would make everything clear. He sought out "books on the themes nearest to [his] life." The fact that each author invited him to subscribe to the truths of his or her particular universe did not satisfy him, and he always seemed to be hoping desperately that the next book he opened would hold the magic formula. Perhaps he would come upon it tomorrow in Jane Austen's work, but no; although he found Little Pedlington "everywhere," he lamented the author's failure to "explore depths of the human soul." Perhaps William James's next book would tell him what he wanted to know, but no, James had become too involved in mysticism for Holmes's taste. Holmes always expected more from Hegel than Hegel offered him. Books on religion lined a shelf in the library, but Holmes discovered no answers in them. He understood the hopelessness of his quest from that early reading of Plato, but he seemed unable to cease his searching. He would fill his correspondence with the scraps he found, but nothing offered the comprehensiveness for which he yearned. He pressed on, made do with truth being what he *"can't help* thinking," and never able to decide whether his "can't helps [had] any cosmic worth."

He looked at pictures in somewhat the same way, although perhaps a little less intensely. For more than forty years, since he had published that little piece on Albrecht Dürer in *The Harvard Magazine,* Holmes had pursued a less-than-consuming but more-than-casual interest in art. It was part aesthetic and part philosophical—he could not help translating the artist's smallest squiggle into abstract terms. When he went to Washington, he continued his pursuit. He cultivated the friendship of the prints curator at the Library of Congress, from whom he occasionally bought a duplicate the Library wanted to dispose of; sometimes, too, he was able to trade one of his for one of theirs. He developed personal relationships with art dealers, subscribed to *Print Collector's Quarterly,* and kept his eyes open for opportunities to add a fine specimen to his growing collection of etchings and engravings. He collected "for the pleasure that the things themselves" gave him; he had "no ambition to be a trustee for posterity," and did not care whether his purchase was a first or third "slate."

To his friends, he would proclaim with a childish joy his latest discovery, and he decorated what wall space remained in his library after the books were arranged with Rembrandts, Van Dykes, Whistlers, Dürers. He loved the old in art as well as in books and preferred prints "that go back two or three hundred years and show one the same human feeling that we have today."

For what appear to be purely aesthetic reasons, Holmes took to observing and documenting Nature's Washington, which proliferated in the parks, especially Rock Creek Park, along the old unused Baltimore & Ohio Canal, and on the carefully tended grounds of government buildings. He delighted in the first signs of spring, those three verdant months before the steamy enervating heat set in in June. Pink and white magnolias, dogwood, and in later years cherry blossoms stunned him with their beauty. The fauna enchanted him equally, and he once scrawled on the back of a court opinion Brandeis had sent him for comment: "This afternoon I was walking on the towpath and saw a cardinal. It seemed to be the first sign of spring. By the way, I concur." Dining outdoors at the Old Mill in Rock Creek Park transported him, and the romance in the natural beauty of the setting overcame his usual terseness of expression. "The birds sang," he reported, "the leaves rustled and made divine green reflections in the water, rivaling the blue sky, and swans and geese pulled up their legs and floated on the shallow (quondam) mill pond, and the burr of the fall behind the other sounds made all life seem a dream and stirred a vague wonder whether I really liked the life one seems to remember."

CHAPTER *18*

Holmes v. Roosevelt

STARTING OVER AGAIN at the age of sixty-one, Holmes was quiet during his early days on the high federal court—as he had been on the state court—and there was no indication that he would develop into a national hero. At first he was intimidated by the

> demi-gods with huge heads and big faces who understand everything with diabolic swiftness,

and it required a little time for his judicial self-confidence to return.

For nearly the first year and a half after Holmes took his seat, the president had little cause for disappointment in his appointee—if, indeed, being preoccupied with the administrative and political business of the presidency and not being a lawyer himself, he even noticed Holmes's opinions. Roosevelt and Lodge were no doubt congratulating themselves that they had assessed Holmes correctly regarding his views on the new American possessions; in the only one of the so-called insular cases to come before the Supreme Court during Holmes's first term,* he followed the example Horace Gray had set for him and joined the five-judge majority that denied to Hawaiian citizens the usual requirements of trial by jury as well as the "due process of law" in the Fifth Amendment to the Constitution. During that idyllic period, Holmes wrote forty-four opinions for the majority and no dissents or concurrences. None of these was a landmark opinion or even particularly significant, and on a Richtér scale measuring public reaction, the effect of Holmes's writings would have been barely noticeable.

* *Hawaii v. Mankichi.* 190 U.S. 197 (1903).

In fact, many of the opinions he wrote during this time described familiar controversies—estates, contracts, land titles, bankruptcy, mortgages—which he had confronted on the state court. Other opinions dealt with public issues—antitrust, civil rights, civil liberties, labor relations, and all the other public questions Americans were trying to answer at the time, few particularly different in principle from those Massachusetts people had been trying to solve during the past two decades when Holmes was a judge there. His jurisprudence did not change much when he came to Washington; the buds only flowered fully. He became more skillful at adapting common-law formulas to the solution of constitutional questions, and his deference to the legislature and denial of judicial supremacy only became more marked.

He never came to believe, however, that his state court work had prepared him for the U.S. Supreme Court. The scope of the questions had broadened between Boston and Washington to nearly intimidating proportions. Here in Washington, Holmes was called on to resolve controversies between the states, between the states and the nation, between the individual and his government—to adjust the ever-shifting built-in tensions among all parts of the American body politic. It all had to be done in accordance with the unspecific and often vague words of the Constitution—"due process of law," "equal protection of the laws," "unreasonable searches and seizures," "speedy . . . trial," and so on. Here there was no tomorrow. The Supreme Court was the final arbiter. Holmes and his brethren had the last word. Less than a month after he took his seat, Holmes told Pollock:

> Yes—here I am—and more absorbed, interested and impressed than ever I had dreamed I might be . . . a new and solemn volume opens. The variety and novelty to me of the questions, the remote spaces from which they come, the amount of work they require, all help the effect. I have written on the constitutionality of part of the Constitution of California, on the powers of the Railroad Commissioners of Arkansas, on the question whether a law of Wisconsin impairs the obligation of the plaintiff's contract. I have to consider a question between a grant of the U.S. in aid of a military road and an Indian reservation on the Pacific coast. I have heard conflicting mining claims in Arizona and whether a granite quarry is "Minerals" within an exception in a Railway land grant and fifty other things as remote from each other as these.

Although the scope of the issues made him "shudder from time to time," he didn't "lie awake over them." He tried to "think of them merely as problems to be handled in just the same way whether they involve[d] $25—or the welfare of a state or people." The variety of the cases, the diversity of their settings, the "unmercifully long" records, briefs, and arguments to be digested dwarfed the demands of his previous work. "There is nothing that you can do that prepares you for this job," declared a later justice, William J. Brennan, who had been schooled in the New Jersey court system. Benjamin N. Cardozo, Holmes's successor on the U.S. Supreme Court, complained—sometimes bitterly—that his experience on the New York State Court of Appeals bore little resemblance to his work on the high federal court.

Some days during those early years, Holmes felt "pretty cocky"; on others, he felt "depressed." Gradually he got the "hang of the work" and the confidence he could handle his share. It was not long before he could write in a patent case—over which state courts had no jurisdiction—"as if [he] had waded in physics all [his] life."

In thirty-five years of lawyering—legal practice, scholarship, judging—Holmes had formulated some ideas on what a court opinion ought to be. It ought, first of all, to begin "where the law left off before you announce it. The principles need to be developed a little further and applied to decide the rights of parties. It should leave off there." Judges who elaborated on those principles, he thought, erred. "The rest will be better done later in the light of the next set of facts."

Since opinions were theoretically spoken, he thought they ought to be "agreeable to the ear when read aloud," and he strove for a "free, unconscious expression of his own spontaneity." He was cavalier about commas but fussy about his "shalls" and "wills." He was so stylistically self-conscious that he tried to end his paragraphs with either a monosyllable or a word accented on the last syllable—"so that the axe may fall and the head drop."

When you end on a polysyllable it gives a squashy feeling.

And he who knew within minutes how a case should be decided would recast an entire opinion for the "sake of a phrase, or even a word."

Brevity, too, was of paramount importance. He feared his own short opinions would make him "seem less weighty." He was finding that a "great opinion indicates itself by padded breast and shoulders." He complained of long records in which the relevant material could have been reduced to a few words, and he himself had learned to trim and prune until he could compress the result of years of reflection into a sentence. Unfortunately, he had a way of occasionally leaving out some of the minor steps, which he considered self-evident, and lawyers sometimes complained to the chief justice not that Holmes's opinions were less weighty but that he sacrificed clarity to brevity. His opinions made one lawyer "think of seeing a man sitting on a roof at the top of a long ladder with perhaps three rungs on it. He has kicked out the intervening rungs and you kind of wonder how he got there."

His own first opinion, which fulfilled his stylistic requirements, he produced less than a month after he had taken his seat. The case, *Otis* v. *Parker,* had come from the Supreme Court of California, and involved the validity of a provision of the state constitution prohibiting the sale of stocks on margin. Was such a prohibition a proper allocation of state power, or did it unduly limit the liberty to make contracts and thus deprive investors of property without the due process of law guaranteed by the Fourteenth Amendment? In specifying stocks and omitting other familiar objects of speculation such as cotton or grain, did the provision discriminate and thus deprive investors of the equal protection of the laws also guaranteed by the Fourteenth Amendment? Holmes's answer was a signpost to the next thirty years of his jurisprudence. He had written in *The Common Law* that the "first requirement of a sound body of law is that it should correspond with the actual feelings and demands of the community, whether right or wrong," and followed it up in his opinions for the Massachusetts court. Now, for his debut on the U.S. Supreme Court, he rewrote it once again. It was not his responsibility as a judge, he said, to decide the desirability of the provision at issue. It was clear to him that it had been included in the state constitution because of the "deep-seated conviction" of Californians, and such a "deep-seated conviction" was "entitled to great respect." If the state believed the prohibition necessary, "courts cannot interfere" unless they could see that it clearly and unmistakably violated the federal Constitution. In this particular case, the Supreme Court could discover no such violations.

When Holmes circulated *Otis* v. *Parker* for comments from the other justices, Brown scribbled on his copy: "I hope your opinion may call the attention of our brethren, including myself, to the value of brevity, in respect to which I think we are all sinners."

Shortly after *Otis* v. *Parker* was handed down, Holmes wrote an opinion for the court in a copyright case, *Bleistein* v. *Donaldson Lithographing Co.,* that more than eighty years later still served as a foundation for American copyright law. It was one of the subjects for which Holmes could not have prepared on the state court; the Constitution made copyright, like patents, strictly a federal matter.

The question the Court had to decide in *Bleistein* was whether an advertising poster for a circus could be copyrighted. Did it meet the standards for the "useful arts" set by Article 1, section 8 of the Constitution and further defined by Congress as pictorial illustrations "connected with the fine arts"?

Bleistein gave Holmes an opportunity not only to quote from a hero of his youth, John Ruskin, and to do some fancy figure-skating in aesthetics, but it also gave him a chance to argue against dependence on absolute standards. His opinion extending copyright protection to an advertising poster regardless of its artistic merit, an entirely subjective matter, elicited from him perhaps as personal a statement on a public matter as he ever made. A picture, whether by Whistler or an unknown lithographer, was, he said,

> the personal reaction of an individual upon nature. Personality always contains something unique. It expresses its singularity even in handwriting, and a very modest grade of art has in it something irreducible, which is one man's alone. That something he may copyright unless there is a restriction in the words of the act.

Holmes could find none, however, and he took the occasion to warn that

> It would be a dangerous undertaking for persons trained to the law to constitute themselves final judges of the worth of pictorial illustrations. . . . At the one extreme some works of genius would be sure to miss appreciation. . . . At the other end, copyright would be denied to pictures which appealed to a public less educated than the judge.

The Court was shorthanded that spring. White came down with a cold that kept him at home for a time. McKenna was "shut up" with some long, unnamed illness, and William R. Day, a close friend of the late President McKinley, appointed recently to replace George Shiras, Jr., on the latter's retirement, spent his early weeks on the job recovering from pneumonia. If Holmes was not already a glutton for work, he would have been forced to become one.

But he still was a glutton for work, and as on the Massachusetts bench, the one or two opinions he was assigned each week were not enough. He developed a routine that served him well for three decades. He examined the briefs and records of a case for the first time during oral argument; at the same time he was taking notes on counsel's salient points, amassing citations of relevant precedents, and jotting down questions he intended to inquire about at greater length. It was during oral arguments that he generally reached his conclusions regarding the disposition of a case.

The Court conference, which he wryly claimed he prepared for with "fasting and prayer," began at 10 A.M. Saturday. Holmes's votes were based on the notes he had taken at oral argument and the answers to whatever inquiries he had made. Late Saturday afternoon, the chief justice decided who should write what, and the messengers arrived at the justices' homes with the assignments between 4 and 5 P.M. Holmes began work immediately. At first, each opinion "loom[ed] a shapeless black immensity." But after he consulted his notes and thought it out,

> it turned out to be the usual old donkey in the lion's skin.

He wrote it mentally before he committed it to paper. By Monday morning he was in a "delirium" and "miserable until his work was done." Fanny always thought he paid for his intensity "by being a little upset physically," and Holmes was inclined to agree. He worked at the opinion until it was time to go to court, which opened at noon, unwound after court adjourned at 4:30 P.M. by walking the two miles back to I Street, and worked again until it was time to dress for dinner, writing painstakingly but illegibly in longhand. By Tuesday, or at latest, Wednesday morning, Holmes had his work ready for distribution to the other judges in accordance with long-standing Court tradition. He seldom, however, solicited suggestions and was inclined to be a little "short" with any that were offered.

Usually he finished ahead of the others, and looked around for more. This constant hustling of opinion-writing assignments which had begun on the Massachusetts court seemed to have some deeper meaning for Holmes than simply his Puritanical compulsions or his desire that a hundred years later, "men who never heard of him" would be "moving to the measure of his thought"; perhaps there was also some complicated combination of an unconscious desire to justify his survival in the war along with a similar desire to compensate for his childlessness. Chief Justice Fuller very shortly became accustomed to Holmes's

> Why don't you send me a real stinker?

> I notice your pile is large. Why don't you unload some of them to me?

Every few weeks the justices adjourned to devote more time to opinion writing. Holmes's were almost always already written, and he spent the recess reading, driving about the local area, and giving assistance to colleagues who wrote less rapidly. His speed, which later became a "vice," was a "point of pride with him," and until his very last years on the Court, Holmes badgered chief justices for more work, anticipating once again the joy of the lonely thinker in the reward of discovery. To "put something better than it has been put before, or that is new and penetrating," made him "walk on clouds."

SHORTLY AFTER THE Holmeses moved to Washington, a woman Wendell had known as a young girl nearly fifty years before in Hagerstown, Maryland, a member of the family that had tended his wound after the Battle of Antietam, arrived in town and invited him to call one evening at her hotel. Fanny, who was still paying out the rope when occasion demanded it, insisted on his wearing his dress clothes and taking with him a large bouquet.

The evening dragged on. He hadn't returned by 10; Fanny went to bed. Finally, about 11, she heard him unlock the front door, and trudge up the steps to his library. She waited, but there was only silence. At last she got out of bed and went to him. She found him sitting at his desk, his face in his hands.

"Wendell!"

"Woman, shut your trap."

Impossible for Fanny. She could not resist asking, "She'd grown fat, hadn't she?"

"Yes, my dear."

THANKS TO THE intransigence of the U.S. Supreme Court after the Civil War, the civil rights of blacks at the turn of the twentieth century were for all intents and purposes nonexistent, at least in the South. Congress had passed and the states had ratified the Thirteenth, Fourteenth, and Fifteenth Amendments to the Constitution, all intended to nationalize blacks' civil rights, but the Supreme Court had put the burden of protecting them on the states,* a hopeless gesture at a time when the Ku Klux Klan was in the ascendancy. In 1875, Congress had passed a Civil Rights Act, one of whose provisions had been

---

* *Slaughter-House Cases.* 16 Wall 36 (1873).

designed to assure blacks "the full and equal enjoyment" of all public facilities—buses, hotels, restaurants, theaters, parks. But the Supreme Court had struck it down, dismantling once and for all the attempts of Reconstruction Congresses to rescue the black from second-class citizenship.* Only John Marshall Harlan dissented, his customary emotional level elevated by the fact that the ink that flowed from his pen came out of the inkwell Chief Justice Roger B. Taney had used in writing the Court's opinion in Dred Scott's case, a treasure Harlan had acquired from the marshal.

Mostly, in the latter two decades of the nineteenth century and the first two decades of the twentieth, the Fourteenth Amendment, which declared that no state may

> deprive any person of life, liberty, or property, without due process of law; nor deny to any person within its jurisdiction the equal protection of the laws.

was invoked in behalf of corporate interests, and the black, whose full first-class citizenship it had been intended to secure, was left judicially stranded. A study in 1960 of 554 Supreme Court decisions that turned on the equal protection clause of the Fourteenth Amendment revealed that 426, or 76.9 percent, involved economic matters and only 78 or 14.2 percent, involved racial questions. (The rest dealt with taxation.)

Partly this had to do with the nature of the nominations to the Supreme Court: a high percentage of corporate lawyers, whose natural interests and sympathies lay with the rapidly developing commerce and industry. And partly it had to do with national political realities. Following the close election of 1876—Republican Rutherford B. Hayes versus Democrat Samuel J. Tilden—Republicans, in return for disputed electoral votes in South Carolina, Florida, and Louisiana, withdrew support of black civil rights in the South, leaving the Democratic South free to hold the black in bondage and a conservative Supreme Court free to utilize the controversial Fourteenth Amendment to further economic laissez-faire. Both sides kept the bargain.

In 1896, the opinion of Henry Brown, a thoroughgoing Republican, for an eight-judge majority in *Plessy* v. *Ferguson* (164 U.S. 537), key to

---

*The Supreme Court's decision in the *Civil Rights Cases* of 1883 (109 U.S. 3) stood for nearly a century. Finally, in December 1964, in *Heart of Atlanta Motel* v. *United States* (379 U.S. 241), the Court upheld the constitutionality of the Civil Rights Act of 1964, which prohibited, under the commerce clause of the Constitution, discrimination on the basis of race, religion, or national origin in accommodations that serve the public.

American jurisprudence in racial matters for sixty years, served to reinforce the political deal made twenty years before. The separate-but-equal formula established by *Plessy*, which encouraged the Jim Crow laws proliferating at the time throughout the South, prevailed until it was overruled by *Brown* v. *Board of Education of Topeka* in 1954. Racial segregation was the law of the land.

When Holmes took his seat on the Supreme Court in 1902, the condition of the southern black was desperate (he was not much better off in the North, the difference being that discrimination in the South was supported and could be enforced by law). The states, to which the Court had delegated the responsibility, were not interested in advancing the black's status or protecting his civil rights, and Congress, thanks also to the Supreme Court, was not allowed to do so. Jim Crow laws, legitimized by *Plessy*, regulated the black's use of public drinking fountains, toilets, buses, waiting rooms, recreation areas, and restaurants. Poll taxes, literacy tests, peonage systems, and separate but *un*equal schools all conspired to reduce the black to second-class citizenship. He remained voteless, vulnerable to white brutality both physical and intellectual, victimized by white judicial and political systems, segregated, ostracized socially, and helpless to remedy any of these conditions.

Holmes's record in civil rights cases during his three decades on the Supreme Court was mixed but leaned toward support of Southern customs and traditional inbred community attitudes; on occasion, however, he could be eloquently civil righteous. Two early cases involving the racial composition of grand juries illustrate his—and the Court's—position, a position that contributed little to the civil rights revolution of the later twentieth century. He was much more tolerant of the revolutions in industrial and financial relationships.

The first civil rights opinion Holmes wrote for the Court, *Brownfield* v. *South Carolina*, reached it early in 1903. Brownfield believed the exclusion of blacks from the grand jury that had indicted him for murder had denied him the equal protection of the laws guaranteed by the Fourteenth Amendment. The Court did not agree. It made good political sense to the chief justice to assign the opinion unanimously rejecting Brownfield's claim to Holmes, fresh from the abolitionist state of Massachusetts. Holmes conceded that the case raised "questions of the gravest character," but in the absence of proof by the plaintiff that the all-white jury had been the result of deliberate racial discrimination, the Court's hands were tied.

Not long afterwards, an Alabama black man brought to the Court a charge similar to Brownfield's,* but he also brought evidence, and the Court paid attention this time. Speaking once again through Justice Holmes, the Court declared that intentional exclusion of blacks from a grand jury was indeed contrary to the Fourteenth Amendment to the Constitution. Quoting his predecessor, Horace Gray, Holmes wrote:

> Whenever by any action of a State, whether through its legislature, through its courts, or through its executive or administrative officers, all persons of the African race are excluded, solely because of their race or color, from serving as grand jurors in the criminal prosecution of a person of the African race, the equal protection of the laws is denied him, contrary to the Fourteenth Amendment of the Constitution of the United States. †

Giles v. *Harris,* involving the denial of voting rights to some five thousand black men living in Montgomery County, Alabama, followed *Brownfield* just over a month later. When, in 1901, Alabama amended its constitution, qualifications for voting were changed. Literacy tests, complicated registration procedures, and minimum property holdings were added to the usual age, sex, and residency requirements. The effect was to disenfranchise large numbers of blacks.

William Giles believed racial discrimination had been the intent and filed suit in federal court accusing the state of violating the Fifteenth Amendment to the federal Constitution, which declared that the "right of citizens of the United States to vote shall not be denied or abridged by the United States or by any State on account of race, color, or previous condition of servitude." Giles asked the court to order the Montgomery board of registrars to enter the names of the disenfranchised blacks on the voting lists, in effect to supervise the electoral process in Alabama. The lower court denied it had jurisdiction, and Giles took his case to the Supreme Court.

Once again, political tactics argued for assigning the opinion rejecting Giles's claims to Holmes. The Court, Holmes declared, writing for the six-judge majority (Fuller, Day, White, Peckham, McKenna, Holmes) found it "impossible" to accede to Giles's requests. If, he reasoned, Alabama's scheme for keeping blacks from voting was as deliberate and

---

* *Rogers* v. *Alabama.* 192 U.S. 226 (1904).

† The question of jury composition was not settled in *Rogers* v. *Alabama,* the forcefulness of the Court's decision notwithstanding. Ignorance of court decisions combined with deliberate defiance of them kept alive the practice of discriminating against blacks in jury selection, and cases kept right on coming to the Supreme Court. Until 1935, judicial disapproval was sporadic. Then, beginning in 1935 with *Norris* v. *Alabama,* the second Scottsboro case, the Supreme Court became substantially more vigilant in protecting the civil rights of blacks in general and of the process of jury selection in particular.

blatant as Giles claimed in his suit, "how," he asked, "can we make the court a party" to it by "accepting it and adding another voter to its fraudulent lists?"

Second, he said, the Supreme Court's jurisdiction did not include the authority to "enforce political rights." And if it did, he wondered, how could the Court enforce an order it might make? Consideration of those "actual feelings and demands of the community, whether right or wrong," was always lurking somewhere about when Holmes wrote his opinions. The Supreme Court, he said, had "little practical power to deal with the people of the State in a body." If, as Giles charged, "the great mass of the white population intends to keep blacks from voting . . . something more than ordering [Giles's] name to be inscribed upon the lists of 1902 will be needed. If," Holmes reasoned, "the conspiracy and the intent exist, a name on a piece of paper will not defeat them." Unless the Court was prepared to actually supervise voting in Alabama, which it was not, a court order would amount to no more than an "empty form." Political wrongs must be righted by the people and the state itself or by the Congress. Judges must not interfere.

Brewer, Brown, and Harlan, the lone dissenter in *Plessy* who made a practice of dissenting in most cases that rejected the civil rights claims of blacks, dissented. These three—a rare alliance: Brewer was a rigid conservative, Brown had written the majority opinion in *Plessy,* Harlan stood firmly for civil rights—clearly believed the Supreme Court could and ought to provide Giles with what he sought, although none offered a way in which it could be done.

Although Holmes's opinion lacks passion—he might have been describing the situation of two competing railroads rather than that of a politically helpless black man—to achieve his usual degree of remoteness had required some effort. He felt the decision was "inevitable," but "it was one of those terrible questions over which one would lie awake if he had not strong nerves." Holmes had the requisite "strong nerves." A veteran of the trenches, he had schooled himself to "think only of the problem and nothing else—to be neither egotist nor altruist according to [his] tiresomely repeated formula." Passion, like grief, detracted from the business at hand.

Holmes always claimed he didn't read newspapers, but he knew down to the final dot over the final "i" what they said about his opinions, and he grumbled, following announcement of *Giles,* that the press was "representing [him] as a second Taney in respect of probing another Dred Scott decision."

Nevertheless, as the 1902 Term wound down and he ordered the first bound volume of his decisions, without which he never felt the term was really over, as he sent the servants north and prepared himself to leave for Beverly Farms, he was content. The "demigods with huge heads and big faces who understood everything with diabolical swiftness" and who had intimidated him back in December had turned into men no larger intellectually than himself.

And "Lord how [he] like[d his] job!" The more he did it the better he liked it. The work was "hard and absorbing—oh how absorbing . . . more filling to the imagination than [he had] dreamed." He "profoundly rejoice[d]" that he "took the chance."

HOLMES DID NOT, however, settle into his customary routine of biking, reading, idle wandering about the North Shore, and enjoying the sea breezes that summer. By the end of the term, his spirit was "flabby" and a vague, unexplained "rumbling uneasiness" possessed him, exacerbated perhaps by a chance meeting in a Washington hotel with Charles Whittier with whom he had served in the Twentieth Massachusetts a half-century ago; Whittier had grown old in the interim, and Holmes had been "shocked" at the sight. His own brain was "dull." He was "tired." The work had been exhausting, the adjustment to unfamiliar people and places enervating. He "need[ed] a change," and, proceeding along "simple principles of hygiene," he sailed for England on June 13. He would miss Beverly Farms, and he did not anticipate a "lark"—he had dined out as much as he cared to—though he intended, of course, to look up old friends.

Recuperation in London, which he "filled as full as it would hold"—at the last he "sawed the days up into hour lengths"—took the usual form of reuning with English men and women to whom he undoubtedly felt closer than the Washingtonians he had so recently met. He visited Henry James at Rye and the Castletowns at Granston Manor and Doneraile. Romance seems no longer to have been a factor in Holmes's relationship with Lady Castletown, and when the bridge parties assembled in the evenings, Holmes was generally "left to some chance lady or book."

It was during this trip to Doneraile that the Castletowns introduced Holmes to Canon Patrick A. Sheehan, parish priest, occasional novelist, and thinker of some erudition whose intellectual attainments and philosophical reflections caught Holmes's imagination, and the two men, the one a man of faith, a mystic, the other a skeptic and supreme rationalist, struck up a firm friendship based on a frank and affectionate exchange of ideas. Despite their different backgrounds, they shared a love of literature, especially the classics, a philosophical habit of mind, and a love of intellectual battle which they carried on in a decade-long correspondence* and which often served to ease mutual feelings of intellectual loneliness. On Holmes's part, he "love[d] an idealist," even while he did not embrace the ideals. On Sheehan's part, the difference in their "interpretation of human life and the universe" around them "in no wise diminish[ed his] esteem" for his new friend.

Holmes and the president were still enjoying a honeymoon in the summer of 1903, and it was to Holmes that Roosevelt entrusted a letter informally outlining his customarily strong views on the drawing of the Alaska-Canada boundaries, which had been ambiguously defined in the Anglo-Russian Treaty of 1825 and were then being discussed by American and British-backed Canadian diplomats in London. Roosevelt had wanted to appoint a Supreme Court justice to the American negotiating team and had approached two, White and Holmes. Both had declined on the grounds of propriety and time. Failing that, Roosevelt had written Holmes his views and instructed Holmes to show the letter "privately and unofficially" to prominent Englishmen with whom he was acquainted and who were involved in the boundary discussions. When matters were settled and the boundaries worked out almost "exactly along the lines" Roosevelt had indicated in his letter, the president told Holmes that Holmes's unofficial diplomacy "was not without its direct effect on the decision." Holmes was less positive, thought it "extremely probable," but really believed "the circumstance [would] remain among the arcana of history."

Socially, the Roosevelts adopted the Holmeses into the ever-widening circle of White House familiars. Although Roosevelt and Holmes remained "Mr. President" and "Judge" to each other—no hint of personal informality colors their correspondence—they came to enjoy each other's company. Holmes sent Roosevelt books and select friends he thought the president would be interested in. Roosevelt, who customarily surrounded himself with the liveliest types America had to offer—cowboys, prizefighters, and big-game hunters mingled at the White House with newspapermen, intellectuals, diplomats, and political figures—told the Holmeses they were the best friends he had made since he arrived in Washington. Holmes suspected the president liked them because neither "Mrs. Holmes or I want to get anything from him." In any case, Roosevelt talked "with a freedom at the White House that would turn

* The *Holmes-Sheehan Correspondence: The Letters of Justice Oliver Wendell Holmes and Canon Patrick Augustine Sheehan,* edited by David H. Burton, was published by Kennikat Press in 1967.

your hair gray." The Holmeses dined often at the White House and easily fell into a regular schedule of theater-going with the Roosevelts and Lodges.

Although Holmes clearly enjoyed the company of both Roosevelts, he equally clearly had reservations about the president from the first. He was "always troubled by a conflict between [his] strong personal liking" for Roosevelt and his "inability to approve some of [Roosevelt's] political doings and sayings." Holmes found the president "great-hearted" and he appreciated the "picturesqueness of Roosevelt's character, his political tact, and the noble side of him." Holmes recognized, however, just how politically unscrupulous Roosevelt could be, and he offered his personal affection only to the degree "it was possible to like a man that you knew would throw over the friendship he professed the moment one allowed one's understanding of one's judicial duty to prevail over what *he* wanted." The halcyon days of the Holmes-Roosevelt friendship lasted until late winter 1904, just until the Northern Securities case was decided by the Supreme Court, when Holmes's "understanding of [his] judicial duty" did in fact prevail over what the president wanted.

In this instance, what Roosevelt, who was anxious to save the country as well as his friends from the more radical reforms blowing in the wind during the early years of the twentieth century, wanted was to use the Sherman Anti-Trust Act to regulate business practices and growth of the enormous monopolies and industrial combinations that were at the time strangling American consumers. To American industrialists, the trust—the secret pooling by manufacturers of processing, production, pricing, and profits—represented the acme of American financial ingenuity, a cleverly devised antidote to the loss of profits resulting from the wastefulness of cutthroat competition inherent in uncontrolled laissez-faire. By 1890, monopolies controlled most of life's major commodities, from sugar and salt to tobacco and transportation.

To the ordinary American, to whom the economies of monopoly did not filter down, the trust represented all that was wrong with the capitalistic system: arbitrary price-fixing that extorted premium prices for necessities as well as luxuries, corruption of municipal and state governments which accepted bribes in return for franchises and other privileges, the flow of money into the hands of the few.

In response to popular demand for control of these runaway corporations, state governments began to outlaw monopolies. Enforcement of the statutes was, however, lackadaisical, and by 1890 it looked as though congressional action was necessary if the evils believed to be inherent in corporate combination were to be banished. In 1890, Republican

Senators John Sherman of Ohio, Hoar of Massachusetts, and Edmunds of Vermont—Roosevelt's unsuccessful candidate for president in 1884— put together and Congress passed what became known as the Sherman Anti-Trust Act. A primitive attempt to limit the overwhelming power of the trusts, it declared illegal every "contract, combination in the form of trust or otherwise, or conspiracy, in restraint of trade or commerce among the several States" and imposed penalties on any who violated it.

To its sponsors, the act looked watertight; in fact it was full of leaks. "The President and the Congress are all very well in their way," Roosevelt was to remark sometime later. "They can say what they think they think, but it rests with the Supreme Court to decide what they have really thought." For the next two decades the Supreme Court kept up a running dialogue over what Congress had meant by the Sherman Anti-Trust Act.

Did the new statute, the Court asked itself, supersede the common law and make *all* combinations in restraint of trade illegal? Small businessmen fervently hoped so.

Or did the new statute, as corporate America hoped it did, formalize the common law which favored laissez-faire economics and allowed certain monopolistic practices and distinguished only between reasonable and unreasonable limits on trade? That part of the common law involving combination had developed in complexity more or less in proportion to the growth of consolidations, monopolies, and pools, and a lot of judicial hairs were split deciding what was reasonable, what unreasonable. In general, the common law supported combinations so long as they accomplished their ends by legal means and did not involve a "wholesale restraint of trade," that is, force prices up or withhold products from the market, put men out of work or contravene public policy. The common law also distinguished between direct and indirect restraint of trade, and between necessities and convenience products.

For the first several years following passage of the Sherman Act, the federal courts, including the Supreme Court, gave it the common-law construction. The landmark case was *United States* v. *E.C. Knight Co.*, the Cleveland administration's case against the sugar trust which by the time the case came to the Supreme Court, had acquired control of 98 percent of all sugar processing in the United States. The Court, 8 to 1 (Harlan dissented), dismissed the case. The sugar refiners, wrote Chief Justice Fuller, a strong individualist with little enthusiasm for paternalistic government, were engaged not in interstate commerce but in manufacturing, an indirect restraint of trade not only permissible and by implication reasonable under the common law, but also a local activity reserved for state control under the Tenth Amendment ("The powers not delegated to the United States by the Constitution, nor prohibited by it to the States, are reserved to the States respectively, or to the people"). Since the combination in *Knight* affected interstate commerce only indirectly, it was permissible under common-law standards.

It was not long, however, before the Court began to march in the other direction. In early 1897, the Court concluded that the Sherman Act erased the common-law distinction between reasonable and unreasonable restraint of trade. In *United States* v. *Trans-Missouri Freight Association,* there was no question of manufacturing that the justices could hide behind; they had to confront the reasonableness of restraint of trade in interstate commerce squarely. They held against the trust and reaffirmed their decision shortly afterwards in a similar case, *United States* v. *Joint Traffic Association,* despite Senator Edmunds's eloquent arguments as defense counsel in the lower court that he and his co-authors had intended a common-law construction of the Sherman Act.

It looked to Roosevelt, when he ascended to the presidency, as if the time might be ripe to unleash the full power of the government against the trusts. He considered the Court's decision in the sugar trust case as damaging to the nation as that in the Dred Scott case had been, and he vowed to reverse it "in the interests of the people."

The biggest and most powerful of the trusts as the twentieth century opened were the railroad trusts, which first knit the fabric of a huge continent together but in the process gained control of all land transportation—and therefore indirectly, all American industry—within the United States until the advent of the automobile. Their directors operated like despots of old, raising and lowering rates as casually as window shades, buying legislators like penny candy—in some states the railroad lobby operated as a fourth branch of government—and generally showing contempt for the public interest.

Just before Roosevelt succeeded to the presidency, a small group of financiers led by J. P. Morgan and Jim Hill had taken control of the entire railroad system of the Northwest, consolidating in the Northern Securities Company all freight and passenger transportation from the Great Lakes to Puget Sound. Roosevelt feared the merger was but prelude to their taking control of the entire continent's railroad systems. He would have preferred only to regulate the trusts, to rid them of their obvious abuses. He believed "great corporations" were "necessary, and only men of great and singular mental power can manage such corporations successfully, and such men must have great rewards. But these corporations should be managed with due regard to the interest of the public as a whole." And since they were not so managed, he forged ahead with the only tool—the Sherman Anti-Trust Act—Congress had provided, restrained only by the reminder of the potential for revolt among Republican businessmen, i.e., campaign contributors.

Early in 1902, some months before Holmes was appointed to the Court, Roosevelt had approached his attorney general, Philander C. Knox, former corporation lawyer and one of the organizers of Andrew Carnegie's steel company, the cabinet member on whom corporate America was relying to be a steadying influence on the impulsive president. Roosevelt wondered whether the Northern Securities Company might be taken to court under the Sherman Anti-Trust Act. Knox thought it probably could. Roosevelt instructed him to go ahead with it.

While the necessary papers were being prepared for filing in the lower federal court, which required some weeks, not even a hint of Roosevelt's intention was leaked; not one rumor got loose in a historically rumor-ridden city. When on February 19, 1902, Knox, carefully waiting until the stock market had closed for the day, announced to the press that "within a very short time," the government intended to file suit against Northern Securities under the Sherman Anti-Trust Act, the business world was astonished. Before the New York stock exchange even opened the next day, telephone orders poured into brokerage offices from stockholders wanting to sell. When the gong sounded on the exchange to begin business on February 20, there was a mad scramble to sell. London, Paris, and Berlin panicked along with New York and shares fell sharply. J. P. Morgan, barometer of business, was reported to have gone "white with fear and rage" when he learned what the government had done. James J. Hill complained that it seemed "hard that we should be compelled to fight for our lives against the political adventurers who have never done anything but pose and draw a salary." Legal advisers to the two magnates rationalized that the president had been misled by "an unknown country lawyer from Pennsylvania," to which Roosevelt replied: "They will know this country lawyer before this suit is ended."

Unable to understand this sudden display of audacity on the part of a Republican administration, Morgan went straight to the White House where he attempted to discuss the matter with Roosevelt, man to man, Republican to Republican. Surely the president could be persuaded to do the gentlemanly thing. After all, a Morgan partner, Robert Bacon, had been at Harvard with the president; another Morgan associate, George Perkins, had recently visited the White House. If his company had misbehaved, Morgan said to the president in innocence and arrogance, "send your man to my man and they can fix it up."

"That can't be done," Roosevelt replied.

"We don't want to fix it up, we want to stop it," said Knox, who also was present and who had warned New York businessmen that if they did not "cheerfully acquiesce in moderate correction at the hands of their friends," they ran the risk of having "the administration of affairs thrown into the hands of those who would not deal gently with them."

As good as his word, Knox filed the suit for the government in federal court in Minnesota. On April 9, 1903, that court handed down its decision declaring that the organization of Northern Securities had indeed violated the Sherman Anti-Trust Act. The company immediately took its case to the U.S. Supreme Court.

Oral arguments opened on December 14, 1903. As was the custom, Monday through Friday, October to June, during Holmes's years on the Court, Capitol policemen stationed themselves in the marble corridor outside the courtroom at a few minutes before noon. A nearby swinging door opened. The policemen stopped traffic in the corridor. Dapper little Chief Justice Fuller appeared first. He was the last public figure in Washington to wear his white hair shoulder length and parted in the middle; his mustaches rivaled Holmes's. Attired in their flowing black robes, the associate justices followed solemnly to the courtroom. Holmes once heard a sightseer remark to a companion as he passed, "Christ, what dignity!"

The justices marched on toward their raised bench. Originally they had sat on the same level with the lawyers who argued before them, but Henry Clay, so legend has it, once helped himself to a pinch of snuff from one of the justices' snuff boxes during his argument, and the justices, dismayed by Clay's casual familiarity, ordered the bench elevated.

Chief Justice Fuller occupied the center chair. He was so short that it had been necessary to raise his courtroom chair to accommodate a hassock for his feet. The "side judges" sat to his right and left in order of seniority. Only eight judges were present on this particular Monday. Henry Brown, whose eyesight had been failing for some years and whom fears of blindness had plagued since childhood, had been kept at home by an eye ailment. He would have to decide *Northern Securities Co.* v. *United States* on the basis of the briefs.

Attorney General Knox, assisted by a phalanx of lower-echelon Justice Department lawyers, was to make the case for the government. He was a typical representative of the public bar in the early decades of the twentieth century. Prosecutors were recruited from the ranks of corporation attorneys and often returned to their Wall Street offices when their political patrons left the White House. The reasoning was that these men knew best the intricate workings of the corporation. From the lawyer's point of view, the corporation was one of the few places where he could achieve the prominence and attract the kind of attention that led to political appointment.

On the other hand, could the president entirely rely on a corporation lawyer to prosecute big business with all the vigor that might be required? Richard Olney, member of a prominent Massachusetts family, distinguished member of the Boston bar, had, as attorney general in 1895, prosecuted the sugar trust less than enthusiastically, practically asked the Supreme Court to decide against him, and later worked for repeal of the Sherman Anti-Trust Act. Solicitor General James M. Beck, as humble a servant of the special interests as ever wrote a brief, distrusted the exercise of national power and once freely confessed he was glad the Supreme Court's decision had gone against him in a case he had argued for the government. *Northern Securities,* the most important government case Knox had argued so far, was a test of his as well as Roosevelt's resolve.

John G. Johnson of Philadelphia, who had argued for the sugar refiners against the government and hoped to repeat his victory, was to present the case for Northern Securities. He was the best counsel corporate America could offer, one of the new type of lawyer, the specialist, whose expertise in the highly technical area of corporation law had made him indispensable to the expanding business community. He had argued many a case in the U.S. Supreme Court—his practice largely involved representing corporate violators of regulatory statutes—and he knew the justices and their prejudices.

Johnson really wanted to win this case. He admired Jim Hill, believed him to be a farsighted planner with more sensitivity to public needs than the usual antitrust defendant, and he was certain the formation of Northern Securities was a positive good for the country. He not only considered consolidation good economic sense for the corporations involved, the cure for the kind of competition that often resulted in corporate ruin, but he also felt the economic well-being and development of commerce in the Northwestern United States depended upon the financial health of these railroads.

The courtroom was filled to capacity. Congressmen, diplomats, and lawyers from all over the country—including James Beck, who had resigned from the Justice Department since presenting the government's case in the lower court and had returned to private practice in New York City—crowded the front benches. Mrs. Roosevelt, Mrs. Cowles (the president's sister), Mrs. Knox, Mrs. Holmes, Mrs. Lodge, and other prominent Washingtonians sat in the audience. Visitors stood in a solid mass behind the bar. The arguments lasted the better part of two days, but there was no flagging of public interest even on the second day. Distinguished guests were in their reserved seats early; others had lined up in the Capitol's halls long before court opened.

Johnson for Northern Securities opened the argument. He began by telling the Court that the decision of the lower court upholding the government's claims had been inconsistent with previous Supreme Court decisions. Then, cheerful and optimistic, he discussed law less and less, economics more and more. His personal conviction that consolidation of the railroads at issue was a valuable economic asset to the expanding commerce of the Northwest dominated his case. Improvement of service had been uppermost in the minds of Morgan and Hill and their partners when they had consolidated their properties; restraint of trade had not crossed their minds, and if it had occurred, it was so little as to be negligible. Johnson described the businessmen's ingenuity in devising trade routes for shipping out Northwestern lumber and bringing back Midwestern steel and Southern cotton as a bold enterprise, comparable to that of those earlier entrepreneurs whose clipper ships had not so very long before carried American trade to the farthest corners of the world. Surely a merger that so expanded trade did not violate provisions of the Sherman law; if it did, the act then must be unconstitutional.

Attorney General Knox had barely begun to reply that first afternoon when the Court adjourned. He resumed his presentation the next day. Compared to Johnson, he appeared severe, gravely concerned about the effects of railroad consolidation, which he believed destroyed the independence of each one involved and removed competition altogether. He outlined in considerable detail the provisions and purposes of the antitrust statute and made it clear that he believed Northern Securities was exactly the sort of combination in restraint of trade that the Sherman law had been intended to prevent.

Questions from the justices were intermittent and did not tip their hands. During most of the time, when he wasn't gnawing on a plug of tobacco as was his custom, White sat back in his chair, his eyes closed. He was not, however, asleep. The movements of a lawyer's face tended to hypnotize him, and only by closing his eyes could he give the argument his full attention. Their public masks of strict neutrality in place, the other justices appeared to listen attentively to both arguments. When the session ended late on Tuesday afternoon, none in the audience had a clue as to which way the decision would go.

Corporate America knew it could depend on Chief Justice Fuller and Associate Justice White, who had indicated in his dissent to the Court's decision in the Trans-Missouri Freight Association case that he felt as strongly about the correctness of the common-law interpretation of the Sherman Act as did the chief justice. Peckham was a foregone conclusion, and they rather anticipated Brewer's vote. Corporate America also knew it could *not* depend on Harlan, whose dissent in the sugar trust case easily matched Fuller's majority opinion for vehemence. Roosevelt undoubtedly was counting on his two appointees, Day and Holmes, to line up behind Harlan. The rest of the justices remained question-marks through the winter of 1903–04, as all America waited tensely for the Court's decision in *Northern Securities*.

As the winter wore on, Harlan assembled a majority to construe the Sherman Act as prohibiting all restraint of trade, whether reasonable or unreasonable under the common law. With him were Brewer, Brown, McKenna, and Day, although the usually conservative Brewer wavered for some time before he finally capitulated, and he did write a separate concurrence.

Although the justices had tried to keep the date of their decision secret, every seat in the courtroom was taken on March 14, 1904; Attorney General Knox, Secretary of War William Howard Taft, and an unusual number of congressmen were present when the senior associate justice, John Marshall Harlan, began reading the Court's decision in the Northern Securities case. As soon as spectators recognized the author of the opinion, they knew which way the Court had gone. The case, however, had been decided by the narrowest of margins, 5 to 4.

Revenge must have been sweet that day for the man who had tried so hard to bring the law to bear on the sugar trust nine years before. As the senior justice in the majority this time, he had assigned the opinion to himself. His reading of it required an hour and a quarter.

In his constitutional jurisprudence, Harlan was in some ways a "premature New Dealer," encouraging the exercise of legislative power in the development of democratic ideals. He revered the new regulatory measures Congress had enacted—the Sherman law, the Interstate Commerce Act of 1887—measures his colleagues often viewed not as reform but as usurpation. "We must not be so unwise," he once told a group of fellow Kentuckians, "or so suspicious or timid as to reject a new policy or a new law simply because it may cover areas not consciously within the mental vision or the thoughts of the framers of the Constitution." The decision in the Northern Securities case could not have fallen into friendlier hands.

In stern and commanding phrases, Harlan declared that, whatever the Court had said in 1895, the Sherman Act had "no reference to the mere manufacture or production of articles or commodities within the limits of the several States." The act was not, he said, "limited to restraints of interstate and international trade or commerce that are unreasonable . . . but embraces *all* direct *restraints* imposed by any combination, conspiracy or monopoly upon such trade or commerce."

Harlan took the opportunity to let American capitalism know what he thought of it. Prediction of financial ruin, he said, usually accompanied enforcement of a statute. He had found, however, "it is the history of monopolies . . . that predictions of ruin are habitually made by them when it is attempted, by legislation, to restrain their operations and to protect the public against their exactions."

The freedom of private business to carry out its operations without government interference—or "liberty of contract" as it had come to be known in legal shorthand—did not, Harlan declared with his accustomed vehemence, "involve a right to deprive the public of the advantages of free competition in trade and commerce." Liberty of contract did not imply the liberty "to defy the national will." All rights "must be exercised in subordination to the law."

Holmes had little use for Harlan's jurisprudence in general; he thought it demagogic, not thoroughly thought out, and, worst of all, long-winded. He used to say Harlan's mind was "like a vise, the jaws of which did not meet. It held only the larger objects." To Holmes, Harlan often seemed stern and humorless; Justice Brewer used to say Harlan went to sleep at night with one hand on the Bible and the other on the Constitution. On Harlan's side, he found Holmes obscure and his jurisprudence unsound. Clashes between the two kept their brethren awake in conference, as Holmes hacked away at Harlan's progressive notions, and Harlan flayed at Holmes's remoteness from the social and economic realities with which the Court had to deal. On one occasion, Holmes was so uncustomarily angry at something Harlan said in conference that he actually interrupted the orderly discussion.

"That won't wash. That won't wash," Holmes roared, and the two antagonists had at it until the gentle little peacemaker among them, Chief Justice Fuller, interjected, "Well, I'm scrubbing away. I'm scrubbing away."

However much Holmes disagreed with Harlan's views on the American Constitution, he could nevertheless respect the man who uttered them; he admitted that Harlan's was a "simple nature—but a formidable intelligence and a personality that it would be hard to replace—under superficial shortcomings a great engine and a noble courage."

In the Northern Securities case, Holmes thought the "great engine" had jumped the tracks and the "formidable intelligence" had failed. Holmes joined White's dissent, which followed the rationale of the Court's decision in the sugar trust case; Fuller and Peckham also joined White's dissent. Holmes's joining with White was a surprise, but the others decided according to expectations.

Then Holmes surprised everybody even more when he read a dissent of his own, which White, Peckham, and Fuller also joined. It was Holmes's first written dissent.*

Used too often, dissent loses its power to persuade. Used frivolously in an insignificant case, it is a waste and may even antagonize the brethren, who will get their revenge in the important opinion the dissenter is also writing. Chief justices generally discourage it as detracting from the authority of the Court, especially in controversial cases. Used sparingly, however, dissent is an effective and time-honored tradition of the Court. On the one hand it serves, because it often is a solo, as a map to the workings of a justice's mind. As Holmes put it,

> one can say what one thinks without having to blunt the edges and cut off the corners to suit someone else.

Dissent may also serve as an educational device to illumine areas of the law not addressed by the majority; and dissent is, as Charles Evans Hughes once wrote,

> an appeal to the brooding spirit of the law, to the intelligence of a future day, when a later decision may possibly correct the error into which the dissenting judge believes the court to have been betrayed.

Holmes didn't like to dissent, though he didn't

> worry very much as to being in a minority if I think my views worth stating in the public interest.

---

* In February 1903, he had joined silently in White's dissent in *Chicago Theological Seminary* v. *Illinois*. 188 U.S. 662, 667.

Although he became known as the Great Dissenter, it was the quality and tenor of his dissents, not the quantity, which amounted only to comparatively few out of the thousands of opinions he wrote, that established his reputation. As he had on the Massachusetts court, he dissented with reluctance and only when a major principle was involved; when his disagreement with the majority was only a matter of construction or some equally minor matter, he was more likely to "shut up," as he usually put it. He sometimes blew off accumulated steam by writing a dissent, then failing to deliver it. When an admirer brought him for autographing a copy of his collected dissents,* he wrote reluctantly and muttered, "I don't seek my reputation as a dissenter."

With his dissent in *Northern Securities,* Holmes defied not only the Court majority but the dominant "feelings and demands of the community," which he generally supported, and the man who had appointed him. When Roosevelt named Holmes to the Supreme Court, his knowledge of the Massachusetts judge was undoubtedly limited to his antecedents—though he may not have been familiar with the family tradition of dissent—his honorable Civil War record, a couple of speeches—one that appealed to Roosevelt, one that didn't—and what Cabot Lodge had told him about Holmes. It seems clear he had not studied Holmes's state court opinions. He saw in Holmes a Brahmin much like himself who could be relied on to confront contemporary public issues in much the same way he himself did and to show some loyalty to his patron in the way Brahmins and political appointees might be expected to. Roosevelt may have been entirely unaware that even as an undergraduate, Holmes had not lacked the courage to defy the Harvard establishment with his unorthodox writings, beside which defiance of the president's wishes by a Supreme Court justice, possessing all the independence a lifetime appointment confers, pales by comparison. Holmes admitted that dissenting in *Northern Securities* was "painful" because it meant going "against what a personal friend [was] hoping for and perhaps expecting." Such considerations, however, had "no effect on the mind of one who is accustomed to weigh questions impersonally." It has even been suggested that he may have bent over backward to demonstrate his independence.

Whatever Holmes and Roosevelt, who was already involved in the government's suit against the Northern Securities Company at the time, discussed that summer day in 1902 when Roosevelt concluded Holmes would make a first-class replacement for Horace Gray, it is highly un-

---

* *The Dissenting Opinions of Mr. Justice Holmes,* arranged by Alfred Lief, foreword by George W. Kirchwey. New York, 1929.

likely that Holmes had even hinted to the president that in the tradition of Adam Smith, he did not like "government meddling with the natural course of events" or that "monopolies on the whole, i.e., the trust and the like—were very much for the public interest—and . . . that the contrary prejudice stands on no reasoned grounds." He could hardly have told Roosevelt he considered the Sherman Anti-Trust Act a "humbug based on economic ignorance and incompetence." If the president had known that Jim Hill's book *Highways of Progress* reinforced Holmes's beliefs "in a striking way," Holmes might indeed have lived out his remaining years as chief justice of the Massachusetts Supreme Court. If Roosevelt had read Holmes's opinions in those Massachusetts labor cases when Holmes observed that "free competition means combination" instead of newspaper articles about them, he might have better understood Holmes's position.

If Holmes was nervous when he delivered his dissent in *Northern Securities,* he did not show it. He had begun to fret over the "growth of his middle register" and felt like "the God Buddha when I try to bend round myself." But expanding girth did not show beneath his robes, and he was the picture of New England dignity when he rose to read his opinion. Chief Justice Fuller, who had joined it, reported that

> you could hear a pin drop, and his sentences were as incisive as the edge of a knife.

Holmes did not like, he said, participating in "great" cases that public interest turned into political crises and inevitably made "bad law." Great cases, he thought, were "called great, not by reason of their real importance in shaping the law of the future, but because of some accident of immediate overwhelming interest which appeals to the feelings and distorts the judgment." He had seen enough of that in the reaction to his dissents in the Massachusetts labor cases. Now, *Northern Securities* had become a contest between the president and Wall Street, and Holmes resented the importance attached to it. Such cases, he felt, were not "half so important as many small ones that involve interstitial development of the law."

Holmes's comprehension of economic realities fell short of his comprehension of political intimations. Trust-busters' accusations that "the great masters of combinations" might also be involved in exploitation he ranked somewhere between cant and drool. He admired Jim Hill and Rockefeller and viewed the large corporation as he viewed the large labor organization: "inevitable," though he thought the former somewhat more desirable than the latter, and considered its efficiencies the key to national prosperity. He had no understanding of the power the trusts had amassed along with the money, no idea how they affected American farmers and small businessmen, no inkling of what uncontrolled growth meant. For years he harped on the same theme:

> that legislation can't cure things—that the crowd now has substantially all there is—that the sooner they make up their mind to it the better—and that the fights against capital are simply fights between the different bands of producers only properly to be settled by the equilibrium of social desires.

Economics bored him and utopian economics bored him absolutely. He had spent practically no time in the study of economics, and it was said that his thinking in the field had stopped at age twenty-five. Some years later, Brandeis "drove a harpoon into [his] midriff" when he suggested "it would be for the good of [Holmes's] soul" to spend the Court's summer recess learning something of economics and shipped him a large crate of scholarly books on the subject. Holmes took one look at it and shipped it right back. Philosophy and law were his fortes as well as his major interests, and he never did familiarize himself with even the basic tenets of economics.

Holmes had no wish to reshape the world, to redistribute wealth, and he was contemptuous and skeptical of those who did. Reformers, he believed, set themselves up as little gods who knew what was good for the universe, and he had distrusted them since his youth in Boston when vociferous Abolitionists had made it clear that "anyone who did not agree with them was a knave or a fool"; he came to "detest a man who knows that he knows." The Sherman Anti-Trust Act, an "imbecile statute" aimed at "making everyone fight" but forbidding "anyone to be victorious," was one of the worst attempts at reform. The question in *Northern Securities,* however, involved not an evaluation of the Sherman Anti-Trust Act, but a judgment on whether or not the big combination had violated it.

It was perfectly clear to Holmes that the financial arrangements among the railroads that made up the Northern Securities Company were entirely compatible with the antitrust law. The lower federal courts and the government at oral argument had made much of the giant combination's effect on competition. Competition, Holmes said, was irrelevant; the act said nothing about competition.

> Much trouble is made [he admonished the majority, which he felt had departed from objective standards of decision-making and injected unwarranted implications into the statute], by substituting other phrases assumed to be equivalent, which then are reasoned from as if they were in the act.

The act, he said, prohibited, quite specifically, only contracts and combinations in restraint of trade.

The seed of his major points in *Northern Securities* had been sown in Massachusetts. In 1887, the Supreme Judicial Court had unanimously allowed a consolidation of three roller-shade manufacturers to live on the common-law grounds that its restraint of trade was not unreasonable.* Holmes's much-discussed labor opinions were essentially paraphrases of the same principle. Agreements in restraint of trade, Holmes reminded the majority in *Northern Securities,* were "dealt with and defined by the common law," and it did not apply to mere combinations, only to those organized to exclude others. Northern Securities Company, Holmes argued, had been organized not to exclude others and restrain trade, but in "community of interest," an expansive concept which the Sherman Act did not forbid and which left the parties "without external restriction."

Of course, he continued, the corporation was a monopoly, but only in the sense that "every railroad monopolizes . . . the trade of some area." A single railroad "down a narrow valley or through a mountain gorge monopolizes all the railroad transportation through that valley gorge." Northern Securities Company was innocent of anything more sinister than that. Followed to its logical conclusion, the majority's interpretation of the Sherman law and the world of small producers that would inevitably result "would make eternal the *bellum omnium contra omnes* and disintegrate society so far as it could into individual atoms," an absurd result contemplated neither by the Constitution makers nor the Congress.

Public announcement of the decision in *Northern Securities* brought about a temporary panic in the stock market, but it recovered quickly and closed higher for the day, although the financial establishment continued to worry about how the Court had affected investors' confidence. Press opinion was generally favorable, and Roosevelt's cabinet was pleased.

---

* *Central Shade-Roller Co.* v. *Cushman.* 143 Mass. 353 (1887).

Attorney General Knox was elated by the Court's decision, and anticipated acceleration of the "return to more sober methods in commercial affairs." He felt the "danger of uncontrolled personal power in railway management" had been averted. In this crucial test of power, the government had ostensibly won, and the Court had given it the wherewithal to deal with the trusts.

Public feeling ran high; at last big business could and would be restrained. Knox was besieged by requests for copies of the Court's opinions, and the Court ordered thirteen thousand printed.

Corporate America was less pleased, at least at first. The decision in *Northern Securities* represented to businessmen a "blow at corporate enterprises," and they set out then and there to prevent Roosevelt's nomination in 1904 on the grounds that he was not a "safe man" for the business interests of the country to have in the White House.

The president himself heard the news while engaged in a conference, which he interrupted to express his satisfaction in the Supreme Court's decision. He was, however, furious with the behavior of his first appointee to the Supreme Court, whose record he had so thoroughly explored and who had betrayed him. Roosevelt, who was said not to "care a damn about law," looked at Holmes as if he were a ward heeler who "didn't deliver the goods." Publicly Roosevelt complained that he could "carve out of a banana a judge with more backbone than that." Holmes, the president told Knox, "will never enter the door of the White House again."

"On the contrary, Mr. President," Knox replied, "you will ask him to dinner within a week or two."

Although experiencing again the "hydraulic pressures" he so disliked, the object of Roosevelt's vituperation was unabashed. He boasted for years that at a White House dinner for labor leaders he told one of them who had been "spouting about Judges: 'What you want is favor—not justice. But when I am on the job I don't care a damn what you want or what Mr. Roosevelt wants.' " He expected the president shortly would "cool down." If he didn't, if Roosevelt's "seeming personal regard for us was based on the idea he had a tool the sooner it is ended the better—we shall see."

The aftermath of *Northern Securities* did in fact destroy the camaraderie between Roosevelt and Holmes; Roosevelt viewed Holmes's dissent as a "political departure (or, I suspect, more truly, couldn't forgive anyone who stood in his way)." When shortly afterwards Lodge sent Roosevelt a news clipping relating how the Emperor of Korea, in a display of his raw power, abolished the Korean supreme court, Roosevelt sent it on to Holmes:

> Respectfully referred to Mr. Justice Holmes, to read, mark, and return. The merit of the suggestion is so obvious that it will at once strike the most headless.

Holmes immediately returned the clipping:

> As to the scurrilous suggestion of Cabot and Bill Bigelow [Sturgis Bigelow who had first discovered the clipping] I shall have to remind these gents that where the Chancellor is, there is the Court of Chancery, and that if I catch them in the New England circuit I will lay them by the heels if they do not keep civil tongues in their heads. The King, of course,—can do no wrong.

The Roosevelts did again invite the Holmeses to the White House, but the old warmth had cooled, and they "talked freely later but it was never the same after that."

The newspapers played up not Holmes's skill in adapting common-law formulas to constitutional problems, but his row with the president; for a defiant gesture Holmes would rather have avoided, the name Holmes became a household word throughout America. He was no longer an obscure "side judge"; he was the man who had gone against Roosevelt's wishes. The Holmes legend was born, though it was hardly the sort of recognition he had so long desired.

The government's victory and subsequent revitalization of the Sherman Act increased the president's popularity enormously. Although the decision was a setback for use of the holding company as a device to circumvent the Sherman Act, the financiers involved—Morgan, Hill, and their partners—did not come out of their little war with the government entirely defeated. The company, of course, had to be dissolved, and the shares of stock returned to the stockholders in the original companies. But Morgan and Hill and their associates, who held large blocks of stock in the original companies, remained in charge of the money. Hill, who had dreamed of Northern Securities as only the beginning of a trading empire extending to Japan, China, and other parts of the Far East, was naturally disappointed that his case had been lost, but for the near future, it meant only that he had to sign two financial statements instead of one. There was even a little something in the decision for men like Holmes's old friend Brooks Adams, who anticipated the rise of real estate prices on West Coast property he owned. As Holmes summed up the case, it

> could not have come out better for all concerned . . . if the whole thing had been arranged and the parts assigned.

CHAPTER *19*

"The Fourteenth Amendment does not enact Mr. Herbert Spencer's Social Statics"

IN THE ANNUAL rush toward summer adjournment, the churning out of the necessary number of opinions in April, May, and June generally resulted in what a later justice called "our cruddiest, our shoddiest work." Holmes took on extra opinions that June, finding them a "relief from the languor that comes on when work is done and the weather very hot." Washington's steamy heat always oppressed Holmes at that time of year; it was "very different from that on the North Shore and takes the life out of you." Like Holmes, those Washingtonians who could fled the city as the heat and humidity rose; those who couldn't lived on their front stoops, trying to catch a passing breath of air. Women defied convention to go hatless, and a local laundry boasted on its delivery wagons that "Colemanized Collars Wilt Slowly."

The euphoria of those early days in Washington was beginning to wear off. Perhaps Holmes still missed the familiar ways of Boston; perhaps the public's response to his work did not satisfy him—newspaper reporters had been more interested in his disagreement with the president than in his arguments in *Northern Securities*. In any case, he was beginning to feel "a good deal of loneliness in the midst of much society here," despite "great companionship" with White, "affectionate relations" with Fuller, and "very pleasant ones with the rest."

His flirtations were attracting attention again. Even the president noticed. After watching Holmes operate seated between two dowagers at dinner, Roosevelt leaned over to Fanny and remarked: "Look at him—the sex instinct is strong enough in him to make him talk to Mrs. _____.

I wish I could do that. Do you suppose it is real or is he putting it on!" Fanny's reply has not survived, but Holmes, when he learned what the president had said, could only quip: *"Si on n'a pas ce qu'on aime il faut aimer ce qu'on a,"* or in idiomatic English, "If you're not near the girl you love, you love the girl you're near."

Fanny was still attending to her social duties, but once again she was beginning to feel that she got "more pleasure from solitude than from society." Roosevelt was still seating her next to him at dinners even after *Northern Securities* and finding she could be no less prickly than her husband. Her reply to his question about Washington women has survived more than eighty years: "Mr. President," she said, "Washington is full of famous men and the women they married when they were young." When Mrs. Roosevelt invited her to tea with Mrs. Stonewall Jackson at the White House, Fanny committed the social equivalent to her husband's dissent in *Northern Securities.*

Sensing some reluctance to attend on Fanny's part, Mrs. Roosevelt purred: "Oh, you know she [Mrs. Jackson] is entirely reconstructed."

Replied Fanny, who had spent some of the best years of her young womanhood poring anxiously over casualty lists: "Well, you know I am not." And she didn't go.

ROOSEVELT'S PLEASURE in the Court's decision against the Northern Securities Company paled somewhat by its proximity, in the spring of 1904, to the approaching presidential election and its potential for alienating large contributors to his campaign, although Knox reassured them there would be no "running amuck" over the corporations. In May 1902, shortly after the government had won its suit against Northern Securities in the lower court, the Justice Department had begun proceedings against the beef trust in the U.S. Circuit Court for the Northern District of Illinois. A year later that court decided in favor of the government. Then the case was stalled on its way to the U.S. Supreme Court, and oral argument was postponed until after the election in November 1904, which required financing by big business.

Corporate America and a good many old guard Republicans would have preferred the old-fashioned conservative, Mark Hanna, as their candidate, but Hanna died before the convention, and Roosevelt won the Republican nomination by acclamation. His Democratic opponent, a New York judge named Alton B. Parker, was a nonentity who, it was hoped, would draw the fearful financiers away from Roosevelt. Convinced, however, that Republican rule was still in their best interest, the businessmen rallied behind Roosevelt after all and financed his campaign handsomely. J. P. Morgan gave $150,000; Standard Oil, which was already on Roosevelt's list of trusts to bust, gave $100,000; Henry Clay Frick, whose U.S. Steel was shortly to be attacked by the government's legal antitrust infantry, gave $50,000. Roosevelt won handily by a margin of 2.5 million popular votes and 196 electoral votes.

Two months after Roosevelt's election, which had also been supported by J. Ogden Armour of the Chicago meatpackers and other members of the beef trust, the case against those very meatpackers was argued in the U.S. Supreme Court. *Swift & Co.* v. *United States,* it was called. The cattlemen were charged on several counts of violating the Sherman Anti-Trust Act, through regulating prices, livestock shipments, and rules of credit, in order to monopolize the meat business in the United States. Altogether they controlled about 60 percent of the American meat trade.

John S. Miller, former corporation counsel for the city of Chicago and prominent lawyer there, argued the case for the meatpackers. Fifty-two-year-old William H. Moody, Massachusetts Republican and Roosevelt crony—Moody had been the president's first choice for the Supreme Court seat to which he ultimately had appointed Holmes—had succeeded Philander Knox as attorney general; he argued for the government. Seven generations of Massachusetts sailors, ministers, and farmers had endowed him with a yeoman's capacity for hard work and a strong New England sense of justice, a perfect combination, in Roosevelt's estimation, for forceful trust-busting.

The case was important enough for the Court to set aside two days, January 6 and 9,* for oral arguments, although these were not particularly imaginative, and questions from the justices were few. Miller argued that the Sherman Act was so general and vague that "a defendant cannot know from its terms what he may or may not do. . . ." In any case, he said, the packers sold their fresh meats to dealers locally and were not therefore involved in interstate commerce, which the Sherman Act required for violation. Attorney General Moody argued that the meatpackers had conspired to "control the market of the nation for fresh meats," that the conspiracy had succeeded, and that this control was "merciless and oppressive." Holmes briefly enlivened the first day's presentation when he asked whether certain stockyards in which he was a shareholder were involved in the suit, and was no doubt relieved when Miller said they were not.

* Volume 196, page 375, of the *United States Reports* gives the dates as January 6 and 7. January 7, however, fell on a Saturday, and arguments were actually concluded on Monday, January 9.

Three weeks later, on January 30, the Supreme Court handed down its decision. The justices were unanimous. The beef trust, in its efforts to exclude competitors and monopolize the meat markets of the nation, had indeed violated the Sherman Anti-Trust Act. Since Holmes had dissented in the last big antitrust case, it made good sense to Fuller to assign the opinion in the beef trust case to him.

Despite his distaste for the Sherman Act, the statute had been upheld by the Court, and the judges, Holmes said, were "bound" to support it. How he detested the condition

> that it should be part of my duty to take part in enforcing laws that I don't believe in.

But of course he couldn't say so publicly. He could only do the majority's bidding when he wrote for it.

In *Swift,* citing *Commonwealth* v. *Peaslee,* one of his own Massachusetts opinions—he was his own "favorite author" of precedent—Holmes again adapted a common-law concept for use in a constitutional problem and explained how the component parts of the meat dealers' operations (fixing beef prices, restricting shipments, blacklisting uncooperative cattlemen, and so on), while perhaps not unlawful separately, when taken together added up to an intentional and thereby unlawful scheme to restrain and monopolize trade among the several states.

He went on and not only declared the beef trust an illegal combination within the meaning of the Sherman Anti-Trust Act, but invented a new term, "current of commerce," in order to demolish the meat dealers' main argument and bring them within the meaning of interstate commerce:

> [C]ommerce among the states is not a technical legal conception, but a practical one, drawn from the course of business. When cattle are sent for sale from a place in one State, with the expectation that they will end their transit, after purchase, in another, and when in effect they do so, with only the interruption necessary to find a purchaser at the stock yards, and when this is a typical, constantly recurring course, the current thus existing is a current of commerce among the States, and the purchase of the cattle is a part and incident of such commerce.

That night in Philadelphia, Roosevelt, reiterating the theme of his administration, urged members of the Union League Club to "lead in the effort to secure proper supervision and regulation of corporate activity by the Government, . . . because in the long run it will be in the interest above all of the very people who often betray alarm and anger when the proposition is first made."

In his first opinion for the U.S. Supreme Court in 1903, *Otis* v. *Parker,* Holmes had indicated his inclination to allow the exercise of state legislative power so long as it did not violate the provisions of the Fourteenth Amendment to the Constitution. As he had in his opinions for the Massachusetts court, he searched his Constitution for the prohibition of a legislative act while his brethren, like those in Massachusetts, searched theirs for a positive grant of power. Of the thousands of Court decisions in which he was to be involved over the next three decades, the Fourteenth Amendment was to figure in an inordinate number, as the Court alternated between Holmes's interpretation of it and that of the judges who gave it a traditional formalistic interpretation.

Of all the controversial provisions of the U.S. Constitution, the Fourteenth Amendment, appended to the document in 1868, must be the most controversial. Its relevant commands are deceptively simple:

> All persons born or naturalized in the United States, and subject to the jurisdiction thereof, are citizens of the United States and of the State wherein they reside. No State shall make or enforce any law which shall abridge the privileges or immunities of citizens of the United States; nor shall any State deprive any person of life, liberty, or property, without due process of law; nor deny to any person within its jurisdiction the equal protection of the laws.

Nevertheless, the intent of its framers has puzzled generations of justices who have utilized it to permit all manner of legislative behavior, from the regulation of slaughterhouses to the sterilization of the feeble-minded. The Fourteenth Amendment served as the main pillar of racial segregation in 1896 and racial *de*segregation in 1954.

The questions surrounding the Fourteenth Amendment involve the relationship between the state and the nation. In the eagerness of its authors to ensure the black's civil rights, did its passage alter the basic structure of American government? Did it require the federal government to preempt the rights and responsibilities of the states? Did the Fourteenth Amendment, for example, impose the Bill of Rights on the states? Prior to 1868, the courts had followed John Marshall's precedent-setting decision of 1833, *Barron* v. *Baltimore,* in which he declared that the Bill of Rights provided no protection against state action. Did the Fourteenth Amendment overrule Marshall?

During the twenty-three years they sat together on the U.S. Supreme Court, Justices Felix Frankfurter and Hugo L. Black carried on a continuous dialogue regarding the meaning of the Fourteenth Amendment. Frankfurter insisted it did not extend the protections of the Bill of Rights to the states; Black argued that it did. As a practical matter, Black's view ultimately prevailed; through a gradual process of incorporation which continued even after Black's death in 1971, the Supreme Court did in fact bring most of the provisions of the Bill of Rights within the purview of the states.

The Court had faced the issue for the first time in 1873 when the *Slaughter-House Cases* came before it. The cases did not involve the rights of blacks, for whose protection the amendment had ostensibly been intended, but rather the privileges of the white butchers of New Orleans. In 1869, the carpetbag legislature of Louisiana, exercising what were known as its police powers—the powers "reserved to the States" by the Tenth Amendment to legislate in behalf of the health, safety, morals, and general welfare of their citizens—passed a law granting a twenty-five-year monopoly of the meat-slaughtering business in three parishes to the Crescent City Live-Stock Landing and Slaughter-House Company. In so doing, the legislature had deprived upwards of a thousand butchers of their livelihood. The butchers immediately challenged the right of the state to establish such a monopoly. Prior to the passage of the Fourteenth Amendment, the matter would have been taken care of in the state courts. After passage, it was possible to translate the issue into federal terms and to involve the federal Constitution. The state statute, argued the butchers, violated the provisions of the Fourteenth Amendment by abridging "the privileges or immunities of citizens of the United States," by denying to the butchers excluded from the monopoly "the equal protection of the laws," and depriving them of "their property without due process of law."

Recognizing the far-reaching significance of the case, the U.S. Supreme Court confronted the question squarely: Did the Fourteenth Amendment really purport to transfer the responsibilities of the states to the federal government? As frequently happens in a difficult and significant case, the Court divided by the narrowest of margins, 5 to 4. The majority could not believe the authors of the Fourteenth Amendment intended so sharp a change in the structure of government and answered the question in the negative. The Louisiana legislature had acted within its rights in creating the monopoly. The power of the state to police the "unwholesome trades, slaughter-houses, operations offensive to the senses, the deposit of powder, the application of steam power to propel cars, the building with combustible materials, and the burial of the dead" had been, in the interest of public health, "always conceded to belong to the States."

Over the next half-century, the Fourteenth Amendment provided a substantial portion of the litigation before the U.S. Supreme Court. Between the decision in the *Slaughter-House Cases* and 1888 when Chief Justice Fuller took his seat, the Court decided more than seventy cases involving that amendment. Over the next thirty years, the number was multiplied ten times, to 725; a very few involved black civil rights.

Citing the *Slaughter-House Cases* as precedent and the public interest as justification, the Court, over the first quarter-century, allowed further expansion of state police powers. The justices upheld Missouri's refusal to grant suffrage to women, tax laws of various states, California's right to dispense with indictment by grand jury in felony cases, San Francisco's anti-Chinese ordinances, a Pennsylvania statute prohibiting the sale of oleomargarine, as well as state railroad regulations including, in 1877, the Granger laws regulating grain elevator and freight rates.

Then in 1897, the Court, which had become increasingly conservative since Melville Fuller had taken his seat in 1888, discovered in the Fourteenth Amendment what certain dissenters had known was there all along: a doctrinal foundation to protect business and industry from just that sort of interference by state governments. In a case called *Allgeyer* v. *Louisiana,* in which the Court struck down a Louisiana law regulating the licensing of insurance companies, former Albany corporation lawyer and New York State judge Rufus Wheeler Peckham wrote for the majority that the Louisiana statute was a clear violation of the Fourteenth Amendment. "The liberty mentioned in the amendment," he explained, "means not only the right of the citizen to be free from the mere physical restraint of his person by incarceration, but the term is deemed to embrace the right of the citizen to be free in the enjoyment of all his faculties; to be free to use them in all lawful ways; to live and work where he will; to earn his livelihood by any lawful calling; to pursue any livelihood or avocation, and for that purpose to enter into all contracts which may be proper, necessary and essential to his carrying out to a successful conclusion the purposes above mentioned." In such humble circumstances was judicial protection for "liberty of contract" born. It was to serve for many years as a powerful weapon against state laws that addressed social and economic matters.

Which is about the way things stood when Holmes took his seat on the U.S. Supreme Court in 1902. Application of the Bill of Rights—the freedoms of speech, press, and assembly, the prohibitions on unreasonable searches and seizures and on self-incrimination, the rights to counsel, trial by jury, and so on—fell under federal jurisdiction; the state legislatures remained in charge of the health, safety, morals, and general welfare, including the civil rights of their citizens, unless the U.S. Supreme Court found such policing in violation of the Fourteenth Amendment.

Late nineteenth- and twentieth-century financial and industrial moguls went to sleep at night secure in the knowledge that their world turned on the principles of economic laissez-faire. They could depend on the constitutional euphemism "liberty of contract" that had, by a simple effort of transference, developed out of the Fourteenth Amendment's protection of a person's life, liberty, and property—with the emphasis on property—to see them through these turbulent times. They could count on the courts not to capitulate to the radical regulatory schemes that were abroad in the land.

At the same time, reformers were attempting to utilize the law for social reconstruction, were arguing for those very regulatory measures the businessmen opposed on the ground they deprived owners of their property without "due process of law." They fought for legislation that would return some semblance of humanity to the victims of industry's ruthless competition: the automatons who worked the factories for pittances, the tenement house drudges, the cigar rollers in their sweatshops, the seamstresses bent over their machines twelve and fourteen hours a day, the children at their looms, the consumers of impure foods, the buyers of short weights, the debt-ridden farmers.

Measuring the new laws against the provisions of the Fourteenth Amendment, the judges sometimes allowed the reforms; more often, particularly in cases involving labor legislation, they rationalized nullification on the ground that it violated "liberty of contract," deprived a corporation of property without due process of law.

Lochner v. *New York,* a classic case of liberty of contract versus state police powers, reached the U.S. Supreme Court in late 1904 and was argued and decided in early 1905. In his dissent, Holmes staked out in the most trenchant terms his judicial territory regarding Fourteenth Amendment cases.

Joseph Lochner, owner of a bakery in Utica, New York, had been convicted in county court and fined $50 for violating an 1897 state law which prohibited bakery employees from working more than sixty hours a week. The state supreme and appellate courts had affirmed the judgment. At the urging of a young baker who had studied law and believed the New York law an unconstitutional infringement on the liberties of bakers, Lochner took his case to the federal Supreme Court. The state law at issue, Lochner's attorney argued, "denies to certain persons in the baking trade the equal protection of the laws" because the legislation did not affect all bakers, only those in the "biscuit, bread or cake bakery, or confectionary establishment." Such an exercise of the state's police power was not a reasonable one; it had nothing to do with the public health or safety; it was "purely a labor law."

The U.S. Supreme Court agreed, although not without some controversy. At the first conference, the majority voted to affirm Lochner's conviction, and the chief justice assigned the opinion to Harlan who wrote that the statute in question plainly had been enacted "in order to protect the physical well-being of those who work in bakery and confectionary establishments . . . the statute must be taken as expressing the belief of the people of New York that, as a general rule, and in the case of the average man, labor in excess of sixty hours during a week in such establishments may endanger the health of those who thus labor." Whether or not the legislation was wise, Harlan believed it was not the province of the Court to inquire; it was not the Court's business. Constitutionality was the only thing that mattered to the justices. Harlan firmly believed the Court, to annul the New York statute, would have to stretch the Fourteenth Amendment beyond all recognition.

At a later conference, one of the justices changed his vote, the majority became a minority, Harlan's Court opinion became a dissent— joined by White and Day—and the Court's opinion was reassigned to Rufus Peckham, who had so adroitly articulated for the majority the "liberty of contract" concept in 1897.

Peckham owed his seat on the U.S. Supreme Court to his long and active involvement in upstate New York Democratic politics and his political intimacy with fellow New Yorker Grover Cleveland who, when he became president, used to say with some regularity, "We'll get you down to Washington yet, Rufus." Peckham himself was less than jubilant over the appointment when it finally came in 1896, commenting to a friend that "If I have got to be put away on the shelf I suppose I might as well be on the top shelf."

Although he never would be numbered among the great justices of the Supreme Court, Peckham made up in consistency and tenacity for his shortcomings in scholarship and creativity. He was outspoken and firm in his judicial creed, a creed that precluded social and economic change. Holmes said, "emotional predilections somewhat governed him on social themes," and his major premise was "God damn it." He came from a long line of New Yorkers who first had trod American soil in the seventeenth century, who had achieved comfortable circumstances if not great wealth, and to whom social change seemed a threat. Peckham never turned his back on his people, but voted again and again against legislative experimentation in social and economic matters.

He could not find in his Constitution any authority for them, and so there was no place in his cosmology for these new labor laws the states seemed to be passing with shameless abandon—Massachusetts had a ten-hour act for women and children employed in factories, New York had attempted to prohibit the manufacture of cigars in tenement houses, although the state court of appeals had invalidated that particular piece of legislation. New York, Illinois, and Washington had enacted statutes regulating the qualifications of blacksmiths; the Kansas legislature had passed and the U.S. Supreme Court had upheld, although over Mr. Justice Peckham's dissent, a statute making it a criminal offense for public works contractors to require employees to work more than eight hours a day. All this had been done in the name of protecting the public welfare, but Rufus Peckham knew these laws had been passed out of "other motives."

The legislation at issue in the Lochner case, Peckham began, "necessarily interferes with the right of contract between employer and employés." He conceded the state possessed certain police powers; they were not, however, unlimited. "Otherwise the Fourteenth Amendment would have no efficacy and the legislatures of the States would have unbounded power, and it would be enough to say that any piece of legislation was enacted to conserve the morals, the health or safety of the people; such legislation would be valid, no matter how absolutely without foundation the claim might be." The Supreme Court, said Peckham, believed the "limit of the police power" had been "reached" and "passed" in this case. The statute was neither "necessary" nor "appropriate" as a health law—it safeguarded neither the health of the public nor that of the bakers. The "real object" had been to regulate the "hours of labor between the master and his employés in a private business, not dangerous in any degree to morals or in any real and substantial degree to the health of the employés." Such interference with the traditional cherished freedom of master and employee to make a contract violated the federal Constitution, and the judgment against employer Joseph Lochner was therefore reversed.

Unable to find in *his* Constitution any prohibition of it, Holmes dissented and upheld the New York statute regulating the hours of bakery workers even though he believed most social and economic legislation was a mistake. He had made it clear over thirty years before in his article for the *American Law Review* on the London gas-stokers' strike that in his opinion reform by legislation did not "get rid of any burden, but only changed the mode of bearing it," and he had not changed his mind. If anything, his ideas had been reinforced. The ills of society were not so readily cured. His private "agreement or disagreement" with such legislation, however, had "nothing to do with the right of a majority to embody their opinions in law."

His dissent was brief—three paragraphs—and to the point. It was also a trenchant critique, perhaps a little imperialist in tone, of judges who read their personal prejudices into the Constitution, and he worried that his strong words might "chafe the majority"; nothing could be "further from his mind." He had expressed similar sentiments in his first opinion for the court, *Otis* v. *Parker,* but his manner had been a little less forceful, even perhaps a little tentative as he felt his way into the Court's rhythms; certainly it was less sharply critical. If his dissent in *Northern Securities* was critical at all, it was more by implication, and Holmes seemed then to be concerned mainly with the intellectual puzzles the case presented to him.

Now, at the outset of his *Lochner* dissent, he declared that the majority had decided the case on the basis of an economic theory "which a large part of the country does not entertain." It was time, he thought, putting into formal constitutional terms what Progressives were saying much more pointedly in their books and pamphlets, that judges faced the fact that regulation in one form or another already touched much of life, was apparently here to stay, and he reminded his brethren that all manner of statutes and state constitutional provisions—Sunday blue laws, usury laws, school laws, the Sherman Anti-Trust Act, the Post Office, the new Massachusetts compulsory vaccination law whose constitutionality had been upheld only six weeks before by this same court,* to name only a few—interfered with somebody's "liberty of contract." He didn't ask judges to change their minds—Lord knows, privately he shared many of their biases—he only asked them not to impose their prejudices

---

* *Jacobsen* v. *Massachusetts.* 197 U.S. 11 (1905).

on their jurisprudence. It should be obvious, he said acidly, neatly separating his own biases from his jurisprudence, because of course he did admire and personally incline to agree with Mr. Herbert Spencer's social Darwinism, that the "Fourteenth Amendment does not enact Mr. Herbert Spencer's Social Statics."

Whether judges shared or were repulsed by the concepts these laws embodied, whether judges thought them "injudicious" and "tyrannical" or wise and helpful, was irrelevant to judicial responsibility. A constitution, he declared, warming to his subject,

> is not intended to embody a particular economic theory. . . . It is made for people of fundamentally differing views, and the accident of our finding certain opinions natural and familiar or novel and even shocking ought not to conclude our judgment upon the question whether statutes embodying them conflict with the Constitution of the United States.

The majority, Holmes said, concluding his little lecture, "perverted" the meaning of the word "liberty" in the Fourteenth Amendment when it was used "to prevent the natural outcome of a dominant opinion" and to invalidate a state statute which did not "infringe fundamental principles as they have been understood by the traditions of our people and our law." This New York statute, he felt, did not by any means qualify for invalidation.

Writing his dissent in the Lochner case had given Holmes not a little joy, and he confided to a friend not long afterward, "What I regard as one of the greatest dangers to our system of giving the last word to judges is the tendency to read into the fundamental instrument one's own economic and social views, when the words don't require it. I regarded the prohibition in the Fourteenth Amendment of a State depriving a man of *liberty* without due process of law as an inadequate foundation for the result and it gave me pleasure to remark that the Fourteenth Amendment does not enact Mr. Herbert Spencer's Social Statics."

Public reception of his dissent, which was politicized in the interpretation, gave Holmes less pleasure. Again, as with previous dissents, he was being appreciated for the wrong reasons. The fact of his dissent, what seemed to some his attitude of independence, even defiance, enlarged his stature in the public eye. With his pungent characterization of his fellow judges and support of a labor law, the Progressives discovered him, and he became a hero to all those Americans who believed that legislation was the key to social and economic reform. Another brick was added to the foundation of the Holmes legend.

HENRY JAMES ARRIVED in Washington with the magnolias that spring for an eight-day stay. Henry Adams put him up at his big house on Lafayette Square. Washington lionized him. The secretary of state, the French ambassador, even the president feted him, although Roosevelt considered him "effete" and a "miserable little snob." Even Admiral Dewey left his card. Washington's cynicism and crassness, however, disgusted James, and he mourned that "poor Wendell" with whom he found time to dine had "chosen success."

Holmes briefly considered going abroad that summer, but thought better of it. He had had enough of dinner parties, hadn't any money after paying for his portrait to be painted—a project Fanny had initiated—and he was reluctant to leave Fanny, who refused to budge. She had seemed "very tired and joyless" that winter, and Holmes had been somewhat worried about her. Idling the summer away in a little biking, a little solitaire, a little Hegel—"an international mystification" occasionally leavened with "apercus and suggestions"—a little nineteenth-century English law, a little *belles lettres* read aloud with Fanny—"Do you know the value of that to make you enter into books which would be tiresome to read alone?" he asked rhetorically—in sum a "happy *solitude à deux*" at Beverly Farms revived the bodies and spirits of both Holmeses.

That summer, John Morse's two-volume biography of Dr. Holmes appeared in print. Wendell pronounced it "admirable," if perhaps a little indiscreet at times in its use of personal names. Whether because Holmes thought the author's insights lacking or because he disliked having his family held up to public scrutiny, Morse apparently had had to prod his cousin into acknowledging the work, and Holmes's note to Morse is almost a dismissal, complete with a lame apology for not getting in touch that summer with the author, although they were practically neighbors at Beverly Farms.

It had been John Chipman Gray's custom to send each year to his half brother, Horace Gray, Holmes's predecessor on the U.S. Supreme Court, a secretary from the Harvard Law School's graduating class. For the first years after Holmes took his seat on the Court, he had no use for a secretary. Then, in 1905, he changed his mind and told Gray's wife, with whom he corresponded regularly, he would indeed "be much obliged if he would have me in mind as he used to have his brother."

Holmes specified a man "presentable, clever, not unwilling or unable to make out my checks for me at the beginning of the month, etc. and up in the latest fashions of the law school." He also required a free man, and although he waived the condition for certain individuals, he stipulated men without outside commitments. Married or engaged men did not "have the freedom of mind and spirit" Holmes liked in his secretaries. After 1912, when he could retire at full pay, he always "reserved the right to die or resign."

The intangibles were important, too. Discretion, for example. A secretary ought to know better than to discuss even the most insignificant aspect of cases before the Court. He must remember he is working for a public figure and not at liberty to reveal personal matters regarding life at 1720 I Street.

Compatibility was another important asset in a secretary. He ought to be able to sense Holmes's moods and "meet them on his ground," to "enjoy what he enjoys," to "play with him," and to understand that every opening conversational gambit did not require philosophical discussion.

The official duties of Holmes's secretaries were at most inconsequential. They kept his docket books up to date, looked up or checked legal citations, and wrote memoranda on the petitions for certiorari (requests for cases to be reviewed by the Court) that streamed into the Court daily. Unofficially, they prepared his tax returns, reconciled his checkbook, accompanied him on his frequent drives, and, after Fanny's death, read to him. Their most important function, however, was to "sit and hear my views . . . on law and economics, not to speak of excursions into the cosmos at large." Having a new secretary every year saved Holmes the embarrassment of repetition; he could repeat himself at least annually.

Holmes did not encourage personal intimacy from these young men, although in all the jaws (Holmes's term for lively intellectual conversations) a certain intellectual closeness was inevitable. He was accustomed to beginning the year with the observation:

> You see, boy, with my secretaries I have all the pleasures of paternity without any of the responsibilities. If there is anything here [and he would touch his temple—] perhaps I can enrich it and you will go away not entirely ungrateful. If not, no harm is done.

Not only his own but the secretaries of other justices bringing messages from their masters were accorded the benefit of the "jaw" or "chin" as it was alternately known, and Dean Acheson, secretary to Brandeis from 1919 to 1921, reported that "one rarely got away from 1720 I Street" without one.

By early 1906, Chief Justice Fuller was beginning to fall asleep on the bench, and Henry Brown had reached the age of seventy. His failing eyesight having become a problem in his work, he resigned from the Court. Roosevelt's first choice to replace Brown was his friend and political crony, Secretary of War William Howard Taft. Taft's wife, however, had presidential ambitions for her husband, and he yielded to her wishes. At his urging, Roosevelt next considered Horace Harmon Lurton of the U.S. Court of Appeals for the Sixth Circuit, upon which Taft had sat. Republican Roosevelt was not unaware of the political advantage to be gained from the appointment of a Southern Democrat. "Nothing," he explained to Lodge, no doubt recalling a lesson he had learned the hard way when he appointed Holmes, "has been so strongly borne in on me concerning lawyers on the bench as that the *nominal* politics of the man has nothing to do with his actions on the bench. His *real* politics are all important." Lurton, he added, had demonstrated that he cared about the things Roosevelt cared about, that he was "right" on the most important issues of the time. Lodge, however, was not convinced; he did not see "why Republicans cannot be found who hold those opinions as well as Democrats." The fact that Roosevelt had been disappointed in the performance of an appointee did not seem to Lodge to "militate against the proposition." Lodge preferred a Republican, "by nature a liberal constructionist," by political inheritance a follower of Alexander Hamilton and Marshall, over a Southern Democrat, heir to the principles of Jefferson and Calhoun "whose disciples carried their doctrines into the practical form of secession." Lodge preferred by all measurements his fellow Republican from Massachusetts, the attorney general and recent successful prosecutor of the beef trust, William H. Moody. Lodge's view prevailed, and Moody was appointed.

In February of 1907, an early environmental case, *Georgia v. Tennessee Copper Co.*, forced the justices to take a hard look at some of the negative aspects of industrialism—in this case, the pollution of large tracts of Georgia air and destruction of the state's forests, orchards, and crops—and to work out a scheme for coping with them—one of those "felt necessities of the time" that Holmes had talked about in *The Common Law*. Fuller assigned the opinion to Holmes, who discovered a rationale in the natural concern of the state for the protection of its citizens. The state, he argued, had "an interest . . . in all the earth and air within its domain. . . . It is a fair and reasonable demand on the part of a sovereign that the air over its territory should not be polluted on a great scale by sulphurous acid gas, that the forests on its mountains . . . should not be further destroyed or threatened by the act of persons beyond its control, that the crops and orchards on its hills should not be endangered from the same source."

The 1906–1907 term* went by "like a flash . . . with the absorbing monotony of successive problems," and on June 11, Holmes sailed for England, although "without gaiety of heart." As he grew older, the idea of leaving Fanny behind "weigh[ed] on [him] more," and he did not believe he would go abroad again unless he could persuade her to accompany him.

Once he reached London, however, his heart lifted, and he entered on the customary round of lunches, dinners, theater parties, and outings in the country with old friends. A brief trip to Paris where he revisited the Louvre and the usual finale at Doneraile with the Castletowns and Canon Sheehan rounded out what he called his "visit of affection," and he sailed for Boston on September 3.

On his return to Washington for the opening of the 1907 term in October, he found the "old boys" with whom he sat had "grown no younger through the lapse of time, but they all seem[ed] in good case and none of them appear[ed] to be loose in the socket."

Shortly before the justices had adjourned for the summer, a significant case involving federal labor legislation reached the Court. It raised the question of an employer's responsibility for his employee's job-related injuries or death. The law had not kept pace with the new industrial occupations in which all manner of complex mechanical instruments held the potential for serious injury. A miner's workplace was a gassy trap, his tools dangerous. On the railroads, brakes failed, switches were not thrown in time; workmen were sideswiped, crushed, and run over. Under the common law, the employer was only rarely held liable for these accidents; like Holmes's as a Massachusetts judge, the prevailing attitude had been that a workman understood the risks of the job when he took it. In 1906, Congress passed the Federal Employers' Liability Act (FELA) which settled responsibility on interstate carriers for injuries to employees caused by supervisors' negligence or defective equipment, and by 1907, the law was being challenged in the Supreme Court.

A badly splintered Court declared on January 6, 1908, that the stat-

---

* The term traditionally opened the first Monday in October and ended in June during Holmes's years on the Court—hence the designation *October Term,* OT, which operated much like an academic year.

ute was unconstitutional because it covered employees of interstate railroads who had been injured in intrastate commerce. White wrote the Court opinion—a tedious, obscure, tortuously reasoned, and prolix affair which did not command a majority. Day concurred with White; Peckham, joined by Fuller and Brewer, wrote a separate opinion concurring only in White's result. Moody and Harlan, the latter joined by McKenna, each wrote separate opinions concurring in part and dissenting in part. It was a Court decision in name only.

Holmes, for whom the issue now was not a particular negligence suit, as the Massachusetts cases largely had been, but the constitutionality of a particular statute duly passed by Congress, wrote a brief solo dissent in which he simply said without elaboration, dicta, or justification that since it was the responsibility of the Court to uphold the constitutionality of acts of Congress whenever possible, the act, with minor adjustments, could—and should—be upheld. He had as much liking for the act as he had for the Interstate Commerce Commission—"a body I don't greatly believe in," and for largely the same reason. He thought "most of the Government meddling with the organization of the world which is happening outside of and in spite of government is probably noxious—but of course [he couldn't] say so."*

Three weeks later, on January 27, the Court announced its decision in another important labor case.

Protesting a wage cut in the spring of 1894, employees of the Pullman car works in Chicago called a local strike which soon escalated to a bloody insurrection with national implications. Both sides overreacted. Management refused to arbitrate, the railroad men refused to handle Pullman cars, transportation and mail delivery were seriously disrupted, and violence was ended only by the use of federal troops. To avoid a recurrence, Congress passed the Erdman Act, which provided means for arbitration of labor disputes and forbade discrimination against employees because they belonged to unions. The act became law on June 1, 1898, and its friends predicted a new era in employee-employer relations. Its enemies, however, viewed section 10 of the act, which held any employer who fired or fined an employee for union membership criminally liable, as a serious violation of "liberty of contract."

A decade later the Supreme Court, in another display of its antipathy to labor organization, found the Erdman Act unconstitutional.† Fuller chose John Marshall Harlan, who generally supported legislative exer-

---

* Congress later amended the act to meet the Court's objections, and in January 1912, a unanimous Court, in the *Second Employers' Liability Cases,* upheld the constitutionality of the new act.
† *Adair* v. *United States.* 208 U.S. 161 (1908).

cise of police power and who had dissented with vigor when the Court struck down New York's ten-hour law for bakers, to write the majority opinion. The choice of Harlan lent more credibility to the opinion than if, say, Brewer or Peckham were to write it. The decision was restricted to the issue of section 10; the Court did not consider other provisions of the act, which involved methods of arbitration. It did not turn on the commerce clause of the Constitution, as expected, but was based on the Fifth Amendment's guarantee of liberty and property rights against deprivation without due process of law.

It was true, Harlan reasoned, that the constitutionally guaranteed protection against deprivation of liberty and property without due process of law was subject to limitation when the common good required it. It was not, however, "within the functions of government . . . to compel any person in the course of his business and against his will to accept or retain the personal services of another, or to compel any person, against his will, to perform personal services for another. The right," Harlan added, assuming in effect the political power of employee and employer to be equal, "of a person to sell his labor upon such terms as he deems proper is, in its essence, the same as the right of the purchaser of labor to prescribe the conditions upon which he will accept such labor from the person offering to sell it . . . the employer and the employé have equality of right, and any legislation that disturbs that equality is an arbitrary interference with the liberty of contract which no government can legally justify in a free land. . . ."

Holmes did not agree. If his economic cosmology seemed naive and simplistic, still he was willing to consider "liberty of contract" not as the absolute some of his brethren considered it but as a fluid concept in the context of the changing realities of his time; he was willing to differentiate the future from the past.

"I confess," he said in his dissent, "that I think that the right to make contracts at will that has been derived from the word liberty in the amendments has been stretched to its extreme by the decisions; but they agree that sometimes the right may be restrained. Where there is, or generally is believed to be, an important ground of public policy for restraint the Constitution does not forbid it, whether," he added, twitting his brethren for, as he believed, injecting their prejudices, "this court agrees or disagrees with the policy pursued." Congress had a legitimate public interest in preventing strikes, and Holmes found it "impossible to say that Congress might not reasonably think that the provision in question would help a good deal to carry its policy along." He did not discuss the effects of labor unions—his assessment of them had not changed since he had supported them publicly in Massachusetts, then sneered at them privately. However, he concluded, he could not "pronounce it unwarranted if Congress should decide that to foster a strong union was for the best interest, not only of the men, but of the railroads and the country at large." He believed the Erdman Act constitutional.

That spring, the Court reiterated—again via Holmes—its environmental views when it supported New Jersey's right to prohibit the diversion to New York of water from its streams.* It appeared to the Court that "few public interests are more obvious, indisputable and independent of particular theory than the interest of the public of a State to maintain the rivers that are wholly within it substantially undiminished, except by such drafts upon them as the guardian of the public welfare may permit for the purpose of turning them to a more perfect use. This public interest is omnipresent wherever there is a State, and grows more pressing as population grows."

That term, too, Holmes welcomed his old friend Louis Brandeis to the I Street house. Brandeis had come down from Boston to argue *Muller* v. *Oregon* before the Supreme Court. The case was a test of Oregon's law that limited women's working hours to ten a day; seventeen other states had similar laws on the books. Brandeis brought to the Court that day a new approach to briefing and arguing a case. It became known as the Brandeis brief, and it persuaded even David Brewer.

Brandeis believed the new social legislation required new techniques for argument. He believed the principles of law ought, of course, to be expounded in his briefs, but he also believed that all the relevant facts that described a situation should be presented to support the legal argument. Hadn't Holmes himself argued that it was experience, not logic, that gave the law its life? Sometimes the legal sections of Brandeis's briefs were but a few pages; the expository sections often ran to hundreds of pages. He introduced a new element into the ecology of constitutional law, imposed a new factor to be considered in decision-making. Its finest flowering occurred a decade after Brandeis's death when NAACP lawyer Thurgood Marshall compiled volumes of psychological and sociological data to illustrate to the Supreme Court that racially segregated public education was harmful to blacks.

Brandeis used this pragmatic approach for the first time in *Muller* v. *Oregon*. With the assistance of the National Consumers League, he had gathered material regarding the effect of fatigue on women, their family

---

* *Hudson County Water Co.* v. *McCarter.* 209 U.S. 349 (1908).

life, their children born and unborn, from anyone whose credibility was dependable—factory workers, physicians, trade unionists, economists, social workers.

When on January 15, 1908, he presented his argument, he addressed the legal side of the issue—that the right to purchase or sell labor guaranteed by the Fourteenth Amendment is subject to restraints the state may impose in the exercise of the police power for the protection of health, safety, morals, and general welfare; that the Oregon ten-hour law had been enacted for the purpose of protecting these very things; and that the law should be upheld. Then he submitted his voluminous collection of facts citing the dangerous aspects of overlong hours and the benefits to both women and industry of regulated work hours for women.

And he convinced the justices. Chief Justice Fuller assigned the opinion to the Court's best-known conservative, seventy-one-year-old David Brewer, who could be relied on to write as narrowly as possible in the case, which he did. He conceded virtually nothing to Brandeis's legal argument that liberty of contract might be limited; rather, overcome by the "copious collection" of data submitted by the lawyer for the state, he concentrated on the "injurious" effect of long hours on women's well-being. The Court upheld the Oregon statute; it specifically did not, however, overrule *Lochner,* and the justices limited application of their decision to "the work of a female in a laundry."

Holmes reached the age of sixty-seven that year. He still owned his father's Beacon Street house, and reminded perhaps of Fanny's homesickness, he told a friend, "When I am 70 I shall retire."

Fanny appears to have had surgery that spring, leaving Wendell to fend for himself at home, a solitude he endured in the usual way: dinner at the British Embassy with the James Bryces—his friend Bryce had been made ambassador to the United States the year before—dinner at the White House, dinner at the homes of various friends; he hardly had a chance to eat the cold ham and cold roast chicken Fanny had arranged for him at home.

Fanny's "pulldown" gave Beverly Farms, in which Holmes had recently bought a two-thirds interest to keep from being evicted, a special urgency that summer. There was no talk of going abroad this year. The Holmeses were "as quiet as possible," their excursions entirely dependent upon Fanny's ability to regain her strength. Wendell spent the mornings reading and writing, afternoons driving with Fanny "in the woods where automobiles could not go," evenings playing solitaire. He got eight hours of sleep each night, drank little or nothing—he had given up champagne the previous year, drank only whiskey and soda on social occasions and nothing at home—and accumulated strength to see him through the next eight months of high pressure in Washington.

A portion of his summer leisure Holmes spent arranging and having bound a "confused mess of papers (mss.)" of his father's which he had been surprised to discover recently. Before he died, Dr. Holmes had suggested making "a little worm of a nephew his library Executor, whatever that may be." But Wendell had argued against the plan and "intimated that perhaps after all I might be trusted not to wish to belittle his reputation!" The doctor had yielded, and nearly a decade and a half after his death, his son was still working his way through the papers. He had had four volumes bound the previous year; this summer he expected to do four or five more.

Theodore Roosevelt did not run for reelection in 1908, but passed the scepter to the crown prince, the jovial Cincinnati Brahmin, Secretary of War Taft who, he was confident, would continue his policies. His attacks on the trusts and his sponsorship of social legislation had provided a safety valve for American indignation, and he was convinced he had saved the country from Socialist revolution.

"I am, after my fashion, a conservative," he told a reporter for a French magazine as his reign was drawing to a close, "and it is for this that I combat the abuses of plutocracy."

Before Roosevelt left, he and Holmes apparently had a heart-to-heart talk during which they at last settled their differences over *Northern Securities*. Holmes did not reveal whether one or the other yielded (doubtful) or whether they simply agreed to disagree; the matter, however, was "finished." Holmes would miss the Roosevelts "personally a good deal," he thought, but he couldn't help thinking, too, that the country was ready for a change.

ALL HIS LIFE Holmes had "sneered at the natural rights of man" and had often thought the "bills of rights in Constitutions overworked." Then in December 1908, he wrote the Court's majority opinion in a case that reminded him of their necessity.

Two years before, the Interstate Commerce Commission, under the guise of developing new legislation, had gone on what amounted to a fishing expedition among railroad entrepreneurs, summoned them as witnesses, and questioned them about their holdings. Some refused to answer, and the Court, via Holmes, supported them. The mandate of the ICC, for which Holmes had as little use as he had the Sherman

Anti-Trust Act—the commission was "always trying to extend its power," he believed, and this case confirmed that belief—was limited to enforcing the laws Congress passed, and it was only when faced with a violation that the commission could subpoena witnesses. He feared the commission's assumption of such broad "autocratic power" in this instance only foreshadowed further aggrandizement for "still vaguer" reasons in the future.* His phrasing was cool and formal as befitted a Court opinion; his customary dispassion dominated his writing. Privately, however, he could not suppress his contempt for the oppressor and allowed that the ICC's behavior had made his "blood . . . boil."

* *Harriman* v. *Interstate Commerce Commission.* 211 U.S. 407 (1908).

CHAPTER 20

The Court Rejuvenated

TAFT'S INAUGURATION ON March 4, 1909, proceeded without incident. Snow drove it into the Senate chamber, and Holmes did not die of pneumonia as he always expected he would from standing on the "windswept platform" at the east front of the Capitol. Shortly afterwards, the mayor of Tokyo promised Mrs. Taft that Washington would have a thousand Japanese cherry trees to adorn its newly opened Potomac Drive. The Holmeses and the Tafts became official friends, but for the Holmeses, there were no more intimate little dinners and theater parties with the White House tenants.

As the new president settled into his job, he began to take the measure of the other branches of government with which he would have to deal. When he looked at the judiciary, he did not like what he saw. Chief Justice Fuller he believed to be "almost senile." Harlan not only did no work, but also slept through the arguments. Brewer, who was "so deaf that he cannot hear" and had gone "beyond the point of the commonest accuracy in writing his opinions," followed Harlan's example. They were, in Taft's estimation, a lot of "old fools" hanging on with a "tenacity that is most discouraging."

Holmes at sixty-eight was frisky by comparison, still a glutton for work and still not satisfied with the recognition he was receiving, although he had received "a good deal more than [he] expected." He consoled himself with the thought that "few men in baggy trousers and bad hats" were recognized as great by those who knew them. They had "to wait as Lincoln did for their myth to grow." Fanny made light of his moods, urging him to describe his "latest plaything" to his friends.

"What do you mean, Dickie Bird? What new plaything are you talking about?" he asked.

"Despair," she answered.

In the spring of 1909, Holmes found an opportunity to refine slightly his old "prediction" theory of law which he had partially developed as a young lawyer and Massachusetts judge. In 1872, he had written that in essence the law was what worked in a given place at a given time. "The only question for lawyers is, how will the judges act?" In 1897, he had rephrased it to define the law as a "prediction that if a man does or omits certain things he will be made to suffer in this or that way by judgment of the court." Now, a decade later, he restated it in a Supreme Court opinion:

> Law is a statement of the circumstances in which the public force will be brought to bear upon men through the courts. (*American Banana Co.* v. *United Fruit Co.*)

For all his complaints about his lack of preparation for the work of the high federal court, he had come to it with his bags packed and had left little room for a new suit—a tie, perhaps, or a pair of cuff links, nothing substantial.

Sheriff Shipp's contempt case* returned to the Supreme Court in the spring of 1909. It had been there three years before for settlement of some preliminary legal questions,† and Holmes had written the majority opinion. Now it was back for a decision on the merits.

The case involved the role of Sheriff John F. Shipp of Chattanooga, Tennessee, in the lynching of Ed Johnson, a black man who had been convicted of raping a white schoolgirl. Johnson had been scheduled to hang, but at the last minute, following the lower federal court's refusal to hear the case, Justice Harlan had granted a stay and allowed an appeal to the U.S. Supreme Court. Nevertheless, on the night before the date set for his execution, a mob had broken into the jail where Johnson was being held, dragged him six blocks to the bridge over the Tennessee River, and strung him up. The rope broke the first time, and Johnson dropped to the ground, still alive. Next time the men made sure; they emptied their revolvers into the swinging figure.

The day after the lynching, an enraged Fuller summoned the justices to his home for an emergency conference. Two months later, as a result of a Justice Department investigation instigated by the Supreme

---

* *United States* v. *Shipp.* 214 U.S. 386 (1909).
† *United States* v. *Shipp.* 203 U.S. 563 (1906).

Court, Shipp and several of his deputies were charged with contempt of court. The information accused them of failing to protect the prisoner, "pretending to do their duty," but really "sympathizing" and "conspiring" with the mob.

Shipp and his co-defendants answered that the Supreme Court did not have jurisdiction in the case. The Court heard his arguments on that question and other related issues in December 1906. Holmes left no doubt where the Court stood. Peckham and McKenna originally thought his opinion was too strong, but ultimately the decision was unanimous.

Johnson's appeal, Holmes declared, had come to the Court "as a matter of right," and the Supreme Court, like all other courts, had an "inherent" power to "punish for contempts. . . . The power and dignity of this court are paramount. This court is preeminent as speaking the last word for the judicial power." Johnson's lynching was "murder by a mob, and was an offense against the State as well as against the United States and this court . . . the United States has complete power to punish, whether the State does or not."

A court-appointed commissioner resumed investigation of the case and took testimony in Chattanooga over the next two years. In early March 1909, the inaugural bands blaring in the background, the Court heard the question of Shipp's contempt argued. Holmes was originally assigned to write the Court's opinion, but perhaps because of the potential for repercussions, Fuller thought the decision required the full authority of the chief justice behind it, and he himself wrote it.

His opinion was as strong as Holmes's had been. He described in detail the events leading up to the lynching as well as Shipp's failure to prevent or stop it and concluded that it did "not admit of question on this record that this lamentable riot was the direct result of opposition to the administration of the law by this court. It was not only in defiance of our mandate, but was understood to be such."

Holmes, who confessed he was "sore distraught" as to the Court's duty in Shipp's case, thought the sheriff deserved a year's imprisonment. Apparently the others thought differently. After giving the Tennesseans time to file a petition for rehearing, which the justices denied, Fuller announced ninety-day prison terms for Shipp and one of his deputies and sixty-day terms for the other three defendants.

The early summer of 1909 found Holmes off on a flying trip to England where he received on June 23 an honorary D.C.L. from Oxford. It was just twenty-three years since his father had been similarly honored. He loved the "striking" show of it all, the scarlet gown, the discourse in Latin—"Can you translate it, Sir?" an undergraduate sang out—but especially the acknowledgment of his contributions to legal history. William Holdsworth, eminent British legal historian, delivered the discourse, and, to Holmes's "surprise and satisfaction," it contained "a few words of the kind that [he] should like to have said." He stayed in England only three weeks seeing old friends, including, briefly, the Castletowns in London, then sped back to Fanny, from whom now he didn't like to be separated any longer than he could help.

The Pollocks came to America later that summer and Holmes took them to see the president, who was vacationing nearby at Beverly Farms that year. Taft, to Holmes's surprise, spoke with a startling freedom and, among other things, remarked that Brewer had said "his wit would not let him resign" from the Court.

The high point of Holmes's summer that year—after Oxford—was not the Pollocks' visit, not anything he read, not the drives through the countryside, but a review put on by the Civil War Veterans of Essex County, for which he was a guest of one of the posts. The advancing age of the men kept the march to a mile, but did not diminish his emotional reaction to sharing a carriage with an old adjutant of the Massachusetts Twentieth, a "thin sweet ghost of the past." Nothing could stop him "feeling the romance of the association" with these men, their faces "twisted by age and work" now, with whom he had shared one of the most profound experiences of life.

When the Court convened on October 11 for the 1909 term, there were 630 cases on the docket and only seven judges to decide them and write the opinions. Peckham was terminally ill at his summer home, Coomore, near Albany, and Moody was incapacitated by chronic rheumatism in New York. He had lost seventy-five pounds while lying flat on his back alone in a private room, and he had "sunk into a state of great depression." Taft was very shortly going to have his chance to rejuvenate the Court.

Peckham died first, on October 24 at Coomore, of angina pectoris complicated by Bright's disease. The Court adjourned for the week, and the justices trekked North for the funeral.

Taft responded by sending to the Senate the nomination of his old comrade on the Sixth Circuit whom he had tried to persuade Roosevelt to appoint to the Court three years before, Horace Harmon Lurton, Democrat of Tennessee. Sensitive perhaps to a growing bitterness against the conservative Court and still not completely free of Roosevelt's progressive influence, Taft as president in 1910 was not the rigid reactionary he later became. He did not test his candidates for the vacant Su-

preme Court seats on their political principles. He had a weakness for
federal judges and successful lawyers, preferably middle-aged, who could
do the demanding work of the Court, but he was willing to risk naming
a qualified Democrat to a court which in any case had compiled a strong
record of protecting property rights—indeed, it might even be politically
wise to do so.

Lurton, a Confederate veteran, was no Rufus Peckham. He was
chunky and gray-haired, a gentle, mild-mannered man—Peckham's ritual "Goddamn it"s were as foreign to his nature as was his predecessor's
rigid conservatism. Lurton's Court opinions more or less followed the
contours of his character, neither judicially flamboyant nor imaginative.
He invented no legal precepts, established no judicial principles. He was
neither as reactionary as some of his brethren nor as progressive as
others, but came down just slightly to the right of center. He had no
compulsion to challenge the rights of property, and he generally put his
faith in precedent over progress. He was not unwilling, however, to join
this or that majority to support on occasion a genteel expansion of federal power.

The seventy-three-year-old David Brewer was the next to oblige the
president. He died suddenly of apoplexy in the bathroom of his Washington home on March 28, 1910. Holmes feared for a moment the justices might be required to go to Leavenworth, Kansas, for the funeral,
"which in view of a blizzard that has been raging would have meant
serious danger to the Chief if not to all," but Mrs. Brewer, who understood the pressures on the Court as well as the frailty of the justices,
"begged them not to do it." Holmes was "glad of his death on his own
account, as well as otherwise." Brewer clearly had begun to fail, and
Holmes had feared "dreadfully" that he "might remain after his mind
had gone," as had his uncle, Stephen J. Field, who had had to be persuaded off the bench.

In record time, Taft settled on the liberal Republican governor of
New York, Charles Evans Hughes, to replace Brewer. Of all the men
who have sat on the U.S. Supreme Court, Hughes probably came closest to the image of a justice. He was a tall man with a well-brushed
graying beard, a resolute step, a somewhat stiff public manner, and
what the *New York Times* called "the most ferocious eyebrows in public
life." When these characteristics combined with his impeccable tailor-
ing and his reputation for rectitude, he personified dignity and authority.

As a young lawyer he had joined a prominent Wall Street firm, married a partner's daughter, and embarked on what became an eminently

successful legal practice. In 1905, at the suggestion of William Howard Taft's brother Henry, he was appointed counsel to a state legislative committee investigating local utility rates. Following his public exposure of financial corruption in that industry, he was appointed to another legislative committee investigating insurance companies, during which he revealed similar scandals in that business. His disclosures resulted not only in certain measures of corporate reform but also in a certain panache attaching to his name, and in 1906, he was elected governor of New York. He was reelected in 1908 and served until his appointment to the U.S. Supreme Court. As governor, Hughes attacked race-track gambling and got it banned from the state, sponsored a workmen's compensation law, and tried, unsuccessfully, to get a child labor law passed. His campaign contributors had, however, little cause for complaint. He also vetoed a reduction in railroad rates and opposed a state constitutional amendment for an income tax. At about the time Hughes was trying to persuade the legislature to pass a bill regulating utilities, Taft offered him a seat on the Supreme Court.

Whether Hughes's appointment was a conspiracy between Taft and New York Republicans who feared for their corporate lives if Hughes remained in Albany, or whether the president feared for his own political life, should Hughes, whose reputation was growing beyond New York's border, oppose him for the presidency in 1912, or whether it was a reward for Hughes's vigorous efforts for Taft in the latter's 1908 campaign, has never been entirely clear. Whatever Taft's motives, Hughes accepted with enthusiasm, and his old friends on Wall Street breathed a long sigh of relief.

Holmes had met Hughes at a White House dinner two years before, had liked him "very much," and was "excited and pleased" with the nomination. Holmes didn't know "how much of a lawyer" Hughes was, but at least he had had "metropolitan experience," had seen "public life," and had the "admirable merit of having told me in former times that my book started him in the law."

During his six years as an associate justice, until he resigned to run for the presidency in 1916, Hughes wrote 151 majority opinions and 32 dissents, nearly all of them contradictions of his conservative predecessor. He was generally classed with the progressive wing of the Court and voted most often to support the reform programs which the legislatures were sponsoring and which were being challenged in the courts.

Holmes's share of the Court's work that term had "not been of remarkable interest," and as the year drew to a close, he was looking forward to final adjournment. At April's end, summer plans were still pending. Fanny had suggested a trip abroad, perhaps, now that they were growing older, to take Holmes's secretary (Leland B. Duer in 1909–10) "to boss the show," but he and she had come to an impasse. Neither was particularly keen on the plan but each would gladly go to please the other. Holmes rather suspected the plan would fall apart, though temporarily they were declining invitations "on the strength of possibilities."

In the end, they went to Beverly Farms for the usual rest and recuperation. They went North in time for Holmes to attend Harvard's commencement where he ran into Roosevelt at the Porcellian dinner, sang the old songs at Alpha Delta Phi, and noted with pride the bronze inscription he had written in honor of Alpha Delta Phi men fallen in America's wars. Reunions, he said, gave him a "pleasant fillip to shake hands with the old fellows and the young ones who present themselves."

Commencement, however, was to be the only bright spot in an otherwise depressing summer. On July 4, Chief Justice Fuller, in his seventy-eighth year, died after a heart attack at his summer home in Sorrento, Maine. He had outlived most of his contemporaries, and, Taft's assessment of his later years notwithstanding, continued to do his share of the Court's work until his last term, when he began to seem, according to Holmes, "less rapid and active than heretofore." Due primarily to Holmes's regular Sunday calls on him, the two judges had developed an affectionate relationship, and Holmes, who attended services for him both in Sorrento and Chicago, expected to "miss him as long as I sit on the Bench."

Taft's first choice for the chief justiceship was himself—to be chief justice of the United States had been his lifelong ambition, and he regretted having to offer the position to another. He dilly-dallied several months before appointing anyone.

Fuller's death was followed about six weeks later by that of William James of heart disease at his country place in New Hampshire. The affectionate intimacy of their youth had not survived the temperamental and philosophical differences between Holmes and James, and they had had little communication for some years except on the few occasions when James sent Holmes copies of his books or articles, and Holmes responded. Still, James's death cut a "root . . . that went far into the past." The funeral was held in Harvard's Appleton Chapel. Holmes thought Henry, who had been visiting his brother when he died, looked "deeply moved and distingue" as he walked up the aisle with William's widow. Henry, however, had "seemed remote the last few years," and Holmes did not attempt to rejuvenate their relationship, but attributed his old friend's coolness to the "vicissitudes of the Irish temperament and the difference of emphasis in our respective interests."

A few weeks later, Captain Gustave Magnitzky, at one time Holmes's first sergeant, later promoted to captain, still later office manager for Shattuck, Holmes, and Munroe, was buried, and perhaps to purge some of the sadness that had characterized the summer, Holmes wrote a moving little tribute to the captain and fired it off to the *Boston Transcript* where it was published.

The sadness of the deaths themselves, combined with the intimations of his own mortality, made Holmes more than ever aware of his age—seventy next birthday. Three deaths on the Court plus Moody's "slowly dying" would make the Court "quite different" from the one he had "grown accustomed to." The deaths of William James and Captain Magnitzky added to his discomfiture. Lady Castletown was losing the sight of an eye, an English friend was seriously ill, and the houses at Beverly Farms where he "used to be at home" were now inhabited by "strangers and ghosts."

He cheered himself up by thinking of the work he still wanted to accomplish and the recognition he might yet gather. He had found "encouraging" a recent honorary degree from the University of Berlin; yet the "heart knoweth its own bitterness" and he wanted "more and louder to be satisfied." He liked to speculate on what he would do in December 1912, when his ten years would be up and he could retire at full pay. He had no intention of deciding yet, but he felt it was "well not to wait until you go under fire to speculate on conduct." Others had counseled him to leave as soon as he could, on general principles, and he believed the counsel "sound." Better to have people ask "why the devil does he than why the devil doesn't he."

When he wearied of his personal problems, he could always speculate on who the next chief justice would be. The New York lawyer Elihu Root would have been Taft's second choice, but Root, sixty-five, Taft felt was too old. He dangled the appointment before Hughes, but Hughes at forty-eight was too young. He might outlive the fifty-three-year-old Taft and thus frustrate Taft's own chances for the chief justiceship later. Common-change gossip in Washington, however, assumed Hughes would be the nominee.

The justices, however, did not like the idea of a young inexperienced man in the highest judicial office in the nation, and they drew up a "round robin" letter to the president, listing their objections to Hughes's appointment. Holmes, who would be quite satisfied with Hughes as chief justice, refused to join the others in their protest. The seventy-seven-year-old Harlan, senior in terms of length of service, wanted it so badly he attempted to bargain for it through the attorney general: a temporary appointment for himself in return for his support of Hughes for the top position permanently. Taft summarily rejected such a trade.

Holmes would have "like[d] the place," although he never thought of it as a possibility. He thought he and McKenna were the only two "who didn't have booms going for [them]." He was too old, and presidents traditionally did not elevate associate justices—it did not do to skip over men who were senior. He believed White, next in seniority to Harlan, "the ablest man" under consideration. White's writing, Holmes felt, was less than brilliant, but his thinking was "profound." While Holmes considered himself a better administrator, White, he thought, would prove "more politic." Holmes feared, however, that White, as an associate justice, had "about as little chance as I." Actually, Holmes didn't care much who was appointed, "if only he is a man who can dispose of the little daily questions with promptitude and decision." Taft, whom Holmes saw on a casual social basis occasionally at Beverly Farms that summer, had told Holmes he meant to send for him to "talk about the new appointments," but there is no evidence that Taft fulfilled the promise.

Finally, after months of deliberation and discussion, Taft surprised the capital and sent to the Senate for confirmation the name of Edward Douglass White of Louisiana. He was the first sitting justice in the Court's history to be named chief. (William Cushing had been offered the position but had declined.)

Politically, White's appointment could not have been improved upon. He was a Roman Catholic, a Democrat, a Southerner, and a Confederate Civil War veteran. An added dividend was the potential of the appointment for mollifying Roosevelt, who had disliked sharing the center stage of reform with Hughes and probably would not enjoy seeing the crusading New Yorker in the nation's highest judicial post. Although the former political intimates had split by 1910, Taft was still hoping for Roosevelt's help in the approaching 1912 presidential campaign.

Holmes and White, who like Holmes had been seriously wounded in Civil War combat, had the soldier's bond in common. Each year on the anniversary of the Battle of Antietam, White brought Holmes a red rose to wear on his robe. The Southern patriot remained a Southern patriot always, but he did not nurse the grudges of wartime, and he frankly admitted the errors of the Confederacy, including the original error of secession.

"My God," he had been heard to say, the horror apparent in his voice, "My God, if we had succeeded."

Many years later, when Holmes had more than two decades of Supreme Court work behind him and White was dead, Holmes discussed with one of his secretaries White's commitment to the Confederacy. "Both of us knew," Holmes explained, "that one reason we were in that fight was because the Supreme Court's Dred Scott decision inflamed sectional passions. White and I knew it was our business so far as the Court was involved, to see that there would never be a Civil War again."

White's opinions, which it was his custom to announce without text or notes, reminded Holmes of "seeing a man on the brink of a roaring chasm. Then you look away for a moment and when you look back he is on the other side." White, on his part, writhed in agony over Holmes's "obscurities" and generalities. The two justices nevertheless had become friends, and on White's "advent to the throne," as Holmes called it, he predicted that the new chief justice's popularity in Washington as well as his "anxiety and far sight as to consequences to the country from our decisions" could only help the Court.

White and Holmes were "apt to agree (with an occasional sharp difference)" on the cases that came before them, but their

> interests were so remote from each other that the sense of companionship was not as great as [Holmes] could wish.

White was a political animal, concerned about the practical effects of a decision. The speculative side, which attracted Holmes's attention, did not interest the chief justice, and intellectual communication between the two men was stifled.

When Taft finally decided to elevate White to the chief justiceship, he then had White's former seat to fill—his third associate justice to appoint in less than two years. Before the end of his term he would replace the fourth "old fool" plus Moody, making a Taft-appointed majority. It was the second largest number of Supreme Court justices appointed by a single president in this century; Taft was surpassed only by Franklin D. Roosevelt, who appointed nine.

For this third vacancy, Taft chose railroad lawyer and federal judge Willis Van Devanter of Wyoming, prominent in territorial—after 1890, state—Republican politics. On the Supreme Court he remained solicitous of corporate interests, but his influence on constitutional jurisprudence during his twenty-seven years as a justice was grounded not in his opinions but in his technical legal expertise. A sufferer from "pen paralysis," he wrote relatively few opinions; his thinking in legal matters, however, was incisive, his skill in ferreting out essential points buried in a legal morass was exceptional, and his skill at negotiation in conference was appreciated by his brethren who made a habit of calling on him for help when the complexities of some case stymied them—help for which he held himself available and which he gave generously to progressive and conservative alike.

"Van Devanter runs the Court now," Louis Brandeis remarked a decade or so after the Westerner joined the Court. "He is like a Jesuit general . . . always helpful to everybody, always ready for the C.J. . . . knows a deal of federal practice, federal specialties, particularly land laws and he is in with all the Republican politicians."

Sure enough, as Holmes had expected, Moody was forced by his failing health to resign shortly after the 1910 term opened—at the comparatively young age of fifty-seven. His successor, fifty-one-year-old former railroad and corporation lawyer Joseph Rucker Lamar of Georgia, descendant of Lucius Quintus Cincinnatus Lamar who had sat on the U.S. Supreme Court from 1888 until 1893, had met the vacationing president-elect, William Howard Taft, on the golf links of Augusta in the winter of 1908. When Moody resigned, Taft was hard-pressed to find still another nominee of high caliber. He had the attorney general inquire about Lamar, whom he had found particularly engaging company. Lamar, a Southern Democrat, had endorsements from congressmen, corporation lawyers, and judges statewide. There was, of course, a good deal more to Lamar than his pleasant manners. He had in fact served on the Georgia Supreme Court and had made a public record—more than two hundred opinions, and Taft's attorney general had read them all—a record that indicated he was not entirely hostile to government regulation in the interests of "the public health, the public morals, or the public safety."

As courts go, the early White Court was a relatively young one. Harlan was the oldest, but he would not be there long. White, McKenna, Day, and Holmes were in their sixties, Van Devanter and Lamar were in their early fifties, and Hughes was only forty-eight.

Eight of the nine—all except Hughes—had had judicial experience before they joined the Supreme Court. Four were Civil War veterans—two Confederate (White and Lurton), two Union (Harlan and Holmes). Three were Southern Democrats (White, Lurton, Lamar), the rest Republicans.

There seemed to be no one on this Court, as there had been no one on the Fuller Court, with whom Holmes could enjoy any sort of deep friendship, no companion to share his solitary reflections. And he cried out:

> Oh my dear Canon [Sheehan] you are lonely, but so am I although I am in the world and surrounded by able men—none of those whom I meet has the same interests and emphasis that I do.

The brethren were pleasant enough, as was Holmes generally, but intellectual intimacy between the detached Olympian who had matured in the company of Emerson and Lowell, the companions of whose young manhood had included William and Henry James, Henry and Brooks Adams, Charles Peirce and John Gray, and these practical men who had matured in the maelstrom of public affairs seemed out of the question; relations remained little more than casually amiable. In the rare references Holmes made to the other justices in his correspondence, he seemed bored with—even, on occasion, contemptuous of—their emanations, oral and written. One letter from Fred Pollock or, later, Harold Laski, gave him more of an intellectual kick than hours in discussion of constitutional complexities at conference with his colleagues.

During the decade of White's stewardship, the Court assumed a more moderate jurisprudential stance than it had for the past two decades under Fuller. The two most rigid conservatives, Peckham and Brewer, had been replaced by the moderate Lurton and the progressive Hughes, the strident Fuller by the less aggressive though often unpredictable White. Lamar would never be as progressive as Moody, but he was tolerant. If Van Devanter's concern for the downtrodden did not stand out, for the time being he was offset by Harlan. Holmes was becoming the darling of the Progressives, not because he sought the honor or because he shared their goals—he certainly didn't—but because in his willingness to tolerate any regulatory measure he did not deem unconstitutional, however absurd he deemed it, he was unintentionally building a reputation as a Progressive.

It was in general a quieter Court; dissents were less shrill, conservatism less rigid. Its posture has been characterized as both mild progressivism and mellow conservatism.

WHITE TOOK THE oath as chief justice—the nation's ninth—on December 19, 1910, relieving Harlan, who had been presiding since Fuller's death and had begun to look "sad and aged." On January 3, 1911, Holmes rang in the new year—and the new Court—with his expansive opinion in *Noble State Bank* v. *Haskell*. In 1907, the Oklahoma legislature had created a Depositors' Guaranty Fund to protect depositors against state bank insolvency. It was financed by a levy of 1 percent—later 5 percent—on the average daily deposits of all state banks. When a bank failed and its cash was insufficient to reimburse all its depositors in full, the Depositors' Guaranty Fund was supposed to make up the deficiency. The bankers objected, and officials of the Noble State Bank took the issue into court on the grounds that the assessment on the daily deposits amounted to confiscation of private property for private use and violated the Due Process Clause of the Fourteenth Amendment to the Constitution.

In deciding against the bankers, Holmes spoke for a unanimous Court, although whether that included Lamar and Van Devanter, who took their seats after the case was argued, is unclear; justices do not usually participate in cases whose arguments they have not heard; the opinion in *Noble State Bank,* however, contains no notation to that effect.

Holmes hinted that strictly speaking, the bankers might be right. Judges, however, he said, must be

> cautious about pressing the broad words of the Fourteenth Amendment to a drily logical extreme. Many laws which it would be vain to ask the court to overthrow could be shown, easily enough, to transgress a scholastic interpretation of one or another of the great guarantees in the Bill of Rights. They more or less limit the liberty of the individual or they diminish property to a certain extent. We have few scientifically certain criteria of legislation, and as it often is difficult to mark the line where what is called the police power of the States is limited by the Constitution of the United States, judges should be slow to read into the latter a *nolumus mutare* as against the law-making power.

It was absolutely true, he admitted, that the statute robbed Peter to pay Paul, who might even be a rival bank, but the considerations on the other side—"an ulterior public advantage"—certainly justified a "comparatively insignificant taking of private property for what, in its immediate purpose, is a private use." Once again, if the state legislature "thinks that the public welfare requires the measure under consideration, analogy and principle are in favor of the power to enact it." A lot of people, including two of his brethren—Harlan and McKenna—thought Holmes's generalizations regarding the state's police power shocking. Could the state then require all corporations or all grocers to help to guarantee each other's solvency? Holmes seemed to have opened Pandora's box, and where would it all end? Holmes thought such questions "futile." With regard to the police power, as elsewhere in the law, "lines are pricked out by the gradual approach and contact of decisions on the opposing sides."

Later the same day, in *Bailey* v. *Alabama* (1911), Progressives were again encouraged when the Court, via the newly arrived Hughes, struck down Alabama's infamous peonage laws. Holmes in dissent, however, demonstrated how his detachment along with his willingness to capitulate to the "feelings and demands of the community" could warp his sensitivity to human tragedy.

Led by Alabama, several Southern states had passed so-called peonage statutes that criminalized a workman's breaking a contract while he still owed the employer money—the breach itself was "prima facie evidence of the intent to injure or defraud" the employer. The practice prevalent at the time was for an employer to advance a laborer a small sum and arrange for repayment over a specified time. During that period, the workman received a monthly wage from which the installment was deducted. If he left the job during the repayment period, he could be fined double the amount he still owed plus court costs. Intent to defraud was assumed by the fact that the employee still owed money when he quit. Poor blacks were the most frequent victims of this system, which in practice was better than slavery but not much.

Lonzo Bailey, an illiterate black man, had received a $15 advance from the Riverside Company in return for which he had agreed to work as a farmhand on its Scotts Bend Place in Montgomery County, Alabama, from December 30, 1907, until December 30, 1908, at the rate of $12 a month, from which $1.25 would be deducted against the $15 advance. Bailey had worked only into early February, then quit, still owing $13.75 to the Riverside Company. He was arrested, tried, and found guilty. The jury awarded damages of $15 to the Riverside Company and fined Bailey $30 plus court costs. The judge in the case, however, privately urged Booker T. Washington to use it as a test case and organize an appeal to the U.S. Supreme Court. White lawyers were found to take the case, Roosevelt was alerted to its importance, the attorney general—Charles J. Bonaparte at the time—was told to investigate it, and Washington's friend Oswald Garrison Villard was persuaded to publicize it in the *New York Evening Post*.

When the case came to the Supreme Court for the first time in 1908, it challenged the constitutionality of Alabama's peonage statute under the Thirteenth and Fourteenth Amendments (*Bailey* v. *Alabama*, 1908). The Court, however, did not decide it on the issues on the ground that Bailey had not followed proper procedures on his way to Washington, but had taken a "short cut." Holmes wrote the brief majority opinion, which did not consider Bailey's peonage, the Thirteenth Amendment, or the Alabama statute at issue, but focused largely on technical procedural matters. At the same time he seemed to encourage Bailey to try again. Harlan was characteristically furious. "It is a curious condition of things," he thundered in dissent, "if this court must remain silent when the question comes before it regularly, whether the final judgment of a State does not deprive the citizen of rights secured to him by the Supreme Law of the Land."

The case was sent back to Alabama for retrial. Again Bailey was found guilty, and fined $30 and court costs of $46.40, which to a poor black in Alabama at that time meant 136 days of hard labor. Again the judge and other whites both in Alabama and the North found funds to appeal. The new attorney general, George Wickersham, put together an *amicus curiae* (friend of the court) brief supporting Bailey's arguments.

The case was argued in October 1910, before a Court substantially reconstituted since 1908. Fuller was dead and Harlan was presiding until the new chief justice could take his seat. Lurton and Hughes had replaced Peckham and Brewer. Moody was absent but had not yet resigned, and the lawyers remembered him as an enemy of peonage. White was still on the Court, but not yet chief justice, although he would be by the time the decision was handed down. Day had joined Harlan's dissent in 1908 and undoubtedly was reliable, as was McKenna, but Holmes was a question mark.

Whether Harlan or White, who did not become chief justice until December 19, assigned the opinion is unclear. When possible, opinions were traditionally assigned at conferences immediately following argument; two months would have been a long time to wait for White, although Hughes's biographer, Merlo J. Pusey, contended that "Hughes emerged in conference as the ablest champion of the view that the Alabama law was unconstitutional," and was asked by White to write it. If Harlan assigned it, on the other hand, it is curious that he did not want to write it himself. Perhaps he feared expression of his strong feelings in the matter might alienate Southerners as well as justices otherwise inclined to strike down the Alabama law. In any event, Hughes wrote it.

Bailey's lawyers and the assistant attorney general who had argued for the Justice Department had urged on the Court the social realities of race and poverty. Perhaps to alleviate sectional tensions, Hughes ignored them and "dismissed from consideration" the fact that Bailey was a "black man." He insisted on viewing the Alabama statute "in the same manner as if it had been enacted in New York or Idaho." Nevertheless, in considering the way the law operated, he found it had been "a convenient instrument for the coercion which the Constitution and . . . Congress forbid; an instrument of compulsion peculiarly effective as against the poor and the ignorant, its most likely victims."

The state could not, he wrote, assume by statute the intent to defraud. Mere nonpayment of a debt could not be criminalized by statute; those who thought it could were talking in effect about involuntary servitude, which had been outlawed by the Thirteenth Amendment and the act of Congress which nullified all state laws "by which it should be attempted to enforce the 'service of labor of any persons . . . in liquidation of any debt or obligation, or otherwise.' " Clearly, Alabama's statute could not stand.

Hughes could not believe his eyes when he saw Holmes's dissent, although to those familiar with Holmes's cold intellectuality, his dissent in *Bailey* would not have come as a surprise. He was, as he always had been, loath to strike down state laws, and he looked no doubt on Alabama's peonage laws with the same objective eyes with which he had viewed New York's maximum hours measure. Only the sanctity of contracts equaled the sanctity of state statutes in Holmes's hierarchy of legal principles, and the consequences to society of tolerating default on contracts were far more serious than the fate of a poor black worker.

He saw Bailey's case as one involving breach of contract and fraud, and Bailey himself as a shiftless, irresponsible fellow, not the victim of a discriminatory peonage system. Peonage, he declared, required "service to a private master at which a man is kept by compulsion against his will." Bailey, however, could and did leave. The law had not compelled him to perform his part in the contract against his will; it did, however, intend to penalize him if he didn't. As he had said in *The Common Law*, the law traditionally interfered only after "a promise has been broken." He saw nothing in the Alabama statute to contradict that tradition. Legal liability for breach of contract was only a "disagreeable consequence which tends to make the contractor do as he said he would." If a state added to "civil liability a criminal liability to fine, it simply intensified the legal motive for doing right"; it did not "make the laborer a slave."

The statute at issue had been intended to punish fraud, said Holmes, exactly the sort of fraud he believed Bailey had committed: the fraud in "obtaining money by a false pretense of an intent to keep the written contract in consideration of which money is advanced." The fact that the breach itself was considered *prima facie* evidence of intent to defraud the employer did not disturb Holmes. "Is it not evidence," he asked, "that a man had a fraudulent intent if he receives an advance upon a contract over night and leaves in the morning?" Holmes thought it "very plainly was." The time of departure—the next day, the next week, the next month—was irrelevant.

Their denials notwithstanding, the justices seemed to have tacitly assumed that the law was not administered in Alabama as it would be in New York and that juries in Alabama acted "with prejudice against the laboring man." Holmes thought his brethren were mistaken and that these cases might quite safely be left to local juries. He had written in *The Common Law* that "The distinctions of the law are founded on experience, not on logic," and in this case, experience meant not men like Bailey, but "the men of the world" who made up an Alabama jury. They had learned that "in certain conditions it is so common for laborers to remain during a part of the season, receiving advances, and then to depart at the period of need in the hope of greater wages at a neighboring plantation"; they knew from long experience when to bring the law to bear. Holmes could not see where the Alabama statute infringed on the Thirteenth Amendment or any act of Congress.

The Progressive press—the *Outlook*, whose editor, Lyman Abbott, had helped finance Bailey's lawyers, the *Nation,* the *Independent*—hailed the Supreme Court's decision in *Bailey* not only as a harbinger of changed relations between laborers and employers, but also as a signal that the times themselves were changing—for the better, finally. Holmes, however, paid no attention, and two months later, on receipt of the new edition of Pollock's book on contracts, he took the opportunity to restate briefly his concept of contractual obligation: a contract at common law, he declared, was "not a *promise* to pay damages on etc. but an act imposing a liability to damages nisi—You commit a tort & are liable—You commit a contract and are liable *unless* the event agreed upon, over which you may have no, and never have absolute, control, comes to pass." What could be simpler, more logical?

Holmes turned seventy on March 8, 1911. A little nosegay of violets appeared at his place on the bench, compliments of the senior associate justice. He was still leaving "to the future" the decision whether he would retire or "keep on." Most judges, he recalled, kept on, and "most of them have made a mistake in doing so, as it was obvious that they no longer were up to their old mark." Friends encouraged him to stay, reassuring him that the quality of his work had not fallen off, but he was "cynically aware of the illusions that we all are ready to drop into with regard to ourselves."

That spring, after a series of delays and postponements, *Standard Oil Co.* v. *United States,* one of the most significant of the antitrust cases, was being considered by the Supreme Court. It had been begun back in 1906 during Roosevelt's administration. Back to back with *United States* v. *American Tobacco Co.,* a similar case, it was argued for the second time in January 1911. The justices took four months to decide it, and it was not announced until mid-May 1911.

For more than a decade, White had been urging on his brethren a "rule of reason" in antitrust cases, a standard for judging the legality of trusts and combinations that distinguished between reasonable and unreasonable consolidations—the basic common-law distinction which Holmes also supported. The Sherman Act, White felt, although he had been in the minority in *Northern Securities,* did not apply to all trusts and combinations, only to those that operated in restraint of trade, that were unreasonable. His dissent in *Northern Securities* had been supported by Holmes; Holmes in fact had implied White's position in his own dissent. By 1911, White had at last put together a solid majority, and the Court decided, 8 to 1, Harlan dissenting, that White's "rule of reason" was indeed the appropriate standard for judging the operations of trusts. The moment Holmes caught the rule-of-reason concept in the twenty-thousand-word draft opinion, he "knew [White] had us. How could you be against that without being for a rule of unreason?" Having got this far, it was no trick at all for the Court to declare unreasonable Standard Oil's discriminatory practices in connection with rebates and rates, its control of pipelines, unfair price cutting, even "espionage" against its competitors.

The unreconstructed author of *Northern Securities,* John Marshall Harlan, his bald dome red with anger, delivered a bench-pounding dissent. Although the big Kentuckian seemed to have recovered from his disappointment at being passed over for the chief justiceship, his dissent in the oil trust case, Hughes observed, was "the roar of an angry lion." Harlan referred, his voice dripping with sarcasm, to "our present Chief Justice" and "my brethren in their wisdom"; he felt "impelled to say that there is abroad, in our land, a most harmful tendency to bring about the amending of constitutions and legislative enactments by means alone of judicial construction." He would with the Court crush Standard Oil, but he would have no part of the Court's distinguishing between reasonable and unreasonable. The Sherman Act, he thundered, restating *Northern Securities,* "prohibited *any* contract in restraint of interstate commerce, it hence embraced all contracts of that character, whether they were reasonable or unreasonable." Harlan's fury notwithstanding, two weeks later, on May 29, 1911, the chief justice applied his rule of reason to the decision against the American Tobacco Company.

Holmes, the economic conservatism in his nature rebelling whenever the Sherman Act was put into play, had mixed feelings about the results in the two antitrust cases. He had gone along with the majority reluctantly, in order to get the "most moderate results," that is, "confining the Sherman Act to unreasonable restraints of trade. . . . If Harlan had his way he would cut all these concerns into inch bits." Old Harlan seemed "incapable of understanding that national wealth is consistent with private ownership." In Holmes's view, "if Rockefeller owned the whole concern, and had committed more imperial crimes than Frederic the Great or Napoleon to produce it, still he has made the nation richer by an imperial result—a great coordinated machine—and that to destroy the machine because you disapprove the builder is folly. . . . Just when other nations, England and Germany, are encouraging unification as manifest destiny and clear gain we persist in our Sherman Act policy, and I think we are fools."

Outside the court, the effects of the decisions in *Standard Oil* and *American Tobacco* turned out to be anticlimactic. As in the aftermath of *Northern Securities,* the corporations reorganized as ordered, but the same men continued to control corporate behavior, and the profits and the oil continued to gush. J. P. Morgan pronounced the decision "very satisfactory," and steel magnate Andrew Carnegie said he was a very happy man. Carnegie wrote George W. Perkins, his opposite number at International Harvester, and forwarded a copy of his letter to the White House: "Standard Oil and Tobacco are laughing at the government. Who isn't? 'Disbandment' is futile."

Taft, who, like his predecessor, had wanted only corporate abuses curbed and had long distinguished between good and bad trusts, called the opinion "good." He regarded Harlan's dissent as "nasty, carping, and demagogic, directed at the Chief Justice and intended to furnish La Follette and his crowd as much pabulum as possible."

La Follette and his Progressive crowd viewed White's opinion as a discouraging setback. Commented the senator: "Every trust will now come into court and claim justification on a special set of facts going to support the claim that it is not restraining trade unreasonably, and it is to be expected that courts will make use of a sliding scale of reasonableness to apply to each case."

In fact these two, *Standard Oil* and *American Tobacco,* were the last of the big antitrust suits decided by the Supreme Court for nearly a decade. The Justice Department began the government's suit against United States Steel in 1911, but the case dragged on for nine years, only to be dismissed in the end. Recognizing the inevitability of corporate consolidation inherent in the economics of the twentieth century, the White Court went easy on those few trusts that did come before the justices after 1911. Many cases did not get that far; on several occasions the attorney general and firms believed to be in violation of the Sherman Act negotiated reorganization plans which would bring the monopolies into conformation with the statute as most recently interpreted. Thus was the way paved for the unopposed development of the big trusts of the 1920s.

HOLMES HAD FOUND the 1910–11 term "hard and anxious and not as agreeable as usual," and in early June he was glad it was over. The results in the Standard Oil and American Tobacco cases did not "satisfy" him; they were, however, "all that [he] could hope for"; in other matters he was, he said, "content." Added to the pressures of Court work that year was anxiety over Clare Castletown's operation for a displaced retina and her husband's recent bankruptcy. He was depressed when he contemplated Doneraile, which had been put into receivership, without her, and he dispatched frantic inquiries to their several mutual friends.

Believing judges should limit their public utterances to their court opinions, and not "meddle with burning themes," Holmes had not made a speech in nearly ten years, almost since he had gone to Washington. But in June 1911, on the eve of commencement, he made an exception for the Harvard Alumni Association and represented the class of 1861, fifty years out. It was not to be a long speech, but he "hate[d] not to do as well as I can," and he began work on it ten days before the event. In a nostalgic mood, inevitable perhaps at seventy, he reminisced about the two training grounds where his life had been fashioned, Harvard College and the Massachusetts Twentieth, and tried to make philosophic sense out of—bring some semblance of unity to—the chaos that seemed to characterize men's days on earth. He talked about materialism, much as he had in "The Soldier's Faith" back in 1895, and reminded his audience that "the root of joy as of duty is to put out all one's powers toward some great end." He had learned about duty through the "stern experience" of war, and he had not changed his mind that man was "born to act." Surprisingly for Holmes, he concluded on the faintly mystical note that

> our only but wholly adequate significance is as parts of the unimaginable whole. It suggests that even while we think that we are egotists we are living to ends outside ourselves.

Attempting to satisfy his incessant hunger for the approval of his peers, Holmes sent a copy of his speech to Henry James, who had remained in the United States following his brother's funeral and had received an honorary degree from Harvard only hours before Holmes gave his speech. James pronounced the speech "beautiful" and apologized for not being there; still recovering from the melancholia of the year before, he had been "quite spent, when the afternoon came, by that horrid and trying day," and had scurried away to Nahant where he was staying with a friend.

Along with the speech, Holmes also sent a letter in which he expressed some concern that the " 'difference in the sphere of [their] dominant interests' might have 'made a gulf [they could] not cross.' " Whatever could Wendell mean after all those years? Of course, they were very different sorts of people. Holmes was a doer, "born to act"; James was a writer, essentially an observer. The war would, of course, always stand between them. Did Holmes perhaps recall how critical he had been of James's expatriation, which Holmes no doubt considered a shirking of duty? But their differences could not erase North Conway and all the other good times they had shared as young men. James was astonished at the tone of Holmes's letter:

> As I look back at any moment of our contact—which began so long ago—I find myself crossing & crossing with a devotedness that took no smallest account of gulfs, or, more truly, hovering & circling & sitting on your side of the chasm altogether (if chasm there were!)—with a complete suspension, as far as you were concerned, of the question of any other side. Such was my pleasure & my affection & homage—& when & where in the world did you ever see any symptom of anything else?

James could never forget "old memories, communities & pieties," and he was "so far from not caring to see" Holmes again that he would make it a point to "motor over to tea" before he sailed for England in August.

John Marshall Harlan's dissents in the Standard Oil and American Tobacco cases, if they were two of his most strident, were also his last. He returned to the Court in the fall of 1911 with a cold. During the first two days of the session—the last he attended—he was restless, alternately talking to himself and sleeping in the courtroom. At the end of the second day, McKenna accompanied him home in a taxi, and, on arrival, had difficulty getting the weakened justice up the stairs. Harlan was running a high fever—103°—which abated only intermittently. His condition worsened over the next few days until he died quietly on Saturday morning, October 14, 1911. It was said of him that he had learned in the "fierce warfare of personal strife during the Civil War and in the intensity of political contests after the war, to beat his brute and human enemies as his fathers had learned to subjugate the wilderness. But he never well learned what it was to follow a leader. . . . Where others agreed with his views he would march with them, but when they differed he marched on alone. His was not the temper of the negotiator." Holmes thought that at seventy-eight "the old boy had outlived his usefulness, but he was a figure the like of which" Holmes did not expect to meet again. "He had some of the faults of the savage, but he was a personality, and in his own home and sometimes out of it he was charming."

Back in 1910, Taft had announced that he expected to appoint a majority of the Supreme Court. At last his expectations were about to be fulfilled. The seat left vacant by Harlan's death gave him the opportunity to name his fifth new man. Five associate justices and a chief justice constituted a record to date; only George Washington surpassed it.

On February 19, 1912, Taft named fifty-four-year-old Mahlon Pitney of New Jersey to Harlan's place. He had met Pitney the week before at a dinner in Newark and been impressed with Pitney's geniality. A tall, handsome man who wore high stand-up collars, Pitney was the descendant of eighteenth-century English settlers, the son of a lawyer, and a classmate at Princeton of the New Jersey governor now on the verge of running for president, Woodrow Wilson. He had matured professionally in the crucible of New Jersey politics, had been elected to the U.S. House of Representatives and the state Senate, and had been rewarded for his political service with an appointment to the New Jersey Supreme Court, where he became known for his antilabor opinions.

Holmes found him an "emotional" man. When Pitney first came to the Court, his incessant talking from the bench and in conference "used to get on [Holmes's] nerves." Either Pitney quieted or Holmes got used to it; Holmes later found him an "honest hardworking Judge and a useful critic" if not a "thunderbolt."

His appointments to the Supreme Court were the few consolations Taft had to see him through the turmoil of the 1912 presidential campaign. He could at least rest secure in the knowledge that he had put five strong men there where they could be relied on to "preserve the fundamental structure of our government as our fathers gave it to us." Should the now radicalized Roosevelt win in 1912, at least the Court would be safe.

In June 1912, Holmes made a "flying visit" to Williams College in Williamstown, Massachusetts, where he collected an honorary degree. That summer he sat—or stood, actually—for his portrait in judicial robes and got for his efforts a "crick in the back." In late September, the Alpha Delta Phi Club at Harvard, to which he had belonged as an undergraduate, gave him a dinner and "did what they could to make me think myself a great man."

Finally, the longed-for moment came. On Sunday, December 8, he turned to volume 187 of the *United States Reports* and reread the notice of his own appointment exactly ten years before. Having reached the age of seventy in 1911, he now had reached the required decade of service and could if he chose "notify the President tomorrow and retire on a pension."

"Ha," he exclaimed, "doesn't that make one feel free!"

Ten years was also the time limit Fanny had set when the Holmeses arrived in Washington in 1902. Her joy may have been somewhat less, however, for "in spite of warnings from some tailless foxes that old men can't trust their judgment," and that he had better leave the Court as soon as possible, he intended "to remain until I am conscious of some warning, or like it less than I do now." During the decade, he had developed a certain comfort in his routine, a familiarity with precedent and some standards for judging; he found "the work easier than ever" and had been "encouraged to believe" that neither his brethren nor the president wanted him to leave.

Washington hostesses still wrote about the Holmeses' entertaining presence at dinner parties, although less often than heretofore. Both Holmeses had in fact largely withdrawn from the social whirl, had given up their official Monday afternoon at-homes, went out less and less, and were "more than content not to." Afternoon drives, especially in spring when Washington came alive, and evenings of reading aloud and solitaire conserved their energies, and Holmes found it an "unmixed joy to escape the White House flagellations."

He felt good physically, and he still noticed petticoats instinctively. But intimations of his mortality were all around him. Colleagues and friends were dying, some younger than he. How hard it was to "realize the irrevocable" and to walk past doors in Boston where he used to turn in.

"Our business," however, he had told the Alpha Delta Phi Club recently, "is to commit ourselves to life," and he was not ready to retire from it. "When I shave and catch my eye," he told a friend a little later, "I try to say; it is not for long—but Lord life is as interesting as ever and I don't feel it in my bones."

CHAPTER 21

"[T]he quiet of a storm center"

HOLMES'S SECOND DECADE on the U.S. Supreme Court coincided roughly with his seventies, and he grieved as old friends vanished, leaving him stranded in life. He fell in with several much younger men, perhaps finding some sense of security in the knowledge they were unlikely to desert him by dying.

The first to enter Holmes's life during this period was Felix Frankfurter, in his early thirties, introduced to Holmes by John Gray under whom Frankfurter had studied at Harvard Law School. The two men should have been antipathetic: Holmes the aristocrat with the aristocratic bearing of his class and many of its social prejudices; Frankfurter, born in Vienna the year Holmes joined the Massachusetts Supreme Judicial Court, bred in the Jewish ghetto on the Lower East Side of Manhattan. Nevertheless, the young Frankfurter and the childless Holmes enjoyed as close a relationship as Holmes ever had with another man. Frankfurter guarded it jealously. He advertised the fact of it, but he published few of its details. He admired Holmes's intellect and his opinions enormously. He often referred to Holmes as the Master and never wearied of quoting him. He often said his feeling for Holmes bordered on reverence. For Holmes's part, he found in Frankfurter "a very vivid, articulate brilliant youngster," a man who "sees the powers that be at so much shorter range than I do that I value his intimations."

The brilliant, ebullient, and totally engaged Frankfurter, who in those days was spending his ever-abundant energies on all manner of social causes and progressive reforms, was the antithesis of Holmes, who in *his* thirties had channeled his energies into philosophical explorations of the legal universe. It perhaps amused the older man to recall his own isolation and loneliness at the time as he watched Frankfurter bounce from political campaigning to the War Department to the Harvard Law School faculty. Frankfurter clearly stimulated Holmes intellectually; he also brought out in Holmes an unusual capacity for fatherly affection. Frankfurter reported a poignant incident that revealed a rarely seen side of the detached, reserved, and sometimes stern judge: One summer night at Beverly Farms, after a typical long "jaw," as Holmes liked to refer to his livelier conversations, the justice escorted Frankfurter to his room to make sure "everything was o.k.," bade the young man goodnight, and left. He returned shortly, put his hand on Frankfurter's shoulder, and said:

My son, it was a piece of good fortune for me when I fell in with you,

then abruptly left the room for the second time.

Pre–World War I Washington saw the pair frequently tramping the broad, nearly autoless streets, the tall man with a thatch of snowy hair, matching mustaches, and a long stride, accompanied by a short man half running to keep up and breathlessly talking. Frankfurter remembered quiet evenings by the fire in Holmes's drawing room or his study, quiet conversation, exciting in its quality—philosophy, law, life—very exhilarating for a young man.

Holmes transmitted to Frankfurter his traditions and his philosophy, made Frankfurter see, as he saw, the Constitution as a way of maintaining a living, continuing government and not as a dead document. He made Frankfurter see, as he saw, the law as an instrument of society, as a way of ordering life, and not as a cold abstraction or an end in itself. Frankfurter became the foremost interpreter of Holmes, the original author of the Holmes legend which began to take shape during this second decade on the Supreme Court.

Holmes began to be noticed during this decade, partly because Frankfurter made sure he was, but also because he himself, no longer a neophyte, was drawing attention to himself. Neither the issues nor his views regarding them had changed, but his now-mature and forceful writing style showed a growing self-assurance and his enlarged command of precedent gave him an increased capacity for getting around in the constitutional universe.

The attention Holmes was attracting during this decade was largely, although not entirely, favorable. Several cases with the potential for reputation-making came before the Court. Although in some cases Holmes showed himself to be less than the egalitarian many Americans thought him, people seemed to remember his support for legislation that promised social and economic reform and his civil libertarian outbursts, which in fact were rarer and less libertarian than was often thought. His private views frequently conflicted with his public utterances; still, he became a hero to Progressives and liberals of various stripes.

His brethren, however, were not so fortunate. Americans, as the first decade of the twentieth century ended and a new decade began, were noisily dissatisfied with the conduct of their courts. As they saw it, court decisions underlay all society's ills, and judicial oligarchies perpetuated them. Popular magazines exploited the widespread discontent and filled their pages with charges and countercharges. Journalists invented all manner of cure-alls. Politicians rallied around the twin banners of judicial recall and legislative review of judicial decisions. In January 1913, a bill to add two judges to the United States Supreme Court was introduced in the Senate, a move Holmes viewed as "the beginning of the end." The court-packing bill ultimately fizzled out, but Holmes's anger didn't, and in a speech to the Harvard Law School Association of New York in mid-February 1913, he tried to put into perspective all those nightmares that were troubling the serenity of judge, lawyer, and layman alike.

Although he had made almost a fetish of judicial celibacy since he took his seat on the Supreme Court, he made an exception for the Harvard Law School Association and had even assumed the presidency of it in 1911, at the age of seventy. Generally, his duties were even less than ceremonial, but when Irving S. Olds, his former secretary (1910–11), invited him to speak to the New York branch, which was comprised of the city's and even some of the nation's most influential lawyers, it seemed perhaps a politically useful forum in which to advance his views.

As he rose to address the Harvard alumni, then lighting up after-dinner cigars, he was reminded of a similar hall at Oxford five years before. He had enjoyed unusual kindness and hospitality since his arrival in New York, and he was feeling a general mellowness toward his audience. He had prepared his talk carefully, as he usually did; leaving it to last-minute jottings on the train was not his style, and he gave the room full of lawyers a little bit of *Vegelahn,* a little bit of "The Soldier's Faith," a little bit of *Lochner,* plus a glimpse of the structure of his personal universe. Henry Cabot Lodge thought it good enough to have reprinted as a public document.

He spoke for a minute or so of his own ambition, then with affection of the Supreme Court, how it was a "very quiet" place, although as everyone in the room knew, it was "the quiet of a storm center." He told the lawyers how his "heart ache[d]" when his mail contained letters accusing him of corruption, painted him as a "tool of the money power," and he dwelt a little on his industry and integrity. He tried, he said, to take the criticism "philosophically" and to "see what we can learn from hatred and distrust."

The attacks on the Court, he felt, were "merely an expression of the unrest that seems to wonder vaguely whether law and order pay." He thought perhaps men who blamed the judges for their misfortunes were preoccupied with detail, particularly economic detail, were missing the larger implications, and he sailed into a brief discussion of his own economic "philosophy," if such it could be called—his frequently repeated conviction that "we need to think things instead of words—to drop ownership, money, etc., and to think of the stream of products; of wheat and cloth and railway travel. When we do it is obvious that the many consume them; that they now as truly have substantially all there is . . . that the great body of property is socially administered now, and that the function of private ownership is to divine in advance the equilibrium of social desires—which socialism equally would have to divine, but which, under the illusion of self-seeking, is more poignantly and shrewdly foreseen."

He had said in *Lochner* and even before that that the law was "behind the times" and that judges, afraid of change, had an unfortunate tendency to translate their fears "into doctrines that had no proper place in the Constitution or the common law." Like everyone else, judges had still to learn "to transcend our own convictions and to leave room for much that we hold dear to be done away with short of revolution by the orderly change of law."

He had no use for panaceas and no interest in the "nostrums now so strenuously urged." He thought rather the "main remedy, as for the evils of public opinion, is for us to grow more civilized."

In his own vision, he did not think about socialism or the legislative treatments so often proposed or the price of flour and train tickets. His vision was larger than that. As he grew older and his perspective lengthened and sharpened, he also grew calm.

If I feel [he told the lawyers] what are perhaps an old man's apprehensions, that competition from new races will cut deeper than working men's disputes and will test whether we can hang together and can fight; if I fear that we are running through the world's resources at a pace we cannot keep; I do not lose my hopes. I do not pin my dreams for the future to my country or even to my race. I think it probable that civilization somehow will last as long as I care to look ahead—perhaps with smaller numbers, but perhaps also bred to greatness and splendor by science. I think it is not improbable that man, like the grub that prepares a chamber for the winged thing it never has seen but is to be—that man may have cosmic destinies that he does not understand. And so beyond the vision of battling races and an impoverished earth I catch a dreaming glimpse of peace.

The old guvnor himself would have been proud of his son's peroration:

> The other day my dream was pictured to my mind. It was evening. I was walking homeward on Pennsylvania Avenue near the Treasury, and as I looked beyond Sherman's Statue to the west the sky was aflame with scarlet and crimson from the setting sun. But, like the note of downfall in Wagner's opera, below the sky line there came from little globes the pallid discord of the electric lights. And I thought to myself the Götterdämmerung will end, and from those globes clustered like evil eggs will come the new masters of the sky. It is like the time in which we live. But then I remembered the faith that I partly have expressed, faith in a universe not measured by our fears, a universe that has thought and more than thought inside of it, and as I gazed, after the sunset and above the electric lights there shone the stars.

ALTHOUGH THE TWO MEN had not been close personally, Holmes had "felt sorry for Taft" after the 1912 election. For the first time since 1856, a Republican candidate had run a poor third, collecting only 8 of the total 531 electoral votes (Bull Moose Roosevelt had received 88, Democrat Woodrow Wilson, 435) and just over half the popular vote cast for Wilson. Holmes thought Taft "the best man," but felt he had made "every political mistake" in the book. After Wilson's inauguration on March 4, 1913, Holmes was frankly pessimistic. He found the new president personally attractive enough; Wilson could "speak English," he had "the manners of a man of the world," and, perhaps most important to Holmes, he "let us out pretty soon" when the justices made their formal call at the White House. His policies, however, were another matter. Holmes perceived "a good deal of apprehension" among his acquaintances regarding what the first Democratic administration since Grover Cleveland's might do. There seemed to Holmes to be "an atmosphere of universal negation and a desire to upset whatever is—that does not command my sympathy or respect."

Despite her husband's assessment of Wilson's social persona, Fanny

Holmes thought Wilson lacked breeding. When, at a White House dinner for the Supreme Court, a waiter spilled soup on Justice Day's shirt, the president fussed until Day was clearly embarrassed. Sitting to Wilson's right, her tongue not the least bit mellowed by age, Fanny turned to him and snapped: "Mr. President, there are some things one doesn't talk about."

Holmes's birthday that year—his seventy-second—was a joyous occasion. The chief justice produced two bottles of champagne at lunch, and when Holmes arrived home after the long, tiring Saturday conference, a cascade of flowers and congratulatory telegrams and letters welcomed him. A little dinner party that included the French ambassador, Jean Jules Jusserand, and his wife, as well as U.S. Army Chief of Staff Leonard Wood and his wife, topped off the day. Jusserand made a little toast to Holmes at dinner, the men retired for their after-dinner smoke to Holmes's library, which they seemed to admire appropriately, and in general "everybody was so pleasant and friendly." It was the sort of celebration Holmes truly enjoyed, and for a time he seems to have soft-pedalled his concerns about aging.

The Washington spring, which came in with "cataracts of flowers . . . large flowering trees and shrubs," further cheered him. The panorama from the first magnolias in March to the laurel at the end of May was "splendid" that year—"really adequate enough to satisfy me."

Along with the magnolias and laurels that spring came the usual biennial hemming and hawing about whether Holmes would return to England during the summer. Fanny thought he needed the change, that seeing new people did him "as much good" as it gave "trouble to her." Holmes was reluctant to go without her, but realized if she accompanied him, she "would anxiously avoid social encounters of every kind, as what she gets here tires her, and she is rather a solitary bird." Fanny suggested she might settle somewhere "incognito" and leave him to be a "butterfly," but he found that arrangement entirely unsatisfactory. As April sought out May, Holmes just didn't know. Perhaps if someone took him in hand, made all the plans and bought all the tickets, he "shouldn't mind so much."

He had about decided to go and had applied for space on the *Mauretania* when, on the day he was writing his last Court opinion for that term, he tripped and fell on his knee, necessitating his confinement at home for a time and causing some uncertainty whether he would be able to sail. As the doctor had prophesied, however, Holmes recovered in time and sailed as scheduled on June 11. Fanny went as far as New York with him, but no farther.

All through the spring, Holmes had wondered whether London would "seem a new place" to him, so many of his old friends having died or "come to grief," and at times he did find himself "a helpless spectator of misery after misery." Faces were missing from his social schedule. Canon Sheehan, whom Holmes visited at Doneraile, was dying; they would not meet again. Lord Castletown was still recovering from the nervous collapse that had followed his financial collapse. It made Holmes feel "wicked" to be happy "when so near misery," but the Stoic in him supposed it was "normal." The Golden Rule meant, he thought, to realize another's "consciousness as vividly as one's own, and so is a vain exhortation to have more imagination than is given to man."

His encounters with "misery" did not inhibit him socially at all. His journal resembled a page from Burke's *Peerage:* Lord McDonald, Lady Falmouth, Lord Haldane, Lady Monson, Lord Cecil, Lady Sheffield, Lord Gray, and so on. He stayed part of the time with the Pollocks and managed to squeeze in lunch with Henry James; it was the last time the two old friends would meet, and James was dead by early 1916. Holmes had hoped to get to Scotland, also France, but reunions with English friends crowded too close together. He lunched and dined out every day for five weeks in London before he went to Ireland. Following the visit to Doneraile, he stayed with the Monsons at Lincoln and the Leslie Scotts in the Cotswolds. The pressure of the trip was so great that he collapsed when he got home—"with the ailment belonging to childhood and green apples." At Beverly Farms, where Fanny had spent the summer and he expected to rest briefly before they returned to Washington, he was put to bed immediately and a nurse was brought in to attend him.

The Holmeses, whose retinue now included a mischievous white kitten—the "tyrant of the house," inclined to walk across and smear the master's writing paper—left for Washington in early October in time for the Court's opening. His first chore upon arrival was always to shelve the bound volumes of his last term's decisions with the others; "then the last term is finished." Then he unpacked the few things he had taken to Beverly Farms—most remained in Washington. Then he entered on the permanent record he kept the list of books he had read over the summer. He paid accumulated bills and answered accumulated letters. His secretary sorted the accumulated books and pamphlets, then set to work to discover and resolve the discrepancies between the bank statements and Holmes's checkbook notations. Only then was he ready for the term to begin.

A bout with lumbago in November housed Holmes briefly, but an invitation to attend the unveiling of the portrait for which he had sat the previous year revived his spirits. The event was to be a high point at the annual meeting of the Massachusetts Bar Association, which had commissioned the portrait, and the picture was to be hung in the Social Law Library, where a several-decades-younger Holmes had done much of his scholarly research for his articles in the *American Law Review* and his book, *The Common Law*. Holmes was unable to go, but sent his regrets, which were read at the exercises. He would have liked to meet again the "friends that remain to Rip Van Winkle" and to "know the younger men who have come in" since he left Boston. He sympathized deeply with the latter in "their anxious interrogation of destiny." The doubts he himself had nursed as a young man had largely been laid to rest, but "in some form," he thought, "youth is sure to be anxious," and he wished he could be there to say a " 'Sursum corda.' " He would have enjoyed the show, at which the prominent and the influential paid him tribute, said a loving "Sursum corda" to *him* for whom life, despite his numerous anxieties, was always just beginning.

HOLMES'S SEVENTY-THIRD BIRTHDAY on March 8, 1914, passed amid a flurry of rumors he would resign and be replaced by former President Taft—rumors the Wilson administration took pains to deny quickly and firmly—and Holmes hastened to inform his correspondents that he was "busier than a witch in a gale of wind . . . and going strong." Holmes had discovered, however, that he was one of the oldest surviving members of Boston's Saturday Club, and friends were dropping like leaves from a tree. Pen Hallowell of Harvard '61 and the Twentieth Massachusetts died that spring. Hallowell had gone into banking, and although he had settled near Boston, he and Holmes had "ceased to have much intercourse." Nevertheless, Hallowell's death left "a great space bare." Holmes did not plan to return to England that summer; he felt, however, "an inward expectation" that he would see his "Beloved Hibernia" again at Doneraile before he died.

The Court was shorthanded again during the late winter and early spring of 1914. The seventy-year-old Lurton had been stricken by pneumonia and asthma the previous December and forced to abandon his work for a couple of months. He returned to the bench in April, just in time to join the judicial melee that had developed over *The Pipeline Cases,* which had been argued in October 1913, before he left. *The*

Pipeline Cases tested the constitutionality of the Hepburn Act of 1906. They also tested Holmes's patience with his brethren and his tolerance for compromise.

Standard Oil of New Jersey had not lost all its tentacles when the Supreme Court ordered the big corporation broken into its component parts in 1911. New monopolies based on ownership of vast networks of pipelines had succeeded the old ones, and for all practical purposes, Standard Oil had gained control of the transportation of domestic oil from the fields east of California to the Atlantic Ocean. These pipelines carried the precious oil, even more in demand since the advent of the automobile, from nearby wells to refinery to market. Standard Oil dictated the prices and the terms. The alternatives for a producer were to transport its oil by the more expensive tank car or go out of business. To fend off charges of public sponsorship that could in the future subject Standard Oil to public control, the company's lawyers in the 1880s and 1890s had taken considerable trouble to ensure that in building the pipelines, the company did not take advantage of any right of eminent domain. They did not want the pipelines to be regarded in any way as common carriers vulnerable to government regulation, as the railroads were. They wanted to keep everything strictly in private hands.

The problem of Standard Oil's unfair terms for transporting oil had been a particularly irritating burr under Roosevelt's saddle during his second term, and he had persuaded Congress to pass, over the strenuous opposition of conservatives known as the "railroad Senators," the Hepburn Act. Except for a diluted pure food and drug act and a similarly altered meat inspection act, the Hepburn Act was the only major White House–sponsored piece of Progressive legislation to survive from the several Roosevelt had proposed in his famous 1904 message to Congress.

As finally approved by the Senate on June 29, 1906, the Hepburn Act in general stopped up holes in the Interstate Commerce Act of 1887 by giving rate-making authority to the Interstate Commerce Commission and empowering the ICC to order the separation of railroad ownership and production industries such as mines—an arrangement that had invited collusion and resulted in monopolistic strangleholds. It also extended the ICC's jurisdiction over methods of interstate transportation, including oil pipelines.

Emboldened by its newly acquired authority, the ICC ordered Standard Oil–owned pipelines to file with the agency schedules of their rates and charges for transporting oil. Standard Oil, considering its lines entirely private, immediately brought suit in Commerce Court to have the commission's order set aside and nullified. That court, a shortlived judicial body recently created to draw off some of the workload from the Supreme Court, decided for the oil company and declared the Hepburn Act unconstitutional. The ICC and the government appealed to the U.S. Supreme Court, where their case was argued by the new solicitor general, John W. Davis, former corporation lawyer and future Democratic candidate for president (1924).

When Davis first scrutinized the case records, he was inclined to agree with the Commerce Court and thought the Supreme Court case would be a "tight squeak." Nevertheless, he pressed the government's case. His brief was forceful and cogent. It was, however, his first oral argument for the government before the Supreme Court, and as the day approached, he was as nervous as a "schoolboy" on the eve of his "commencement day oration"; he did not even want his wife to come to court.

The eminent corporation lawyer John G. Milburn, with the usual entourage of assistants that accompanied corporate legal talent, argued for the oil company along the predictable lines that the ICC, via the Hepburn Act, had been wrongly empowered to deprive "persons and corporations of their property without due process of law" and to take it "for public use without just compensation."

It was not a particularly complicated case, but it brought into play one of some justices' strongest biases—the sanctity of private property—and eight months of discussion followed. While the brethren may have been inclined to uphold the constitutionality of an act of Congress, they did not want to jeopardize traditional concepts of ownership by encouraging such legislation, and they appear to have had difficulty resolving their conflicts. The period between argument and decision was one of unusually extended and acrimonious debate. Chief Justice White wanted to hold the case over for the 1914 term.

Despite the pressure from White, however, the Court, on June 22, 1914, the last day of the 1913 term, handed down its decision to uphold the government and to reverse the Commerce Court. The decision, written by Holmes, was nearly unanimous; only his archrival, McKenna, dissented.

"Vanity" compelled Holmes, who had his own conflicts between his inclination to support congressional legislation and his distaste for the ICC, to recount the story for his former colleague, Moody, some three months after the decision was handed down. "[O]thers"—Holmes did not specify which others—had attempted to put together an opinion for the Court. Apparently a majority could not be assembled or possibly wording did not satisfy at least five, and just about a week before the end of the term, Holmes, who was known for his quick comprehension of issues and rapid writing, was assigned to write it. Caught in the end-of-term rush, he "shoved an opinion into the printer's hands" and in due time distributed it to the justices. It was a strong opinion declaring the pipelines to be common carriers in all but name and authorized Congress to regulate them in the "common weal," all accompanied by explanations, elaborations, and, with a nod to his own opinion in *Noble State Bank* v. *Haskell* three years before, invocation of the federal police power as justification for the taking of private property. This last was exactly what his colleagues had wanted to soft-pedal, and they objected.

Despite the exigencies of time, Holmes had his drafts returned by only two justices. On the Thursday before Monday, June 22, when the opinion was to be announced, one of the others called on him at about 8 P.M. and suggested additions he was sure would command a majority. Holmes rewrote his opinion as requested and had it ready for redistribution late Friday. On Saturday, another judge called and suggested striking out a sentence or two, and still another called for additional deletions. As late as Monday morning on the bench, one of them approached the beleaguered author with requests for still more changes. He was willing to

> strike out anything between title and conclusion that would enable [him to] get the case off per contract.

The final decision was a mere skeleton of Holmes's original opinion. It brought the pipelines under the Hepburn Act as common carriers and declared the act constitutional, thus reversing the Commerce Court. But the explanations and elaborations had disappeared along with the references to the police power of Congress, and in their stead there was extended discussion of the monopoly issue. All he had considered "reasoning to justify the conclusion," Holmes grumbled to Moody, had disappeared, and he had "put his name to something that [did] not satisfy or represent [his] views without explanations that made [him] able to say what [he] did." He "never was so disturbed," but he had thought it his "duty to let it go as the majority was content and the case had hung along in other hands for months."

Solicitor General Davis called on Holmes socially not long after the decision was announced. Holmes asked him what he thought of it. Davis answered that he was, of course, pleased by the outcome, but somewhat puzzled by the justification.

"Well," Holmes replied, "that's the way it is. I circulate an opinion to my brethren. One of them pulls out a plum here, another a plum there and they send me back a mass of shapeless dough."

THE SUMMER PASSED quietly at Beverly Farms with the usual correspondence, afternoon drives, reading, and solitaire pleasantly interrupted by callers, including Johnny Morse of whom Holmes "wish[ed he] saw more." A new face, that of former Senator Albert J. Beveridge of Indiana, appeared at Beverly Farms that summer, and a new friendship began. Justice Lurton died of a heart attack at his hotel in Atlantic City in July. He was replaced by Wilson's attorney general, fifty-two-year-old James C. McReynolds, who had been a government special prosecutor in its case against the American Tobacco Company; he was a bachelor so handsome that sculptors wanted to cast his head in bronze and a justice so mean-spirited that he refused to sign Court farewell letters to two of the other justices on their resignations.

James C. McReynolds has to be one of the strangest men ever to have sat on the U.S. Supreme Court. He disliked blacks, Jews, women lawyers, red fingernail polish, tobacco, men's wristwatches, relatives who tried to borrow money, and some of his brethren on the Court—in particular, Pitney, whose voice irritated him, and two later appointees: Brandeis, who was Jewish, and John Clarke, whom he thought stupid and to whom he simply stopped speaking. He made offensive remarks to counsel in court and once made a point of being rude to the president by remaining seated at a Gridiron Club dinner, his back to the chief executive, while the rest of the audience stood. He habitually left the conference room when Brandeis spoke and the bench when a woman lawyer rose to present a case.

There was, however, another side to McReynolds. He could be courteous and kind as easily as mean and sarcastic. When, in the absence of his seniors, presiding in court fell to him, he was the soul of courtesy, graciously greeting and raptly listening to the arguments by lawyers of both sexes. During World War II, he adopted thirty-three children who had been victims of the Nazi blitzkrieg in 1940; he willed his money to charity.

He was a life-long bachelor and dismissed with a chuckle rumors connecting him with Washington women, though they served some purpose:

They do at least indicate that I am not supposed to be inhuman after all. That is something.

At seventy-five, a note of sadness crept into his tone: "[W]ith such children you have much to live for," he told his brother. "[T]here is precious little to live for when there is no family . . . the shadows are growing longer for us all."

His progress to the Supreme Court had followed the usual pattern— through politics. As a young man in Nashville, he had run unsuccessfully for Congress. Although a Democrat, his politics had been acceptable to Theodore Roosevelt, and the president had appointed him an assistant attorney general in Philander Knox's trust-busting Justice Department. In 1907, nonsmoker McReynolds began the donkey work that resulted in the government's winning its case against the tobacco trust in 1911. He resigned in 1912 following a dispute over the final dissolution of the tobacco trust, and thus brushed the contaminating dust of Republicanism off his public clothing. He campaigned for Woodrow Wilson in 1912, made friends with Wilson's political factotum, Colonel Edward M. House, and was rewarded with appointment as attorney general in 1913. His alienation of key senators and his poor management of the Justice Department persuaded administration officials to look for a way to get rid of him. The timely death of Horace Lurton in 1914 provided the opportunity, and shortly afterwards Wilson kicked Attorney General McReynolds upstairs to the Supreme Court.

He was not a productive member of the Court, and his voting in the conference room was as contradictory as his personality: for and against trust-busting, for and against civil rights, for and against civil liberties, for and against state and federal police powers.

What particularly irritated Holmes was his preference for duck hunting over court sessions. He was frequently absent so that arguments sometimes had to be rescheduled, and he held up for months opinions the other justices were anxious to announce.

Although sitting on the Supreme Court appealed to his "vanity" and "love of assured position," he disliked the work; it was too "exacting" and tended to "cut one off" from friends or associates. Nevertheless, displaying a last contradictory characteristic, near the end of his life he wrote to the marshall of the Supreme Court asking to be buried in his robes. Holmes summed him up as "poor McReynolds":

a man of feeling and of more secret kindliness than he would get the credit for. But as is common with Southerners, his own personality governs him without much thought of others when an impulse comes, and . . . without sufficient regard for the proprieties of the Court.

* * *

HOLMES WAS SADDENED by the outbreak of World War I in August of 1914, although he thought the international rivalries at the time had made it "inevitable." His political loyalties were in conflict. He "admire[d] the Germans so much" that it gave him "real pain . . . to have to wish their defeat." He also believed, however, in "'my country right or wrong' and next to my country my crowd—and England is my crowd." It was not long before England had his full support. He fretted about Clare Castletown, who was doing war work at Doneraile, and her husband, who was involved in military recruiting. The misfortunes of Holmes's English friends, their husbands, sons, and brothers wounded, missing, even dead, were such that he "simply dare[d] not write them." He could "offer no consolation but only groan."

When the Supreme Court convened in October, 632 cases crowded the docket. No serious business was conducted that day, however. Chief Justice White eulogized the late Justice Lurton; the new justice, McReynolds, took his constitutional oath; and the Court paid its official call on the president.

Six weeks later, Leo Frank's nationally debated case had made its well-publicized way to the U.S. Supreme Court. Although the case was eventually to be written into the early chapters in the history of the application of the Fifth and Fourteenth Amendments' "due process of law" clauses to state criminal trials, in November of 1914, it had become so mired in technical legal swamps that the guilt or innocence of the defendant had become irrelevant.

Frank's story began the year before, on Saturday, April 26, 1913, the day fourteen-year-old Mary Phagan, a millhand's daughter, was murdered. The city of Atlanta, Georgia, was in a party mood that day, despite the unseasonably cold weather. It was Confederate Memorial Day, a legal holiday in Georgia. Businesses had closed, and a parade of six thousand marchers including two hundred surviving Confederate veterans was planned for early afternoon. Confederate flags whipped in the cold, blustery wind over Peachtree Street, blue and gray bunting draped the buildings along the parade route, and the shell-ripped battle flags of the Georgia regiments surrounded the reviewing stand. No one had seen an American flag in Atlanta for years.

They found Mary's little body, bruised, mutilated, her hair matted with blood, her lavender dress blood- and urine-stained, her throat cut by the cord that had garroted her, in the dark hours of Sunday morning lying prone in the basement of the National Pencil Factory where she had stopped on her way to the parade to collect a day's wages owed her: $1.20, or twelve cents an hour.

At that point the press and the mobs took charge of the case. The party mood of the day before dissipated; vengeance took control of Atlantans' minds. Their outrage—and fears—whipped up by newspapers, engaged at the time in a circulation war and prone to exaggeration and hyperbole, Atlantans crowded into Mary's funeral, gathered on street corners at night to discuss developments in the case, and when the time for trial came, stomped and cheered as if they were at the movies and not in a court of law.

The police, inclined under pressure to be careless of proper criminal procedure and less than meticulous in the gathering of evidence, soon arrested Leo Max Frank, twenty-nine-year-old superintendent of the National Pencil Factory, where Mary had been employed. Frank was perfectly cast in the role of scapegoat. He was a Jew, an alien in a hostile land. He was a Northerner—it was Yankee capitalists like Frank's family in New York that were keeping Georgia millhands like Mary's father poor. And he was an employer, a highly resented representative of the new industrialization which encroached—at the same time it brought Northern capital to an impoverished South—on some of the richest farmland in America, forcing farmers to leave that land and to work in the dark and grimy factories where the air was foul, the hours, long, and the wages, low. The reality was bad enough; the psychological factors—Southern awareness of its impotence, the nature of Southern humiliation—heightened the resentment.

Leo Frank was a thin, nervous, bespectacled milquetoast of a man, but he was made out to be a lascivious brute because white Georgians believed that sending their women—revered out of all proportion, at least in the abstract—to work in the factories, although an economic necessity, was somehow akin to prostitution, and if Leo Frank had not literally deflowered Mary Phagan, he had done so figuratively.

Frank's trial was held in a fan-cooled makeshift courtroom in the old City Hall because the new million-dollar county courthouse was not finished. Testimony consisted of rumors and unsubstantiated charges. But what really convicted Leo Frank was the crowd: the crowd in the courtroom which made no secret where its sympathies lay, the crowd gathered just outside the courtroom door, an unruly group of hecklers waiting to get in, and the crowd outside the building—so large it blocked traffic in the streets, so loud its chanting of "Hang the Jew or we'll hang you!" could be heard in the courtroom through the open windows by lawyers, judge, jury, witnesses, and the defendant himself. Frank had, as the Atlanta *Journal* had prophesied, the chance "of a snowball in hell."

The judge believed Frank was innocent, but commented to one of the defense lawyers: "Why, if Christ and all his angels came to show this man innocent, they would still vote him guilty." As the end of the month-long trial approached, spectators were threatening to lynch Frank if the jury acquitted him, and newspaper editors warned the judge that a verdict of acquittal would certainly cause a riot as bloody as Atlantans had ever seen. Court and counsel both agreed that it was too dangerous for Frank to remain in the courtroom when the jury announced its verdict, and Frank, unaware of the agreement, remained in his cell at the county jail during the final stages of the trial.

Following the certain verdict of "guilty," the party mood of the previous April returned to Atlanta. Men threw their hats in the air, women wept and hugged each other. The crowd outside the courtroom hoisted the prosecutor on their shoulders in triumph. The verdict was posted at the ball park, and hundreds of men and women did the cakewalk in front of the National Pencil Factory.

The following day, Leo Frank was sentenced to death by hanging.

The minute Leo Frank's arrest back in April had become known, every millhand in Georgia had prophesied, "Frank will never hang. He is rich and Mary Phagan has no friends." It was true that Frank's family back in New York as well as his Atlanta in-laws were well-to-do, and his uncle, owner of the pencil factory, was probably a millionaire; he contributed $50,000 to his nephew's defense. Chicago philanthropist Albert J. Lasker not only gave in the neighborhood of $160,000, but persuaded some of his wealthy friends to help. The case attracted nationwide attention. The *New York Times* adopted it as a crusade, and contributions came also from churches, civic groups, and other ordinary Americans.

Citing the disturbances by the crowds and the defendant's absence from the courtroom when the verdict was announced, Frank's lawyers filed a motion for a new trial. Despite lingering doubts regarding Frank's guilt, the trial judge felt bound by the jury's verdict and refused to grant a new trial. He was upheld by the Georgia Supreme Court. The fact that his counsel had agreed to Frank's absence from the courtroom at a critical juncture in his trial constituted, in effect, said the justices, Frank's waiver of his right to be present. As for the incidents of disorder charged, they were, the Georgia judges declared, "but an irregularity not calculated to be substantially harmful to the defendant." Furthermore, Frank's lawyers had filed their motions too late.

They then went to the U.S. Supreme Court in the person of Mr.

Justice Lamar, a native Georgian and circuit justice for the Fifth Circuit which included Georgia—the usual route in such cases. Lamar turned them down on the ground that no federal question was involved; local procedural issues belonged in the Georgia Supreme Court, which had made its decision. The lawyers next approached Holmes, who echoed Lamar.

Holmes, who had seen one telling example of mob rule in the lynching of the black man Ed Johnson, of Chattanooga, Tennessee, the previous decade * and thought Frank probably "had not had due process of law seeing that he was tried in a Southern State with a violent and hostile crowd around the Courthouse and in the Court," wrote a brief memorandum explaining his denial of jurisdiction, which he had felt bound to issue in light of the limitations imposed on the Supreme Court regarding state procedures. At the same time he expressed profound doubts that Frank could have received due process of law "in the presence of a hostile demonstration and seemingly dangerous crowd, thought by the presiding judge to be ready for violence unless a verdict of guilty was rendered." He had written the memorandum for the other judges' eyes only, a "suggestion to my brethren if any of them could see a way to giving relief." He was "surprised" and irritated when his private memorandum was leaked to the press and there it was on page one of the *New York Times* and page ten of the *Washington Post* alongside the war news and hailed on the editorial page of the *Times* as the first expression of interest in the "human as apart from the technical considerations of the case."

Heartened by Holmes's doubts and believing they might be able to use them to establish a constitutional question, Frank's lawyers, who now included in addition to the Atlantans Louis Marshall of New York City, prominent in legal and Jewish circles as well as experienced in Supreme Court practice, applied to the federal district court for the northern district of Georgia for a writ of habeas corpus—a court order frequently sought to release a person from unlawful custody; it forces the prisoner and his captor into court. Not only did the district judge deny them the writ, but he refused, too, to sign a certificate of probable cause for appeal, the ticket of admission to the U.S. Supreme Court.

Undismayed, Marshall went back to the Georgian Lamar, who seems to have changed his mind. Where the month before he had discerned no federal question, now at the end of December 1914, he found several of them, some involving the constitutionality of the defendant's invol-

---

* *United States* v. *Shipp.* 214 U.S. 386 (1909) and 215 U.S. 580 (1909).

untary absence from the courtroom when the jury gave the verdict, others involving federal jurisdiction over certain state practices. He would allow Frank's appeal. Whether he was influenced by Holmes's memorandum or whether he had come to his decision alone is not known.

Feeling his position was "legally and morally impregnable," Marshall was confident he would win in open court. Leo Frank's family was jubilant. Frank himself remained stoical and calm, his only comment: "It's a long lane that has no turning."

At the same time Leo Frank's case was bouncing between the courts, other, less notorious cases were being heard and decided by the U.S. Supreme Court. In the fall of 1914, a little less than four years after the Court in *Bailey* v. *Alabama* struck down Alabama's basic peonage statutes, the justices confronted, in *United States* v. *Reynolds,* a test of the constitutionality of a variation on the same theme. This second version was called the "criminal-surety system." It was supported by statute both in Alabama and Georgia, and it worked, like the basic peonage laws, to hold blacks in a self-perpetuating bondage. Holmes's position on such matters had not changed in the interim between *Bailey* and *Reynolds;* if anything, it had solidified.

Operation of the surety system was simple enough. When a black was convicted of a petty crime in a court of law, and assessed a fine plus, usually, court costs, a white employer—the surety—paid the assessment, then contracted with the black man to work off the debt, generally over a longer period than a prison term would have entailed. Fear of the chain gang made the system palatable to the black man, who was often sponsored by an employer for whom the rest of his family worked. The system was popular among white farmers who got cheap labor out of it, and often two or three competed for the services of a single black. To keep the system running, fines were sometimes inflated to keep the periods of servitude sufficiently long, and serious crimes were deflated to misdemeanors. The idea was to convict as many blacks as possible—demand far outran supply.

In the eyes of the U.S. Department of Justice, the system had become an "engine of oppression" against blacks, and it was decided, following a broad-based investigation of criminal-surety operations in Alabama, to bring a test of the system's constitutionality to the U.S. Supreme court.

In return for a promise that their own punishments would be nominal if they were convicted, J. A. Reynolds and G. W. Broughton, neighboring planters from Monroeville, Alabama, agreed to be the defendants. The case revolved around one Ed Rivers, a black man who had been convicted of petty larceny in May 1910, fined $15, and assessed court costs of $43.75. He was penniless, and sentenced to hard labor for fifty-eight days—ten days to work off the fine, and forty-eight days to work off the court costs. Reynolds appeared as surety for Rivers and paid the black man's debt to the state. Rivers then entered into a written contract with Reynolds to work for him as a farmhand for nine months and twenty-four days at the rate of $6 a month to pay back his debt—already Rivers was committed to working for Reynolds more than four times as long as his original sentence by the court.

Rivers worked for his surety about a month, then quit. He was rearrested and charged with breach of contract. He was convicted, fined one cent, but assessed additional court costs of $87.05. He could pay it or work 115 days in a chain gang. This time Broughton appeared as surety, paid Rivers's debt, and contracted to hire Rivers as a farmhand at the same rate for fourteen months and fifteen days. Rivers was now liable for ten times his original sentence by the court.

United States v. *Reynolds* and *United States* v. *Broughton* were argued in tandem October 23, 1914. Broughton had stood surety not only for Rivers but also for others, including E. W. Fields, a white workman whose story was similar to Rivers's, and it was Fields's indenture that was the subject of the government's case against Broughton. Solicitor General Davis appeared for the government. The oral arguments have not survived, but the brief for the defendants was written by William L. Martin, presumably a local Alabama lawyer, and Robert C. Brickell, Alabama attorney general who had helped the Justice Department in its search for a viable case.

Less than six weeks later, on November 30, the Court handed down its decision. Day wrote the opinion for the majority—all except Mc-Reynolds, who as attorney general had been involved in the Justice Department's efforts to put the case together, and Holmes, who concurred separately. Day found the Alabama criminal-surety system in violation of the Thirteenth Amendment and the congressional enactments designed to implement it—that is, intended to strike down all laws passed "to maintain and enforce, directly or indirectly, the voluntary or involuntary service or labor of any persons as peons, in the liquidation of any debt or obligation."

Holmes's concurrence was as grudging as it was brief—one paragraph. In another time it would have been called racist. He reversed the position he had taken in *Bailey* v. *Alabama* and allowed that the surety system did, as Day had said, violate the law. But he could not resist reiterating his view of the sanctity of contract as well as his contempt for those who violated it—"impulsive people with little intelligence or foresight." They may be expected, he declared, "to lay hold of anything that affords a relief from the present pain even though it will cause greater trouble by and by." The community whose "actual feelings and demands, whether right or wrong," were represented by Southern law remained for Holmes the dominant white community.

That same day the Court handed down its decision in *McCabe* v. *Atchison, Topeka & Santa Fe Railway*, another case involving the civil rights of blacks and featuring a concurrence by Holmes which, read alongside a sharply worded note from Hughes while the case was still being discussed within the Court, adds to the record still another instance of Holmes's early judicial astigmatism when faced with the realities of the black's position in American life.

McCabe addressed the constitutionality of a 1907 Oklahoma statute called the Separate Coach Law requiring separate but equal railroad accommodations for black and white passengers; section 7 of the act, however, decreed that the railroads might provide sleeping, dining, and "chair" cars for whites but was under no obligation to provide these luxuries for blacks. The reasoning was that there probably would not be sufficient demand for such accommodations by blacks to warrant the outlay in providing them.

Days before the law went into effect, five black Oklahomans sought an injunction to restrain five railroads operating within the state from making any distinction in service based on race. *McCabe* was the first case involving state Jim Crow laws to come to the Court since the death of Harlan, the Court's long-time unofficial advocate of black civil rights. Hughes, however, beginning with his majority opinion in *Bailey* v. *Alabama,* was slowly taking Harlan's place on race issues. He was not, like Harlan, a stump speaker, but applied a cooler, more analytical hand to the problems at issue. When the justices voted to uphold the Oklahoma statute, it perhaps made good political sense to White to assign the opinion to Hughes, who three years before had written the opinion for the majority in *Bailey* v. *Alabama* supporting black claims against the Alabama peonage laws. By the same token, Hughes perhaps agreed to write *McCabe* in the belief that if any justice could blend into a rejection of civil rights claims some word of encouragement to blacks, he was the man to do it.

Citing *Plessy* v. *Ferguson,* still the authority for the "separate but equal" formula, Hughes gave the Supreme Court's imprimatur to the Oklahoma statute, but he took strong issue with section 7. That provision made, he said, a "constitutional right depend upon the number of persons who may be discriminated against, whereas the essence of the constitutional right is that it is a personal one. . . . It is the individual who is entitled to the equal protection of the laws." If a railroad, acting under the authority of state law, denies "a facility or convenience . . . which under substantially the same circumstances is furnished to another traveler, he may properly complain that his constitutional privilege has been invaded." The states had been warned; let them not underestimate the power of the Supreme Court.

And then Hughes braked so suddenly that his own passengers must have been thrown through the windshield. There was, he said, an "insuperable obstacle" to granting the injunction McCabe and his fellow plaintiffs sought. In effect, their case was a trumped-up one. First of all, they had applied for relief before the law had gone into effect. Second, none of the plaintiffs had traveled on any one of the five railroads, none had requested transportation on any of them, and none had tried to reserve accommodations in sleeping, dining, or chair cars. Although they had predicted that 50,000 blacks in Oklahoma would be deprived of their civil rights under the new law, no complainant could succeed in the U.S. Supreme Court "because someone else may be hurt." The Court required specific examples of injury; the allegations of *McCabe* were "too vague and indefinite." As harsh as the opinion may have sounded, however, it was in fact an invitation. Beneath all the rhetoric, Hughes was telling McCabe and his associates: Bring us a proper case and we'll be able to help.

Holmes, along with Lamar and McReynolds—neither of whom was particularly sympathetic to the legal aspirations of blacks—concurred only in the result of the decision, which undoubtedly meant they dissociated themselves from Hughes's encouragement of legal challenges by blacks. Holmes wrote a memorandum on the case which was subsequently lost. Reconstruction of it in terms of Hughes's answer to it indicates Holmes apparently considered section 7 a reasonable provision. Perhaps certain arguments made by the railroad companies in their brief had caught his attention:

> The public sentiment of the state . . . demands a separation of the white and Negro races by transportation companies.

and

> The matter of the separation of the races in public places and especially in transportation facilities is vital to the people of the southern states. It is a

practical condition with them and not a theoretical question. It is a situation that can be dealt with only from a practical standpoint.

It was Holmes's practice to recommend resolution of local questions to local officials, just the way he had advocated leaving Lonzo Bailey's economic bondage and William Giles's political bondage to the good people of Alabama who had supported enactment of the peonage and disenfranchisement laws that had brought the two men into the U.S. Supreme Court. The perceived racial injustices connected with luxury accommodations on the Oklahoma railroads he undoubtedly felt could be resolved by Oklahomans at what he would have called the point of contact, Oklahoma.

Hughes could say to Holmes privately what he could not say publicly in the Court's opinion. Returning Holmes's memorandum, he categorically rejected the idea that "a black man must sit up all night—just because he is black, unless there are enough blacks to make a 'black sleeping car' pay." Hughes did not see *McCabe* as a case "calling for 'logical exactness' in enforcing equal rights," as Holmes may have suggested—critically—was Hughes's overly principled interpretation. Hughes saw it as a "bald, wholly unjustified discrimination against a passenger solely on account of race." Holmes's only recorded reaction was his dissociation from Hughes's opinion. The two justices did not often clash, and even less often did they clash with such vehemence. But, pitting practice, which had long been a cornerstone of Holmes's jurisprudence, against principle, which Hughes supported equally vigorously, *McCabe* had elicited the strongest responses from both men.

As 1914 NEARED ITS END and worlds Holmes had known were shattering in the noise of the guns, never to be whole again, he tried to recapture some intimations of his past in a melancholy note to his "Beloved Hibernia" which he wrote on Christmas Eve:

> The night before last I dreamed that you were just as fond of me as ever and it made me ever so happy.

He wanted to send her

> every wish in spite of the misery that weighs upon the world.

CHAPTER 22

The Young Turks

THE SHERMAN ANTI-TRUST Act of 1890 did not specify any particular kind of organization that could be held in violation of its provisions, and it was an unimaginative businessman who did not recognize the potential of the statute for use against labor unions during the early years of the century. Congress was frequently importuned to exempt labor unions and farmers' organizations from its restrictions, but the efforts all failed, and the act remained, after a quarter century, unmarred by amendment. Overall, in fact, the Sherman Act may have been considerably more dangerous to labor than to capital. Business was imperiled largely when the federal government took the time and trouble to bring suit, though the Sherman Act allowed small businessmen to sue the trusts, but any employer could, under section 7 of the act, sue a troublesome union for triple damages. As the courts were constituted in the early part of the century, the employer's chances of victory were high—a victory that often destroyed the union itself.

In January 1915, in the case of *Lawlor* v. *Loewe,* otherwise known as the Danbury Hatters case, the U.S. Supreme Court began firing a new round of shots at American labor unions, whose membership was constantly growing, and, along with it, the unions' potential for paralyzing commerce. *Lawlor* v. *Loewe* had been in the courts for nearly fifteen years. In 1901, the local branch of the United Hatters of North America, an affiliate of the American Federation of Labor (AFL), led by one Martin Lawlor, demanded that Dietrich Loewe and his partners allow them to unionize Loewe's hat factory in Danbury, Connecticut. When Loewe refused, the hatters struck, and organized a boycott of Loewe's hats, which were sold to wholesalers nationwide. The boycott was successful, and converted Loewe's 1901 profit of $27,000 to losses of $17,000 in 1902 and $8,000 in 1904. Loewe brought suit under the Sherman Anti-Trust Act against the union. The case went to the U.S. Supreme Court for the first time in the fall of 1907 on a question of whether the suit was properly brought under the Sherman Act. That court decided unanimously in February 1908 that it was. Citing *United States* v. *Trans-Missouri Freight Association, United States* v. *Joint Traffic Association,* and *Northern Securities Co.* v. *United States,* Chief Justice Fuller declared that the "Anti-Trust law has a broader application than the prohibition of restraints of trade unlawful at common law" and brought the Danbury Hatters squarely under it. Holmes did not dissent.

The situation in the Danbury Hatters case was different from the one he had confronted in *Vegelahn* v. *Guntner,* from which he had dissented nearly twenty years before as judge in Massachusetts and which had incorrectly identified him as a friend to labor. *Vegelahn* was a local situation involving a little peaceful picketing that could be covered under the common law's tolerance for reasonable restraints of trade; it was just as reasonable, Holmes had said then, for workingmen to combine "with a view, among other things, to getting as much as they can for their labor," as for capital to combine "with a view to getting the greatest possible return. . . ." In the Danbury Hatters case, he was dealing with substantial financial losses suffered by a manufacturer involved in interstate commerce, plus the limitations imposed by the Sherman Act, by which he was bound, however hostile he felt toward it.

Now, in January 1915, the Danbury Hatters had returned to the Supreme Court to challenge the validity of the $252,130 of damages assessed. Again the justices were unanimous, and Holmes, the so-called friend of labor, was assigned to write for the Court. In a brief, straightforward opinion, he reaffirmed all the chief justice had said in 1908 and validated the assessment of financial damages. The company eventually settled for $235,000 from the AFL, although not before local hatters' homes and bank accounts had been attached. Shortly after Holmes announced the decision, he received a notice from the post office that a letter was being held in Danbury for two cents postage. He "felt warranted in assuming it was abuse from a hatter and did not send the two cents."

Just under three weeks after *Lawlor* v. *Loewe* was handed down, on January 25, in *Coppage* v. *Kansas,* the Supreme Court, under the ever-expanding umbrella of "liberty of contract" implied by the due process clause of the Fourteenth Amendment, gave constitutional sanction to the notorious anti-union "yellowdog" contract, which had become a potent weapon in employers' hands. A six-year-old Kansas statute had made unlawful such contracts, which allowed employers to condition a man's employment on his agreement not to join a union. Citing *Adair* v. *United States*, in which the Supreme Court had annulled a similar act of Congress seven years before, Pitney, who had made a reputation as an enemy of labor on the New Jersey courts, invalidated Kansas's law and with it similar laws enacted by thirteen states and Puerto Rico.

Day and Hughes dissented together, Holmes dissented separately, finding analogies between *Coppage* and the Massachusetts labor cases which had made him famous. Paraphrasing them, he wrote that a workman "not unnaturally may believe that only by belonging to a union can he secure a contract that shall be fair to him. If that belief, whether right or wrong, may be held by a reasonable man, it seems to me that it may be enforced by law in order to establish the equality of position between the parties in which liberty of contract begins." Whether in the long run Kansas's law was wise was not Holmes's concern, but he strongly believed, as he had said from the beginning of his time on the Court, that "there is nothing in the Constitution to prevent it," and that both *Adair* and *Lochner* v. *New York* ought to be overruled. Citing his own dissents in *Vegelahn* and *Plant* v. *Wood,* he added: "I still entertain the opinions expressed in Massachusetts."

EVERY SEAT IN the little courtroom was occupied during the oral arguments in Leo Frank's case on February 25 and 26; each side was allowed two and a half hours to make its case. Arguments for both sides focused on the issue of mob violence—a point, Holmes remarked on the first afternoon, that "impresses me very much"—and on the defendant's right to be present at all stages of trial proceedings. The justices' questions to counsel both days seemed to indicate that the Court attached more importance to the charges of public disorder during the trial and its effect on the jury than to the defendant's absence when the verdict was announced.

Louis Marshall's confidence in his ability to win over the justices, however, had been misplaced. On April 19, 1915, the Supreme Court, in a ten-thousand-word opinion, declared that Leo Frank had not been denied due process of law.

Pitney spoke for the Court. He looked at Leo Frank's case with a detachment that not even the usually detached Holmes could summon. Frank, Pitney wrote, had gotten all that he was entitled to from the state; the federal courts could do no more. Frank, said Pitney, had been tried publicly before a court of "competent jurisdiction, with a jury law-fully constituted," he had had counsel for his defense, had been found guilty and sentenced, all in proper legal order; he had taken advantage of the opportunities to ask for a new trial, to have the verdict set aside, and to be heard by the state's highest court; his arguments had been rejected. Georgia, through its courts, had afforded Frank "the fullest right and opportunity to be heard according to the established modes of procedure. . . ." In the Court's opinion, he was

> not shown to have been deprived of any right guaranteed him by the Four-teenth Amendment or any other provision of the Constitution or laws of the United States; on the contrary, he has been convicted, and is now held in custody, under "due process of law" within the meaning of the Consti-tution.

Holmes had his reply ready—one of the most forceful he ever wrote, a cornerstone of the future Holmes legend. He had no idea whether Frank was guilty or innocent—he had never read the evidence and didn't care. Guilt or innocence was irrelevant in Leo Frank's case. The "due process of law" issue in his case involved not some ephemeral economic or social arrangement—a peonage law, antitrust statute, or maximum hours measure—that could be modified or repealed tomorrow. The "due process of law" here involved one of the eternal verities of the Consti-tution, one which reckoned its age from Magna Carta. Although origi-nally constrained by the legal proprieties that governed acceptance of state cases by the Supreme Court—he had left it to others to find some way, as Lamar subsequently did—Holmes felt free to have his say about Frank's case now that it was before him. Hughes assisted him. In fact, Holmes scribbled on Hughes's copy of their joint draft dissent that if it was all right with Hughes, he thought "it would be fair to say . . . that you and I think the judgement should be reversed and to put we for I all through." Hughes replied that he would be "proud to be associated" with Holmes. Holmes circulated the dissent, hoping to attract support. Van Devanter told him parts of the opinion appealed to him "very strongly and are admirably put," but he believed the "charge of mob influence was not true." Not even Lamar, who had worked out the constitutional grounds on which the Court might hear Frank's case, could be per-suaded. Only Hughes, with whom Holmes had begun to discover a ju-dicial compatibility, would join with him. Hughes, Holmes believed, had a "non-conformist conscience" combined with "what is rarely con-gruous with that, wit," and "certain abysses of melancholy skepticism."

Hughes perhaps supplied the emotion and Holmes the style, although Holmes seems to have been unusually involved in this case and described it to friends in a kind of detail he rarely approached. The aroused authors first brushed aside the question of whether Frank should have been present during the verdict—the Court never had been "impressed" by the argument that the Constitution required the defendant's presence—and concentrated on the issue of the hostile environment in which the trial was conducted. They recited chronologically the incidents of disorder, then spelled out their mortification at the way events had transpired in and around the Atlanta courtroom. It was clear to them the trial had been a "farce":

> Whatever disagreement there may be as to the scope of the phrase "due process of law," there can be no doubt that it embraces the fundamental conception of a fair trial, with opportunity to be heard. Mob law does not become due process of law by securing the assent of a terrorized jury.

Specifically refuting the rationale of the Georgia Supreme Court, they added:

> We are not speaking of mere disorder, or mere irregularities in procedure, but of a case where the processes of justice are actually subverted.

The state's attempts to correct the injustices had amounted only to going through the motions—form without substance. Under these circumstances, the federal court was empowered to act without undermining state authority.

There was no doubt in the minds of Holmes and Hughes that Frank had been the victim of a legal lynching. Every experienced judge, they noted, understood the susceptibility of juries to the atmosphere around them. When the trial judge declared that neither the defendant nor his counsel could be safe from the crowd, the dissenting justices believed the "presumption overwhelming that the jury responded to the passions of the mob." Lynch law, they concluded,

> was as little valid when practiced by a regularly drawn jury as when administered by one elected by a mob intent on death.

Frank's case had been a worrisome one, and Holmes was relieved when it was over. A few months later, he received a letter from Frank which he described as "very well written, with a surprising moderation of tone." Confessing in his old age to a youthful fascination with the grotesque—his thrill at seeing "the last quid of tobacco, chewed by some well-known criminal before execution"—Holmes thought he would save the letter.

Georgia Governor John L. Slaton commuted Frank's sentence to life imprisonment, and for his courage lost his chance to be elected to the U.S. Senate. Finally, a band of men from Marietta, Mary Phagan's home town—including a clergyman, two former superior court judges, and an ex-sheriff, Marietta's "best citizens"—stormed the prison farm at Milledgeville where Frank was being held, seized him, drove him to a grove outside Marietta, escorted him to a big oak tree, and, just before dawn, hanged him. His swinging body became an immediate tourist attraction. Souvenir hunters ripped off pieces of clothing and cut strands from the rope around his neck. Cameras clicked. Some came just to gape. One man wanted to mutilate and burn Frank's body, but was restrained. Obscenities polluted the cool country air. The *Marietta Journal* editorialized: "We are proud, indeed, to say that the body hanged for more than two hours amid a vast throng and no violence was done. Cobb county people are civilized. They are not barbarians." *

As Holmes wrestled with the issues presented by Leo Frank's case in the winter of 1915, John Gray had died in Boston. He had been Holmes's oldest friend. Their lives had run parallel, and they had shared the experiences of war, Harvard College and Harvard Law School, private legal practice in Boston for which Gray, slightly ahead of Holmes professionally, had helped prepare Holmes by quizzing him before the bar examination, and the *American Law Review* in which Gray had given Holmes his first chance to test his scholarship and in which Holmes had deepened enormously his interest in legal philosophy. In the early 1870s, Gray had returned with Holmes to teach at Harvard; then they had parted; Gray had stayed on for some forty years—until he retired in 1913—and Holmes had left to give his full attention to private practice and the scholarship that had led to the writing of *The Common Law*. They had kept in touch, partly through their own efforts and partly through Gray's wife, Nina, with whom Holmes corresponded regularly. Holmes had not seen his friend for the past couple of years, but Gray had told him his—Gray's—"clock was running down," and his death did not come as a shock. The news had reached Holmes too late for him

---

* In 1982, a witness said that as a fourteen-year-old office boy at the National Pencil Factory, he had seen a man other than Leo Frank carrying Mary Phagan's body. He had not spoken out at the time, he said, because the real murderer had threatened to kill him. At first the Georgia Board of Pardons and Paroles refused to grant Frank a pardon on the grounds that the evidence was inconclusive. Later the board reversed its position and in 1986 granted him a posthumous pardon.

to get to Gray's funeral, and he mourned by writing an appreciation of Gray for the Massachusetts Historical Society.

Holmes's morale continued to sink as he passed his seventy-fourth birthday in March. "A very well mannered old party, time," he thought. "He doesn't speak loud, or come bulging in on you as some ingenuous young secretaries will, but he comes up as soft-footed as a cat . . . and by a by he lays a soft paw on your sleeve, so gently. And then slowly, like the dog in Faust's study, he begins to swell, and grow more like a tiger. And the door is locked and one must await his doings." Holmes sighed. "The horizon grows pretty bare of all those who gave character to life when I was younger." Tangible reminders of the intangible were numerous. Younger men got up to give him a seat in the trolley, his teeth were disintegrating, and he found it hard "not to turn into the doors in Boston where those [he] knew used to be"—

> a thousand trifles [gave him] each a little sting of a reminder that . . . [he was] getting near the end.

He considered rereading Casanova's memoirs to "freshen [him] up"; things of that sort brought back "gaiety to life when one feels a little slack." He had been intending for some years, however, to reread the work that had "put a wiggle" into him during the depression that followed his completion of *The Common Law,* and he was not at all sure he had time to do it now. Almost on the verge of planning his funeral, he would then sit up and refuse to believe his age:

> most of the time [I] feel as I did fifty years ago except that I am much happier.

Whatever hopes blacks had nursed for improvement in their status and which had been shattered by the Court's reaffirmation of the "separate but equal" concept eight months before in *McCabe* were revived in June 1915 by the Court's decisions in the *Grandfather Clause Cases* and *United States* v. *Mosley.* The former challenged the constitutionality of the grandfather clauses which had been added to the constitutions of the Southern states in late nineteenth century to disenfranchise blacks by imposing strenuous educational and property tests for voting, then exempting those qualified to vote in 1866, 1867, and 1868 *and* their descendants, which could not include blacks. *Mosley* involved a Justice Department suit against a pair of Oklahoma election officials, Tom Mosley and Dan Hogan, who had effectively disenfranchised blacks in eleven precincts of Blaine County by not counting their votes. Both Democrats, they had discarded some 1,200 Republican ballots, many of them cast by blacks and Indians, and had thus defeated several Republican candidates.

Both the *Grandfather Clause Cases* and *Mosley* had been argued back in the fall of 1913, while Horace Lurton was still on the Court, and held over until June 1915, an unusually long gestation period. It has been suggested that the Georgian Lamar and Lurton had threatened to dissent in the *Grandfather Clause Cases,* and Chief Justice White, who by far preferred unanimous courts, particularly in politically sensitive cases, was angry. Lurton died in July 1914, and still the decisions were not announced. Possibly Lamar's continued determination to dissent delayed decision; perhaps the Court thought it wise to hold back controversial cases until the end of the term when the justices were leaving town for the summer—a time-honored Court tradition. In any event, the *Grandfather Clause Cases* and *Mosley* were announced on June 21, 1915, the last day of the term.

As the chief justice had wanted, Lamar withheld his dissent, and the *Grandfather Clause Cases* were unanimous. Notwithstanding the reluctance to interfere in local political matters which he had shown in *Giles* v. *Harris* during his early days on the Court, Holmes joined the majority, which declared unflinchingly that Oklahoma's method of disenfranchising voters violated the Fifteenth Amendment and was therefore unconstitutional. To give the opinion the utmost force, Chief Justice White, Louisianan and former Confederate officer, wrote it himself.

Holmes wrote *Mosley*—for which Lamar had saved his dissent. The issue involved construction of section 19 of the Criminal Code enacted by Congress in 1909: whether it applied to conspiracy by election officials not to count votes, or, as the defense had contended in the lower federal court, only to forcible prevention of voting. The U.S. Supreme Court had actually heard only one side of the controversy; counsel for the defense had not submitted his brief on time, and had failed to appear at oral argument. Solicitor General Davis, on the other hand, although privately he was not convinced that black suffrage was wise, argued that the right to vote "consists not merely of the right to cast a ballot but likewise of the right to have that ballot counted. Otherwise the vote is no vote at all, but simply so much paper."

Although he cavalierly omitted some steps in the evolution of section

19 from a provision of the Civil Rights Act of 1870 to its present language, Holmes must have taken no little pleasure in pointing out how this particular concept of law had responded to the "felt necessities of the time. . . ." He explained how in the days of the Ku Klux Klan's disturbing presence, Congress had indeed emphasized a prohibition against acts of violence; forty-odd years later, when the Ku Klux Klan had "passed away," Congress had subordinated that aspect and placed its emphasis on prohibiting peaceful conspiracies to deprive citizens of their constitutional rights.

Times change and with them the considerations that affect legislation. In 1915, the Tom Mosleys of the world were more of a threat than the Ku Klux Klan, and Congress, Holmes believed, had foreseen that possibility when it engineered the changes in the law:

> We cannot allow the past so far to affect the present as to deprive citizens of the United States of the general protection which on its face section 19 most reasonably affords.

The routine at Beverly Farms was enlivened that summer not only by the rumors that Justice Hughes might run for president but also by the presence of former Senator Albert J. Beveridge of Indiana who had been defeated for reelection in 1911, had bought a house not far from Holmes's, and was writing a biography of John Marshall. It was Beveridge's custom to submit his manuscript for criticism to historians and other authorities before it was submitted to his publisher, and Holmes, who found Beveridge a "man of ideas" and "enthusiasm"—they made "each other sing like canary birds"—and who had grown closer to the former senator at Beverly Farms than he ever was in Washington, was one who agreed to read it. There was a reunion, too, with Johnny Morse who took Holmes for drives in good weather and frankly confessed to astonishment at his cousin's persistent intellectuality, which seemed to alienate him from the realities of life. Morse had been "struck with the fact" that Holmes lived "wholly upon & among words." The words conveyed ideas, Morse admitted, but they were

> ideas wh. have no substance or value beyond that of being merely expressed . . . wh. concern themselves with no reality in life; when they have once struggled into intelligible utterance, they have fulfilled the whole function & end of their existence. They *mean* nothing & do no good in any possible way to mankind. Wendell & I wld. have a poor time of it, if we were shipwrecked together on a desert island.

The summer ended with the disturbing news that Lamar, while vacationing in White Sulphur Springs, West Virginia, had suffered a stroke; his left arm and leg were paralyzed. Initially, the prognosis was optimistic; the justice should be ambulatory in a week or two. He did not, however, improve as scheduled. He returned to Washington in October, but not to the Court. *Mosley* had been his last dissent. On January 2, 1916, he died of heart failure. He was only fifty-eight and belonged to the junior group of sitting justices.

Less than four weeks later, President Wilson stunned the entire country when he named to Lamar's place not Taft, from whose friends had come great pressure, nor a Southerner as Lamar had been, and not one of the state judges or politicians whose names had been urged on him. Instead he nominated his unofficial advisor and Holmes's old friend from Boston days, Louis Dembitz Brandeis. Over the next six months, nationwide debate as well as that in the U.S. Senate heated well beyond the boiling point as Brandeis's professional record, his judicial qualifications, his temperament, ethics, and allegiances were dissected, and digested.

Brandeis was Jewish—no Jew had yet sat on the U.S. Supreme Court, although Judah P. Benjamin had been offered a seat which he refused—and anti-Semitism played at least some role in Brandeis's long struggle for confirmation by the Senate. His penchant for disaffecting men in high places played perhaps a more significant part. While Holmes had sat more or less serenely on the bench during the past three and a half decades, Brandeis had been making enemies in his role as the People's Attorney. Having acquired a fortune in Boston as a corporation lawyer, he had been able to take on public interest cases—cases like Oregon's ten-hour day for women, which he had argued and won in the U.S. Supreme Court. He had attacked public transportation franchises, fought for lower gas rates and reorganized the structures of public utilities, investigated insurance company practices, even invented an insurance system of his own which eventually went into effect in Massachusetts, and had virtually brought the New Haven Railroad to its corporate knees. In 1909, he had seriously embarrassed the Taft administration when he politically disemboweled Taft's secretary of the interior, Richard A. Ballinger, for allegedly sacrificing public lands to Western mining and timber interests. At each step into public advocacy, which frequently included exposure of corruption and scandal, Brandeis inevitably had antagonized entrenched interests, and he had become known as a dangerous radical. Fanny Holmes herself was not fond of her husband's friend. It was said she was anti-Semitic. That, however, was unlikely, since she seemed fond enough of Wendell's other Jewish friends. The more likely explanation was that Fanny, as Bostonian and aristocrat, and having in her stubborn soul a strong streak of loyalty to old friends and traditions, could not forgive this People's Attorney for working against the Boston establishment, the very people who had welcomed him, invited him into their homes, elected him to their clubs when he arrived in Boston to practice law; they happened to be Fanny's friends.

Although they were hidden behind charges of wrongdoing in the controversial cases in which Brandeis had been involved, the senators' intuitions were not very different from Fanny Holmes's. The senators seemed to sense in Brandeis a breed of man to which they were not accustomed, one who didn't play by the usual gentlemen's rules or respect the traditions the Court had been at such pains to uphold against the challenges born of the new industrialism. Brandeis seemed in truth to be part of the assaults, had involved himself in the seamy problems of laboring men and other manifestations of shifting social and economic standards. He represented a new order they did not quite understand and which in their ignorance they feared.

Holmes professed not to understand the rancor of the debates. He genuinely like Brandeis, thought him a "good man," a man he "respected and admired." Yet long before Brandeis had been nominated for the Court, Holmes was "made aware of an adversely critical attitude on the part of some whose opinions [he] respected." How, he asked himself, could "other good men" be "down on" one he believed quite as good? He did say he thought Brandeis's nomination a "misfortune for the Court." If the Senate rejected him, "the proletariat will say only tools of the plutocrats get in"; if he was confirmed, "many people will think that the character of the Court is no longer above question." In either case, half the country would be dissatisfied.

A few weeks after the president had sent Brandeis's nomination to the Senate, Holmes's serious preoccupations were suppressed temporarily and his spirits revived in the celebration of his seventy-fifth birthday. First the Illinois and Harvard law reviews dedicated their current issues to him, making him "feel that the long struggle had not been in vain." Then Fanny invited a group of young men and women to assemble at the house on I Street for a birthday party. Holmes was surprised out of his wits. The first inkling he had was hearing the "house filled with the song of birds"—Fanny had provided the guests with bird calls she had bought from a "faker" on F Street. Just as Holmes realized who was there and had begun to think "in dismay" that no preparations had been made for their call, the dining room doors opened to reveal a sumptuous supper, complete with a bowl of "very judicious punch."

For all her good humor and funny practical jokes, however, Fanny apparently was worried. Perhaps she had absorbed Holmes's fears; perhaps she had constructed some of her own. She took Felix Frankfurter aside quietly and unobtrusively, saying: "I want you to promise me something." Frankfurter replied that he could not think of any promise she asked that he would not fulfill.

"Promise me," she demanded, "that when you see the slightest drop in the quality of his opinions that you will let me know. That day he will get off the bench."

The party continued, the guests unaware of Fanny's concerns. They "giggled and made giggle" until after midnight, and Holmes went to bed "touched and pleased."

The progress of Brandeis's nomination could not recede from the Court's consciousness for long. Charges and countercharges echoed through the Senate chamber. Administration figures, including the president himself, exerted on senators every pound of pressure they could. IOUs were collected. When the flames seemed to flicker, the press kept the controversy alive. Finally, on May 24, the Senate Judiciary Committee voted to confirm Brandeis, ten Democrats for, eight Republicans against. A week later, on June 1, the full Senate followed suit, 47 to 22, almost but not quite as strictly along party lines.

Whatever Holmes's doubts, they evaporated once Brandeis was confirmed, and he immediately shot off a telegram as eloquent as it was brief. "Welcome," he simply said.

As soon as Brandeis took his seat on June 5, 1916, he and Holmes resumed their old camaraderie, which was strictly a professional and intellectual relationship, not a social one. They walked or rode home from court together, but their wives were not friends and they did not visit back and forth or share the casual diversions of life. The ascetic Brandeis avoided the available distractions such as the theater, restaurants, the receptions and dinners that were a staple of Washington's social life, even movies and radio, all of which Holmes enjoyed.

Their relationship was deep and enduring, and Holmes wondered whether "loveableness is a characteristic of the better class of Jews." He suspected it was. Brandeis seemed to

> have this quality and always gives me a glow, even though I am not sure he wouldn't burn me at a slow fire if it were in the interest of some very possibly disinterested aim.

That summer Holmes discovered another young Jew who would "warm [his] heart" over the next two decades. In July 1916, Felix Frankfurter brought to Beverly Farms the twenty-three-year-old Harold J. Laski, a frail, bespectacled, and entirely agreeable Englishman recently arrived at Harvard where he had been appointed a junior instructor in the department of government. Laski was not yet the Socialist he later became, but even then his mild liberalism—identification with trade unionists and other economic underdogs—made him stand out in the still conservative university set down in a region known for its aristocratic inclinations. A half century separated the man Frankfurter revered as "one of the most impressive personalities of his day" from this youngster who was to co-author the Holmes legend. As Frankfurter undoubtedly had known they would, however, Laski's intellectual gifts astonished and appealed to Holmes, who found him "one of the most learned" fellows he had ever seen "at any age." Laski was appropriately worshipful, writing in his bread-and-butter note to Holmes after their first meeting that it had been

> the realisation of one of my dreams—and if I could write a fairy-story of the happiness men hope for I should try to analyse the vigorous refreshment you gave to all I hold most dear. I do not say "thank you"—not merely because it is inadequate but because from one's master one learns that it is simply duty to receive. You teach our generation how to live.

Laski set in this first note to Holmes, whose reply began their intellectual conversations and invited response as well as a return visit, the tone that dominates Laski's side of the correspondence, a flattering and reverential one, every letter a genuflection.

Laski saved Holmes's replies, sent him books and articles, and dedicated his own books to "the master." For nearly twenty years, until Holmes was too weak to reply, they carried on a wide-ranging, intellectually adventurous, almost weekly correspondence, sharing common interests in law, politics, history, literature, and gossip concerning the great and near-great of America and England.* They did not indulge in "much abstract philosophical talk" and Holmes did not care for Laski's later embrace of Socialism, which aimed to destroy Holmes's sort of world, his "passion for equality." Holmes saw "no injustice in our being made with different degrees of power" and thought Laski's thesis that "the rich exploit the poor" pure "drool." He "admire[d]," however, his

---

* *Holmes-Laski Letters: The Correspondence of Mr. Justice Holmes and Harold J. Laski 1916–1935,* edited by Mark DeWolfe Howe, was published by Harvard University Press in 1953.

young friend's writing on the subject, found it "penetrating," and he looked forward to reading all Laski wrote. When in 1921 Laski, who had visited the Holmeses at Beverly Farms and in Washington on numerous occasions, told Holmes he was leaving Cambridge and returning to England, Holmes wrote: "I shall miss you sadly. There is no other man I should miss so much."

Shortly before he met Laski, Holmes had begun corresponding with another young Jew, the philosopher Morris R. Cohen, who had been Frankfurter's roommate at Harvard, the correspondence leading naturally in time to occasional visits by Cohen to Beverly Farms and Washington—especially Beverly Farms, where Holmes had the leisure to indulge in the long and heated discussions he so enjoyed with men who enjoyed the kind of intellectual "jaws" he did. Cohen, a member of the philosophy faculty at The College of the City of New York, and Holmes exchanged letters less frequently than did Laski and Holmes, although discussions by Cohen and Holmes of their common interest—the mysteries of life and the universe—approached the intellectual intimacy of that between Laski and Holmes. They exchanged observations on their readings in philosophy and compliments on their work. They shared an occasional premise, but more than that, they shared the unadulterated joy of twisting "the tail of the cosmos till it squeaks." Cohen dedicated his *Reason and Nature,* published in 1931, to Holmes; "to have known Holmes," he wrote shortly after the justice's death, "was to have had a revelation of the possibilities of . . . human personality." Holmes, who in 1919 had joined some of Cohen's friends to subsidize a sabbatical year for him, told Cohen he was one of the "few for whose judgment I care so much."

Lewis Einstein, a young American diplomat whom Clare Castletown had sent to Holmes, and Walter Lippmann, a young American writer whose work Holmes once described as "devilish well-written, full of articulation of the impalpable and unutterable . . . not without the superstitions of a young come-outer as to capital, and quoting foolish things about the Courts—altogether a delightful fresh piece of writing and thinking," both enjoyed long and rewarding friendships with Holmes, and the correspondence between Holmes and Einstein was later published.*

Much has been made of the fact that these young men were Jewish. Holmes himself was not unaware of it and remarked on it, although he dismissed it as a factor of no importance except to some of his Brahmin

---

* *The Holmes-Einstein Letters: Correspondence of Mr. Justice Holmes and Lewis Einstein 1903–1935,* edited by James Bishop Peabody, was published by St. Martin's Press in 1964.

friends who were "savage" about it. It never occurred to him "until after the event" that a man he liked was a Jew, nor did he "care." He realized, however, that he seemed to be attracted to Jews and to the "hopeful attitude toward the future that seems characteristic of [Brandeis's] race." Frankfurter, Holmes thought, had "the encouraging tone that seems to be a point of consciousness with the Jews." Holmes could not embrace their schemes for social reform, one of the manifestations of his friends' "hopeful attitude toward the future," but he could enjoy their explorations, not so different in kind from those he and William James had embarked on those many years ago. Writing about the Holmes-Laski relationship, Edmund Wilson thought the connection could be explained in terms of a cultural affinity between Old Testament Jews and early New England Puritans, whose theology had adapted Hebrew elements and whose stern way of life imitated biblical discipline.

The Jewishness of these young men, however, may have been less significant in their relationships with Holmes than other shared characteristics—the Harvard connection, for example. Frankfurter, Laski, Lippmann, and Cohen each had some connection with Holmes's Harvard. Laski, Lippmann, and Cohen were connected to Frankfurter.

Not all Holmes's young friends were Jewish. John C. H. Wu, a young Chinese scholar at Michigan Law School who caught Holmes's attention with an article he had written, brought out the paternal instincts in the older man, who fretted over Wu's academic progress, freely offered advice, and later contributed to a scholarship for Wu at Harvard Law School. Ultimately Wu returned to China where he became a prominent figure in the judicial community. Holmes also kept in touch for many years with a Japanese count, Kentaro Kaneko, who had been at Harvard Law School from 1876 until 1878, and returned frequently to the United States for visits.

On his way home from court in the afternoon, Holmes often stopped for an intellectual gambol or a game of double solitaire at a place he had wryly named the House of Truth, a house on 19th Street shared by Lippmann, Frankfurter during his various missions in Washington during the war years, and other young men-about-town, not all of them Jewish. The atmosphere was not unlike that of the Cambridge house shared by Owen Wister and John Jay Chapman and their friends where Holmes had enjoyed dropping in for stimulating talk and occasional meals when he was still a state judge. Like the young men in Massachusetts, those at the House of Truth made Holmes "laugh consumedly."

Jews perhaps had the edge in "loveableness" and optimism, but the common characteristic that Jews, Japanese, Chinese, some of Holmes's secretaries, and all the other young men who wandered into Holmes's orbit brought him was their youth: their capacity for making "life seem large and free," a quality not always appreciated by the Bostonians he had known. Heaven knows, Johnny Morse didn't understand Holmes anymore. Perhaps he never had. Even as a child, Johnny hadn't taken Wendell seriously and had brushed off his questions glibly, as if such matters had long been settled and did not concern him. Henry Adams, who presided over one of the most brilliant intellectual salons in America at his house on Lafayette Square opposite the White House, "chilled" Holmes's "soul" with his talk about "how futile it all was" and "everywhere was dust and ashes," and Holmes stopped calling on his old friend on his way home from court; he was too old and tired for that kind of talk. Holmes's relations with the other justices were "most friendly," but his interests didn't mesh with theirs, and he was often "lonely." The young men filled the gap. They were friends, students, the sons he never had—he may have been the father they would have liked, one they did not feel compelled to "swallow and digest."

The youngsters were intellectually exciting, adventurous; their minds were unfettered, their spirits soared. Fearing perhaps the mental and spiritual stagnation that so often accompanies old age, he prized their youthful qualities more and more as he grew older. They amused and stimulated him, quenching his thirst for intercourse with men of ideas. They "put [him] onto books" they thought would be "good for [him] and pleased [him] by their . . . enthusiasm, and their talent." They sent him their own books, the formal products of their minds, and autographed them in the extravagantly worshipful prose that characterized their relations with him. They marked his birthdays, judicial anniversaries, and opinions in the *New Republic,* a young organ of Progressivism published in Washington to which several of them contributed regularly and to which he subscribed. He did not share their social or economic views or their utopian dreams, but all he asked was a challenging intellectual run for his money and a devil-may-care sense of fun. He relished their playfulness and participated in it wholeheartedly. He might meet a group of them in the street and spontaneously treat them to a bottle of champagne.

> It is pleasant to play the benevolent old uncle to young ones who are working for their living but have the spirit of larkiness.

He wallowed in their "unction," which men of his own age did not offer. Unquestioning and unthreatening, leaving control of the relationships in Holmes's hands, they clearly adored him, relished his wit, admired his intellect, and envied his worldly wisdom. He listened to them, encouraged them, and showed his delight in them. Not the least of his attractions for them was the opportunity for close contact with a figure of stature.

As old friends disappeared, these young people helped Holmes conquer the feelings of loss, afforded him perhaps some sense of continuity which, childless, he may have lacked. Summing it all up, with his customary brevity, he explained:

The young fellows of my acquaintance keep me hopeful. When left to myself I should get gloomy. I had a visit from two yesterday that restored my circulation.

CHAPTER *23*

Child Labor

LESS THAN A WEEK after Brandeis had taken his seat on the Supreme Court, on June 10, 1916, the Republicans, meeting in Chicago, nominated Justice Charles Evans Hughes for president. Chief Justice White and Justice Van Devanter had advised Hughes, who had tried to discourage efforts to secure his nomination, that he could not turn it down if made, Hughes's wife had agreed, and Hughes immediately resigned from the Court. Even the usually skeptical Holmes believed it had been Hughes's "sense of duty" that had convinced him to accept the nomination. Holmes expected to miss his colleague "consumedly, for he is not only a good fellow, experienced and wise, but funny, and with doubts that open vistas through the wall of a non-conformist conscience." They had enjoyed their six-year association; they had often walked home together after court had adjourned for the day, speaking pig Latin. Holmes had responded to Hughes's humor by writing amusing rhymes and comments on Hughes's draft opinions:

Wee—Musoo—I float in a fairy bark to the bight and serenely anchor there with you.

Yes, with humility. I now see what you have been about when I was giving parties their constitutional right to jaw while I slept.

Hughes had admired the sparkling and incisive style of Holmes's opinions, had been entertained by the Bostonian's fresh and "pungent" utterances, and stimulated in their joint efforts on opinions such as their dissent in *Frank* v. *Mangum*.

William H. Taft's supporters once again besieged Wilson to fill the vacant Supreme Court seat with the former president—unsuccessfully; it was hardly to be expected that a Progressive Democrat would choose a conservative Republican, however "gracious" a gesture it might appear to be. On July 14, Wilson nominated a fifty-eight-year-old millionaire bachelor, John Hessin Clarke of Ohio, a locally prominent Democratic politician and for the past two years a judge of the U.S. District Court for the Northern District of Ohio. There was some grumbling by the press that Wilson had appointed another "radical" like Brandeis, but the *New Republic* and the equally liberal *Nation* rejoiced, seeing in Clarke the third member of a Holmes/Brandeis/Clarke trinity. He took his seat on the opening of the Court term on October 9, 1916.

The following month, on November 7, Hughes was defeated in the presidential election, and Wilson was narrowly reelected. There was, however, no going back, and Hughes, ex-governor of New York, ex-justice of the Supreme Court, ex-candidate of the Republican Party, resumed the practice of law with his old firm in New York City. Holmes was "deeply grieved" at the outcome, partly because of his "personal affection" for Hughes but mostly because he thought Hughes "would have been a better President than the incumbent."

Holmes did not go out socially much any more, but when he did, the people who sat next to him at dinner never forgot his handsome presence or his humorous antics—his profanity delivered "in the old-fashioned aristocratic way that is never cheap or offensive," his poetic renditions of

> The bells of hell go ting-aling-ling
> For you, but not for me.
> The Angel choirs they sing-aling-ling
> That's the goods for me.
> Oh, death where is thy sting-aling-ling
> Where grave thy victoree?
> When the bells of hell go ting-aling-ling
> For you but not for me.

The news of Clare Castletown's stroke, which affected her left side and her speech, did nothing to improve Holmes's morale. It was "lucky," he thought, "that most of the time [he had] too much work to do to realize [his] own sadness—not to speak of the world's."

Felix Frankfurter, who could always cheer Holmes up, bounced into town in mid-January 1917 to argue before the Supreme Court the state of Oregon's latest legislative schemes for regulating working conditions. *Bunting* v. *Oregon* involved the state's new ten-hour law, which applied to men and women both who worked in the mills and factories; overtime was limited to three hours and required extra pay. *Stettler* v. *O'Hara* and *Simpson* v. *O'Hara* were both minimum-wage cases. In the nine years between the Court's decision in *Muller* v. *Oregon,* which upheld Oregon's ten-hour law for women, and Brandeis's appointment to the Supreme Court, the People's Attorney had spent much of his professional time defending the constitutionality of similar legislation that had been passed by the states in the euphoria following *Muller.*

Brandeis had argued all three of these latest cases previously, the minimum-wage cases in December 1914, *Bunting* in April 1916. Turnover on the Court, however, delayed decision; the cases were restored to the docket and scheduled for reargument in January 1917. In the meantime, Brandeis was appointed to the Court, and he handed the responsibility for reargument to his willing pupil, Frankfurter. Once on the bench, Brandeis could not participate in the cases at all, because he had been counsel.

Frankfurter was at ease in the courtroom—he had argued there before as a War Department lawyer. Feeling was running high in the United States on wages and hour laws, however, and he found the two days over which the arguments were spread "regular trench warfare." He had to "fight step by step."

Continuing in the style set by his mentor, Frankfurter presented, in addition to the legal argument, the social one: the detrimental effects of long hours and low wages on laborers and the conditions which had led to the passage of the legislation in Oregon and other states. At one point McReynolds turned on him:

"Ten hours! Ten hours! Ten! Why not four?"

Frankfurter paused for a moment, then made his way slowly and dramatically to where McReynolds was sitting.

"Your honor," Frankfurter replied, "if by chance I may make such a hypothesis, if your physician should find that you're eating too much meat, it isn't necessary for him to urge you to become a vegetarian."

Holmes was delighted with his young friend. "Good for you!" he exclaimed loudly and "embarrassingly," as Frankfurter remembered it.

McReynolds was less delighted and retaliated during subsequent court sessions by alternately interrupting Frankfurter excessively, then ignoring him and ostentatiously reading the brief for the other side while the lawyer talked. He also voted to strike down the state statutes.

Shortly before Frankfurter's appearance in court, Holmes had told Laski that he was "mighty sceptical" of minimum-wage and other such regulations, but, he speculated, "it may be that a somewhat monotonous standardized mode of life is coming." Protective legislation amounted simply to taking "out of one pocket to put into the other," a theme Holmes had been developing tirelessly into a concerto since he had first articulated it publicly, apropos of the London gas-stokers' strike, in the *American Law Review* in 1873. Holmes thought the "courageous thing to say to the crowd, though perhaps the Brandeis school don't believe it"—nor did Laski, Holmes might have realized—"and you'd better face it instead of trying to lift yourselves by the slack of your own breeches." He sighed. "[A]ll our present teaching is hate and envy for those who have any luxury, as social wrongdoers." He had told Frankfurter himself more or less the same thing the summer before. Nevertheless, when it came time for the Court to make its decision, Holmes once again acquiesced to the "actual feelings and demands of the community." On April 9, the Court decided narrowly (5 to 3 in *Bunting,* 4 to 4 in *Stettler* and *Simpson,* which in the latter two allowed the lower-court decision supporting minimum wage to stand) to validate both the maximum-hour and minimum-wage laws at issue. Apparently, in the early discussions of *Stettler* and *Simpson,* support for the minimum-wage law wavered, and Holmes, believing himself in the minority, had written a dissent not a lot less sharply accusatory than his dissent a decade before in *Lochner.* Whoever among the justices had been uncertain at first, however, ultimately decided in favor of affirmation, and Holmes's dissent survives only in his own files.

America's entry in April 1917 into the three-year-old war in Europe turned judicial attention temporarily from the domestic social and economic issues cases like *Bunting* involved and focused it on questions arising out of the extraordinary conditions of wartime, which required extraordinary measures. Its actions ultimately upheld by the Supreme Court, the government assumed control of the railroads, the communications systems, and the lives of its male citizens between the ages of eighteen and forty-five. Congress attempted, not always successfully, to silence dissent via the Espionage and Sedition Acts, and the exigencies of the emergency were often sufficient to bend the usual legal rules of behavior. Holmes, in whom victims of the Alabama peonage system had elicited only contempt, was even willing to modify regulations governing the behavior of parties to a contract when a wartime emergency seemed to require it. In *North German Lloyd* v. *Guaranty Trust Co. of New York,* decided in May 1917, Holmes, speaking for the Court, had no trouble justifying the failure of Captain Polack, master of the *Kronprinzessin Cecilie,* to deliver his cargo when threatened with capture and detention of his passengers. Brandeis, who was "not convinced" but withheld dissent, "darkly intimated" that Holmes "neglected principles that he heard [Holmes] lay down 30 years ago."

During the first week of June 1917, as nearly thirty-five thousand young Washingtonians registered for the draft, the United Confederate Veterans held their twenty-seventh annual reunion in Washington, the first one held in the nation's capital, which fifty-six years before they had besieged and from which they were thrown back by Union forces. Their ranks thinned now by death, their faces marked by age, they sang the old songs, renewed old friendships, and paraded in a body down Pennsylvania Avenue. Their convention was an orgy of patriotism as well as a reunion, an announcement to the world that North and South stood together and their support for America in the grim days ahead would not falter. They solemnly watched movies of the battles recently fought in Europe and cheered the president when he urged rededication to the principles that had made America great. The sign that caught Holmes's attention and pleased him almost more than he could find words for stated flatly: *"Damn a man who ain't for his country right or wrong."*

Except for Holmes's discovery of "the pleasure of soft shirts and collars during the undress season" and the joy he always got from Harold Laski's weekend visits, the summer at Beverly Farms seems to have been uneventful that year. At "odd minutes" after he returned to Washington for the new Court term, he read a critically acclaimed "war book" which he found "generically familiar . . . though different in detail and greater in degree." He was "sad" to be out of this one and he could not help but recall the "mixed emotions" he had felt when the Massachusetts Twentieth "went over with the first brigade to cross at Fredericksburg," and he had been hospitalized with dysentery; he remembered the tears he shed at the same time he had rejoiced that his "hide was safe."

In early November, the Court decided *Buchanan* v. *Warley,* a landmark case involving residential racial segregation. For the first time, the Court was unanimous in a case involving Jim Crow laws, although Holmes at one point threatened to shatter what must have been a hard-won unity.

Following the examples of Atlanta, Georgia, Winston-Salem, North Carolina, and Baltimore, Maryland, where the scheme originated, the segregationists of Louisville, Kentucky, in 1914 had gotten an ordinance enacted requiring "the use of separate blocks for residences, places of abode and places of assembly by white and colored people respectively." It was unlawful for blacks to move into any neighborhood occupied by a majority of whites, and vice versa, a not particularly subtle device of imposing equal restrictions on both races in order to circumvent the Fourteenth Amendment's "equal protection of the laws" requirement. At the same time it effectively confined blacks to specific well-defined— and less desirable—areas of the city.

Following race riots in Springfield, Illinois—the city of Lincoln—in 1908, the National Association for the Advancement of Colored People (NAACP) had been organized with precipitating social change through legal challenge among its priorities. Its Louisville branch had been organized specifically to challenge the city's 1914 residential segregation law. The case that was put together was so obviously contrived that its justiciability was threatened.

William Warley, the black chief of the Louisville NAACP, arranged with Charles Buchanan, a white real estate agent sympathetic to NAACP goals, to buy a lot in a predominantly white neighborhood with the intention of building his residence on it. Citing the Municipal Segregation Ordinance, as these schemes had come to be known, Warley defaulted on the contract to buy, and Buchanan sued for nonperformance, creating the anomalous situation in which a black officer of the NAACP was supporting the ordinance to get him out of a contract he had entered into in order to get the ordinance declared invalid. Refusing to enforce the contract, the trial court judge dismissed the case and ruled that the ordinance was valid. The Court of Appeals of Kentucky similarly held the ordinance constitutional and a valid defense against Buchanan's suit.

The case was argued in the U.S. Supreme Court for the first time in April 1916, but only seven justices heard it—Day was ill and Brandeis had not yet taken the seat vacated by Lamar. It was argued before the full bench a year later. Ironically, the white Buchanan was represented by the Bostonian Moorfield Storey, president of the national NAACP in 1916; in his young adulthood he had belonged to the same social and professional circles Holmes had, had in fact succeeded Holmes as editor of the *American Law Review*. The black officer of the Louisville NAACP was represented by Louisville city attorneys.

There was considerable concern among those involved in the case regarding what the two Southerners on the Court, White and McReynolds, would do. Storey was more concerned that the Court might, as it often did, find a way to avoid such a "disagreeable" question as the case of *Buchanan* v. *Warley* asked, and Day in his opinion for the Court, announced on November 5, 1917, acknowledged that the justices had indeed pondered whether they had to dismiss the case because "attacks upon the validity of laws can only be entertained when made by those whose rights are directly affected by the law or ordinance in question." The principle was a settled one, and in this case, a white man was asserting the denial of constitutional rights to blacks.

Holmes had objected to the Court's decision on that very ground. Caught between his reverence for contractual obligations and his inclination to let the legislature have its way—and perhaps agreeing with the Kentucky appeals court which had indicated black neighborhoods could be made as desirable as white ones with the application of a little elbow grease, an attitude that would have been consistent with comments he had made in *Bailey* and *Reynolds*—he took the justiciability way out and wrote a dissent in which he wondered whether the suit ought even to be "entertained without some evidence" that it was not a "manufactured case." Brushing this problem to one side, he went on to challenge Buchanan's right to use this method to attack "a wrong to some one else." On balance, he thought the case ought to be dismissed or the judgment of the Kentucky courts affirmed.

The Court, having pondered the problem, rejected Holmes's objection to deciding the case on its merits. But the justices shifted the ground for decision from the constitutionality of residential racial segregation to the Fourteenth Amendment's old, reliable guarantee of property rights, including "the right to acquire, use, and dispose of it," a hook that practically assured the capture of the Court's conservatives, including the Southerners. The question to be decided became: "May the occupancy, and, necessarily, the purchase and sale of property of which occupancy is an incident, be inhibited by the States, or by one of its municipalities, solely because of the color of the proposed occupant of the premises?" No, the Court answered emphatically. Louisville's "attempt to prevent" the sale of the property in question "to a person of color was not a legitimate exercise of the police power of the State, and is in direct violation of the fundamental law enacted in the Fourteenth Amendment of the Constitution preventing state interference with property rights except by due process of law." The ordinance could not stand. The Kentucky Court of Appeals was reversed, and *de jure* residential segregation lay mortally wounded. Jim Crow was still alive and well in the South, but the White Court's decisions like the *Grandfather Clause Cases, Buchanan*, and Hughes's warnings in *McCabe* had at least prevented its growth into full-blown apartheid.

In the normal course of events, Day's concluding sentences would have signalled Holmes to prepare for announcing his dissent. Holmes, however, had a surprise for his brethren. Possibly White's passion for unanimity influenced him. Perhaps his friend Brandeis, who had a well-developed sense of racial injustice, dissuaded him. He may have arrived at his decision independently, simply decided in the face of such strong opposition to "shut up" as he sometimes did. But he did not read his dissent. Since Day had addressed Holmes's concerns in the Court's opinion, the latter's decision to withdraw his own was probably a last-minute one. In any event, Holmes ultimately joined the majority to make the Court's decision unanimous.

The Progressive press as well as the black press exulted; the more realistic Southern press predicted residential patterns would not change, that custom and usage would effect what law had frustrated. The Southerners were right. *De facto* segregation, in many places supported by private covenants, continued as if nothing had happened, its momentum maintained by social and economic pressures.

A FREQUENT PRESENCE in the White Court was the American Indian. Most of the litigation involved rights to lands; some cases, however, addressed the status of the Indian under federal law. On May 20, 1918, Holmes for a unanimous Court wrote *Carney* v. *Chapman,* exempting Chickasaw tribal marriage customs from strictures of civil law.

On the same day he announced the Court's unanimous decision in *Western Union Telegraph Co.* v. *Foster,* a "matter not without difficulty," although eventually it succumbed, like others over the years, to the usual principles of legal analysis. Holmes always said "there is no such thing as a hard case. Five hundred times," he had thought when confronted with what appeared to be a complicated issue,

> now I shall see what a damned fool I am—I never shall understand this— And when you tackle it the lion's skin comes off and the old donkey of a question of law is underneath.

Foster involved an attempt by the state of Massachusetts to stop the transmissions by telegraph of stock quotations between the New York Stock Exchange and one Calvin H. Foster of Boston, owner of a string of illegal gambling establishments where betting relied on current market quotations. The case presented some nice distinctions between intra- and interstate commerce, the former vulnerable to state regulation, the latter insulated from it. After he had stripped the case of its "lion's skin," however, Holmes seemed to answer the questions effortlessly. He concluded that the transmissions at issue were in interstate commerce until received by the subscriber to the quotation service and thus frustrated the state's attempt to choke them off. A fine point, but in effect the decision closed off interstate telegraph messages to state regulation.

The case that caught the public's attention in 1918 was *Hammer* v. *Dagenhart,* a constitutional test of the Keating-Owen Act of 1916, which prohibited the transportation across state lines of all goods manufactured with child labor.

In the early 1900s, children as young as ten, much cheaper than adult labor, hunched over factory machines and descended into mines nights as well as days for six and seven days a week. Led by Massachusetts, where a law to limit child labor had been passed after the Civil War, several states had attempted to forbid or reduce child labor, but their efforts had been neither uniform nor effective. Manufacturers in those states where it had been abolished or limited were put at a disadvantage in the competition with manufacturers in states that allowed it, and in 1910, nearly two million youngsters under fifteen years of age were employed in American industry. Explained a spokesman for the cotton mill owners of North Carolina: "I think children, especially boys ten years of age, should be allowed to work in mills." Hard work, he added, was "the savior of the people, religiously, educationally, and . . . physically."

Earlier in the decade, before he had made friends with Holmes, Senator Beveridge, recognizing the futility of state action, proposed that Congress, although it was not empowered to deal directly with matters such as child labor, act under the Commerce Clause of the Constitution, which commanded the national legislature "To regulate Commerce with Foreign Nations, and among the several States, and with the Indian tribes." Beveridge believed this catchall provision which already held a potpourri of federal regulatory legislation—the Interstate Commerce Act, Sherman Anti-Trust Act, Wilson Tariff Act of 1894—could easily find room for another with its broad authority. Federal child labor legislation, however, had not been a high priority of the Roosevelt and Taft administrations—Roosevelt favored the "securing of approximately uniform legislation of the proper character among the several states"—and it was not until Woodrow Wilson, with his proposals for a New Freedom, his vision of a more egalitarian world on which he had based his presidential campaign, moved into the White House in March 1913 that Congress at last swung into action. Congress was in a progressive mood and had passed, just days before Wilson's inauguration, the Sixteenth Amendment, permitting the levying of income taxes, and shortly afterwards, the Seventeenth Amendment, providing for the direct election of senators. The House passed a child labor bill in 1915; the president, however, had some doubt about its constitutionality, did not support it, and the Senate killed it. Then child labor legislation was written into the platforms of both parties in 1916, and when the original bill was resubmitted to Congress that year, it passed with the support of the president, who perhaps had changed his mind about its constitutionality in the light of its political desirability.

No sooner had Wilson signed the bill, known as the Keating-Owen Act (for its sponsors, Edward Keating, Democratic congressman from Colorado, and Robert L. Owen, Democratic senator of Oklahoma) than David Clark of the Executive Committee of Southern Cotton Manufacturers began to search for someone to test its constitutionality. He found him in the person of Roland H. Dagenhart, an employee of a small Charlotte, North Carolina, cotton mill whose two sons, aged thirteen and fifteen, were also employed by the mill. Under the Keating-Owen Act, the family income would be reduced dramatically. Clark found lawyers and raised the funds to finance a suit against the local U.S. attorney, W. C. Hammer, who was charged with enforcing the new law, and the mill owners who had announced to their employees that they intended to comply with it. Dagenhart won in the local federal district court, where the act was declared unconstitutional and the U.S. attorney enjoined from enforcing it. The government took the case to the U.S. Supreme Court.

When oral argument opened on the afternoon of April 15, 1918, Solicitor General John W. Davis, who as Congressman Davis of West Virginia—a state that relied heavily on child labor—had opposed passage of child labor legislation, handled the case for the government. Morgan J. O'Brien, prominent member of the New York bar, active in Democratic politics, and former New York State judge, had been engaged, with four associates, to appear for the appellees, the Dagenharts, father and sons.

Admission of lawyers to practice before the Court was the first order of business. Eighteen attorneys, including William Hendren of Winston-Salem, North Carolina, one of the Dagenharts' legal team, were admitted.* Next came the announcement of opinions—twenty-one in

---

*When an experienced Supreme Court lawyer like Morgan O'Brien is engaged to argue a case in that court, it is customary for him to bring along a local lawyer familiar with local conditions. Frequently, this local lawyer has not previously argued in the Supreme Court and must be admitted to practice there before he or she may participate. Leading lawyers from areas remote from Washington in fact are often admitted to Supreme Court practice on the day of their first arguments.

all. Finally the Court was ready to hear the arguments scheduled for that day.

Solicitor General Davis opened for the government. His good conservative states-rights soul must have trembled when he declared: "The time has gone by when the power of Congress to close the channels of interstate commerce to articles which it chooses to regulate can be questioned." He reminded the justices that "the decisions of the court have upheld its power when used for the far broader purposes of protecting the health, welfare, moral and economic situation of the people of the United States."

Adopting the Brandeis style of argument, he reiterated the "evil effects" of working around machinery on the well-being of "persons of tender years," the dangers of the machinery itself, as well as the potential for arresting a child's development and decreasing his or her resistance to disease. He touched on the adverse effect on natural competitive forces provoked by nonuniform legislation from state to state; "the slightest difference in the cost of production," he argued, "or what amounts to the same thing, a belief on the part of manufacturers in the existence of such differences, alters the development of an industry." Unbalanced forces of competition, created by nonuniform labor laws, clearly made that competition unfair and obstructed development of the industry.

Although Davis had not concluded his argument, court, as was its custom, adjourned promptly at 4 P.M., and the solicitor general had to hold his closing paragraphs until the following afternoon, coincidentally at the same time that upstairs in the Capitol a House subcommittee was hearing appeals from national leaders in child welfare work for a law to protect women and children wage earners in the District of Columbia.

Davis drew a running fire of questions from the justices when he stated that "underlying this statute is the conviction that child labor is always and everywhere inherently an evil thing and all statutes are a reflection of the prevailing opinion in the public mind." He concluded: "Congress was attempting to regulate commerce in good faith. . . . It sought only to prevent the evil resulting from the interstate transportation of child-made goods. The court is confined to the purpose expressed in the act. Nor is it concerned with questions of the wisdom, expediency, or oppressive character of legislation."

O'Brien replied that Congress, in passing the Keating-Owen Child Labor Act, already had overstepped its bounds. James Madison himself, said O'Brien, would agree. The Commerce Clause, the author of the Constitution had explained, "was intended as a negative and preventive provision against injustices in the states themselves, rather than as a power to be used for the positive purposes of the general government." In attempting to do "indirectly what it can not do directly," Congress had intruded upon the domain of the states. The Court's decision in 1895 to allow the sugar trust to continue on the ground that the mere production of sugar had no relevance to interstate commerce had, of course, been weakened since then. Nevertheless, that decision's "distinction between production and commerce is still effective to prevent direct congressional regulation of production as distinguished from sale and transportation." In regulating commerce, he argued, Congress regulated traffic in "things, vehicles of transport and things *in transitu,* but not the things themselves. Before and after the *transitus* they are beyond the power of regulation." The production and use of the articles at issue were subjects not "of the commercial power, but of the States from which and to which they are transported."

In conclusion, O'Brien posed the question on everyone's mind: "Has Congress absorbed the police power of the States? If Congress has the power here asserted, it is difficult to conceive what is left to the States." In 1824, a time when interstate commerce amounted to little more than a trickle, John Marshall, in a case called *Gibbons* v. *Ogden,* had appeared to give Congress carte blanche when he declared the power given Congress by the Commerce Clause "may be exercised to its utmost extent, and acknowledges no limitations, other than are prescribed in the Constitution." That same Constitution, however, had allotted the states a portion of power, too, and Marshall had declared in that same *Gibbons* v. *Ogden* that while the Commerce Clause had given Congress the "power to regulate," that is, "the power to control the means by which commerce is carried on," the document had not granted the national legislature the authority "to forbid commerce from moving," that is, the power to "destroy." Politically, *Hammer* v. *Dagenhart* was one more skirmish in the ongoing struggle for control between the nation and the states which the Founding Fathers had built into the Constitution.

Hammer v. *Dagenhart* was also another incident in the struggle for supremacy between the Congress and the Court. The attitude of the justices toward federal legislation had not been consistent or predictable since Holmes had joined the Court. During that decade and a half, they had struck down ten congressional enactments, a fourth of all the federal legislation voided during the 127 years of the Court's existence. Holmes, who would have been satisfied judicially if the Court lost its "power to declare an Act of Congress void" and who did his best to save what legislation he could in good conscience save, dissented in four of the ten.

Most of the federal statutes that had displeased the justices during Holmes's time on the Court had been annulled during the Fuller years. The White Court had shown itself slightly more favorably disposed toward progressive legislation. In 1911, in *Hipolite Egg Co.* v. *United States,* the Court had upheld the Pure Food and Drug Act of 1906, which authorized the seizure of adulterated goods in interstate commerce. In 1912, in *Savage* v. *Jones,* it had sustained a statute requiring certain standards for the importation of dog food. In 1913, in *Hoke* v. *United States,* the justices upheld the so-called White Slave Traffic Act of 1910, which prohibited the transportation of a woman in interstate commerce for purposes of prostitution. In 1914, in *The Pipeline Cases,* Holmes had written the Court's affirmation of the Hepburn Act which extended the authority of the ICC to regulation of pipelines, and in 1917, in *Clark Distilling Co.* v. *Western Maryland Railway,* the Court upheld the Webb-Kenyon Act and thereby the power of Congress over the transportation of intoxicating liquors in interstate commerce. Holmes had been with the majority in all but *Clark Distilling Co.,* in which he dissented without opinion, although he later regretted it.

Holmes was not satisfied with his performance in the last-named case. *Clark Distilling Co.* involved the constitutionality of the Webb-Kenyon Act and its relationship to state prohibition laws. Chief Justice White worked it all out for the Court in his customary tortured manner. Originally Holmes had not intended to dissent, but "at the last minute was stirred to do so by dissatisfaction with [White's] opinion." He was sorry he "didn't either say a few words or shut up."

Looking at the Court's record in recent years, some observers expected the justices to have difficulty in striking down the Keating-Owen Child Labor Act. Some thought—perhaps hoped—Woodrow Wilson's appointees to the Court—McReynolds, Brandeis, and Clarke—would change the Court's attitude toward labor legislation, which—state and national both—had not fared well under either the Fuller or White Courts.

When the Court's decision was announced on June 3, 1918, the prophets had been fooled and those who had worked so many years for passage of Keating-Owen were disappointed. Keating-Owen was declared unconstitutional. It was the forty-second act of Congress the Court had declared in violation of the Constitution since Marshall had established the principle of judicial review in *Marbury* v. *Madison* in 1803.

Writing for the five judges who made up the majority, Day first tried to distinguish between previous Court decisions in which regulation of interstate commerce had been supported by the Court. In *Hipolite Egg Co., Hoke,* and *Clark Distilling Co.,* "the use of interstate transportation was necessary to the accomplishment of harmful results," and prohibiting the use of it had been the only way "to effect the evil intended." That element was "wanting" in *Hammer* v. *Dagenhart.* Keating-Owen did not regulate transportation among the states, but aimed "to standardize the ages at which children may be employed in mining and manufacturing within the states." The goods shipped were "harmless." Production, the step objected to, ended at the factory loading dock, had nothing to do with interstate commerce, and was a matter for local regulation. It was almost as if the Court had turned back the calendar to 1895 and the justices were discussing whether or not the sugar trust violated the Sherman Anti-Trust Act.

The so-called unfair competition that the solicitor general had insisted resulted from nonuniform child labor laws was irrelevant, said Day; Congress had no power to "require the States to exercise their police power so as to prevent possible unfair competition." Minimum-wage laws put some states at an economic disadvantage, too, but the fact did not give Congress the authority to deny transportation in interstate commerce in those states. The grant of power to Congress over interstate commerce had been intended to enable the legislature to regulate such commerce; it had not been intended as authorization for federal control of matters "carefully reserved" to the states by the Tenth Amendment to the Constitution. However desirable the imposition of strict limitations on child labor, and however beneficial uniformity of such laws, the problem belonged to the states alone. "[I]f," Day concluded, "Congress can thus regulate matters entrusted to local authority by prohibition of the movement of commodities in interstate commerce, all freedom of commerce will be at an end, and the power of the State over local matters may be eliminated, and thus," as Marshall had predicted, "our system of government be practically destroyed."

O'Brien had the final answer to his question: "Has Congress absorbed the police power of the States?" The Supreme Court had replied, "Yes." The ten and twelve year olds would go on working, their backs hunched over factory machinery, their thin arms loading coal from mines and quarries. The Commerce Clause could not be used to right social wrongs.

Holmes did not agree, and circulated a strong dissent among the justices with which Clarke "cordially" concurred and which Brandeis joined without comment. Pitney studied it carefully but was not persuaded; he had found Day's arguments "sound," and, not surprisingly, joined the majority. McKenna originally had reservations.

The only question in *Hammer* v. *Dagenhart,* Holmes began, was whether Congress had "power to prohibit the shipment in interstate or foreign commerce of any product of a cotton mill situated in the United States" in which child labor prohibited by Keating-Owen was employed. Applying the old reliable objective standard he had worked out nearly a half century before, he ruled the social and moral aims of Keating-Owen irrelevant and declared that if a statute was "within the powers specifically conferred upon Congress," it seemed to him it was not made "any less constitutional because of the indirect effects that it may have, however obvious it may be that it will have those effects," and the Court was not "at liberty upon such grounds to hold it void." Citing, as Day had, *Hipolite Egg, Hoke,* and *Clark Distilling Co.*—some of the "most conspicuous" decisions of the Court in this area—he painstakingly demonstrated how these had sustained regulation of interstate commerce that had had ulterior motives.

Inspired possibly by former Senator Beveridge, his friend and neighbor at Beverly Farms, he even indulged uncustomarily in a bit of moral outrage. "[I]f," he wrote, "there is any matter upon which civilized countries have agreed—far more unanimously than they have with regard to intoxicants and some other matters over which this country is now emotionally aroused—it is the evil of premature and excessive child labor. I should have thought that if we were to introduce our own moral conceptions where in my opinion they do not belong, this was preëminently a case for upholding the exercise of all its powers of the United States."

Finally Holmes distinguished between state and federal concerns:

The act does not meddle with anything belonging to the States. They may regulate their internal affairs and their domestic commerce as they like. But when they seek to send their products across the state line they are no longer within their rights. If there were no Constitution and no Congress their power to cross the line would depend upon their neighbors. Under the Constitution such commerce belongs not to the States but to Congress to regulate. It may carry out its views of public policy whatever indirect effect they may have upon the activities of the States. Instead of being encountered by a prohibitive tariff at her boundaries the State encounters the public policy of the United States which it is for Congress to express. It is a good deal better off than it would be if it stood alone, but it cannot have things all its own way when it attempts to leave the domestic domain.

The last sentence disturbed McKenna. "You have already referred," he told Holmes, "to the power of Congress as a substitute for states acting antagonistic to one another, and why emphasize it." He suggested Holmes add something positive about congressional power to regulate commerce. Holmes followed his suggestions:

The public policy of the United States is shaped with a view to the benefit of the nation as a whole. . . . The national welfare as understood by Congress may require a different attitude within its sphere from that of some self-seeking State. It seems to me entirely constitutional for Congress to enforce its understanding by all the means at its command.

McKenna was delighted. "You have grasped my idea and executed it well," he scribbled on Holmes's next draft. "If you could catch another vote the opinion would be epochal. It would make the commerce clause truly independent not subservient to some state purpose or limited or restrained as you say, by some state purpose."

Holmes did not "catch" another vote; nevertheless he was pleased with his work. He "flattered" himself that he "showed a lot of precedent and also the grounds in reason." He was less pleased that his reputation as a liberal/progressive judge was growing when it was as a judicial philosopher he wanted to be recognized. *Hammer* v. *Dagenhart* was beset by the same misunderstandings that had surrounded *Vegelahn* and *Plant* two decades before.

In Congress, reaction to the Court's decision was loud and angry. Keating-Owen's sponsor, Senator Owen, submitting an amended bill to his fellow senators, spoke at some length against the whole concept of judicial review as well as against child labor. "The slavery of children is wrong," he roared, "and the child-labor act was intended to prevent the slavery of children, even by their own parents, in so far as the United States could prevent it by the exercise of its control over interstate commerce." He had amended the original bill, adding provisions that removed from all federal courts, including the Supreme Court, the power to declare it unconstitutional. In the House, Representative Meyer London of New York complained that if *Hammer* v. *Dagenhart* remained the law of the land, it would be impossible for the Congress "to take up child-labor legislation, legislation on behalf of women, legislation cal-

culated to modify or to change or to improve conditions in industry."
Although disappointed and angry, Congress was not, however, defeated,
and the lawmakers were not without imagination. Perhaps prohibition
of child labor could somehow be read into Webb-Kenyon's prohibition
of intoxicating liquors; could the products of child labor perhaps be denied the use of the mails? Several avenues remained to be explored.

The president also was disappointed, and although preoccupied at
the time with German attacks on American shipping and other war
matters, he sought out an opportunity for a private talk with Postmaster
General—and former Congressman—Albert S. Burleson, an adroit political operator, although conservative in outlook.

"Burleson," Wilson said, "I want a child labor law that will stand.
How can I get one?"

"I'll tell you," Burleson replied, "but if I were in Congress I should
vote against it. I am not in sympathy with you on it, but I'll help you."

Meanwhile, down the street and around the corner at the War Labor Policies Board, Felix Frankfurter, then its chairman, was writing
into federal contracts a provision making requirements of Keating-Owen
binding on all manufacturers who sold their products to the government.

COURTS DECIDE HOW people may behave, but they have no police or soldiers to enforce their decisions. These belong to other branches
of the government. The only means courts have of maintaining order
and enforcing their decrees is the contempt power, the authority to
punish whoever defies them. On June 10, 1918, the final session of
what Holmes called "not a specifically interesting term," the Supreme
Court virtually erased an early nineteenth-century law that limited the
contempt power of the federal judiciary.

Responding to a lower federal court judge's misuse of the contempt
power—he had disbarred and imprisoned a man who had criticized one
of his opinions publicly—Congress in 1831 had enacted a statute limiting that authority to punishing only conduct that directly obstructed the
administration of justice. The statute had stood unscathed for eighty-
seven years, until the Supreme Court in 1918 announced its decision
in *Toledo Newspaper Co.* v. *United States.* In deciding it, the justices—
including Holmes in dissent—also announced their priorities in dealing
with questions that involved the First Amendment's command that
"Congress shall make no law . . . abridging freedom of speech, or of
the press. . . ."

Toledo Newspaper Co. involved publication by the *Toledo* (Ohio) *News-Bee* of a number of articles and cartoons professionally derogatory to the presiding federal judge in a pending street railway fare dispute that had excited substantial "public agitation and discussion." John M. Killits, U.S. District judge for the Western Division of the Northern District of Ohio, had found the material personally intimidating as well as calculated to provoke the public's resistance to his rulings, and he cited the *Toledo News-Bee* for contempt. He tried the case himself, without a jury, and imposed a large fine.

A majority of the Supreme Court approved Judge Killits's action. Speaking for the Court, Chief Justice White declared that the Constitution and the congressional enactment of 1831 notwithstanding, "however complete . . . the right of the press to state public things and discuss them, that right, as every other right enjoyed in human society, is subject to the restraints which separate right from wrong-doing."

Holmes, however, who "would go as far as any man in favor of the sharpest and most summary enforcement of order in Court and obedience to decrees," found Killits's behavior "wholly unwarranted" and dissented. Brandeis joined him. Holmes did not directly address the issues of free speech and press presented in *Toledo Newspaper Co.;* his concern was for the dignity of the court, which he thought had been compromised by Killits's behavior. But his permissive stance regarding the *News-Bee,* combined with the clear implication he thought Killits had acted foolishly, foreshadowed his positions in a series of freedom-of-expression cases with which he would have to deal shortly.

Holmes expected more from a federal judge in whom resided, he assumed, "ordinary firmness of character," and he found it "impossible to believe" that a man who possessed it could have been affected by what the *News-Bee* had published. Holmes had found in the material "nothing that would have affected a mind of reasonable fortitude"; still less could he discover "anything that obstructed the administration of justice." Killits, the implication was, had been entirely too thin-skinned and his performance counterproductive, "the last thing that could maintain respect for the courts."

CHAPTER 24

"Clear and Present Danger"

EVEN HOLMES, ISOLATED, detached, remote in his intellectual aerie, could not have failed to notice the changes in the atmosphere that occurred upon America's entry into World War I. The economic and social reformers of the recent past had been silenced while the national will concentrated on winning the war against Germany. The centrifugal forces that generally accompany a national emergency had been released, and almost every activity that touched American life—labor relations, transportation, housing, communications, foreign trade, the price of food—had been put in control of the federal government.

With the exceptions of a treason statute which proved useless and an internment statute which affected only alien enemies, however, the United States had entered World War I with practically no law on the books to protect the country against opposition to its policies. For that reason, Congress passed the Espionage Act on June 15, 1917. In addition to dealing with matters such as actual espionage and protection of military secrets, the statute set penalties of twenty years' imprisonment and/or a $10,000 fine for obstruction of military recruitment or operations. The attorney general, Thomas W. Gregory, was not satisfied with the scope of the act and asked Congress to expand it. An aroused Senate Judiciary Committee put together an amendment directed at suppressing virtually all dissent, which sailed through the Congress in May 1918. Also known as the Sedition Act, it set similar penalties for obstruction of Liberty Bond sales, discouragement of recruiting, and utterances in "disloyal or abusive language" about the government, the conduct of the war, the Constitution, even the flag or the uniform. Together, these two statutes, as extreme as any European measures taken to discourage disloyalty, effectively criminalized nearly all dissent in connection with public affairs. Under these two laws, more than 1,900 men and women were prosecuted for offenses involving speeches, books, newspaper articles, and pamphlets; one U.S. attorney estimated that at least 90 percent of the alleged pro-German plots never existed.

Such repression may seem an aberration in a country where John Adams was considered a hero for defending in court British participants in the Boston Massacre, where Alexander Hamilton is honored for representing Loyalists, and Ulysses S. Grant demanded amnesty for Robert E. Lee. The legislation of 1917 and 1918, however, reflected national public sentiment. War hysteria was abroad in the land, as contagious as the flu that was ravaging American cities in the winter of 1918 and even had shut down the Supreme Court briefly. Americans were indulging themselves in an orgy of hate against all things German. German operas were barred from concert halls, German books from public libraries. It was forbidden to teach the German language in some public schools. It was not safe to have a German name; sauerkraut was even renamed "Liberty Cabbage." Witch hunts proliferated, encouraged by Attorney General Gregory himself, who announced that "complaints of even the most informal or confidential nature are always welcome." A government-approved private vigilante group known as the American Protective Association sniffed out instances of disloyalty.

Germans were the main victims of American wrath, but not the only ones. To the ordinary undiscriminating eye, a pacifist might as well be a German. Pacifists' magazines were banned from the mails and their editors harassed. Scores of citizens were imprisoned for avowals of pacifism.

The growth of competing ideologies abroad in the early years of the twentieth century frightened a good many Americans who saw Socialists, Communists, and Bolsheviks as threats to prosperity, to free enterprise, and to the orderliness of the "American way of life" in general, and with only a slight effort of transference, "Lenin," "labor," and "liberal" soon became synonymous. Fear of the strange and incomprehensible ideas bred intolerance and intolerance, suppression. A reign of terror against the Red Menace, fully as ugly as that against things German, ensued. Dissident writers were suppressed. Anarchists were hounded. And genteel Bostonians like Holmes's old friend Brooks Adams were writing to their senators to complain that Herbert Hoover, whose attempts to stabilize prices as food administrator during the war had included curbing excess profits, was the "chief Bolshevik."

It was in this atmosphere of hostility to dissent, representing perhaps the epitome of disorder to fearful Americans, that beginning in the spring of 1918 with *Schenck* v. *United States,* filed in the court clerk's office on May 3 as the 1917 term was winding down, a group of cases involving freedom of expression reached the U.S. Supreme Court. Holmes's definition of First Amendment freedoms in the first case served as the linchpin of First Amendment jurisprudence long after his death. His subsequent eloquence in behalf of those same freedoms became a rallying cry for civil libertarians in every age thereafter. His opinions in all these post–World War I free-expression cases, both for the Court and in dissent, when read alongside other freedom-of-speech cases he had written beginning in 1907 when he was still something of a rookie and dependent on Blackstone's formulas, show Holmes in the stages of jurisprudential growth and development that culminated in further dramatization of the Holmes legend. After his dissent in *Abrams* v. *United States* in 1919, Bostonians gathered in their drawing rooms on Beacon Hill could only shake their heads ruefully over their strayed lamb and wonder, perhaps like orthodox parents whose offspring has suddenly embraced some eastern mystic ritual, why he had gone wrong. Holmes's cousin, contemporary, and childhood co-conspirator, Johnny Morse, on the other hand, had remained a model citizen of the local aristocracy, much in demand for elite club memberships and institutional trustee-ships.

The definition of freedom of the press in fashion when Holmes was in law school and which American states, including Massachusetts, had adapted to their constitutions was Blackstone's: liberty of the press, Blackstone had said in his *Commentaries on the Laws of England,* was "essential to the nature of a free state." It consisted, however, only "in laying no previous restraint upon publications"; it did not include "freedom from censure for criminal matter when published." Every man, Blackstone reasoned, had an "undoubted right to lay what sentiments he pleases before the public; but if he publishes what is improper, mischievous, or illegal, he must take the consequences of his own temerity." Blackstone being the authority at the time, most people assumed that his interpretation of a free press was the one the Founding Fathers referred to when in 1791 they added the First Amendment to the American Constitution. It reads: "Congress shall make no law . . . abridging the freedom of speech, or of the press. . . ."

Only once since then and prior to the passage of the Espionage Act of 1917 had Congress attempted to curtail free expression. The national emergency generated by the threat of war with France in 1798 had produced the Alien and Sedition laws, which allowed arbitrary deportation of aliens considered dangerous and punished citizens for criticizing the government. Passage of these two laws, however, was one of the biggest mistakes the Federalists ever made. Harassment and imprisonment of Republican writers and editors rallied public opinion against the Federalists, wrecked the party, and helped substantially to elect Republican Thomas Jefferson president in 1800. For the next century, the nation was largely preoccupied with taming a continent, and few cases involving freedom of expression arose. Even the national emergency of civil war did not produce anything as repressive of speech—although there were other repressions—as the Espionage and Sedition acts of 1917 and 1918.

Passage of the Sedition Act, the filing of *Schenck,* and the Supreme Court's refusal to review the case of Frederick Kraus, one-time Socialist candidate for governor of New Jersey who had been convicted under the Espionage Act of 1917 for an antiwar speech he had made in Newark, almost all at once at the end of the 1917 term, perhaps opened Holmes's inner debate on the issues raised by the concept of free speech, which until World War I was largely taken for granted: the age-old conflict between the individual's right to free expression, to unrestricted discussion of public matters, versus the government's right to protect itself. A chance meeting with one who had recently staked his career on his belief in the former and had lost could only have heightened Holmes's awareness of this conflict with which he realized he was to be confronted in his official capacity shortly.

On the train bound for Massachusetts in early June 1918, Holmes fell into conversation with Learned Hand, federal district judge in New York who was en route to *his* summer place in Cornish, New Hampshire. Hand's reputation at the time was still suffering from wounds sustained after his decision in *Masses Publishing Co.* v. *Patten,** one of the first cases to be decided under the new Espionage Act, in which Hand had made the fatal mistake of marching too far ahead of his followers. In a rare display of courage at the time, Hand had held that Thomas G. Patten, the local postmaster, could not under the Espionage Act ban from the mails the magazine *Masses,* which had carried articles critical of the government, the draft, and the war effort. Hand made no quarrel with the act itself. But he insisted that so long as one stopped short of "urging upon others that it is their duty or their interest to resist the law, . . . one should not be held to have attempted its viola-

---

* *Masses,* some scholars believe, may have contributed to Hand's failure to be promoted to a vacancy on the federal court of appeals for which he had been recommended; he was ultimately appointed, but not until 1924.

tion." Unless words incited to unlawful action, they could be published; if that was not the test, Hand could "see no escape from the conclusion" that under the Espionage Act "every political agitation" which could be shown "to be apt to create a seditious temper" was illegal. He was "confident" that Congress had had no such "revolutionary" purpose in mind. He acknowledged the government's right to protect itself; he believed, however, that the best defense was not suppression but "tolerance of all methods of political agitation which in normal times is a safeguard of free government." When he and Holmes met on the train that summer, Hand was still undoubtedly smarting from his reversal by the court of appeals.

Matters involving freedom of expression being perhaps on both judges' minds, it was only natural that they should venture into a discussion of it, even though Holmes had not yet read *Masses*. Hand and Holmes had known each other for several years. Hand was in the habit of calling on the Holmeses when he visited Washington, and Holmes "value[d] Hand's good opinion very highly," thought him "one who really counts." Nevertheless, the two men came at the freedom-of-expression issue from different intellectual positions: Hand the advocate of allowing the broadest interpretation of this "hard-bought acquisition in the fight for freedom"; Holmes the old soldier, who hoped he would die for it, but was disenchanted with freedom of speech as a theory. Reconstructing the main points of their conversation, it seems likely that Hand talked of unrestricted discussion as the route to truth, of criticism as essential to formulation of public policy, while Holmes talked of forcible suppression in the name of national safety, perhaps paraphrased what he had written in *The Common Law*:

> It seems clear that the *ultima ratio* . . . is force, and that at the bottom of all private relations, however tempered by sympathy and all the social feelings, is a justifiable self-preference. If a man is on a plank in the deep sea which will float only one, and a stranger lays hold of it, he will thrust him off if he can. When the state finds itself in a similar position, it does the same thing.

The superior force had won at Fair Oaks, and the superior force would win in the battle of ideas.

Hand was stunned and "gave up rather more easily" than he thought later he should have. Mulling over the conversation at home, Hand decided to continue it by mail and wrote Holmes a long letter whose meaning would come to haunt Holmes in the not-too-distant future:

You say that I strike at the sacred right to kill the other fellow when he disagrees. The horrible possibility silenced me when you said it. Now I say "not at all, kill him for the love of Christ and in the name of God, but always realize that he may be the saint and you the devil. Go your way with a strong right arm and a swift shining sword, in full consciousness that what you kill for, or what you may die for, some smart chap like Laski may write a book and prove it is all nonsense."

Patiently Hand explained his rationale, which seemed to coincide with Holmes's frequently expressed skepticism, but it was after all still wartime, and a thrice-wounded veteran of the Civil War who interpreted his soldier's duty in this current war as requiring him to put all the money he could spare into U.S. bonds was an unlikely champion of dissent.

Opinions [Hand wrote] are at best provisional hypotheses, incompletely tested. The more they are tested, after the tests are well scrutinized, the more assurance we may assume, but they are never absolutes. So we must be tolerant of opposite opinions or varying opinions by the very fact of our incredulity of our own.

It was Holmes's turn to be astonished. "Rarely," he told Hand, did a "letter hit me so exactly where I live as yours." He claimed to have no quarrel with his antagonist, yet countered that "free speech stands no differently than freedom from vaccination. The occasions would be rarer when you cared enough to stop it but if for any reason you did care enough you wouldn't care a damn for the suggestion that you were acting on a provisional hypothesis and might be wrong." As Holmes had said so often since the war, "man's destiny is to fight";

Therefore take thy place on the one side or the other, if with the added grace of knowing that the Enemy is as good a man as thou, so much the better, but kill him if thou Canst.

On arriving at Beverly Farms that summer and indulging in the usual "fortnight of emptiness and collapse that comes upon stopping work," Holmes had begun to trudge through volume two of the recently published *Science et Technique en Droit Positif Privé.* In it, François Gény, a French professor and legal philosopher whose dynamic vision of the law bore some similarities to Holmes's own, discussed prevalent concepts of natural law. Gény's philosophy combined empiricism with natural law in a complex and sometimes ambivalent fashion, and Holmes was inspired by his reading of Gény's work to write a brief—less than two thousand words—article, "Natural Law." In it, he deplored "the philosopher's effort to prove that truth is absolute and the jurist's search for criteria of universal validity which he collects under the head of natural law," but acknowledged that while tolerance of heresy in the abstract was all very well, as a practical matter, it was force that decided which truths survived and which did not. As he had told Hand, "deep-seated preferences can not be argued about . . . and therefore, when differences are sufficiently far reaching, we try to kill the other man rather than let him have his way." Holmes finished the article in August, then for relaxation fell into a study of Virgil that Johnny Morse had loaned him. On a visit to Laski, then vacationing in Rockport, Massachusetts, Holmes showed him a draft of "Natural Law"—in longhand. Laski wanted it for the *Harvard Law Review,* of which he was book editor at the time. Holmes took it home and copied it "in the attempt to secure legibility for a cold world in which chirography seems to be an almost forgotten art." He returned it to Laski, and it appeared in the *Harvard Law Review* in November.

That same November, the *New Republic* published an article on "Freedom of Speech." It had been written at the urging of Laski by Zechariah Chafee, Jr., a young Harvard Law School professor with impeccable Yankee credentials who had recently begun an independent study of the subject in connection with a course he was teaching on problems of injunctions against torts, including libels. What *was* this liberty of the press? he had asked himself, and had undertaken to find out. Ironically, this little article, along with others Chafee wrote on the same subject, was eventually to make Chafee himself one of the issues raised by the debates on freedom of expression and to jeopardize his academic standing at Harvard. Such was the temper of the times.

Chafee's contribution to the free speech debate, in which he quoted Hand's *Masses* opinion and which Holmes undoubtedly read when it appeared in mid-November—days after the Armistice ended World War I—argued the simple political wisdom of recognizing the worth of nearly absolute free expression, even in wartime. Short of causing "direct and dangerous interference with the conduct of the war," speech ought to be free, Chafee believed, to discover and disseminate information "on subjects of general concern." The national welfare demanded "that this just war be pushed to victory," but it also demanded that "an unjust war" be stopped. The only way to find out whether a war is just or unjust is "to let the people say so." Once force was "thrown into the argument," Chafee explained, it became "a matter of chance whether it is thrown on the false side or the true, and truth loses all its natural advantage in the contest." Furthermore, Chafee suggested, those sections of the Espionage Act that dealt with abridgment of speech might well be unconstitutional. If there was one thing which the First Amendment had been meant "by our ancestors to protect," he reminded people, "it was criticism of the existing form of government, the kind of criticism which George III's judges punished."

With Hand's and Chafee's reflections ringing in his ears, Holmes listened, on January 9 and 10, 1919, to the oral arguments in *Schenck* v. *United States,* which had reached the Court the previous spring along with *Baer* v. *United States.* The plaintiffs were in this together, and their cases were argued and decided in tandem.

As both antiwar propagandists and officials of the Socialist Party, Charles T. Schenck and Elizabeth Baer were doubly handicapped. Their crime was publication and distribution to draftees of some fifteen thousand leaflets urging opposition to military conscription, in the view of the Justice Department a clear violation of the Espionage Act. "A conscript is little better than a convict," their leaflet declared, then asked, "Are you one who is opposed to war, and were you misled by the venal capitalist newspapers, or intimidated or deceived by gang politicians and registrars into believing that you would not be allowed to register your objections to conscription? . . . In a democratic country each man must have the right to say whether he is willing to join the army. . . . Conscription laws belong to a bygone age. . . . Come to the headquarters of the Socialist Party . . . and sign a petition for the repeal of the Conscription Act. Help us wipe out this stain upon the Constitution!" Schenck and Baer were convicted under the act and sentenced to six months in jail. They took their cases to the U.S. Supreme Court. There their lawyers, supported by those few federal cases in which the First Amendment was upheld, based their arguments on Judge Hand's distinction between criticism, which he believed was protected by the First Amendment, and incitement to action, which he was sure was not. Schenck and Baer, their lawyers declared, were guilty only of the former.

All of a sudden the discussion Holmes had had with Hand the previous summer became more than a bull session. The issue in *Schenck* bore considerable resemblance to that in *Masses,* and now it was Holmes himself who was sitting in the seat of judgment. Privately, he didn't understand why the government had pressed its prosecution of Baer and Schenck. Had they started draft riots like those during the Civil War when Holmes was risking his life on the firing line, he might have had misgivings. But he thought it silly to make an example of these impotent little propagandists with their feeble fists raised in futile fury against a strong and healthy democratic society.

Holmes was also contemptuous of Socialism, but he hardly felt threatened by it, or by any of the other isms that some of his acquaintances believed were fouling the air in 1919. He thought Americans were "too far along for the chaos suggested by Russia and have too many small property owners for anything more socialistic than more stringent regulations of one sort or another—or state ownership of this or that." Holmes would not have made such an issue out of Schenck's and Baer's puny efforts, had *he* been running the Justice Department.

Now that the cases confronted him, however, what the law required would have to be decided, and he was faced with a serious dilemma which he may not have resolved immediately. Outwardly, he seems to have maintained his Olympian detachment and did not communicate to his regular correspondents the inner debate that could not but have disturbed him, as deep feelings on both sides vied for supremacy.

On a personal level, some of his oldest memories involved his own experiences as a youthful intellectual renegade. He could hardly have forgotten his warning to his fellow undergraduates not to avoid "books of an agitating tendency" or his defiance of the college administration's sly efforts to suppress the agitating tendencies of the *Harvard Magazine*. Scenes of 1861 Boston, when intolerance of abolition provoked him to join a "little band intended to see Wendell Phillips through if there was a row after the meeting of the Anti-Slavery Society," were never far from his field of vision. Although the possibility that someone might attempt to obstruct the raising of troops must have appalled the old soldier, he could not have forgotten that it was the copperheads of the Twentieth Massachusetts, fighting as vigorously and dying as courageously as the believers, who had taught him not only about patriotism but also about tolerance.

On an intellectual level, he might have remembered Emerson's "Whoso would be a man, must be a non-conformist" and the sage's willingness to risk the consequences of speaking out. He reread *On Liberty* by John Stuart Mill whom he had met and admired more than a half century before; now Mill's defense of " 'liberty of the press' as one of the securities against corrupt or tyrannical government"—a liberty Mill would restrain only when it became a "positive instigation to a mischievous act"—was not just an abstraction but held concrete implications for Holmes's own jurisprudence. Frankfurter, Laski, Lippmann—

Holmes had not yet met Chafee but he knew Chafee was thick with the others—all his high-spirited young friends with their civil libertarian talk and their soaring hopes for a democratic society had often moved if they had not always persuaded him.

Perhaps recalling his discussion with Hand, possibly even reviewing Hand's letter, Holmes at last read Hand's *Masses* opinion in February, the month after *Schenck* and *Baer* were argued. He admired the opinion's "force" and "admirable form"; he still would, however, he thought, after all was said and done, have "come to a different result"; he did not say what. Holmes's casual comments to Hand regarding the use of force to achieve goals represented more accurately his mature thinking, the way he had felt at least since he himself had carried a gun to silence his Confederate opponents. Truth, he had said then, "was the majority vote of that nation that could lick all others." Only a year or so ago he had exclaimed to Frankfurter that patriotism was no more than the "demand of the territorial club for priority, and as much priority as it needs for vital purposes, over such tribal groups as the churches and trade unions." Holmes went "whole hog for the territorial club," and he didn't "care a damn if it interferes with some of the spontaneities of the other groups." He thought the Puritans had been "quite right when they whipped the Quakers" and that war was the "ultimate rationality."

The same applied to individual rights, whether they involved free speech or free enterprise, antiwar propaganda or child labor. He had no patience with the extremists, whether they shouted for liberty of expression or liberty of contract. He scoffed at rights, hardly ever used the word except contemptuously. Society held the superior weaponry, and Holmes still believed, as he had written in *The Common Law*, that

> No society has ever admitted that it could not sacrifice individual welfare to its own existence. If conscripts are necessary for its army, it seizes them, and marches them, with bayonets in their rear, to death. It runs highways and railroads through old family places in spite of the owner's protest, paying in this instance the market value, to be sure, because no civilized government sacrifices the citizen more than it can help, but still sacrificing his will and his welfare to that of the rest.

Then there was Holmes's own judicial record to consider, which was hardly protective of free expression. The First Amendment did not apply to the states when Holmes was a Massachusetts judge, and although the Massachusetts constitution protected free speech in the Blackstone fashion, Holmes had avoided invoking it, deciding *McAuliffe*

v. *New Bedford* on the basis of employment regulations for public officials and *Commonwealth* v. *Davis* on the basis of the Boston Common's rules for its use. When in 1907 he had faced for the first time as a federal judge a freedom-of-expression issue in *Patterson* v. *Colorado,* a contempt-of-court case, he had left undecided whether the Fourteenth Amendment imposed the First Amendment on the states, then, surprisingly for a legal Darwinist, had chosen to ride the dinosaur in his stable and cited Blackstone's definition of free speech which he had learned forty years before at Harvard Law School. Ironically, this decision, written by the man who later became known for his protection of free speech, revived the broad authority of judges over contempt which had been limited by Congress three-quarters of a century before. Eight years later, writing for a unanimous Court in *Fox* v. *Washington,* he had upheld the constitutionality of a statute enacted by the Washington legislature that penalized publication of matter encouraging disrespect for the law. There is no evidence that he seriously considered the freedom-of-expression issue in any of these cases or that he thought of them as anything more than ordinary criminal cases. Had he not had that chance meeting with and subsequent communication from Judge Hand which had hit him "so exactly where [he] live[d]," Holmes might have tossed off the 1919 cases as glibly as he had their predecessors.

At some point during the two months following oral argument of *Schenck* v. *United States,* eight justices of the Supreme Court, most of whom saw an unacceptable potential for disorder in open criticism of public policy, decided to affirm Schenck's and Baer's convictions. Holmes made it unanimous. Chief Justice White assigned the opinion to Holmes. Holmes always said he had been chosen because the chief justice believed he, Holmes "would go farther probably than the majority in favor" of free speech. This is highly unlikely. White, whose conservatism in his later years was actually exceeded by his patriotism, was not looking for a champion of free speech. Holmes and White had sat together on the court for seventeen years; White was not only familiar with Holmes's record, but undoubtedly had heard him discuss his theories of individual rights in the conference room and could not but have been intimately acquainted with Holmes's rather negative views. It probably did not matter to White that Holmes had dissented in *Toledo Newspaper Co.,* the most recent case in which White had made clear his opposition to unrestrained freedom of the press, because Holmes in his dissent had skirted that issue and had concentrated on the question of judicial decorum. White probably did not know of Holmes's recent private interchanges with Judge Hand, and it is likely that Holmes's opinions in

Patterson and *Fox,* in which White had concurred, sprang to mind when the chief justice was looking for an author for *Schenck.*

Holmes himself had told Hand he was not in complete agreement. But there were other factors that affected the writing of the Court's opinion and may have contributed to Holmes's failure to take into consideration Hand's views. Given the temper of the times—Hand, after all, had been reversed—and the composition of the Supreme Court in 1919, Holmes may have gone as far as he dared if he was to maintain judicial unanimity, which was important in a potentially divisive case like *Schenck.* An author who had to please Louis Brandeis and James McReynolds sailed between Scylla and Charybdis in every paragraph. McReynolds loved Holmes's opinion and scribbled on the back of the first draft that was circulated: "Direct as you usually are and as strong as direct—concur." Brandeis joined the Court's opinion, but indicated later he might have been jostled by Holmes. "Admirably well put," noted the chief justice, obviously satisfied with his choice of author. "Yes, verily," said Day.

Holmes read the Court's decision on March 3, 1919. Mill was a major contributor, but the opinion was mostly Holmes, who once again had discovered a common-law formula to resolve a constitutional problem.

First he disposed of minor evidentiary issues the case had presented, then, with a meticulousness unusual for Holmes (old Harlan, on the other hand, would have written pages and pages of angry rhetoric; White would have presented a lengthy dissertation, remarkable for its convoluted reasoning; Brandeis would have gone back to the invention of language), he addressed the question of free expression the case raised. It was the first time he had grappled with it publicly.

Hand, Chafee, the old guvnor, and his bright young friends notwithstanding, Holmes had not yet reached Hand's conclusion that it was to society's advantage to tolerate political dissent, discussion, and criticism. The opinion Holmes wrote in *Schenck* moved forward, away from Blackstone's vague standards of "improper" and "mischievous" behavior as grounds for punishment, and set more specific standards, making it a little more difficult for government to indulge in the fishing expeditions which were popular at the time. Holmes stopped short of Hand, however.

The document which Schenck and Baer had distributed to the draftees, Holmes declared, could only have been intended to persuade young men to avoid conscription. He didn't say the pamphlet actually incited them to obstruct the draft—as Hand would have required to justify curtailing First Amendment rights. He said only that it had been *intended* to influence them to do so; that was enough for Holmes.

> If the act, (speaking, or circulating a paper,) its tendency and the intent with which it is done are the same, we perceive no ground for saying that success alone warrants making the act a crime.

In Holmes's view, as he later explained his reasoning, Schenck and Baer had performed the equivalent of holding a lighted match near a haystack; although, Holmes had said in *The Common Law*—he loved fire imagery, and back in Boston had been in the habit of chasing fire engines whenever the fire-bells rang—the match was blown out when the potential arsonist discovered he was being watched, his behavior had been considered a criminal attempt to burn the haystack. He had explained then:

> The reasoning for punishing any act generally must be to prevent some harm which is foreseen as likely to follow that act under the circumstances in which it is done.

He had followed this up two decades later, in 1901, when as chief justice of Massachusetts, he had written in *Commonwealth v. Peaslee* that a man could be convicted for a scheme, only half completed, to set fire to a building, even though at the last minute the potential arsonist had changed his mind. He recalled, too, his "favorite author's" similar reasoning in *Swift & Co. v. United States* when he brought down the beef trust, also using *Peaslee.*

Holmes admitted that in "many places and in ordinary times," Schenck and Baer would have been within their rights. But he reiterated what he had said in *The Common Law;* the

> character of every act depends upon the circumstances in which it is done.

The limitation on freedom of expression that followed protected it considerably better than Blackstone had:

> The most stringent protection of free speech would not protect a man in falsely shouting fire in a theatre and causing a panic. It does not even protect a man from an injunction against uttering words that may have all the effect of force. The question in every case is whether the words used are used in circumstances and are of such a nature as to create a clear and

present danger that they will bring about the substantive evils that Congress has a right to prevent. It is a question of proximity and degree.

This was just what Mill had said in *On Liberty*:

An opinion that corn-dealers are starvers of the poor . . . ought to be unmolested when simply circulated through the press, but may justly incur punishment when delivered orally to an excited mob assembled before the house of a corn-dealer, or when handed about among the same mob in the form of a placard.

Circumstances mattered to Mill and circumstances mattered to Holmes. War, for example, changed the rules. Although nearly half a century before Holmes had noted exceptions to Kent's rule that "all contracts with the enemy, made during war, are utterly void," in 1917, when a wartime emergency appeared to require it, Holmes had been quick, in *North German Lloyd* v. *Guaranty Trust Co. of New York,* to allow the contract between a steamship company and the bank which had hired it to deliver a cargo to enemy country to be nullified. Now, in the spring of 1919, he declared that "when a nation is at war many things that might be said in time of peace are such a hindrance to its effort that their utterance will not be endured so long as men fight and that no Court could regard them as protected by any constitutional right."

Holmes thus reaffirmed the state's right to protect itself and his view of force as the arbitrator. He seemed not even to wonder whether suppression or free discussion—points made by Mill, Hand, and Chafee—offered the best protection. *Schenck,* however, replaced Blackstone as the standard measurement of free expression, and the phrases "falsely shouting fire in a theatre" and "clear and present danger" became cultural as well as legal shibboleths, part of the American language.

Some years later, Chafee asked Holmes whether the definition of free speech the justice had enunciated in *Schenck* had been an original one or whether he had read it somewhere. Holmes replied that it was original—"not helped by any book that I know." He thought it probably had evolved out of something Chafee had said in the *New Republic*—perhaps that Blackstone's definition "ought to be knocked in the head once for all"—which had made him realize that his own dependence on Blackstone for his opinion in *Patterson* "surely was ignorant." After that, all he had to do was think back to *The Common Law, Peaslee,* and *Swift,* and review what he had said about the law of attempts. Then he had thought out the connections "unhelped."

A few days after he announced *Schenck* in court, Holmes celebrated his seventy-eighth birthday—"the foothills of 80" he called it—and made up a little limerick to commemorate it:

> I will sit in the seats of the mighty
> If I can until I am eighty (pronounce *ity*)
> And what I'll do then
> In the following ten
> I leave to the Lord God Almighty.

He felt fine, was working as well as ever, was even able to help former Senator Beveridge with his biography of John Marshall. He was a little concerned because the brethren "shake their heads and say you oughtn't to do it" when he ran to catch a trolley car. But Brandeis, who "for many years . . . [had] from time to time, at critical moments, said things" that had given Holmes "courage," once again responded to Holmes's doubts and said "some very comforting things" when Holmes confided to the younger man his "apprehensions whether [he] was doing right in holding on to [his] place."

A week after Holmes announced *Schenck,* on March 10, 1919, he delivered the Court's decisions in two more cases falling under the Espionage Act: *Frohwerk* v. *United States* and *Debs* v. *United States.* He "greatly regretted having to write them—and . . . that the Government pressed them to a hearing." He hoped the president would pardon the "poor fools," whom Holmes "should have been inclined to pass over if [he] could."

The first case involved one Jacob Frohwerk of Kansas City, who had published articles in the Missouri *Staats Zeitung* urging resistance to recruitment for the military; Frohwerk had been convicted and sentenced to ten years in prison. The second case involved a speech by the labor leader and frequent Socialist candidate for president Eugene V. Debs, who also had been convicted and sentenced to ten years' imprisonment for what the Justice Department and the federal trial court considered incitement to "insubordination, disloyalty, mutiny and refusal of duty in the military and naval forces of the United States. . . ." The speech in question, which Debs had given not to draftees, but at a Socialist convention in Canton, Ohio, the year before, while the war was still on, was less definable than Schenck's pamphlet or Frohwerk's articles, which pointed out it had been a "monumental and inexcusable mistake" to send American soldiers to France to fight a war "to protect some rich men's money." Frohwerk painted a dismal picture of a draftee's sufferings and asked, "who then . . . will pronounce a verdict of guilty upon him if he stops reasoning and follows the first impulse of nature: self-preservation. . . ." Debs's appeal was less direct. He talked of Socialism, its growth, and prophesied its ultimate success; he discussed the cases of several men and women who had been jailed for their opposition to the war, people he obviously considered martyrs in a worthy cause; and he talked of the war as a class war, declared by the "master class" and fought by the "subject class." His criticism of government policy was bitter, but pales beside the opposition to a war expressed, for example, during the Vietnam conflict. At his trial, Debs addressed the jury, and although, he contended, his speech at Canton did not warrant the charges against him, he said, "I have been accused of obstructing the war. I admit it. Gentlemen, I abhor war. I would oppose the war if I stood alone."

Finding Debs's behavior akin to falsely crying fire in a theater, the Supreme Court, via Holmes, affirmed his conviction,* along with Frohwerk's. Again the Court acted in concert, and again the justices applauded the author of the opinions.

"I agree and may he enjoy many days," McReynolds wrote on the back of his copy.

"Yes," said Van Devanter, "I think you have happily disposed of a bunch of unattractive cases."

"Right again," said Day.

All except Brandeis, to whom free expression was an important ethical end in itself. He joined the majority opinions, as he had joined the majority in *Schenck*, but he never was "quite happy" about his concurrence in any of them.

"I thought at the subject," he told Felix Frankfurter some years later, "not through it." The result reached by the majority disturbed him less than its justification. Holmes's "clear and present danger" test was too broad, he thought; had the Court invoked the war power—the extraordinary power of Congress to meet a national emergency—"then the scope of espionage legislation would be confined to war. But in peace the protection against restrictions of freedom of speech would be unabated. You might as well recognize that during a war—"

"All bets are off," Frankfurter interjected.

"Yes," Brandeis replied, "all bets are off. But we would have a clear

---

* Debs served two years of his ten-year sentence. In 1920, he ran on the Socialist ticket for president from his prison cell, receiving nearly 900,000 votes. In 1921, President Warren G. Harding commuted his sentence.

line to go on. I didn't know enough in the early cases to put it on that ground. Of course," he observed wryly, "you must also remember that when Holmes writes, he doesn't give a fellow a chance—he shoots so quickly—"

By late March, Judge Hand had read Holmes's opinions in *Schenck, Debs,* and *Frohwerk.* In his letter to Holmes, he promised that what he had to say was "positively" his "last appearance in the role of liberator." In what he called his "dying words," he restated what he had said in *Masses:* The Espionage Act prohibited only "positive impediments to raising an army," and responsibility for speech "only began when the words were directly an incitement." Holmes's "test of motive" might well be a "dangerous test" and "serve to intimidate . . . many a man who might moderate the storms of popular feeling."

Holmes could not for the life of him see where he and Hand differed and determinedly restated his own position in these cases. He claimed lack of time prevented him from reviewing *Masses;* he assumed, however, Hand agreed that "words may constitute an obstruction within the statute, even without proof that the obstruction was successful to the point of preventing recruiting." Holmes thought they were haggling over words and guessed they would just have to agree to disagree. He sent his "blessing" and promised not to hold Hand "bound by [his] adieu."

A few weeks later, Harold Laski called Holmes's attention to Ernst Freund's article in the latest *New Republic,* "The Debs Case and Freedom of Speech." Was Holmes influenced by Freund's analysis, Laski asked. Freund was a highly respected legal scholar and professor of law at the University of Chicago at the time; previously he had sent Holmes copies of his books, *The Police Power, Public Policy and Constitutional Rights* (1904) and *Principles of Legislation* (1916).

In his article for the *New Republic,* Freund was clearly outraged by Holmes's decision in *Debs.* In Freund's view, there had been no evidence to show that Debs had been responsible for "actual obstruction or an attempt to interfere with any of the processes of recruiting." Following the Court's decision in *Debs,* freedom of speech was compelled to rely on arbitrary judicial interpretation which itself was based on decisions made by juries that could only guess at "motive, tendency and possible effect" and that were vulnerable to the tides of majority opinion. Holmes, Freund thought, had set the nation "adrift in a sea of doubt and conjecture" at a time when the Court ought to have reestablished a national sense of what was and was not permitted under the First Amendment. A "wise government," of course, Freund suggested— the only place where his and Holmes's viewpoints converged, although

Holmes could not say so publicly—would have resisted pressures to punish opinion. "As in the case of all political persecution," Freund concluded, "the cause of government has gained nothing, while the forces of discontent have been strengthened. . . . Toleration of adverse opinion is not a matter of generosity, but of political prudence."

To answer Laski's query, Holmes sent him a letter he had written in strict confidence to Herbert Croly, editor of the *New Republic*. He had not mailed it because "some themes may become burning," and in fact still another case under the Espionage Act, *Abrams* v. *United States*, had been filed in the Court on March 12, only two days after Holmes had delivered the Court's opinion in *Debs*.

Holmes had wanted to tell Croly how much he objected to Freund's article. He resented Freund's description of juries as "guessing at motive, tendency and possible effect"; if Freund really believed that, he must object to "pretty much the whole body of the law." Other than to elaborate on this point, however, Holmes did not in his letter to Croly address Freund's major criticisms of *Debs* but rather concentrated on the conditions of wartime to justify his position. Holmes had wanted to emphasize to Croly that *Debs* had been decided by *Schenck*, and, as he had told some of his close friends, he had "hated to have to write the Debs case and still more those of the other poor devils before us the same day and the week before"; Holmes never had seen the "wisdom of pressing the cases, especially when the fighting was over," and he thought it "quite possible" he would have voted "for acquittal" had he served on the jury that had convicted Debs. In addition, he believed the sections of the Espionage Act at issue in these cases "not only were constitutional but were proper enough while the war was on." He continued:

> When people are putting out all their energies in battle I dont think it unreasonable to say we wont have obstacles intentionally put in the way of raising troops—by persuasion any more than force.

Chafee stood next in the line of sophisticated and intelligent critics of Holmes's recent opinions. He had expanded his *New Republic* article into a long and detailed piece, "Freedom of Speech in War Time," for the June 1919 *Harvard Law Review*. In it, he examined the major events and documents that had led to the writing of the freedom-of-speech clause in the federal Constitution and explained the issues and interests involved in the past as well as in 1919. He concluded that "one of the most important purposes of society and government is the discovery and spread of truth on subjects of general concern." There were, however, other purposes of government, such as "order, the training of the young, protection against external aggression. Unlimited discussion sometimes interferes with these purposes, which then must be balanced against freedom of speech, but freedom of speech ought to weigh very heavily in the scale." He had hoped that Holmes, when confronted with the recent cases under the Espionage Act, "would concentrate his great abilities on fixing the line" between these two interests. Holmes, however, had turned in a disappointing performance, and had told those who had anxiously awaited his decisions that "certain plainly unlawful utterances are, to be sure, unlawful." It was "regrettable," in addition, that Holmes "did nothing to emphasize the social interest behind free speech, and show the need of balancing even in wartime."

Laski gave Holmes a copy of Chafee's article, then invited both men to tea. Chafee and Holmes discussed it, but Chafee found Holmes unreconstructed—committed to allowing Congress "a very wide latitude" in carrying on the war.

The subtle and even the not-so-subtle distinctions between Blackstone's and Holmes's definitions of free expression, and the implications of the scholarly discussions, escaped most ordinary Americans who saw only the convictions, particularly Debs's. The decision in Debs's case, Holmes discovered, seemed "to have let loose every damned fool in the country." He received a lot of "stupid letters of protest" from "fools, knaves, and ignorant persons" who insisted Debs had been convicted because he "was a dangerous agitator and that obstructing the draft was a pretence."

Not all the criticism of Holmes was so genteel. About six weeks after the Court handed down *Debs,* opposition assumed a more concrete form. Holmes, and Attorney General A. Mitchell Palmer, who had succeeded Gregory, Postmaster Burleson, and others, were mailed bombs; a bomb actually exploded on the front doorstep of Palmer's home. The one meant for Holmes was discovered at the post office in New York and defused. Nevertheless, police guards were posted for a time at 1720 I Street. Holmes claimed to be unconcerned and tried to reassure Fanny: if he "worried over all the bullets that [had] missed [him he] should have a job."

In the meantime, he was anxiously watching developments at Harvard, where his two close friends, Felix Frankfurter and Harold Laski, along with Dean Roscoe Pound of Harvard Law School, were personally experiencing the side effects of the Red Menace hysteria. At the university, it took the form of a "general crusade against all things liberal."

Tory Boston—much of it alumni who remained influential in Harvard's affairs—feared labor unrest the way white Southerners once had feared slave uprisings. Any threat to property tended to bring the New Englanders together, and organized labor was perceived as the single biggest threat to the community's well-being. A quarter century before, Holmes had felt the local establishment's hostility when he had dared to uphold labor's legal rights; now, a generation later, his young friends were feeling it.

Frankfurter, as a member of the president's Mediation Commission during the recent war, had investigated labor conditions in the oil fields, lumber mills, and copper mines of the West and in his official report had recommended that negotiation and arbitration replace strike and lockout in industrial disputes. The very fact that he recognized the legitimacy of organized labor as a participant in industrial affairs branded him, on his return to the Harvard Law School faculty, a dangerous radical in Boston and unleashed a campaign to "push [him] out of the school." The pressures were not explicit, Holmes was told; Frankfurter would merely be made to feel uncomfortable until he left of his own accord. Laski was still not the Socialist he later became, but he was, like Frankfurter, Jewish; Holmes thought that might be behind the drive to oust both men. He was also a foreigner. In Boston, the combination was fatal. His defense of the Boston police strike during the summer of 1919 only served to alienate him further from the ruling class. Pound had made the indefensible mistake of publicly supporting Brandeis's nomination to the Supreme Court, when most of patrician Boston, including the Harvard president, Abbott Lawrence Lowell, bitterly opposed it. Bostonians had long memories for heresy. When Pound's newfangled teaching method—sociological jurisprudence it was called, easily confused with Socialism by politically sensitive members of the local establishment—was added to his sins, Pound's enemies howled for his blood.

Considerable pressure was put on the university president to get rid of this trio of agitators—it was suggested that Frankfurter be deported—rumors of which reached Holmes in Washington. He was "full of helpless anxiety." He brooded. He fretted. The law school would "lose its soul" if Pound and Frankfurter left. He had heard that Pound's presence had prevented contributions to the school; he found it hard to believe that the "spark of inspiration" was not "worth more than dollars."

"By Jove," he would say just that to Lowell. He was, after all, still president of the law school alumni association, a figurehead to be sure, but his opinions ought nevertheless to carry some weight. He was reluctant to use his position in that way, uncertain what he ought to do. *Should* he write Lowell? he asked Brandeis, whom Pound had kept informed about the deteriorating situation at Harvard. Brandeis rather thought he should.

Holmes did write Lowell. He tried to mention his presidency of the alumni association in a way that did not seem as if he were throwing his weight around. But he minced no words and told Lowell plainly that Frankfurter and Pound "have and impart the ferment which is more valuable than an endowment and makes of a Law School a focus of life." Pound, in addition, was "one of the very few men whose work on legal subjects is referred to by Continental writers." Far from being driven out, he ought to be given an LL.D.

Lowell's reply has been lost. But Holmes need not have worried. Lowell himself had the highest standards of academic freedom and had indicated in a recent annual report his wholehearted commitment to "personal liberty from constraint" for his professors. Despite his own wholehearted disapproval of their convictions, he kept Frankfurter, Laski, and Pound on the Harvard faculty.

It had been a sobering spring for Holmes. These men were not poor, powerless pacifists of the sort whose cases were coming before the Supreme Court. These men were respected intellectuals, Harvard faculty members, Holmes's friends. The cost of suppressing free speech was beginning to take on a personal meaning Holmes might not have anticipated when he had discussed it philosophically with Judge Hand that day on the train.

Holmes's concern with matters of free expression, while consuming intellectually and emotionally, could not be allowed to absorb him entirely. Other questions continued to confront the Court in the usual rapid-fire succession, the most significant of which in the late spring of 1919 were the *Arizona Employers' Liability Cases*. These were a group of five cases through which several Arizona copper companies were challenging the constitutionality under the Fourteenth Amendment of an Arizona statute that made employers financially liable for the injury or death of employees in hazardous occupations and gave these victims the option of taking their cases to court—betting that a jury would award them more in damages than the prescribed workmen's compensation scale would. As a Massachusetts judge, Holmes had been bound by the common law's requirement that it was employees who assumed the risks of their occupations, and he had written in that vein in a number of industrial accident cases then. Now, two decades later, states were discarding old formulas and coming to terms with the realities of modern life. Arizona's law shifted the burden of risk from the employee to the employer.

Carefully deciding the cases on the narrowest grounds, the Court in recent years had upheld several state statutes altering old common-law relationships between labor and capital, including workmen's compensation schemes. Largely due to Holmes's impetuosity, the Court was so badly splintered in the *Arizona Employers' Liability Cases* that it nearly undid what it had done to date.

The cases had been argued back in January 1918. At the conference afterwards, a majority apparently decided to uphold the law as compatible with protection of the public interest under the state's police power— better to recompense the injured workman or the deceased's relatives, who probably had not saved against a rainy day, thus preventing "pauperism, with its concomitants of vice and crime," than to force the public to support them. Chief Justice White assigned the opinion to Holmes.

As he had in *Noble State Bank* v. *Haskell* back in 1911, Holmes opened a Pandora's box of possibilities for the future for which his brethren were not prepared. He failed, first, to include the usual disclaimers regarding the wisdom of the law in question. Although he privately believed that "any rearrangement of property, while any part of the world propagates freely, will prevent civilization from killing its weaker members" was "absurd," there hangs about his opinion in the *Arizona Employers' Liability Cases* an unusual air of approval of the state's behavior, as if he might have enjoyed writing it, or as if it fit into his scheme of the way things ought to be. He no doubt rather liked the principle of self-interest in the thought that there was

> no more certain way of securing attention to the safety of the men, an unquestionably constitutional object of legislation, than by holding the employer liable for accidents . . . they probably will happen a good deal less often when the employer knows that he must answer for them if they do.

It seemed eminently fair to him that in the commercial jungle

> If a business is unsuccessful it means that the public does not care enough for it to make it pay. If it is successful the public pays its expenses and something more. It is reasonable that the public should pay the whole cost of producing what it wants and a part of that cost is the pain and mutilation incident to production. By throwing that loss upon the employer in the first instance we throw it upon the public in the long run and that is just.

He concentrated on the principles involved in the shift of responsibility from employee to employer, which he found unbarred by the Constitution. But his generalities did not distinguish between hazardous and nonhazardous occupations, and when he circulated his draft opinion, it looked like a mine field to some of the brethren—even Brandeis considered dissenting and prepared an opinion, although he never published it.

Pitney, for one, thought the implications that the law might be reconstructed to include other occupations were "dangerous." It may have been at this point that the chief justice deserted the majority and joined McKenna in dissent, leaving Holmes the senior justice in the majority. Day, too, was wavering. A majority seemed to want the Court to continue on the mildly progressive road it was at the time traveling, but Holmes's opinion went too far. The cases were held over for the next term.

In the interests of harmony, Holmes suggested that Pitney, who could be relied on to confine the labor-sensitive Court's decision to the facts of the specific Arizona cases and would not erect signposts to the future, write the Court's opinion. Brandeis said later that had it not been for Pitney, "we would have had no workmen's compensation laws." Even Pitney's restraint, however, could not hold the Court together. When the decision was announced on June 9, he was joined only by Day and Holmes. Holmes's former Court opinion was also published as a concurrence, which Brandeis and Clarke joined. McKenna's dissent was joined not only by White but also by Van Devanter and McReynolds. McReynolds wrote a dissent of his own.

It may have been Holmes's opinion in the *Arizona Employers' Liability Cases* that inspired Brandeis to suggest Holmes spend the summer acquiring a sense of industrial operations.

"You talk about improving your mind," Brandeis had said, but "you only exercise it on the subjects with which you are familiar. Why don't you try something new, study some domain of fact. Take up the textile industries in Massachusetts and after reading the reports sufficiently you can go to Lawrence and get a human notion of how it really is."

Although he did not doubt "it would be good for [his] immortal soul to plunge into them, good also for the performance of [his] duties," Holmes hated facts. He much preferred to "meditate on the initial push and the following spin." He protested to Brandeis that he was "too old" to do all the younger man asked.

Brandeis replied that Holmes was indeed "too old to acquire knowledge in many fields of fact but not too old to realize through one field what the world of fact was and to be more conscious and understanding of it."

Brandeis's little summer school never materialized, however. Fanny had another "pull down" just about the time they reached Beverly Farms and had to be hospitalized. Her formerly full features became gaunt and drawn. Her recovery was slow, and she was still weak and easily tired on the eve of their return to Washington. They stayed at the Shoreham Hotel while the servants made the house on I Street comfortable. Even after her return, she spent most of her time in her room, to which only a few of her most intimate friends penetrated. Sometimes, when weather permitted, she drove with Wendell to the Court, then returned to I Street alone. Reporting "apologetically" to Brandeis in the fall, Holmes told his would-be mentor that Fanny had occupied too much of his mind for the suggested study program to be the "new interest and . . . relaxation" that Brandeis had hoped for.

Holmes had his priorities, however, and his concern for Fanny did not prevent his fretting over the issues surrounding free speech which were to be argued again before the Court shortly after it reconvened in October. Sandwiched between the escape books he consumed during that period—Scott's *The Talisman,* Robert Louis Stevenson's *An Inland Voyage,* essays by Charles Lamb, and others of that ilk—he was consuming at the usual quick-step significant works on government and history which included commentaries on freedoms of various shapes. Several he read at the instigation of Laski, who had gently and deferentially suggested that in *Schenck,* Holmes might have drawn the line "a little tighter about executive discretion" and who now plied him with both books and recommendations for reading.

Laski had dedicated his latest work, *Authority in the Modern State,* to Holmes and Frankfurter, the "two youngest" of his friends, and had made certain a copy got to Holmes in time for his seventy-eighth birthday. "[S]urprised and moved" by Laski's gesture, Holmes could hardly wait until he should have time to read it, and when he did, nearly swallowed it whole. He had difficulty digesting Laski's socialistic premises and found his friend somewhat more optimistic than he himself was, but rejoiced that both he and Laski were "ideasts rather than thingsters." He did not comment on Laski's observation that

> We . . . insist . . . that the mind of each man . . . pass judgment upon the state; and we ask for his condemnation of its policy where he feels it in conflict with the right.
> That, surely, is the only environment in which the plant of liberty can

flourish. It implies, from the very nature of things, insistence that the allegiance of man to the state is secondary to his allegiance to what he may conceive his duty to society as a whole. . . . The discovery of right is, on all fundamental questions, a search, upon which the separate members of the state must individually engage.

Not long afterwards, Laski recommended F. S. Marvin's A *Century of Hope,* and Holmes sent for it. The author did not deal specifically with political freedoms, but it is clear that without the uninhibited clashes of ideas by which he measured the nineteenth century, the social progress that gave Marvin his high hope for civilization's future could not have been made. Holmes found the book uplifting, though he could not "follow it with entire belief." Laski had recently read G. P. Gooch's *English Democratic Ideas in the Seventeenth Century,* and Holmes, perhaps seeking illumination of contemporary freedoms in their early stages of development, followed suit. Before Holmes returned to Washington that fall, Laski sent him E. S. P. Haynes's *The Decline of Liberty in England,* in which the author expressed his fears that wartime tendencies toward suppression of civil liberties might continue after the necessity for them disappeared. Haynes's book, which demonstrated the ease with which freedom of discussion and others could be curtailed, elicited from Holmes a comment indicating he might be revising his own view of the matter:

The whole collectivist tendency seems to be toward underrating or forgetting the safeguards in bills of rights that had to be fought for in their day and that are still worth fighting for.

CHAPTER 25

"Free Trade in Ideas"

THE FOURTH—AND crucial in terms of Holmes's jurispru-
dence—case involving freedom of expression in wartime, *Abrams* v. *United
States,* was argued in the Supreme Court on October 21 and 22, 1919.
Holmes hoped it was the "last, or nearly the last, of the Espionage Act
cases." It seemed to him now that not only the government prosecutors
but also "some of our subordinate Judges . . . have been hysterical
during the war."

Abrams was Jacob Abrams's final challenge of the government's case
against him. With four others, he had been convicted under the Espionage Act of unlawfully inciting and encouraging resistance to American war policies. All five were Russian-born, self-confessed "Rebels,"
"revolutionaries," and "anarchists." In August 1918, they had published
and distributed—by throwing them out of an open factory window on
the Upper East Side of Manhattan—several thousand inflammatory circulars critical of the president personally as well as of his conduct of
the war, particularly his sending American troops to Vladivostok, which
Abrams and his friends interpreted as an overt threat to the Russian
Revolution. Although there was no evidence that their propaganda had
persuaded a single person to abandon his factory bench or that the leaflets had reached a single munitions worker, Abrams had been tried,
convicted, and sentenced to twenty years in prison. Two of his co-con-
spirators received the same sentence, one received fifteen years, and the
last, three. Had they actually shut down every munitions factory in
America, their sentences would have been the same. Even Holmes came
to believe such a heavy penalty indicated that Abrams and his colleagues

were being "made to suffer not for what the indictment alleges but for the creed that they avow."

Relying primarily on their previous decisions in *Schenck* and *Debs,* seven justices of the Supreme Court voted to affirm the convictions. Holmes, however, was not available to write the majority opinion this time; he was planning to dissent. The contentions of critics he respected combined with the provocative books he had read during the past few months and possibly with the gentle persuasions of Brandeis as they strolled home together after court adjourned for the day—a convincing combination unusual in Holmes's judicial experience—undoubtedly had contributed to Holmes's deepening appreciation for the meaning of the First Amendment. He came to *Abrams* in a more thoughtful mood than that with which he had approached *Schenck* and *Debs,* when he had shot too quickly, at least for Brandeis's peace of mind.

Less than a week after he listened to the arguments in *Abrams,* Holmes hinted to Laski that perhaps the young man's efforts had not been futile. He seemed to be taking another step away from Blackstone, although he had not abandoned his old formula of force as a dominant factor in human affairs:

> I fear we have less freedom of speech here than they have in England. Little as I believe in it as a theory I hope I would die for it and I go as far as anyone whom I regard as competent to form an opinion, in favor of it. Of course when I say I don't believe in it as a theory I don't mean that I do believe in the opposite as a theory. But on their premises it seems to be logical in the Catholic Church to kill heretics and the Puritans to whip Quakers. . . . When you are thoroughly convinced that you are right— wholeheartedly desire an end—and have no doubt of your power to accomplish it—I see nothing but municipal regulations to interfere with your using your power to accomplish it.

It occurred to Holmes that at conference he might "be persuaded to shut up," although he didn't "expect it." Surely he never expected the sort of pressure that was applied. In an unusual attempt to stifle Holmes's dissent, three of the justices—Van Devanter, Pitney, and one other whose name could not be recalled—with no less influential a figure than Fanny Holmes in tow, called on him together. Appealing to his sense of an old soldier's duty to close ranks against the common enemy, they urged him not to lend his prestige to common subversives. Holmes had stationed his secretary—Stanley Morrison that year—within discreet eavesdropping distance, and the young man reported that the conversation remained friendly at all times. Holmes, however, was unmoved.

Not for nothing was he the grandson of Abiel and son of the first Oliver Wendell Holmes. It would have been appropriate for the third-generation dissenter to recall at this point Dr. Holmes's warning that

> fear of open discussion implies feebleness of inward conviction and great sensitiveness to the expression of individual opinion is a mark of weakness.

Though he may have recalled the doctor's warning privately, he apparently did not offer it to his callers. He simply said he regretted he could not do as they wished. They did not press, and he retired to his library to write one of the most memorable pieces of libertarian prose in American constitutional history. Brandeis could not allow his friend to die so soon for his newly developed ideas regarding free speech, and he joined Holmes's dissent "heartily" and "gratefully."

Abandoned by Holmes, Chief Justice White chose his second-best justice in terms of credibility to write *Abrams* for the Court. John H. Clarke was a strong and recognized liberal; in a recent discussion with friends, however, he had alluded to Reds as "murderous." No doubt in White's view, Clarke could be relied on not only to garner what little liberal support there might be for the Court's decision, but also to write a strong opinion affirming the radicals' convictions. White was not disappointed.

Abrams was announced on November 10, 1919, coincidentally the same day hearings began in several American cities in cases involving the deportation of so-called radicals rounded up a few days before during the first of Attorney General Palmer's "Red Raids"—Palmer's revenge for the bomb scares of the previous spring. Clarke quoted extensively from the pamphlets in question, which probably gave them more circulation than had their original distribution through the factory window, and he concluded that "the language of those circulars was obviously intended to provoke and to encourage resistance to the United States in the prosecution of the war."

Holmes could not go along with the majority. In his dissent he made light of the exhortations in the circulars, even made the authors sound a little silly. "Poor and puny anonymities," he called them.

As he had had to write *Debs*, he thought it now in *Abrams* his "duty" and his "right" to explain what he "thought the limits were to the doctrine that condemned him and some others." Without saying so explicitly, Holmes explained in some detail his previous reference to "falsely shouting fire in a theatre and causing a panic," and rehashed the way the law satisfied standards of civil and criminal liability when intent was involved. He retraced the trail he had laid through the law of attempts in *Schenck,* and he concluded that *Schenck, Frohwerk,* and *Debs,* which had been based on these principles, had been "rightly decided." He did not doubt "for a moment" that the United States was authorized to "punish speech that produces or is intended to produce a clear and imminent danger that it will bring about forthwith certain substantive evils that the United States constitutionally may seek to prevent."

This doctrine, however, had its limits—those imposed by the First Amendment—and here Holmes proceeded to condense those eight months of what appears to have been substantial inner turmoil—which he could not describe publicly—into a statement of free expression which had not been evident in his previous writings in the Espionage cases, but which approached considerably nearer to the principles endorsed by Hand, Freund, Chafee, and Mill, even the old guvnor. In *Schenck,* Holmes had stressed what the First Amendment did not protect; using almost the same words in *Abrams,* he stressed what it *did* protect. And in conclusion, the unlikely combination of intellectual Darwinism, Holmes's own aversion to dogma, and his impulse to settle matters by combat came together. Two decades before, he had described in one of his addresses "the struggle for life among competing ideas, and of the ultimate victory and survival of the strongest." Two decades before, the phenomenon was a simple fact of life. Holmes obviously had not thought about positive political or social value, as had been pointed out to him since. He still did not attach any moral meaning to it; there was no nonsense about individual rights. In line with his longest-held concepts of law, his reasoning was objective, rooted in history and extrapolated from experience. His critics would see that he had listened attentively to all but adopted none. As his pen scratched across the page, he set down one of the afterwards most-quoted justifications for freedom of expression in the English-speaking world:

> [W]hen men have realized that time has upset many fighting faiths, they may come to believe even more than they believe the very foundations of their own conduct that the ultimate good desired is better reached by free trade in ideas—that the best test of truth is the power of the thought to get itself accepted in the competition of the market, and that truth is the only ground upon which their wishes safely can be carried out. That at any rate is the theory of our Constitution. It is an experiment, as all life is an experiment. Every year if not every day we have to wager our salvation

upon some prophecy based upon imperfect knowledge. While that experiment is part of our system I think that we should be eternally vigilant against attempts to check the expression of opinions that we loathe and believe to be fraught with death, unless they so imminently threaten immediate interference with the lawful and pressing purpose of the law that an immediate check is required to save the country. I wholly disagree . . . that the First Amendment left the common law as to seditious libel in force. History seems to me against the notion.

Judge Hand was "greatly pleased . . . especially with the close." He thought Holmes's views must in the end "prevail, after people get over the existing hysteria." He was a little disappointed that Holmes had not backed off his "clear and present danger" standard, but it was a good deal of comfort for Hand to discover himself "not in a judicial minority of one." Laski found *Abrams* a "fine and moving document" for which he was "deeply and happily grateful."

"Respectable citizens" of Boston "cursed out" their strayed lamb. Chafee, however, who ranked Holmes's *Abrams* dissent with the writings of Mill, Thomas Erskine, and John Milton, invited him to speak at a meeting of the Harvard Liberal Club. Holmes was unable to attend, but he sent on a letter which was read to the assembled group:

For obvious reasons I should not care to speak upon your subject, except as from time to time I have to. I see no impropriety, however, in suggesting the isolated reflection that with effervescing opinions, as with the not yet forgotten champagnes, the quickest way to get them flat is to let them get exposed to the air.

NOT EVERYONE HAD forgotten the taste of champagne. Even before the Eighteenth Amendment went into effect, Washingtonians were motoring to Baltimore to buy bootleg liquor, loading their automobiles "with barrels and boxes of stuff, enough to last an ordinary man a life time." Holmes had had the foresight to "lay in a good cellar" of slow-maturing wines which he could enjoy legally during the long ban on the sale of liquor.

The Eighteenth Amendment was scheduled to go into effect in January 1920. Speed was of the essence when *Hamilton* v. *Kentucky Distilleries Co.,* challenging the constitutionality of the War-Time Prohibition Act, a temporary measure, was argued in the Supreme Court on November 20, 1919, lest it be mooted by the Eighteenth Amendment. Even more important was unanimity in a matter that many Americans ranked in importance with free speech. But the Court was badly splintered. Early indications were that five justices, including Holmes, whose distaste for Prohibition was matched only by his distaste for the precedents on which validation of the War-Time Prohibition Act would be based, wanted to strike down the act, and four intended to uphold it. Chief Justice White, along with Brandeis, whose alliance with Holmes was beginning to solidify, were in the minority. Holmes, however, was believed to be shaky. Then White and Holmes met on the street one day and Holmes confessed his doubts. He wouldn't mind, he told the chief justice, seeing a draft "written the other way to see how it would go." White, realizing his majority was about to materialize, lost no time getting to Brandeis. He suggested Brandeis write the opinion because he, White, thought Brandeis "could get Holmes more easily." Brandeis did "get Holmes," and McReynolds and Pitney as well. In the end the desired unanimity was achieved, and the constitutionality of the War-Time Prohibition Act was upheld.

The increasingly frequent agreement between Holmes and Brandeis made some of Holmes's friends back home in Boston uneasy. Nina Gray, John's widow, said it for the whole Boston establishment: "If only you stay thoroughly Anglo-Saxon." Holmes in his reply demonstrated just how thoroughly Anglo-Saxon he could be. "I take the inference to be," he told her, "that I am under the influence of the Hebs." He denied it. He had, after all, been deciding cases for thirty-five years before Brandeis came to the Supreme Court. "I am confident," he continued, eager to establish his intellectual independence in her—and Boston's—eyes, "that I am under no influence except that of thoughts and insights. Sometimes my brother B. seems to me to see deeper than some of the others—and we often agree." Holmes could recall, however, only a single case in which Brandeis's argument "convinced me contrary to my first impressions." In two or three other cases Brandeis had "perhaps turned the scale on the question whether I should write—but in each of those I was and am glad that I did." Regarding the cases his correspondent cited, Holmes declared emphatically that he had reached his conclusions independently.

"I don't suppose," he concluded, knowing the long memories of Bostonians for sinners and their sins, "that I shall change your prepossessions by what I say, but I am confident that you need not be uneasy on that score."

Holmes's disclaimers to Mrs. Gray notwithstanding, he frequently confided his judicial kinship to Laski, who knew and liked Brandeis and was apt to show more understanding:

> I have sent round an opinion in which I take three pages to say what should be said in a sentence, but which Brandeis thought ought to be put in solemn form because of its importance.

> On that day came down an opinion that stirred the innards of Brandeis and me and he spurred me to write a dissent.

> Brandeis . . . made me put in a passage explaining a decision of Harlan's . . . that rather impeded the course of what I thought necessary but I didn't care very much.

> Brandeis who was the other way said he'd agree if I'd cut off its tail.

> I did not dissent from Brandeis in a case when I thought of it—and he came in with me in one of mine when at first he was the other way.

> [A] dissent that the ever active Brandeis put upon my conscience awaits.

> I am catspawed by Brandeis to do another dissent on burning themes.

A few years after Mrs. Gray had reminded Holmes of his origins, the accord between Holmes and Brandeis had become so noticeable that Holmes himself remarked regarding a case in which their conclusions did not correspond: "Brandeis and I are so apt to agree that I was glad to have him dissent in my case, as it shows that there is no preestablished harmony."

Their relationship was anomalous. Holmes the New England patrician, descendant of the earliest American settlers, reared in the traditions of a *Mayflower* aristocracy; Brandeis the son of recent immigrants—refugees from the continental revolutions of 1848—reared in the traditions of nineteenth-century European liberalism. Holmes the dispassionate scholar, isolated in his thought, the skeptical philosopher, his only faith that of the soldier in superior force, contemptuous of "come-outers"; Brandeis the moral man and passionate advocate, the reformer, full of faith in the perfectibility of human society. When Holmes supported a legislative enactment, he was leaving the cosmos alone to work itself out—the measure was not unconstitutional; when Brandeis upheld the same statute, it was desirable and expedient. Holmes the objective man suspected his friend of "letting partisanship disturb his judicial attitude" and of having "hobbies that sometimes deflect his judgment a little." Generally, Holmes agreed with Brandeis that social experiments ought to be tried, but Holmes was less enthusiastic; he saw it as robbing Peter to pay Paul.

Holmes the intuitive, Brandeis the rational. Holmes the thinker, politically innocent; Brandeis the practitioner, unafraid of getting his hands dirty. Holmes talking of battle in the abstract, Brandeis flailing away in the middle of it. Holmes the stylist, elegant and literary, Brandeis the technician, portrayer of naked social and economic realities. Holmes the detached observer, Brandeis burning with moral righteousness.

Holmes, who avoided "loading up the wagon" with factual knowledge, was often baffled by the background complexities of cases that came before the Court and confessed he sometimes wanted only "to sit down and cry or tell them to ask Brandeis." The way, Holmes said, in which "that cuss is loaded with facts on all manner of subjects leaves me gawping." Nevertheless, Holmes continued to resist Brandeis when the latter "bullie[d]" him to put away his philosophy books—he had "improved his mind that way as far as it can go"—and learn the economic facts of life. Holmes clung steadfastly to the principle of wanting to know "as little about a case as I can safely go on."

Interestingly enough, it was Brandeis the judicial technician, consistent in his thinking, meticulous in his prose, who became a legend among the members of the legal profession, and it was Holmes the philosophical and literary, his meaning and method not always clearly set down, who became the popular legend.

Still they found common ground. The man from the *Mayflower* aristocracy was not its typical product—he left that role to Johnny Morse and his friends. Intellectually—though not always socially—Holmes was as much of a loner, and an outlander, as Brandeis. They shared an independence of thought that tended to alienate them from both the Boston establishment and their old-school brethren on the Court.

Most important perhaps was their common concept of constitutional law as fluid, experimental, *alive,* the document itself not a straitjacket but a garment that must fit each succeeding generation, must respond to the "felt necessities of the time." Unlike most of their brethren, who were holding fast against upheaval and disorder in American society, Holmes and Brandeis were not afraid of change. Holmes, though, saw it as inevitable, the product of evolutionary forces; Brandeis saw it as desirable, something men might effectuate and governments advance. It is entirely conceivable that the immutability and dogmatism of the Court majorities with whom they sat served to push Holmes closer to Brandeis and so accounted for the gradually increasing frequency of their accord, which reached its peak during the latter part of the 1920s.

Their reputations as dissenters has been exaggerated. In fact they concurred with the majority more often than not. Their dissents were, however, important both for what they said and for what they prophesied. Holmes and Brandeis wrote at a critical juncture in constitutional history—at the point where nineteenth-century laissez-faire had some of its most violent clashes with twentieth-century tendencies toward collectivism. Together they raised their voices in protest against the judicial arrogance that had allowed the Court for nearly three-quarters of a century largely to ignore the explosive social and economic forces that were changing the American persona and to cling to constitutional shibboleths no longer invested with the power to deal with contemporary reality. As such, these two justices heralded the Court of the 1930s when, confronted with the threat of dilution of its power, the "Nine Old Men" humbled themselves, changed their ways, and so refrained from institutional suicide.

FELIX FRANKFURTER GAVE Holmes some uncomfortable moments that fall of 1919. Presiding over an Armistice Day meeting at Faneuil Hall in Boston, he urged a "sensible policy as to Russia," anathema to Tory Boston, at the time enduring the ominous presence of large numbers of "radical" laborers in its industrial suburbs. Frankfurter had been reluctant to chair the assembly and had asked the organizers to find "some leader with a good Back Bay name"; in the present "ferment," they should "avoid having a Jew of alien origin preside at a meeting concerned with Russia." When none came forth, Frankfurter succumbed to their persuasions. He carefully talked along lines a certain few statesmen had already talked: Russia ought to be allowed to solve its own problems; the rest of the world ought to stay out of the Revolution; it was patience and help, not military and political interference, that would aid Russia in convalescence. As Frankfurter had feared, his speech plunged him into another quarrel with the Tories at Harvard. Holmes fretted—not for the last time—wondered if this time his young friend might not have overdone his enthusiasms: "Of course," Holmes believed in "academic freedom." Hadn't he written Lowell on the subject, defended Frankfurter's position only a few months before?

[O]n the other hand it is to be remembered that a professor's conduct may affect the good will of the institution to which he belongs. It may turn aside gifts that otherwise would have come to it, or students that it would like to have. I don't think a man would do his whole duty if he merely indulged his spontaneity—even in a case where he had opinions that required courage to state and that he thought it desirable to make known. He must weigh the harm that he may do to his employer while he takes his employer's pay. Suppose for instance that you knew that if while a professor you presided over the meeting you would cause a rich old bird to knock out a legacy of a million to this college. I don't think you would have a right to do it. I think it would be a question between resignation and silence.

Holmes didn't presume to judge the participants in the argument—he didn't know all the particulars, but he hoped Frankfurter was "too level headed to be looking for martyrdom." The spat between Frankfurter and the university was not fatal, and Frankfurter was not fired, although his appointment to an endowed chair was delayed. Holmes's gentle warning had no visible effect on the little professor, who hardly broke his pace.

Frankfurter did, however, give Holmes some joyous as well as uncomfortable moments. He announced his engagement that fall to Marion Denman of Springfield, Massachusetts. He had brought her to call on the Holmeses previously; Holmes had liked her at sight and always thereafter referred to her as Luina because she looked like one of Luini's portraits. When Frankfurter bubbled his good news to Holmes, the justice could hardly wait to tell Fanny.

"Dickie!" he shouted, joy apparent in his voice. "Dickie bird!" Fanny dutifully shuffled into the room. Advanced age had slowed her step, and she moved only with effort.

"Tell her! Tell her!" Holmes cried.

"I'm going to marry Miss Denman," Frankfurter said.

Fanny received the news expressionlessly and shuffled out of the room wordlessly. Surprised and embarrassed, the two men shifted the conversation to more general subjects. Shortly, Fanny returned, her expression unchanged, her hands clenched. She approached Frankfurter.

"Which do you think she would like? This," and she opened one fist to reveal a piece of jade, "Or this?" and she opened the other, which held a piece of amber. Frankfurter somberly chose the amber. Fanny gave it to him and slunk out of the room, emerging no more that day.*

---

* Felix Frankfurter and Marion Denman were married on December 20, 1919, by Benjamin N. Cardozo, then judge of the New York State Court of Appeals. In 1932, Cardozo replaced Holmes on the U.S. Supreme Court. In 1939, Frankfurter replaced Cardozo.

* * *

HOLMES'S HOPE THAT he had seen the last of the cases coming to the Court under the Espionage Act proved futile. In the fall of 1919, two more appeared on the docket. The first, *Schaefer* v. *United States*, which was argued on October 21, 1919, and announced on March 1, 1920, appealed the convictions of several officers of a German-language association that published, among others, the *Philadelphia Tageblatt* and *Philadelphia Sonnenblatt*.

The editors were in the habit of assembling their paper every day by cutting and pasting articles from other newspapers, necessarily shortening the originals and frequently distorting their meanings. The finished products generally glorified the German war effort and undermined the American. Five officers of the parent association were convicted under the Espionage Act. The Supreme Court affirmed the convictions of three.

Subversion, like beauty, is in the eye of the beholder. McKenna, who wrote for the Court's majority of six, knew of "no other more powerful or effective instruments of evil than [the] German newspapers organized and conducted as these papers were organized and conducted." Brandeis, to whom Holmes left the dissenting this time, found the additions and omissions from the original news items, as Holmes undoubtedly did, "harmless" and the editorial opinions "impotent."

Citing Holmes's "clear and present danger" test as the "rule of reason" in determining the permissibility of speech, Brandeis appealed for calm judgment and good sense "in times of deep feeling and on subjects which excite passion." Hysteria had no place in such deliberations. He could not bring to *Schaefer* perhaps the objectivity Holmes had brought to *Abrams,* and he concluded on a moral note:

> The constitutional right of free speech has been declared to be the same in peace and in war. In peace, too, men may differ widely as to what loyalty to our country demands; and an intolerant majority, swayed by passion or by fear, may be prone in the future, as it has often been in the past, to stamp as disloyal opinions with which it disagrees. Convictions such as these, besides abridging freedom of speech, threaten freedom of thought and of belief.

The last, finally, of the free speech cases brought under the Espionage Act, *Pierce* v. *United States*, followed *Schaefer* closely both in time and judicial impact. Argued in November 1919 and announced March

8, 1920, it involved the convictions of Socialists who during the war had distributed an antiwar pamphlet written by a prominent Episcopal clergyman. Again the Court majority affirmed the convictions. Pitney's opinion was so strong it made Chafee, who was finishing his book, *Free Speech in the United States,* rub his eyes and wonder "whether he ha[d] dreamed himself back into the eighteenth century." And again, Brandeis, "heartily" joined by Holmes, dissented.

These half-dozen cases, beginning with *Schenck,* that had come to the Court under the Espionage Act had broken Blackstone's grip on the First Amendment, thanks to Holmes. His opinions assumed a prominent place in American constitutional history. But for the moment, as the postwar hysteria raged on and Attorney General Palmer, in the name of sniffing out Communist conspiracies, conducted another of his infamous Red Raids while the Court had been pondering *Schaefer* and *Pierce,* Holmes's little odyssey from *The Common Law* to *Abrams,* via Chafee, Hand, Laski, Mill, and other points on his intellectual compass, may have seemed to have been for naught. Ironically, after Holmes had outlined for the majority in *Schenck* what people could and could not say and applied his rule to *Debs* and *Frohwerk,* he then had had to become a dissenter in order to utilize it as precedent. The majority in *Abrams,* *Schaefer,* and *Pierce* steered well clear of Holmes's "clear and present danger" test, almost as if the justices had forgotten it had been written into a majority opinion affirming the convictions of alleged subversives. As the chief and McReynolds, McKenna and Pitney, Day, Van Devanter, and even the usually liberal Clarke found criticism of the government and its war effort more and more unpalatable, and the potential arsonist with his match could be prosecuted standing farther and farther away from the haystack, the "free trade in ideas" came to a virtual standstill.

Despite the unfavorable climate at the time, Brandeis did not see his and Holmes's dissents as the exercises in futility they may have appeared to be. On the contrary. He believed they would over the long haul prove to have been well worth the effort. He hoped, he told Dean Acheson, his secretary that year,

> to educate the country. We may be able to fill the people with shame, after the passion cools, by preserving some of it on the record. The only hope is the people; you cannot educate the court.

CHAPTER 26

"Still the dash
of a D'Artagnan"

THE BUSTING OF the trusts begun by Theodore Roosevelt during the early years of the century ended with a whimper on March 1, 1920, when the Supreme Court dismissed the government's case against the powerful United States Steel Corporation. Despite its monopolistic practices, the big company, the Court said, had not violated the Sherman Anti-Trust Act. The case had been initiated by President Taft's Justice Department in 1911, and the records had grown almost to the height of Holmes himself. The Court was split, 4 to 3—McReynolds had been attorney general during part of the time the case was dragging through the courts; Brandeis, who had testified at the House Judiciary Committee hearings on trust legislation in 1911 and 1912 and had made some sharp comments regarding the monopolistic structure of U.S. Steel, also had felt obliged to disqualify himself.

It had been sixteen years since Holmes had disappointed Roosevelt with his dissent in the Northern Securities case—twice as long since he had expounded for the first time as a judge his theories of monopoly in *Central Shade-Roller Co.* v. *Cushman.* Even now he had not changed his mind, and in the intervening years he had flown from majority to majority, depending upon each one's proximity to his own position that size alone did not constitute a crime under the Sherman Anti-Trust Act. Although Holmes thoroughly approved the result in the steel case, he "deeply regretted" the way the decision had been made, thought it unrepresentative of the full Court and contrary to what the justices might have decided had all nine of them participated in the deliberations. He hoped and believed, he said, that he had not been persuaded to join the majority by his private view that the Sherman Anti-Trust Act was "a foolish law."

The steel case was the last of the big antitrust prosecutions Holmes would judge. Between the Court's decisions in the *Standard Oil* and *American Tobacco* cases in 1911 and its dismissal of the steel case in 1920, the Court had handed down opinions in twenty-seven antitrust cases; settlements were negotiated with several of the larger corporations—American Telephone and Telegraph and the New York, New Haven, and Hartford Railroad, for example. The object lessons had been largely taught, the worst of the trusts humbled, and the government was running out of targets as well as support, both public and presidential.

Reluctant though Holmes was to overturn state statutes, he did think "the Union would be imperiled" if the Court was prohibited from doing so, for one in his place saw "how often a local policy prevails with those who are not trained to national views and how often action is taken that embodies what the Commerce Clause was meant to end." The interests of the states, in short, were parochial, too often oblivious of the national interest. In *Missouri* v. *Holland,* decided April 19, 1920, he had an opportunity to explain what he meant.

In 1916, the United States and Great Britain had signed a treaty to protect various species of migratory birds in danger of extinction. The state of Missouri objected and tried to prevent federal game wardens from enforcing the statute which implemented the treaty. The Supreme Court upheld the national interest; Holmes wrote for the majority:

> Wild birds are not in the possession of anyone. . . . The whole foundation of the State's right is the presence within their jurisdiction of birds that yesterday had not arrived, tomorrow may be in another State and in a week a thousand miles away. . . .
>
> Here a national interest of very nearly the first magnitude is involved. It can be protected only by national action in concert with that of another power. . . . But for the treaty and the statute there soon might be no birds for any powers to deal with.

At the same time he seized the opportunity to put forth some of his ideas on the living Constitution:

> [W]hen we are dealing with words that are a constituent act, like the Constitution of the United States, we must realize that they have called into life a being the development of which could not have been foreseen

completely by the most gifted of its begetters. It was enough for them to realize or to hope that they had created an organism; it has taken a century and has cost their successors much sweat and blood to prove that they created a nation.

Evans v. *Gore* had been argued on March 5, 1920, then held for announcement until the end of the term, probably because of its potential for embarrassing the justices who had to decide it. The previous year Congress had passed a general revenue statute that included a provision for taxing the salaries of certain federal officials, including judges. Several of the judges were disturbed by this sudden drop in their income, and Walter Evans, Federal District Judge for the Western District of Kentucky, officially challenged it in court on the ground that Article III, Section 1, of the Constitution specifically stated that the compensation of judges "shall not be diminished during their continuance in office." Evans's claim was rejected in the lower court, and he took his case to the Supreme Court, which upheld it, via Van Devanter.

The subject didn't interest Holmes particularly, and he couldn't get the "blood of controversy in [his] neck," but he decided to dissent anyway. He believed the tax would have been valid under the original Constitution, but if not, the Sixteenth Amendment, ratified in 1913, which authorized Congress to establish an income tax, made it lawful. "The exemption of salaries from diminution," he told his brethren in his draft dissent, was "intended to secure the independence of judges on the ground, as it was put by Hamilton in the Federalist, (No. 79,) that 'a power over a man's subsistence amounts to a power over his will.' That is a very good reason for preventing attempts to deal with a judge's salary as such, but seems to me no reason for exonerating him from the ordinary duties of a citizen, which he shares with all others."

Bostonians were not the only ones to notice the frequent Holmes-Brandeis accord. The justices had noticed it, too, and McReynolds, an announced anti-Semite, thinking Brandeis must have been behind Holmes's dissent, scribbled on it: ". . . for four thousand years the Lord tried to make something out of Hebrews, then gave it up as impossible and turned them out to prey on mankind in general—like fleas on the dog for example." Holmes considered McReynolds a "savage" with "all the irrational impulses of a savage," and undoubtedly paid no attention to the point implied. Another's criticism, however, did make him hesitate to publish his dissent. One of the justices suggested to Holmes he was helping "to make the position of the majority embarrassing—as deciding in their own interest." He reconsidered carefully. In the end, the old detachment emerged to make deciding easier. If, he reasoned, his "opinion were the unpopular one," he would be "but a poor creature if [he] held back . . . you get lost in morasses if you think of anything except the question, the answer, and whether the public interest is that both sides should be stated." He published his dissent; it was joined only by Brandeis.

Abbott Lawrence Lowell had been a professor of government at Harvard in 1895 when Holmes spoke about "The Soldier's Faith" there. Now, a quarter century later, he was president of the institution, and he invited Holmes to return on Memorial Day and speak again at the commemoration the university was planning to honor the Harvard men who had given their lives in America's latest war. Recalling "The Soldier's Faith," he explained to Holmes, "there is no Harvard graduate who can speak so well on this occasion as you can. The gleam of high devotion with which we entered the war, the aspiration for a better world, has been fading into a materialist revulsion. . . . it is important to say that these men have not died in vain, and that we will not allow their spirit to slumber." Holmes did not accept Lowell's invitation. His reply has not survived; if he ran true to form, he excused himself on the grounds of age and his duties in Washington, although it must have been sorely tempting to update what he had said on Lowell's themes twenty-five years before. Nothing, it seemed, had changed.

In the summer of 1919, Holmes and Laski had discussed the possibility of Laski's editing a collection of Holmes's extrajudicial writings for publication in book form. That fall, Holmes supplied his young friend with his personal copies of his speeches and articles from the *American Law Review*, the *Harvard Law Review*, and other periodicals. Before he sailed for England in June 1920, to become a professor at the London School of Economics, Laski attended to preparing the manuscript for publication and reading the galleys. That summer, Holmes wrote a little preface, and all of a sudden in the fall of 1920, *Collected Legal Papers* was published by Harcourt, Brace and Company. Holmes told one reviewer he had been as pleased to have it appear before he reached eighty as he had been on publishing *The Common Law* before he reached forty. He called the collection "little fragments of my fleece that I have left upon the hedges of life." In due time the reviews began to come in: feature articles in the book-review sections of the Harvard, Columbia, Yale, University of Pennsylvania, and Cornell law reviews, the *Nation*, the *New York Times*, and one by Morris Cohen in the *New Republic*, all flattering to the man, the judge, the scholar. This sort of public recognition gratified him, and he gave warm expression to the "great pleasure to an old warrior who cannot expect to bear arms much longer, that the brilliant young soldiers still give him a place in their councils of war."

The issue of free expression just would not go away, although Holmes considered *Gilbert* v. *Minnesota* less a case of free expression than another yank in the unending tug-of-war between the nation and the states. Between the Revolution, when Massachusetts and Virginia had passed antisedition laws, and America's entry into World War I, state interest in punishing opposition to the country's wars was virtually nonexistent. Following the American declaration of war in 1917, several states devised their own espionage acts similar to the federal statute, and in 1920, the Supreme Court upheld their right to do so under the Constitution.

Shortly after Minnesota passed its espionage act, which made teaching or advocating obstruction of the war effort a crime, Joseph Gilbert, an official of Jackson County's Non-Partisan League, an organization suspected locally of sedition, made an antiwar speech and was duly indicted and convicted. The Supreme Court affirmed his conviction.

The Minnesota statute, McKenna declared for the Court's majority of seven, was a measure designed to enhance cooperation between the states and the United States, and did not undermine federal authority. Holmes, who "disagreed . . . with most that McK. said," concurred, although only in the result. White and Brandeis, who believed the constitutional guarantee of freedom of speech could not be curtailed by any state, and the latter of whom sent his draft opinion to Frankfurter and Chafee at Harvard Law School to be checked for factual errors, dissented. Ironically, White, the former Confederate officer, supported the supremacy of the national government, and Holmes, the Union officer, supported states' rights.

Holmes lumped Minnesota's law suppressing speech with all the other state statutes he had upheld during his two decades as a Supreme Court justice. Had he chosen to write a concurrence, he probably could have done it without looking up a single precedent. He believed *Otis* v. *Parker*, his first opinion for the Supreme Court in 1903, in which he had upheld California's right to prohibit the sale of stocks on margin, applied here. To Holmes, Minnesota's right to prohibit seditious discussion was "a matter that the states may deal with by their general powers unless they run across something that necessarily excludes them. . . . They have the same right to deal with this general subject that they have with murder." What, he implied, could be clearer?

* * *

THE FAT YEARS of the Babylonian twenties—years of uncontrolled industrial expansion, financial hijinks, and political corruption—succeeded the lean years of war—of high taxes, low fuel supplies, wheatless Mondays and meatless Tuesdays. Holmes noticed the renewal of optimism in a war-weary dispirited America that marked the inaugural on March 4, 1921, of Warren G. Harding, former small town newspaper editor and United States senator, who had promised in his campaign for the presidency to return the nation to normalcy.

Holmes saw it in the inaugural audience, "the most beautiful crowd" he had ever seen, and rhapsodized to a friend: "A heather of human faces filled full the whole space from the capital [*sic*] to the Library of Congress and up the street beyond to the Representatives Building and I should think to the Senate Building . . . bands of color, and a medley of tints from the women near to. . . ." Holmes hoped for "some gain from the present administration, though of course more is expected than possibly can come to pass."

Festivities marking his eightieth birthday, which had been duly noted by the *Harvard Law Review* in its dedication and Dean Roscoe Pound's lead article, "Judge Holmes's Contribution to the Science of Law," followed closely behind Harding's inauguration. Fanny took him completely by surprise. Unbeknownst to him, she had invited his secretaries, past and present, to dinner on the Sunday evening nearest March 8, had even persuaded him to dress—tails and all—in honor, she said, of "our last Sunday in the 79s," and had calmly dispelled his suspicions when minor alterations had to be made in the usual Sunday schedule. A few minutes after 8 P.M., dinner was announced. Fanny and Wendell descended from the second-story library where they had been waiting. Suddenly the folding doors to the dining room swung open, revealing nearly all the justice's former secretaries gathered around the table.

"Ghosts!" he muttered, then added for all to hear, "Well, I'll be damned."

When the champagne, of which the Holmeses still had a pre-Prohibition case or two, began to flow, he was heard to whoop for joy. There was grape juice for "conscientious objectors," but Holmes spotted none in the crowd.

> We and I think all [Holmes reported afterwards] had a ripping time—and they were so affectionate and kind that it went to my heart.

In the following day's *New Republic,* Lord Richard Haldane's tribute to Holmes as America's finest example of legal scholarship and intellectual achievement "put the *comble* to [Holmes's] happiness."

It was the best he would feel for some time.

Holmes's judicial life had begun 1921 somewhat less auspiciously than had his personal life. Days after the new year opened, the Court in *Duplex Printing Press Co.* v. *Deering* had seriously compromised the effectiveness of the Clayton Anti-Trust Act, which Samuel Gompers had hailed as "Labor's Magna Carta" when it was passed in 1914 and Holmes pronounced "legislative humbug," and which had been thought by many people to exempt labor unions from the prohibitions of the older Sherman Anti-Trust Act. Whether Holmes, who had joined the majority to uphold labor's liabilities under the Sherman Act in the *Danbury Hatters' Case* thirteen years before, was persuaded by his perceptions of the Clayton Act or whether Brandeis's carefully researched opinion for the minority seduced him, he had felt compelled to risk the charge of inconsistency and join Brandeis's dissent.

The day before Holmes's eightieth birthday, the Court in *Milwaukee Publishing Co.* v. *Burleson* had gone farther than ever before in restraining freedom of the press when it had upheld Postmaster General Burleson's exclusion of the *Milwaukee Leader* from the mails for violation of the Espionage Act. The use of the mails, Holmes thundered in dissent, displaying his usual contempt for those who suppressed speech, was "almost as much a part of free speech as the right to use our tongues, and it would take very strong language to convince me that Congress ever intended to give such a practically despotic power to any one man."

The circumstances surrounding the announcement of *Block* v. *Hirsh* on April 18 were not calculated to raise Holmes's spirits. He saw the issue in the case as a not particularly complicated challenge of congressional authority to enact a rent control law for the District of Columbia, where the war emergency had caused a crisis in housing. The senior justice in the majority, Holmes took on the opinion himself, seeing it perhaps as an interesting example of balancing public and private interests, although he may not have been prepared for the scorn heaped on him by the minority.

He recognized that "tangible property" tended to "give a rigidity to our conception of our rights in it"; he also recognized, however, that precedent had long before established that a "public exigency" justified the "legislature in restricting property rights in land to a certain extent without compensation." Once again, it was a question of knowing where to draw the line. He had insisted so often on the proposition that the "question of degree runs through the law" that his benchmates both in Massachusetts and Washington had "smiled and smiled." Regarding the rent control law, Congress had chosen to draw the line where "unquestionable embarrassment to the Government" and "danger to the public health" converged to produce an emergency situation. He could find nothing unreasonable about either Congress's estimate of conditions or its method of coping with them.

Between them, McKenna—the official author—the chief justice, Van Devanter, and McReynolds put together what can only be considered a polemic. Holmes, they feared, had done exactly what he had tried to do in *Arizona Employers' Liability Cases* decided more than a year before. Then they had asked themselves how soon it would be before not just the "dangerous" occupations, but all occupations, could be regulated. Now they asked themselves how long it might be before rent control became national socialism.

McKenna pounded away at familiar themes, arguing that if "the public interest may be concerned, as in the statute under review, with the control of any form of property, it can be concerned with the control of all forms of property. . . . The security of property, next to personal security against the exertions of government, is the essence of liberty." Not only had Holmes rubbed raw the minority's sensitivities to the sacred rights of property, he also had sullied their Constitution. "Has it suddenly become weak," they asked, "become, not a restraint upon evil government, but an impediment to good government? Has it become an anachronism, and is it to become an 'archaeological relic,' no longer to be an efficient factor in affairs but something only to engage and entertain the studies of antiquarians? Is this not to be dreaded—indeed will it not be the inevitable consequence of the decision just rendered?"

Strong words are hardly uncommon in the opinions of Supreme Court justices. It was undoubtedly the potential for discord inherent in cases like *Block* v. *Hirsh* that lay at the bottom of the justices' custom of shaking hands before each conference: "No hard feelings," they implied. The dissent in *Block* v. *Hirsh,* however, was a little harsh even for Holmes, and he told Frankfurter he thought the minority's acrimonious criticism of his opinion was "bad form."

Pleading judicial duty, Chief Justice White had been postponing for months what in a younger man would have been a simple bladder operation. Finally, in mid-May 1921, he entered Garfield Hospital in Washington to undergo the necessary surgery. He made arrangements for reassigning the opinions he had been scheduled to write, and entered the hospital not without optimism. At first his doctors considered his postoperative progress "satisfactory." Then his heart gave out. Last rites of the Church were administered shortly after midnight on May 19, and White died later that day. He was seventy-six. He had served on the Supreme Court for twenty-seven years, more than ten of them as chief justice.

Before White had become chief justice, Holmes had thought a "close companionship" between them might have developed. But White's enlarged duties had prevented it. Still, there had been "points of keen mutual understanding," never any "alienation or coldness," however divergent their professional judgments. Aware that for the past year White had been "laboring against infirmities and pain and . . . could not have looked forward to much else," Holmes found the chief's death endurable, thought it probably a "release." He would miss White "a good deal personally." He doubted, however, given those "infirmities," whether White "could have been very useful to the Court if he had recovered."

Holmes was not sanguine about the prospects for White's successor. He assumed he himself was too old and certainly Harding owed him no favors, though he considered himself capable, believed he knew his place "with regard to the higher aspects of the law." He thought Harding would look for "political experience" and "popular prominence." Brandeis's chances, Holmes felt, had departed with Wilson. From the available Republicans, Holmes would have chosen Hughes, but speculation was centering on former President Taft, who had been impatiently biding his time as a professor of law at Yale and had made no secret of his judicial ambitions. Nearly twenty years before, when Taft was still governor general of the Philippines and Melville Fuller was still chief justice, Mrs. Fuller had warned a young Army officer bound for the Far East:

> And when you get to the Philippines you tell Willie Taft not to be in too much of a hurry to get into my husband's shoes.

Now, in 1921, Taft had gone so far as to call on the ailing chief justice to assess his health. White complained of poor eyesight, failing health, and the heavy burdens of the chief justiceship, but not a word about retirement. In fact, in a letter to McReynolds three days before he entered Garfield Hospital, he said he expected to return to work "before the Court rises"; in the unlikely event that he did not, he wished his brethren a "happy vacation" and hoped they would meet in the fall "sound and well."

After White's death, Taft accelerated his campaign, dispatching a friend to lobby within the administration hierarchy for his appointment. There seemed to him a poetic justice in the prospect of White, whom President Taft had appointed chief justice, being succeeded by former President Taft.

Harding did not notice the connection and vacillated, settling now on ex-Senator George Sutherland of Utah who had been his campaign manager and to whom Harding had promised a Supreme Court seat the first chance he got, and now on Taft, unable to decide between the two Republicans. There was even talk that Day, although junior to Holmes, might be named chief justice on the understanding he would resign in six months so that Taft could succeed him. Holmes wondered "how many men are pulling wires now."

On the last day of June 1921, after more than a month of rumor, negotiation, lobbying, and intrigue, Harding finally chose the sixty-four-year-old Taft. He was only a year short of the age limit Taft himself as president had set for a chief justice. He had been endorsed not only by Republicans but also by Democrats, by bar associations, judges, and businessmen. The former president was confirmed by the Senate with dispatch and only four dissenting votes.

A few weeks later a friend commented to the newly appointed chief justice that she could not yet think of him in that office. Replied Taft, who had himself appointed a majority of a previous Court and had watched while high judicial office slipped away so many times in the interim, pining for it all the while, "I can't think of myself in that position." It was all too good to be true: the culmination of a career in public service that had begun forty years before and included an unusual number of high offices—prosecuting attorney, municipal judge, solicitor general of the United States, federal circuit judge, governor general of the Philippines, secretary of war, president, and, at last, chief justice of the United States. Taft was the only man in American history to hold the offices of both president and chief justice.

On the personal side, he struck people as well-groomed (unlike many large men), kindly, optimistic, and dignified. He was also as jovial a man as Washington had ever seen. His laugh was famous, "a form of physical enjoyment," as one observer put it. It began quietly even before he came to the point of his story and grew in volume until he had moved his audience to deep laughter. He loved laughter. He loved to laugh and he loved others to laugh with him. He spread goodwill and kindliness wherever he walked. "He is," Holmes said, "just natchally loved by everyone."

Even so, Holmes was not looking forward to working with Taft, whom he had heard was "indolent" and "hard to get along with if you don't agree with him." But he shot off his usual welcoming letter, promising to "cooperate" and "to make the work agreeable."

What Holmes had heard about Taft proved inaccurate. Taft did "two men's work." He rose at 5 A.M., worked a twelve-hour day, and virtually gave up social life. He could work long hours at a stretch, had extraordinary powers of concentration, and unique abilities to exclude nonessentials. He realized, too, that the chief justice "goes into a monastery and confines himself to his judicial work."

It was certainly true that Taft liked the brethren to see constitutional issues as he did, and beneath the jollity lurked the will to bend the others his way. Like other chief justices before and after, he felt dissent undermined the authority of the Court, and he especially hoped to put an end to the long chain of 5 to 4 decisions, with their implications of divisiveness and rancor among the justices. But hard to get along with he was not. He tried to distribute the cases fairly, claiming for himself enough important and interesting ones to compensate for the leftovers he took because other justices didn't want them. He demanded a "good" product from the Court—opinions that would provide clear guidance to the bar and the lower courts. His gold-rimmed glasses astride his nose, his big white mustache drooping, Taft presided over court and conference with authority and efficiency, and even Brandeis had to admit that the chief justice was adept at "smooth[ing] out difficulties instead of making them."

Presiding over that first conference after he took his oath of office on October 3, 1921, Taft could only have singled out Brandeis as the biggest problem he would face in bringing the sweet harmony he sought out of the discord he had inherited. Dislike of the man he blamed for bringing the taint of scandal to his administration still lingered, even though he had partly avenged himself when he publicly opposed Brandeis's appointment to the Supreme Court. Taft had said then that Brandeis was a "muckraker, an emotionalist for his own purposes, a Socialist . . . a man who has certain high ideals in his imagination . . . of great tenacity of purpose, and, in my judgment, of much power for evil."

Over the years, as he came into daily association with Brandeis, Taft would grow "to like [him] very much indeed," even admire certain of Brandeis's qualities: his capacity for hard work, his analytical mind, and his quiet pride in the Court which Taft himself so loved. On the few occasions on which Taft and Brandeis concurred, Taft was apt to write flowery comments on Brandeis's draft opinions:

This is a most useful opinion and straightens out the law not only for the public but for your colleagues. WHT.

I congratulate you on your opinion. . . . It is [illegible], compact, forcible and clear. It relieves me greatly to get rid of such a case so satisfactorily. I thank you for your promptness.

I like this opinion very much. It works the result out most satisfactorily. . . .

Substantial judicial accord between the two men, however, could hardly have been possible. Brandeis the crusader for Progressive reforms whom Taft considered a radical at best would only rarely concur with Taft the spokesman for an earlier generation, economic Tory, and political reactionary.

The rest of the Court over which Taft was presiding presented other sorts of problems for the new chief justice. McKenna, the senior justice, was not only physically in decline at seventy-eight, but he had also added the irascibility common to very old men to his mental failings, which were all too apparent now. Taft soon found himself taking over McKenna's opinions because the older man refused to write what the Court had ordered.

The chief justice soon dismissed Day and Pitney as the other "weak members of the court." McReynolds he held in even lower esteem, found him "a continual grouch" and offensive to the other justices. Van Devanter he called his "mainstay," found his legal learning had made him "the most valuable man in our court," and recommended Yale give him an honorary degree.

He had mixed feelings about Holmes. Holmes's friend John Gray had suggested Taft's son Robert go to Washington as Holmes's secretary in 1913–14, but the ex-president had vetoed the idea. He wanted Robert to "get started permanently" in Cincinnati, and he didn't think a year with Holmes would do anything for his son that Harvard Law School hadn't.

It was at the first conference of Taft's chief justiceship or one shortly after that Taft announced he had been "appointed to reverse a few decisions," and he "looked right at old man Holmes when [he] said it." Holmes seemed sometimes to puzzle Taft, who found him personally a "delight" and the "life of the court," but professionally unreliable. At eighty, Holmes fell automatically into the chief justice's criterion for retirement; yet Taft was surprised to find Holmes had not "lost his mental acumen" and was considerably sharper than McKenna, although McKenna was two years younger.

Taft had bought a house on Wyoming Avenue in the northwest quadrant of Washington, about three miles from the Court, and made a point of walking in every day. For the first few years, until both men began to fail physically, he often picked up Holmes on the way and they walked together. Taft became "fond of the old gentleman," but grieved that Holmes seemed "so completely under the control of Brother Brandeis that it gives to Brandeis two votes instead of one." Taft didn't think much of Holmes as a constitutional lawyer in general, thought Holmes lacked the "experience of affairs in government that would keep him straight on constitutional questions," which is only to say, Holmes didn't agree with Taft. The chief justice also despaired of Holmes's work habits, particularly the fact that he seemed to give more attention to his dissents than to his opinions for the Court, which troubled Taft because the latter were often "very short and not very helpful."

The fundamental constitutional differences that were to separate the Holmes/Brandeis axis from the Taft forces were pointed up during Taft's first year as chief justice, in the case of *Truax* v. *Corrigan*. It was the new chief justice's first major labor case, and he learned right away that the sweet harmony among the justices that he longed for was not going to be easy to produce, his loveableness, fairness, and large executive abilities notwithstanding.

In April 1916, the cooks and waiters at William Truax's nonunion restaurant, the English Kitchen in Bisbee, Arizona, had struck for higher wages, an eight-hour day, and recognition of their union. Bisbee was the center of copper mining in the Southwest where local labor strife had disrupted copper production during the recent war, and sympathy for the demands of working men was scarce to nonexistent. When Truax rejected their demands, his employees picketed the restaurant.

Truax and his partners sought to enjoin the employees from picketing and otherwise harassing them. It all must have sounded so familiar to Holmes, bringing the twenty-five-year-old case of *Vegelahn* v. *Guntner* immediately to mind. The antiunion atmosphere in which the Massachusetts case had been decided had not changed much by 1921, but the law had. Following the example of several other states, Arizona, in its first civil code enacted under statehood, had passed a statute prohibiting use of the injunction in labor disputes, and the state supreme court had upheld the anti-injunction law against Truax. Truax appealed to the U.S. Supreme Court where the case was argued first in April 1920.

Afterwards, Holmes, Brandeis, and Clarke walked home together from the Court.

"Well," said Holmes, who often made up his mind on a case even before oral argument ended, "at least in this case no one will vote for reversal."

Brandeis was less certain. "We'll be lucky if we can sustain it 5 to 4," he said.

The Court voted, 6 (Chief Justice White with Justices McKenna, Day, Van Devanter, Pitney, McReynolds) to 3 (Holmes, Brandeis, Clarke) to reverse the Arizona Supreme Court and to hold the state anti-injunction law unconstitutional. White assigned the majority opinion to Pitney, who had heretofore been swatting at protective labor legislation like flies. Before Pitney finished writing it, however, Brandeis sent around his dissent, his usual lengthy dissertation that went back practically to the invention of money. Pitney actually was persuaded to change his vote. After reading Brandeis's opinion, he could "find no grounds for declaring that the State's action is so arbitrary and devoid of reasonable basis that it can be called a deprivation of liberty or property without due process of law" and concluded he could not "write in accordance with the vote."

Which left the decision in *Truax* v. *Corrigan* at 5 to 4. Then Chief Justice White died, and the Court was evenly divided, which would have allowed the state supreme court judgment to stand. The bitterly divided Court restored the case, which had national implications, to the docket for reargument in October 1921, after Chief Justice Taft had taken his seat. No friend to labor, Taft joined the four who would strike down the anti-injunction law. He himself would write this important opinion.

Taft had no argument with labor's right to organize, to bargain collectively, even to stop work and strike. As a federal judge in the 1890s, when workmen's compensation laws were widely held in disrepute and Holmes seemed to have no special interest in modifying the common law's doctrine that wage earners assumed the risks of their occupations, Taft had been known to bend over backwards to uphold workmen's compensation laws and to protect individual laborers from abuse.

He also believed that labor should enjoy no special protections or privileges, and he considered that the anti-injunction statutes being passed discriminated against the employer by overprotecting labor. Less than a year after he wrote *Truax,* he was to tell his brother Horace: "The only class which is distinctly arrayed against the court is a class that does not like the courts at any rate, and that is organized labor. That faction we have to hit every little while, because they are continually violating the law and depending on threats and violence to accomplish their purpose." He expected union men, whose arguments had been consistently rejected by the courts, to behave like gentlemen, like the men he knew in the banks, on the bench, in the political arena, in academe.

Beginning what would become a custom, Taft had Van Devanter edit his opinion in *Truax* before he circulated it to the other justices. Satisfied with it at last, the chief justice announced it on December 19, 1921, just before the Christmas recess. Calling on the ubiquitous Fourteenth Amendment, the Court invalidated Arizona's anti-injunction law. To Taft and the other four justices in the majority, the statute clearly authorized the taking of property without the due process of law guaranteed by that amendment. Any law which allowed behavior such as the strikers' at the English Kitchen could not be held valid under the Fourteenth Amendment, or, as the Court had declared in a recent case, "peaceful picketing [is] a contradiction in terms" (*American Foundries* v. *Tri-City Council*). Because the statute applied only to labor controversies—it overprotected workers, the Court implied—it was discriminatory and denied businessmen not only due process of law, but its Fourteenth Amendment companion, equal protection of the laws.

"At Brandeis's request," Holmes wrote a brief dissent, and at Brandeis's urging, published it. Holmes was fond of expanding what seemed like simple words into larger concepts—as in 1905 in *Swift & Co.* v. *United States,* he had expanded the meaning of "commerce" from simple acts of buying and selling into "stream" or "current" of commerce which included buying, selling, production, transportation, and any other activity involved in the movement of goods. "Delusive exactness," he declared now in 1921, "is a source of fallacy throughout the law," and he similarly attempted to expand the meaning of business from mere pecuniary value to "a course of conduct" which, he said, was "subject to substantial modification according to time and circumstances both in itself and in regard to what shall justify doing it a harm." To claim it was unconstitutional to allow modification by the boycott and picketing allowed by the Arizona statute, Holmes said, rejected precedent.

Further, he failed to discern, as the majority had, discrimination in the statute in question. "Legislation," he declared testily, "may begin where an evil begins. If, as many intelligent people believe, there is more danger that the injunction will be abused in labor cases than elsewhere I can feel no doubt of the power of the legislature to deny it in such cases."

He concluded with a reiteration of his view of the Fourteenth Amendment:

There is nothing that I more deprecate than the use of the Fourteenth Amendment beyond the absolute compulsion of its words to prevent the making of social experiments that an important part of the community desires, in the insulated chambers afforded by the several states, even though the experiments may seem futile or even noxious to me and to those whose judgment I most respect.

Although it had been Brandeis's dissent that had persuaded Pitney to abandon the Court majority, Pitney did not join Brandeis's final opinion, but wrote his own which Clarke, who thought Brandeis's "too discursive & expanded," joined. The Arizona legislature, Pitney had decided, knew what was best for Arizona, and if its members had concluded that prohibition of the use of the injunction in labor controversies suited local conditions, he would not try to second-guess them.

Brandeis joined the dissents of both Pitney and Holmes and also filed his own. He expressed sentiments more or less similar to Pitney's and included a detailed history of the development in England and the United States of "the rules governing contests between Employer and Employed."

The divergence of opinion in this difficult field of government action [he wrote] should admonish us not to declare a rule arbitrary and unreasonable merely because we are convinced that it is fraught with danger to the public weal, and thus to close the door to experiment within the law.

Through *Truax* v. *Corrigan,* the Supreme Court resuscitated the injunction as a viable weapon against labor just when the states had begun to weaken its hold on life. But the issue here was much more than that. The real issue that was settled in this case, which set the judicial tone for more than a decade of industrial warfare and other economic and social conflicts accompanying the ferment of the time, was the inflexibility in the 1920s and 1930s of words written in the 1780s. The pattern had been set for the Tafts and McReynoldses and Van Devanters and others still to come to stubbornly oppose all legislative experimentation with the immutable property rights they believed had been cast in cement by the Founding Fathers. Those justices like Holmes and Brandeis who attempted to adapt the Constitution to fit the fluid contours of American society could only remain for the next several years a weak if vocal minority.

DECEMBER 8, 1922, marked Holmes's twentieth anniversary on the United States Supreme Court and a full forty years since his appointment to the Massachusetts bench. Instigated by Frankfurter, the editors of the *New Republic* noted the double anniversary publicly in somber congratulatory tones. Brandeis noted it with a brief message:

For O.W.H.
Twenty years after—
Still the dash of a D'Artagnan.

The editorial in the *New Republic* "went to [his] heart," made Holmes feel "the long day's task had not been in vain." It also scared him a little, gave him occasion to contemplate what the fall from "the top of the hill" might be like. But he knew better than to take Brandeis's comment seriously. There was not much dash left in a fellow who coughed "half the night," whose asthmatic breathing even during the day was "stertorous," and whose younger brethren had adopted the custom of reminding him to ride rather than walk home when the pavements were icy. Fanny made a "row" when he wanted to go for a walk and fussed over him the way she would over a child.

The better part of the summer, 1922, Holmes had spent at Corey Hill Hospital in suburban Brookline, Massachusetts, recovering from prostate surgery. (Still deeply Victorian, Holmes talked freely of his surgery, but never gave it a name in public. A man's prostate remained a private matter in his world.) Stricken just before he was to leave for Amherst College where he had been invited to receive an honorary degree, he underwent the two-operation treatment that was standard at the time, the first one almost immediately, the second nearly a month later. In 1922, it was a dehumanizing procedure, replete with postoperative risks including pneumonia, cerebral thrombosis, heart disease, and intestinal cancer. It was most dangerous for men over seventy-five.

Hospital routine revolutionized the Holmeses' lives temporarily. He "suspended intellectual functions," though he read voraciously—"largely drool"—and lived from medical bulletin to medical bulletin. He and Fanny had hoped to celebrate their fiftieth wedding anniversary in grand style, but they had spent it instead among catheters, little black pills, and the apprehensions that surgery imposes, becoming "absorbed in the egotism of the sick room." Holmes tried to remain cheerful, or at least philosophical, though he recognized that "such things are serious." He was not after all a young man, and surgery in the early 1920s was not something to be tossed off lightly.

All went well, however, and the patient awoke to contemplate a long convalescence, including some five weeks more in the hospital, during which he devoured every letter from Frankfurter, Laski, and all his other correspondents, regarding each as evidence that "birds still sing outside." Johnny Morse, who had dressed his cousin's war wound sixty years before, called regularly. It was mid-August before Holmes was strong enough to "lollup round on beds and couches" at Beverly Farms, and he began to realize how weak he really was and that it would take time "for an old fellow to build up." On his return to Washington in time for the Court's opening, he "blushed but submitted" when he was met at the train by a wheelchair which conveyed him to his taxi.

The Holmeses lived for several weeks at the Powhatan Hotel while an elevator was installed at 1720 I Street, a project that brought "chaos" to Fanny's customary orderliness and usurped a good deal of space formerly occupied by Holmes's books and papers. He solved the latter problem by putting a match to the papers and giving the overflow of books to the public library at Pittsfield, Massachusetts, where he had spent all those delicious summers in his youth.

He worried a lot about the weakness in his legs. He used the elevator "as in duty bound," but insisted on testing himself on the stairs, sorely trying Fanny no doubt. After one of his bouts with illness, she remarked: "He was sick—but he is worse now, he is convalescing."

There was the usual urging by friends that he "drop the job and take [his] ease"; to them he gave the usual reply: "I want to produce as long as I can and think that I shall be intellectually honest in judging my condition and product." His young Chinese friend suggested he write his autobiography, but Holmes preferred to put whatever energies he still possessed into the work of the Court. "A man's spiritual history," he explained to Wu, "is best told in what he does in his chosen time— Life having thrown me into the law I must try to put my feeling of the infinite into that. To exhibit the detail with such lines of a vista as I can—to show in it the great line of the universal."

That fall, Laski reported to Frankfurter from London that he heard from Holmes "as regularly and joyously as ever"; Laski discerned "no diminution in quality or vigor." Taft, however, who was on the spot,

thought Holmes had lost "his jaunty appearance of youth"; he was physically weak and intellectually "unresilient." Taft hoped his "very sensible wife . . . would . . . soon conclude to influence him to lay down
his office." Brandeis reserved judgment for a while; he wanted to make
up his mind. Finally, he reported to Frankfurter, he had decided Holmes
was "in good form & able to carry the load." Even as a convalescent,
Brandeis thought Holmes looked "well"; he had not missed a conference
or court session and was turning out opinions with his "customary speed."
He "tired physically & at times mentally"; Brandeis thought, however,
that he would "work easily" once he returned to the familiar library at
home, a prophecy that proved to be accurate. Indeed, during the 1922
term, Holmes, although he did not, as had been his custom, beg for
extra assignments, did his share of the work, proudly reporting that his
doctor thought him "remarkable" for being able "to carry through [his]
share of the team's work without asking for any allowances."

Life at 1720 I Street soon normalized. Not long after Brandeis made
his first report to Frankfurter, he spotted Holmes walking along K Street
with his secretary, and Holmes himself could see that his legs were
growing stronger. He and Fanny soon resumed their daily drives about
what was becoming a car-clogged city; they avoided such newfangled
inventions and continued to hire an "old fogey one-horse vehicle."

While Holmes was struggling to keep pace with the "team" that
year, the team itself was limping along. First, the old rivalry between
McKenna and Holmes erupted at conference one day, temporarily shattering the veneer of decorum the justices so solemnly wore. Taft put it
down to McKenna's jealousy of Holmes exacerbated by a "peevish vanity
and irritability and a subconsciousness of losing grasp." McKenna's intransigence was pushing Taft to the limits of his capacity for tolerance.
The chief justice worried that a man who missed the point in case after
case should be in a position to cast a deciding vote in them. McKenna,
however, refused to resign. "[W]hen a man retires," he said, "he dis-
appears and nobody cares for him."

The seventy-three-year-old Day, Taft complained, "has been doing
no work"; Van Devanter, never much of an opinion writer, was having
trouble with his eyes, McReynolds had the gout, and Pitney had had a
nervous breakdown. The Court had been "shot to pieces."

Privately despairing of spending his last years "determining whether
a drunken Indian has been deprived of his land before he died or whether
the digging of a ditch in Iowa was constitutional or not," Clarke, in the
pink of good health at sixty-five except for a worsening deafness, was
the first to resign. In his letter to the president, he cited a long-held

desire to read, travel, and "serve . . . some public causes in ways in which I cannot serve them while I hold public office." The "public causes" turned out to be public appeals for American participation in the League of Nations. Clarke died in March 1945, ironically only three months before the major countries of the world met in San Francisco to create the United Nations.

Clarke was succeeded by Harding's former campaign manager, sixty-year-old ex-Senator and corporation lawyer George Sutherland of Utah. Although Taft had advised Harding to name Governor Nathan L. Miller of New York to Clarke's seat, he pronounced Sutherland, for whom Harding had been seeking a place ever since the election, "a very excellent appointment," and gave him a warm welcome. "Our views are very much alike," he told the nominee, "and it is important that they prevail."

Day was the next to leave. Enfeebled after nineteen years on the bench, he resigned in October 1922. He accepted an appointment as umpire to a war-claims commission, but found even that overly taxing. He and his son set out for their summer fishing camp in northern Michigan as usual the next year, but it was too late for the aging justice, and he died on July 9, 1923.

To all appearances, Holmes had fully recovered from his surgery by December 1922. Citing Holmes's opinion in *Pennsylvania Coal Co.* v. *Mahon,* Brandeis had begun to think, however, that perhaps his friend's physical struggles had weakened his intellectual capacities.

The case represented one of the first of the Taft Court's decade-long attacks on state statutes enacted in the name of the public welfare under the state police power. This one involved Pennsylvania's Koehler Act, which prohibited the mining of anthracite coal in a manner to cause cave-ins and had been intended to protect the public from reckless entrepreneurs. The property in question had been bought from the Pennsylvania Coal Company in 1878, the company reserving the right to remove coal from beneath the surface, the buyer assuming the risk that the ground on which his home stood could be weakened and the structure damaged. The risk seemed minimal in 1878. Coal companies at the time mined only about two-thirds of what lay beneath, leaving the rest to support the surface.

Times, however, had changed during the decades following. "Pillar robbing," which further weakened the surface, had become prevalent; a million people now lived over the undermined land which covered nine counties in northeastern Pennsylvania, and large areas of the city of Scranton were near collapse. The politics of cave-in dominated debate in the Pennsylvania legislature during the first two decades of the century, and in 1921, the lawmakers sought to resolve the issue with the Koehler Act. Following its passage, the Mahons, a local lawyer and his wife who owned property the Pennsylvania Coal Company intended to mine, as well as a house on it, tried to stop the company's underground operations; the Koehler Act, they insisted, had nullified the company's rights.

The Mahons had lost in the lower Pennsylvania court and won in the Pennsylvania Supreme Court; the coal company had taken its case to the U.S. Supreme Court, where its arguments were presented by no less a figure than John W. Davis, former solicitor general and soon-to-be-nominated candidate of the Democratic Party for president. The question the Court faced was: When did the state's authority to regulate land use spill over into confiscation of property?

It would appear that on a Court led by Taft and made up of McKenna, Holmes, Van Devanter, McReynolds, Brandeis, and Sutherland (Day's successor had not yet taken his seat, and Pitney had been incapacitated by a stroke, although he had not yet officially resigned), Holmes and Brandeis were the Mahons' only hope for support. Brandeis alone did not disappoint them. Holmes, who generally supported legislative authority as the voice of the people, deserted one of his firmest principles, surprised everyone, and voted with the majority to kill the Koehler Act; the state had exceeded the speed limit. Shrewdly, Taft assigned the majority opinion to Holmes who was becoming the darling of the Progressives. His opinion in *Pennsylvania Coal Co.* must have shocked them. It might have been written by Peckham or Brewer, were they still on the Court. Holmes acknowledged that "some values . . . must yield to the police power" and "property may be regulated to a certain extent." If, however, "regulation goes too far it will be recognized as a taking." As he had said so many times before, it was a question of degree; in his and the majority's opinion, the Koehler Act crossed the line, imposing restrictions well beyond anything previously sanctioned by the Supreme Court. In conclusion he fell back on an old theme, one that subtly undergirded the entire opinion:

> So far as private persons or communities have seen fit to take the risk of acquiring only surface rights, we cannot see that the fact that their risk has become a danger warrants the giving to them greater rights than they bought.

Brandeis was clearly disappointed in the position Holmes took, thought a "refined man" had become "gross," a "sensitive and just man" had done an "injustice." But the younger man had sat through the conferences, participated in the exchanges of notes, and knew his friend well enough to weigh the factors Holmes had considered when he cast his vote with the majority. Brandeis was well aware of Holmes's detached view toward imminent disaster in Pennsylvania's coal-mining communities, which lawyers for the city of Scranton as *amicus curiae* had described in lurid detail. He was well aware of the conflict that besieged Holmes when his usual deference to legislative authority was pitted against his reverence for contractual obligations. Brandeis concluded that Holmes's apparent turnabout should be attributed to a "heightened respect for property" he believed had become part of Holmes's growing old, a reversion to "views not of his manhood but childhood." Brandeis was one of Holmes's few friends who realized how hard it always had been for Holmes "to rid himself of undue regard for property" intellectually and that emotionally Holmes was entirely incapable of it.

But even more, Brandeis ascribed Holmes's vote in *Pennsylvania Coal Co.* to an unaccustomed intellectual weakness that followed Holmes's surgery of the previous summer. The majority in this case had caught Holmes "when he was weak & played him to go whole hog." It was, after all, Holmes himself who had noted more than forty years before in *The Common Law* that "the life of the law" depended upon experience, including the "prejudices judges share with their fellow-men."

Predictably, the opinion was unpopular in Pennsylvania, and the *New Republic* was a lot less flattering when it deconstructed *Pennsylvania Coal Co.* v. *Mahon* than it had been when it celebrated Holmes's judicial anniversaries just weeks before, declaring now that "Justice Brandeis's view seems the superior statesmanship." Frankfurter, who generally commented on Holmes's opinions, maintained an austere silence, probably, Holmes thought, because he was "feeling an unnecessary delicacy about saying that he disagrees." Laski, too, was silent, although Holmes sent him the opinion and not very subtly solicited his comments.

As the new year opened, however, Holmes was optimistic. Taft had reassured him that he "more than carries his load." He and Fanny didn't "go about, dine out or give dinners" much anymore, but on the rare occasions they did, they attracted admiring attention, like that of the British ambassador's wife:

I like to see an old lady like that with her white hair still dining out.

But Holmes tired easily, his persistent cough, which finally had been diagnosed as asthma—the Holmes family disease—enervated him, he had come to the point where he never stood when he could sit and now drove to and from the Court. But most of his physical difficulties appeared now to be history. He could walk stairs with reasonable ease now, he had resumed at least a short daily constitutional, and had even written an introduction to Professor Wigmore's new book, *Introduction to Rational Basis of Legal Institutions,* which he swore was his "last appearance in public except in the reports." His mustache had been "curled . . . to beat the Kaiser" and his hair cut "to rival Bond Street." He was feeling "very fine *pro tem*" and waving his sword as he advanced on the earthworks of his third and final decade on the Court. Bugler, blow the charge.

CHAPTER 27

Upholding the "right of a donkey to talk drool"

HOLMES WAS READY for the final charge. His intellectual powers intact, he organized his work efficiently so that little time was wasted. Distresses were minor. He volunteered less often to relieve others of their caseload, and he sometimes had to be reassured of his usefulness. But in general he seemed to function well. His doctor gave him a clean bill of health, told him his heart was "a good pump," and that very few men of Holmes's age were "as well off" as he was—to which Holmes drily replied that "most of them are dead." But he was pleased that the "main machinery" was "in good running order," and he frequently felt "perky" enough to get out of the carriage part way home from court and walk the remaining blocks with Brandeis.

Social life, though, had entirely ceased. The invitations still came, but Holmes turned down "everything except an invitation to a White House reception to which I say yes and don't go." Formerly one of Washington's most popular couples, the Holmeses stayed home alone now, and Johnny Morse was disappointed when he called and received only a "general" invitation to dinner *"some day."*

Holmes acknowledged he wasn't getting any younger or stronger, that his memory for names and faces was deteriorating, and he had begun to shop for a cemetery plot, but his routine conceded nothing to his advancing age. On days when court sat, having as usual retrieved a delicacy from the worm barrel in the basement for Fanny's baby starling or the Japanese robin, Holmes, informal in slippers and mohair jacket, arrived in his library soon after 9:30 A.M., and sat down at the big desk. Arthur Thomas, his messenger, then brought in the mail. Holmes liked to speculate on how Thomas knew when the justice was at his desk, finally concluded that the messenger stood ready just on the other side of the door and opened it when he heard Holmes's chair squeak.

Holmes's library was the center of his life, and the desk was the center of his library. There he wrote his opinions with a sputtering ink-encrusted pen, smoked his "Between the Acts Cigars," kept his will and his treasures such as the cork from the bottle of champagne he and Shattuck had shared the day *The Common Law* was published. Sometimes he stole a quick nap there. When he wanted a real sleep, he moved to his leather-upholstered chair with its adjustable mechanical foot rest. His secretary covered his legs with a shawl, turned on the electric heater, and the old man took his rest.

He loathed "conveniences," refused to use a typewriter, wrote his letters in his chronically illegible hand, and teased Fanny for buying "one of those dust devourers that swallow everything into a bag." Occasionally Fanny wandered in.

"Holmes! Holmes, J." she cried.

He answered politely, then tried to chase her with a "Now, Dickie, see here, you run along, I've got to work."

Undaunted, she then tried to engage the secretary in conversation while Holmes, J., fidgeted.

Shortly before 11:30, when he was scheduled to depart for court, Holmes slipped out of his mohair jacket and into his dress uniform—cutaway coat and stiff shirt. Thomas helped him on with his highly polished black shoes, and handed over the Morocco-bound docket book. A final conference with Fanny, and the justice left in his hired car for work.

On days when court was not sitting, the routine began similarly, but instead of leaving for Capitol Hill at 11:30, Holmes worked on opinions and petitions for certiorari, making notes on a big unlined pad which he would have ready for conference the following Saturday. Messengers came and went, bringing the other justices' draft opinions for Holmes's comments. "The goddam fecundity of my brethren," he complained, "will kill me yet."

Afternoons, Wendell and Fanny, sometimes accompanied by the secretary, adventured out into the city for drives. Spring was the favored season. Holmes's heart never failed to leap at the "thousand veils of green and brown and red mists from the just opening buds in March," the "symphony of silver bells from the little tree toads," the sight of little boys, released from the penitentiary of winter, shooting marbles on streetcorners. He thrilled at the first crocus on the White House lawn, the first cherry blossoms beside the Tidal Basin, the walls of tulip trees, dogwoods, and magnolias in Rock Creek Park.

After dinner—summer and winter at 7 P.M.—he enjoyed an hour or two of solitaire, while Fanny read to him: "[A] hypnotic rest at the end of a day's work." He played five games successively, each until he won. He didn't cheat, but had devised "certain rules of [his] own which mitigate troubles."

It was not a particularly arduous existence. The Supreme Court then was not so demanding a taskmaster as it later became. The total annual workload per man during Holmes's time has been estimated as the writing of fewer than 150 pages in a volume of the *United States Reports*. Even when twenty hours a week of open court sessions for seventeen or eighteen weeks, Saturday conferences, and several hours each week examining the petitions for certiorari are added, the time expended still totals no more than that expended by a modern-day law student. It was, though, more than it used to be. In the earliest days, the Court's demands were so small that John Jay could serve as chief justice and secretary of state simultaneously; Oliver Ellsworth served as minister to France during his chief justiceship. During Holmes's years on the Court, Brewer gave lectures and White taught at Georgetown University Law School.

His eagerness to reach ninety on the Court notwithstanding, Holmes by this time had begun to function at least partially fueled by his ample reserves of judicial adrenalin. Many of the cases now, when the debris was swept away, came down to familiar principles and precedents that triggered ingrained responses in him. When he hauled out, as he often did, his long-held belief that questions of law were but questions of degree, the brethren who did not stifle yawns smiled tolerantly. When the justices rambled on at conference about liberty of contract, Holmes tuned them out and contemplated all the beautiful women he had known. There were a few surprises left, but only a few.

SEVERAL OF HOLMES's dissents from the Supreme Court bench became the law of the land after his death. In *Moore* v. *Dempsey*, he enjoyed his triumph while he was still alive. He was there at the conference when the judges agreed that legal lynching, the sort which Holmes's dissent in Leo Frank's case eight years before had condemned, had no place in the American system of criminal justice. Appropriately, Taft assigned Holmes to write the Court's opinion.

The make-up of the Court had changed over the years since it had decided *Frank* v. *Mangum* in 1915. Four of the men who had made up the majority in *Frank* had since left the Court: Chief Justice White, Day, the Georgian Lamar who had opened the way for the Court to hear the case, then decided against Leo Frank, and Pitney who had written the Court's opinion in *Frank* and had recently resigned from the Court following a stroke. Brandeis, who had replaced Lamar, was predictable in a case involving mob law, but the new chief justice was not. Nor were the two newest justices, Pierce Butler, the Minnesota railroad lawyer who had replaced Day, and Edward T. Sanford, the former federal district judge and southern Republican who had replaced Pitney.

Moore v. *Dempsey* involved the questionable convictions of several blacks for the murder of a white man in Phillips County, Arkansas. Witnesses had been whipped and tortured. The trial had lasted less than an hour; the jury had required five minutes to reach a verdict. It was Leo Frank's case all over again. Appeals to the governor of Arkansas had elicited only threats and protests by the local American Legion post, the Rotary Club, the Lions Club, and other of Phillips County's "best citizens." Appeal to the state supreme court had been futile.

The U.S. Supreme Court, however, over the dissents of only McReynolds and Sutherland, reversed the position it had taken in Leo Frank's case and now in 1923 supported federal correction of the state's misbehavior. In the dissent he and Hughes had put together in *Frank*, Holmes had written that the due process of law guaranteed by the Constitution was bypassed in any trial where the overall "processes of justice are . . . subverted." Now, eight years later, in *Moore* v. *Dempsey*, he elaborated on that same theme—triumphantly, it may be assumed. With the authority of the Supreme Court behind him at last, he declared firmly that when in a case "the whole proceeding is a mask—that counsel, jury and judges were swept to the fatal end by an irresistible wave of public passion, and that the State Courts failed to correct the wrong," the U.S. Supreme Court stood ready to secure men's constitutional rights.

On economic issues, the Taft Court majority was substantially less liberal. Thanks at least partly to Taft's intervention with the Harding White House, well-known judges with liberal tendencies were passed over when Supreme Court vacancies occurred. Taft warned Harding against Learned Hand who, he feared, "would almost certainly herd with Brandeis and be a dissenter." The chief justice denounced Cuthbert W. Pound of the New York State Court of Appeals as a potential troublemaker and Benjamin N. Cardozo of the same court as a "Jew

. . . a Democrat and . . . a progressive." The president and the chief justice were looking for men with safe and sound views on the rights of property—the property of bankers, industrialists, transportation moguls, and other businessmen, and they found exactly what they were looking for in at least two of the three newcomers: Sutherland who found it unsettling that Americans were abandoning "the methodical habits of the past" to go "careening after novel and untried things," and Butler who insisted that the Court construe the Constitution "in the light of the principles upon which it was founded." With Van Devanter and the ever-inflexible McReynolds, these two new arrivals rehearsed during the 1920s for their starring roles in the 1930s as the Four Horsemen of Conservatism who set out systematically to dismantle FDR's New Deal legislation by judicial fiat.

Taft had prepared the way for them. In *Truax* v. *Corrigan,* in which he had virtually read labor out of the American political spectrum, he had oiled up the old Fourteenth Amendment for use as a weapon in sabotaging legislative reforms in the states. A year and a half later, in *Bailey* v. *Drexel Furniture Co.,* again writing for the majority, the chief justice had let the national legislature know what he thought of its attempts at social and economic reform when he prohibited it from using the taxing power to redress the evils of child labor,* thus affirming *Hammer* v. *Dagenhart.*

In April 1923, the future four horsemen combined with McKenna to invalidate a five-year-old minimum wage law for women in the District of Columbia, a federal enclave under federal law. Congress had enacted the law in order to put District of Columbia employees on an economic par with employees in other localities protected by similar state laws. The challenge to its constitutionality was called *Adkins* v. *Children's Hospital,* and it came to the Court in the spring of 1923, but it might as well have been called *Lochner* v. *New York* and come to the Court in 1905, when liberty of contract carried the day with ease. Holmes was weary of the whole issue, of hearing his fellow judges mouth the liberty of contract proprieties for all those years, and he had nearly exhausted his supply of answers. He had heard them all; what more was there to say?

Holmes and even Taft thought that the issue of minimum wages for women had been settled fifteen years before when the Court, in *Muller*

---

* Congress next tried constitutional amendment as a device to limit child labor, but not enough state legislatures ratified it. Finally, in 1941, Harlan Fiske Stone, using Holmes's twenty-three-year-old dissent in *Hammer* v. *Dagenhart,* wrote the Court's opinion upholding the Fair Labor Standards Act of 1938, which included prohibition of child labor (*United States* v. *Darby Lumber Company*).

v. *Oregon*, had upheld Oregon's maximum hours statute, via Justice Brewer, than whom not even Taft, Butler, or Sutherland was more protective of property rights. In principle, the District of Columbia's minimum wage law was remarkably similar to Oregon's hours law through which Justice Brandeis in his previous incarnation as Lawyer Brandeis had educated the Court in 1908. Brandeis, unfortunately for the appellants in *Adkins*, felt compelled to disqualify himself from the case because his daughter was secretary to the District of Columbia minimum wage board which was involved in the case—Jesse Adkins was its chairman.

Nevertheless, the law at issue seemed to have a favorable prognosis. The Court had not actually upheld a minimum wage law, but the justices, evenly divided in *Stettler* v. *O'Hara* and *Simpson* v. *O'Hara*, had allowed Oregon's to stand, and they had supported the constitutionality of the same state's extension of maximum hours legislation to men in *Bunting* v. *Oregon*. Heartened, twelve states had passed legislation requiring minimum wages for women which had been upheld by their courts; three other states had included provisions for them in their constitutions. *Adkins* had drawn five state attorneys general as well as nine prominent lawyers to file *amicus curiae* ("friend of the court") briefs in support of the District of Columbia statute's constitutionality.

The National Consumers League, which had sponsored the Oregon cases in the Supreme Court and was supporting the Adkins case, had secured the services of Felix Frankfurter, who frequently took on public causes in addition to his academic duties at Harvard Law School. Having argued *Stettler*, *Simpson*, and *Bunting* for the National Consumers League, Frankfurter was a practiced advocate for wage and hour laws by 1923. He had had the commission which administered the minimum wage law in each state that had one prepare for him a report on the operation of the law, the positive good accomplished by it, the lessening of industrial evils under it, and the frustration of all the dire prophecies. He added to this a section on European experiences under minimum wage legislation, compiling in the end a thousand persuasive pages, another regular Brandeis brief. Fortified by an evening with the Holmeses and "one of the very best talks" he and the justice had ever had, Frankfurter bounced into court well prepared and confident; nevertheless, he wished he could have had a cocktail before he spoke to the justices.

Lawyers for Children's Hospital brought out of storage, once again, the arguments that had persuaded the Court for years to see social realities in terms of property rights. Minimum wage legislation, they said, deprived both employer and employee of property and freedom of contract rights without due process of law, points that Brewer had rebutted fifteen years before. Nevertheless, they convinced the Court.

The justices turned back the clock to 1905 and *Lochner* v. *New York.* They decided to strike down the District of Columbia's minimum wage statute, the forty-fifth act of Congress they had struck down. Sutherland was chosen to write the Court's opinion.

His personal appointments belied the seriousness of his jurisprudence. He was a tall, slender man with a closely trimmed beard which was parted in such a way as to give the appearance of a perpetual smile. He had a reputation as a raconteur, and it became a regular routine for Holmes, on arriving at the weekly conference, to approach Sutherland and plead: "Sutherland, J., tell me a story." Complying, the junior justice unfailingly sent the assembled brethren into roars of laughter.

His jurisprudence, however, was not a laughing matter. He had been born in Utah into poverty and conquered it. He had studied law at the University of Michigan under Thomas McIntyre Cooley, distinguished conservative scholar of the Constitution. He had ridden horseback over mountain trails to try cases before justices of the peace as a young lawyer, had watched the pioneers create a civilization out of a vast wilderness with no help from government, and he had become an unreconstructed individualist. Whatever enhanced the freedom of the individual was his conception of a positive good; whatever restrained it, he despaired of.

Constitutionally disposed as he was to protest all application of federal power to the regulation of industrial evils, Sutherland was a perfect choice to write the majority opinion in the Adkins case. He abhorred any interference by the state with what were considered the competitive forces of nature and the free marketplace. He believed these forces, though often harsh, ultimately achieved the best result—the survival of the fittest, economically, socially, politically. He was deeply convinced that ill-considered experimentations in government—as represented by minimum wage legislation—would ultimately prove to be the real enemy of democracy. Holmes's personal universe in many ways resembled Sutherland's, but Holmes liked to remind people it was his duty to help them go to hell if that's what they wanted.

Sutherland's opinion in *Adkins,* which was announced April 9, 1923, and from which Van Devanter, who had a cooler, more analytical head, had extracted some of Sutherland's more extreme observations, accurately reflected Sutherland's Darwinian views. Beginning with the concession that the "judicial duty of passing upon the constitutionality of an act of Congress is one of great gravity and delicacy," he went on to rehash the concept of liberty in "liberty of contract," the concept of power in "police power," and the concept of justice in "social justice." At each step the minimum wage legislation was found to be wanting. He dredged up *Lochner* v. *New York,* which most observers and some of the justices had assumed had been overruled *sub silentio,* and concluded that in the light of women's new status under the Nineteenth Amendment, which, he said, made protection unnecessary, the District of Columbia's minimum wage legislation was unconstitutional. He fretted, like most conservatives—and not for the last time—about where government regulation would end. "If," he wrote, "in the face of the guaranties of the Fifth Amendment, this form of legislation shall be legally justified, the field for operation of the police power will have been widened to a great and dangerous degree." If Congress could require a minimum wage, could it also require a maximum wage?*

Chief Justice Taft was torn. In his universe, stability was paramount, and precedent, as stability's handmaiden, weighed heavily on his constitutional scale. His tolerance for economic regulation, however, was as low as his respect for precedent was high. Ultimately the chief justice opted for precedent and reluctantly dissented from the majority in *Adkins.* He thought Holmes's dissent "very strong," but was unable to agree with certain of Holmes's observations, and elected to write his own dissent. Dissent was a rare experience for Taft. He disliked dissent and indulged in it only about twenty times in the nine years he sat on the Court. He was apt to remind justices that "the continuity and weight of our opinions on important questions of law should not be broken anymore than we can help by dissent."

For Taft, whose dissent was joined by the newcomer Sanford, *Muller* v. *Oregon* controlled *Adkins.* The Nineteenth Amendment "did not change the physical strength or limitations of women upon which the decision in *Muller* v. *Oregon* rests. The Nineteenth Amendment did give women political power and makes more certain that legislative provisions for

* Nearly fourteen years later, on the last Monday of March 1937, the Court finally reversed itself regarding state minimum wage laws for women, in *West Coast Hotel Co.* v. *Parrish.* The Court at the time faced the possibility that Congress, angry at the justices' hostility to New Deal social and economic measures, would approve FDR's plan to pack it. The original vote in the case was 5 to 4 to declare the legislation at issue unconstitutional. Then Justice Owen J. Roberts, one of the five, changed his mind—the famous "switch in time that saved nine," as it came to be known—and the Court upheld Washington state's minimum wage law for women. Sutherland, unrepentant, dissented. The case, he wrote, was "in every substantial respect identical with the statute involved in the Adkins case. Such vices as existed in the latter are present in the former. And if the Adkins case was properly decided, as we who join in this opinion [Van Devanter, McReynolds, and Butler, who also had joined Sutherland in *Adkins*] think it was, it *necessarily* follows that the Washington statute is invalid."

their protection . . . will be in accord with their interests as they see them."

Holmes's weariness with the issue *Adkins* involved notwithstanding, his dissent revealed no diminution of Holmes's judicial powers. That Congress had the power to enact the statute in question he thought was "absolutely free from doubt." Its purpose, "to remove conditions leading to ill health, immorality and the deterioration of the race, no one would deny to be within the scope of constitutional legislation." The means had been approved by Congress, several states, and various foreign governments. In Holmes's mind the matter was settled.

Next he turned to that shibboleth so often employed by the Court's majority, liberty of contract. Nearly all law, he said, recalling his own rationale in his *Lochner* dissent, "consists in forbidding men to do some things that they want to do, and contract is no more exempt than other acts"; he cited in support usury laws, fraud statutes, Sunday laws, regulation of insurance rates, and others the justices had upheld.

The test of constitutionality, as he had said so many times before in similar circumstances, was not "whether we believe the law to be for the public good." If reasonable men reasonably believed a minimum wage statute to be a viable expedient, and if the Constitution did not prohibit it, the Supreme Court had no authority to prohibit it. Holmes himself had some doubts about this one, as he often did, but they involved "whether the bill that has to be paid for every gain . . . was not greater than the gain was worth." The Court, however, did not have to decide that question. He believed the statute was a valid exercise by the legislature, and the lower court, which had said it wasn't, should be reversed. Holmes commented afterwards:

> The C.J. and Sanford seemed to think I said something dangerous or too broad. . . . I think that what I said was plain common sense. It was intended . . . to dethrone Liberty of Contract from its ascendency in the Liberty business.

The Court's invalidation of the District of Columbia minimum wage law affected 12,500 women wage earners there. They could now return to living on $8 and $10 a week instead of the munificent $16.50 which the Minimum Wage Board had required. On the national level, the body language of the Supreme Court had indicated, once again, that legislation which did not conform to the majority's social and economic views would not be tolerated, a gesture that gave rise to considerable

public criticism and demands for Court-curbing legislation. Senator La
Follette carried the issue into his unsuccessful independent campaign
for the presidency in 1924, urging popular election of federal judges and
a constitutional amendment granting Congress power to reenact legislation struck down by the Court. Senator William E. Borah, liberal
Republican of Idaho, proposed legislation to require the approval of no
fewer than seven justices before an act of Congress could be invalidated.
None of these schemes to handcuff the Court was adopted, although
the effect of Borah's threat was to reduce the number of 5 to 4 decisions
temporarily; even Holmes complied and did not dissent so often, at least
for a time. But the Court did not substantially change its direction; the
two branches of government were on their course toward collision in
1937.

PUBLIC RECOGNITION OF his achievement made the spring of
1924 memorable for Holmes. Bertrand Russell's mid-April call on him
and the "jaw" they had together gave him "unmixed joy." He showed
the "joy of a child" when in early June the president conferred on him
the Roosevelt Memorial Association's gold medal for his service to the
law:

> In peace and in war [said Calvin Coolidge, who had succeeded to the pres-
> idency on the death of Harding] as a soldier and as a jurist, you have won
> the gratitude of a nation by your uniformly gracious and patriotic devotion
> of great talent to its service. One can but well feel very confident that
> President Roosevelt would have been peculiarly gratified to know that this
> distinction was to be conferred upon you. This medal will be to you as a
> testimony to the universal recognition of your great public contributions.

These were words Holmes had waited a very long time to hear. They
made a nice addition to the growing Holmes legend. Deeply moved, he
replied:

> For five minutes, Mr. President, you make the dream of a life seem true.
> But one who is still on the firing line cannot dream long. I hope that the
> short time that is left to me will not dim the honor of today.

Summer at Beverly Farms that year was quiet and uneventful. Fanny
was recovering from a severe attack of rheumatism, Holmes from a spring
cough and cold that had taken "the stuffing" out of him. No longer

"oppressed by the thought that [he] ought to be doing something," though he knew not what, Holmes seemed to relax more completely than ever. Even the "bloody shirts" did not seem to agitate him unduly. He visited "one or two ladies for transitory jaws," indulged in the usual summer reading, and took regular drives up and down the coast, renewing his "delight in the rocks and ever changing sea and windswept downs."

At Beveridge's request, Holmes again helped him with his writing, a biography of Lincoln this time. Holmes's concept of biography was not surprisingly a typical nineteenth-century one, and he urged the author to delete references to "belittling things," including the uncertainty surrounding Lincoln's paternity, as well as "dirty words" at which "we have ceased to laugh . . . as we did when little Boys."

The Puritan in him would not allow Holmes to relax too completely, and he began the last of what he called the "Day of Judgment Books": Thucydides, although in a concession to age, he read only three books in Greek, the rest in translation "with only an occasional eye to the original." He feared, he said by way of explaining such a prodigious undertaking, that when he appeared before "le Bon Dieu," he would be asked, "Holmes, can you recite on Thucydides?" Suppose he couldn't? Suppose he had to answer "No, Sire"? Think, he would say, "what a fool I'd feel."

The only interruption of this lovely idyll—and it was more a contribution than an interruption—was a visit from Felix Frankfurter who "delighted" Holmes and was in turn delighted by the long and fruitful talks they had. Following his visit, the ebullient little Harvard Law School professor reported both Holmeses to be "frisky & young as years ago, he better than I've seen him for years."

Term time was something else. Brandeis discerned "no impairment" of his friend's "working powers," but Taft appeared to have begun an attempt to persuade Holmes "as painlessly as possible" that "his usefulness had ceased" and assigned the older man "all of the Court's junk." Some believed the chief justice may have been responsible for the rumors that led newspapers to predict Holmes's resignation, although Holmes himself rather suspected Chief Justice Arthur Rugg of Massachusetts, who perhaps viewed the U.S. Supreme Court as destiny for one in his position since two of his predecessors had been appointed to it. Holmes considered people who started "such yarns" "S.O.Bs" and he denied them all. Like Fuller before him, Holmes refused "to be paragraphed out of [his] office." His biggest worry in the summer of 1924, he told friends, was his "getting a little fat . . . his stored up trousseau may not fit him."

Unable to exile Holmes, Taft did finally in the fall of 1924 convince the pathetically aging McKenna to resign. Then, anxious to shape the Court in his own image, the chief justice persuaded President Coolidge, who had recently defeated the Democrat John Davis and the independent Republican Robert La Follette to become president in his own right, to name his old friend from Amherst College and present attorney general, Harlan Fiske Stone, to McKenna's place.

Descendant of early New England settlers and the son of a New Hampshire farmer, the squarely built Stone had all the square virtues of the self-made man: ambition, determination, stamina, prudence, intellectual vigor, moderation, and frugality. He had put himself through Amherst and Columbia University Law School where he later became dean. While dean, he had divided his time between the school and private law practice in lower New York where he was a partner in a small but influential firm. Shortly after Stone joined one of the big Wall Street legal organizations, the new President Coolidge fired his predecessor's attorney general, Harry M. Daugherty, who was awash in a sea of scandals, and replaced him with Stone, who had helped Coolidge's campaign for the presidency in 1924, speaking particularly against Senator La Follette's proposals to diminish the power of the U.S. Supreme Court. Stone barely had time to disinfect the Justice Department when Coolidge elevated him to the Supreme Court.

Progressives in the Senate were not pleased with Stone's nomination. The smog of the 1924 presidential election, in which Coolidge had defeated one of their own, still clung to the chamber. They accused Stone of unethical professional conduct as attorney general, of harassing another of their own, Senator Burton K. Wheeler of Montana, with trumped-up charges, and of being allied with J. P. Morgan's interests. Finally, in February 1925, after a lengthy and acrimonious debate in the Senate, Stone was confirmed.

On his nomination the *New York Times* predicted that Stone would be "entirely regular on fundamental issues that come before the court." The *New York Times,* however, and a lot of other people, including Stone's sponsor, the president, were scheduled for some surprises. In his early days, Stone was "entirely regular" in his voting patterns, herding with the chief justice and the four horsemen. His stolidity of appearance coincided with a stolidity of mind that came to conclusions slowly and cautiously, if independently, and he required some time to acclimate himself to the political and constitutional weather in the Supreme Court. He had been on the Court less than a year when this justice with the mien of a businessman, this former neighbor of Dwight

W. Morrow, Thomas W. Lamont, and other Morgan partners, prompted
Holmes to caution Harold Laski:

> Don't make a mistake about Stone. He is a mighty sound and liberal-minded
> thinker.

And Brandeis urged Frankfurter:

> As to Harlan's liberalism—wait.

In the meantime, Taft wooed him by inviting him to the chief justice's informal Sunday afternoon conferences during which Taft, Van
Devanter, Sutherland, Butler, and Sanford devised strategies to frustrate the Holmes-Brandeis axis. The former group was in the ascen-
dency now, and the chief justice hoped to keep it that way. He answered complaints that the Court stifled legislative initiative by blaming
the "recklessness" of lawmakers who "refused to consider the question
of their powers at all" and passed "any law that seemed popular." Society, he warned, would not be saved by an "overwhelming mass of ill-
digested legislation."

The Progressive era had ended. The American people had returned
conservative majorities to Congress and sent conservative men to the
White House. The latter, in turn, had appointed conservative judges to
the federal courts, including the U.S. Supreme Court, so that all three
branches of government were for most of the 1920s captives of conservatism.

No one even seemed to mind. The decade of prosperity bred a co-
ordinate complacency. The coming of the automobile, which revolutionized American life more than mere political dogma ever could, diverted
attention from social concerns. By 1927 Ford had put fifteen million
Model Ts on the new roads that were striping the land, and the price
was down to $260, putting a car within reach of a lot of ordinary Amer-
icans. Farmers used it for work and play, factory workers became com-
muters, blacks could drive right off the plantations and out of the South
where they had been penned for centuries and right on into Northern
cities to look for better-paying work. Eyes were blind and ears deaf to
the growing slums, as subsidiary industries—gas stations, tourist cabins
(called motels after World War II), roadside restaurants, highway construction, shopping centers, billboards—blossomed almost as splendidly
as traffic jams.

New luxury goods—cosmetics, gourmet foods, fancy clothing, telephones, radios, movies, electric labor-saving machines—were revolutionizing domestic life. Conspicuous consumption was replacing subsistence economics, installment buying was replacing the use of cash. And all of the new arrangements were sustained by a burgeoning multi-million-dollar advertising industry, which was continuously urging Americans to buy, buy, buy and spend, spend, spend.

Private philanthropy papered over poverty. The social responsibility of the rich for the poor, a noblesse oblige originally articulated by Andrew Carnegie as justification for laissez-faire, allocated a billion dollars to private charity by 1925, including the newly organized community chests operated by middle-class donors, but individual efforts could hardly keep pace with need. A billion dollars was but a drop in the bucket, and the bucket was full of holes.

Bootlegging was the national sport. The speakeasy was living room to millions of Americans, homemade brews and bathtub gin their sustenance. In Washington, illicit liquor flowed freely into the houses of the very men who had written and passed the Eighteenth Amendment. Crime was at a historic high.

Sexual behavior underwent a revolution. The corset and chastity were out, the Charleston was in. The Nineteenth Amendment had given women a psychological as well as a political lift considerably beyond what the married women's property rights laws of the nineteenth century had accomplished. The automobile offered a convenient courting site, suggestive movies and nightclub dance floors dissipated whatever inhibitions remained. Pornography, permissiveness, and promiscuity, the raw materials of the young novelist F. Scott Fitzgerald, were as widespread as he said they were.

Euphoric Americans were even further buoyed by the songs and rhythms of George Gershwin; they laughed with Will Rogers and Robert Benchley, savored the comedies of "Amos 'n Andy." They were less pleased, however, with their portraits in Sinclair Lewis's *Main Street* and *Babbitt*.

Like the rest of the country, the small Southern city that served as the nation's capital was in a manic phase. By mid-decade, demographers estimated that despite postwar demobilization and a substantial exodus, Washington's population stood at nearly half a million. The construction business, then as later, was the biggest business in town outside government. Private dwellings, luxury hotels, apartment houses, and office buildings were rising as fast as contractors could find space for them.

The bulldozer was at work on the H. H. Richardson–built twin houses of John Hay and Henry Adams at 16th and H Streets just across Lafayette Square from the White House. Long before Adams's death in 1918, Holmes had stopped going there for an after-work tete-à-tete and a cup of tea with the dispirited intellectual himself. A new luxury hotel, appropriately named the Hay-Adams, was to rise where these two fine old mansions had stood. Such a slaughter would not have happened in Holmes's Boston, where stately homes, like their stately inhabitants, were in the habit of facing down the bulldozers of progress.

National organizations, beginning with the Chamber of Commerce and the Parent-Teachers Association (PTA), reflecting the increasing centralization of power, were moving their headquarters to Washington, the start of a long-continuing trend. New government buildings to house the Internal Revenue Service and the Department of Commerce were going up just below Pennsylvania Avenue. A convention bureau was established; its first clients, in the summer of 1925, were twenty-five thousand hooded, white-robed Ku Klux Klansmen. After several false starts, Nellie (Mrs. William Howard) Taft's three thousand Japanese cherry trees planted around the Tidal Basin, the gift in 1912 of the mayor of Tokyo, had finally taken hold and blossomed. By 1927 they were so handsome, such a tourist attraction, that a Cherry Blossom Festival was held. It became an annual fete, interrupted only by the war in the 1940s between Japan and the United States.

Like the rest of the country, Washington had adopted the automobile. Gas fumes and "vehicular casualties"—9,400 in 1925—deterred all but the most determined pedestrians, and parking problems—the entire Mall had become an open-air garage—dominated cocktail party small talk. Traffic congestion mounted. The opening of Memorial Bridge connecting Washington with suburban Virginia encouraged many more families to settle in the suburbs and commute to work by automobile. Holmes resisted the automobile for some years and continued to take his daily drives in a hired horse and buggy, catching cabs for longer jaunts and, always, the train to Beverly Farms in summer. He finally succumbed to the "inevitable," but he never owned an automobile; he hired it by the month, complete with driver; that way, Holmes reasoned, he couldn't be sued.

To the comfortable and well-to-do—the people with automobiles, central heating, indoor plumbing, and plenty of food on the table—the United States at mid-decade seemed a second Eden, the New World utopia of which old John Winthrop had dreamed. For those thus blessed, God was in His heaven, and the United States Supreme Court stood guard at the gates, making sure all was indeed right with the world.

Benjamin Gitlow was exactly the sort of fellow against whom the Supreme Court's majority felt America needed protection: a Socialist, author of *The Left Wing Manifesto,* and business manager of *The Revolutionary Age,* official organ of the Socialist Party's Left Wing section which advocated Communist revolution and proletarian dictatorship. His activities had brought him into conflict with the section of New York's penal code which prohibited criminal anarchy, defined as "the doctrine that organized government should be overthrown by force or violence or by assassination of the executive head or of any of the executive officials of government, or by any unlawful means." He had been convicted in 1920, sentenced to five to ten years at hard labor, and his conviction had been upheld by the New York State Court of Appeals. He based his Supreme Court challenge of his conviction on the ground that it violated the "due process of law" guaranteed by the Fourteenth Amendment.

The U.S. Supreme Court's record was inconsistent regarding the relationship of the Fourteenth Amendment to personal liberties, as was Holmes's. In 1920, in *Gilbert* v. *Minnesota,* the justices, including Holmes, had allowed Minnesota's espionage act to stand. Two years later, in *Prudential Insurance Company* v. *Cheek,* they—including Holmes—had declared categorically that "the Constitution . . . imposes on the States no obligation to confer upon those within their jurisdiction . . . the right of free speech." Then, in 1923, in *Meyer* v. *Nebraska,* the Court, Holmes dissenting, had struck down state laws prohibiting the teaching of foreign languages below the high school level. Only a week before the Court was to announce its decision in Benjamin Gitlow's case, Holmes had joined its decision * to strike down Oregon's law forbidding parents to send their children to private schools. The "liberty" protected by the Fourteenth Amendment seemed to some observers to be expanding a little, at least enough to embrace the right of parents to bring up their children as they saw fit. Was the Court also beginning to clear the way for protecting free expression in the states?

No. The Court's majority, which rarely hesitated to use the Fourteenth Amendment against disagreeable social and economic measures enacted by state legislatures, viewing them as inroads against property rights, had developed a keen solicitude for state-sponsored legislation that made inroads against human rights, especially those of Socialists and their ilk who appeared to threaten traditional values. In *Gitlow,*

---

* *Pierce* v. *Society of Sisters.* 268 U.S. 510 (1925).

"every presumption is to be indulged in favor of the validity of the statute." The majority upheld the constitutionality of the operative section of the New York penal code; it was, the justices said, a valid exercise of the state's police power. Taft assigned the majority opinion to Sanford, who adapted Holmes's imagery of fire to fit the facts in *Gitlow,* but rejected Holmes's reasoning. For Sanford, the danger from incitement to unlawful behavior need not be so "clear and present," as Holmes had required in *Schenck;* its vagueness made it no less threatening:

> A single revolutionary spark may kindle a fire that, smoldering for a time, may burst into a sweeping and destructive conflagration. It cannot be said that the State is acting arbitrarily or unreasonably when in the exercise of its judgment as to the measures necessary to protect the public peace and safety, it seeks to extinguish the spark without waiting until it has enkindled the flame or blazed into the conflagration. It cannot reasonably be required to defer the adoption of measures for its own peace and safety until the revolutionary utterances lead to actual disturbances. . . . It may . . . suppress the threatened danger in its incipiency.

Holmes did not agree—eloquently, even though it had been his custom to let the work of local lawmakers live whether their efforts involved ephemeral economic arrangements or the more enduring liberties of the person. From *Patterson* v. *Colorado* in 1907 to *Gilbert* v. *Minnesota* in 1920, Holmes's scheme of federalism allowed the states the same freedom to deal with seditious discussion as with murder.

What changed his mind? He did not write for publication in *Gilbert* v. *Minnesota,* but only confided his view of state power privately to Felix Frankfurter. Possibly he was influenced by the fact that Minnesota's espionage act was a wartime precaution, not intended to be permanent. Possibly Gilbert's antiwar speech seemed a clearer and more imminent threat to the republic than Gitlow's Socialist propaganda, which Holmes called "drool." If he

> didn't believe that socialism rested on dramatic contrasts and not on a serious consideration of what changes it could be expected to make in the nature of distribution of the stream of products, [he] should listen to it with more respect—But the argument never gets much farther than look at the big house and the little one—It never becomes quantitative—asking how much does the tax levied by the rich for the pleasures of the few

amount to—Also it never proposes to begin by taking life in hand—which seem[ed] to [Holmes] the only possible starting point for an attempt at social revolution.

Brandeis alone* joined Holmes's dissent in *Gitlow*. Although Brandeis undoubtedly would have liked Holmes to include in his dissent some soaring statement about the sanctity of freedom of speech, he knew better; he understood Holmes's antipathy toward abstract civil libertarian concepts, Holmes's disdain for men's rights. Brandeis had a certain sympathy for the oppressed; Holmes had little; what he had was contempt for the oppressor. Brandeis was content this time to let his friend speak for him.

Socialism disputed everything Holmes valued, but where others saw even wage and hour legislation as a threat to individual freedom, an opening of the road to Socialism, Holmes dismissed such fears lightly. Talk of class war he thought "humbug," and he ranked Benjamin Gitlow with Jacob Abrams and his friends—"poor and puny anonymities," he had called the latter. He thought Gitlow's efforts almost a joke with the slimmest "chance of starting a present conflagration."

Although Holmes had agreed with the majority in the Prudential Insurance Company case three years before that the states were under no obligation to honor the First Amendment's guarantee of free speech, he now declared categorically that the "general principle of free speech . . . must be taken to be included in the Fourteenth Amendment," and that his own opinion in *Schenck* was the operative precedent here. Gitlow, he declared, had presented "no present danger of an attempt to overthrow the government by force."

For the rest, he relied largely on the Darwinian concept of free expression he had developed for *Abrams* in 1919:

> It is said that this manifesto was . . . an incitement. Every idea is an incitement. It offers itself for belief and if believed it is acted on unless some other belief outweighs it or some failure of energy stifles the movement at its birth. The only difference between the expression of an opinion and an incitement in the narrow sense is the speaker's enthusiasm for the result. Eloquence may set fire to reason. . . . If in the long run the beliefs expressed in proletarian dictatorship are destined to be accepted by the

---

* *Gitlow* had been argued before Stone took his seat on the Court and he did not participate in the decision. The court reporter, however, omitted that fact in his notes, and it does not appear in the *United States Reports*.

dominant forces of the community, the only meaning of free speech is that they should be given their chance and have their way.

Zechariah Chafee at Harvard Law School was ecstatic. In the next edition of his book *Free Speech in the United States,* he ranked Holmes and Brandeis with Milton and Mill, rhapsodizing:

> The victories of liberty of speech must be won in the mind before they are won in the courts. In that battlefield of reason we possessed in 1925 new and powerful weapons, the dissenting opinions of Justices Holmes and Brandeis. . . . The majority opinions determined the cases, but these dissenting opinions will determine the minds of the future.

One subject of all this admiration was weary of the issue and bored by the case. Holmes insisted that his performance in *Gitlow* conferred only "the right of a donkey to talk drool about the proletarian dictatorship, etc.," then added contemptuously, "In practice the sacred right of free speech means that I will let you say anything that does not shock *me.*"

As for Benjamin Gitlow, he had been nominated in 1921, while in prison, by the Workers' League for mayor of New York, but was denied a place on the ballot on the grounds that he would not be available to serve. In the end he was pardoned by Governor Alfred E. Smith after serving three years of his five- to ten-year sentence.

CHAPTER 28

"Three generations of imbeciles are enough"

HOLMES CELEBRATED HIS eighty-fifth birthday on March 8, 1926, with the usual deluge of cards, letters, and telegrams plus an outpouring of felicitations in the press that "surprised" and "pleased" him. Frankfurter planted another paean of praise in the *New Republic,* noting that the "tender, wise and beautiful being who is Mr. Justice Holmes" was "one of those unique gifts, whose response to life is so transforming that he vivifies life for all who come within his range." Ironic how the men responsible for Holmes's being where he was—Lodge, who had died sixteen months before, leaving "a blank" for Holmes; Roosevelt, who had died, half deaf and blind in one eye, seven years ago—had passed into history, and here was Holmes, his work increasingly noticed and honored, his intellect still functioning, his domestic life with Fanny serene. He confided to Brandeis shortly after his birthday that the last fifteen years, what Holmes defined as his "old age," had been "unquestionably the happiest period of [his] life."

By 1926, many of the cases that came to the Supreme Court were only restatements of old familiar questions that required little digging through the layers of precedent. In most of them Holmes joined the Taft-led majority, as was his custom unless the justices dented one of his judicial fenders, in which case he was often able to merely rephrase familiar principles he had been advancing for more than two decades, largely without success:

> [In] dealing with state legislation upon matters of substantive law we should
> avoid with great caution attempts to substitute our judgment for that of the
> body whose business it is in the first place, with regard to questions of

domestic policy that fairly are open to debate . . . the great body of the law consists in drawing such lines, yet when you realize that you are dealing with a matter of degree you must realize that reasonable men may differ widely as to the place where the line should fall . . . the law allows a penumbra to be embraced that goes beyond the outline of its object in order that the object may be secured. (*Schlesinger* v. *Wisconsin,* 270 U.S. 230, 241, 1926)

[I]f the Legislature regarded the danger [from the use of unsterilized shoddy in comfortables] as very great and inspection and tagging as inadequate remedies, it seems to me that in order to prevent the spread of disease it constitutionally could forbid any use of shoddy for bedding and upholstery. (*Weaver* v. *Palmer Brothers Co.,* 270 U.S. 402, 415, 1926)

If a State speaking through its legislature should think that, in order to make its highways most useful, the business traffic upon them must be controlled, I suppose that no one would doubt that it constitutionally could, as, I presume, most States or cities do, exercise some such control. The only question is how far it can go. (*Frost Trucking Co.* v. *Railroad Commission of California,* 271 U.S. 583, 601, 1926)

We fear to grant power and are unwilling to recognize it when it exists. . . . [W]hen legislatures are held to be authorized to do anything considerably affecting public welfare it is covered by apologetic phrases like the police power, or the statement that the business concerned has been dedicated to a public use. The former expression is convenient, to be sure, to conciliate the mind to something that needs explanation: the fact that the constitutional requirement of compensation when property is taken cannot be pressed to its grammatical extreme; that property rights may be taken for public purposes without pay if you do not take too much; that some play must be allowed to the joints if the machine is to work. But police power often is used in a wide sense to cover and . . . to apologize for the general power of the legislature to make a part of the community uncomfortable by a change.

I do not believe in such apologies. I think the proper course is to recognize that a state legislature can do whatever it sees fit to do unless it is restrained by some express prohibition in the Constitution of the United States or of the State, and that Courts should be careful not to extend such prohibitions beyond their obvious meaning by reading into them conceptions of public policy that the particular Court may happen to entertain. . . . The notion that a business is clothed with a public interest and has been devoted to the public use is little more than a fiction intended to beautify what is disagreeable to the sufferers. The truth seems to me to be that, subject to compensation when compensation is due, the legislature may forbid or restrict any business when it has a sufficient force of public opinion behind it. Lotteries were thought useful adjuncts of the State a century ago; now they are believed to be immoral and they have been stopped. Wine has been thought good for man from the time of the Apostles until recent years. But when public opinion changed it did not need the Eighteenth Amendment, notwithstanding the Fourteenth, to enable a State to say that the business should end. . . . What has happened to lotteries and wine might happen to theatres in some moral storm of the future, not because theatres were devoted to a public use, but because people had come to think that way. (*Tyson & Brother* v. *Banton*, 273 U.S. 418, 445–446, 1927)

Even 1926's battle between the legislature and the presidency, *Myers* v. *United States*, with its cumbersome baggage of complicated political history and potential for disturbing relationships between the branches of government, when Holmes got hold of it boiled down to the old familiar question of judicial deference to legislative authority, to the "actual feelings and demands of the community."

The Constitution conferred on the president the power to appoint various officials of the government with the advice and consent of the Senate, but it was silent on the subject of removing them. *Myers* asked whether the president could remove one of his appointees without the approval of the Senate. Had Woodrow Wilson acted unlawfully when he fired Postmaster Frank S. Myers of Portland, Oregon, before the end of the latter's term, without Senate permission? Was the legislation enacted in 1876 which set postmasters' terms and provided for their removal with the advice and consent of the Senate, unconstitutional? Myers's heirs—both he and Wilson had died in the interim—sued in the Court of Claims to recover his salary for the unexpired part of his term. When that court rejected the claim, they turned to the Supreme Court, which had never settled the issue, although it had begged for settlement at intervals over the past century and a half.

Taft, with an ex-president's concern for executive power in general, over hiring and firing specifically, and a patrician's fears of congressional excesses, had no doubt that Wilson had acted within his rights. He hoped to establish the presidential prerogative via this "most important case," preferably with a unanimous Court. No sooner had he circulated the first draft of his opinion, the writing of which was too important to entrust to any of the others, than Brandeis announced his intention to dissent. Taft was disappointed, but not surprised:

> Brandeis puts himself where he naturally belongs. He is in favor evidently of the group system . . . opposed to a strong Executive. . . . His ideals do not include effective and uniform administration unless he is the head. That of course is the attitude of the socialist. . . .

Perhaps recalling Brandeis's role in bringing down members of his own administration, Taft added:

> He loves the kicker, and is therefore in sympathy with the power of the Senate to prevent the Executive from removing obnoxious persons, because he always sympathizes with the obnoxious person.

Taft was also not surprised when Holmes declared his plan to dissent; he rather suspected Holmes's advanced age was breeding an increased dependence on Brandeis. But McReynolds's dissent shattered him. He put it down to "cantankerous[ness]," and confided bitterly to his brother that

> McReynolds and Brandeis belong to a class of people that have no loyalty to the Court and sacrifice almost everything to the gratification of their own publicity and wish to stir up dissatisfaction with the decision of the Court, if they don't happen to agree with it.

For Taft, writing *Myers* was sheer agony. He took a long historical trip back to the First Congress, where the issue originally had been debated, and followed the trail through the nineteenth century. He analyzed the separation of powers. He reassured the men and women of the Civil Service whom he said would not be affected by the *Myers* decision.

As he wrote, he worried about his logic, his organization of the voluminous material, and what the dissenters were going to say. He sought the advice of the justices who had voted with him, invited them to Sunday editorial sessions at his home "to run [the opinion] over"; he wanted "to get it into shape so that it will be ready for [all the justices'] careful consideration." *Myers* was his last thought before he dropped off to sleep at night. Revision followed revision. The original twenty-eight pages more than doubled. It took Taft a year to write them, and when he had finished, he felt "like a woman who has given birth to a large child."

The result, however, was worth the agonizing hours at his desk. Taft had high hopes for his offspring. In ascending order of importance, the Court's decision affirmed the judgment of the Court of Claims—there had been nothing improper in Wilson's dismissal procedure; it declared that section of the 1876 legislation that required Senate approval of presidential firings unconstitutional; and it preserved the power of the executive, made it practically unlimited in the hiring and firing of almost all presidential appointees except judges.* Taft thought it ought to stem "the advance of Congress" which he felt had been trying to dilute presidential authority.

Holmes joined in the conclusions of both McReynolds's and Brandeis's dissents and spoke admiringly of their "exhaustive research," although in private he undoubtedly resented having to plow through it—together they totaled 117 pages. He wished, though, he told them, to add a "few words" of his own.

And a few words it was. He alone was brief—three paragraphs. He accused Taft of weaving "spider's webs inadequate to control the dominant facts." Stripped down to its skeleton, the issue for Holmes proved to be the simple matter of recognizing Congress as the official lawmaker for the nation, including the president and the judiciary. The office of postmaster, he said, owed

> its existence to Congress and . . . Congress may abolish it tomorrow. . . . The duty of the President to see that the laws be executed is a duty that does not go beyond the laws or require him to achieve more than Congress sees fit to leave within his power.

Congress giveth and Congress taketh away.

Brahmin Boston had been quiescent about its maverick judge in recent years. Perhaps Holmes had outlived the critics whose teeth had been set on edge by his writings in *Vegelahn* and *Plant* nearly three decades before. He had not, however, outlived Johnny Morse, who undoubtedly had long chafed at what he considered his cousin's deference to, even championship of, labor, anarchists, and economic regulation of all sorts. Like Taft, he perhaps saw something socialistic about subor-

---

* Taft's "large child" remained the law of the land for nine years. He did not live to see Sutherland, writing in 1935 for a unanimous Court in *Humphrey's Executor* v. *United States,* substantially narrow the scope of *Myers* by denying the president authority to dismiss members of the independent regulatory agencies and other inferior offices without Senate approval.

dinating the president to the Congress, and he couldn't resist saying so. Holmes replied affectionately but firmly:

Dear Johnny
Your letter is delightful. . . . You . . . probably know that I listen respectfully to any opinion of yours. . . . [T]hough I don't share your opinion as to the evils of the power of Congress, yet if I did it could make no difference. I think one of the most subtle dangers of giving the last word to the Court is that judges read into the Constitution their notions of what is desirable instead of coldly interpreting the document. It has given me pleasure to sustain the Constitutionality of laws that I believe to be as bad as possible, because I thereby helped to mark the difference between what I would forbid and what the Constitution permits.

In 1927, BLACKS all over the country, not only in the South, were vying for the money and attention of the NAACP, which had stepped up its efforts to remodel a social system through legal challenges. Letters begging help for blacks in trouble with the law, their neighbors, or their governments were delivered daily to NAACP headquarters in New York City. Some were typed legibly on proper stationery; others were scribbled by unlettered hands on scraps of soiled paper; all were pathetic. The NAACP, after some months of discussion and deliberation, decided to sponsor the case of Dr. A. L. Nixon, a prominent El Paso, Texas, physician, who had been denied the right to vote in primary elections. A case like Dr. Nixon's held the potential for influencing voting rights of blacks throughout the South.

The case, known as *Nixon* v. *Herndon,* was argued in early January 1927. Holmes's old friend Moorfield Storey had originally been scheduled to appear, but had begged off; he was eighty-two years old now, and the trip to Washington was time-consuming as well as tiring. He had suffered a serious setback only a few months before when the property-sensitive Supreme Court had unanimously approved a racially restrictive covenant drawn up by a group of white neighbors in midtown Washington, D.C.*Storey had argued the case. The decision had reopened gates that had seemed to be closed ten years before. Now resi-

---

* *Corrigan* v. *Buckley.* 271 U.S. 323 (1926).

It required two decades and a climate more favorable to civil rights for the U.S. Supreme Court to put a stop to the old reliable restrictive covenant which had effectively imprisoned blacks in the ghetto. Finally, in 1948, Chief Justice Fred M. Vinson wrote for a unanimous Court in *Shelley* v. *Kramer* that judicial enforcement of a racially restrictive covenant amounted to state action and as such was prohibited by the Fourteenth Amendment.

dents who wanted to keep their neighborhoods white need not resort to restrictive ordinances, which *Buchanan* v. *Warley* had ruled unconstitutional in 1917; they had only to draw up private agreements. Storey was more sanguine about *Nixon* v. *Herndon,* however, which he viewed as a "simple case and one the court will have no trouble . . . in dealing with."

The Court's record was slightly more favorable to blacks in cases involving their civil rights than in those involving property rights. *Nixon* v. *Herndon* fell squarely into the former category. It had grown out of the schemes and subterfuges local governments had devised to deny blacks the vote, lest they enlist their superior numbers in some areas to take over politics. Encouraged by a previous Supreme Court decision that had approved disenfranchisement of blacks in primary elections, which often were not thought to be "basic" to the electoral process, Texas did not even bother with subterfuge but enacted a blatantly discriminatory white primary law in 1923: "In no event shall a Negro be eligible to participate in a Democratic Party election in the State of Texas." Since the primary elections when Democrats battled each other for city, county, and state offices were the only elections that counted in Texas and other parts of the South, a white primary effectively deprived the black of a voice in government.

Dr. Nixon was challenging the constitutionality of the Texas law. He had lost in the lower federal court, which had held that state primaries were exempt from federal jurisdiction. He had turned to the Supreme Court where a local El Paso lawyer actually argued the case, guided by the brief submitted by Storey and other NAACP lawyers. Texas election officials against whom the suit had been brought did not bother to appear for oral argument.

Taft had been assigning "a pretty interesting lot of cases" to Holmes this term. Holmes sometimes feared the "Chief" might be "considering his age &c" and giving him the "easy ones," though Brandeis on consultation thought not. In any event, Taft gave Holmes the Court's unanimous opinion in Dr. Nixon's case.

Certainly Holmes's advancing age had had no effect on the speed with which he worked. He still had the cases assigned to him on Saturday to the printer on Monday and in the hands of the brethren on Tuesday. He announced the Court's decision in *Nixon* v. *Herndon* on March 7, 1927, the eve of his eighty-sixth birthday, which would be marked at 1720 I Street by the arrival of flowers, congratulatory telegrams, and letters, including one from President Coolidge. On the night before he announced this politically sensitive case, which state legislatures all over the South were monitoring closely, he had "rollicked" with laughter at Douglas Fairbanks in *The Black Pirate,* and when he began to read for the Court in the Nixon case, whispered comments on his still firm voice circulated through the courtroom.

The Court had decided to unequivocally support Dr. Nixon's suit and to invalidate the Texas white primary law. In a surprise move, the justices relied not on the Fifteenth Amendment, which prohibits denial of the right to vote by the United States "or by any State on account of race, color, or previous condition of servitude," but on the Fourteenth Amendment, which guarantees "equal protection of the laws." The Court had found it "unnecessary," Holmes explained, to consider the Fifteenth Amendment, "because it seems to us hard to imagine a more direct and obvious infringement of the Fourteenth," which, while it "applies to all," had been passed "with a special intent to protect the blacks from discrimination against them." Quoting from the late Justice Day's opinion in *Buchanan* v. *Warley,* he described that amendment as not only giving "citizenship and the privileges of citizenship to persons of color," but also as denying "to any State the power to withhold from them the equal protection of the laws. . . . What is this but declaring that the law in the States shall be the same for the black as for the white; that all persons, whether colored or white, shall stand equal before the laws of the States . . . ?" He made no apologies for failing to make his usual bow to the state legislature this time; rather, he told Texas in firm, lucid language that its government had exceeded the speed limit:

> States may do a good deal of classifying that it is difficult to believe rational but there are limits, and it is too clear for extended argument that color cannot be made the basis of a statutory classification affecting the right set up in this case.

James Weldon Johnson, secretary of the NAACP, expressed keen pleasure in the Court's decision. Governor Dan Moody of Texas observed that "some legislation will be necessary to protect the ballot and give the guaranty of good government which the voided statute was designed to offer." The Texas legislature did in fact perform a series of legislative gymnastics which were not brought under control until 1944, in *Smith* v. *Allwright,* in which the U.S. Supreme Court uncompromisingly and leaving no room for further stunts, condemned all racial discrimination in the electoral process.

Nixon v. *Herndon* was the last major case of discrimination against blacks in which Holmes participated. His own record over the past quarter century, like the Court's, was mixed. There were exceptions, but in general, his judgments had been a little more favorable to blacks when civil rights were involved than when property rights were the issue. Ever since he had written, in 1903, his first year on the Court, that the justices could not enforce political rights (*Giles* v. *Harris*), he had begun to tilt the other way. He had joined in the Court's nullification of racially discriminatory state voting rights laws (*Grandfather Clause Cases*), had even written two of them (*United States* v. *Mosely, Nixon* v. *Herndon*), and he had been particularly adamant in condemning the legal lynching of blacks by the state courts (*United States* v. *Shipp, Moore* v. *Dempsey*). But, inclined to recommend local problems to local solutions and loathe to disturb the work of state legislatures, he had upheld Alabama's blatantly discriminatory economic measures as set down in the peonage statutes (*Bailey* v. *Alabama, United States* v. *Reynolds*) and Oklahoma's railroad accommodations law (*McCabe* v. *Atchison, Topeka and Santa Fe Railway Co.*); he had threatened to dissent when the Court decided to invalidate Louisville's racially restrictive covenant ordinance (*Buchanan* v. *Warley*), and he had uncomplainingly joined the Court in approving the private scheme for residential segregation which Washingtonians had put together (*Corrigan* v. *Buckley*).

It is in this area of racial discrimination that Holmes's commitment to the permanent values of the American political system—suffrage, fair trial, and other personal liberties outlined in the Bill of Rights—stands out in high relief against what he considered the ephemeral values implied in social and economic legislation, of which he was merely tolerant. Encroachment on the former seemed more likely to move him to action than did encroachment on the latter, and he was not unwilling to curb state power when a man's right to vote was at stake. But, isolated and insulated, he seemed unaware of the depths of economic and social discrimination, and he looked at peonage laws through the same spectacles he wore for reading wage and hour statutes, found them subject to society's frequently changing whims, and aggressively left them alone.

At the end of the third decade of the twentieth century, the black man was not much better off than he had been at the end of the nineteenth century. The justices went to the funerals of their court messengers, but they were miserly about wielding the full power of the Constitution. *Plessy* v. *Ferguson,* with its separate-but-equal formula, was still *the* precedent, and Jim Crow was still the leading character in black life.

*   *   *

As MARCH SLIPPED into April 1927, a long letter from Doneraile Court informed Holmes his "Beloved Hibernia" had died. She had been ill—her heart—for several months. He had last said goodbye to her fourteen years before, not knowing it would be forever. He often wondered what had become of "the other," whose name Holmes could never remember, although "the other" had put his "nose out of joint." Before and even during the war he had kept alive the hope that he would one day return, and glimpse her once again. After the war he stopped talking about such a trip. Then last year he had heard she was ill. Now she was gone, and another "gap" had appeared in his "horizon," this one looming perhaps larger than most, a gap not even the double-flowering cherry blossoms and the pink and white dogwood that signalled April's bringing of new life could fill.

Albert Beveridge died, too, that spring—in mid-sentence, as it were, leaving his life of Lincoln unfinished. He, too, would be missed, and Holmes cried out to Frankfurter in anguish: "Kindly remain alive. Even my haircutter is dead."

Holmes's commitment to legislative power reached its apogee in the spring of 1927 in the famous eugenics case, *Buck* v. *Bell,* a case that disappointed admirers of Holmes and threatened to tarnish the growing Holmes legend. Such reactions, however, were of no consequence to him. The fact that at last he had been assigned to write the Court's opinion in a case in which he could combine support for legislative authority with personal approval of the social measure at issue was a rare occurrence, and it gave him "pleasure."

The case began with the admission of Carrie Buck, a white unwed mother, to the Virginia Colony for Epileptics and Feebleminded at Lynchburg, later known as the Central Virginia Training Center. Carrie's mother, Emma Buck, was already a resident there. Standard intelligence tests in vogue at the time had established that Carrie had achieved only a mental age of nine—within the definition of moron—Emma, about eight. Carrie's illegitimate daughter, Vivian, although only seven months old at the time, was pronounced "not quite normal." Under a Virginia statute of 1924 that allowed the sterilization of men and women "afflicted with hereditary forms of insanity, imbecility, &c," plans were made to sterilize eighteen-year-old Carrie "in the best interests of patient and society." Carrie's court-appointed guardian immediately began legal proceedings to stop the sterilization. At her trial in 1924, "experts" testified that the feeblemindedness of the three Bucks—mother, daughter, daughter's daughter—conformed to the Mendelian laws of inheritance and upheld the order for her sterilization. The case made its way through the Virginia courts, where the order for sterilization was also upheld, to the U.S. Supreme Court.

The American public was at the time caught up in a eugenics craze. Since the earliest years of the twentieth century, lecturers, books by enthusiastic laymen as well as scientists, articles in law journals, newspapers, and magazines had popularized the idea that selective breeding could vastly improve the composition of the human race. Physical, mental, even social defects could over many years be bred out, and a world of superior beings achieved—a world free of crime, mental disabilities, such hereditary abnormalities as epilepsy, and other defects believed to run in families the same way color ran through generations of cows. Eugenics societies had sprouted up, state fairs featured Fitter Families Contests, Gregor Mendel became a household name, the Mendelian laws of heredity the subject of samplers.

Tests of intelligence were devised and given to draftees during World War I, incorporated into the personnel practices of businesses, and administered to school children on a national scale. And state legislators rushed to enact sterilization laws, most of which in the early days were found by the courts to be unconstitutional. Virginia's law had been designed to meet judicial objections, and Carrie Buck had been chosen to test it.

Holmes was a true believer. Thirty years before he had urged law students at Boston University to think deeply about such "fundamental questions" as whether the criminal law did "more good than harm":

> Do we deal with criminals on proper principles? . . . If the typical criminal is a degenerate, bound to swindle or to murder by as deep seated an organic necessity as that which makes the rattlesnake bite, it is idle to talk of deterring him by the classical method of imprisonment. He must be got rid of; he cannot be improved, or frightened out of his structural reaction. If, on the other hand, crime, like normal human conduct, is mainly a matter of imitation, punishment fairly may be expected to help keep it out of fashion.

Statistics describing the high incidence of crime in crowded cities where example had "the greatest chance to work" supported the latter view. "[W]eighty authority," however—a new school of continental criminologists who had shifted their investigations from the study of crime to the study of the criminal—also supported the former view, as did Holmes's personal prejudices: his Boston Brahmin's instincts for racial purity combined with recollections of Dr. Holmes's investigations of the relationship between heredity and moral responsibility, which is the theme of the doctor's first novel, *Elsie Venner*—in which, incidentally, a rattlesnake's bite is the cause of all the trouble. The theme had long interested Dr. Holmes, and in 1872, he had written in one of his regular columns for the *Atlantic Monthly:*

> When [the traditionalists] have come across a moral monster they seemed to think that he put himself together, having a free choice to all the constituents which make up manhood, and that consequently no punishment could be too bad for him.
>
> I say, hang him . . . if that is the best thing for society; hate him, in a certain sense, as you hate a rattlesnake, but if you pretend to be a philosopher, recognize the fact that what you hate in him is chiefly misfortune, and that if you had been born with his villainous low forehead and poisoned instincts, and bred among creatures of the *Races Maudites* whose natural history has to be studied like that of beasts of prey and vermin, you would not have been sitting there in your gold bowed spectacles and passing judgment on the peccadilloes of your fellow creatures.

Taking everything he had read, heard, and remembered into consideration, the younger Holmes had decided in 1897 that " 'not the nature of the crime, but the dangerousness of the criminal, constitutes the only reasonable criterion to guide the inevitable social reaction against the criminal.' "

When in 1914 a new edition of the English political economist Thomas Malthus's *Essays on Population* appeared, Holmes bought it, consumed it eagerly, was persuaded of the potential for disaster in population pressures, and became a "devout Malthusian." Over the next decade, he synthesized the thoughts he had thrown out to the young men in 1897 and those Malthus had thrown out to the world a century before. Using Malthusian terms and concepts, he began to talk like a eugenicist. The idea that humankind might "secure an economic paradise by changes in property alone" seemed to him "twaddle." He could better understand "legislation that aims rather to improve the quality than to increase the quantity of the population." He could understand saying "we will keep certain strains out of our blood," and in his private utopia, Holmes would impose a "systematic prevention of the survival of the unfit." He would congratulate, not condemn, a physician who refrained from performing life-saving surgery on an "idiot." Eugenics, he had long believed, was the "true beginning, theoretically, of all improvement." Humankind must stop "tinkering with the institution of property," and begin "taking in hand life and trying to build a race."

When the U.S. Supreme Court, assembled in conference, took under consideration the constitutionality of Virginia's sterilization law, no fewer than eight justices voted to uphold it. McReynolds, Van Devanter, Sutherland, Butler, and Taft at last had found a piece of contemporary social legislation they could support—something with implications for preserving tradition and order instead of disrupting them, as most modern measures attempted to do. Only Butler, a Roman Catholic and friend of members of the American Catholic hierarchy, voted to strike down the Virginia law, although he did not divulge his reasons.

Taft assigned the majority opinion to Holmes; Holmes's authorship of an opinion that might appear to some to encroach on personal liberties could provide a sugar coating for the bitter medicine. When he gave the job to Holmes, Taft advised caution:

> Some of the brethren are troubled about the case, especially Butler. May I suggest that you make a little full the care Virginia has taken in guarding against undue or hasty action, the proven absence of danger to the patient, and other circumstances tending to lessen the shock many feel over such a remedy? The strength of the facts in three generations of course is the strongest argument for the necessity for state action and its reasonableness.

Holmes heeded the chief justice's advice, and Taft pronounced the finished opinion "admirably put." Holmes had tiptoed around implications that Virginia's sterilization statute denied personal liberties and concentrated on the legal and medical safeguards constructed around the person:

> the rights of the patient are most carefully considered.

Carrie Buck had had every consideration required under "due process of law."

Next he addressed the social justification for such an order, rephrasing the principle he had laid down in *The Common Law* that

> no society has ever admitted that it could not sacrifice individual welfare to its own existence.

He put it similarly in *Buck* v. *Bell:*

We have seen more than once that the public welfare may call upon the best citizens for their lives. It would be strange if it could not call upon those who already sap the strength of the State for these lesser sacrifices, often not felt to be such by those concerned, in order to prevent our being swamped with incompetence.

The social engineer took over from the soldier:

It is better for all the world, if instead of waiting to execute degenerate offspring for crime, or to let them starve for their imbecility, society can prevent those who are manifestly unfit from continuing their kind. The principle that sustains compulsory vaccination is broad enough to cover cutting the Fallopian tubes. . . . Three generations of imbeciles are enough.

Buck v. *Bell*, which he announced on May 2, 1927, as the term was winding down, was one of Holmes's strongest, most pungent opinions. Maximum hours, regulation of theater ticket prices, of coal mining procedures—in these he easily glossed over the regulation itself and concentrated on the use of constitutional authority. Not so regarding Virginia's sterilization statute. Here there was no softening of the argument with the usual doubts involving the wisdom of the law at issue—his belief in its wisdom is apparent in the rhetoric. He felt in fact that he had gotten, in *Buck* v. *Bell*, "near to the first principle of real reform." He didn't want to imply that the "surgeon's knife" was the "ultimate symbol," but he did feel he was "getting near."

Shortly after the Court's opinion was announced, Carrie Buck was sterilized. She was eventually discharged from the Virginia Colony for Epileptics and Feebleminded. She married twice—her first husband died after twenty-four years of marriage—sang in the Methodist Church choir, and took work helping a family in Front Royal, Virginia, to care for an elderly relative. She died in a state-operated nursing home near Waynesboro, Virginia, in 1983, at the age of seventy-seven.

Considerable doubt surrounds her imbecility today. In fact, she was said to display substantial intelligence as well as kindness, to be an avid reader and a lucid conversationalist, even in her last days. Her daughter, Vivian, lived only eight years, but she, too, contradicted institutional and judicial estimates of her mental capacities. She went through the second grade in school and was considered by her teachers to be "very bright."

Following the Supreme Court's decision in *Buck* v. *Bell*, state legislators once more rushed to enact sterilization laws, and by the end of the decade, no fewer than twenty-four states had done so. Approximately a thousand inmates of the Virginia Colony for Epileptics and Feebleminded were sterilized over the ten years following the Court's decision; some twenty thousand men and women were sterilized during that time throughout the United States.

CHAPTER 29

Sacco and Vanzetti

THE USUAL SERENITY of the summer at Beverly Farms was disrupted in August of 1927 by the intrusion of the Sacco and Vanzetti case, which was permanently dividing not only Boston but also much of the Western world into two opposing camps: those who believed the two Italians had in truth robbed the South Braintree, Massachusetts, shoe factory and killed the guard and paymaster that mid-April day in 1920, and those who had been persuaded that the two men had been railroaded, persecuted for their political beliefs, were really the innocent victims of the anti-Red hysteria of the early 1920s. Holmes had avoided reading about the case for the six years it had been bouncing around the Massachusetts courts, as the defendants' lawyers struggled unsuccessfully to get their clients a new trial, but he could not escape it. Ultimately he was involved personally as well as professionally.

Holmes's friend Felix Frankfurter was one of those who had been instrumental in stirring up the wasps' nest when he wrote an article on the case for the March 1927 *Atlantic Monthly*. In it he charged that the case against Sacco and Vanzetti for murder "was part of a collusive effort between the District Attorney and agents of the Department of Justice to rid the country of these two Italians because of their Red activities." By "systematic exploitation of the defendants' alien blood, their imperfect knowledge of English, their unpopular social views, and their opposition to the war, the District Attorney had invoked against them a riot of political passion and patriotic sentiment; and the trial judge connived—one had almost written, cooperated—in the process." In the men's defense, Frankfurter wrote that they had never been positively identified as the murderers, that they both had alibis for the day on which the robbery and murders occurred, and that overall the evidence against them had been inconclusive. Frankfurter expanded the article into a book, *The Case of Sacco and Vanzetti,* also published in 1927. He sent Holmes a copy, which the justice read immediately and which "moved [him] much." In a terse and unforthcoming thank-you note to his friend, Holmes confessed the book was the only source of his knowledge about the case. Fearing he might have to act in the case officially, he did not want to say more.

Holmes admired Frankfurter's "heroism," but thought the ebullient little law professor was "potently abetting" with his writing "the row that has been kicked up" over the case, and he confided to their mutual friend Laski that while he would be the last to depreciate Frankfurter's "self-sacrifice in his excursions and alarums," he felt Frankfurter was "so good in his chosen business . . . that he helps the world more in that way than he does by becoming a knight-errant or martyr."

The atmosphere in America, and especially in Boston, was tense as Sacco and Vanzetti awaited their execution, scheduled, after several delays, for August 22, 1927. Bombs were exploded in various cities and on the front lawn of a juror in the original trial. Demonstrators took over Boston Common for their protest meetings. Extra guards were posted at government buildings here and abroad, and the Boston police force, armed with riot guns, was put on twenty-four-hour emergency duty.

As Holmes had feared, he was drawn into the controversy in his official capacity. The defendants' legal team had decided to try to persuade the Supreme Court to hear the case, and since the Court had adjourned for the summer, the route lay through individual justices. Holmes seemed the logical first step. Not only was he the justice in charge of the New England circuit, but his firm condemnation of legal lynching in the case of a group of Arkansas blacks in *Moore* v. *Dempsey* only four years before was encouraging.

"Stirred," Holmes supposed, by Frankfurter, his friend and fellow Brahmin Arthur Dehon Hill had joined the Sacco and Vanzetti case as chief counsel for the defense and, accompanied by other of the defendants' lawyers and a platoon of reporters, marched on Beverly Farms in the early evening of August 10, "exciting the apprehension of friendly neighbors." They wanted Holmes to issue a writ of habeas corpus and pled with him for two and a half hours. Holmes listened patiently.

He saw their situation much the way he had seen Leo Frank's situation before Lamar had changed his mind and agreed to give the lawyers in the Georgia case a full-court hearing. Holmes found Sacco and Vanzetti a "lamentable" case, and privately his "prejudices were all with

[Frankfurter's] book," and "against the convictions." But he could not stretch the jurisdiction of the federal courts so far.

He had, he told Hill and the others, changing the words but not the meaning of his early memorandum regarding Leo Frank's case,

> no authority to take the prisoners out of the custody of a State Court having jurisdiction over the persons and dealing with a crime under State law— that the only ground for such an interference would be want of jurisdiction in the tribunal, or,

he added, recalling *Moore* v. *Dempsey* and at the same time differentiating it from Sacco and Vanzetti,

> where a mob in and around the court ready to lynch the prisoner, jury, counsel and possibly the judges if they did not convict, made the trial a mere form.

These facts, the lawyers countered, "went only to motives." What was the difference, they asked, "whether the motive was fear or the prejudices alleged in this case?"

Most differences, Holmes answered, were "differences of degree." He thought "the line must be drawn between external force, and prejudice—which could be alleged in every case," and which was all the lawyers had offered him. He could not grant their request.

As his visitors were leaving, Holmes whispered to one of them:

> I am convinced that these men did not get a square deal, but we cannot take the United States government into State affairs and undermine the basic principles of the separate sovereignties of the State and Federal Governments.

Fearing for Holmes's safety in the emotionally charged atmosphere of the moment, a young male cousin offered to stand guard on the piazza that night, but the Holmeses declined. Shortly afterwards a police guard was mounted and stayed several weeks.

When the commotion seemed to be over for the night, Holmes's secretary—Thomas G. Corcoran that year—challenged his action. "But has justice been done, Sir?" he complained.

It was just the kind of opening Holmes loved, and he proceeded to lecture the young man as if he were still a student at Harvard Law School:

Don't be foolish, boy. We practice law, not "justice." There is no such thing as objective "justice," which is a subjective matter. A man might feel justified in stealing a loaf of bread to fill his belly; the baker might think it most just for the thief's hand to be chopped off, as in Victor Hugo's *Les Miserables*. The image of justice changes with the beholder's viewpoint, prejudice or social affiliation. But for society to function, the set of rules agreed on by the body politic must be observed—the law must be carried out.

A week and a half later, just two days before Sacco and Vanzetti were scheduled for execution, their lawyers returned to Beverly Farms to ask Holmes for a stay. Holmes again refused "to meddle" in the affairs of a state:

> I have received many letters from people who seem to suppose that I have a general discretion to see that justice is done. They are written with the confidence that sometimes goes with ignorance of the law. . . . I have no such power. The relation of the United States and the courts of the United States to the States and the courts of the States is a very delicate matter that has occupied the thoughts of statesmen and judges for a hundred years and cannot be disposed of by a summary statement that justice requires me to cut red tape and to intervene.

Recalling perhaps his grant just the previous month of a stay in the case of two blacks convicted, of rape, in a courtroom protected by machine guns, he added:

> Far stronger cases than this have arisen with regard to the blacks when the Supreme Court has denied its power.
> A State decision may be set aside by the Supreme Court of the United States—not by a single justice of that court—if the record of the case shows that the Constitution has been infringed in specific ways. An application for a writ of certiorari has been filed on the ground that the record shows such an infringement; and the writ of habeas corpus having been denied, I am asked to grant a stay of execution until that application can be considered by the full court. I assume that under the statute my power extends to this case, although I am not free from doubt. But it is a power rarely exercised and I should not be doing my duty if I exercised it unless I thought that there was a reasonable chance that the court would entertain the application and ultimately reverse the judgment. This I cannot bring myself to believe.

The evidence the lawyers had offered that the judge in the case had allowed his prejudices to color the trial was just too flimsy. Holmes was not convinced.

Undeterred, the defendants' legal team returned again at 9 P.M. on the very eve of the scheduled execution, and again Holmes rejected their pleas. Time being of the essence, they sped away to Brandeis's summer home at Chatham on Cape Cod. Unlike Holmes, Brandeis had followed the case closely and praised Frankfurter's book as "an event of importance with bench & bar; perhaps the turning point." The party of lawyers reached Chatham at 2 A.M., and called on the justice after breakfast. He met them on the porch, but did not invite them in. Because of his "personal relations to some of the people who had been interested in the case," Brandeis told them, he must disqualify himself from acting on any matter connected with Sacco and Vanzetti. He did not elaborate, but it was understood that his daughter had taken an interest in the case, Frankfurter was a close friend, and Mrs. Elizabeth Glendower Evans was a family friend. Prominent in Boston society and active in social causes, including the defense of Sacco and Vanzetti, Mrs. Evans not only had lived in the Brandeis home but some years earlier had brought Mrs. Sacco there while the Brandeises were away. The lawyers did not linger, but headed north, for the Isle of Haut off the Maine coast where Justice Stone was vacationing. He, too, refused to grant a stay, and the two men were executed on schedule.

Intellectually, as a professor of law, Frankfurter could understand Holmes's refusals. He told a friend much later:

> Mr. Justice Holmes wrote me appreciatively about my little book on the Sacco and Vanzetti case. . . . But as a Justice of the Supreme Court he could not stay the execution of Sacco and Vanzetti.*

Emotionally, Holmes's rejections may have been more difficult for Frankfurter to cope with. He had invested so much of himself in the case of Sacco and Vanzetti—not in trying to establish their innocence,

---

*Some years later, in 1946, when Frankfurter was sitting in Holmes's Supreme Court seat, he himself was the "swing vote" in Willie Francis's case (*Francis* v. *Resweber*, 329 U.S. 459, 1947). The seventeen-year-old black man, convicted of killing a druggist in a holdup and sentenced to die in the electric chair, had been strapped into the chair at the scheduled time, but the chair had malfunctioned and Francis had walked away. The Supreme Court had to decide whether a second attempt to execute Francis was "cruel and unusual punishment" prohibited by the Eighth Amendment to the Constitution or whether the state of Louisiana could lawfully order another execution. The Court decided, 5 to 4, in favor of the state. "Something inside of [Frankfurter] was very unhappy," and he had to "hold on to [him]self" not to dissent. But duty overrode personal feelings, and he joined the majority, explaining his behavior much the way Holmes had explained *his*.

on which he did not comment publicly, but in trying to win a new trial for them. Not only had he poured his sense of injustice into his book, but he had once more had to withstand the wrath of the Harvard establishment because of it. He had used up a good deal of political capital lobbying among the great and near great in his circle of acquaintances. And Holmes was his idol. Before Holmes there was Henry L. Stimson, Frankfurter's boss in the U.S. attorney's office; after Holmes there would be Franklin Roosevelt; but Holmes would always be the Zeus in Frankfurter's pantheon, and on one level Zeus had failed him. Whether the two men had discussed the case during Frankfurter's visit to Beverly Farms in July is not known. They may have; Holmes was a little more open on Court matters with Frankfurter than he was with others, and they had discussed it previously. Frankfurter did not mention the case either in his own reminiscences, which were recorded during the latter part of his life and published in 1960, or in his *Mr. Justice Holmes and the Supreme Court,* published in 1938. Perhaps it was still too painful.

On the official level, Holmes maintained his customary detachment—he might have been ruling on compulsory vaccination in Massachusetts or the application of the Sherman Anti-Trust Act to a new arrangement of railroad routes. Privately, however, he was agitated, not by the issues of the case, but by the "shriekers" who had elevated the defendants to the status of "heroes" and transformed what he considered minor judicial indiscretions—perhaps he could stretch it to prejudice—in an ordinary murder trial to an international cause célèbre, though he was always careful to except Frankfurter's book from his criticisms. Cases that excited public feeling always disturbed him; he had made that plain in *Northern Securities* nearly a quarter century before. Too, he could not but have been troubled by what was being said about the Massachusetts judiciary, of which he had been a member for twenty years; it has even been suggested that this was the real reason for his rejection of the defense lawyers' pleas. To impugn the integrity of Georgia or Arkansas justice was one thing. But Massachusetts? Added to all that, he undoubtedly feared for his friend Frankfurter's professional life, which had been endangered by the law professor's extracurricular activities, and conversely, for the school which he perhaps thought had again been damaged financially by Frankfurter's outspokenness.

Holmes wrapped his deeply felt concerns in grumbling that "the world cares more for red than for black," complaints about public ignorance regarding federal/state relations, or charges that the media had been attempting to retry the case by public opinion. He was glad when "the echoes of Sacco and Vanzetti [grew] fainter" that fall, though "abusive" letters continued to come in, and he was positively relieved when Arthur Hill told him Frankfurter intended to "write nothing more about Sacco and Vanzetti for a year." He hoped it might be "longer than that." The further he got from the events of that 1927 summer, the "more . . . convinced" he was that the case "was hardly the occasion for kicking up a row that the facts did not justify." Rather, he thought it only had given "the reds a chance to howl."

THE EXCLUSIONARY RULE—which requires that illegally obtained evidence in criminal cases cannot be admitted in court—is a peculiarly American invention for which there was no equivalent in Roman or the English common law. The Constitution of the United States says nothing about an exclusionary rule, either. It is a judge-made device given constitutional dimension through judicial decision. It surfaced for the first time in 1886 when the U.S. Supreme Court, supported by quotations from the writings of James Otis and John Adams, declared a man's private papers inadmissible as evidence in court because they had been seized illegally, in violation of the Fourth Amendment to the Constitution, which prohibits "unreasonable searches and seizures.* Over the next couple of decades its fortunes declined, and few restrictions were placed on the prosecution's methods of obtaining evidence. Warrantless searches and extorted confessions—the third degree—were common and judicially tolerated.

Then it reappeared in 1914 when the U.S. Supreme Court, speaking through Justice Day and with the tacit concurrence of Justice Holmes, reversed the conviction of a Kansas City, Missouri, express company employee accused of illegal use of the mails. He had been arrested without a warrant, his house had been ransacked, also without a warrant, and police had made off with his files, which were introduced as evidence at his trial.† The decision, which held intimations of the revolution in criminal justice to come half a century later, is usually cited as the modern origin of the exclusionary rule. It applied, however, only in federal court; it was not until 1961 that the Supreme Court ruled it must apply in state courts, too.‡

Since its conception, the exclusionary rule has been one of the most controversial rules of legal evidence. Its application has been blamed for the collapse of countless cases against men and women believed to be

* *Boyd* v. *United States.* 116 U.S. 616 (1886).
† *Weeks* v. *United States.* 232 U.S. 383 (1914).
‡ *Mapp* v. *Ohio.* 367 U.S. 643 (1961).

guilty, and periodically, during times of high crime rates, public opinion, pandered to by political figures, demanded dilution of the exclusionary rule. It was, thought many people, including former Chief Justice Warren E. Burger, that letting "the criminal go free because the constable blundered" was too high a price to pay for constitutional rights. Burger's Court indeed began in the early 1970s to emasculate the exclusionary rule until it existed practically in name only.

The original statement of the rule, however, had not been subjected to a legal cost accounting, but had involved matters of ethical principle, lofty restatements of constitutional underpinnings. Said Day for the Court in 1914: "The efforts of the courts and their officials to bring the guilty to punishment, praiseworthy as they are, are not to be aided by the sacrifice of those great principles established by years of endeavor and suffering which have resulted in their embodiment in the fundamental law of the land." Holmes had continued that tradition. In 1921, speaking for the Court, he had expanded the exclusionary rule to cover a second generation of evidence.* The government could not, he said, use as evidence any knowledge that was an offspring of evidence gained through illegal behavior, or, as it is called in lawyers' jargon, "the fruit of the poisonous tree." The use of such ill-gotten gain, Holmes explained, "reduces the Fourth Amendment to a form of words. The essence of a provision forbidding the acquisition of evidence in a certain way is that not merely evidence so acquired shall not be used before the court, but that it shall not be used at all."

As the 1920s wore on, violations of the Eighteenth Amendment, which had gone into effect on New Year's Day, 1920, and since then had made criminals out of a lot of ordinary Americans, were straining the resources of law enforcement officers almost to the breaking point. The rumrunners ruled America's coast lines, Maine to Florida, Washington to Baja, California. Despite a half million arrests and more than three hundred thousand convictions for bootlegging, it went right on increasing. As often happens when criminals appear to gain ascendancy over law and order, police, in response to the public outcry, were taking shortcuts in the gathering of evidence against them.

In 1928, the Supreme Court agreed to hear the case of Roy Olmstead, a Seattle, Washington, police officer and bootlegger, who had been convicted by evidence obtained through wiretapping—a new factor introduced into the ecology of law enforcement, a result of the recent advances in communications.

---

* *Silverthorne* v. *United States.* 251 U.S. 385 (1921).

Olmstead had constructed a particularly elaborate smuggling operation. He had begun his professional life as a police patrolman and risen through the ranks of the Seattle Police Department; by 1920 he was a lieutenant. During that year he was arrested with a crew of rumrunners who were unloading liquor from a launch near Seattle. Evidence later indicated he was protecting the rumrunners. He was dismissed from the force.

Overnight he became known as the "King of the Bootleggers" in the Pacific Northwest. He had a staff of fifty, two seagoing vessels for the transport of liquor to British Columbia, and several small boats for coastal shipments in the state of Washington. He had a ranch house outside Seattle with a large underground cache for storage and a number of small warehouses within the city. He operated like any modern corporate executive, employing account executives, salesmen, deliverymen, dispatchers, scouts, bookkeepers, collectors, and an attorney. His annual net ran around two million dollars. He also operated a radio broadcasting station over which his wife, known as "Aunt Vivien," told bedtime stories each evening for local children—believed to be in reality a clever code system to warn radio-equipped rumrunners, plying the waters of Puget Sound and the Northern Pacific, where government ships were waiting.

In 1901, the state of Washington had enacted a law making the interception of telephone messages a misdemeanor; nevertheless, federal prohibition officers gathered evidence against Olmstead by tapping his telephone and eavesdropping on his and his partners' business conversations. Their notes and records of the conversations consumed 775 pages.

Along with his accomplices, Olmstead was convicted in federal court of conspiracy to violate the National Prohibition Act. The circuit court of appeals affirmed the conviction, and Olmstead turned to the U.S. Supreme Court. Tapping his telephone, he argued, violated the Fourth Amendment's guarantee of the right of the people "to be secure in their persons, houses, papers, and effects, against unreasonable searches and seizures"; using his own words from the telephone conversations as evidence violated the Fifth Amendment's guarantee of the right not to be "compelled in any criminal case to be a witness against himself."

The case was argued in February 1928. Olmstead was supported not only by his lawyers but by Pacific Telephone and Telegraph, American Telephone and Telegraph, and other telephone companies, which filed a joint *amicus curiae* brief condemning the use of wiretapping on the grounds that it was an invasion of privacy:

It is better that a few criminals escape than that the privacies of life of all the people be exposed to the agents of government, who will act at their own discretion, the honest and the dishonest, unauthorized and unrestrained by the courts.

Chief Justice Taft, a long-time crusader against crime as well as a zealous supporter of police and prosecutors in their uphill efforts to enforce Prohibition, took the opinion himself, perhaps, Holmes thought, as a "rhetorical device to obscure the difficulty," perhaps "merely because he did not note the difference" between honest and dishonest enforcement of the law. Three years before, Taft had upheld the convictions of a pair of bootleggers in Michigan when he wrote for the Court that federal Prohibition agents might lawfully stop automobiles and other vehicles to search them when there was reasonable ground for believing they contained contraband liquor.* The decision elicited a "great howl" but Taft defended it vigorously on the ground that it was "good law," and he hoped it would be "a useful means of rendering the prosecution of crime through automobiles more possible." He fretted over "the problems presented by new inventions. Many of them are most useful to the criminals in their war against society."

In putting together the Court's opinion in *Olmstead* v. *United States,* Taft clucked like a mother hen trying to get her brood into the henhouse. He knew he would never get Brandeis who, contrary to an agreement among the justices at conference, had insisted upon expanding the scope of his dissent beyond the specific issues of the case and upon discussing the ethics of law enforcement. "Where we make a limitation," Taft thundered to Sanford who had helped to make a majority in *Olmstead,* "we ought to stick to it, and I think anyone would have done so but the lawless member of our Court." At first the chief justice had had some hope of holding Holmes, who had initially voted with the majority, but "Brandeis," Taft grumbled, "got after him and induced him to change." Butler's dissent was a sharp blow.

Taft could absorb Butler's straying as a rare aberration, but Stone's was still another signal that he was irretrievably lost to the majority. The indefatigable McReynolds tried to alert the newest member against the one of their number, presumably Brandeis, who was "consciously boring from within," and Taft had cautioned Stone some time ago regarding the importance of unanimity. But it had been no use. For a time Stone had capitulated to Taft's powerful and persuasive personality

---

* *Carroll* v. *United States.* 267 U.S. 132 (1925).

and had joined in the chief justice's efforts to have the Court speak with one voice—fulfilling the dire predictions of the liberals who had fought his confirmation. But his allegiance to the majority was short-lived. Sharing their outlook on the necessity for flexibility in matters of constitutional jurisprudence, Stone shortly joined Holmes and Brandeis, and "Holmes, Brandeis, and Stone dissenting" became a regular tail to the announcement of Court decisions. Taft dismissed what he called Stone's "subservience to Holmes and Brandeis" contemptuously; the turncoat simply "hunger[ed] for the applause of the law-school professors [presumably Frankfurter, with whom he corresponded regularly and for whose comments on his opinions he waited anxiously] and the admirers of Holmes." Taft was outspokenly "disappointed" when Stone and Butler diluted the power of Taft's opinion in *Olmstead* by joining the Holmes/Brandeis axis and making the majority's margin slimmer. It could have been 6 to 3; with Stone's desertion, it would be 5 to 4.

Desperately trying to hold the four others he had, Taft invited them to the usual informal conferences at his home and accepted their suggestions for the Court's opinion graciously. His health had begun its final decline, but no diminution of his power was apparent when he announced the Court's decision on June 4, 1928, the last day of the 1927 term.

In it, he reviewed the applications of the Fourth and Fifth Amendments since 1886 when the exclusionary rule was invented, and concluded that the Fourth did not cover telephone wires and the Fifth, which prohibits a person from being "compelled in any criminal case to be a witness against himself," did not cover the eavesdropping at issue in Olmstead's case. Of course, Taft admitted, Congress could legislate the inadmissibility of intercepted telephone messages as evidence in criminal trials. But, he declared,

> the courts may not adopt such a policy by attributing an enlarged and unusual meaning to the Fourth Amendment. The reasonable view is that one who installs in his house a telephone instrument with connecting wires intends to project his voice to those quite outside, and that the wires beyond his house and messages while passing over them are not within the protection of the Fourth Amendment.

Crime-fighter Taft added:

> Our general experience shows that much evidence has always been receivable although not obtained by conformity to the highest ethics. . . . A

> standard which would forbid the reception of evidence if obtained by other than nice ethical conduct by government officials would make society suffer and give greater immunity than has been known heretofore.

Taft would adhere to the common law's rule that the

> admissibility of evidence is not affected by the illegality of the means by which it was obtained.

Except to say that a state law could not affect the rules of evidence applicable in federal courts, Taft was reluctant to comment on Washington's law prohibiting wiretapping.

Holmes confessed privately that he would not have written a dissent if Brandeis had not asked him to. He was a little embarrassed because he had "scattered [dissents] more copiously than [he] could wish this last term," but it was the only way he knew to respond to the Court's decisions which he "deeply regret[ted]." His words and manner, as he read the brief opinion, were "disdainful," as if he were "obliged to hold something unpleasant in his hands," and he did in fact characterize wiretapping as a "dirty business."

He dismissed Taft's reference to the common-law rule regarding the use of illegally obtained evidence with the observation that it had been overruled in 1914 by *Weeks* v. *United States.* He realized the states could not control the rules of evidence in federal courts, but the state had "authority over the conduct in question," and he hardly thought the United States "would appear to greater advantage when paying for an odious crime against State law than when inciting to the disregard of its own." He was not prepared, he said, to decide the applicability of the Fourth and Fifth Amendments to wiretapping. He was prepared, however, to comment on the spurious behavior of the government, and it was clear that the contempt in his manner had sprung from his deep feelings about integrity in government. He cited no precedents and invoked no laws. Where was the statute that covered what he was about to say?

> It is desirable that criminals should be detected, and to that end all available evidence should be used. It is also desirable that the Government should not itself foster and pay for other crimes, when they are the means by which the evidence is to be obtained. . . . We have to choose, [he added, articulating what has become one of the most quoted statements in American constitutional law, second only to Holmes's own pronouncements nearly

a decade before in the free speech cases] and for my part I think it a less evil that some criminals should escape than that the Government should play an ignoble part.

Taft was furious with Holmes, accused him of writing "the nastiest opinion." But, he sighed, Holmes was a "law unto himself if Brandeis says yes." Taft, the former Yale law professor, worried what "the academic lawyers who write the college law journals" were going to say— newspaper editorials already had been hostile—but if they thought he would be "frightened in our effort to stand by the law and give the public a chance to punish criminals, they [were] mistaken, even though we are condemned for lack of high ideals." On further consideration, he thought "the more the case is read and understood, the less effective will be the eloquence and denunciation of Brandeis and Holmes."

Brandeis also wrote an epilogue to *Olmstead*:

I suppose some reviewer of the wire tapping decision will discern that in favor of property the Constitution is liberally construed—in favor of liberty, strictly.

CHAPTER **30**

Duty Done

IN SHARP CONTRAST to the summer of 1927, which had brought the pain and turmoil of the Sacco and Vanzetti affair, the summer of 1928 at Beverly Farms allowed the kind of relaxation the eighty-seven-year-old Holmes required. That summer he was as "near bliss" as he ever got. The lightening of professional pressures, the drives along the North Shore where the rocks and sea were "divinely beautiful," restored his vitality quickly. The usual reading kept him occupied: a little Bertrand Russell, a volume of Vernon Parrington's intellectual history of America, Samuel Eliot Morison's *Oxford History of the United States,* and, not the least uplifting, Anita Loos's *But Gentlemen Marry Brunettes.* He found to his surprise he liked the work of young Ernest Hemingway despite what he ordinarily would have considered obvious literary drawbacks: Fanny "backed out" when she had to read about the bullfights in *The Sun Also Rises,* but Holmes trudged on. The experience was "singular":

> An account of eating and drinking with a lot of fornication accompanied by conversations on the lowest level, with some slight intelligence but no ideas, and nothing else—and yet it seems a slice of life, and you are not bored with details of an ordinary day.

When he returned to Washington in October, Holmes succeeded to the title of oldest man to sit on the Supreme Court, breaking Chief Justice Roger B. Taney's record of eighty-seven years, six months, and twenty-five days. He was beginning to fall asleep over the certioraris at times, felt "stupid and muddle-headed at the oral arguments" and had to ask Brandeis's help to understand the issues, and "felt a queer nervousness" until the brethren returned the drafts of his opinions, lest they "betray some symptom of decline that [he] had not noticed."

> Rum business, this growing older [he thought]—nature withdraws here a raisin and there a plum from your pudding—until one doubts if anything is left but sodden dough.

In the spring of 1929, domestic life as Holmes had known it for nearly sixty years came to an end—abruptly and without warning. Just as Fanny, eighty-eight years old, was recovering from a bout with "the grippe," she had the classic accident of the old: a bad fall in the bathroom that fractured her hip. At first it was thought that "no serious harm" had been done, and the doctor put her in a proper cast. But at her age she could hardly hope that the bone would knit, and she was in a great deal of pain.

There was, however, no diminution in the old soldier's attention to his work. "There seems to be," he explained, "a distinct compartment in one's mind that works away no matter what is going on with the rest of the machinery." He had, of course, the momentum of nearly fifty years to keep the machinery turning. He could almost write opinions in his sleep; he need, at this point, only to choose the proper principle from the large inventory he had built up, continue living out of habit and according to schedules laid out decades before. At least for the first half of April, when Fanny seemed to be "slowly improving," he attended conferences regularly, sat in court for oral argument, and wrote his opinions more or less as usual. At home he kept up his regular correspondence, writing the customary chatty letters about books and people and politics, saying nothing about his own misfortune.

Then in mid-April, Fanny's health further declined, and Holmes began to miss court sessions. On his return he seemed "crushed—fully twenty years older than he has been for months—actually the old man." Nevertheless he finished his assigned opinions and delivered them on schedule—with a "smile." Brandeis reported to Frankfurter: "O.W.H. is making a grand fight, but it is a very hard one."

Finally, on the last day of April 1929, Fanny Holmes, who could make "roses bloom on a broomstick," could hold her weakening body together no longer and died in her sleep. "Exhaustion following fracture of the left femur," her doctor said it was.

Fellow Unitarian Chief Justice Taft, who knew "how to run a Unitarian funeral," and had an instinct for kindness as well as a keen personal understanding of his brethren, who knew how desolated and help-less Holmes would be, hurried to 1720 I Street and took charge of ar-rangements for her funeral, which was private. "How," asked the grieving Holmes, "can one help loving a man with such a kind heart?" She was buried in Arlington National Cemetery where Holmes some time before had chosen a "lovely spot" in a grove of pines and tulips and where he planned to join her later.

> In her way [said Marion, Felix Frankfurter's wife] she was as great a per-sonality as the Justice.

For a long time to come, Holmes necessarily expended a good deal of his thought, energy, and emotion in simply adjusting to the most deeply felt event to occur in his life since the Civil War. At the same time, however strong the urge to look back, he struggled to look for-ward, and to take his changed life in hand. The mechanical chores were the easiest—sending the traditional black-bordered cards, putting Fan-ny's affairs in order—and kept him occupied for a time, leaving less time for grief.

Shortly after Fanny's death, he confided to Laski that it "seemed like the beginning of my own." But he did not dwell on it. He begged Laski to keep on sending his cheerful letters and Holmes would do his best to respond. Soon the justice's letters resumed, even though he was "confused and hardly [knew] what [he thought] about anything."

Finally, he was "reconciled," because he believed prolonged life would have meant "only . . . longer suffering and pain, and the time had come." He was "ready . . . to follow her." But he kept up his "interest in [his] work while it last[ed]":

> If I last a year or more longer I shall hope to die in harness, but all that remains of these side activities seem to me like a man's beard growing after he is dead.

It was better, too, he thought, that he was the one left alone. Fanny "would have been more at a loss," had she been the survivor. Holmes liked "solitude with intermissions"; Fanny just liked solitude, had been "almost a recluse," and there was "no one except me with whom she was very intimate."

One of the reasons Holmes could get along alone was the capable and cheerful presence of young Mary Donellen whom Fanny, in antic-ipation of her own death, had trained in her last years to take charge of

Wendell and the house at 1720 I Street. Mary took over, just as Fanny had planned, catering to Wendell's whims and wants, watching him "tigerishly," trying to prevent his seeing too many people and tiring himself out, making the last six years of his life as comfortable domestically as she could.

Following Fanny's death, the normally gregarious Holmes had not wanted to see anyone at first, and his secretary—John Lockwood that year—fended off the inevitable well-intentioned callers.

Before May's end, Holmes was inviting Owen Wister to "share [his] solitary chicken and rather poor home made ice cream" at Sunday lunch. He already had been on the telephone to Brandeis to discuss an opinion, and Taft was loading him up with opinions to write. He was, Brandeis reported joyfully to Frankfurter, "in fine form again, working as of old." He was reading his opinions in court, attending conferences regularly, and joining in the dissents of his usual allies. At the end of May, he delivered his own dissent in Rosika Schwimmer's case.

The postwar intolerance for alien beliefs ought to have worn off by 1929. Americans, however, still persisted in persecuting those who espoused them. As Rosika Schwimmer's case* was to demonstrate, there had not been a lot of progress since the Abrams case, decided a decade before, had let loose the hornets.

Rosika Schwimmer was a forty-nine-year-old Hungarian-born author, feminist, and internationally known pacifist when she applied for citizenship in 1926. It was she who had persuaded Henry Ford, near the end of 1915, to sponsor a peace ship to bring "the boys out of the trenches by Christmas." A few years after the expedition aborted, she left her native Budapest and immigrated to the United States, "a country which is based on principles and institutions more in harmony with my ideals." She got as far as question 22 on the citizenship application form: "If necessary, are you willing to take up arms in defense of this country?" Firmly, she answered, "No." (Ordinarily, women were exempt from answering question 22; in Miss Schwimmer's case, the women's auxiliary of the American Legion had asked that she be required to answer.) She assured the authorities that she could take the oath of allegiance without reservations; she did not see "that a woman's refusal to take up arms is a contradiction to the oath of allegiance." Civic-minded as well as intellectually inclined, Miss Schwimmer also assured them she would conceive it her duty to defend America and American institutions publicly, both orally and in writing. Should American women

* *United States* v. *Schwimmer.* 279 U.S. 644 (1929).

be drafted, she expected to be treated like any other conscientious objector. She was, however, she also assured the authorities, an "uncompromising pacifist," and she paraded her contempt for national borders as well as her religious convictions, which bordered on atheism.

She was denied citizenship by naturalization. When a federal appeals court granted it, the United States took the case to the Supreme Court. It was the last significant civil liberties case to come before the Court in the 1920s.

A majority (six) of the Court found Rosika Schwimmer's ideas undesirable in a citizen of the United States. Butler, who wrote the Court opinion, did not say in so many words that she presented a "clear and present danger" to the republic, though he implied it strongly:

> Whatever tends to lessen the willingness of citizens to discharge their duty to bear arms in the country's defense detracts from the strength and safety of the Government. And their opinions and beliefs as well as their behavior indicating a disposition to hinder in the performance of that duty are subjects of inquiry under the statutory provisions governing naturalization and are of vital importance, for if all or a large number of citizens oppose such defense the "good order and happiness" of the United States can not long endure.

The American experience with conscientious objectors and pacifists during the recent Great War had been almost entirely negative. Several hundred had been convicted and imprisoned "for offenses involving disobedience, desertion, propaganda and sedition." It was obvious, Butler wrote, "that the acts of such offenders evidence a want of attachment to the principles of the Constitution." American citizenship was not to be Miss Schwimmer's; her ilk was not welcome.

Holmes was certain it was memories of the "anti-draft talk" during the war that had pushed the majority into its rigid stance. But Miss Schwimmer's "flamboyant" atheism had not helped her cause. Holmes, however, thought the majority wrong in its conclusions and intended to say so.

He stood alone in life now. He had outlived his entire family and most of his contemporaries. He knew his days on the Court were numbered, that his stamina and mental agility were not what they once had been. Still, he was able to summon from his reserves the strength to write a dissent in which he abandoned, positively and with finality, his class and all that patrician Boston stood for. Though Holmes's emotional attachment to the place of his birth seemed indissoluble, and in his own personal life he reflected the Boston Brahmin's gentlemanly code, he had over the years fought his way to intellectual independence. He chuckled when he read an early draft of his dissent to a friend:

> This is designed to occasion discomfort in certain quarters.

Holmes always said a man's education begins two hundred years before his birth. It was the Jackson genes that were tutor to his dissent in Rosika Schwimmer's case, some cultural memory that brought back into play Grandfather—Judge—Jackson's willingness as a member of the Massachusetts Supreme Judicial Court a century before to defy the Calvinist majority as well as his own theological liberalism:

> [S]ome persons, and I confess I am one of their number, would never say they could not conscientiously attend on the preaching of almost any one. But such persons would think it somewhat hard to be obliged to hear a preacher as often as the Legislature might think proper to enjoin, or submit to whatever penalty might be provided for the neglect. . . .
>
> Would it not be best to prohibit the Legislature from passing any laws of the compulsory nature. . . . ?
>
> If any one, neither for religious motives, fancy, curiosity or any other motive, is disposed to attend public worship on Sundays, I should think it would be somewhat worse than doing nothing, to compel his attendance or subject him to a penalty for non-attendance. . . .

By the time Holmes was an undergraduate, he himself was condemning those who "burnt men's bodies for not agreeing with our religious tenets" and lamenting that "we still burn their souls." What he was writing, alone in his study, no longer cheered by Fanny's playful interruptions, he had also implied in *Vegelahn*—for what did his judicial support of labor's legal rights mean but that personal prejudices had no place in the American constitutional scheme?

Personally and politically, Holmes had no more use for pacifism than he had for social and economic reform:

> If there is a thing I loathe, it is the sentimental squashiness of a big minority of our time—Religious squeams about taking human life . . . the notion that war is about to be abolished by the sacred influence of woman and all the rest of it. The Universe is predatory . . . all life except the very lowest is at the expense of other life . . . I do despise the upward and onward. . . .

But that was the point of what he had to say. Frankfurter had once come upon him at Beverly Farms grumbling about book censorship, specifically about the deletion of a chapter in a book he was reading.

Is there nobody in Boston who's got any guts?

Frankfurter replied:

Practically no one except an old gentleman 30 miles north of Boston.

Holmes's entire adult life had argued against the attitudes pacifism promoted. For the man who, personally, had found in war a divine message, whose reading of history had confirmed the inevitability of war, whose experiences had confirmed the necessity of conflict to the national character, for the author of "The Soldier's Faith" who at eighty-eight, his country right or wrong, would willingly "throw away his life in obedience to a blindly accepted duty" if his country asked it of him, his dissent in Rosika Schwimmer's case must have required nearly all the strength he had left.

He began in a quietly ironic vein. He did not see the point in denying the applicant citizenship "in as much as she is a woman over fifty years of age, and would not be allowed to bear arms if she wanted to." She had indicated that she held "none of the now-dreaded creeds" but believed thoroughly in "organized government" and preferred that of the United States to any other. "Surely," Holmes twitted the majority which had inferentially equated pacifism with Socialism and its kin, "it cannot show lack of attachment to the principles of the Constitution that she thinks it can be improved. I suppose," he sighed, "that most intelligent people think it might be." He did not view Miss Schwimmer's commitment to the abolition of war as different in principle from a "wish to establish cabinet government in England, or a single house, or one term of seven years for the President."

The fear she might advocate resistance to military recruitment, should war come, seemed silly to Holmes. "Her position and motives are wholly different. . . . She is an optimist and states in strong and . . . sincere words her belief that war will disappear and that the impending destiny of mankind is to unite in peaceful leagues." Holmes did not share her optimism, although he shared her horror, and, with most people, he welcomed "any practicable combinations that would increase the power on the side of peace." Ideas like Miss Schwimmer's or the seven-year presidential term, like the minimum wage, were expedients, timely remedies for temporal conditions. Censorship, capitulation to political bias, was a permanent threat which the framers of the Constitution had hoped to prevent. He concluded quietly but firmly with his statement of the concept that had driven millions to American shores and that would live long in America's conscience: "Some of [Miss Schwimmer's] answers might excite popular prejudice, but"

> if there is any principle of the Constitution that more imperatively calls for attachment than any other it is the principle of free thought—not free thought for those who agree with us but freedom for the thought that we hate.

Only Brandeis joined Holmes's dissent. Sanford dissented separately, and Stone, so often a dependable ally of Holmes and Brandeis, unexpectedly joined the majority. Though he agreed with all Holmes had said, he did not think it applied to Rosika Schwimmer; he firmly believed she not only would disobey the law but would encourage disobedience in others and that Congress had, "rightly or wrongly . . . prescribed" that she and others like her should not be admitted to the coveted American citizenship.

The majority decision was widely criticized—"a lot of foolish comments . . . by editors and others whose ambition is roused to give judgment in a case, the first principle of which they do not understand," Taft complained. It also inspired immigration officers to take greater pains in excluding the politically unorthodox from citizenship. It stood as the law of the land until 1946 when the Supreme Court finally overruled it, noting that the oath of citizenship did not specifically require an applicant to swear to bear arms.[*]

"At the risk of violating legal etiquette," Rosika Schwimmer herself wrote Holmes to express her "deep-felt gratitude" for his dissent. Its magnificence had "helped [her] to take the blow of refusal without loss of faith in the inherent idealism of your nation." Such effusion could only make one who prided himself on his detachment blush. Politely and gently but nonetheless firmly, he admonished her, beginning a sporadic personal relationship with a party to a Supreme Court case—his first one. "You are too intelligent," he replied, "to need explanation of the saying you must never thank a judge. . . . If his decision was of a kind to deserve thanks, he would not be doing his duty. A case," Holmes explained, "is simply a problem to be solved, although the considerations

[*] *Girouard* v. *United States.* 328 U.S. 61 (1946).

are more complex than those of mathematics. After which protestation, I must add that of course I am gratified by your more than kind expression." A few days later Miss Schwimmer sent Holmes some books; a couple of years later she visited him at 1720 I Street.

Holmes's dissent in Rosika Schwimmer's case was his last of enduring significance either to the Holmes legend or American constitutional jurisprudence. Creativity had largely ended. The play itself was over. Only the chorus waited in the wings to speak the epilogue.

Accompanied by the household staff, all of whom refused the usual month's vacation that year, Holmes went as usual to his summer home at Beverly Farms following the term's end in June. Wisps of Fanny lurked in every room; wherever he turned, he found "memories and ghosts." His secretary arrived in mid-July to "help [him] in [his] work and drive [him] in [his] play." Women came to lunch—he thought people came "to see a survivor"—and sent books. He was "not allowed to be lonely." Someone turned up nearly every day, oftener than he wanted, and were "apt to stay longer than [he could] well endure." Being on intellectual parade at his age was not easy, and there was a limit to the amount of time he could still stand at attention. He tired more easily than usual, although he managed to process the bulging bags of certioraris dispatched to Beverly Farms by the Supreme Court clerk's office. Neighbors saw him taking regular short walks, chatting with the railroad stationmaster who periodically brought him up to date with the latest local gossip. As the shadows began to lengthen in September, thoughts of death encroached on his idyll, and he thought he would like some small insight into the meaning of the universe before he died. But, he sighed,

> one who thinks as I do perceives that he has no right to make the demand, but should shut up and go quietly under like a good soldier.

Later that year he sat for a portrait to be hung at Harvard Law School. He had been pleased and flattered by Harvard's interest in the project but embarrassed to inspect it. Still, he wanted "one more glimpse" of the law school. Frankfurter and his wife finally took him to see it hanging at the school late one afternoon after the students had left. His eyes roved critically over his own image:

> I have shaved this face for more than 70 years and I don't know what it looks like. But that looks like a smart fellow.

As 1929 melted into 1930, the noticeable slippage in Chief Justice Taft's health made it impossible for him to continue on the Court; by early January 1930, his final illness was keeping him off the bench, and on February 3, he resigned. From January 6 until his successor took the oath in mid-February, the responsibility for presiding over the Court and conferences fell to the senior associate justice, the eighty-eight-year-old Oliver Wendell Holmes. He was nervous but not inexperienced. Three decades before he had presided over the Massachusetts high court. Over the past few years, as Taft's deteriorating health kept him at home increasingly often, Holmes had been forced to fill in, and Stone was moved to comment on the "admirable manner" in which the "young man" was presiding; conferences were a "joy," and the justices were "dispatching business with great rapidity."

On March 8, coincidentally Holmes's eighty-ninth birthday, first Sanford—unexpectedly—then, within hours, Chief Justice Taft died. Sanford had collapsed in the dentist's chair; Taft, who had complained of bladder, digestive, and cardiovascular ailments for a decade, succumbed after a long illness. The double shock paralyzed the Court, which heard the news during a conference. Another judicial era had ended.

Within five hours after receiving Taft's resignation on February 3, President Hoover had surprised court-watchers, who had expected Stone to succeed Taft, and nominated former justice Charles Evans Hughes, whom Taft himself had urged on the president. The president shrewdly sought to smoothe Holmes's feathers by having lunch with him, during which Hoover explained politely that he would have liked to appoint Holmes but thought that at Holmes's age he ought not to be "burdened." Passed over twice before, Holmes had seemed then to smart a little, as if he had been slapped. This time Holmes seemed to be satisfied to be spared, claiming that "in all seriousness," Laski's flattering article in the most recent *Harper's Magazine* pleased him far more than appointment to the chief justiceship.

In March 1930, the president also replaced the late Justice Sanford of Tennessee. Originally, he had looked to the South and found federal circuit judge John J. Parker of North Carolina. But Parker was not confirmed—he was the last senatorial veto of a Supreme Court nominee until 1969, when the lawmakers rejected Clement Haynsworth for chief justice. Hoover next nominated the Philadelphia Brahmin Owen J. Roberts, who had earned a reputation for his prosecution of scandals involving the Harding administration.

The summer of 1930, except for a last visit by Sir Frederick Pollock and his wife, passed quietly. Holmes accepted no invitations, but confined his social life to a few friends who came to lunch, the secretary and staff looking after him "as if [he] were porcelain and liable to break." In September, shortly before he returned to Washington, he paid a visit to the state supreme court on which he had sat for two decades, a call he had been accustomed to making annually but in recent years had not felt up to.

In October, he told a friend he must try to live four or five months longer to reach ninety. Then, he confessed, he thought he would be "ready to depart," although Brandeis was urging him to "hang on" two more years to round out fifty years of judicial service. He didn't "care for that particularly." He knew he couldn't say his job was done until he stopped working at it, but he had begun to "feel anxious whether [he should] be up to the mark much longer."

The year 1931 brought further decline in Holmes's health. He walked more slowly now, and he had a slight stoop. Lumbago and fatigue enfeebled him and his bed at Beverly Farms was moved downstairs. Friends had begun to notice his growing weakness, though they insisted "his brain and spirit are as alert, comprehensive and acute as ever." They noticed, too, that he seemed to require encouragement in a measure he never had before and conversely, "the irritations and tribulations of the world, when they impinge on him are less easy to throw off."

Holmes himself had noticed his body weakening and described himself as "a kind of well invalid." His handwriting, never really legible, had shrunk, and he found the physical act of putting pen to paper hard; "all life [came] harder." He was thinking "too much about death and the futility of life," and his letters had assumed a "wistful" coloration. He was cheered whenever he was able to read his opinions out in court, and he responded as he always had to the appearance of the first bloodroot and white magnolias in Rock Creek Park. Though his doctor was encouraging, thought Holmes might live to be one hundred, Holmes himself doubted it, rather suspected the "old hulk" was "going to pieces."

The high point of that year for him was the radio broadcast on his ninetieth birthday, when all those men he admired admitted him to their Olympian circle. He welcomed their praise, accepted it with pride and pleasure, but it could not dispel all his doubts. He wondered whether he really ought to continue on the Court. The brethren were "all kind"; they gave "no hint" that they wanted him to leave, and Holmes was certain some sincerely wanted him to stay. But he was uneasy and feared he was not doing his full share of the work. He suspected Chief Justice Hughes of giving him easy cases, although Holmes had "put in a caveat against it," and he was depending more and more on Brandeis's judgment. In the end, the decision was made for him.

As the 1931 term opened as usual the first Monday in October, it was apparent that Holmes was "slipping." He frequently had to be helped in mounting the bench, and it became clear in the conferences that he was not capable of taking on a full load. A group of justices approached Hughes, who consulted Brandeis. Reluctantly, for he thought there was still "some more good law" to be gotten out of Holmes, Brandeis agreed the time had come for his friend to resign. The "highly disagreeable duty" of informing Holmes fell to the chief justice.

Holmes, however, made Hughes's task easier by accepting Hughes's suggestion without "the slightest indication of resentment or opposition," as if the old soldier, his duty done, had just been waiting for the command to "fall out." Hughes took from Holmes's book shelves the applicable statute, and Holmes, understanding neither the plan of campaign nor the tactics any better than he had three decades before but obedient to the end, wrote out his resignation in his shaky hand then and there:

The time has come and I bow to the inevitable.

He postdated it so he could read his last opinion from the bench the following day.*

When on Monday morning he entered the hushed courtroom for the last time, spectators, unaware of Holmes's resignation, noticed only his bristling mustache and pink cheeks under his heavy mop of white hair. But as he read his opinion his voice faltered. Soon his words were barely audible beyond the first row of benches. He returned after the lunch recess to hear the arguments in pending cases, although he would have no part in deciding them. When the Court adjourned that afternoon, he was seen to glance for a last time around the semicircular chamber under the Capitol dome, then march out as purposefully as ever. As a Court attendant helped him on with his overcoat, Holmes said simply:

I won't be down tomorrow.

*Dunn v. United States. 284 U.S. 390 (1932).

The next day's mail brought the president's answer to Holmes's letter of resignation: an appropriate mix of regret that Holmes was leaving and gratitude for his long public service:

> I know of no American retiring from public service with such a sense of affection and devotion of the whole people.

The same mail brought the customary farewell message from the other justices. Previously the unofficial spokesman for the Court in these circumstances, Holmes had written several similar letters, the latest one going to Chief Justice Taft shortly before he died. Now Holmes was on the receiving end. As his own letters had been, the justices' note was appreciative of Holmes's work and affectionate to the man. The justices had emphasized those contributions for which they knew Holmes wanted to be remembered: his "profound learning" and "philosophic outlook" which had "enrich[ed] the literature of the law as well as its substance." The brethren would miss his "daily companionship," but rejoiced that their friend, "relieved of the burden that had become too heavy," would undoubtedly experience a "renewal of vigor," enabling him to find "satisfaction in [his] abundant resources of intellectual enjoyment." Moved, Holmes answered in kind:

> My dear brethren:
> You must let me call you so once more. Your more than kind, your generous letter touches me to the bottom of my heart. The long and intimate association with men who so command my respect and admiration could not but fix my affection as well.
>   For such little time as may be left for me I shall treasure it as adding gold to the sunset.
>
> Affectionately yours,
O. W. Holmes*

The following day, the U.S. Senate paused in its deliberations while Senator David Walsh of Massachusetts said a few words in honor of Holmes, and the justices of the U.S. Supreme Court set aside a time to read the recent correspondence between Holmes and his brethren. Newspapers nationwide recounted the events of his public career on the news pages and his contributions to constitutional jurisprudence on the

---

*Retirement at full pay, however, turned out to be a fiction. An economy bill passed by Congress, intended to reduce the largest federal deficit in American history—almost a billion dollars—halved Holmes's pension.

editorial pages. None, however, could have pleased him so much as his young friend Walter Lippmann's column in the *New York Herald Tribune*:

> There are few who, reading Judge Holmes's letter of resignation, will not feel that here they touch a life done in the grand style. This, they will say, is how to live, and this is how to stop, with every power used to the full, like an army resting, its powder gone but with all its flags flying.

Holmes could not have put it better himself. Lippmann continued:

> [H]e is one of that small number who have determined not merely the course of the law but the premises and quality of legal thinking. For this great judge is one of the true philosophers of the English-speaking world, and it is the part of the philosopher to show men not so much what to think as how. This is his immortality. He has altered the casts of thought.

Which was what he had set out to do.

He had tried to persuade men to jettison—as he had during those long lonely nights when he had sailed into the uncharted waters of ancient legal history—their preconceived notions of law, to abandon old loyalties to rigid ideologies grounded in theory or superstition or dogma:

> It is revolting to have no better reasons for a law than that so it was laid down in the time of Henry IV. It is still more revolting if the grounds upon which it was laid down have vanished long since, and the rule simply persists from blind imitation of the past. ("The Path of the Law," 1897)

He had wanted men to see, as he had seen, their legal tradition with the eyes of a skeptic when they had been accustomed to accepting it passively:

> Certitude is not the test of certainty. We have been cock-sure of many things that were not so. ("Natural Law," 1918)

He had tried to teach them what he had learned from his own investigations: that the law was not static, but that like the natural world it responded to the ever-changing pressures of its environment:

> The development of our law has gone on for nearly a thousand years, like the development of a plant, each generation taking the inevitable next step,

mind, like matter, simply obeying a law of spontaneous growth. ("The Path of the Law," 1897)

He urged the study of legal history as anthropology; he hoped men would adapt the law to life: to

> resort to it to discover what ideals of society have been strong enough to reach that final form of expression, or what have been the changes in dominant ideals from century to century. . . . Who could fail to be interested in the transition through the priest's test of truth, the miracle of the ordeal, and the soldier's, the battle of the duel, to the democratic verdict of the jury! ("Law in Science and Science in Law," 1899)

Himself the product of the nineteenth century's faith in reason and science, he had urged men to look at the law scientifically and objectively when they had been accustomed to looking at it from the subjective perspective of the moralist:

> An ideal system of law should draw its postulates and its legislative justification from science. As it is now, we rely upon tradition, or vague sentiment, or the fact that we never thought of any other way of doing things, as our only warrant for rules which we enforce with as much confidence as if they embodied revealed wisdom. ("Learning and Science." Speech, June 25, 1895)

He had taught both by exhortation and by example. He did not write—he was rarely chosen to write—many of the Court's landmark opinions; he preferred to make his points in the less significant cases that contained the knotty little puzzles of law that always had intrigued him, and his brethren no doubt preferred it that way—in Holmes's constant search for universals, he had a disconcerting habit of giving small words the capacity to grow into large concepts, a practice that often involved expanding the scope of a decision beyond the other justices' expectations. He admitted in his old age that it had been

> just as well to have McKenna, Day and others cut out some of my exuberances from opinions of the Court—but in general I think what I have said is true.

His inclination to dissent has been exaggerated. Of the total 5,950 cases in which he participated between 1902 and 1932—excluding the *per curiam* on which all the justices agreed and the opinions, usually brief, were written under no one justice's name—Holmes dissented in only 173. But those few, in which he had urged men to deal with contemporary realities, had drawn public attention out of all proportion to their quantity.

He had sat serenely above the crowd, had found its passing fancies hardly worth his notice, its felt necessities ephemeral. His concern was for the centuries, not the moment. Whether pharmacy owners ought to be trained pharmacists did not interest him, but if the people of Pennsylvania decided, via their state legislators, that a "divorce between the power of control and knowledge" was an "evil" and should not be allowed, he could find nothing in the Constitution to gainsay it.* The provision was just one more facet of an increasingly complicated modern society which the law was reflecting. He cared nothing for the specific measures he sustained; indeed he thought most of them humbug: peonage laws, minimum wage and maximum hour laws, antitrust legislation. Today's emergency would be gone tomorrow when some new economic pressure was felt. Judges, he thought, ought to take the long view. What he cared about was that the legislature, as spokesman for the people, was not silenced, that judges did not arbitrarily cut off experiment, for that was what these expedients amounted to. The principle mattered in the twentieth century, and it would matter in the twenty-fifth.

He had happened on the judicial scene at a crucial moment in American life. The Supreme Court's stubborn opposition to the forces in society and its active interference with them were carrying it toward its own destruction. Holmes's posture of nonintervention played an important part in the Court's voluntary about-face when in 1937 the president tried to force it into submission. He had never aspired to authorship of a school of jurisprudence, but this very policy of nonintervention became known some years later as "judicial restraint," and his disciple, Felix Frankfurter, was its major practitioner.

He had only wanted to persuade judges to make the first rule of judging that the judge keep his own preferences and prejudices out of his decisions and maintain his thought processes detached and disinterested:

I have considered the present tendencies and desires of society and have tried to realize that its different portions want different things, and that

---

* *Liggett Co.* v. *Baldridge*. 278 U.S. 105, 114 (1928).

my business was to express not my personal wish, but the resultant, as nearly as I could guess, of the pressure of the past and the conflicting wills of the present. ("Twenty Years in Retrospect." Speech, December 3, 1902)

He differentiated, however, between legislative fashions and certain enduring democratic values he believed crucial to the health and vitality of the republic. He dismissed all talk of individual rights, claimed he had no use for them. But he protected them, not as rights in the way people were accustomed to thinking about them, but as benefits to the larger society. Mob violence in or around a courtroom could not, for example, but preclude the emergence of truth out of the clash between the parties, and prevented the discovery of guilt or innocence, might well rescue the real criminal from conviction. Suppression of speech and thought cut off the "free trade in ideas" and was far more of a threat to the continued well-being of the republic than the spread of the isms Americans so feared. The shelf-life of an ism was short, lasting only until another ism superseded it. Speech and thought were enduring values, essential to the excavation of truth. And what sort of example was set by a government that resorted to criminality to enforce its laws? In Holmes's judicial cosmology, Roy Olmstead's crime was petty compared to the government's. Holmes had only contempt for oppression and its perpetrators.

As Holmes interpreted his work, his judicial posture was essentially negative—to decide whether a law was *un*constitutional—and he offered, during his half century on the bench, no coherent programs for the betterment of human life, no directives, no social or economic panaceas, and was impatient with those who did. He was equally contemptuous of the conservative who feared change and the reformer who thought redistribution of property would create the longed-for utopia. He was not eager for change, but unlike many Americans he did not fear it. He spoke neither for the socialist nor the individualist. He had no loyalties to any group, and he led no crusades to a constitutional holy land.

He didn't pretend to know the answers to the questions that plagued the society in which he lived. If there was a constant strain running through his thought, private as well as public, it was that the universe, of which he was but an insignificant part, was capable of working out its own destiny without his interference, as was the Congress, the state legislature, and the electorate. In all humility—he had learned early in life that he was not God—he did not fiddle with the law, and he did not fiddle with the cosmos. He would like to have better understood his old friend the cosmos, whose tail he had twisted so mercilessly as a young man, but he realized now the futility of those midnight conversations. All a man could do was to live. In awe and wonder:

Life seems to me like a Japanese picture which our imagination does not allow to end with the margin. We aim at the infinite and when our arrow falls to earth it is in flames.

At times the ambitious ends of life have made it seem to be lonely, but it has not been. . . . [D]ear friends have helped to keep alive the fire in my heart. If I could think that I had sent a spark to those who come after I should be ready to say Goodbye.

Part *VIII*

 *BENEDICTION*

After his death, when we opened his private safety deposit box, we found therein . . . a little paper parcel, the size of one finger, which, when opened, was found to contain two musket balls and on the paper was written in his handwriting "These were taken from my body in the Civil War." In the closet in his bedroom we found two old Civil War uniforms . . . and to them was pinned a piece of paper, on which he had written "These uniforms were worn by me in the Civil War and the stains upon them are my blood."

—John S. Flannery to Mark DeWolfe Howe, May 13, 1942

CHAPTER 31

Finishing Canter

HOLMES'S OWN "LITTLE finishing canter," to which he had alluded during the radio broadcast on his ninetieth birthday, lasted just over three years—time enough for him to see the cherry trees around the Tidal Basin and the magnolias in Rock Creek Park blossom and to summer at Beverly Farms three times more. Although friends had feared Holmes might "go into a decline" following his resignation from the Court, which had given purpose to his life for three decades, he gave no outward "sign of distress." The justices took turns calling, making the transition from one way of life to the other less abrupt, giving time a chance to work. Felix Frankfurter, former secretaries, family, Washington figures, all followed in their turn to the shrine. On his ninety-first birthday, NBC broadcast the tributes offered at the annual banquet of the Federal Bar Association; Holmes "listened in" from his study, but did not attempt to answer them as he had the year before. He sent instead his answer in writing.

He was seen occasionally passing the Capitol on his daily drives, but he did not return to the courtroom and did not keep up with affairs of the Court. That chapter was closed. What he wanted, he told one caller, was for his days to pass "as a rock in a bed of a river, with water flowing over it." He did, however, contribute a short introduction to Felix Frankfurter's collection of tributes to Brandeis, which was published in 1932 as *Mr. Justice Brandeis*. And the secretaries continued to arrive each fall, dispatched from Harvard by Frankfurter, who recognized the continuing value of their companionship to the aging Holmes. They drove with him and read to him while he listened or dozed. One of them estimated they had read four and a half million words during the first

eight months of his term. "[P]reparing for his last examination," Holmes
still trudged through the heaviest tomes, but at ninety-one, he felt he
had "outlived duty," and Oswald Spengler and Aristotle shared his attention with Agatha Christie and Dashiell Hammett for whose work he
had in late years developed a "consuming weakness." These authors had
"no style—no insight into life—no characterization, but there is something doing all the time." Holmes's reading list for 1932 includes the
works of E. Phillips Oppenheim, John Dickson Carr, Mignon Eberhart,
and Dorothy L. Sayers. He once hornswoggled one of the secretaries
into reading *Macbeth,* not for the high drama and poetry but for the
blood and thunder. Bulldog Drummond was a favorite, and Holmes would
willingly stay up until the early hours of the morning listening to a
murder tale.

Friends who called at Beverly Farms that summer found Holmes
"melancholy" and preoccupied with thoughts of death. "It's all very remote to me," he told the Frankfurters when they tried to divert him
with talk of affairs and events. "I'm dead. I'm like a ghost on a battlefield with bullets flying through me."

His body was weakening fast, and he apologized for not rising when
women entered the room. He resented the incapacity, which he considered a breach of etiquette, and on at least one occasion he compensated by pulling himself up to his full height as his callers drove out
through his gate and waving a last determined salute. But the "hard
case of O.W.H." had "melted"; now he required "petting" and "tender
affection."

Johnny Morse made his usual call. In a wistful mood, Johnny had
told Holmes not long ago that he had become "accustomed to being the
cousin and old-time comrade of 'Mr. Justice Holmes.' " Their paths had
"separated after college days," and while "Leany" Holmes was closeted
alone with his books as he searched out antiquity for beginnings, "Fatty"
Morse was writing his bland little biographies of America's heroes: Benjamin Franklin, John Quincy Adams, Thomas Jefferson, Abraham Lincoln, and a two-volume work on his uncle, Dr. Oliver Wendell Holmes.
When "Leany" challenged the economic framework supporting the Boston establishment, "Fatty" and his fellow Brahmins, convinced disaster
was imminent, were reviling the new forces that threatened their position.

You had greater—much greater, abilities than I had [Morse had told Holmes].
Yet mine, I think were fairly good. The really great difference was that
you had ambition as well as a distinct purpose. I had neither. You worked

hard and well. I certainly did neither. While you toiled splendidly along the paths of learning and of thought, I amused myself with my horses and my goats. Had I worked as you did, I could by no means have achieved, even along different lines, any result at all approaching those which you have accomplished. But along different lines I might have done a little something,—(I flatter myself!)—Well, the game is played to an end now, and . . . I confess that I don't *much* regret my own non-performance . . . I admire and am glad of, your brilliant success . . . But horses, & dogs, and goats help me through the job of life pretty well.

Some years before, Johnny had asked Holmes why Holmes's mustache was so much fuller than his own, and Holmes had replied:

"Mine was nourished in blood."

On March 8, 1933, Holmes's ninety-second birthday, a festive lunch with Felix Frankfurter, down from Harvard for the occasion, Holmes's secretary—Donald Hiss that year—and a former secretary, Thomas Corcoran, marked the event. Hiss had gotten hold of some bootleg champagne, and Holmes drank three or four glasses.

"Young fellow," he told Frankfurter, "I don't want you to misunderstand things; I do not deal with bootleggers but I am open to corruption."

The usual cards, gifts, and telegrams had been coming in all day; there seemed to be no letup, and the telegraph boy was complaining. The court clerk had brought flowers, and Chief Justice Hughes had arrived with his wife shortly after luncheon. At about dusk, America's First Family itself pulled up in front of 1720 I Street, and the new president, Franklin Delano Roosevelt, helped by his son James and his wife, Eleanor, emerged from the car and negotiated the front steps of the red brick house while a crowd gathered to watch. At Frankfurter's instigation, he had interrupted his work on the economic emergency—the banks closed, millions unemployed—to pay a birthday call on the former justice and while away a half hour in the library with him. As the chief executive was about to leave, he turned to Holmes and said:

"Justice, you are the greatest living American. For half the history of the Republic you have seen its greatest events and known its greatest men. What is your advice to me?"

"Mr. President," Holmes replied, "you are in a war; I, too, was in a war. There is only one rule in a war. Form your battalions and fight."

Holmes had entertained the president in his second-floor library. He didn't come downstairs much any more, but sat in his chair with a shawl over his feet. The physical act of writing was harder now; ultimately the secretaries wrote his letters for him, and his correspondence fell off. Friends called, but were warned not to stay too long, and, Holmes confessed, "I am pretty idle and find it easy to be for I am tired."

Owen Wister came to see him and told him a story that ordinarily would have produced a guffaw. But Holmes didn't get it.

"Sorry, Whiskers," he said, "I'm living behind a cloud, Whiskers, I'm sorry. But," he added, his eyes flashing in the old way, "I can still pull my brains together and call a man a son-of-a-bitch if I have to."

He made a new will. He had no children and no close relatives except Ned's son, on whom he had never spent much affection and who in any case was in comfortable circumstances. He hardly ever contributed to charity and had serious doubts on the few occasions when he did. After making a few small bequests to the servants, his nephew, a cousin, and one or two of Fanny's kin, he left his library and prints to the Library of Congress and the bulk of his estate—a little more than a quarter of a million dollars—to the United States government without explanation. A lot of people thought it was a queer thing to do. But he may have felt the gesture was some small compensation for his leaving the Army before the war was over, for surviving when so many had not. At last, perhaps, his duty was done. This was his final salute.*

Through the end of 1933 and most of 1934, Holmes's health appeared good. Then, in the late winter of 1934, he caught a cold. He had survived several over the past couple of years, and there seemed no reason to believe he would not survive this one. Plans were made to celebrate his ninety-fourth birthday on March 8, 1935. Then the cold turned into bronchial pneumonia—the "old man's friend," as one of the secretaries described it. He weakened steadily. On March 5, an oxygen tent was brought in.

"Every soldier to his tent, Captain Holmes," said the secretary, James Rowe, in the gentle way he had, and saluted. Holmes returned the salute with a vigorous thumbing of his nose. Hours later, at 2:15 A.M., March 6, he breathed his last. The final entry he had added to the list

---

* Unaccustomed as it was to such largesse, the government had no idea what to do with the money. A committee was appointed by Congress to study the matter, and after some years of sporadic deliberations, the members offered such proposals as a memorial library, publication of Holmes's own writings, and a memorial garden to be placed near the Supreme Court. Finally, in 1955, Congress created a permanent Committee for the Oliver Wendell Holmes Devise and assigned it the task of supervising the production of the definitive multivolume history of the United States Supreme Court. The first target date was 1965, and leading American constitutional scholars were recruited to write it. Delays, deaths, and resignations have beset the project from the first. New target dates were set. Gradually, beginning in 1971, the volumes were published, one after the other. By late 1990, eight of the projected eleven volumes had come out, a ninth was nearly complete, and the other two were expected to be out in 1993.

of books he had read that year was Thornton Wilder's *Heaven's My Destination.*

A Unitarian funeral service was held at All Souls' Church in Washington on that very birthday for which the small celebration had been planned and to which some of the mourners had been invited. The justices of the Supreme Court served as honorary pall bearers, secretaries, past and present, as ushers. The church was filled; outside a crowd waited behind the police lines.

The flag-draped coffin was carried on a caisson to Arlington National Cemetery, where Fanny already lay and where he had chosen to be buried among soldiers, far from home and the graves of his people who lay so close to the shadow of the State House dome. Muffled drums set the slow cadence.

Ceremonies at the grave were delayed briefly until the White House car arrived. An aide supported the president as he walked through the crowd. A group of infantrymen shot off the ceremonial triple volley. A soldier blew taps. A soft spring rain was falling. As Mary Donellen, who had cared for him since Fanny's death, watched the soldiers unload his coffin from the caisson, she turned to the man standing next to her and said quietly:

"Soldiers don't mind the rain."

ABAJ: American Bar Association Journal

AJH: Amelia Jackson Holmes, OWH's sister

ALH: Amelia Lee Jackson Holmes, OWH's mother

ALJ: Albany Law Journal

ALR: American Law Review

AM: Atlantic Monthly

BB: Black Book (OWH's reading lists)

BDA: Boston Daily Advertiser

BET: Boston Evening Transcript

BG: Boston Globe

BH: Boston Herald

BP: Boston Post

BPL: Boston Public Library

CC: Clare Castletown

CEH: Charles Evans Hughes

CLP: Collected Legal Papers

CM: Charlotte Moncheur

CR: Congressional Record

DAB: Dictionary of American Biography

EJH: Edward Jackson Holmes, OWH's brother

EJH, Jr.: Edward Jackson Holmes, Jr., EJH's son

ES: Ethel Scott

FDH: Fanny Bowditch Dixwell Holmes, OWH's wife

FF: Felix Frankfurter

FP: Frederick Pollock

HCL: Henry Cabot Lodge

HFS: Harlan Fiske Stone

HGM: Harvard Graduates' Magazine

HJL: Harold J. Laski

HLR: Harvard Law Review

HLSA: Harvard Law School Association

HLSL: Harvard Law School Library

HM: Harvard Magazine

HU: Harvard University

HUA: Harvard University Archives, Pusey Library

HUh: Houghton Library, Harvard University

JTM: John T. Morse, Jr.

LC: Library of Congress

LCRB: LC Rare Books Room, where OWH's library is stored

LDB: Louis Dembitz Brandeis

LE: Lewis Einstein

LJ: Law Journal

LQ: Law Quarterly

LQR: Law Quarterly Review

LR: Law Review

MADH: Mark Antony DeWolfe Howe

MDH: Mark DeWolfe Howe

MHS: Massachusetts Historical Society

NA: National Archives

NAACP: National Association for the Advancement of Colored People

NAR: *North American Review*

NEH&GR: *New England Historical and Genealogical Register*

NEQ: *New England Quarterly*

NG: Nina Gray

NR: *New Republic*

NYT: *The New York Times*

O.T.: October Term

OWH: Oliver Wendell Holmes (1841–1935), the younger

OWH, Sr.: Oliver Wendell Holmes (1809–1894), the elder

PAS: Patrick A. Sheehan

TCL: *The Common Law*

TR: Theodore Roosevelt

WHT: William Howard Taft

WJ: William James

WP: *Washington Post*

WS: *Washington Star*

YLJ: *Yale Law Journal*

SOURCES AND BIBLIOGRAPHY

1. Interviews

Edgar J. Bellefontaine
Mary E. Grant
Jeffrey M. Haskins, M.D.
Alger Hiss
James Hutson
Jean M. Kennett

Max Lerner
John Monagan
Paul C. Reardon
Joann Reiss
H. Chapman Rose
Sylvia Stein

2. Manuscript depositories and collections

Henry Adams, HUh
Berkshire Athenaeum, Pittsfield, Massachusetts
Boston Athenaeum, Boston, Massachusetts
Catherine Drinker Bowen, LC
Louis Dembitz Brandeis, HLSL and University of Louisville
David J. Brewer, LC
Henry B. Brown, Burton Historical Collection, Detroit Public Library
Hampton L. Carson Law Collection, Free Library of Philadelphia
Richard Cary, MHS
Zechariah Chafee, HLSL
Joseph H. Choate, LC

James Freeman Clarke, HUh
Thomas M. Cooley, Michigan Historical Collections, Bentley Library, University of Michigan
Thomas G. Corcoran, LC
Dana family papers, MHS
William R. Day, LC
James T. and Annie A. Fields, HUh
Felix Frankfurter, HLSL and LC
Melville W. Fuller, LC and Chicago Historical Society
Elmer Gertz, LC
Grant Gilmore, HLSL
Robert Grant, HUh
Hale family papers, MHS
Norwood P. Hallowell, MHS

Learned Hand, HLSL

John Marshall Harlan, University of Louisville and LC

Harvard University Archives

Thomas Wentworth Higginson, HUh

George Frisbie Hoar, MHS

Abiel Holmes, HUh

John Holmes, HUh

Oliver Wendell Holmes, HLSL, LC, and Schimmel Collection, Columbia University

Oliver Wendell Holmes, Sr., HUh and LC

Mark DeWolfe Howe, HLSL

Charles Evans Hughes, LC

James family papers, HUh

Philander C. Knox, LC

Joseph Rucker Lamar, Hargrett Rare Book and Manuscript Library, University of Georgia

Little, Brown, HUh

Henry Cabot Lodge, MHS

John Davis Long, MHS and Massachusetts State Archives

Abbott Lawrence Lowell, HUA

James Russell Lowell, HUh

Horace H. Lurton, LC

James C. McReynolds, Arthur J. Morris Law Library, University of Virginia

Massachusetts State Archives

Agnes Meyer, LC

Middlebury College Library, Middlebury, Vermont

William H. Moody, LC

John T. Morse, Jr., MHS

National Archives, Waltham, Massachusetts, and Washington, D.C.

National Association for the Advancement of Colored People, LC

Charles Eliot Norton, HUh

John G. Palfrey, HUh

Roscoe Pound, HLSL

Theodore Roosevelt, LC

Edward T. Sanford, University of Tennessee

Stuart Schimmel Collection, Rare Book and Manuscript Library, Columbia University

George Otis Shattuck, MHS

Social Law Library, Boston, Massachusetts

Harlan Fiske Stone, LC

Suffolk County Probate Court, Boston, Massachusetts

George Sutherland, LC

William Howard Taft, LC

W. R. Thayer, HUh

Annie H. Thwing, MHS

Twentieth Massachusetts Volunteer Infantry Regiment, BPL

United States Supreme Court case files, NA

Willis Van Devanter, LC

Wendell family papers, New York Public Library

Wigglesworth family papers, MHS

Owen Wister, LC

Alfred E. Zimmern, Bodleian Library, Oxford University

3. Documents: proceedings, reports, catalogues, and other records

Boston Athenaeum. *Report to the Proprietors of the Boston Athenaeum in Relation to the Issuing of New Shares*. Boston, 1853.

Catalogue of the Porcellian Club of Harvard University. Cambridge, Mass., 1867 and 1936.

Congressional Record. Issues as cited.

Controversy Between the First Parish in Cambridge and the Rev. Dr. Holmes Their Late Pastor. Cambridge, Mass., 1829.

Harvard College. *Class of 1861 Fiftieth Anniversary and Final Report.* Boston, 1915.

———. Class of 1867: *Secretary's Report No. 3.* Cambridge, Mass., 1870.

———. *The Statutes and Laws of Harvard College.* Cambridge, Mass., 1860.

Harvard Law School. Faculty Minutes: 1870–1928. HLSL.

———. *Quinquennial Catalogue of the Law School of Harvard University: 1817–1924.* Cambridge, Mass., 1925.

Harvard University. *Annual Report of the President and Treasurer of Harvard University.* Cambridge, Mass., volumes as cited.

———. *Catalogue.* Cambridge, Mass., volumes as cited.

———. College Records. HUA, volumes as cited.

———. Corporation Records. HUA, volumes as cited.

———. Monthly Returns, Examinations and Term Aggregates. HUA, volumes as cited.

———. Orders and Regulations of the Faculty. HUA, volumes as cited.

———. Overseers' Records. HUA, volumes as cited.

———. Presidents' Papers. HUA, volumes as cited.

———. *Quinquennial Catalogue of the Officers and Graduates: 1636–1925.* Cambridge, Mass., 1925.

———. Scale of Merit, 1849–61. HUA, volumes as cited.

———. Weekly Absences. HUA, volumes as cited.

Massachusetts Historical Society. *Collections;* volumes as cited.

———. *Proceedings;* volumes as cited.

The Medical and Surgical History of the War of the Rebellion: 1861–1865; part 1, volumes 1, 3; part 2, volume 1. Washington, D.C., 1870.

New England Historical and Genealogical Society. *New England Historical and Genealogical Register.* Boston, volumes as cited.

Roosevelt, Theodore. *Message of the President to Congress, December 6, 1904.* United States House Documents, volume 1, number 1; 58th Congress, 3d Session, 1904–05.

United States War Department. *The War of the Rebellion. A compilation of the official records of the Union and Confederate Armies.* Washington, D.C., volumes as cited.

4. Unpublished material

Belknap, Chauncey. Some Words of Justice Holmes. OWH papers, HLSL.

Brandeis-Frankfurter Conversations. FF papers, LC.

Cleveland, Richard F. Mr. Justice Holmes. FF papers, LC.

Corcoran, Thomas G. Rendezvous with Democracy: The Memoirs of "Tommy the Cork" (with Philip Kopper), Thomas G. Corcoran papers, LC.

Crowninshield, Caspar. Journal. Twentieth Massachusetts Volunteer Infantry Regiment papers, BPL.

Dixwell, Epes Sargent. Dixwell Pedigree. OWH papers, HLSL.

Ely, Richard T. My Recollections and Connections with Mr. Justice Oliver Wendell Holmes. OWH papers, HLSL.

Estate of Justice Oliver Wendell Holmes, The Library: A list compiled at his late residence, 1720 I Street, NW, Washington, D.C. LCRB.

Estate of Justice Oliver Wendell Holmes, The Library: Beverly Farms, Massachusetts. LCRB.

Harlan, Malvina S. Some Memories of a Long Life. John Marshall Harlan papers, LC.

[Hiss, Alger]. Observations on the processes followed by Justice Holmes in carrying out his judicial duties during the October Term 1929. Grant Gilmore papers, HLSL.

Holmes, Oliver Wendell. BB, a year-by-year list of Holmes's reading, 1876–1935, and his notes for *TCL;* personal collection of H. Chapman Rose.

———. "Regimental Veteran Association's Resolutions on the Late Colonel Lee." Twentieth Massachusetts Volunteer Infantry Regiment Collection, BPL.

Howe, Mark DeWolfe. Howe Diary. MDH papers, HLSL.

Hughes, Charles Evans. Autobiographical Notes. CEH papers, LC.

Lee, William R. Memoir of Colonel Paul Joseph Revere. Twentieth Massachusetts Volunteer Infantry Regiment papers, BPL.

Lockwood, John E. Justice Holmes: Year 1928–29. OWH papers, HLSL.

"Meeting of Holmes's Secretaries"; OWH papers, HLSL.

Mr. Justice Holmes's opinions, O.T. 1902–32 (drafts, include notations by other justices); OWH papers, HLSL.

Ropes, Henry. Letters, 1859–63. Twentieth Massachusetts Volunteer Infantry Regiment papers, BPL.

Sutherland, Arthur E. Recollections of Justice Holmes. Sutherland papers, HLSL.

Whittier, Charles A. Journal. Twentieth Massachusetts Volunteer Infantry Regiment papers, BPL.

Woollcott, Alexander. Lecture on Mr. Justice Holmes. FF papers, LC.

5. Published material: books, articles

Abraham, Henry J. "John Marshall Harlan: The Justice and the Man." 46 *Kentucky LJ* 448 (1958).

———. *Justices and Presidents.* New York, 1985.

Acheson, Dean G. *Among Friends: Personal Letters of Dean Acheson.* Edited by David S. McLellan and David C. Acheson. New York, 1980.

———. *Morning and Noon.* Boston, 1965.

————. "Reminiscences of a Supreme Court Law Clerk." 103 *Pittsburgh Legal Journal* 3 (1955).

————. "Speech." American Law Institute *Proceedings,* 1956, 732.

Adams, Charles Francis. *Charles Francis Adams, 1835–1915.* New York, 1916.

————. *Memoirs of John Quincy Adams.* Philadelphia, 1876, volumes as cited.

————. *Richard Henry Dana.* Boston and New York, 1890, volumes 1, 2.

Adams, Edward B. "Oliver Wendell Holmes." 15 *Green Bag* 1 (1903).

Adams, Frederick Upham. "Are Great Fortunes Great Dangers?" 40 *Cosmopolitan* 392 (1906).

Adams, Henry. *The Education of Henry Adams.* New York, 1918.

————. "The Great Secession Winter of 1860–61." 43 MHS *Proceedings* 660 (1910).

————. *The Letters of Henry Adams.* Cambridge, Mass., 1982, volumes 1, 2.

Adams, Marian (Hooper). *The Letters of Mrs. Henry Adams.* Edited by Ward Thoron. Boston, 1936.

Adams, Mildred. "In the Supreme Court Law Is Majesty." NYT, 11/10/29, v, 10.

————. "Three Venerable Justices Who Refuse to Grow Old." *NYT,* 12/8/29, v, 12.

Agassiz, Louis. "Evolution and Permanence of Type." 33 *AM* 92 (1874).

Aichele, Gary J. *Oliver Wendell Holmes, Jr. Soldier, Scholar, Judge.* Boston, 1989.

Aitcheson, Clyde B. "Justice Holmes and the Development of Administrative Law." 1 *George Washington University LR* 165 (1933).

Alger, George W. "The Courts and Legislative Freedom." 111 *AM* 345 (1913).

Allen, Alexander V. G. *Life and Letters of Phillips Brooks.* New York, 1900, volume 1.

Allen, Francis A. "Criminal Law." 31 *University of Chicago LR* 257 (1964).

American Academy of Arts and Sciences, Boston. *Memorial of Joseph Lovering.* Cambridge, Mass., 1892.

Anderson, Isabel. *Presidents and Pies: Life in Washington 1897–1919.* Boston, 1920.

Anderson, Thornton. *Brooks Adams: Constructive Conservative.* Ithaca, N.Y., 1951.

The Athenaeum Centenary: The Influence and History of the Boston Athenaeum from 1807 to 1907. Boston, 1907.

Atiyah, Patrick. "The Legacy of Holmes Through English Eyes" in *Holmes and The Common Law: A Century Later,* 27 (see below).

Auchincloss, Louis. "Mr. Justice Holmes." 29 *American Heritage* 68 (1978).

Auerbach, Jerold S. *Unequal Justice.* New York, 1976.

Austin, James C. *Fields of the Atlantic Monthly: Letters to an Editor 1861–1870.* San Marino, Cal., 1953.

Austin, John. *The Province of Jurisprudence Determined.* New York, 1970.

Baier, Paul R. "Dedication of a Portrait: Edward Douglass White: Frame for a Portrait." 43 *Louisiana LR* 1001 (1983).

Bail, Hamilton Vaughan. "Harvard's Commemoration Day: July 21, 1865." 15 *NEQ* 256 (1942).

Bailey, Thomas A. "Theodore Roosevelt and the Alaska Boundary Settlement." 18 *The Canadian Historical Review* 123 (1937).

Baker, Leonard. *Brandeis and Frankfurter: A Dual Biography.* New York, 1984.

Baker, Liva. *Felix Frankfurter: A Biography.* New York, 1969.

Baldwin, Elbert F. "The Supreme Court Justices." 97 *Outlook* 156 (1/28/11).

Bander, Edward J. "Holmespun Humor." 10 *Villanova LR* 92 (1964).

Barbour, Thomas. *Naturalist at Large.* Boston, 1943.

Barnes, Harry Elmer. *A History of Historical Writing.* New York, 1937.

Bartol, C. A. *Our Sacrifices.* Boston, 1861.

Bartosic, Florian. "The Constitution, Civil Liberties, and John Marshall Harlan." 46 *Kentucky LJ* 407 (1958).

Barzun, Jacques. *A Stroll with William James.* Chicago, 1983.

Basch, Norma. *In the Eyes of the Law: Women, Marriage, and Property in Nineteenth Century New York.* Ithaca, N.Y., 1982.

Batchelder, Samuel F. "Old Times at the Law School." 90 *AM* 642 (1902).

Beard, Charles A. "Justice Oliver Wendell Holmes." 33 *Current History* 801 (1931).

Beck, James M. *The Constitution of the United States.* Garden City, N.Y., 1924.

———. "The Federal Power over Trusts." 24 American Academy of Political and Social Science *Annals* 89 (1904).

———. "Justice Holmes and the Supreme Court." 1 *Federal Bar Association Journal* 36 (1932).

———. *May It Please the Court.* Atlanta, 1930.

———. "Nullification by Indirection." 23 *HLR* 441 (1910).

———, and Merle Thorpe. *Neither Purse nor Sword.* New York, 1936.

Beebe, Lucius. *Boston and the Boston Legend.* New York, 1935.

Belknap, Chauncey. "A Retrospective Note." 28 *University of Florida LR* 392 (1976).

Benjamin Peirce. Reminiscences by Charles W. Eliot, A. Lawrence Lowell, W. E. Byerly, and Arnold B. Chace. Oberlin, Ohio, 1925.

Bent, Silas. *Justice Oliver Wendell Holmes.* New York, 1932.

Beringause, Arthur F. *Brooks Adams: A Biography.* New York, 1955.

Berle, A. A., Jr. "A Friendship of Opposing Minds." *NYT,* 3/15/53, vii, 1.

Bernstein, Irving. "The Conservative Mr. Justice Holmes." 23 *NEQ* 435 (1950).

Bickel, Alexander. "Mr. Taft Rehabilitates the Court." 79 *YLJ* 1 (1969).

———. *The Unpublished Opinions of Mr. Justice Brandeis.* Chicago, 1957.

———, and Benno C. Schmidt, Jr. *The Judiciary and Responsible Government, 1910–1921.* New York, 1984.

Biddle, Francis. "The Aging of Justice Holmes." 151 *NR* 19 (12/19/64).

———. "The Friendship of Holmes and Brandeis." 216 *AM* 86 (1965).

————. *Justice Holmes and Natural Law*. New York, 1961.

————. "Mr. Justice Holmes." 72 *NR* 105 (9/7/32).

————. *Mr. Justice Holmes*. New York, 1942.

————. "Mr. Justice Holmes: Notes Toward a Biography." 185 *Harpers* 470, 593 (1942).

Birrell, Augustine. *Frederick Locker-Lampson*. London, 1920.

Bishop, Joseph B. *Theodore Roosevelt and His Time*. New York, 1920, volume 1.

Blackstone, William. *Blackstone's Commentaries . . . .* Edited by St. George Tucker. Philadelphia, 1803, volumes as cited.

Bogen, David S. "The Free Speech Metamorphosis of Mr. Justice Holmes." 11 *Hofstra LR* 97 (1982).

Boorstin, Daniel J. "The Elusiveness of Mr. Justice Holmes." 14 *NEQ* 478 (1941).

Boudin, Leonard. "Justice Holmes and His World." 3 *Lawyers Guild Review* 24 (1943).

Bowditch, Charles P. "War Letters of Charles P. Bowditch." 57 MHS *Proceedings* 414 (1924).

Bowen, Catherine Drinker. *Yankee from Olympus*. Boston, 1945.

Bowen, Clarence Winthrop. *The History of Woodstock, Connecticut*. Norwood, Mass., 1935, volumes 1–6.

Bowen, Francis. *The Principles of Metaphysical and Ethical Science Applied to the Evidences of Religion*. Boston, 1855.

————. *The Principles of Political Economy*. New York and London, 1974.

[————]. "Review of On the Origin of Species by Means of Natural Selection, or the Preservation of Favored Races in the Struggle for Life. By Charles Darwin." 187 *NAR* 474 (April 1860).

————. *A Theory of Creation*. Boston, 1845.

Bowen, James L. *Massachusetts in the War: 1861–1865*. Springfield, Mass., 1889.

Boyden, Albert. *Ropes-Gray: 1865–1940*. Boston, 1942 (privately printed).

Braeman, John. *Albert J. Beveridge, American Nationalist*. Chicago, 1971.

Brewer, David J. "Organized Wealth and the Judiciary." 57 *The Independent* 301 (8/11/04).

————. "The Supreme Court of the United States." 33 *Scribner's Magazine* 273 (1903).

Briggs, Charles W. "Justice Holmes Was Not on a Ladder to Hitler." 32 *ABAJ* 631 (1946).

Brooks, Van Wyck. "Dr. Holmes: Forerunner of the Moderns." 14 *The Saturday Review of Literature* 3 (6/27/36).

————. *The Flowering of New England, 1815–1865*. New York, 1936.

————. *New England: Indian Summer*. New York, 1940.

Brown, Abram English. "Beacon Hill." 28 (n.s.) *The New England Magazine* 631 (1903).

Brown, Francis H. *Harvard University in the War of 1861–1865*. Boston, 1886.

Bruce, George A. *The Twentieth Regiment of Massachusetts Volunteer Infantry, 1861–1865.* Boston and New York, 1906.

Bryce, James T. *The Nation's Capital.* Washington, D.C., 1913.

Bullough, Vern L. *Sexual Variance in Society and History.* New York, 1976.

Burlingham, C. C. "The Holmes-Pollock Letters." *WP,* 3/23/41, 10.

Burton, David H. "The Friendship of Justice Holmes and Canon Sheehan." 25 *Harvard Library Bulletin* 155 (1977).

———. "Justice Holmes and the Jesuits." 27 *American Journal of Jurisprudence* 32 (1982).

———. *Oliver Wendell Holmes, Jr.* Boston, 1980.

———. *Oliver Wendell Holmes, Jr.: What Manner of Liberal?* Huntington, N.Y., 1979.

Butler, Charles Henry. *A Century at the Bar of the Supreme Court of the United States.* New York, 1942.

Callcott, George H. *History in the United States, 1800–1860: Its Practice and Purpose.* Baltimore and London, 1970.

Capen, Oliver Bronson. "Country Homes of Famous Americans. XV. Oliver Wendell Holmes." 8 *Country Life in America* 308 (1905).

Cardozo, Benjamin N. "Mr. Justice Holmes." 44 *HLR* 682 (1931).

Castletown, Bernard. *Ego: Random Records of Sport, Service, and Travel in Many Lands.* London, 1923.

Cater, Harold D. *Henry Adams and His Friends.* New York, 1970.

Catton, Bruce. *Mr. Lincoln's Army.* Garden City, N.Y., 1951.

———. *This Hallowed Ground.* Garden City, N.Y., 1956.

———. *A Stillness at Appomattox.* Garden City, N.Y., 1953.

Chafee, Zechariah, Jr. "A Contemporary State Trial: The United States Versus Jacob Abrams et al." 33 *HLR* 747 (1920).

———. *Free Speech in the United States.* Cambridge, Mass., 1942.

———. "Freedom of Speech." 17 *NR* 66 (11/16/18).

———. "Freedom of Speech in Wartime." 32 *HLR* 932 (1919).

———. "Liberal Trends in the Supreme Court." 35 *Current History* 338 (1931).

———. "Thirty-five Years with Freedom of Speech." 2 *Kansas LR* 2 (1952).

Chamberlain, Joshua L., ed. *Harvard University: Its History, Influences, Equipment and Characteristics.* Boston, 1900.

Chase, Philip Putnam. "A Crucial Juncture in the Political Careers of Lodge and Long." 70 *MHS Proceedings* 102.

Cheever, David W. "Dr. Holmes, the Anatomist." 3 *HGM* 154 (1894).

Child, Maude Parker. "Capital Society." 198 *Saturday Evening Post* 12 (2/20/26).

Child, Rilla. "A Story of Brave Women." *The Congregationalist and Christian World* 245 (2/22/08).

Chused, Richard H. "Married Women's Property Law: 1800–1850." 71 *Georgetown LJ* 1359 (1983).

Clark, Champ. *My Quarter Century of American Politics.* New York, 1920, volumes 1, 2.

Clarke, Edward H. *Sex in Education, or a Fair Chance for the Girls.* Boston, 1873.

Clarke, John H. "Observations and Reflections on Practice in the Supreme Court." 8 *ABAJ* 263 (1922).

Cohen, Jeremy. *Congress Shall Make No Law: Oliver Wendell Holmes, the First Amendment, and Judicial Decision Making.* Ames, Iowa, 1989.

Cohen, Morris R. "Justice Holmes." 82 *NR* 206 (4/3/35).

———. "Justice Holmes and the Nature of Law." 31 *Columbia LR* 352 (1931).

Collins, Ronald K. L., and Jennifer Friesen. "Looking Back on *Muller v. Oregon.*" 69 *ABAJ* 294 and 472 (1983).

Commager, Henry Steele. *The American Mind.* New Haven, Conn., 1950.

———. "Justice Holmes in His Letters." *NYT*, 3/23/41, vii, 1.

Congressional Quarterly. *Guide to the Supreme Court.* Washington, D.C., 1979.

Conway, Moncure Daniel. *The Autobiography of Moncure Daniel Conway.* New York, 1969, volumes 1, 2.

Cooke, Alistair. "The Late Captain Holmes." 104 *NR* 401 (3/24/41).

Coolidge, Louis A. "On the Streets at the Nation's Capital." 28 *Cosmopolitan* 365 (1900).

Corwin, Edward S. "Judicial Review and the 'Higher Law.' " 19 *Think* 3 (1953).

Cover, Robert M. "The Left, the Right and the First Amendment." 40 *Maryland LR* 349 (1981).

Cowles, Anna Roosevelt. *Letters from Theodore Roosevelt to Anna Roosevelt Cowles, 1870–1918.* New York and London, 1924.

Cramer, John Henry. *Lincoln Under Enemy Fire.* Baton Rouge, 1948.

Crawford, Mary Caroline. *Famous Families of Massachusetts.* Boston, 1930, volumes 1, 2.

"Critical Notices." 118 *NAR* 383 (1874).

Croly, Herbert. *The Promise of American Life.* Indianapolis, 1965.

Crompton, Henry. "Class Legislation." 19 (n.s. 13) *Fortnightly Review* 205 (1873).

Crothers, Samuel M. "The Autocrat and His Fellow-Boarders." 104 *AM* 237 (1909).

Crowninshield, Benjamin W. *A Private Journal, 1856–58.* Cambridge, Mass., 1941.

Curti, Merle. *The Growth of American Thought.* New York, 1951.

Curtis, Laurence. "From a Personal Point of View." 28 *University of Florida LR* 392 (1976).

Cushing, Carolyn Kellogg. "The Gallant Captain and the Little Girl." 155 *AM* 545 (1935).

Cutter, William R. *Genealogical and Personal Memoirs in Relation to the Families of the State of Massachusetts.* New York, 1910, volumes 1–4.

Dalzell, Robert F., Jr. *Enterprising Elite: The Boston Associates and the World They Made.* Cambridge, Mass., 1987.

Dana, Richard Henry, Jr. *The Journal of Richard Henry Dana, Jr.* Edited by Robert F. Lucid. Cambridge, Mass., 1968, volumes as cited.

Danelski, David. *A Supreme Court Justice Is Appointed.* New York, 1964.

Dapping, William O. *Susan Dixwell Miller.* Boston, 1924.

Dart, Henry Plauché. "Edward Douglass White." 5 *Louisiana History Quarterly* 144 (1922).

Davies, Joseph E. *Trust Laws and Unfair Competition.* Washington, D.C., 1916.

Davis, Horace B. "The End of the Holmes Tradition." 19 *University of Kansas City LR* 53 (1951).

Davis, William T. *Bench and Bar of the Commonwealth of Massachusetts.* New York, 1974, volumes as cited.

———. *History of the Judiciary of Massachusetts.* Boston, 1900.

Day, Gardener M. *The Biography of a Church.* Cambridge, Mass., 1951.

Degler, Carl N. "American Political Parties and the Rise of the City: An Interpretation." 51 *Journal of American History* 41 (1964).

———. *At Odds.* New York, 1980.

D'Emilio, John, and Estelle B. Friedman. *Intimate Matters.* New York, 1968.

Denby, Charles. "An Extraordinary Man." 28 *University of Florida LR* 393 (1976).

De Normandie, James. "Some Notes from an Old Parish Record Book." 38 MHS *Proceedings* 340.

Derby, Augustin. "Recollections of Mr. Justice Holmes." 12 *New York University LQR* 345 (1935).

Dewey, John. "Justice Holmes and the Liberal Mind." 53 *NR* 210 (1/11/28).

Dilliard, Irving. "An Immortal Makes His Mark." 46 *Saturday Review* 22 (8/17/63).

Dinnerstein, Leonard. *The Leo Frank Case.* New York and London, 1968.

Dixwell, Epes Sargent. *An Autobiographical Sketch.* Edited by Mary C. D. Wigglesworth. Boston, 1907.

Dobyns, Fletcher. "Justice Holmes and the Fourteenth Amendment." 13 *Illinois LR* 71 (1918).

Drake, Samuel Adams. *Historic Mansions and Highways Around Boston.* Boston, 1899.

———. *The History and Antiquities of Boston.* Boston, 1856.

———. *Old Landmarks and Historic Personages of Boston.* Detroit, 1970.

DuBin, Alexander, ed. *Wendell Family.* Philadelphia, 1939.

Duffus, R. L. "At Ninety, Justice Holmes Marches On." *NYT,* 3/8/31, v, 3.

———. "Mr. Hughes the Chief Justice Emerges." *NYT,* 6/28/31, v, 3.

———. "The Remarkable Career of Justice Holmes." *NYT,* 3/13/32, iv, 7.

Dupree, A. Hunter. *Asa Gray, 1810–1888.* Cambridge, Mass., 1959.

Duyckinck, Evert A. and George L. *Cyclopaedia of American Literature.* Philadelphia, 1877, volume 1.

Early, Jubal A. *War Memoirs.* Bloomington, Ind., 1960.

Edel, Leon. *Henry James*. Philadelphia, 1953–72, volumes 1–6.

Einstein, Lewis. *A Diplomat Looks Back*. New Haven, 1968.

Eitzen, D. Stanley. *David J. Brewer, 1837–1910*. Emporia, Kan., 1964.

Eldridge, F. Howard. "Justice Holmes: Another Aspect of His Life and Philosophy." 20 *University of Chicago LR* 417 (1943).

Eliot, Charles W. *Harvard Memories*. Freeport, N.Y., 1969.

———. *A Late Harvest*. Boston, 1924.

———. "Oliver Wendell Holmes." 31 *HGM* 457 (1923).

Elliott, E. Donald. "Holmes and Evolution: Legal Process as Artificial Intelligence." 13 *Journal of Legal Studies* 113 (1984).

Ely, John Hart. *Democracy and Distrust: A Theory of Judicial Review*. Cambridge, Mass., and London, 1980.

Emerson, Edward Waldo. *The Early Years of the Saturday Club, 1855–1870*. Boston and New York, 1918.

Emerson, Ralph Waldo. *The American Scholar*. New York, 1901.

———. *Heroism*. New York, 1906.

———. *Selected Prose and Poetry*. New York and Toronto, 1950.

Epstein, Barbara L. *The Politics of Domesticity*. Middletown, Conn., 1981.

"Ernst Freund and the First Amendment Tradition." 40 *University of Chicago LR* 235 (1973).

Essary, J. Frederick. "The Human Side of the Supreme Court." 86 *Scribner's Magazine* 498 (1929).

"An Evolutionist on the Bench: The Story of Justice Holmes." 14 *The World Tomorrow* 219 (1931).

Ewing, Cortez A. M. *The Judges of the Supreme Court, 1789–1937*. Minneapolis, 1938.

Farnum, George R. "Holmes—the Mystic Philosopher." 2 *American Lawyer* 12 (1937).

———. "Holmes—the Soldier-Philosopher." 2 *The Lawyer* 9 (1939).

———. "Holmes—the Solitary Scholar." 1 *The Lawyer* 13 (1938).

———. "Justice Holmes—Philosopher and Humanitarian." 3 *The Law Society Journal* 3 (1930–31).

———. "Oliver Wendell Holmes." 29 *ABAJ* 17 (1943).

Farrelley, David G. "Harlan's Formative Period: The Years Before the War." 46 *Kentucky LJ* 367 (1958).

Feinstein, Howard M. *Becoming William James*. Ithaca, N.Y., 1984.

Fiechter, Frederick C., Jr. "The Preparation of an American Aristocrat." 6 *NEQ* 3 (1933).

Field, David Dudley. "The Codes of New York and Codification in General." 19 *ALJ* 192 (1879).

Fields, Annie. *Authors and Friends*. Boston, 1896.

———. "Oliver Wendell Holmes: Personal Recollections and Unpublished Letters." 49 (n.s. 27) *Century Magazine* 505 (1895).

Fields, James T. *Barry Cornwall and Some of His Friends*. Boston, 1876.

Findlay, Anna Howell Kennedy. "Where the Captain Was Found." 33 *Maryland Historical Magazine* 109 (1938).

Fisch, Max H. "Justice Holmes, the Prediction Theory of Law, and Pragmatism." 39 *Journal of Philosophy* 85 (2/12/42).

———. "Was There a Metaphysical Club in Cambridge?" In *Studies in the Philosophy of Charles Sanders Peirce*. Edited by Edward C. Moore and Richard S. Robin. Amherst, Mass., 1964.

Fiske, John. *The Letters of John Fiske*. New York, 1940.

Fitzsimmons, Matthew A., and Alfred G. Pundt. *The Development of Historiography*. Harrisburg, Pa., 1954.

Follansbee, Mitchell D. "Oliver Wendell Holmes: A Judge with Imagination." 22 *American Lawyer* 766 (1903).

Foote, Henry W. *Annals of King's Chapel*. Boston, 1882–1904, volumes 1–3.

Foraker, Julia B. *I Would Live It Again: Memories of a Vivid Life*. New York, 1932.

Forbes, A[bner]. *The Rich Men of Massachusetts*. Boston, 1852.

Ford, John C. "The Totalitarian Justice Holmes." 159 *Catholic World* 114 (1944).

Foster, John W. *Diplomatic Memoirs*. Boston and New York, 1909, volume 1.

Fox, Jabez. "Constitutional Checks upon Municipal Enterprise." 5 *HLR* 30 (1891).

Frank, John P. "The Appointment of Supreme Court Justices: Prestige, Principles, and Politics." 1941 *Wisconsin LR* 173, 343, 461 (1941).

———. "Harlan Fiske Stone: An Estimate." 9 *Stanford LR* 621 (1957).

Frankfurter, Felix. *The Case of Sacco and Vanzetti*. New York, 1961.

———. "The Constitutional Opinions of Mr. Justice Holmes." 29 *HLR* 683 (1916).

———. "The Early Writings of Oliver Wendell Holmes, Jr." 44 *HLR* 771 (1931).

———. *Felix Frankfurter Reminisces*. Garden City, N.Y., 1960.

———. " 'Moral Grandeur' of Justice Brandeis." *NYT*, 11/11/1956, vi, 26.

———. "Mr. Justice Holmes." 48 *HLR* 1279 (1935).

———. *Mr. Justice Holmes and the Supreme Court*. New York, 1965.

———. "October Days." 3 *Today* 5 (3/9/35).

———. *Of Law and Life and Other Things That Matter*. Edited by Philip B. Kurland. Cambridge, Mass., 1965.

———. *Of Law and Men*. Edited by Philip Elman. Hamden, Conn., 1956.

———. "Twenty Years of Mr. Justice Holmes's Constitutional Opinions." 36 *HLR* 909 (1923).

———, ed. *Mr. Justice Brandeis*. New York, 1932.

———, ed. *Mr. Justice Holmes*. New York, 1931.

Frederickson, George M. *The Inner Civil War*. New York, 1965.

Freund, Ernst. "The Debs Case and Freedom of Speech." 25 *NR* 13 (5/3/19).

Frey, Sylvia R. *The British Soldier in America*. Austin, Tex., 1981.

Friedman, Lawrence M. *A History of American Law*. New York, 1973.

———. "A Search for Seizure: *Pennsylvania Coal Company* v. *Mahon* in Context." 4 *Law and History Review* 1 (1986).

Friedman, Leon, and Fred L. Israel. *The Justices of the United States Supreme Court, 1789–1969*. New York, 1978, volumes 2, 3.

Friendly, Henry J. "A Shattering Book from Beacon Hill." *NYT Book Review*, 8/11/63, vi, 6.

Fuller, Lon L. *The Law in Quest of Itself*. Chicago, 1940.

Gabriel, Ralph H. *The Course of American Democratic Thought*. New York, 1940.

Garraty, John A. *Henry Cabot Lodge: A Biography*. New York, 1953.

———. "Holmes's Appointment to the United States Supreme Court." 22 *NEQ* 291 (1949).

Garrison, Lloyd McKim. *An Illustrated History of the Hasty Pudding Theatricals*. Cambridge, Mass., 1897.

Gengarelly, W. Anthony. "The Abrams Case: Social Aspects of a Judicial Controversy." 25 *Boston Bar Journal* 19, 9 (3, 4, 1981).

Gilmore, Grant. *The Ages of American Law*. New Haven, 1977.

———. *The Death of Contract*. Columbus, Ohio, 1974.

Golden, Harry L. *The Lynching of Leo Frank*. London, 1966.

Goldsmith, Arnold L. "Oliver Wendell Holmes: Father and Son." 48 *Journal of Criminal Law and Criminology* 394 (1957).

Goodwin, Doris Kearns. *The Fitzgeralds and the Kennedys*. New York, 1988.

Gordon, Robert W. "Holmes' *Common Law* as Legal and Social Science." 10 *Hofstra LR* 719 (1982).

Gossett, Elizabeth Hughes. "Charles Evans Hughes: My Father the Chief Justice." 1976 Supreme Court Historical Society *Yearbook* 7.

Grant, Robert. *Fourscore: An Autobiography*. Boston and New York, 1934.

Gray, George Arthur. *The Descendants of George Holmes of Roxbury, 1594–1908. To which is added the Descendants of John Holmes of Woodstock, Connecticut*. Boston, 1908.

Gray, John Chipman, and John C. Ropes. *War Letters, 1862–1865, of John Chipman Gray and John Codman Ropes*. Boston, 1927.

Gray, Russell. "Historical Sketch of the Supreme Judicial Court of Massachusetts." 13 *Medico-Legal Journal* 225 (1895–96).

"Great Span." 51 *New Yorker* 29 (4/14/75).

Green, Constance McLaughlin. *Washington*. Princeton, N.J., 1962, volume 2.

Green, Martin. *The Problem of Boston*. London, 1966.

Greenberg, Jack. *Race Relations and American Law*. New York, 1959.

Greenslet, Ferris. *The Lowells and Their Seven Worlds*. Boston, 1946.

Gregg, Paul L. "The Pragmatism of Justice Holmes." 31 *Georgetown LJ* 262 (1943).

Gresham, Matilda. *Life of Walter Quintin Gresham*. Chicago, 1919, volume 2.

Grey, Thomas C. "Holmes and Legal Pragmatism." 41 *Stanford LR* 787 (1909).

Griswold, Harriet Ford. "Justices of the Supreme Court of the United States I Have Known." 8 *The Supreme Court Historical Society Quarterly* 1 (1987).

Gunther, Gerald. "Learned Hand and the Origins of Modern First Amendment Doctrine: Some Fragments of History." 27 *Stanford LR* 719 (1975).

Haldane, Richard B. "Mr. Justice Holmes." 26 *NR* 34 (3/9/21).

Hale, Edward Everett. "Memories of a Hundred Years." 72 *Outlook* 301 (10/4/02).

———. *A New England Boyhood*. Boston, 1900.

Hale, Richard Walden. *Some Table Talk of Mr. Justice Holmes and 'The Mrs.'* Privately printed, 1935.

Hallowell, Norwood P. *Selected Letters and Papers*. Peterborough, N.H., 1963.

Hamilton, Walton Hale. "The Legal Philosophy of Justices Holmes and Brandeis." 33 *Current History* 654 (1931).

———. "On Dating Mr. Justice Holmes." 9 *University of Chicago LR* 1 (1941).

Hamm, Margherita A. *Famous Families of New York*. New York and London, 1901, volume 2.

Hammond, John Hays. *The Autobiography of John Hays Hammond*. New York, 1974, volumes 1, 2.

Hand, Learned. "Review: Collected Legal Papers by Oliver Wendell Holmes." 36 *Political Science Quarterly* 528 (1921).

Handlin, Oscar. *Boston's Immigrants*. Cambridge, Mass., 1959.

Hapgood, Norman. "Justice Brandeis: Apostle of Freedom." 125 *Nation* 330 (10/5/27).

Harbaugh, William H. *Lawyer's Lawyer: The Life of John W. Davis*. New York and London, 1973.

Harmond, Richard. "Troubles of Massachusetts Republicans During the 1880s." 56 *Mid-America* 85 (1974).

Harris, Robert J. *The Quest for Equality*. Baton Rouge, 1960.

Hart, Henry M., Jr. "Holmes' Positivism—An Addendum." 64 *HLR* 929 (1951).

Harvard Law School Association. *The Centennial History of the Harvard Law School: 1817–1917*. Cambridge, Mass., 1918.

Harvard Memorial Biographies. Edited by Thomas W. Higginson. Cambridge, Mass., 1866, volumes 1, 2.

Hay, John. *Lincoln and the Civil War in the Diaries and Letters of John Hay*. New York, 1939.

Hayakawa, Samuel I. "Holmes's Lowell Lectures." 8 *American Literature* 281 (1936).

Hedge, Frederic H. "University Reform. An Address to the Alumni of Harvard at Their Triennial Festival, July 19, 1866." 18 *AM* 296 (1866).

Heffron, Paul. "Theodore Roosevelt and the Appointment of Mr. Justice Moody." 18 *Vanderbilt LR* 545 (1965).

Hess, James W. "John D. Long and Reform Issues in Massachusetts Politics 1870–1889." 33 *NEQ* 57 (1960).

Heuser, Herman J. *Canon Sheehan of Doneraile*. New York, 1917.

Hicks, Frederick C. "Lincoln, Wright, and Holmes at Fort Stevens." 39 *Journal of the Illinois State Historical Society* 32 (1946).

Higginson, Thomas W. *Contemporaries.* Boston, 1899.

———. "George Frisbie Hoar." 40 *Proceedings of the American Academy of Arts and Sciences* 761 (1905).

———. *Massachusetts in the Army and Navy During the War of 1861–1865.* Boston, 1896, volumes 1, 2.

———. *Old Cambridge.* New York, 1899.

———. "Republican Aristocracy." 117 *Harper's Monthly Magazine* 202 (1908).

Hill, Arthur Dehon. "Oliver Wendell Holmes." 39 HGM 265 (1931).

Hiss, Alger. "Paragon Without Peer." 28 *University of Florida LR* 304 (1976).

Hoar, George Frisbie. *Autobiography of Seventy Years.* New York, 1903.

Hoffheimer, Michael H. "Justice Holmes: Law and the Search for Control." 1989 Supreme Court Historical Society Yearbook, 98.

Holbrook, Stewart H. *The Age of the Moguls.* Garden City, N.Y., 1953.

[Holbrook, William A.]. "A Review." 7 HM 243 (1860).

Holmes, Abiel. "Address." 5 *American Antiquarian Society Proceedings* 57 (1815).

———. *An Address . . . 5 July 1813.* Cambridge, Mass., 1813.

———. *American Annals.* Cambridge, Mass., 1805, volumes 1, 2.

———. *A Discourse . . . XVII September MDCCCXVIII.* Cambridge, Mass., 1818.

———. *A Discourse . . . August 29, 1803. . . .* Boston, 1807.

———. *A Family Tablet.* Boston, 1796.

———. *The History of Cambridge.* Boston, 1801.

———. *Life of Ezra Stiles.* Boston, 1798.

———. *A Sermon on the Freedom and Happiness of America . . . February 19, 1795, the day appointed by the President of the United States for a National thanksgiving.* Boston, 1795.

———. *A Sermon . . . June 7, 1799.* Boston, 1799.

———. *A Sermon . . . December 19, 1799, occasioned by the Death of George Washington.* Boston, 1800.

———. *A Sermon . . . January 4, 1801, the first Lord's Day in the Nineteenth Century.* Cambridge, Mass., 1801.

———. *Sermon . . . April 6, 1809. . . .* Cambridge, Mass., 1809.

———. *A Sermon . . . January 19, 1814.* Cambridge, Mass., 1814.

Holmes, John. *Letters of John Holmes to James Russell Lowell and Others.* Edited by William Roscoe Thayer. Boston and New York, 1917.

Holmes, Oliver Wendell. "Agency." 4 HLR 345 (1891).

[———]. "The Arrangement of the Law: Privity." 7 ALR 46 (1872).

[———]. "Books." 4 HM 408 (1858).

[———]. "Codes, and the Arrangement of the Law." 5 ALR 1 (1870).

———. *Collected Legal Papers.* New York, 1920.

[———.] "Common Carriers and the Common Law." 13 ALR 609 (1879).

———. *The Common Law.* Boston, 1938.

Holmes, Oliver Wendell. *The Dissenting Opinions of Mr. Justice Holmes.* Arranged by Alfred Lief. New York, 1929.

[————]. "The Gas-Stokers' Strike." 7 *ALR* 582 (1873).

————. "Grain Elevators: On the Title to Grain in Public Warehouses." 6 *HLR* 450 (1872).

————. *His Book Notices and Uncollected Letters and Papers.* Edited by Harry C. Shriver. New York, 1936.

————. "Holdsworth's English Law." 25 *LQR* 412 (1909).

[————]. "Impeachment." 2 *ALR* 547 and 747 (1868).

————. "In Memoriam: Fredric William Maitland." 23 *LQR* 137 (1907).

————. Introduction to *Mr. Justice Brandeis.* Edited by Felix Frankfurter. New York, 1932.

————. Introduction to *Rational Basis of Legal Institutions.* Edited by J. H. Wigmore and A. Kocourek. New York, 1923.

————. Introduction to Charles Louis de Secondat Montesquieu's *The Spirit of the Laws.* New York, 1900.

————. *The Judicial Opinions of Oliver Wendell Holmes.* Edited by Harry C. Shriver. New York, 1940.

————. "Just the Boy Wanted." 62 *The Youth's Companion* 73 (2/7/1889).

————. "Law in Science and Science in Law." 12 *HLR* 443 (1899).

————. "Memoir of George O. Shattuck, LL.B." 14 MHS *Proceedings* 361.

————. *The Mind and Faith of Justice Holmes: His Speeches, Essays, Letters, and Judicial Opinions.* Edited by Max Lerner. New York, 1943.

[————]. "Misunderstandings of the Civil Law." 6 *ALR* 37 (1871).

————. "Natural Law." 32 *HLR* 40 (1918).

[————]. "Notes on Albert Durer." 7 *HM* 41 (1860).

————. *The Occasional Speeches of Justice Oliver Wendell Holmes.* Compiled by Mark DeWolfe Howe, Jr. Cambridge, Mass., 1962.

————. "The Path of the Law." 10 *HLR* 457 (1897).

————. "Plato." 4 *The University Quarterly* 205 (1860).

[————]. "Possession." 12 *ALR* 688 (1878).

[————]. "Pre-Raphaelitism." 7 *HM* 345 (1861).

[————]. "Primitive Notions in Modern Law." 10 *ALR* 422 (1876) and 11 *ALR* 641 (1877).

————. "Privilege, Malice and Intent." 8 *HLR* 1 (1894).

[————]. Review of *The Code of Iowa. . . .* 7 *ALR* 318 (1873).

[————]. Review of *Digest of the Law of Evidence in Criminal Cases.* 1 *ALR* 375 (1867).

[————]. Review of *Essays in Anglo-Saxon Law.* 11 *ALR* 327 (1877).

[————]. Review of *The Law Magazine and Review.* 6 *ALR* 723 (1872).

[————]. Review of *The Law of Torts.* 5 *ALR* 341 (1871).

[————]. Review of *A Manual of Medical Jurisprudence.* 1 *ALR* 376 (1867).

[————]. Review of *Reports of Cases in Law and Equity, determined in the Supreme Court of the State of Iowa.* 3 *ALR* 357 (1869).

[————]. Review of *The Science of Legal Judgment*. 6 ALR 134 (1871).

————. "The Soldier's Faith." 4 HGM 179 (1895).

————. *Speeches*. Boston, 1913.

————. "The Theory of Legal Interpretation." 12 HLR 417 (1899).

[————]. "The Theory of Torts." 7 ALR 652 (1873).

————. *Touched with Fire, Civil War Letters and Diary of Oliver Wendell Holmes, Jr., 1861–1864*. Edited by Mark DeWolfe Howe. Cambridge, Mass., 1946.

[————]. "Trespass and Negligence." 14 ALR 1 (1880).

[————]. "Ultra Vires: How Far Are Corporations Liable for Acts Not Authorized by Their Charters." 5 ALR 272 (1871).

————, and Morris R. Cohen. "Holmes-Cohen Correspondence." 9 *Journal of the History of Ideas* 3 (1948).

————, and Lewis Einstein. *The Holmes-Einstein Letters*. Edited by James Bishop Peabody. New York, 1964.

————, and Franklin Ford. *Progressive Masks*. Edited by David H. Burton. Newark, N.J., 1982.

————, and Harold J. Laski. *Holmes-Laski Letters*. Edited by Mark DeWolfe Howe. Cambridge, Mass., 1953, volumes 1, 2.

————, and Frederick Pollock. *Holmes-Pollock Letters*. Edited by Mark De-Wolfe Howe. Cambridge, Mass., 1946, volumes 1, 2.

————, and Patrick A. Sheehan. *Holmes-Sheehan Correspondence*. Edited by David H. Burton. Port Washington, N.Y., 1976.

Holmes, Oliver Wendell, Sr. "Four Letters of Dr. Holmes." 14 (n.s.) *Yale Review* 410 (1925).

————. Introduction to Clarence W. Bowen's *The History of Woodstock, Connecticut* (see above).

————. "Letters of Dr. Holmes to a Classmate." 54 *Century Magazine* 946 (1897).

————. "Letters of Dr. Oliver Wendell Holmes." 30 *Harvard Alumni Bulletin* 374 (1927).

[————]. "My Hunt After the Captain." 10 AM 738 (1862).

————. Review of *The Study of Sociology*. 89 *Boston Medical and Surgical Journal* 587 (1873).

————. *The Works of Oliver Wendell Holmes*. Boston and New York, 1892, volumes 1–13.

Holmes, Richard. *Acts of War*. New York, 1988.

Holmes and The Common Law: A Century Later. Cambridge, Mass., 1983.

"Holmes, Peirce and Legal Pragmatism." 84 YLJ 1123 (1975).

"Holmes's American Annals." 29 NAR 428 (1829).

"Holmes's Common Law." 15 ALR 331 (1881).

Holt, George C. "The New Justice of the Supreme Court." 54 *The Independent* 2361 (1902).

"Honorable Charles Jackson." 8 *Monthly Law Reporter* 601 (1856).

Hovey, Richard B. *John Jay Chapman—An American Mind*. New York, 1959.

Howe, Julia Ward. *Reminiscences: 1819–1899.* New York, 1969.

———. "Social Boston Past and Present." 43 *Harper's Bazaar* 195 (1909).

Howe, Mark Antony DeWolfe. "The Boston Religion." 91 *AM* 729 (1903).

———. *Boston: The Place and the People.* New York, 1903.

———. "Boston—Why Is It and What?" 52 *Harper's Weekly* 8 (11/21/08).

———. *Holmes of the Breakfast Table.* Mamaroneck, N.Y., 1972.

———. *John Jay Chapman and His Letters.* Boston, 1937.

———. *Memories of a Hostess: A Chronicle of Eminent Friendships (from the diaries of Mrs. James T. Fields).* Boston, 1922.

———. *Moorfield Storey: Portrait of an Independent.* Boston, 1932.

———, ed. *Later Years of the Saturday Club.* Freeport, N.Y., 1968.

Howe, Mark DeWolfe. "Choosing the Law." 28 *University of Florida LR* 398 (1976).

———. "The Creative Period in the Law of Massachusetts." 69 MHS *Proceedings* 232.

———. *Justice Oliver Wendell Holmes: The Proving Years, 1870–1882.* Cambridge, Mass., 1963 (hereafter cited as *Proving*).

———. *Justice Oliver Wendell Holmes: The Shaping Years, 1841–1870.* Cambridge, Mass., 1957 (hereafter cited as *Shaping*).

———. "The Letters of Henry James to Mr. Justice Holmes." 38 *Yale Review* 410 (1949).

———. "Mr. Justice Holmes and His Secretaries." *NYT* 4/8/51, vii, 15.

———. "Mr. Justice Holmes Seeks His Friends." 199 *AM* 71 (1957).

———. "Oliver Wendell Holmes at Harvard Law School." 70 *HLR* 410 (1957).

———. "The Positivism of Mr. Justice Holmes." 64 *HLR* 529 (1951).

Howells, William Dean. *Literary Friends and Acquaintances.* New York and London, 1900.

Hughes, Charles Evans. "Mr. Justice Holmes." 44 *HLR* 677 (1931).

———. *The Supreme Court of the United States.* New York, 1966.

Huntington, Arria S. *Memoir and Letters of Frederic Dan Huntington.* Boston, 1906.

Hurst, J. Willard. *Justice Holmes and Legal History.* New York, 1964.

———. Review of *Justice Oliver Wendell Holmes: The Proving Years, 1870–1882.* 77 *HLR* 382 (1963).

Hutcheson, Joseph C. Review of *The Judicial Opinions of Oliver Wendell Holmes.* 10 *George Washington University LR* 247 (1941).

Ipswich Historical Society. "Thomas Dudley and Simon and Ann Bradstreet." 12 *Publications of the Ipswich Historical Society* 3 (1902).

Jackson, James. *Reminiscences of the Honorable Jonathan Jackson.* Boston, 1866.

Jaher, Frederic C. "The Boston Brahmins in the Age of Industrial Capitalism." In *The Age of Industrialism in America.* Edited by Frederic C. Jaher. New York, 1968, 188.

———. "Nineteenth-Century Elites in Boston and New York." 6 *Journal of Social History* 32 (1972).

James, Alice. *The Diary of Alice James.* Edited by Leon Edel. New York, 1964.

James, Henry. *Charles William Eliot.* Boston, 1930, volume 1.

———. *Nathaniel Hawthorne.* New York, 1879.

———. *Notes of a Son and Brother.* New York, 1914.

———. "Poor Richard." 19 *AM* 694 (1867); 20 *AM* 32, 166 (1867).

James, William. *Letters of William James.* Edited by Henry James. Boston, 1920, volumes 1, 2.

———. "The True Harvard." In William James's *Memories and Studies.* New York, 1911, 348.

Jenks, W. "Memoir of the Rev. Abiel Holmes, D.D., LL.D., &c." 7 MHS *Collections* 270 (1838).

Jerrold, Walter. *Oliver Wendell Holmes.* London, 1893.

Jessup, Philip C. *Elihu Root.* New York, 1938, 1964, volumes 1, 2.

Jones, Leonard A. "Oliver Wendell Holmes, the Jurist." 36 *ALR* 710 (1902).

Josephson, Matthew. *The Robber Barons.* New York, 1962.

Joyce, Walter E. "Edward Douglass White: The Louisiana Years." 41 *Tulane LR* 751 (1967).

"Judge Putnam's Recollections of Chief Justice Fuller." 22 *Green Bag* 526 (1912).

Kalven, Harry, Jr. "Torts." 31 *University of Chicago LR* 263 (1964).

———. *A Worthy Tradition.* Edited by Jamie Kalven. New York, 1988.

Kanin, Garson. "Trips to Felix." 213 *AM* 55 (1964).

Kaplan, Benjamin. "Encounters with Oliver Wendell Holmes." In *Holmes and The Common Law: A Century Later* (see above).

Kaplan, Harold I., Alfred M. Freedman, and Benjamin J. Saddock. *Comprehensive Textbook of Psychiatry/III.* Baltimore, 1980, volume 2.

Keller, Morton. *In Defense of Yesterday: James M. Beck and the Politics of Conservatism, 1861–1936.* New York, n.d.

Kelley, Patrick J. "A Critical Analysis of Holmes's Theory of Torts." 61 *Washington University LQ* 681 (1983).

———. "Oliver Wendell Holmes, Utilitarian Jurisprudence, and the Positivism of John Stuart Mill." 30 *American Journal of Jurisprudence* 189 (1985).

Kellogg, Augusta W. "The Boston Athenaeum." 29 (n.s.) *New England Magazine* 167 (1930).

Kellogg, Charles Flint. *NAACP: A History of the National Association for the Advancement of Colored People.* Baltimore, 1967, volumes 1, 2.

Kellogg, Frederic Rogers. *The Formative Essays of Justice Holmes.* Westport, Conn., 1984.

———. "Law, Morals and Justice Holmes." 69 *Judicature* 214 (1986).

Kennedy, William Sloane. *Oliver Wendell Holmes: Poet, Litterateur, Scientist.* Boston, 1883.

Kent, Charles A. *Memoir of Henry Billings Brown.* New York, 1915.

Kent, James. *Commentaries on American Law.* Boston, 1873 (12th edition, edited by Oliver Wendell Holmes), volumes 1–4; 1884 (13th edition, edited by Charles M. Barnes), volume 1.

Kevles, Daniel J. "Annals of Eugenics." 60 *New Yorker* 52 (10/15/84).

Keyes, Francis Parkinson. *Capital Kaleidoscope: The Story of a Washington Hostess.* New York, 1937.

———. *Letters from a Senator's Wife.* New York, 1924.

King, Willard L. *Melville Weston Fuller.* Chicago and London, 1950.

Klinkhamer, Sister Marie Carolyn. *Edward Douglass White, Chief Justice of the United States.* Washington, D.C., 1943.

Kluger, Richard. *Simple Justice.* New York, 1976.

Knox, John. "Some Correspondence with Holmes and Pollock." 21 *Chicago Bar Journal* 219 (1940).

Konefsky, Samuel J. "Holmes and Brandeis: Companions in Dissent." 10 *Vanderbilt LR* 269 (1957).

Kraus, Michael. *The Writing of American History.* Norman, Okla., 1953.

Krislov, Samuel. "Oliver Wendell Holmes: The Ebb and Flow of Judicial Legendry." 52 *Northwestern University LR* 514 (1957).

Kuklik, Bruce. *The Rise of American Philosophy: Cambridge, Massachusetts, 1860–1930.* New Haven and London, 1977.

Kulikoff, Allan. "The Progress of Inequality in Revolutionary Boston." 28 *William and Mary Quarterly* 375 (1971).

Kurland, Phillip B. "Portrait of the Jurist as a Young Mind." 25 *University of Chicago LR* 206 (1957).

Lamar, Clarinda Pendleton. *The Life of Joseph Rucker Lamar.* New York and London, 1926.

Lane, Franklin K. *Letters of Franklin K. Lane.* Edited by Annie W. Lane and Louise H. Wall. Boston and New York, 1922.

Laski, Harold J. *Authority and the Modern State.* New Haven, 1919.

———. "Ever Sincerely Yours, O. W. Holmes, One of the Greatest of Letter Writers." *NYT*, 2/15/48, vi, 11.

———. "The Judicial Function." In *The Danger of Being a Gentleman.* New York, 1940, 105.

———. "Memories of a Great American." 25 *The Listener* 359 (3/13/41).

———. "Mr. Justice Holmes—For His 89th Birthday." 160 *Harper's Magazine* 415 (1930).

———. "The Political Philosophy of Mr. Justice Holmes." 40 *YLJ* 683 (1931).

———. "A Statesman of the Law." Review of *Mr. Justice Brandeis*, edited by Felix Frankfurter. 168 *NR* 50 (8/24/32).

Lavery, Emmet. "Justice Holmes and Canon Sheehan." 172 *Catholic World* 13 (1950).

Lawrence, William. *Henry Cabot Lodge: A Biographical Sketch.* Boston and New York, 1925.

Leach, W. Barton. Review of *Touched with Fire.* 56 *YLJ* 427 (1947).

LeClair, Robert C. "Henry James and Minny Temple." 21 *American Literature* 35 (1949).

Leder, Lawrence, ed. *The Colonial Legacy.* New York, 1973, volumes 3, 4.

Le Duc, Alice Sumner. "The Man Who Rescued 'The Captain.' " 180 *AM* 80 (1947).

Lee, Henry and Mary. *Letters and Journals with Other Family Letters.* Compiled by Frances Rollins Morse. Boston, 1926.

Leech, Margaret. *Reveille in Washington: 1860–1865.* New York, 1941.

Lerner, Max. "Holmes and Frankfurter." 147 *The Nation* 537 (11/19/38).

———. The Mind and Faith of Justice Holmes. New York, 1954.

———. "Mr. Justice Brandeis." In *Ideas Are Weapons.* New York, 1939, 70.

———. "Mr. Justice Holmes." In *Ideas Are Weapons* (see above), 54.

———. "The Scar Holmes Leaves." 46 *YLJ* 904 (1937).

"Letter from Chancellor Kent to Edward Livingston. . . ." 16 *American Jurist* 361 (1837).

Levitan, David M. "The Jurisprudence of Mr. Justice Clarke." 7 *University of Miami LQ* 44 (1952).

———. "Mahlon Pitney—Labor Judge." 40 *Virginia LR* 733 (1954).

Linde, Hans A. "Courts and Censorship." 66 *Minnesota LR* 171 (1981).

Little, Eleanor N. "The Early Reading of Justice Oliver Wendell Holmes." 8 *Harvard Library Bulletin* 163 (1954).

Llewellyn, Karl N. "Holmes." 35 *Columbia LR* 485 (1935).

———. "On Philosophy in American Law." 82 *University of Pennsylvania LR* 205 (1934).

Lockwood, John E. "I Always Prefer the Original." 28 *University of Florida LR* 394 (1976).

Lodge, Henry Cabot. *An Address upon Chief Justice Marshall.* Washington, 1901.

———. *Early Memories.* New York, 1913.

———. *Theodore Roosevelt.* New York, 1919.

Lombardo, Paul A. "Three Generations, No Imbeciles: New Light on *Buck* v. *Bell.*" 60 *New York University LR* 30 (1985).

Long, John Davis. "Reminiscences of My Seventy Years' Education." 42 MHS *Proceedings* 348.

Longworth, Alice Roosevelt. *Crowded Hours: Reminiscences of Alice Roosevelt Longworth.* New York, 1933.

Loring, Katherine P. "The Earliest Summer Residents of the North Shore and Their Houses." 68 *Essex Institute Historical Collections* 193 (1932).

Lovett, James D'Wolf. *Old Boston Boys and the Games They Played.* Boston, 1906.

Low, A. Maurice. "Society in Washington." 104 *Harper's Monthly Magazine* 689 (1902).

———. "Washington: The City of Leisure." 86 *AM* 767 (1900).

Lowell Putnam. Cambridge, 1863.

Lowry, Edward G. "The Men of the Supreme Court." 27 *World's Work* 629 (1914).

Luce, Henry R. "Reverse Mr. Justice Holmes." 17 *Vital Speeches* 596 (7/15/51).

Lucey, Francis E. "Holmes—Liberal—Humanitarian—Believer in Democracy?" 39 *Georgetown LJ* 523 (1951).

———. "Jurisprudence and the Future Social Order." 16 *Social Science* 211 (1941).

———. "Natural Law and American Legal Realism: Their Respective Contributions to a Theory of Law in a Democratic Society." 30 *Georgetown LJ* 493 (1942).

Lurie, Edward. *Louis Agassiz: A Life in Science*. Chicago, 1960.

Lurton, Horace H. "A Government of Law or a Government of Men?" 193 *NAR* 9 (1911).

McCormack, Alfred. "A Law Clerk's Recollections." 46 *Columbia LR* 710 (1946).

McDevitt, Matthew. *Joseph McKenna*. New York, 1974.

McLean, Joseph E. *William Rufus Day*. New York, 1946.

Maguire, J. M. Review of Catherine Drinker Bowen, *Yankee from Olympus*. 57 *HLR* 1118 (1944).

Main, T. F. "Impotence." In *Psycho-Sexual Problems*. Baltimore, Md., 1975, 101.

Maine, Henry Sumner. *Ancient Law*. New York, 1864.

Maitland, Frederic W. *The Life and Letters of Leslie Stephen*. London, 1906.

Marke, Julius J. "A Law Student's Guide to Mr. Justice Holmes." 28 *University of Florida LR* 376 (1976).

Marquand, John P. *The Late George Apley*. New York, 1940.

Martin, Kingsley. *Harold Laski (1893–1950): A Biographical Memoir*. London, 1953.

Mason, Alpheus T. *Brandeis: A Free Man's Life*. New York, 1946.

———. *Brandeis: Lawyer and Judge in the Modern State*. Princeton, N.J., 1933.

———. *Harlan Fiske Stone: Pillar of the Law*. New York, 1956.

———. *William Howard Taft: Chief Justice*. New York, 1964.

Massachusetts Bar Association. *The Supreme Judicial Court of Massachusetts: 1692–1942*. Boston, n.d.

Maxwell, Robert S. *La Follette*. Englewood Cliffs, N.J., 1969.

May, Samuel. "Dr. Holmes with His Classmates." 3 *HGM* 159 (1894).

Mayda, Jaro. *François Gény and Modern Jurisprudence*. Baton Rouge, 1978.

Meigs, Charles D. *The History, Pathology and Treatment of Puerperal Fever and Crural Phlebitis*. Philadelphia, 1842.

———. *On the Nature, Signs, and Treatment of Childbed Fever; A Series of Letters Addressed to His Class*. Philadelphia, 1854.

Men of Progress: One Thousand Biographical Sketches and Portraits of Leaders in Business and Professional Life in the Commonwealth of Massachusetts. Compiled by Richard Herndon; edited by Edwin M. Bacon. Boston, 1896.

Mendelson, Wallace. "Mr. Justice Holmes—Humility, Skepticism and Democracy." 36 *Minnesota LR* 343 (1952).

Meyer, Agnes E. *Out of These Roots*. Boston, 1953.

Meyer, Balthasar H. "A History of the Northern Securities Case." *Bulletin of the University of Wisconsin* (Economic and Political Science Series, no. 3) 219 (1906).

Milano, Anthony J. "A Study in Crimson: Letters from the Harvard Regiments." 13 *Civil War* 15 (1988).

Mildmay, Susan, and Herbert St. John, eds. *John Lothrop Motley and His Family: Further Letters and Records.* London, 1910.

Mill, John Stuart. "Austin on Jurisprudence." In *Dissertations and Discussions.* London, 1867, iii, 206.

———. *On Liberty.* Edited by David Spitz. New York, 1975.

Miller, Loren. *The Petitioners: The Story of the Supreme Court of the United States and the Negro.* New York, 1966.

Miller, Perry. *The New England Mind.* New York, 1939.

Monagan, John S. "The Enigmatic Fanny Holmes." *BG*, 11/29/81, 14.

———. *The Great Panjandrum: The Mellow Years of Justice Holmes.* Lanham, Md., 1988.

———. "The Love Letters of Justice Holmes." *BG*, 3/24/85, 15.

Morison, Samuel Eliot. *The Maritime History of Massachusetts: 1783–1860.* Boston, 1979.

———. *The Oxford History of the American People.* New York, 1965.

———. *Three Centuries of Harvard: 1636–1936.* Cambridge, Mass., 1936.

Morris, George P. "Jurist and Stylist." 54 *The Independent* 2058 (8/28/02).

Morse, John T., Jr. "Incidents Connected with the American Statesmen Series." 64 MHS *Proceedings* 370.

———. *Life and Letters of Oliver Wendell Holmes.* Boston, 1896, volumes 1, 2.

———. *Memoir of Colonel Henry Lee.* Boston, 1905.

———. "Memoir of Henry Lee Higginson." 53 MHS *Proceedings* 105.

———. "Moorfield Storey: A Memoir." 63 MHS *Proceedings* 288.

———. "Recollections of Boston and Harvard Before the Civil War." 65 MHS *Proceedings* 150.

Motley, John Lothrop. *The Correspondence of John Lothrop Motley.* New York and London, 1900, volumes 1–3.

Murstein, Bernard I. *Love, Sex, and Marriage Through the Ages.* New York, 1974.

Musmanno, Michael Angelo. *After Twelve Years.* New York, 1939.

National Geographic Society. *Equal Justice Under Law.* Washington, D.C., 1965.

Nellis, Walter, and Samuel Mermin. "Holmes and Labor Law." 13 *New York University LQR* 517 (1936).

"The New Justices of the Supreme Court." 47 *Harper's Weekly* 212 (2/7/03).

Noonan, John T., Jr. *Persons and Masks of the Law.* New York, 1976.

Norton, Charles Eliot. *Considerations on Some Recent Social Theories.* Boston, 1853.

———. Review of *Memoirs of John, Lord of Joinville. . . .* 98 NAR 419 (1864).

Novick, Sheldon M. *Honorable Justice.* Boston and New York, 1989.

O'Brian, John Lord. *Civil Liberty in Wartime.* Washington, D.C., 1919.

O'Connell, Jeffrey, and Nancy Dart. "The House of Truth: Home of the Young Frankfurter and Lippmann." 35 *Catholic University LR* 79 (1985).

O'Connor, Thomas H. *Bibles, Brahmins, and Bosses.* Boston, 1984.

One Hundred and Twenty-five Years of Publishing: 1837–1962. Boston, 1962.

One of a Thousand: A Series of Biographical Sketches of One Thousand Representative Men Resident in the Commonwealth of Massachusetts A.D. *1888–89.* Compiled under the supervision of John C. Rand. Boston, 1890.

Our First Men (containing a list of those persons taxed in Boston, credibly reported to be worth $100,000). Boston, 1846.

Palfrey, Francis Winthrop. *Memoir of William Francis Bartlett.* Boston, 1881.

Palmer, Benjamin W. "Defense Against Leviathan." 32 *ABAJ* 328 (1946).

———. "Hobbes, Holmes, and Hitler." 31 *ABAJ* 569 (1945).

———. "Reply to Mr. Charles W. Briggs." 32 *ABAJ* 635 (1946).

Parker, Joel. *The Law School of Harvard College.* New York, 1871.

Parrington, Vernon L. *Main Currents in American Thought.* New York, 1927, 1930, volumes 2, 3.

Paschal, Joel F. *Mr. Justice Sutherland: A Man Against the State.* New York, 1969.

Patch, Joseph D. *The Battle of Ball's Bluff.* Leesburg, Va., 1958.

Pearson, Drew, and Robert S. Allen. *The Nine Old Men.* Garden City, N.Y., 1937.

Perry, Bliss. *Richard Henry Dana: 1851–1931.* Boston and New York, 1933.

———. *Life and Letters of Henry Lee Higginson.* Freeport, N.Y., 1972.

Perry, Ralph Barton. "The Common Enemy. Early Letters of Oliver Wendell Holmes, Jr., and William James." 156 *AM* 293 (1935).

———. *The Thought and Character of William James.* Boston, 1935, 1936, volumes 1, 2.

———. "William James." 19 *HGM* 212 (1910).

Persons, Stow. *The Decline of American Gentility.* New York and London, 1973.

Phisterer, Frederick. *The Army in the Civil War.* New York, 1885, volume 13.

Plucknett, Theodore F. T. "Holmes: The Historian." 44 *HLR* 712 (1931).

Pohlman, H. L. *Justice Oliver Wendell Holmes and Utilitarian Jurisprudence.* Cambridge, Mass., 1984.

Polenberg, Richard. *Fighting Faiths.* New York, 1987.

Pollard, Joseph P. "Hughes the Humanitarian." 229 *NAR* 444 (1930).

———. "Justice Holmes Dissents." 85 *Scribner's Magazine* 22 (1929).

———. "Opinions of Mr. Justice Holmes." *NYT*, 11/19/31, v, 5.

Pollock, Frederick. "Abrams v. United States." 36 *LQR* 334 (1920).

[———]. "Holmes on the Common Law." 51 *The Saturday Review of Politics, Literature, and Science* 758 (6/11/1881).

———. "Mr. Justice Holmes." 48 *HLR* 1277 (1935).

Pollock, John. "The Pollock-Holmes Correspondence." 277 *The Quarterly Review* 44 (1941).

Porter, Kenneth Wiggins. *The Jacksons and the Lees*. New York, 1937, volumes 1, 2.

"A Portrait of Mr. Justice Holmes." 32 *Harvard Alumni Bulletin* 741 (1930).

Pound, Roscoe. "The Call for a Realist Jurisprudence." 44 *HLR* 693 (1931).

———. "Justice Holmes's Contribution to the Science of Law." 34 *HLR* 449 (1921).

Powell, Thomas Reed. "Holmes and Pollock." 152 *Nation* 580 (5/17/41).

Pringle, Henry F. *The Life and Times of William Howard Taft*. New York, 1939, volumes 1, 2.

———. *Theodore Roosevelt: A Biography*. New York, 1931.

Pusey, Merlo J. *Charles Evans Hughes*. New York, 1952, volumes 1, 2.

Putnam, Elizabeth Cabot, and James Jackson Putnam. *The Honorable Jonathan Jackson and Hannah (Tracy) Jackson: Their Ancestors and Descendants*. Privately printed, 1907.

Putnam, James Jackson. *A Memoir of Dr. James Jackson*. Boston and New York, 1905.

Ragan, Fred D. "Justice Oliver Wendell Holmes, Jr., Zechariah Chafee, Jr., and the Clear and Present Danger Test for Free Speech: The First Year, 1919." 58 *Journal of American History* 24 (1971).

Reeder, Robert P. "Chief Justice Fuller." 59 *University of Pennsylvania LR* 1 (1910).

Reid, Sydney. "Oliver Wendell Holmes: A Biographical Sketch." 54 *The Independent* 2057 (8/28/02).

Review of *American Annals*. 2 *The Quarterly Review* 319 (1809).

Rhodes, James Ford. *The McKinley and Roosevelt Administrations: 1897–1909*. New York, 1922.

Richardson, William A., and George P. Sanger, eds. *The General Statutes of the Commonwealth of Massachusetts*. Boston, 1860.

———. *Supplement to the General Statutes of the Commonwealth of Massachusetts: 1860–1872*. Boston, 1873.

Rodell, Fred. "Justice Holmes and His Hecklers." 60 *YLJ* 620 (1951).

Roe, Gilbert E. "Our Judicial Oligarchy." 22 *Hearst's Magazine* 109 (1912).

Rogat, Yosal. "The Judge as Spectator." 31 *University of Chicago LR* 213 (1964).

———. "Mr. Justice Holmes: A Dissenting Opinion." 15 *Stanford LR* 3 (1962) and 254 (1963).

———, and James M. O'Fallon. "Mr. Justice Holmes: A Dissenting Opinion—The Speech Cases." 36 *Stanford LR* 1349 (1984).

Roosevelt, Theodore. *An Autobiography*. New York, 1985.

———. "Nationalism and the Judiciary." 97 *Outlook* 532 (3/11/11).

———, and Henry Cabot Lodge. *Selections from the Correspondence of Theodore Roosevelt and Henry Cabot Lodge*. New York, 1925, volumes 1, 2.

Ropes, John C. *The Story of the Civil War*. New York, 1933, volumes 1, 2.

Rosenthal, James M. "Massachusetts Acts and Resolves Declared Unconstitutional by the Supreme Judicial Court of Massachusetts." 1 *Massachusetts LQ* 301 (1916).

Roth, Larry Martin. "Touched with Fire, Forged in Flame: Holmes and a Different Perspective." 28 *University of Florida LR* 365 (1976).

Rovere, Richard H. "Sage." 33 *New Yorker* 157 (4/6/57).

Samuels, Charles and Louise. *Night Fell on Georgia*. New York, 1956.

Samuels, Ernest. *Henry Adams: The Middle Years*. Cambridge, Mass., 1958.

———. *The Young Henry Adams*. Cambridge, Mass., 1948.

Sandburg, Carl. *Abraham Lincoln: The War Years*. New York, 1940, volume 3.

Schildt, John W. *Drums Along the Antietam*. Parsons, W. Va., 1972.

Schwarz, Joan I. "Oliver Wendell Holmes's 'The Path of the Law': Conflicting Views of the Legal World." 29 *American Journal of Legal History* 235 (1985).

"Scotch Prisoners Deported to New England, 1651–52." 61 MHS *Proceedings* 4.

Sedgwick, John. *Correspondence of John Sedgwick Major-General*. Privately printed, 1903.

Sergeant, Elizabeth Shepley. "Oliver Wendell Holmes." 49 *NR* 59 (12/8/26).

———. "Oliver Wendell Holmes." In *Fire Under the Andes*. Port Washington, N.Y., 1966, 307.

Services at the Celebration of the Two Hundred and Fiftieth Anniversary of the Organization of the First Church in Cambridge, February 7–14, 1886. Cambridge, 1886.

Sharp, Malcolm P. "Contracts." 31 *University of Chicago LR* 268 (1964).

Sheedy, Morgan M. "Justice Holmes." 22 *The Commonweal* 97 (5/24/35).

Sherman, Stephen O., and Weston F. Hutchins. "The Massachusetts Bench and Bar." 34 *New England Magazine* 433, 529, 643 (1906).

Shriver, Harry C. "Great Dissenter—Whose Dissents Now Prevail." *NYT*, 3/9/41, vii, 13.

———. "Oliver Wendell Holmes: Lawyer." 24 *ABAJ* 157 (1938).

Shyrock, Richard H. "Philadelphia and the Flowering of New England." 64 *The Pennsylvania Magazine of History and Biography* 305 (1940).

Sketches of Some Historic Churches of Greater Boston. Boston, 1918.

Sklar, Martin J. *The Corporate Reconstruction of American Capitalism, 1890–1916: The Market, the Law and Politics*. Cambridge, England, 1988.

Skotheim, Robert A. *American Intellectual Histories and Historians*. Princeton, N.J., 1966.

Slayden, Ellen. *Washington Wife. The Journal of Ellen Mary Sladen from 1897–1919*. New York, 1962.

Smalley, George W. *Anglo-American Memories*. New York, 1911.

Smith, Donald L. *Zechariah Chafee, Jr.: Defender of Liberty and Law*. Cambridge, Mass., 1986.

Smith, J. E. A. *History of Pittsfield (Berkshire County) Massachusetts*. Boston, 1869–76.

Smith, Joseph M. *Puerperal Fever: Its Causes and Modes of Propagation.* New York, 1857.

Smith, Reginald H. *Justice and the Poor.* New York, 1919.

Solomon, Barbara M. *Ancestors and Immigrants.* Cambridge, Mass., 1956.

Sprague, William B. *Annals of the American Pulpit.* New York, 1857, volume 2.

Stearns, Frank P. *Cambridge Sketches.* Freeport, N.Y., 1968.

Stechow, Wolfgang. "Justice Holmes's Notes on Albert Durer." 8 *Journal of Aesthetics and Arts Criticism* 119 (1949).

Steel, Ronald. *Walter Lippmann and the American Century.* Boston, 1980.

"Sterilization of the Mentally Defective in State Institutions." 28 *YLJ* 189 (1918).

Stevens, George T. *Three Years in the Sixth Corps.* Albany, 1866.

Story, Ronald. "Class and Culture in Boston: The Athenaeum: 1807–1860." 27 *American Quarterly* 178 (1975).

————. *The Forging of an Aristocracy.* Middletown, Conn., 1980.

Sullivan, Mark. *Our Times.* New York, 1926–35, volumes as cited.

Sutherland, Arthur E. *The Law at Harvard.* Cambridge, Mass., 1967.

[————]. "Sutherland's Recollections of Justice Holmes." Edited by David M. O'Brien. *1988 Supreme Court Historical Society Yearbook,* 18.

Swindler, William F. *Court and Constitution in the 20th Century: i, The Old Legality, 1889–1932.* Indianapolis, 1969.

Thayer, William R. *Theodore Roosevelt: An Intimate Biography.* Boston and New York, 1919.

Tilton, Eleanor M. *Amiable Autocrat: A Biography of Dr. Oliver Wendell Holmes.* New York, 1947.

Tittle, Walter. "Glimpses of Interesting Americans II: Oliver Wendell Holmes." 110 *Century Magazine* 181 (1925).

Touster, Saul. "Holmes a Hundred Years Ago: The Common Law and Legal Theory." 10 *Hofstra LR* 673 (1982).

————. "Holmes: The Years of *The Common Law.*" 64 *Columbia LR* 230 (1964).

————. "In Search of Holmes from Within." 18 *Vanderbilt LR* 437 (1965).

Tufts, James H. "The Legal and Social Philosophy of Mr. Justice Holmes." 7 *ABAJ* 359 (1921).

Tushnet, Marc. "The Logic of Experience: Oliver Wendell Holmes on the Supreme Judicial Court." 63 *Virginia LR* 975 (1977).

Umbreit, Kenneth B. *Our Eleven Chief Justices.* New York, 1938.

Urofsky, Melvin I., and David L. Levy. *Letters of Louis D. Brandeis.* Albany, 1971–78, volumes 1–5.

Vetter, Jan. "The Evolution of Holmes, Holmes and Evolution." In *Holmes and The Common Law: A Century Later* (see above), 75.

Voorhees, Oscar M. *The History of Phi Beta Kappa.* New York, 1945.

Vose, Clement E. "State Against Nation: The Conservation Case of Missouri v. Holland." 16 *Prologue* 233 (1984).

Wadell, Helen. *Medieval Latin Lyrics.* New York, 1949.

Wagner, Charles A. *Harvard: Four Centuries and Freedoms*. New York, 1950.

Waite, Edward F. "How 'Eccentric' Was Mr. Justice Harlan?" 37 *Minnesota LR* 173 (1953).

Wales, Robert W. "Some Aspects of Life with Mr. Justice Holmes in His 90th Year." 28 *University of Florida LR* 395 (1976).

Warbasse, Elizabeth B. *The Changing Legal Rights of Married Women: 1860–61*. New York, 1987.

Warner, Frances Lester. "Transferred to Washington." 62–64 *House Beautiful*, pages as cited (9/27–7/28).

Warren, Charles. *History of the Harvard Law School and of Early Legal Conditions in America*. New York, 1908, volumes 1–3.

———. "The Progressiveness of the United States Supreme Court." 13 *Columbia LR* 294 (1913).

———. *The Supreme Court in United States History*. Boston, 1926, volumes 1, 2.

Warren, Robert Penn. *The Legacy of the Civil War*. New York, 1961.

Welch, Richard E., Jr. *George Frisbie Hoar and the Half-Breed Republicans*. Cambridge, Mass., 1971.

———. "Opponents and Colleagues: George Frisbie Hoar and Henry Cabot Lodge, 1898–1904." 39 *NEQ* 182 (1966).

Weld, Stephen Minot. *War Diary and Letters of Stephen Minot Weld, 1861–1865*. Privately printed, 1912.

Westin, Alan F. "The First Justice Harlan: A Self-Portrait from His Private Papers." 46 *Kentucky LJ* 321 (1958).

Whately, Richard. *Introductory Lessons on Morals and Christian Evidences*. Cambridge, Mass., 1857.

White, G. Edward. *The American Judicial Tradition*. New York, 1976.

———. "The Integrity of Holmes's Jurisprudence." 10 *Hofstra LR* 633 (1982).

———. "Looking at Holmes in the Mirror." 4 *Law and History Review* 439 (1986).

———. "The Rise and Fall of Justice Holmes." 39 *University of Chicago LR* 51 (1971).

White, Morton. *Social Thought in America: The Revolt Against Formalism*. Boston, 1963.

White, William Allen. "What About Our Courts?" 69 *American Magazine* 499 (1910).

Wiener, Philip. *Evolution and the Founders of Pragmatism*. Cambridge, Mass., 1949.

Wigdor, David. *Roscoe Pound: Philosopher of Law*. Westport, Conn., 1974.

Wigmore, John H. "Justice Holmes and the Law of Torts." 29 *HLR* 601 (1916).

Williams, Alexander. *A Social History of the Greater Boston Clubs*. Barre, Vt., 1970.

Wilson, Carroll A. *Thirteen Author Collections of the Nineteenth Century and*

Five Centuries of Familiar Quotations. Edited by Jean C. S. Wilson and David A. Randall. Privately printed for Scribner's, 1950, volume 2 .

Wilson, Edmund. "Justice Holmes and Harold Laski: Their Relationship." 27 *New Yorker* 132 (5/16/53).

———. *Patriotic Gore.* New York, 1962.

[Wilson, Thomas L.]. *One Who Knows Them: The Aristocracy of Boston; Who They Are, and What They Were.* Boston, 1848.

Wilson, Woodrow. "The Lawyer and the Community." 192 *NAR* 604 (1910).

Winkelman, Barnie F. *John G. Johnson.* Philadelphia, 1942.

Winsor, Justin. *The Memorial History of Boston.* Boston, 1881, volumes 1–4.

Wister, Owen. *Roosevelt: The Story of a Friendship, 1880–1919.* New York, 1930.

Woollcott, Alexander. "Get Down, You Fool." 161 *AM* 169 (2/38).

———. *Long, Long Ago.* New York, 1943.

———. "The Second Hunt After the Captain." 170 *AM* 48 (1942).

Wu, John C. H. *Beyond East and West.* London, 1952.

———. "The Mind of Justice Holmes." *China LR,* 8/35, 136. OWH papers, HLSL.

Wyzanski, Charles E., Jr. "Brandeis." 198 *AM* 66 (1956).

———. "In Defense of Oliver Wendell Holmes." *Harvard Law Record,* 9/17/82, 4.

Yntema, Hessel E. "Mr. Justice Holmes's View of Legal Science." 40 *YLJ* 696 (1931).

Zobel, Hiller B. "Enlisted for Life." 37 *American Heritage* 56 (1986).

SOURCE NOTES

Part I: SAINT

Chapter 1: "The Magnificent Yankee"

Page
3   The canonization . . . "in Washington": Hill, "OWH," 265. BP, 3/9/31,
           1; NYT, 3/9/31, 1.
           Chief Justice . . . "our hearts": CEH, CBS; CEH papers, LC.
4   "Not now" . . . together: NYT, 3/9/31, 1.
           asthma: WHT to Horace D. Taft, 4/17/22; WHT papers, LC.
           lumbago: OWH to NG, 12/27/30; OWH papers, HLSL.
           The years . . . wit quick: Duffus, "At Ninety," 3. WP, 3/3/35, 1. Suth-
           erland, "Recollections," 1 ff.
           missed . . . justices: NYT, 1/23/31, 27.
           most exhausting: OWH to E. A. Curtis, 4/12/41; OWH papers, HLSL.
           he wondered . . . resign: OWH to FF, 1/27/31; OWH papers, HLSL.
           "the greatest . . . judge": NYT, 3/9/31, 1, 18.
5   Lincoln's Inn . . . membership: NYT, 3/5/31, 14.
           The Tavern . . . resolutions: OWH to CM, 4/5/31; OWH papers, HLSL.
           The March . . . honored him: 44 HLR 677; 40 YLJ 685; 31 Columbia LR
           349.
           Robert Marshall . . . after Holmes: Biddle, Mr., 191.
           "for . . . vanishing.": Jacob Billikopf to FF, 2/8/39; OWH papers, HLSL.
           "the presence . . . that day": Robert W. Wales to R. W. Hale, 1/2/31;
           OWH papers, HLSL.
           "reverence" . . . commissioned: unsigned note in MDH's hand to OWH,
           3/8/31; OWH to CM, 4/5/31; OWH papers, HLSL.
           "plunge . . . coming" ' ": OWH to E. A. Curtis, 1/13/31; OWH papers,
           HLSL.
           He sat . . . study: WP, 3/9/31, 1.
           cold: OWH to E. A. Curtis, 1/23/31; OWH papers, HLSL.

cleared . . . accent: tape of CBS broadcast; LC.
5–6   In this . . . " 'coming' ": ibid.
6   As Holmes . . . would: interview with H. Chapman Rose.
the line . . . Virgil: Waddell, *Medieval*, 2–3.
When . . . fire: HJL, "Ever Sincerely," 56.
6   comfortable . . . ceiling: appraisal of 1720 I Street, 4/35; OWH papers, HLSL. Derby, "Recollections," 346. Bowen, Catherine Drinker, memorandum, undated; Bowen papers, LC.
fourteen thousand . . . knowledge: Estate . . . 1720 I Street . . . ; LCRB.
Beginning . . . diaries: OWH, diaries for 1866, 1867; OWH papers, HLSL.
1876 . . . philosophy: OWH, BB, 23 ff.
6–7   Holmes's young . . . "nose at him": HJL, "Ever Sincerely," 56.
7   *"After . . . School": FF, memorandum, 9/28/31; FF papers, LC.
distaste for law: OWH, Sr., *Works*, viii, 324; iii, 124.
he . . . School: Tilton, *Amiable*, 60.
despite . . . spinning: Martin, *Harold*, 13.
The younger . . . War: Fiechter, "Preparation," 5. MDH, *Shaping*, 76.
"clarity . . . outlook": *NYT*, 3/9/30, 28.
"swamped . . . personally": Alger Hiss to FF, 3/20/30; FF papers, LC.
A few . . . Marshall: "A Portrait," 741.
8   "My . . . Washington": ibid., 748.
Now . . . 1929: *NYT*, 9/30/31, 20; 10/29/40, 21.
"Oh . . . again!": *WP*, 3/6/35, 1.
"I really . . . civilization": Hale, Richard W., *Some*, 17.
trips . . . burlesque house: *WP*, 3/6/35, 1.
asked your . . . Holmes: Pollard, "Justice," 22.
P-TA: pamphlet found among Holmes's books; LCRB.
"tried . . . plan": OWH to HJL, 12/3/24; OWH papers, HLSL.
"touched . . . fire": Sergeant, "Oliver," 59.
8–9   The first . . . *Olympus*: see Bibliography.
9   "regard . . . detachment": OWH to Franklin Ford, 2/8/08; OWH papers, HLSL.
9–10   Over . . . peak: Gilmore, *Ages*, 48–51.
10   academic . . . speech: Lucey, "Holmes," 254.
detractors: see Burton, "Justice"; Gregg, "The Pragmatism"; Lucey, "Holmes," "Jurisprudence," "Natural Law"; White, G. Edward, "Integrity," "Looking," "The Rise"; Palmer, "Defense," "Hobbes," "Reply."
World: Ford, "The Totalitarian," 114 ff.
"cynical . . . cult": Rodell, "Justice," 260.
"for . . . mind": Luce, "Reverse," 596.
10–11   Holmes . . . weak: Gilmore, *Ages*, 48–49.
11   heap scorn . . . dollar: Corcoran, Rendezvous, 16–17.
turn around . . . champagne: OWH to LE, 1/15/15; OWH papers, HLSL.
weep . . . crusts: John S. Flannery to MDH, 5/13/42; OWH papers, HLSL.
"passion for equality": OWH to HJL, 5/12/27; OWH papers, HLSL.
12   "how many . . . looks": OWH to ES, 9/24/10; OWH papers, HLSL.
"poetry": OWH to FP, 5/24/29; OWH papers, HLSL.
visited . . . fingers: interview with H. Chapman Rose.
"Beloved Hibernia": OWH to CC, 6/7/1898; OWH papers, HLSL.

grave . . . Ireland: *Cork Examiner,* 3/15/28, unpaged clipping, OWH papers, HLSL.
13   Lindbergh . . . Washington: *NYT,* 3/24/28, 7.
    "in the atmosphere . . . Massacre": Adams, Henry, *Education,* 43.
15   "Nature . . . genius": OWH to Alice S. Green, 11/9/13; FF papers, LC.
    Beverly . . . shirt: OWH to Eleanor N. Little, 2/4/29; OWH papers, HLSL.
16   "breathe . . . virtues": OWH to FF, 12/31/15; OWH papers, HLSL.
    "wouldn't play . . . mind": 11 *DAB* 417.
    wrote . . . point: Acheson, *Morning,* 58.
17   Every person's . . . already: OWH, Sr., *Works,* i., 128–30.
    listed . . . "strangers": OWH to NG, 6/22/18; OWH papers, HLSL.
    "queerly . . . envelope": OWH to Georgina Pollock, 7/2/1895; OWH papers, HLSL.
    "best . . . documents": OWH to LE, 9/30/32; OWH papers, HLSL.
18   "I forget . . . slippers": OWH to FF, 11/26/21; OWH papers, HLSL.
    wrote similarly: OWH to HJL, 12/22/21; OWH papers, HLSL.
    "solemn . . . hope to have": HJL to OWH, 12/31/21; OWH papers, HLSL.

Part II: BRAHMIN

Chapter 2: Family

21   "There is . . . clownish": OWH, Sr., *Works,* v, 3.
    "harmless" . . . learning: ibid., i, 20–22.
    "hub . . . system": ibid., i, 125.
    "the Common . . . yardstick": MADH, *Holmes,* 4.
21–22   New York . . . Pennsylvania: Shyrock, "Philadelphia," 305 ff.
22   "more . . . equality": Green, *Problem,* 59.
    Dr. Holmes . . . Hooper: OWH, Sr., Letterbook; OWH, Sr., papers, HUh.
    Holmes . . . Cabot: see OWH, *Touched.*
    "His mother . . . average": OWH to Herbert Hoover, 12/23/31; OWH papers, HLSL.
23   "interlocking directorates": Story, *Forging,* 4.
    The same . . . affairs: ibid., 10–19.
    "the way . . . revolt": OWH to HJL, 7/10/24; OWH papers, HLSL.
    "the people . . . classes": Norton, *Considerations,* 158.
24   Olivers . . . 1632: 19 *NEH&GR,* 100.
    Young . . . Boston: 36 *NEH&GR,* 242.
    Dr. Holmes . . . "acquaintance": JTM, *Life,* i, 12–13.
24–25   Evert's . . . aristocracy: ibid., 14.
25   "feel . . . shirtsleeves": ibid., ii, 199.
    The Holmeses . . . Massachusetts: Bowen, Clarence W., *History,* vi, 83 ff.
    "Scotch Prisoners," 29.
    At nearby . . . Connecticut: Bowen, Clarence W., *History,* i, 14.
    "probably . . . crown": JTM, *Life,* i, 4–5.
25–26   "Boundary . . . committee": Bowen, Clarence W., *History,* i, 3.
26   Old John . . . Philip's War: ibid., vi, 83.

grandson . . . Army: Bowen, Catherine Drinker, *Yankee,* 5.

Fifty years . . . ended: Bowen, Clarence W., *History,* vi, 89.

great-grandson . . . Wars: OWH to LE, 12/26/21; OWH papers, HLSL.

Abiel . . . First Church: 5 *DAB* 160 ff. JTM, *Life,* i, 6 ff.

155-year-old . . . 1792: *Sketches,* 232–33. *Controversy,* 4.

27 Now, mama . . . can now: Higginson, *Old,* 8, 11–18.

She never . . . behind: JTM, *Life,* i, 15. OWH, Sr., *Works,* viii, 6.

sit for . . . cap: MADH, *Holmes,* 9.

She brought . . . Calvinist homes: Tilton, *Amiable,* 12–15. Brooks, *Flowering,* 27.

Abiel's calm . . . gentle: Duyckinck, *Cyclopedia,* i, 530. JTM, *Life,* i, 15. Sprague, *Annals,* ii, 246.

"possessed . . . affections": Sprague, *Annals,* ii, 244–45.

joined . . . Society: 1 MHS *Proceedings* 117.

28 "a labor . . . pleasure": Duyckinck, *Cyclopedia,* i, 530.

Abiel . . . historiography: Brooks, *Flowering,* 27, 131. Calcott, *History,* 199.

liberals . . . to one: Tilton, *Amiable,* 144.

28–29 no Jonathan . . . revivals: Sprague, *Annals,* ii, 245.

29 For some . . . stripe: *Controversy,* 41.

Official . . . clergymen: *Christian Register,* 8/30/1828, 138.

Gradually . . . pleased: *Controversy,* vi.

July 20 . . . "constitute them": ibid., 1.

"difficulties . . . to alter": ibid., 4.

29–30 escalated . . . "unto you": Tilton, *Amiable,* 45–46. *Sketches,* 252–59.

30 "paralytic affliction": Wilson, Carroll A., *Thirteen,* ii, 507.

Darwin . . . dominance: JTM, *Life,* i, 20.

"I am just . . . dinner": ibid., 168.

"man can see . . . world": OWH, Sr., *Works,* ii, 217.

five feet . . . tall: JTM, *Life,* i, 54.

stood . . . read it: Higginson, *Old,* 83.

31 inherited . . . "spoon": *BET,* 10/8/1894, 3.

"did more . . . Hottentot": OWH, Sr., *Works,* iii, 17.

paid ten . . . "changed": JTM, *Life,* i, 45.

"set of . . . not help": ibid., 38.

31–32 gambrel-roofed . . . billeted: Tilton, *Amiable,* 4–5. Drake, *Historic,* 257–62. OWH, Sr., *Works,* iii, 23–25. Brooks, *Flowering,* 353.

32 Girlish . . . wrist: OWH, Sr., *Works,* xiii, 47.

"The holes . . . 1776": Wilson, Carroll A., *Thirteen,* ii, 608.

Abiel's . . . periodicals: JTM, *Life,* i, 41–42.

"what tasted . . . 'happy' ": Tilton, *Amiable,* 6–7.

"I was born . . . horses": OWH, Sr., *Works,* i, 131.

32–33 formal education . . . gathering: Tilton, *Amiable,* 16–80. Morse, *Life,* i, 53–75.

33 "tempted . . . or later": OWH, Sr., *Works,* ix, 423–24.

"it will have . . . meridian": JTM, *Life,* i, 55.

Holmes, of . . . applause: Wilson, Carroll A., *Thirteen,* ii, 454–55.

Tentatively . . . *Galaxy:* Tilton, *Amiable,* 61–63. JTM, *Life,* i, 68.

"I know . . . threshold": OWH, Sr., to Phineas Barnes, 1/13/1831; OWH, Sr., papers, HUh.

33–34   In the summer . . . famous work: JTM, *Life,* i, 79–81. Hale, Edward
         Everett, "Memories," 310.
         Ay . . . high: OWH, Sr., *Works,* xii, 2.
         Next day . . . poet: Tilton, *Amiable,* 65.
34   "I know . . . the other": JTM, *Life,* i, 70.
         Holmes prepared . . . Louis: Tilton, *Amiable,* 69 ff. Morse, *Life,* i, 82–83.
         Holmes finished . . . years: Tilton, *Amiable,* 134, 142.
         Dr. Walter Channing . . . "for boys": Higginson, *Old,* 84.
35   The white . . . faint: OWH, Sr., *Works,* ix, 424. Morse, *Life,* i, 81.
         students remembered . . . squeak: Cheever, "Dr.," 155–57.
         From Paris . . . steadily: Tilton, *Amiable,* 137, 140–142, 152, 165.
36   "not to . . . sick": OWH, Sr., to parents, 8/13/1833, Letterbook; OWH,
         Sr., papers, HUh.
         Holmes concluded . . . physicians: OWH, Sr., *Works,* ix, 112.
         published first . . . member: ibid., xvi–xvii.
         The *American* . . . excerpts: 6 (n.s.) *American Journal of Medical Science*
         260–62 (7/1843).
37   "the jejune" . . . clear idea: Meigs, *On the Nature,* 113.
         Hugh . . . said: Tilton, *Amiable,* 174–75.
         I am too much . . . forgive him: OWH, Sr., *Works,* ix, 127–28.
37–38   Gradually . . . criticized: Tilton, *Amiable,* 176.
38   "Of course . . . their eyes": OWH, Sr., *Works,* ix, xvii.
         "I think . . . labor": JTM, *Life,* i, 225–26.
         He was not . . . " 'worms' ": Howells, *Literary,* 171.
39   "contented . . . petticoat": JTM, *Life,* i, 65.
         "complement . . . tired of": OWH, Sr., *Works,* ii, 170.
         descendant . . . Wendell: Putnam, *Memoir,* 25.
         Jacksons . . . 1643: ibid., 3.
         thirty-eight . . . Revolution: ibid., 14.
         old Jonathan . . . sea: Porter, *Jacksons,* 318–22.
         Patrick . . . system: Jaher, *Age,* 192.
         Amelia . . . moved in: Putnam, *Memoir,* 115–16.
         Amelia's father . . . law: Story, *Forging,* 47.
         "Of all . . . Blackstone": "Honorable," 607.
39–40   Much later . . . actions: MDH, *Shaping,* 179.
40   widely . . . antiquities: LCRB.
         successful . . . effort: *Aristocracy,* 22.
         Our First . . . $200,000: *Our First,* 28. [Wilson], *One Who,* 22. Forbes,
         Rich, 37.
         who left . . . Court: "Honorable," 608.
         "profound . . . purpose": BDA, 12/14/1855, 2.
         1820 . . . public law: Putnam, *Memoir,* 106–09.
         Charles . . . Corporation: ibid., 112.
         prime mover . . . trade: ibid., 118.
         kindly . . . gum balls: ibid., 116.
         serious . . . "Wit" (0): ibid., 125.
40–41   known Frances . . . "Mr. Jackson!": ibid., 104–05.
41   "I almost . . . exerting myself": Lee, *Letters,* 269–70.

fewer . . . study: Degler, *At Odds,* 152.
41–42   "more . . . world": Tilton, *Amiable,* 161.
42   Justice . . . from her: interview with Alger Hiss.
French . . . dictionaries: LCRB.
"quiet . . . beloved": EJH, Jr., to HFS, n.d., 1944; OWH papers, HLSL.
"absorbed . . . impossible": Fields, Annie, *Authors,* 109.
"her delicate . . . child": JTM, *Memoir,* 390.
an ideal . . . doctor: JTM, *Life,* i, 170–71.
43   To you . . . remembrance: OWH, Sr., *Works,* iii, 349.

Part III: YOUTH

Chapter 3: Beginnings

47   My dear . . . forefinger: OWH, Sir., to Ann Holmes Upham, 3/9/1841;
OWH, Sr., papers, HUh.
A few . . . Jr.: MDH, *Shaping,* 1.
48   *Boston . . . park: *NYT,* 11/14/89, 18.
unself-conscious . . . "view": OWH, Sr., *Works,* v, 128.
big house . . . dowry: ALH, marriage settlement; OWH, Sr., papers, HUh.
When in 1843 . . . Physiology: OWH, Sr., to Boston Athenaeum, 2/21/
1843; Athenaeum archives.
The deal . . . members: Trevor Johnson to Liva Baker, 10/1/87.
"gentlemen's libraries": Story, *Forging,* 124.
Henry . . . camaraderie: Adams, Henry, *Education,* 3–39.
49   "almost genius": OWH to E.A. Curtis, 12/24/20: OWH papers, HLSL.
snowball . . . outmaneuvered: HCL, *Early,* 18–20; Adams, Henry, *Education,* 41 ff.
"tiddledies" . . . paused: OWH to HJL, 12/24/27; OWH papers, HLSL.
"devils . . . doors": OWH, speech, 11/4/02; OWH papers, HLSL.
daughter . . . at her: Jenny R. Holmes to OWH, 3/7/31; OWH papers,
HLSL.
fished . . . Street: MDH, diary, 2/22/34; MDH papers, HLSL.
spent . . . microscope: OWH to LE, 12/8/27; OWH papers, HLSL.
"shrink" . . . ride: OWH to NG, 8/20/1891; OWH papers, HLSL.
49–50   *The Child's* . . . reading habits: LCRB.
50   melodramas . . . thrilled: MDH, *Shaping,* 11.
"periodic . . . commerce": OWH to CM, 8/28/11; OWH papers, HLSL.
"all the evil . . . boy": OWH to JTM, 3/9/21; OWH papers, HLSL.
son . . . side: 11 *DAB,* supplement 2, 475.
office . . . Hamilton Place: *Boston City Directory,* 1849–50, reel 158:2, 212.
Known as . . . "Leany": JTM to Thomas Sergeant Perry, 9/13/18; Morse
papers, MHS.
"afraid . . . door": OWH to JTM, 11/24/22; OWH papers, HLSL.
Roving . . . Cousin Fatty: Fiechter, "Preparation," 7–8.
swindling . . . wanted: OWH to JTM, 11/24/22; OWH papers, HLSL.

"Suppose . . . a lie?": Fiechter, "Preparation," 7–8.

51   decent student . . . "talks too much": Report of Recitations and Deportment During the Week Ending 14 June 1847; OWH papers, HLSL.

"Wendell . . . to say": EJH, Jr., to HFS, n.d., 1944; OWH papers, HLSL.

51–52   sad-faced . . . his school: HCL, *Early*, 64 ff.

52   He himself . . . little school: MDH, *Shaping*, 3.

School Plan . . . creative writing: OWH, Copybook, unpaged; OWH papers, HLSL.

Natural . . . described: LCRB.

53   O.W. Holmes, Jr . . . his age: T.R. Sullivan to E.S. Dixwell, 9/29/1851; OWH papers, HLSL.

Mr. Dixwell had . . . suburban areas: Dixwell, *Autobiographical*, 29–40.

"must . . . bounds": *The Commonweal*, 7/18/1851.

Mr. Dixwell . . . admissions: Dixwell, *Autobiographical*, 51–53.

Dicky . . . law and order: Eliot, *Late*, 18–19. HCL, *Early*, 84 ff.

53–54   he had little . . . "breadth & depth": Dixwell, *Autobiographical*, 43.

54   It included : . . "needless": Dixwell, *Autobiographical*, 53. HCL, *Early*, 83.

reputation . . . college: MDH, *Shaping*, 6–7.

Cousin Johnny . . . Dixwell's: JTM to William Gannett, 11/6/21; JTM papers, MHS.

"a delightful . . . Greek": Eliot, *Late*, 18.

Adams . . . knowledge: Adams, Henry, *Education*, 54.

"walk . . . topics": E. S. Dixwell to OWH, 12/10/1882; OWH papers, HLSL.

Wendell developed . . . "second mother": OWH to Mary I. Dixwell, 7/22/1861, with notation by Mary Dixwell Wigglesworth; Wigglesworth papers, MHS.

Canoe Meadow . . . deed: Kennedy, *Oliver*, 123.

Hawthorne . . . *Book:* Stone, Geoffrey. *Melville.* New York, 1976, 137–38.

"gruff . . . man": OWH to NG, 3/23/21; OWH papers, HLSL.

54–55   Arrowhead . . . *Dick:* visit to Melville's home, June 1985.

55   Feminist . . . Stockbridge: Bell, Millicent. *Edith Wharton and Henry James.* New York, 1965, 81.

Longfellows . . . Holmeses: Longfellow, Fanny. *Mrs. Longfellow, Selected Letters and Journals.* Edited by Edward Wagenknecht. New York, 1956, 54.

Emerson . . . frequently: Kennedy, *Oliver*, 123.

they all . . . thesis: Arvin, Newton. *Herman Melville.* London, 1950, 135–36.

"baronial" . . . 1835: Smith, J. E. A. *History*, 583.

deed . . . house: JTM, *Life*, i, 197.

hunt arrowheads: OWH, Sr., *Works*, ii, 245.

Oliver . . . Parish Church: *Proceedings in Commemoration of the Organization of the First Church of Christ, February 7, 1889.* Pittsfield, Mass., 1889, 35–36.

"Don't you . . . it is so": "Letters of Dr. Holmes," 947.

Beginning . . . tend; JTM, *Life*, i, 197, 200–02.

Standing five . . . Dr. Holmes: "Letters of Dr. Holmes," 947.

55–56   In a picture . . . emerged: MDH, *Shaping,* 66.
56   read . . . pickerel: OWH to Sarah W. Holmes, n.d.; OWH to unnamed correspondent, 7/11/n.d.; OWH papers, HLSL.
    imaginative . . . west: JTM, *Life,* i, 197.
    "Then . . . sold it": Capen, "Country," 309.
    Mrs. Holmes . . . available to her: will of Charles Jackson, codicil of 3/15/1855; Suffolk County Probate Court.
    sold . . . August 1856: Berkshire Middle District Registry, Deeds book 170, 430; book 177, 67.
    "couldn't . . . time": Capen, "Country," 309.
    "very . . . Hebrew": JTM, *Life,* i, 198.
57   Harvard . . . 1805: MADH, *Boston,* 196.
    divinity . . . cathedral: Story, *Forging,* 79–80.
    By 1850 . . . déclassé: ibid., 7–8.
    "Oh—the *ennui* . . . from it": OWH to HJL, 5/8/18; OWH papers, HLSL.
    Although progressive . . . conservatives: JTM, *Life,* i, 303–04.
    "dingy-linened . . . progress": Stearns, *Cambridge,* 153.
    Industrial . . . system: MADH, *Boston,* 257–60.
    "gentlemen" . . . protection: O'Connor, *Bibles,* 96.
    Two years . . . meetings: Foote, *King's,* ii, 473–74.
    Intellectual . . . cousin: Adams, Henry, *Education,* 42, 48. Tilton, *Amiable,* 192. MADH, *Holmes,* 43–44.
    "pestilent abolitionist": 52 MHS *Proceedings,* 153.
58   Dr. Holmes . . . with the South: Tilton, *Amiable,* 224.
    placards . . . in wait: O'Connor, *Bibles,* 102.
    mob . . . Savannah: MADH, *Boston,* 174–80.
    Anthony Burns . . . hisses: ibid., 277–80.
    Dr. Holmes . . . lynched: Tilton, *Amiable,* 224 ff.
58–59   argument . . . Stowe: files of the Boston Athenaeum library, 1856.
59   extremists . . . slave states: Novick, *Honorable,* 20. Morison, *Oxford,* 602.
    In 1863 . . . Proclamation: Pearson, Henry G. "The Emancipation Concert in Music Hall on January First, 1863." 20 (2nd series) MHS *Proceedings,* 247.
    The struggle . . . remedy: OWH, Sr., *Works,* viii, 83.
    In 1883 . . . "friends": OWH, Sr., to American Anti-Slavery Society, 11/30/1883; American Anti-Slavery Society. *Commemoration of the 50th Anniversary of the American Anti-Slavery Society.* Philadelphia, 1884, 61.
60   Henry . . . "shoulders": James, Alice, *Diary,* 12/14/1889.
    civilized . . . "knowest": OWH, Sr., *Works,* viii, 312.
    "made . . . conceited": OWH to FF, 5/21/26; OWH papers, HLSL.
    "lonely": OWH to Sarah W. Holmes, 9/16/n.d.; OWH papers, HLSL.
    "no love . . . *fils*": MDH, *Shaping,* 18.
    "didn't care . . . name": OWH to JTM, 2/8/07; OWH papers, HLSL.
    Ned's son . . . exciting: EJH, Jr., to HFS, n.d., 1944; OWH papers, HLSL.
61   "iron" . . . Sabbath eve: JTM, *Life,* ii, 245 ff.
    One of . . . "lived": OWH to HJL, 11/29/23; OWH papers, HLSL.
62   autobiography . . . pride: Fiechter, "Preparation," 4.
    While . . . foretell: OWH, Copybook, unpaged; OWH papers, HLSL.
    "my guv'nor": [Sutherland], "Sutherland's," 23.

"the damned fool": Corcoran, Rendezvous, 32.

"Are you . . . vanished": OWH to HJL, 3/27/23; OWH papers, HLSL.

pleasure . . . America: OWH to LE, 4/28/23; OWH papers, HLSL.

62–63   "fertile . . . the clever": OWH to unnamed correspondent, 7/26/14; OWH papers, HLSL.

63   "little" . . . bound: OWH to ES, 8/22/08; OWH papers, HLSL.

he presented . . . Washington: NYT, 9/13/32, 19.

a thousand . . . place: Pittsfield Evening Journal, 1/19/1895.

"would take . . . alive"; OWH to ES, 8/22/08; OWH papers, HLSL.

The justice . . . administration: copy, FF papers, LC.

64   I look . . . cheek: JTM, Life, ii, 314.

"too sacred": Edel, Henry, i, 48.

kiss . . . morning: ALH to OWH, 6/11/1866; OWH papers, HLSL.

"God . . . mouth": OWH to ALH, 9/6/1861; OWH papers, HLSL.

help him . . . destroyed: MDH, Touched, viii–xi.

"what does . . . very much": ALH to OWH, 7/2/1866; OWH papers, HLSL.

She listened . . . lessons: OWH to unnamed correspondent, 7/11/n.d.; OWH papers, HLSL.

helped . . . examinations: OWH, diary, 2/1, 2/4, 2/11/1867; OWH papers, HLSL.

took . . . Pittsfield: OWH to Sarah W. Holmes, 9/16/n.d.; OWH papers, HLSL.

65   She owned . . . Fénelon: LCRB.

In the society . . . bodies: Persons, Decline, 85 ff.

reputation . . . Brooks: Bowen, Catherine Drinker, Yankee, 425.

letters . . . teasing: AJH to OWH, 7/16/1866, 5/7/1866; OWH papers, HLSL.

"Buster . . . in voice": Tilton, Amiable, 223.

"Favorite": AJH to OWH, 5/8/1866; OWH papers, HLSL.

"children": OWH to Sarah W. Holmes, 9/16/n.d.; OWH papers, HLSL.

Fanny . . . afar: EJH, Jr., to FDH, 1881–82; OWH papers, HLSL.

66   "as happy . . . with": ALH to OWH, 7/2/1866; OWH papers, HLSL.

Uncle John . . . ninety-three: BET, 1/17/1899, 5.

Appian Way . . . mon frère: MADH, Holmes, 11.

whimsical . . . Grandmother Holmes: Bowen, Catherine Drinker, Yankee, 111–12.

taught . . . swearing: CEH, Autobiographical, 227; CEH papers, LC.

His entertaining . . . Mass: Holmes, John, Letters, 46–59.

"with . . . eagerness": Tittle, "Glimpses," 285.

"whatever . . . hate": OWH to FF, 2/17/20; OWH papers, HLSL.

67   "scientific . . . antecedents": OWH to Morris R. Cohen, 2/5/19; OWH papers, HLSL.

68   When by 1857 . . . breakfast: Morse, Life, i, 195–96.

As a boy of eleven . . . Louisville: Tilton, Amiable, 212 ff. LCRB.

in 1847 . . . the country: Tilton, Amiable, 189–91.

69   As a boy of seven . . . "than gold": OWH, Copybook, unpaged; OWH papers, HLSL.

Beginning . . . "renaissance": Brooks, Flowering, 539.

Money . . . institutions: ibid., 539.

Local . . . satellites: ibid., 122.
70   Fields . . . Street: Fields, *Authors,* 113.
At the monthly . . . mattered: Persons, *Decline,* 106. MADH, *Holmes,* 92–96.
"a weary . . . 'event' ": OWH, speech, 11/14/02; OWH papers, HLSL.
"melancholy . . . yearnings": OWH to ES, 5/21/23; OWH papers, HLSL.

Chapter 4: Harvard College

72   Mr. Danforth's boardinghouse: OWH, speech, 9/27/12; OWH papers, HLSL.
*What is . . . purpose: Morison, *Three,* 7.
Wendell . . . appearance: MDH, *Shaping,* 66.
"sadden[ing] . . . life": OWH, Introduction to Montesquieu's *Spirit,* iv.
besides . . . Cambridge: HU, *Quinquennial,* 952.
The Lowells . . . half: Greenslet, *Lowells,* 7, 76.
Jacob . . . 1733: HU, *Quinquennial,* 154.
Oliver . . . 1753: ibid., 160.
Edward . . . benefactors: Putnam, *Memoir,* 11.
72–73   Great-grandfather . . . Overseer: HU, *Quinquennial,* 10, 14.
73   Cambridge . . . streets: OWH, Sr., *Works,* iii, 22–26.
Harvard . . . settled there: Higginson, *Old,* 14–15.
boys amused . . . cemetery: ibid., 7–8.
The object . . . oppose them: Brooks, *Flowering,* 34–35.
73–74   John Harvard . . . baptized: Morison, *Three,* 9 ff.
74   to explain . . . disturbing questions: Eliot, *Harvard,* 4.
the members . . . medical Boston: Story, *Forging,* 160 ff.
Eliot . . . career: *Benjamin,* 2.
Henry . . . Comte: Adams, Henry, *Education,* 60.
The curriculum . . . decades before: Morison, *Three,* 201, 235.
Based . . . culture: Story, *Forging,* 59.
74–75   course of study . . . religious instruction: HU, *Catalogue,* 1857–58, 28.
75   A former . . . every day: 20 *Dictionary of National Biography,* 1334 ff.
75–76   in the fall . . . "Brethren": Fiechter, "Preparation," 4.
76   Theological . . . universe: [OWH], "Books," 43–44. OWH to Alice S. Green, 12/27/13; FF papers, LC.
"bettabilitarian[ism]": HJL, "Mr. Justice," 418.
"largely personal": OWH to LE, 12/13/29; OWH papers, HLSL.
"I can't . . . thinking": OWH to Alice S. Green, 8/20/09; FF papers, LC.
He also felt . . . supremacy: OWH to John Chipman Gray, 9/3/05; OWH to LE, 5/21/09; OWH papers, HLSL.
No reason . . . kerosened: OWH to HJL, 7/2/21; OWH papers, HLSL.
"humility . . . truth": OWH to ES, 11/28/08; OWH papers, HLSL.
I think . . . is any: OWH to Albert J. Beveridge, 7/8/16; OWH papers, HLSL.
77   "filial . . . Descartes": OWH, speech, 2/12/1886; OWH papers, HLSL.
On the . . . science: Meyer, Agnes, diary, 12/4/19; Meyer papers, LC.
In Boston . . . can be: Corcoran, *Rendezvous,* 10.
Grammar . . . not take it: HUA, Monthly Returns . . . 1857–58, unpaged.

physics . . . anatomy: HU, *Catalogue*, 1860–61, 30–33.

Consistent . . . science: Barbour, *Naturalist*, 150.

Holmes . . . Greek: HUA, Monthly Returns . . . 1860–61, unpaged.

That so . . . undergraduate years: Samuels, *Young*, 12.

grading system . . . behavior: Morison, *Three*, 260.

77–78   a student . . . graduation: HUA, Orders and Regulations of the Faculty, xv, 12.

78   18,681: HUA, Scale of Merit, 1849–62.

"to recite . . . with the other": Hedge, "University," 301.

Any other . . . stamped: Adams, Henry, *Education*, 54–55.

The faculty . . . classes: See HU, *Catalogue*, 1857–58; *DAB*; Morison, *Three*; alumni memoirs.

Among a group . . . loved his: Adams, Charles Francis, *Autobiography*, 35.

78–79   His head. . . large: Wagner, *Harvard*, 116–17.

79   He burned . . . cheated: Morison, *Three*, 299.

He appears . . . Noble: HUA, Monthly Returns . . . 1857–61, unpaged.

Sophocles liked . . . "nothing": MDH, *Shaping*, 41.

"When he . . . College": American Academy, *Memorial*, 11.

"only a spurt": Morison, *Three*, 355.

79–80   "I have . . . flood": Bowen, Francis, *Principles of Political*, ix; *Principles of Metaphysical*, vii.

80   "for repeated . . . Bowen": HUA, Orders and Regulations of the Faculty, xvi, 69.

prided . . . school: HU, *Annual Report*, 1859–60, 4.

New Englanders . . . plantation South: HU, *Catalogue*, 1857–58, 21–24. JTM, "Recollections," 154.

Preparation . . . elitists: Story, *Forging*, 107.

Most of . . . Andover: HC, *Class of 1861 . . . Final Report*.

80–81   Only one . . . professions: 7 *HM* 361–62.

81   "The whole spirit" . . . inflicted: Weld, *War*, 14. Crowninshield, *Private*, 7. Fiske, *Letters*, 48.

"it was a growing . . . force": HU, *Annual Report*, 1859–60, 32.

Smoking . . . petty crimes: Weld, *War*, 38. HUA, Orders and Regulations of the Faculty, infractions cited throughout the volumes, 1857–61.

"Your son . . . college": James Walker to Hugh Gelston, 7/22/1857; HUA, College Letters, iv, 265.

Hallowell . . . freshmen: James Walker to Morris Hallowell, 5/26/1859; HUA, College Letters, iv, 362–63.

Cousin . . . "Rooms": James Walker to J.T. Morse, 6/30/1859; HUA, College Letters, iv, 371–72.

Wendell . . . sophomore year: HUA, Orders and Regulations of the Faculty, xv, 118–19, 258, 266.

82   senior year . . . leniency: Cornelius C. Felton to OWH, Sr., 4/23/1861; HUA, College Letters, v. 144.

The faculty . . . vacation: HUA, Orders and Regulations of the Faculty, xv, 317.

He was rarely . . . classes: HUA, Weekly Absences, 1857–61.

"playing": ibid., 1857–58.

whispering . . . unprepared: ibid., 1860–61.

Dr. Holmes . . . undergraduate: Tilton, *Amiable*, 37.

Wendell's class . . . senior year: HUA, Monthly Returns . . . 1857–61, unpaged.

His overall . . . students: HU, *Catalogue*, 1858–59, 40.

In recognition . . . June 1861: 6 *HM* 286; 7 *HM* 357.

elected to Phi Beta Kappa: Bowen, Catherine Drinker, *Yankee*, 131.

more of a . . . those days: Voorhees, *The History*, v, 54 ff., 202 ff.

82–83   shared . . . composition: HU, *Annual Report*, 1860–61, 32.

83   Johnny . . . before: HU, *Annual Report*, 1858–59, 38.

first professors . . . microscope: Tilton, *Amiable*, 149.

Professor Bowen . . . Christian principles: [Bowen, Francis], "Review," 474 ff.

Josiah . . . morals: Morison, *Three*, 308.

Louis Agassiz . . . disturbing conclusions: Lurie, *Louis*, 252 ff.

Asa Gray . . . scientific knowledge: See Dupree, *Asa*, 238 ff.

84   "noble . . . answered": [OWH], "Notes," 43–44.

"all . . . true": OWH to Kentaro Kaneko, 1/6/08; OWH papers, HLSL.

"in the air": OWH to Morris Cohen, 2/5/19; OWH papers, HLSL.

"almost the first . . . doubt answered": [OWH], "Books," 410.

He read . . . his death: LCRB.

he read little . . . physical: Barbour, *Naturalist*, 151.

"firebrand": OWH to FP, 5/20/30: OWH papers, HLSL.

85   "spark . . . flame": OWH to G.H. Kahn, 3/22/30; OWH papers, HLSL.

"If I ever . . . to you": OWH to PAS, 10/27/12; OWH papers, HLSL.

Wendell's seventeenth . . . "Scholar": LCRB.

[T]he best books . . . never see: Emerson, *American*, 54.

I think it not . . . understand: OWH, speech, 2/15/13. 15 *Harvard Alumni Bulletin* 609 (6/18/13).

Wherever Macdonald . . . table: Emerson, *Selected*, 61.

86   I once heard . . . table: OWH, "The Soldier's," 179.

Dr. Holmes . . . Independence: OWH, Sr., *Works*, xi, 88.

"to go alone . . . mediocrity": Emerson, *Selected*, 84–85.

"Whoso would . . . nonconformist": Emerson, *Selected*, 168.

87   Cousin . . . "Gentleman": 4 *HM* 431.

Wendell . . . "inculcate":[OWH], "Books," 408 ff.

Although . . . undergraduate: Tilton, *Amiable*, 50.

"I have not . . . rhetorically": OWH, Sr., to unnamed correspondent, 12/12/1859; OWH, Sr., papers, LC.

Book reviews: 7 *HM* 111, 235.

editorials: 7 *HM* 26, 37.

chosen . . . 1860: 5 *HM* 365.

In a major . . . "written": [OWH], "Notes," 41 ff.

87–88   It had published . . . "religion": 7 *HM* 31 ff.

88   A hundred . . . their souls: [OWH], "Books," 410.

"Woman in College" . . . reforms): 6 *HM* 353, 102, 1.

"the writers . . . proper tone": Cornelius C. Felton to OWH, Sr., 1/17/1861; HUA, College Letters, v, 106–08.

88–89   The *Harvard* . . . unsoftened: 4 *HM* 438, 7 *HM* 201.

89   In an inoffensive . . . "Emerson": 7 *HM* 201, 205.
"fired": OWH to Elsie Sergeant, 12/7/26; OWH papers, HLSL.
"to find . . . revealed": OWH to Learned Hand, 5/8/24; OWH papers, HLSL.
"I'm going . . . please me' ": Belknap, Some Words, 3.
Beginning . . . mystics: files of the Boston Athenaeum library, 1859, 1860.
eighteenth birthday . . . *Morals:* LCRB.
89–90   essay on Plato . . . "apsides": OWH, "Plato," 205 ff.
90   "laid it . . . do for the young": Belknap, Some Words, 3.
Wendell . . . tools: Fiechter, "Preparation," 12.
doubtful . . . career: Sutherland, "Recollections," 13.
no "ecstacy": OWH to CM, 8/31/10; OWH papers, HLSL.
91   one of his . . . framed: OWH to CM, 8/20/08; OWH papers, HLSL.
"what my . . . my youth": OWH to LE, 1/1/16; OWH papers, HLSL.
In March . . . followed: LCRB.
Records . . . *Art:* files of the Boston Athenaeum library, 1857–61.
The first . . . immersed: [OWH], "Notes," 41 ff.
92   Upon reading . . . "His work": [Holbrook], "A Review," 143–46.
"magnificent . . . restraint": Stechow, "Justice," 119–20.
92–93   Life at Harvard . . . literary interests: Fiechter, "Preparation," 4–5.
93   members frequently . . . "began": OWH, speech, 9/27/12; OWH papers, HLSL.
Hasty Pudding . . . extravaganzas: Garrison, *An Illustrated,* unpaged.
"Harvard . . . bone": interview with H. Chapman Rose.
"aroma . . . faculties": OWH, speech, Harvard commencement, 6/25/1884; *BDA,* 6/26/1884, 8.
"invisible . . . sons": WJ, speech, Harvard Commencement dinner; papers of W.R. Thayer, HUh.
Even into . . . Phi: OWH to CM, 7/20/10; OWH papers, HLSL.
93–94   Shortly after . . . "at Yale": interview with H. Chapman Rose.
94   At first . . . for home: Morse, "Recollections," 155.
Asa . . . abolitionist: Dupree, *Asa,* 153.
The late Reverend . . . institution: Morison, *Three,* 254–55.
Louis . . . South: Lurie, *Louis,* 260–62.
George . . . came: MDH, *Shaping,* 72, note.
94–95   Outside . . . green: Brooks, *Flowering,* 399 ff.
95   "Brother . . . Caroline": OWH, Sr., *Works,* xii, 284 ff.
"pretty . . . Abolitionist": OWH to HJL, 11/5/26; OWH papers, HLSL.
"devoutly": OWH to LE, 4/5/19; OWH papers, HLSL.
"belittling . . . race": OWH to J.C.H. Wu, 6/21/28; OWH papers, HLSL.
Pen . . . spoke in public: MDH, *Shaping,* 65–66.
fifty-cent contribution: *The Liberator,* 2/15/1861, 28.
he joined . . . Temple: OWH to HJL, 11/5/26; OWH papers, HLSL.
"I am . . . did": OWH to J.C.H. Wu, 6/21/28; OWH papers, HLSL.
95–96   "gave . . . progress": OWH to LE, 4/5/19; OWH papers, HLSL.
96   suspicious . . . others: OWH to HJL, 8/7/25; OWH papers, HLSL.
"who were free . . . their task": OWH to NG, 9/22/14; OWH papers, HLSL.

"for not loving . . . feels about it": OWH to LE, 7/17/09; OWH papers, HLSL.

"sometimes . . . good": 3 *DAB* 139.

"sense of . . . whole north": Wilson, Carroll A., *Thirteen*, 535.

97 four . . . Baltimore: *BET*, 4/20/1861, 4.

bank . . . $4 million: *BET*, 4/18/1861, 2.

Thursday Club . . . knapsacks: *BET*, 4/26/1861, 2.

Wendell . . . Infantry: Fiechter, "Preparation," 5.

"as life . . . have lived": OWH, speech, 5/30/1884; OWH papers, HLSL.

"Christian crusade": OWH to Charles Eliot Norton, 4/17/1864; OWH papers, HLSL.

98 "this unique . . . created": Corcoran, Rendezvous, 30.

On April . . . training: *BP*, 4/26/1861, 2.

*By May . . . Union: 7 *HM* 318.

The fort . . . 150: *BP*, 4/26/1861, 2.

A mildly . . . dashed: *BP*, 5/25/1861, 2; Excerpts from the 1861 Diary of William F. Bartlett; OWH papers, HLSL.

When he joined . . . south: Fiechter, "Preparation," 5.

"pity . . . delicacy": Henry Lee to OWH, 6/10/1884; OWH papers, HLSL.

98–99 Of those . . . institution: Cornelius C. Felton to OWH, Sr., 7/20/1861; HUA, College Letters, v, 201.

99 On June 10 . . . class: HUA, Orders and Regulations of the Faculty, xvi, 81.

Forfeiture . . . exercises: Cornelius C. Felton to OWH, Sr., 7/20/1861; HUA, College Letters, v, 201.

Dr. Holmes . . . mediocrity: OWH, Sr., to Cornelius C. Felton, 7/24/1861; OWH, Sr., papers, LC.

President . . . alone: Cornelius C. Felton to OWH, Sr., 7/26/1861; HUA, College Letters, v, 201.

"Alma Mater": 7 *HM* 48.

100 senior class . . . poet: 7 *HM* 237.

"patch[ed] . . . orator": Fiechter, "Preparation," 5.

Be brave . . . rolls: *Cambridge Chronicle*, 6/22/1861, 4.

"excellent" . . . received: *BET*, 6/21/1861, 4.

"student . . . Poet": NY *Tribune*, 7/8/1861, 5.

traditional smashing: *BET*, 6/21/1861, 4.

101 Dr. Holmes was spotted . . . temporarily: Tilton, *Amiable*, 265. John Lothrop Motley to OWH, Sr., 8/31/1862; OWH, Sr., papers, HUh.

Wendell finished . . . "fitter": Fiechter, "Preparation," 4–5.

He checked . . . Library: MDH, *Shaping*, 76.

The doctor . . . unbelief: OWH to HJL, 5/8/18; OWH papers, HLSL.

Dr. Holmes went . . . for Wendell: Tilton, *Amiable*, 265.

Wendell was on his way . . . unread: OWH to FF, 11/2/16; OWH papers, HLSL. Hale, Richard Walden, *Some*, 13.

First Lieutenant . . . camp: Adjutant General to OWH, Sr., 7/23/1861; OWH papers, HLSL.

102 "almost" . . . 2nd Lieut: OWH to Mary I. Dixwell, 7/22/1861; Wigglesworth papers, MHS.

Part IV: SOLDIER

Chapter 5: Ball's Bluff

105   "a very noisy boy": ALH to Emily Hallowell, 2/1/1863; OWH papers, HLSL.
not unlike . . . each other: MDH, *Shaping*, 66.
"coxcomb": FF, memorandum, 8/30/32; FF papers, LC.

106   He marched . . . their men: Whittier, Journal, 12; Twentieth Massachu-
setts papers, BPL.
*Apparently Holmes . . . to see: OWH, *Touched*, ix.
*"The enclosed . . . *fail*": OWH, Civil War Scrapbook; OWH papers,
HLSL.
Dr. Holmes . . . evenings: ALH to Emily Hallowell, 8/5/1863; OWH pa-
pers, HLSL.

107   His regiment . . . Massachusetts: Bruce, *Twentieth*, 1 ff.
His gray . . . determination: Crowninshield, Caspar, Journal, 15; Twentieth Massachusetts papers, BPL.
Others . . ."trumpets"; OWH, Regimental Veteran Association's Resolution on the late Colonel Lee, Twentieth Massachusetts papers, BPL.
Palfrey . . . Whittier: Bruce, *Twentieth*, 445–49.
"the sooner . . . regiment": Higginson, *Massachusetts*, i, 135.

108   "Thine" . . . barn: Hallowell, *Selected*, 24–25.
"I told . . . light' ": ibid., 125.
"savage . . . knew": OWH to LE, 4/17/14; OWH papers, HLSL.

109   Several . . . copperhead: MDH, *Shaping*, 82–83.
Future industrial . . . army service: Josephson, *Robber*, 50, 51.
J. Pierpont . . . banking firm: 7 *DAB* 175 ff.
James J. . . . steamboat line: 5 *DAB* 36 ff.
Jim . . . Marsh: 3 *DAB* 414 ff.
Andrew . . . Railroad: 2 *DAB* 449 ff.
Life . . . Village: Bruce, *Twentieth*, 3–7.

109–10 Less than . . . the war: OWH, Medical Records, NA.

110   On August . . . the other: Bruce, *Twentieth*, 9.
The regiment . . . stop: Higginson, *Massachusetts*, i, 4.
"anxious . . . well": Crowninshield, Caspar, Journal, 7; Twentieth Massachusetts papers, BPL.
old smooth-bore . . . England: Bruce, *Twentieth*, 9.
"reflection . . . accomplish": Sutherland, Recollections, 9.
"how many . . . beginning": OWH, speech, 5/30/1884; OWH papers, HLSL.
At last . . . capacity: Bruce, *Twentieth*, 9–12.

111   Baltimore . . . inscrutable: Crowninshield, Caspar, Journal, 7; Twentieth
Massachusetts papers, BPL.
September . . . Capitol: Bruce, *Twentieth*, 12–15. OWH to ALH, 9/11/
1861; OWH papers, HLSL.
"very . . . pulverized": OWH to ALH, n.d.; OWH papers, HLSL.

111–12 On September . . . Virginia: Bruce, *Twentieth*, 14–15.

112   Stone liked . . . inauguration: Catton, *This*, 81–82.

He was a strict . . . inadequate: Crowninshield, Caspar, Journal, 1; Twentieth Massachusetts papers, BPL.

After three . . . fight: Bruce, *Twentieth,* 18–22. Milano, "Letters," 18.

They could see . . . "drums": OWH to ALH, 9/23/1861; OWH papers, HLSL.

113   "They have . . . smiles": Raymond H. Lee to OWH, Sr., 10/7/1861; OWH papers, HLSL.

The idyll . . . nearby Maryland: Catton, *Mr.,* 76–80.

113–14   "perhaps . . . command": United States War Department, *The War,* section 1, v. 5, 290.

114   Nevertheless . . . woods: Bruce, *Twentieth,* 26 ff.

114–15   "What a long . . . directions": Palfrey, *Memoir,* 20–29.

115   mismanagement . . . over: Bruce, *Twentieth,* 26 ff. Catton, *Mr.,* 6–7. Whittier, Journal, 3; Twentieth Massachusetts papers, BPL.

116   "they looked" . . . swimmer: Bruce, *Twentieth,* 55.

"Here was . . . bank": Palfrey, *Memoir,* 26–27.

The battle . . . open: Bruce, *Twentieth,* 48.

"keyed . . . unknown": OWH to Alfred Zimmern, 1/22/18; Zimmern papers, Bodleian Library, Oxford University.

The first sergeant . . . more serious: OWH to ALH, 10/23/1861; OWH papers, HLSL.

116–17   "I felt . . . agony": OWH, undated memorandum, "Wound at Ball's Bluff"; afterwards cited as "Wound"; OWH papers, HLSL.

117   *"shot . . . same way": LCRB.

"What should" . . . William Lowell Putnam: OWH, "Wound"; OWH papers, HLSL.

whose grandfather . . . constitution: Higginson, *Massachusetts,* i, 35.

between groans . . . mortal: OWH, "Wound"; OWH papers, HLSL.

118   "Scott's . . . the house": anonymous undated letter found among the Hallowell papers, MHS.

Presently . . . gave in to sleep: OWH, "Wound"; OWH papers, HLSL.

"fought . . . brick": OWH to ALH, 10/23/1861; OWH papers, HLSL.

118–19   coming in . . . laudanum: OWH, "Wound"; OWH papers, HLSL.

119   mother . . . battle: Tilton, *Amiable,* 267.

"pretty . . . sure": OWH to ALH, 10/23/1861; OWH papers, HLSL.

"so patient . . . spirit": Nathaniel P. Banks to OWH, Sr., 10/25/1861; OWH papers, HLSL.

"of a piece . . . tent": Francis W. Palfrey to OWH, Sr., 10/26/1861; OWH papers, HLSL.

"recollection . . . leave": OWH, "Wound"; OWH papers, HLSL.

Dr. . . . call: Higginson, *Old,* 93.

"on the right . . . danger": OWH, Sr., to J.L. Motley, 11/14/1861; OWH papers, HLSL.

Others did . . . command: Bruce, *Twentieth,* 59–61. Catton, *Mr.,* 80–83.

119–20   The depleted . . . four months: Palfrey, *Memoir,* 19–30.

120   Pen . . . comrades: Hallowell, *Selected,* 21.

"has been . . . presence": William Hunt to OWH, Sr., 11/3/1861; OWH papers, HLSL.

The day . . . Philadelphia: Tilton, *Amiable*, 267.
"looking . . . spirits": OWH, Sr., to ALH, 11/8/1861; OWH papers, HLSL.
The doctor . . . "well": MADH, *Holmes*, 12.

120–21   Mrs. Holmes . . . donors: "Visitors to the Wounded Lieutenant"; OWH papers, HLSL.

121   "a great pet . . . again": Morse, *Life*, ii, 157–58.
"organized bore": OWH to FP, 2/1/20; OWH papers, HLSL.
Philosophy . . . winter: files of the Boston Athenaeum library, 1861–62.
"The young . . . before": MADH, *Memories*, 21.
Despite . . . previous May: Phisterer, *Army*, 4.
"made love . . . girls": OWH to FP, 9/13/1895; OWH papers, HLSL.

122   "very modest": MDH, *Shaping*, 114.
"Don't . . . that way": OWH to J.C.H. Wu, 1/26/22; OWH papers, HLSL.
"I envy . . . pray": Caroline Dehon to OWH, undated; OWH papers, HLSL.
On November . . . requests: Higginson, *Massachusetts*, ii, 588–89.

123   During . . . circle: *BP*, 10/8/1894, 6.
"the *necessity* . . . something": Lee, *Letters*, 269–70.
A recently . . . handkerchiefs: Higginson, *Massachusetts*, 588–89. MDH, notes; OWH papers, HLSL.
"impressed us . . . manager": *BP*, 10/8/1894, 6.
she kept . . . public: undated, untitled clipping; OWH papers, HLSL.
"It is very . . . more": ALH to Emily Hallowell, 2/1/1863; OWH papers, HLSL.

Chapter 6: Antietam

125   With Ralph . . . send: Ralph Waldo Emerson to OWH, 3/26/1862; OWH, Civil War Scrapbook, OWH papers, HLSL.
captain's bars: Captain's commission, 3/23/1862; OWH papers, HLSL.
"God . . . you": OWH, Sr., to C.E. Norton, 3/25/1862; Norton papers, HUh.
CAPT H——KEEDYSVILLE: William G. Le Duc to OWH, Sr., 9/17/1862; OWH papers, HLSL.
this second . . . jugular: OWH to Ellen Askwith, 9/17/19; OWH papers, HLSL.
"devilish . . . unknown": OWH to Alfred Zimmern, 1/2/18; Zimmern papers, Bodleian Library, Oxford University.
"God . . . rest": MDH, diary, 1/30/34; MDH papers, HLSL.

126   On March 27 . . . "small ship": Bruce, *Twentieth*, 78 ff.
126–27   "The town . . . ruins": Sedgwick, *Correspondence*, 41–42.
127   "We are on . . . nothing": OWH to parents, 4/7/[1862]; OWH papers, HLSL.
The Virginia roads . . . into position: Catton, *Mr.*, 109.
"The men" . . . rain fell: OWH to parents, 4/7/[1862]; OWH papers, HLSL. Bruce, *Twentieth*, 83–84.
"It is very unpleasant" . . . amputated: William F. Bartlett to mother, 4/25/1862; OWH to ALH, 4/25/1862; OWH papers, HLSL. Palfrey, *Memoir*, 40–41.

127–28   Malaria . . . at one time: *The Medical and Surgical,* Part 1, v. 1, 47. Stevens, *Three Years,* 45–46.

128   On May 2 . . . was over: Bruce, *Twentieth,* 85–86. Ropes, Letters, unpaged; Twentieth Massachusetts Papers, BPL.
The Twentieth missed . . . June 1: Bruce, *Twentieth,* 86 ff.
"nearly tired" . . . by shot: OWH to parents, 6/2/1862; OWH papers, HLSL.
"no good . . . force": OWH to LE, 3/10/18; OWH papers, HLSL.

128–29   He described . . . "you both": OWH to parents, 6/2/1862; OWH papers, HLSL.

129   "ten days . . . or two": *Harvard Memorial,* i, 431–32.
For twelve days . . ."& tear": OWH to ALH, probably 7/4/1862; OWH papers, HLSL.
Dr. Holmes was . . . anything else: OWH, Sr., "Four," 410.
Just before . . . afterwards: OWH, speech, 5/30/1884; OWH papers, HLSL.
Greenslet, *Lowells,* 282.
"We have had . . . possible": OWH to ALH, n.d.; OWH papers, HLSL.
Lee had . . . ringing: Catton, *Mr.,* 126.

130   Lee having . . . August 28: Bruce, *Twentieth,* 142–43.
Grandmother . . . "end": *BDA,* 8/22/1862, 1. Morse, *Life,* ii, 164–65.
The valley . . . the enemy: Stevens, *Three,* 142–43.
A Confederate . . . peace: Schildt, *Drums,* 98.
"plethora": OWH to parents, 9/17/1862; OWH papers, HLSL.
Twentieth . . . September 15: Bruce, *Twentieth,* 157.

130–31   "The number . . . marches": Schildt, *Drums,* 102.

131   "Dearest . . . once more": OWH to parents, 9/17/1862; OWH papers, HLSL.
"it would . . . the enemy": OWH to J.C.H. Wu, 6/16/23; OWH papers, HLSL.
*In 1990 . . . years: *NYT,* 7/1/90, 1, 20; *WP,* 4/9/90, B6.
"one . . . hospital": Gray and Ropes, *War,* 15.
Every . . . hospital: Stevens, *Three,* 155.

132   "We have . . . all together": OWH, speech, 12/11/1897; OWH papers, HLSL.
"bolting . . . newspapers": OWH to FP, 6/28/30; OWH papers, HLSL.
"Usual . . . fatal"; OWH to parents, 9/18/n.d.; OWH papers, HLSL.
Thinking . . . "Boston": OWH, Civil War scrapbook; OWH papers, HLSL.
*Some years . . . $20 in compensation: Hallowell, *Selected,* 16–18, 21.

132–33   Surgeons . . . feather bed: Le Duc, "Man," 80 ff.

133   *"I have . . . hostess": OWH to HJL, 12/14/22; OWH papers, HLSL.
He washed . . . wound: Le Duc, "Man," 80 ff.
Rumors . . . his son: [OWH, Sr.], "My Hunt," 748 ff.
"to meet . . . way": OWH to parents, 9/22/n.d.; OWH papers, HLSL.

133–34   the elder . . . awaited him: [OWH, Sr.], "My Hunt," 738–48.

134   On the afternoon . . . to travel: Findlay, "Where," 117 ff.
"womanly . . . home what it is": OWH to Fanny H. Kennedy, 9/30/1862; FF papers, LC.
He frolicked . . . about her: Findlay, "Where," 118 ff.

134–35   Meanwhile . . . "dropped": [OWH, Sr.], "My Hunt," 748 ff.

135   "insane . . . reed": C. W. Walton to OWH, Sr., 10/1/1862; OWH papers, HLSL.

135–36   At Harrisburg . . . "Dad?": [OWH, Sr.], "My Hunt," 754 ff.
136   * "Boy, nothing": Woollcott, "Second," 50.

          ## Chapter 7: Second Fredericksburg

137   *Considerations:* LCRB.
          Lectures: files of the Boston Athenaeum library, 1962–63.
          he cast . . . conduct of the war: notated flyer; OWH, Civil War scrapbook;
          OWH papers, HLSL.
          A general . . . the dead: Lovett, *Old,* 119. Morse, *Life,* ii, 169–70. Ropes,
          Letters, unpaged; Twentieth Massachusetts Papers, BPL.
137–38   Wendell had felt . . . "civilized nation": OWH to AJH, 11/n.d./1862; OWH
          to parents, 11/n.d./1862; OWH papers, HLSL.
138   "flabby . . . fish": OWH to CM, 10/23/16; OWH papers, HLSL.
138–39   "a stronger . . . lowest ebb": Bruce, *Twentieth,* 184, 188.
139   The Union . . . wounded): Morison, *Oxford,* 656. Bruce, *Twentieth,* 221–
          22.
          Little Abbott . . . "like a cane": OWH, speech, 5/30/1884; OWH papers,
          HLSL.
          "feels . . . reproach": Emerson, Ralph Waldo, *Heroism,* 9.
          Ironically . . . Rappahannock: MDH, *Shaping,* 141.
          "stretched . . . assure you": OWH to ALH, 12/12/1862; OWH papers,
          HLSL.
          As weak . . . "safe": OWH to LE, 8/27/17; OWH papers, HLSL.
139–40   he considered . . . "my feelings": OWH to ALH, 12/12/1862; OWH pa-
          pers, HLSL.
140   After . . . visited him: MDH, *Shaping,* 146.
          He checked . . . 1863: OWH, Medical Records, NA.
          "in recognition" . . . marshal: Bruce, *Twentieth,* 228.
          "In a week . . . do things": OWH to CM, 10/23/16; OWH papers, HLSL.
140–41   The men . . . letters home: Bruce, *Twentieth,* 223 ff.
141   Holmes visited . . . transfer: OWH to parents, 3/18/1863; OWH papers,
          HLSL.
          At the end . . . respond: MDH, *Shaping,* 151–53.
          "Drawn . . . fate": N.P. Hallowell to OWH, 2/7/n.d.; OWH papers, HLSL.
          The regiment . . . "niggers": 8 *National Cyclopedia of American Biography,*
          143. N.P. Hallowell to OWH, 2/7/n.d.; OWH papers, HLSL.
142   "We cannot . . . humanity": Birrell, *Frederick,* 93–94.
          "I never . . . my duty": OWH to OWH, Sr., 12/20/1862; OWH papers,
          HLSL.
          "Dear Old" . . . fight again: OWH to OWH, Sr., 3/29/1863; OWH pa-
          pers, HLSL.
142–43   On May 2 . . . peppered them: Bruce, *Twentieth,* 236 ff. MDH, *Shaping,*
          92.
143   THE CAPTAIN . . . SERIOUSLY: telegram, Pemberly Poor to OWH, Sr., 5/5/
          1863; OWH papers, HLSL.
          "Pleasant" . . . his foot: OWH to AJL, 5/3/n.d.; OWH papers, HLSL.
          What he did . . . the front: C. A. Whittier to OWH, 5/15/1863; OWH
          papers, HLSL.

"He lies . . . exposures": [OWH, Sr.], "Letters," 376.

143–44   Dr. William . . . usefulness: William Hunt to OWH, Sr., 5/12/1863; OWH papers, HLSL.

144   "doing very . . . was my response": Morse, *Life,* ii, 24–25.

He later . . . visitor: Sutherland, Recollections, 12.

The books . . . biography: files of the Boston Athenaeum library, 1863.

He also . . . time: ALH to Emily Hallowell, 8/5/[1863]; OWH papers, HLSL.

Little . . . regiment: MDH, *Shaping,* 157.

145   Sumner . . . Ropes . . . killed: MDH, *Shaping,* 157, 292 n. 12.

"not in a state" . . . funeral: J. C. Ropes to OWH, 7/7/1863; OWH, Civil War Scrapbook; OWH papers, HLSL. Ropes and Gray, *War,* 141–42.

The regimental . . . ribbons: Lovett, *Old,* 119.

Following . . . accepted it: MDH, *Shaping,* 157.

"stern . . . title": Mildmay, *John,* 188.

When he . . . Twentieth: MDH, *Shaping,* 159 ff.

"I find . . . properly": OWH to Agnes Pomeroy, 6/21/1864; OWH papers, HLSL.

On January 29 . . . Sixth Corps: MDH, *Shaping,* 159 ff.

146   Holmes had said . . . position: OWH to parents, 3/18/1863; OWH papers, HLSL.

The best . . . tobacco: Sutherland, Recollections, 12.

"Every battle . . . bowled out": MDH, *Shaping,* 161.

"Christian . . . sword": OWH to C.E. Norton, 4/17/1864; OWH papers, HLSL.

Sixth Corps . . . "go in": J.S. Anderson to OWH, 1/16/03; Letters, 1841–1905, LCRB.

Shortly . . . directions: OWH, diary, 5/3, 4, 6/1864; OWH papers, HLSL.

147   On May 6 . . . killed: MDH, *Shaping,* 164.

"noble . . . day!": clipping, *BET,* 10/17/1864; OWH papers, HLSL.

"always" . . . life also: OWH, speech, 5/30/1884; OWH papers, HLSL.

147–48   "May 7 . . . bullets": OWH, diary, 5/7, 9, 12, 13/1864; OWH papers, HLSL.

148   "Before . . . campaign": OWH to parents, 5/16/1864; OWH papers, HLSL.

148–49   "not to spare . . . time": OWH, diary, 5/29/1864; OWH papers, HLSL.

149   "Yet no . . . can know": Marquand, *The Late,* 267.

149–50   "I wish . . . formerly": OWH to parents, 5/30/1864; OWH papers, HLSL.

150   "The campaign . . . to God": OWH to ALH, 6/7/1864; OWH papers, HLSL.

There was no . . . capital: OWH, diary, 6/7, 8–9, 12/1864; OWH papers, HLSL.

"I tell . . . body": OWH to parents, 6/24/1864; OWH papers, HLSL.

"prepare . . . startler": OWH to ALH, 7/8/1864; OWH papers, HLSL.

151–52   The great . . . Stevens: See Woollcott, *Long,* 15. FF to John H. Cramer, 5/19/43; FF papers, LC. Cramer, *Lincoln,* 123. Leech, *Reveille,* 343. Hicks, "Lincoln," 323 ff. MDH, *Shaping,* 168; diary, 10/30/33; MDH papers, HLSL. Sutherland, Recollections, 9–11. interview with H. Chapman Rose. Irving S. Olds to Catherine Drinker Bowen, 7/31/44; Bowen papers, LC.

152   "in '64 . . . guns going": OWH to LE, 3/21/12; OWH papers, HLSL.

Alger . . . himself: interview with Alger Hiss.

"a soldier . . . off": Hay, *Lincoln,* 208.

David Donald . . . students: S. L. Carson to *WP*, 7/22/89, A21.
"was not . . . pressure": OWH to Agnes Pomeroy, 6/21/1864; OWH papers, HLSL.
"Citizen . . . C.A.W.": OWH, scrapbook; OWH, Sr., papers HUh.
Two days . . . reunion dinner: MDH, *Shaping*, 175.

152–53   How fought . . . shall sing: OWH, poem; OWH papers, HLSL.

Chapter 8: *Life Is War*

154   "great . . . fortune": OWH, speech, 5/30/1884; OWH papers, HLSL.
The sight . . . eyes: OWH to unnamed correspondent, 7/26/14; OWH papers, HLSL.
A military . . . "him first?": OWH, speech, 5/30/1884; OWH papers, HLSL.

155   In 1912 . . . "half an hour": OWH to LE, 3/21/12; OWH papers, HLSL.
didn't really . . . Lincoln: OWH to LE, 10/21/18; OWH papers, HLSL.
Mosby . . . *Campaign*: OWH to CM, 2/18/11; OWH papers, HLSL.
Mrs. Mark . . . *War*: OWH to LE, 4/5/19; OWH papers, HLSL.
"recur[ring] . . . times": OWH to FP, 4/27/19; OWH papers, HLSL.
Stephen . . . histories: LCRB.
"those days": OWH to LE, 10/31/19; OWH papers, HLSL.
Other . . . art history: LCRB.
"more or . . . profanity": OWH to unnamed correspondent, 10/11/26; OWH papers, HLSL.
Iliad aloud: OWH, BB, 152; OWH papers, HLSL.
Explorers . . . boats: LCRB.

156   "man who . . . skill": OWH to LE, 6/14/27; OWH papers, HLSL.
"the terrors . . . spirit": OWH to FF, 9/10/28; OWH papers, HLSL.
"Ball's . . . 1922": OWH to HJL, 10/22/22; OWH papers, HLSL.
"(contrary . . . the dead": OWH to PAS, 9/22/08; OWH papers, HLSL.
After . . . birthday: OWH to Leslie Scott, 5/23/10; OWH papers, HLSL.

156–57   He was pleased . . . button it: OWH to CC, 5/28/1897; OWH papers, HLSL.

157   He marched . . . banquets: OWH to PAS, 9/13/09; OWH, speech, 12/10/1892; OWH papers, HLSL.
"nights . . . order": OWH to J.C.H. Wu, 6/16/23; OWH papers, HLSL.
"terrible . . . body": OWH to parents, 6/24/1864; OWH papers, HLSL.
tall . . . thin lips: MDH, *Shaping*, 66.
Despite . . . little hard: Biddle, *Mr.*, 34.
Much later . . . question: MDH, diary, 12/18/33; MDH papers, HLSL.

158   "stripped . . . working force": OWH to LE, 3/10/18; OWH papers, HLSL.
whether any . . . commonplace: Adams, Henry, *Letters*, i, 371.
[T]he Civil War . . . knowledge: James, Henry. *Nathaniel Hawthorne*. New York and London, 1907, 139–40.

159   "carried . . . charge": OWH, speech, 5/29/1897; OWH papers, HLSL.
"soldiers . . . court": OWH, speech, 5/2/1898; OWH papers, HLSL.
"combat . . . ago": OWH, "Soldier's," 184–85.
"*ultima* . . . worlds": OWH to FP, 2/1/20; OWH papers, HLSL.
"second . . . skirmishers": OWH to Melville W. Fuller, 2/29/09; OWH papers, HLSL.

160 "Fight to . . . same text": OWH to E. O. Holland, 2/24/31; Bowen papers, LC.

"the unutterable": OWH, speech, 5/29/1897; OWH papers, HLSL.

"putting out . . . will go": OWH, "Soldier's," 184.

"touch[ing] . . . superlative": Wilson, *Patriotic,* 789.

"fighter . . . envelope": Wolfe, Tom. *The Right Stuff.* New York, 1979, 12.

"[T]he real . . . war": OWH to FP, 12/21/1886; OWH papers, HLSL.

Part V: SCHOLAR

Chapter 9: Harvard Law School

163 in July . . . war: Fiechter, "Preparation," 5.

in the summer . . . "philosophy": FF, memorandum, 9/28/32; FF papers, LC.

Shortly after . . . final slam: Biddle, *Mr.,* 35–36.

164 "in a vague way": FF, memorandum, 9/28/32; FF papers, LC.

165 "be watched . . . barbarism": OWH, Sr., *Works,* ii, 105–06.

"humanizing . . . innocent": OWH, Sr., *Works,* iii, 124.

No lawyer . . . ambition: HJL, "Ever Sincerely," 56.

Dr. Holmes's . . . diplomacy: 7 *DAB* 282 ff.

Lowell . . . literature: HLS, *Quinquennial,* 179.

And what . . . dazzle: 31 *ALJ* 419 (5/23/1885).

I suppose . . . man: OWH to Elsie Sergeant, 12/7/26; OWH papers, HLSL.

166 Thomas . . . Court: HLS, *Quinquennial,* 9, 14, 18, 16.

In 1864 . . . lists: Harvard Law School Association, *Centennial,* 379 ff.

Although . . . boardinghouse: Tilton, *Amiable,* 68.

Wendell . . . law school: MDH, *Shaping,* 196.

Amelia . . . garrulousness: Tilton, *Amiable,* 305.

courted . . . caught: ALH to OWH, 5/8/1866; OWH papers, HLSL.

Porcellian: *Catalogue,* 56.

past April . . . occasion: Emerson, Edward Waldo, *Early,* 37–43.

166–67 the custom . . . faculty: Batchelder, "Old," 648.

167 Students . . . "character": HU, *Catalogue,* 1864–65, 60.

Emory . . . administration: ibid., 64–65.

Before . . . state: 10 *DAB* 499.

Genial . . . legal matters: Warren, Charles, *History,* ii, 307.

Even Henry . . . "tenderness": James, Henry, *Notes,* 348.

"detestable . . . style": Fiske, *Letters,* 116.

167–68 As a teacher . . . frequently: Warren, Charles, *History,* ii, 116.

168 "than . . . ardor": OWH, speech, "The Use of Law Schools"; *The Daily Crimson,* 11/6/1886, 3.

Joel . . . professorship: 7 *DAB* 230 ff. HU, *Catalogue,* 1864–65, 64–65.

"dignified . . . trivialities": Warren, Charles, *History,* ii, 306.

His intention . . . reasonably: Smalley, *Anglo,* 26.

"represented . . . deadliest": James, Henry, *Notes,* 348.

Joseph . . . "follow": Warren, Charles, *History,* ii, 305.

"one of . . . bench": OWH, speech, "The Use of Law Schools"; *The Daily Crimson,* 11/6/1886, 3.

"Chitty's . . . Novel": Warren, Charles, *History,* ii, 308.

Blackstone's . . . partnerships: HU, *Catalogue,* 1864–65, 64–65.

168–69   Parsons was known . . . gossipy: Smalley, *Anglo,* 26; 7 *DAB* 273 ff.

169   his treatise . . . subject: MDH, *Shaping,* 186–87.

"profundity . . . story": Warren, Charles, *History,* ii, 304–05.

"almost if . . . equalled": OWH, speech, "The Use of Law Schools"; *The Daily Crimson,* 11/6/1886, 3.

Greek . . . Dane Hall: Sutherland, *Law,* 121.

the law school . . . their students: ibid., 152–53.

169–70   No course . . . commercial jurisprudence: HU, *Catalogue,* 1865–66, 60–61.

170   "no new . . . instruction": Sutherland, *Law,* 153.

171   the period . . . Constitution: Warren, Charles, *History,* ii, 260–61. HU, *Catalogue,* 1865–66, 68–71.

Sir Henry . . . viewpoint: Little, "Early," 169.

he persuaded . . . to read it: Adams, Henry, *Letters,* 115.

Defence . . . Jurisprudence: Little, "Early," 169.

Holmes got . . . "swagger": OWH to HJL, 11/22/17; OWH papers, HLSL.

171–72   If Holmes . . . criminal law: HU, *Catalogue,* 1865–66, 61.

172   "a very . . . conservatives": OWH to Elmer Gertz, 3/1/1899; Gertz papers, LC.

"ragbag . . . for itself": OWH, *CLP,* 301–02.

John . . . "interested in it": Gray and Ropes, *War,* 450.

"both as . . . interest": OWH to H.H. Brownell, 5/9/1865; quoted in J.A. Brownell to MDH, 4/22/47; OWH papers, HLSL.

172–73   "forget . . . on to fight": OWH to Elmer Gertz, 3/1/1899; Gertz papers, LC.

173   Friends . . . charm: Hill, "OWH," 268.

The victims . . . tongue: Meyer, Agnes, *Out of,* 171.

She was . . . "earnest": OWH to WJ, 12/15/1867; James family papers, HUh.

"decidedly . . . known": WJ, *Letters,* i, 76.

"that villain . . . years": WJ to G.W. James, 3/21/1866; James family papers, HUh.

"beloved . . . better": OWH to WJ, 12/15/1867; James family papers, HUh.

173–74   For James's interests and background, see Barzun, *Stroll,* 6–19.

174   Holmes would stand . . . whiskey: Fiechter, "Preparation," 19.

"the facetiously . . . argumentative": WJ, *Letters,* i, 125.

The only . . . with him: ibid., 75–76.

174–75   On July . . . tearful: Bail, "Harvard's," 265 ff. Allen, Alexander V.G., *Life,* i, 525.

175   Eleven days . . . military men: Edel, *Henry,* i, 184–85, 229–35. MDH, "Letters," 411–12; *Shaping,* 201. Frederickson, *Inner,* 156–58. James, Henry, "Poor".

Still . . . "our view": James, Henry, *Notes,* 457 ff.

176   Again, if . . . insolvency: HU, *Catalogue,* 1865–66, 62.

"going down . . . pursuit": OWH to H.H. Brownell, 10/31/1865; quoted in J.A. Brownell to MDH, 4/22/47; OWH papers, HLSL.

Holmes's reading . . . experience: Little, "Early," 168–69. LCRB.

Although . . . at it: J.A. Lowell to OWH, 6/29/17; OWH to FF, 5/29/30; OWH papers, HLSL. LDB to FF, 5/25/27; FF papers, LC.

176–77   Ostensibly . . . of thought: 5 *ALR* 177 (10/1870).

177   "to most . . . cases there": OWH, diary, 9/27/1866; OWH papers, HLSL.

"illmanner[ed] . . . ascertained": Parker, *Law,* 5.

Harvard . . . prescribed work: HLS, *Quinquennial,* 95.

178   Dr. Holmes . . . 1830s: Tilton, *Amiable,* 81 ff.

Boston's . . . "standards": Green, *Problem,* 58. Story, *Forging,* 166. Adams, Henry, *Education,* 19.

178–79   His first . . . "everywhere": OWH, diary, 5/8, 9/1855; OWH papers, HLSL.

179   Henry . . . "on horseback": OWH, diary, 5/10/1866; OWH papers, HLSL.

"felt . . . loud": OWH, diary, 6/5/1866; OWH papers, HLSL.

"very . . . gaze": Fields, James T., *Barry,* 118.

Henry . . . Wendell retorted: HCL, *Early,* 147–48.

"stiff . . . believe": OWH, diary, 5/13/1866; OWH papers, HLSL.

180   He met . . . "great gun": OWH, diary, 5/26/1866; OWH papers, HLSL.

Ten days . . . "in London": OWH, diary, 6/7/1866; OWH papers, HLSL.

Holmes dined . . . "a smile": OWH, diary, 5/24/1866; OWH papers, HLSL. clipping, *BET,* 9/6/30; FF papers, LC.

He visited . . . "civil": OWH, diary, 5/28/1866; OWH papers, HLSL.

Four days . . . "Eh?" OWH, diary, 6/1, 11/1866; OWH papers, HLSL.

He met . . . Vernon Gallery: OWH, diary, 5/10, 11, 14, 22, 29/1866; 6/9/1866; OWH papers, HLSL.

180–81   Wendell nevertheless . . . Jowett: OWH, diary, 1866, various entries; OWH papers, HLSL.

181   In his first . . . "&c &c": OWH to ALH, 5/26/1866; OWH papers, HLSL.

Letters for him . . . weekly turn: OWH, Sr., to OWH, 7/29/1866; OWH papers, HLSL.

final examinations . . . Mountains: ALH to OWH, 7/3/1866; OWH papers, HLSL.

"Well Favorite . . . my family": AJH to OWH, 5/8/1866; OWH papers, HLSL.

Dr. Holmes . . . "read it": OWH, Sr., to OWH, 6/18/1866; OWH papers, HLSL.

Mrs. Holmes . . . "about it": ALH to OWH, 5/2/1866, 7/3/1866, 6/11/1866, 7/3/1866; OWH papers, HLSL.

182   "each time . . . the last": OWH, diary, 6/8/1866; OWH papers, HLSL.

"a dangerous flirt": Katherine Loring to MDH, 6/4/42; MDH papers, HLSL.

"the Peninsular . . . tear": OWH, Sr., to OWH, 6/11/1866; OWH papers, HLSL.

The list . . . eminences: Samuels, *Young,* 126.

Leslie Stephen . . . purpose: Maitland, *Life,* 111, 116.

At the time . . . recovery: J.M. Thorington to Catherine Drinker Bowen, 5/26/42; Bowen papers, LC.

Stephen . . . youthful at thirty-three: J.M. Thorington to Catherine Drinker Bowen, 6/24/42; Bowen papers, LC.

183   "as if they . . . and rest": Maitland, *Life*, 103.

"[T]here he is . . . before him": Maitland, *Life*, 322.

The two . . . Leicester Square: OWH, diary, 6/12/1866; OWH papers, HLSL.

"sword-slashed . . . sport": OWH, speech, "Soldier's," 184.

"saw one . . . Matterhorn": OWH, diary, 6/12/1866; OWH papers, HLSL.

*Holmes referred . . . survived: *London Times*, 7/21/1865, 10; *Alpine Club Journal*, 9/1865, 148–53.

Stephen and Holmes planned . . . to Switzerland: Leslie Stephen to OWH, 6/28/1866; OWH papers, HLSL.

183–84   In the meantime . . . Louvre: OWH, diary, 6/12–15/1866; OWH papers, HLSL.

184   He wandered . . . "shone before me": OWH, diary, 6/15/1866–7/1/1866; OWH papers, HLSL.

On July 2 . . . "squirts": OWH, diary, 7/2, 3/1866; OWH papers, HLSL.

185   Holmes climbed . . . honor: J.M. Thorington to Catherine Drinker Bowen, 6/2/42; Bowen papers, LC.

"in labor": OWH to HJL, 12/3/18; OWH papers, HLSL.

They began with . . . followed: J.M. Thorington to Catherine Drinker Bowen, 6/2/42; Bowen papers, LC.

"the silence . . . of life": OWH to CC, 6/24/1897; OWH papers, HLSL.

His face . . . crawled over rocks: OWH, diary, 7/6–19/1866; OWH papers, HLSL. MDH, diary, 12/5/33; MDH, papers, HLSL.

185–86   "When we were . . . reaches of snow": OWH, diary, 7/4, 6/1866; OWH papers, HLSL.

186   "[T]he romance . . . la la": OWH to CC, 8/9/1897; OWH papers, HLSL.

"understood . . . misunderstand": Maitland, *Life*, 187.

Stephen got him elected . . . 1866: J.M. Thorington to Catherine Drinker Bowen, 5/26/42; Bowen papers, LC.

A week . . . in Scotland: OWH, diary, 7/26/1866–8/31/1866; OWH papers, HLSL.

"the sanction . . . primogeniture": Maitland, *Life*, 182.

On September 1 . . . captain: OWH, diary, 9/1, 4/1866; OWH papers, HLSL

Chapter 10: Lawyer/Scholar

188   By 9 . . . Library: OWH, diary, 10/18/1866; OWH papers, HLSL.

knowledge . . . office: OWH, speech, 3/7/1900; OWH papers, HLSL.

"endless" . . . Dixwell: OWH, diary, 10/18/1866; OWH papers, HLSL.

188–89   Boston Railroad . . . Works: list of firm's clients; OWH papers, HLSL.

189   Peleg . . . 1855: MDH, *Shaping*, 245–48.

The two lawyers . . . own briefs: OWH, diary, entries for 1867, 1/5, 6, 11, 25; 2/2, 6, 15; 3/23; 4/13; 5/1, 2; OWH papers, HLSL.

"a master . . . for me": OWH, "Memoir," 367.

190   He hated . . . "cases": OWH to James Bryce, 6/17/1879; OWH papers, HLSL.

"permissible" . . . hand: OWH to Hayes, n.d.; OWH papers, HLSL.

"academic . . . cloister": OWH to FF, 7/15/13; OWH papers, HLSL.

He criticized . . . hours: OWH to WJ, 4/19/1868; OWH papers, HLSL.

From Great . . . "idleness": Morse, *Life,* i, 10.

190–91 "Puritanical . . . hand": OWH to LE, 7/23/10; OWH papers, HLSL.

191 "men who . . . thought": OWH, speech, 1/17/1886; OWH papers, HLSL.

"hard" . . . chocolates: Biddle, "Aging," 19, 21. OWH to LE, 6/27/17; OWH papers, HLSL.

"as if . . . to die": OWH to HJL, 8/22/30; OWH papers, HLSL.

191–92 William . . . jury: 177 Mass. 612 (1900).

192 "debauch[ery]": OWH, diary, 11/24/1866; OWH papers, HLSL.

The social . . . law books: OWH, diary, 12/1866; OWH papers, HLSL.

192–93 Socially . . . "past eleven": OWH, diary, 1866/67; OWH papers, HLSL.

193 "in spite . . . feelings": OWH to WJ, 12/15/1867; OWH papers, HLSL.

As the date . . . "all day": OWH, diary, 2/1867; OWH papers, HLSL.

"a wise . . . affairs": OWH, Answer prepared to resolutions on the death of Asaph Churchill (Not delivered because of postponement—Feb. 21, 1898); OWH papers, HLSL.

"satisfactory": OWH, diary, 2/26/1867; OWH papers, HLSL.

193–94 On Saturday . . . "weather": OWH, diary, 3/2, 4, 5/1867; OWH papers, HLSL.

194 Following the bar . . . wrote her: OWH, diary, 2/22/1867–7/26/1867; OWH papers, HLSL.

"farewell . . . last time": Perry, Ralph Barton, "Common," 293.

Although his brief . . . "distinction": OWH, diary, 11/19, 24/1867; OWH papers, HLSL.

194–95 "debauched" . . . demands: OWH to WJ, 12/15/1867, 4/19/1868; James family papers, HUh.

195 "filthy lucre": OWH, diary, 5/1/1867; OWH papers, HLSL.

"the men who . . . Everywhere": OWH to James Bryce, 8/17/1879; OWH papers, HLSL.

"Had they . . . years before": Adams, Henry, *Education,* 237.

Adamses and . . . legislature: Samuels, Ernest, *Henry,* 7.

196 Louis Agassiz's . . . oranges: Brooks, *New England,* 184 ff.

Even at this . . . U.S. Supreme Court: George B. Upham to MDH, 1/27/36; OWH papers, HLSL.

"hopelessly swamped . . . character": WJ to Henry James, 11/14/1875; Perry, Ralph Barton, *Thought,* i, 360.

196–97 the membership . . . that ilk: MADH, *Portrait,* 241.

197 "scarcely" . . . him there: Henry James to OWH, 11/5/n.d., OWH papers, HLSL.

When William . . . cosmos: Fiechter, "Preparation," 19.

James, however . . . in his friend: Perry, Ralph Barton, *Thought,* i, 290.

The more . . . here tonight: WJ to Henry James, 10/2/1869; James family papers, HUh.

more influential: MDH, *Shaping,* 264.

197–98 One otherwise . . . their journal: OWH, diary, 11/21/1866; OWH papers, HLSL.

198 His unsigned . . . Fitzjames Stephen: 1 *ALR* 375 (1/1867).

he had read . . . abroad: OWH, diary, 11/25/1866; OWH papers, HLSL.

In the same issue . . . legal one: 1 *ALR* 376 (1/1867).

having solicited . . . Sumner: OWH to Charles Sumner, 3/18/1867; OWH papers, HLSL.

he put . . . of 1868: [OWH], "Impeachment," 547.

"moralizing . . . of courts": 1 *ALR* 554 (4/1867).

199   "adapting . . . ways": 3 *ALR* 357–58 (1/1869).

During . . . published: OWH, diary, 8/1–8/1867; OWH papers, HLSL.

At the same time . . . sometimes not: OWH, diary, fall 1867; OWH papers, HLSL.

"never known . . . Court.)": WJ to Henry Bowditch, 5/22/1869; James family papers, HUh.

That same . . . Temple: OWH, diary, summer 1867; OWH papers, HLSL. MDH, *Shaping*, 274.

"Poor . . . *Monthly:* James, "Poor."

199–200   Olivia . . . years ago: Olivia Murray Cutting, memorandum, given to MDH by Learned Hand; FF papers, LC. OWH to LE, 2/7/03; OWH, diary, 8/1867; OWH to E.A. Curtis, 2/7/03; OWH papers, HLSL.

200   He had defended . . . "pocket": OWH, diary, 6/14/1867; OWH papers, HLSL.

Then . . . war: George B. Upham to MDH, memorandum, 1/27/36; OWH papers, HLSL.

201   I have just . . . melancholy: Ebenezer Rockwood Hoar to OWH, Sr., 11/14/1867; OWH, Sr., papers, HUh.

However impressed . . . against them: *Richardson* v. *New York*, 89.

*The issue . . . by name: *Dennick* v. *Central Railroad*, 21.

In the summer . . . chickens: MDH, *Shaping*, 274.

Henry . . . declined: Henry James to OWH, 7/29/1868, 8/n.d./1868; OWH papers, HLSL.

The summer . . . Connecticut: MDH, "Letters," 411–15.

"charmingly . . . recreation": Mary James to Henry James, 8/n.d./1869; James family papers, HUh.

"in very" . . . none: WJ to Henry Bowditch, 8/12/1869; James family papers, HUh.

"go" . . . away: Mary James to Henry James, 8/n.d./1869; James family papers, HUh.

202   In 1870 . . . Sedgwick: MDH, *Shaping*, 273.

who had fought . . . matters: 8 *DAB* 546.

"manual . . . matter": OWH to HJL, 12/18/29; OWH papers, HLSL.

"play[ing] . . . and bar": 5 *ALR* 1 (10/1870).

204   "well-settled . . . formula": [OWH], "Codes," 1.

"practical . . . remarkable": ibid., 2, 3, 4.

"about as vague . . . 'peculiar' ": 2 *ALJ* 323 (10/22/1870).

*Nearly three . . . article: Pollock, Frederick. *Encyclopedia of the Laws of England*. London, 1897, 7, note.

205   for two years . . . brother, Ned: HC, *Class of 1867*, 20.

Ned had graduated . . . "in History": HU, *Catalogue*, 1869–70, 63–64.

He had then spent . . . could breathe: HC, *Class of 1867*, 20.

recommended . . . legal community: MDH, *Proving*, 62.

Harvard had not been . . . reverse the trend: Morison, *Three*, 323 ff.

206   "turned the whole . . . born President": Morse, *Life*, ii, 190–91.

"this cool . . . to admire": ibid., ii, 187–88.

"little or . . . judged wisely": R.H. Dana to OWH, Sr., 2/n.d./1870; OWH, Sr., papers, LC.

"increase of . . . his advantage": A.G. Sedgwick to Henry James, 1/30/1870; James family papers, HUh.

In the same crop . . . law school: HUA, Overseers' Records, x, 394–95.

207   "I am to teach" . . . paid $300: OWH to Charles W. Eliot, 1/25/1870; OWH papers, HLSL.

He had 158 . . . a Warren: HU, *Catalogue*, 1869–70, 13–17.

The college . . . gradually: HU, *Catalogue*, 1869–70, 9, 10.

The text . . . "man's nature": Alden, Joseph. *The Science of Government in Connection with American Institutions*. New York, 1866, 12, 10, 13.

"such matters . . . instructive": OWH to Charles W. Eliot, 1/25/1870; OWH papers, HLSL.

The examination . . . constitutional government: copy of examination; OWH papers, HLSL.

208   "delightful . . . opinions": OWH to FP, 8/27/1883; OWH papers, HLSL.

"the ease . . . those days": "Portrait," 747.

"very successful . . . pupils": MDH, *Proving*, 28–29.

In April . . . 1871–72: HU, *Catalogue*, 1871–72, 11.

new category . . . elsewhere: Morison, *Three*, 334–36.

When the scheme . . . medicine: MDH, *Proving*, 61.

Holmes was reappointed . . . for eighteen lectures: HUA, Overseers' Records, xi, 67.

As dean . . . case method: HLS *Bulletin*, 4/81, 16. Sutherland, *Law*, 162 ff.

Coinciding with . . . legal principles: Sutherland, *Law*, 174 ff.

The common law . . . he could: OWH to James Bryce, 5/17/1871; OWH papers, HLSL.

208–9   "misspent . . . darkness": OWH to FP, 4/20/1881; OWH papers, HLSL.

209   "wanting . . . sense": OWH to FP, 7/6/08; OWH papers, HLSL.

In the winter . . . Thayer: James B. Thayer to James Kent, 12/n.d./1869; OWH papers, HLSL.

Holmes spent . . . "lawyer": OWH to James B. Thayer, 2/10/1869; OWH papers, HLSL.

Brooks . . . Library: Beringause, *Brooks*, 50.

210   too much . . . spectator: OWH, Sr., *Works*, iii, 238.

Wendell began . . . above all: Fiechter, "Preparation," 21–22.

His whole . . . at home: Mary James to Henry James, 2/2/1873; James family papers, HUh.

"an aversion to innovation": "Letter," 361, 171.

keep . . . "book": OWH to J.N. Pomeroy, 5/22/1872; OWH papers, HLSL.

210–11   deleted . . . "error": OWH to Thomas M. Cooley, 4/16/1873; Michigan Historical Collections, University of Michigan.

211   Neither . . . arrogance: James Kent to James B. Thayer, 12/17/1873; James Kent to OWH, 12/16/1873; OWH papers, HLSL.

"abundance . . . delight": BDA, 12/18/1874, 2.

The immense . . . space: "Critical," 386.

212   "if, indeed . . . newer": ibid., 388.

"law—law—law": OWH to WJ, 4/19/1868; James family papers, HUh.
anthropology . . . repertory now: Little, "Early," 179–85.

212–13   For his second . . . "interest": [OWH], "Misunderstandings," 37, 41–42, 38.

213   In his third . . . privity: [OWH], "The Arrangement," 46 ff.

214   a means . . . long run: [OWH], "Gas-Stokers'," 582–83.

214–15   When I . . . years: WJ to OWH, 1/3/1868; James family papers, HUh.

215   Such a society . . . homes: Fisch, "Was There," 3 ff. Perry, Ralph Barton, *Thought,* i, 534.

"late . . . smoke": Mary James to Alice James, n.d.; James family papers, HUh.

Wright . . . meetings: Fisch, "Justice," 88, n. 9.

"the highest . . . forever": Mary James to Alice James, n.d.; James family papers, HUh.

"longheaded . . . about it": Henry James to Charles E. Norton, 2/4/1872; Norton papers, HUh.

215–16   "Boxing" . . . practical: Fisch, "Justice," 92.

216   "courts enforce": [OWH], "Codes," 5.

217   What more . . . judges act?: [OWH], "Review of *The Law,*" 724.

"trusting to . . . time": OWH, speech, 6/18/1897; *Providence Journal,* 6/19/ 1897, 5. Martha Mitchell to Liva Baker, 3/9/89.

he sent proofs: MDH, *Proving,* 83–84.

disappointed: OWH to J.H. Wigmore, 1/4/10; OWH papers, HLSL.

A dissent . . . *American Law Review:* 7 ALR 146–47 (10/1872)

Chapter 11: Marriage

218   "watcher . . . antiquity": OWH, Sr., *Works,* iii, 58–59.

218–19   "burning away . . . looks in it": OWH, Sr., *Works,* iii, 141–42.

219   "most intimate . . . years": OWH to Fanny H. Kennedy, 3/11/1872; OWH papers, HLSL.

Fanny's pedigree: Dixwell, Dixwell Pedigree, OWH papers, HLSL.

trustee . . . Athenaeum: *The Athenaeum,* 118.

Harvard Overseer: HU, *Quinquennial,* 43.

first actuary . . . America: Story, *Forging,* 45–46.

220   Much later . . . textile mills: Wilson, *Patriotic,* 770.

The proprietor . . . flute: Dixwell, *Autobiographical,* 21.

Epes . . . Scientific Club: Dupree, *Asa,* 122–23.

Her sister . . . Sewing School: Dapping, *Susan,* 12.

Higher education . . . or so later: Clarke, *Sex.*

Fanny's adult . . . an adult: LCRB.

"the great thing . . . her mind": FF to Catherine Drinker Bowen, 4/19/63; FF papers, LC.

220–21   "never trust[ed] . . . you want": ALH to Fanny Holmes, 12/24/1877; OWH papers, HLSL.

221   "hated": MDH, *Shaping,* 200, note g.

"I'm getting . . . own life: Adams, Marion (Hooper), *Letters,* 437.

Wendell never . . . first edition: Hale, Richard W., *Some,* 13.

"with a sort . . . interval": OWH to Fanny H. Kennedy, 3/11/1872; OWH papers, HLSL.

Cambridge . . . young man: Katherine Loring to MDH, 5/4/42; MDH papers, HLSL.

Two of . . . already married: OWH, diary, 10/18/1866; OWH papers, HLSL. Dapping, *Susan,* 16.

"very superior . . . very much": OWH, Sr., to Ann Holmes Upham, 3/11/1872; OWH, Sr., papers, HUh.

222   "We love Fanny . . . daughter-in-law": ALH to Mary I. Dixwell, 3/12/1872; OWH papers, HLSL.

Fanny Dixwell . . . 17, 1872: Cambridge, Mass., Record of Marriages, vii, 107. *BG,* 6/18/1872, 4.

the ninety-seventh . . . fireworks: *BG,* 6/18/1872, 8.

Wendell sandwiched . . . translation): Little, "Early," 184–85.

Fanny's family as Unitarians: *BET,* 12/2/1899, 5.

"for reasons . . . own": Phillip P. Chase to Richard W. Hale, 2/13/43; Bowen papers, LC.

they were married . . . Brooks: *BG,* 6/18/1872, 4.

The First . . . at the time: C. Conrad Wright to Liva Baker, 5/16/88.

The minister there . . . pastor: Day, *Biography,* 51–53.

Phillips Brooks's . . . before: Allen, Alexander V. G., *Phillips,* 115–16.

William James . . . father: WJ to Robertson James, 9/20/1874; James family papers, HUh.

June . . . *Rev.:* Little, "Early," 184.

The couple . . . fever: Novick, *Honorable,* 133.

223   Following . . . entertainment: Butler, *A Century,* 178–79.

Their finances . . . "fun we had": Foraker, *I Would,* 206.

By 1872 . . . grandmother: *Massachusetts Constitution. Massachusetts General Statutes,* 1860, title vii, Chapter 106, 528 ff. Warbase, *The Changing,* introduction.

224   "dry . . . grace": James, Henry. *The Bostonians.* New York, 1984, 36.

225   "[H]is wife . . . impossible": Fields, Annie, *Authors,* 109.

Why are . . . pillows?: Marian Frankfurter to FF, 10/15/25; FF papers, LC.

As to bosoms . . . Lords' needs: FF to Marian Frankfurter, 10/17/25; FF papers, LC.

Despite . . . children: OWH to HJL, 3/27/18; OWH papers, HLSL.

In private . . . mortal: Hale, Richard W., *Some,* 11. Thomas Corcoran to FF, 11/4/26, 12/9/26, and one undated; OWH papers, HLSL.

"she-devil": Hale, Richard W., *Some,* 12.

225–26   "to throw . . . long for": FDH to OWH, 6/11/07; OWH papers, HLSL.

226   "devoted . . . enchantment": OWH to PAS, 4/1/11; OWH papers, HLSL.

"human being . . . dress coat": OWH to Margaret Bevan, 9/7/13; OWH papers, HLSL.

227   "roses . . . broomstick": MDH, undated note; OWH papers, HLSL.

Fanny . . . vacuum cleaner: OWH to ES, 6/5/11; OWH papers, HLSL. Monagan, "Enigmatic," 82.

Despite Victorian . . . and possible: D'Emilio and Friedman, *Intimate,* 55 ff.

Fanny . . . loved children: MDH, *Shaping,* 20, note h.

She partially . . . cats: FDH to ES, 11/9/09; OWH papers, HLSL.

"unlimited . . . lark": OWH to CC, 6/9/1897; OWH papers, HLSL.

He doted . . . Washington: OWH to EJH, Jr., 12/4/04; OWH papers, HLSL.

wrote . . . years ago: OWH to Esther Owen, 6/8/1892, 1/6/05, and other undated Valentines; OWH papers, HLSL.

228   "I am so . . . up something": OWH to LE, 8/31/28; OWH papers, HLSL.

On an earlier . . . "else into' ": Learned Hand to MDH, 4/29/59; OWH papers, HLSL.

a vague . . . impotence: interviews with Joann Reiss and Jeffrey M. Haskins. See also Bullough, *Sexual*; Kaplan, *Comprehensive*; Main, "Impotence": Murstein, *Love*.

230   "I believe you . . . best in us": OWH to Owen Wister, 1/22/1898; OWH papers, LC.

"two-thirds": OWH to PAS, 4/1/11; OWH papers, HLSL.

Chapter 12: Scholar/Lawyer

231   On March 3 . . . year was out: Little, "Early," 186–87.

"The Theory": [OWH], "The Theory," 652.

That same . . . belonged: MADH. *Portrait*, 1–10, 162, 241.

Samuel Hoar . . . appointed: *The National Cyclopaedia of American Biography, xx,* 369. OWH to HJL, 4/5/25; OWH papers, HLSL.

did not return: HU, *Catalogue*, 1873–74, 24 ff.

he leavened . . . Spencer: Little, "Early," 186.

Study of Sociology . . . Journal: OWH, Sr., Review, 587.

"the necessity . . . thankful:" OWH to James Bryce, 8/17/1879; OWH papers, HLSL.

232   When he joined . . . at night: Irving S. Olds to Catherine Drinker Bowen, 8/31/44; Bowen papers, LC.

"quite . . . over": Mary James to Henry James, 12/8/1873; James family papers, HUh.

the young . . . dined together: OWH to Mrs. Charles Hamlin, 10/12/30; OWH papers, HLSL. Fiechter, "Preparation," 21.

The usual . . . flower bed: OWH to HJL, 11/25/26; OWH papers, HLSL.

"very pleasant" . . . a sort of lens: WJ to Henry James, 7/5/1876; James family papers, HUh.

"No, . . . father": Pollock, John, "The Pollock-," 52.

233   felt twice . . . superlatives: OWH to Winifred Burghclere, 9/17/1898; OWH papers, HLSL.

That summer . . . illuminati: FDH, diary; OWH papers, HLSL.

Pollock's son . . . the meeting: Pollock, John, "The Pollock-," 46.

"made a . . . meet him": OWH to Winifred Burghclere, 12/2/1898; OWH papers, HLSL.

He had commented . . . "Notices": [OWH], Review of *The Law Magazine,* 723.

"there was no stage . . . speculative interest": Pollock, Frederick, "Mr.," 1277.

"never got . . . indifference": OWH to Winifred Burghclere, 2/2/1898; OWH papers, HLSL.

234 At first blush . . . the page: Pollock, John, "The Pollock-," 48.
"grieve[d] . . . to it": OWH to Franklin Ford, 8/3/17; OWH papers, HLSL.
"to more things . . . Bible": Hamilton, "On Dating," 2.
A ball at . . . "back with him": FDH, diary; OWH papers, HLSL.
235 Holmes talked . . . game, too: Pollock, John, "The Pollock-," 51.
Holmes admitted . . . "life": Elizabeth Glendower Evans to OWH, 1/28/32; FF papers, LC.
On July 11 . . . Milan: FDH diary, OWH papers, HLSL.
Among . . . death: Max Ernst to FF, 10/19/43; FF papers, LC.
In early . . . September 8: FDH, diary; OWH papers, HLSL.
sixty cents: C.D. Clement to Elsie Sergeant, n.d.; OWH papers, HLSL.
"beautiful": FDH, diary; OWH papers, HLSL.
236 "in all-round . . . questions of law": OWH, "Memoir," 367.
William . . . native: *Men of Progress,* 163.
The firm . . . legal Boston: OWH to *BET,* 9/10/10; OWH papers, HLSL.
Shattuck's social . . . University: OWH, "Memoir," 365.
236–37 *Pro bono* . . . 1892: Smith, Reginald H., *Justice,* 134, 140. Auerbach, *Unequal,* 53.
237 Litigation . . . corporation law: 3 *DAB* 60. MADH, *Moorfield,* 164, 266. Baker, Leonard, *Brandeis,* chapter 3.
Although . . . retreated from it: JTM to OWH, 3/5/31; OWH papers, HLSL. Jaher, *Age,* 210–11.
"hated": JTM, "Incidents," 370.
devoting . . . "no effort": JTM to OWH, 3/5/31; Jaher, *Age,* 210–11.
238 one of the greatest . . . success: OWH to FP, 9/1/10; OWH papers, HLSL.
"deal with . . . law": 178 Mass. 624, 626 (1901).
241 He made a . . . other side: Journal of R.H. Dana and E.L. Dana, 1, 298; Dana family papers, MHS.
Following the death . . . expected: John C. Gray to Charles C. Beaman, 11/29/1878; judicial papers, NA.
A group . . . "qualifications": 8 lawyers to Charles Devens, n.d.; judicial papers, NA.
"no man . . . satisfactory": J.P. Putnam to William Maxwell Evarts, 12/17/1898; judicial papers, NA.
"able . . . lawyer": Godfrey Morse to Rutherford B. Hayes, 12/5/1878; judicial papers, NA.
Chief Justice . . . scenes: Urofsky, *Letters,* i, 47.
"solicited . . . profound": John C. Gray to Charles Cotesworth Beaman, 11/29/1898; judicial papers, NA.
241–42 "in a mild . . . settled": OWH to FP, 12/9/1878; OWH papers, HLSL.
242 The scenario . . . concluded: Hoar, *Autobiography,* ii, 416–19.
"men . . . thought": OWH, speech, 2/17/1886; OWH papers, HLSL.
243 "only . . . Veronese": OWH, speech, 12/3/02; FF papers, LC.
was admitted . . . 1879: Charles E. Cropley to FF, n.d.; FF papers, LC.
244 thirty-two . . . eighteen: *Massachusetts Reports,* vols. 115–34.
"The only . . . act": OWH, "The Theory," 724.
Judge Lowell's . . . justice: 6 *DAB* 467.
Judge Gray's . . . dressed: 4 *DAB* 518–19; OWH to George Wharton Pepper, 12/6/30; FF papers, LC.

245   Mr. Evans . . . all day: Elizabeth Glendower Evans to OWH, 1/28/32; FF
          papers, LC.
          It often . . . details: OWH, Introduction to Charles, xi.

          Chapter 13: The Common Law

246   "black years": OWH to J.C.H. Wu, 3/3/30; OWH papers, HLSL.
          "Always . . . to do": Emerson, Ralph Waldo, *Heroism,* 23.
          sitting . . . scholar: George B. Upham, memorandum to MDH, 1/27/36;
          OWH papers, HLSL.
          Elected . . . School: Secretary of the Board of Overseers to OWH, 6/28/
          1876; OWH papers, HLSL.

247   He was listed . . . 1879: Garraty, *Henry,* 61.
          He entertained . . . Englishmen: Holmes, John, *Letters,* 144.
          was willing . . . call: Fiske, *Letters,* 357.
          His reason . . . chance: OWH to FP, 9/1/10; OWH papers, HLSL.
          John Gray . . . relationship: OWH to John C. Gray, 7/13/1877 and 7/18/
          1877; OWH papers, HLSL.

247–48   Young Louis . . . Club: Baker, Leonard, *Brandeis,* 25–26. Mason, *Brandeis:
          A Free,* 63–64; *Brandeis: Lawyer,* 16. Urofsky, *Letters,* i, 45.

248   "descended . . . vernacular": Biddle, "The Friendship," 87.
          The two began . . . articles: Urofsky, *Letters,* i, 33–34, 49.
          "politico-legal . . . to come": OWH to J.N. Pomeroy, 5/22/1877; OWH
          papers, HLSL.

248–49   "black gulf . . . sink": OWH, speech, 6/18/1897; *Providence Journal,* 6/19/
          1897, 5. Martha Mitchell to Liva Baker, 3/9/89.

249   "fogs . . . compass": OWH to Albert J. Beveridge, 11/17/26; OWH papers,
          HLSL.
          "black frozen . . . months": OWH to _____ Stevens, 2/21/26; Schimmel
          Collection, Columbia University.
          "the meanest . . . fruit": *The Daily Crimson,* 11/6/1886, 2.
          "established rule . . . master": *Temple* v. *Turner,* 128.

250   His expanded . . . reports: Little, "Early," 187–203.
          "reflected . . . have been!": 3 *ALJ* 420 (5/3/1885).
          "supplant . . . Commentaries": Upham, George B., memorandum, 1/27/
          36; OWH papers, HLSL.
          "for the day . . . law": [OWH], Review of *The Law of Torts,* 341.
          "answer" . . . then): OWH to HJL, 6/1/22; OWH papers, HLSL.
          "sources . . . write": [OWH], Review of *The Science,* 134.

251   "New First . . . Jurisprudence": OWH to Arthur G. Sedgwick, 7/12/1879;
          OWH papers, HLSL.
          The results . . . centuries: See 12 *ALR* 688 (7/1878); 13 *ALR* 609 (7/
          1879); 14 *ALR* 1 (1/1880); 10 *ALR* 422 (4/1876); 11 *ALR* 641 (7/1877).
          If the clothing . . . mind: OWH to Ralph Waldo Emerson, 4/16/1876;
          OWH papers, HLSL.
          "much" . . . critique of it: FP to OWH, 11/26/1876, OWH papers, HLSL.
          "position . . . book": FP to OWH, 5/2/1876, 7/26/1876; OWH papers, HLSL.
          "without" . . . *Nation:* OWH to Arthur G. Sedgwick, 7/12/1879; OWH
          papers, HLSL.

252   Sedgwick complied . . . *Nation:* 29 *Nation* 42 (7/17/1879).

"pleased . . . much": OWH to Arthur G. Sedgwick, 7/21/1879; OWH papers, HLSL.

Later . . . series on the law: Abbott Lawrence Lowell to OWH, 3/31/09; OWH papers, HLSL.

The beneficiary . . . in town: Green, *The Problem,* 53 ff. Story, *Forging,* 14 ff.

"weight . . . life": OWH to CM, 1/9/15; OWH papers, HLSL.

Wendell immediately . . . series: Little, "Early," 202. OWH, *TCL,* iii.

"very hard . . . puts one": OWH to FP, 6/17/1880; OWH papers, HLSL.

The lectures . . . the audience: *BDA,* 11/24/1880, 1. Beringause, *Brooks,* 68.

252–53   Holmes delivered . . . subject: Jones, "Oliver," 713.

253   "no other . . . interest them": *BDA,* 1/1/1881, 1.

"to do what . . . I did so": OWH, *TCL,* iii.

champagne . . . safekeeping: OWH to Mrs. Charles Hamlin, 10/12/30; OWH papers, HLSL.

"ordinary . . . ourselves)": OWH to James B. Thayer, 3/19/1893; OWH papers, HLSL.

The first edition . . . late 1890s: *One Hundred,* 10, 20. Little, Brown papers, HUh.

254   "made the thread . . . on the other": OWH to LE, 12/13/29; OWH papers, HLSL.

"should be . . . study": [OWH], "Books," 410.

"association . . . past": OWH to HJL, 4/18/24; OWH papers, HLSL.

"among the . . . soul": OWH to LE, 9/10/16; OWH papers, HLSL.

"the most . . . can show": OWH to William F. Barry, 4/1/30; OWH papers, HLSL.

254–55   "every brick . . . to forget": OWH, speech, 7/31/02; OWH papers, HLSL.

255   President George . . . Jackson: Putnam, *A Memoir,* 51.

He treasured . . . Indian Wars: OWH to LE, 12/26/21; OWH papers, HLSL.

Occasional . . . Boston's past: OWH to ES, 7/12/24; OWH papers, HLSL.

He liked . . . to tears: OWH to HJL, 6/26/28, 7/9/25, and 8/7/25; OWH papers, HLSL.

He owned . . . "see it?": "Great," 31.

He recognized . . . "emerged": OWH to LE, 6/11/22; OWH papers, HLSL.

Old friend . . . "investigations": LCRB. Henry Adams to OWH, 11/3/1881; OWH papers, HLSL.

256   "the rationale . . . doctrines": OWH to J.N. Pomeroy, 6/8/1881; OWH papers, HLSL.

257   "with bayonets . . . death": OWH, *TCL,* 43.

"forever adopting . . . other": ibid., 36.

The life . . . every stage: ibid., 1.

258   "now a man . . . evenings": OWH to LDB, 3/9/1881; LDB papers, University of Louisville.

"the end . . . world": OWH to Ellen Askwith, 3/3/15; OWH papers, HLSL.

"extraordinary" . . . wants them: 15 *ALR* 332–33 (5/1881).

258–59   "welcomed" . . . parent: 23 *ALJ* 380 (5/7/1881).

259   "master . . . progress": 26 *ALJ* 484 (12/16/1882).
       much that . . . value: 32 *Nation* 465 (6/30/1881).
       "exceedingly . . . obliged": OWH to FP, 7/5/1881; OWH papers, HLSL.
       a searching . . . legal history: [Frederick Pollock], "Holmes," 758–59.
       "the most . . . *Law*": 55 *Spectator* 745 (6/3/1882).
260   Rufus . . . miffed: MDH, *Proving*, 84–85.
       It is not merely . . . mind: OWH to Thomas M. Cooley, 9/22/1882; OWH papers, HLSL.
       "I am surprised" . . . the work: Rufus Waples to Thomas M. Cooley, 10/6/1882; Michigan Historical Collections, University of Michigan.
       In the spring . . . York City: P.T. Rathbone to MDH, 3/23/62; OWH papers, HLSL.
261   Her work . . . "individual": *BDA*, 4/19/1881, 2. 32 *Nation* 286 (4/21/1881). *The American Architect and Building News* 211 (4/30/1881).
       she destroyed . . . 1902: MDH, *Proving*, 255 n. 5.
       "the conversation . . . 'No. 1' ": Morison, *Three*, 358.
261–62 "urgent" . . . house: HU, *Annual Report*, 1880–81, 26. Sutherland, *Law*, 195–96.
262   Dr. . . . five years: OWH, Sr., to Charles W. Eliot, 1/26/1871; HUA, Presidents' Papers, Charles W. Eliot.
       In his 1880–81 . . . of law: HU, *Annual Report*, 1880–81, 27.
       in the fall . . . professor: Thayer, James B., memorandum D; OWH papers, HLSL.
       Harvard Class . . . June of 1881: Reunion program, LCRB.
       he had not changed . . . Langdell: 14 *ALR* 156 (3/1880).
262–63 "not inclined . . . my friends": OWH to Charles W. Eliot, 11/1/1881; OWH papers, HLSL.
263   "no difficulty . . . few days": Charles W. Eliot to OWH, 11/4/1881; HUA, Presidents' Papers, Charles W. Eliot. Garraty, *Henry*, 53.
       "unwilling" . . . Eliot's offer: OWH to Charles W. Eliot, 11/18/1881; OWH papers, HLSL.
263–64 Thayer suppressed . . . accomplished: Thayer, James B., memorandum D; OWH papers, HLSL.
264   On January 23 . . . of law: Charles W. Eliot to OWH, 2/11/1882; OWH papers, HLSL.
       "considerations . . . member": OWH to the Overseers of Harvard College, 3/30/1882; OWH papers, HLSL.
       annual catalogue . . . evidence: HU, *Catalogue*, 1882–83, 138.
       "weary" . . . for England: Adams, Henry, *Letters*, i, 454. OWH to FP, 4/8/1882; OWH papers, HLSL.
265   The same names . . . itinerary: OWH, diary, 1882; OWH papers, HLSL.
       Citing . . . September 9: OWH, Sr., to Charles W. Eliot, 9/9/1882; HUA, Presidents' Papers, Charles W. Eliot.
       November 28 . . . with effort: *BET*, 11/29/1882, 2.
       Judge Lord . . . December 1: *BG*, 12/9/1882, supplement, 1.
       Solomon . . . list: MDH, *Proving*, 259 n. 10.
       "one versed . . . the law": W.G. Russell to John Davis Long, 12/7/1882; OWH papers, HLSL.
265–66 Senator Hoar . . . appointed: OWH to HJL, 4/5/25; OWH papers, HLSL.

266   Robert R. Bishop . . . "appointment": George O. Shattuck to John Davis Long, 12/7/1882; Massachusetts State Archives, Executive Letters, 231, 135.

James Bradley . . . 1881: MDH, *Proving,* 259.

Holmes himself . . . father's house: OWH to John Davis Long, 2/7/1880; Long papers, MHS.

He was a social . . . reform politics: Hess, "John," 57 ff.

descendant . . . "circumstances": Long, "Reminiscences," 348.

In late-nineteenth-century . . . impenetrable: O'Connor, *Bibles,* 121 ff.

267   On Friday . . . the appointment: Thayer, James B., memorandum D; OWH, speech, 3/7/1900; OWH papers, HLSL. MDH, diary, 2/18/34; MDH papers, HLSL.

"every member . . . hands": Long, Journal, 190–91; Long papers, MHS.

267–68   A surprised . . . of others: Thayer, James B., memorandum D; OWH papers, HLSL.

268   "powerful . . . through life": WJ to Henry James, 7/5/1876; James family papers, HUh.

Regarding . . . Overseers: MDH, *Proving,* 270.

"the most . . . show often": OWH to HJL, 3/31/27; OWH papers, HLSL.

Parker . . . responsibility: MDH, *Proving,* 270.

268–69   "was expressly . . . recollections": F.W. Parker to OWH, 12/1/1882; OWH papers, HLSL.

269   There is no indication . . . the law school: HUA, Treasurer's Statement, 1882, 8.

"buried . . . not fair": OWH to FP, 7/2/1895; OWH papers, HLSL.

"fill . . . his years": *BG,* 12/9/1882, supplement, 3. *BDA,* 12/9/1882, 4.

"cloister . . . thinks": OWH to CM, 8/14/10; OWH papers, HLSL.

270   My motives . . . manly course: OWH to James Bryce, 12/31/1882; OWH papers, HLSL.

"appeared . . . intellect": George O. Shattuck to FDH, 1/3/1883; OWH papers, HLSL.

"everything . . . view of the law": OWH to FP, 8/27/1883; OWH papers, HLSL.

Part VI: **JUDGE IN MASSACHUSETTS**

Chapter 14: The Fallow Years

273   To think . . . myself: OWH, Sr., to Carolyn Kellogg, 12/13/1882; OWH, Sr., papers, HUh.

his mind . . . sound: 298 Mass. 575, 595 (1937).

274   One . . . *point:* Esmond Schapiro to MDH, 8/4/42; OWH papers, HLSL.

I want . . . liked it: Lee M. Friedman to MDH, 6/2/55; OWH papers, HLSL.

1,290 . . . years: 298 Mass. 575, 606 (1937).

"attentive . . . notes": OWH to CC, 3/26/1897; OWH papers, HLSL.

He once . . . innuendo: *WP,* 3/6/35, 1.

"always" . . . there you are: Belknap, "Some," 4–5.

275   "to confirm some theories": OWH to FP, 11/2/1884; OWH papers, HLSL.
"the practical . . . life": OWH to James Bryce, 8/18/1879; OWH papers, HLSL.

277   [A]ffairs . . . atrophied: Marquand, *The Late*, 149.

278   as Felix . . . solo: FF, *Of Law and Men*, 108.
"become . . . command": OWH, speech, 6/3/1890; OWH papers, HLSL.
"long . . . Commandments": OWH to CC, 5/20/1897; OWH papers, HLSL.
"cut . . . views": OWH to FP, 3/22/1891; OWH papers, HLSL.
"sharp . . . convictions": OWH to CC, 5/18/1898; OWH papers, HLSL.
"almost . . . silence": *Vegelahn* v. *Guntner*, 104.
"most varied": OWH to FP, 3/25/1883; OWH papers, HLSL.
we are . . . down: OWH to FP, 8/27/1883; OWH papers, HLSL.

279   "to assign . . . me": OWH to CC, 3/26/1897; OWH papers, HLSL.
"to write . . . wind": OWH to Owen Wister, 4/30/1891; OWH papers, HLSL.
so absorbed . . . explorations: OWH to FP, 1/17/1891; OWH papers, HLSL.
it occupied . . . Square: Paul C. Reardon to Liva Baker, 2/8/88.
Five . . . week: OWH to FP, 3/9/1884; OWH papers, HLSL.
Holmes kept . . . covered: *Massachusetts Reports*, LCRB.
the judges . . . court fashion: Paul C. Reardon to Liva Baker, 2/8/88. 2 *Massachusetts LQ* 425–26 (3/17).

280   a note indicating . . . attendance: Putnam, *Memoir*, 106–09.

281   financial . . . mills: Story, *Forging*, 47.
judicial best . . . the better: MDH, "Creative," 240 ff.
he cares . . . people: Adams, Charles Francis, *Memoirs*, xi, 228.

282   Between 1813 . . . construction: Rosenthal, "Massachusetts," 301–09.

283   "high ambition . . . life": OWH to CC, 9/5/1896; OWH papers, HLSL.
"lean . . . horse": Wister, *Roosevelt*, 129.
"desultory": OWH to NG, 7/20/1891; OWH papers, HLSL.
poetry . . . to himself: OWH to FP, 1/17/1887; OWH papers, HLSL.
He made . . . Tuesdays: OWH to E.A. Curtis, 1/7/01; OWH papers, HLSL.
Owen . . . living: OWH to Sarah B. Wister, 5/24/1887; OWH papers, HLSL.
he periodically . . . Appian Way: OWH to Sarah B. Wister, 9/25/1887; OWH papers, HLSL. Biddle, *Mr.*, 70 ff.
Friday . . . habit: OWH to J.H. Wigmore, 2/23/1893; OWH papers, HLSL.

284   "of great . . . dull": OWH to Owen Wister, 3/25/1887; OWH papers, HLSL.
For the first . . . his court: *Haley* v. *Bellamy*, 137 Mass. 357 (1884); *Sears* v. *Fuller*, 137 Mass. 326 (1884); *Lathrop* v. *Thayer*, 138 Mass. 466 (1885); *Barnard* v. *Coffin*, 141 Mass. 37 (1886).
"objects": OWH to Harry H. Edes, 1/10/1887; OWH papers, HLSL.
he refused . . . "Peace": OWH to FF, 8/11/24; OWH papers, HLSL.
He hesitated . . . "familiarities": Wister, *Roosevelt*, 130.
In the early . . . into shape: OWH to LE, 3/31/22; OWH papers, HLSL.
It stood . . . courthouse: Bowen, Catherine Drinker, *Yankee*, 304–05.
Before Holmes . . . Bay: OWH to FP, 7/5/1881; OWH papers, HLSL.
"center . . . delight": OWH to Mrs. Charles Hamlin, 10/12/30; OWH papers, HLSL.

285   His talk . . . improvisations: Wister, *Roosevelt,* 129.
            "artichoke . . . neglected": OWH to FP, 1/17/1887; OWH papers, HLSL.
            Shortly after . . . nomination: *BH,* 9/2/1883, 4.
            His friend . . . "being Senator": OWH to FP, 3/9/1884; OWH papers,
            HLSL. Garraty, *Henry,* 72. FF to Emmet Lavery, 11/12/45; FF papers, LC.
285–86   At the invitation . . . to read: Bowen, Catherine Drinker, *Yankee,* 308.
            BDA, 5/31/1884, 4.
286   The fete . . . "their cause": *BET,* 6/26/1884, 2.
286–87   A month . . . Holmes name: *NYT,* 7/29/1884, 5. HC, *Class of 1867,* 16.
            EJH, Jr., to FDH, 1881–82; OWH papers, HLSL.
287   "to the bottom . . . theories": OWH to FP, 11/2/1884, 11/26/21; OWH
            papers, HLSL.
            "pain and" . . . few days: *Commonwealth* v. *Pierce,* 168–69.
            "to constitute . . . prescription": *Commonwealth* v. *Thompson,* 139.
            Holmes suspected . . . grant it: *Commonwealth* v. *Pierce,* 177.
288   "that a man . . . ensues": ibid., 175.
            "only to . . . to rule": OWH, *TCL,* 49.
            The court . . . criminal: *Commonwealth* v. *Pierce,* 179.
            When a workman . . . at all: OWH, *TCL,* 60; cf. 4 *Blackstone's,* 192.
            "pain . . . distress": *Commonwealth* v. *Pierce,* 168.
289   he described . . . pride: OWH to FP, 11/2/1884; OWH papers, HLSL.
            Which did not . . . harm done: OWH, "Privilege," 3.
            As to your . . . promises: OWH to HJL, 12/17/25; OWH papers, HLSL.
290   "stream of life" . . . social life: *BET,* 2/6/1885, 2.
            With obvious . . . Pollock: OWH to FP, 2/6/1885; OWH papers, HLSL.
            editors . . . issue: 30 *ALJ* 419 (5/23/1885).
            "started eye glasses": OWH to FP, 12/21/1886; OWH papers, HLSL.
290–91   For the first . . . heritage: *Services at the Celebration.* Tilton, *Amiable,* 395.
291   It was reported . . . intimately: Bowen, Catherine Drinker, *Yankee,* 309.
            Of course . . . unattainable: BDA, 2/17/1886, 8.
            Holmes received . . . Oxford: OWH to FP, 12/21/1886; OWH papers, HLSL.
            "our . . . degrees": OWH to Simeon E. Baldwin, 7/15/1886; OWH papers,
            HLSL.
            The judge . . . New Haven: Class of 1861, 25th anniversary program,
            LCRB.
            (Fanny's . . . to fail.): OWH to Simeon E. Baldwin, 5/27/1886; OWH
            papers, HLSL.
            "like the . . . known": *New Haven Palladium,* 7/1/1886, 2.
291–92   "deafening" . . . professions: *The Daily Crimson,* 11/6/1886, 2–4. Baker,
            Leonard, *Brandeis,* 30.
292   You argue . . . being: OWH, speech, n.d.; OWH papers, HLSL.
            "shaping the future": OWH, speech, 6/3/1890; OWH papers, HLSL.
292–93   At about . . . murder: notes of MDH; OWH papers, HLSL. Hovey, *John,*
            47–49. MADH, *John,* 50.
293   In the summer . . . "affairs": OWH to FP, 12/21/1886; OWH, Sr., to
            ALH, 7/11/1884; OWH papers, HLSL. OWH, Sr., to Julia Dorr, 5/29/
            1887; Middlebury College Library. Tilton, *Amiable,* 369. OWH, Sr., to
            James Freeman Clarke, 9/28/n.d.; James Freeman Clarke papers, HUh.
            "a tug . . . roots": OWH to FP, 3/4/1888; OWH papers, HLSL.

"good . . . sweetest": OWH to ALH, 9/23/1861; OWH papers, HLSL.
"Dear Mammy": OWH to ALH, 7/1/1864; OWH papers, HLSL.
Shortly after . . . burned down: OWH to Mrs. Charles Hamlin, 10/12/30; OWH papers, HLSL.

293–94   spent most . . . recuperation: WJ to Henry James, 10/13/1888; James family papers, HUh. OWH, speech, 10/21/03; FF papers, LC. OWH, BB, 155.

294   Following . . . herself: JTM to HCL, 2/25/1887; Morse papers, MHS.
Cousin . . . "father-in-law": ibid.
Whatever . . . comfortable: Tilton, *Amiable,* 376.
"Mrs. . . . woman": JTM, *Life,* ii, 236–64.
demeanor . . . melancholy: OWH to Owen Wister, 3/30/1889; OWH papers, HLSL.

295   "the ideal . . . conquer": *BDA,* 2/17/1886, 3.
he confessed . . . "reign": OWH to CC, 9/5/1896; OWH papers, HLSL.
154 Mass. 116 (1891).
"melancholy . . . die for": OWH to Owen Wister, 3/30/1889, 4/14/1889; OWH papers, HLSL.
"make . . . father": OWH to Owen Wister, 4/14/1889; OWH papers, HLSL.

295–96   he was still . . . War: OWH, Sr., to Henry Willett, 6/21/1889; to William Priestly, 6/21/1889; OWH papers, HLSL.

296   "a most . . . to say": Alice James, *Diary,* 6/16/1889.
"sprightly . . . etc.": OWH to FP, 2/23/1890; OWH papers, HLSL.
leisure-time reading . . . read aloud: OWH, BB, 152.
"every word" . . . points: OWH to WJ, 11/10/1890; OWH papers, HLSL.

297   "*presumed* . . . contemplate it": OWH to FP, 3/22/1891; OWH papers, HLSL.
"great crime . . . responsibility": *Tasker* v. *Stanley,* 150.

297–98   In his early . . . "contemplated": OWH to FP, 3/22/1891; OWH papers, HLSL.

298   "for imperfections . . . material": *Commonwealth* v. *Perry,* 117.
"essential . . . community": ibid., 121.

298–99   Holmes's dissent . . . opinion: Derby, "Recollections," 348–49.

299   Only the . . . exploitation: *Commonwealth* v. *Perry,* 123–24.
"first . . . community": OWH, *TCL,* 41.
It may very . . . "ground": *Commonwealth* v. *Perry,* 124.
"respect . . . property": OWH to HJL, 9/16/24, 8/6/17; OWH papers, HLSL.
the state . . . employer: Tushnet, "The Logic," 1031.

300   On October . . . the same year): OWH, BB, 151.
I am dying . . . is: OWH to NG, 8/7/1891; OWH papers, HLSL.

Chapter 15: Practice Flights

301   A younger . . . change: Katherine Loring to Catherine Drinker Bowen, 11/11/40; Bowen papers, LC.

302   "may have . . . policeman": *McAuliffe* v. *New Bedford,* 220.
"respectable classes": OWH to James Bryce, 7/17/1892; OWH papers, HLSL.
"dangerous radical": OWH to FP, 4/2/1894; OWH papers, HLSL.
The Massachusetts . . . of law: Gray, Russell, "Historical," 235.

In the spring . . . fuel: 155 Mass. 598 (1892).

302–3   "a step . . . other side": OWH to FP, 4/15/1892; OWH papers, HLSL.

303   In a dissent . . . thought: 155 Mass. 598 (1892).

"some follower . . . to be": OWH to NG, 5/10/1892; OWH papers, HLSL.

But he failed . . . of life: 155 Mass. 598, 607 (1892).

The majority . . . education: ibid., 603 ff.

only two . . . citizens: 150 Mass. 592 (1890).

"no less . . . proposed": 155 Mass. 598, 607 (1892).

"blooming communist": OWH to NG, 5/10/1892; OWH papers, HLSL.

303–4   "squarely . . . of time": *BP*, 5/10/1892, 4.

304   "We know . . . merchandise": 155 Mass. 598, 602 (1892).

"command . . . power": OWH to James B. Thayer, 11/2/1892; OWH papers, HLSL.

305   "I don't know . . . bottom": OWH to FP, 11/26/21; OWH papers, HLSL.

grippe: OWH to FP, 4/2/1894; OWH papers, HLSL.

Was it constitutional . . . option: 160 Mass. 586 (1894).

The judges . . . constitutional: ibid., 589 ff.

Once again . . . unconstitutional: ibid., 593–95.

"[A]mong . . . score": OWH to FP, 4/2/1894; OWH papers, HLSL.

"queer . . . fish": FF to Arthur D. Hill, 3/27/31; FF papers, LC.

306   in late . . . August: John Hinckley to Thomas M. Cooley, 5/11/1894; Michigan Historical Collection, University of Michigan.

Harvard's . . . what was said: JTM, *Life*, i, 78.

And the names . . . tomb: *BET*, 10/8/1894, 1.

Wendell still . . . strides: *BG*, 10/8/1894, 5.

306–7   He could . . . eighty-five years old: *BET*, 10/8/1894, 1, 4.

307   A funeral . . . Cemetery: *BP*, 10/11/1894, 1.

burying . . . plot: visit to Mount Auburn Cemetery.

"rather . . . for him": OWH to FP, 10/21/1894; OWH papers, HLSL.

Wendell's inheritance: OWH, Sr., will no. 97053, filed in Suffolk County Probate Court, 10/11/1894; *Athenaeum Centenary*, 139.

308   Wendell was not . . . from it: OWH to James Bryce, 11/5/1894; OWH papers, HLSL.

The portrait . . . years later: Bowen, Catherine Drinker, *Yankee*, 426.

But Fanny . . . appeared: workmen's bills; OWH papers, HLSL.

For the . . . house: *Commonwealth* v. *Davis*, 511.

308–9   "combat" . . . society: OWH, "The Soldier's," 179–80.

309   The *Harvard* . . . delayed: OWH to W.R. Thayer, 8/29/1895, 8/31/1895; OWH papers, HLSL.

"sentimental . . . land": 61 *Nation* 440–41 (12/19/1895).

309–10   "the struggle" . . . commerce: OWH, "The Soldier's," 179–86.

310   "not intended . . . self": OWH to Margaret Bevan, 7/19/1895; OWH papers, HLSL.

It was not war . . . of money: OWH, "The Soldier's," 179–86.

"rarely . . . high key": Henry James to WJ, 7/3/1895; James family papers, HUh.

310–11   "the great . . . use it": Henry James to OWH, 10/13/95; OWH papers, HLSL.

311   "By Jove . . . fine": TR to HCL, 6/5/1895; TR, *Selections*, i, 146.

Less than . . . judgeship: OWH to Georgina Pollock, 7/2/1895; OWH papers, HLSL.

A healthy . . . factory: OWH to Georgina Pollock, 7/2/1895 and 7/10/1897; OWH to EJH, Jr., 2/18/1890; OWH papers, HLSL. *Beverly Times*, 3/7/35, 1. Sullivan, *Our,* i, 241.

After his . . . from it: OWH to FP, 8/11/1895; OWH to NG, 9/2/1895; OWH papers, HLSL.

311–12   Judge Grant . . . overrule him: Grant, *Fourscore,* 212–13.

312   The bicycle . . . "Cavours": OWH to NG, 9/2/1895; OWH to Georgina Pollock, 8/12/1895; OWH to HJL, 8/14/19; OWH papers, HLSL.

Fanny's eye trouble: John Holmes to FDH, 9/10/1892; OWH papers, HLSL.

natural shyness . . . Dixwells: Katherine Loring to MDH, 6/10/42; MDH papers, HLSL.

"Things . . . mind": OWH to LE, 6/16/29; OWH papers, HLSL.

Boston matrons . . . call: Katherine Loring to MDH, 6/10/42; MDH papers, HLSL.

It was said . . . at home: MDH, notes; OWH papers, HLSL. Interview with John Monagan.

313   To add . . . rarely: MDH, *Shaping,* 200 n. 1. Monagan, "The Enigmatic."

He was not above . . . jaw: OWH to NG, 6/16/1897; OWH papers, HLSL.

A well-known . . . tea table: OWH to CC, 5/26/1898 and 3/26/1897; OWH to NG, 8/29/1899; OWH to CC, 11/21/1896; OWH papers, HLSL. Bowen, Catherine Drinker, *Yankee,* 326.

"much . . . thought": OWH to NG, 6/16/1896; OWH papers, HLSL.

313–14   He arrived . . . Pollock: OWH, 1896 diary; OWH papers, HLSL.

314   "tremendous . . . fatiguing": OWH to NG, 7/17/1896; OWH papers, HLSL.

He replenished . . . opera hat: shopkeepers' bills; OWH papers, HLSL.

Henry . . . Ireland: OWH, 1896 diary; OWH papers, HLSL. MDH, "Letters," 419.

In early . . . townhouse: OWH, 1896 diary; OWH papers, HLSL.

They apparently . . . speeches: CC to OWH, 2/19/1892; CC to OWH, n.d., probably 1896; OWH papers, HLSL.

In mid-August . . . Ireland: OWH, 1896 diary; OWH papers, HLSL.

"an enchanting . . . experience": OWH to NG, 10/2/1896; OWH papers, HLSL.

"It is the stopping . . . does it seem": OWH to CC, 8/22/1896, 8/23/1896, 8/24/1896, and 8/25/1896; OWH papers, HLSL.

314–15   "[A]lthough . . . time": OWH to CC, 9/5/1896; OWH papers, HLSL.

315   "jump . . . from you": OWH to CC, 9/17/1896, 12/29/1896; OWH papers, HLSL.

"tender . . . remember?": OWH to CC, 10/17/1896, 1/11/1897, 5/7/1897, and 9/6/1896; OWH papers, HLSL.

Clare . . . Conqueror: Castletown, *Ego,* 154.

Bernard . . . places: *Ego.*

"address" . . . with his: OWH to CC, 9/30/1896, 2/3/1898, 9/5/1898; OWH papers, HLSL.

*Fortunately . . . papers: Inventory to the OWH collection at HLSL, 21. Monagan, *The Great,* 90–91.

Fanny knew: Monagan, *The Great,* 93–94.

316 "Beloved Hibernia": OWH to CC, 6/7/1898; OWH papers, HLSL.
"dying, Egypt, dying": OWH to NG, 8/7/1891; OWH papers, HLSL.
The old armor . . . Court: *The Times World,* 4/12/1899, 11.
She shared . . . linguist: London *Times,* 3/22/27, 16. *Irish Times,* 3/26/27, 7.
She had stalked . . . Morocco: Castletown, *Ego,* 83 ff.
"missed . . . Doneraile": OWH to CC, 1/10/1898, 9/17/1896, and 9/30/1896; OWH papers, HLSL.

317 Back on . . . Savoy: OWH to CC, 12/8/1897, 5/19/1899, 11/21/1896, 12/4/1896, and 8/9/1897; OWH papers, HLSL.
"a little cool . . . inmost soul": OWH to CC, 10/17/1896, 1/11/1897, 5/7/1897, 11/21/1896, 3/3–4/1898; OWH papers, HLSL.
"got accustomed . . . again?": OWH to CC, 9/17/1896 and 5/14/1897; OWH papers, HLSL.

318 Word comes . . . is true: Pringle, *William,* i, 128.
The issues . . . raised: *Vegelahn* v. *Guntner,* 92–96.

318–19 "unlawful . . . them": ibid., 97.

319 "almost . . . law": ibid., 104.
"with . . . profit": OWH to FP, 1/20/1893; OWH papers, HLSL.
courts . . . "consequences": OWH, "Privilege," 7–9.

319–20 *Vegelahn* required . . . "for life": *Vegelahn* v. *Guntner,* 106–08.

320 One of the . . . way: ibid., 108.
"painful . . . not more": OWH to CC, 10/20/1896, 11/21/1896; OWH papers, HLSL.
Shortly after . . . "time": OWH to FF, 9/3/21; OWH papers, HLSL.
"revolting . . . past": OWH, "Path," 469.

321 "adequately . . . ago": ibid., 467–68.
"fired . . . satisfying": OWH to CC, 3/5/1897; OWH papers, HLSL.
"anyone else . . . heart": OWH, *Speeches,* 70.
Not everyone . . . "the last": OWH to CC, 12/8/1897; OWH papers, HLSL.
Brown . . . "the pole": OWH to CC, 6/10/1897; OWH papers, HLSL. OWH, BB. 147. OWH, speech, 6/18/1897, in *Providence Journal,* 6/19/1897, 5. Martha L. Mitchell to Liva Baker, 3/9/89.

321–22 Ned's son . . . beginning: OWH to NG, 7/25/1897; OWH to FP, 7/20/1897; OWH papers, HLSL.

322 At Beverly . . . responsibility: Brooks Adams to Henry Adams, 8/8/1897; Adams papers, HUh. OWH to NG, 8/12/1897; OWH papers, HLSL. Anderson, Thornton, *Brooks,* 110.
By August . . . "balled up": OWH to CC, 8/17/1897, 5/7/1897; and 12/3/1897; OWH papers, HLSL.

322–23 "When you . . . precisely?": OWH to CC, 1/10/1898; OWH papers, HLSL.

323 Ten days . . . "my heart": OWH to CC, 1/18/1898, 2/3/1898, 2/17/1898, 3/18/1898; OWH papers, HLSL.

324 the possibility . . . submission: OWH to CC, 3/27/1898, 4/1/1898, 4/8/1898, 4/29/1898; OWH papers, HLSL.
"Dewey's . . . Atlantic": OWH to CC, 5/3/1898, 6/7/1898, 6/9/1898; OWH papers, HLSL.
By mid-June . . . Mackellars: OWH to Georgina Pollock, 6/17/1898; OWH papers, HLSL.

324–25 "Mrs. Holmes . . . get off": OWH to NG, 6/20/1898; OWH papers, HLSL.
325 He landed . . . Sussex: OWH, 1898 diary; OWH papers, HLSL. MDH, "Letters," 420.

wonderful . . . repeating: OWH to Margaret Clifford, 6/24/27; OWH papers, HLSL.

"visible . . . ashamed": OWH to CC, 9/8/1898; OWH papers, HLSL.

tormented . . . months: OWH to FP, 12/9/1898; OWH papers, HLSL.

Although . . . immediately: OWH, 1898 diary, OWH papers, HLSL.

"curly . . . angel": OWH to CC, 12/9/1896; OWH papers, HLSL.

325–26 I am here . . . "lawful lady": OWH to CC, 9/5/1898; OWH papers, HLSL.
326 "My life . . . repudiate": OWH to CC, 10/7/1898; OWH papers, HLSL.

"by aid . . . my love": OWH to CC, 9/8/1898; OWH papers, HLSL.

326–27 "devoutly . . . not there": OWH to CC, 9/10/1898, 9/11/1898; OWH papers, HLSL.

327 "before reaching . . . about you": OWH to CC, 9/16/1898; OWH papers, HLSL.

She was obviously . . . mistress: Monagan, The Great, 72.

"impossible . . . still the same": OWH to CC, 5/19/1899; OWH papers, HLSL.

328 "revolting . . . the past": OWH, "Path," 469.
328–29 Shortly after 10:30 . . . in Massachusetts: Commonwealth v. Cleary, 176–77. OWH, "Law in Science," 453.

330 "Judges . . . the other": OWH, "Law in Science," 455, 460.

In advising . . . "your hands": OWH to P.E. Mason, 3/1/1899; Schimmel collection, Columbia University.

In the summer . . . "early residence": BG, 8/2/1899, 2. BH, 7/27/1899, 2. Berkshire Eagle, 9/12/1899; OWH papers, HLSL.

The succession . . . "the show": OWH to CC, 5/19/1899; OWH papers, HLSL.

Chief Justice . . . before: BDA, 7/17/1899, 1.

331 firing . . . wine: MDH, "Letters," 424.
331–32 In September . . . must stand: Plant v. Wood, 495 ff.
332 "no illusions . . . their fellows": Plant v. Wood, 505. Vegelahn v. Guntner, 108.

332–33 The last . . . "wishes of the bar": BH, 3/6/01, 3. BG, 3/5/01, 1. 2 Massachusetts LQ 425–26 (5/17/01). OWH to Horace Gray, 2/20/10, FF papers, LC. Alfred R. Hussey to MDH, n.d.; OWH papers, HLSL.

333 he sailed . . . "banished": OWH, 1901 diary; OWH to NG, 7/15/01; OWH papers, HLSL.

He had kept . . . reunion: Henry James to OWH, 11/13/1891; OWH to Henry James, 12/24/1900; OWH, 1901 diary; OWH papers, HLSL.

Holmes on his . . . life: Wilson, Patriotic, 757.

333–34 After several . . . routine: OWH to NG, 7/15/01; OWH papers, HLSL.
334 "talk[ed] . . . convince": OWH to CC, 6/3/1897; OWH papers, HLSL.

we judges . . . judge: OWH to CC, 7/15/1897; OWH papers, HLSL.

A thousand . . . supposed: BDA, 3/8/1900, 1.

"to see . . . present": OWH, speech, 12/3/02; OWH papers, HLSL.

335 "no illusions . . . of life": Plant v. Wood, 505.

"whether . . . tails": Bowen, Catherine Drinker, Yankee, 343.

Part VII: THE WASHINGTON YEARS

Chapter 16: Appointment

339   the question . . . resign: 298 Mass. 575, 594–95 (1937).

340   speculation . . . Hemenway: ibid., 595. 36 *ALR* 238 (4/02).

For some . . . court: Richard Olney to OWH, 5/3/02; OWH papers, HLSL.

the deterioration . . . resign: Horace Gray to TR, 7/9/02; TR papers, LC.

I hear . . . decide: HCL to TR, 6/5/02; TR papers, LC.

The eighteen-year-old . . . morality: Garraty, *Henry,* 78 ff.

"dislike[d] . . . thoroughly": HCL, Journal, 2/14/1876; HCL papers, MHS.

340–41   Lodge—unlike . . . personally: Garraty, *Henry,* 83 ff.

341   former history . . . severely: Pringle, *TR,* 36–37.

"I saw him . . . lived": OWH to HJL, 11/29/24; OWH papers, HLSL.

342   Holmes had in fact . . . College: HCL, *Early,* 178.

the two . . . together: MDH, *Proving,* 274.

It was rumored . . . them off: *Philadelphia Times,* unpaged clipping, 8/15/02; OWH papers, HLSL.

The incident . . . otherwise: Garraty, *Henry,* 80–85. OWH to HCL, 11/29/24; OWH papers, HLSL.

*Holmes . . . of state: Garraty, *Henry,* 82.

342–43   He called on . . . next best: Garraty, *Henry,* 294–95. HCL to TR, 7/7/02; TR papers, LC.

343   "most eminently . . . mistake": Eben S. Draper to George F. Hoar, 2/28/02; Hoar papers, MHS.

Lodge replied . . . Holmes: HCL to Eben S. Draper, 3/3/02; HCL papers, MHS.

There is no . . . position: Eben S. Draper to HCL, 3/7/02; HCL papers, MHS.

perfectly . . . state: Eben S. Draper to HCL, 6/13/02; HCL papers, MHS.

344   Roosevelt seriously . . . him: TR to HCL, 8/15/02; TR papers, LC.

It would be . . . "promotion": HCL to TR, 7/7/02; TR papers, LC.

"in entire . . . views": TR to HCL, 7/10/02; TR papers, LC.

When the news . . . contemplate: Pringle, *TR,* 237.

345   "incumbent . . . hard": TR to Philander C. Knox, 11/10/04; Knox papers, LC.

Physiologically . . . Diana: Longworth, *Crowded,* 65.

He was to call . . . being: Pringle, *TR,* 208.

"They had . . . roughshod": Wister, *Roosevelt,* 211.

"as difficult . . . be": Cowles, *Letters,* 252.

"More . . . nation": TR to Philander C. Knox, 11/10/04; Knox papers, LC.

346   "strong point . . . earnestly believe": TR to HCL, 7/10/02; TR papers, LC.

Many people . . . desirable: Swindler, *Court,* i, 86.

347   How . . . "standing": TR to HCL, 7/10/02; TR papers, LC.

Hadn't he . . . United States: 178 Mass. 619 (1901).

"unworthy . . . did": TR to HCL, 7/10/02; TR papers, HCL.

At one . . . of life: HCL, *An Address,* 22.

if American . . . Marshall: 178 Mass. 619, 627 (1901).

347–48   While Roosevelt . . . immediately: TR to HCL, 7/10/02; TR papers, LC.
348   Lodge agreed . . . Oyster Bay: HCL to TR, 7/19/02; TR papers, LC.
Lodge . . . "through": HCL to TR, 7/26/01; TR papers, LC.
Richard Olney . . . capital: Richard Olney to OWH, 5/31/02; OWH papers, HLSL.
tried to relax: OWH to Georgina Pollock, 7/31/02; OWH papers, HLSL.
Horace Gray . . . president: Horace Gray to OWH, 7/24/02; Fuller papers, Chicago Historical Society.
He rode . . . "torture": OWH to Georgina Pollock, 7/31/02; OWH papers, HLSL.
dabbled . . . father: OWH to Owen Wister, 5/8/02; OWH to Houghton Mifflin, 7/n.d./02; OWH papers, HLSL.
348–49   He journeyed . . . poet: OWH to Georgina Pollock, 7/31/02; OWH papers, HLSL.
349   "agreeably" . . . Civil War: OWH to NG, 8/17/02; OWH papers, HLSL.
"entirely" . . . views: TR to HCL, 7/25/02; TR papers, LC.
"regard" . . . time being: OWH to FP, 9/6/02; OWH to HCL, 7/25/02; OWH papers, HLSL.
July . . . Judgeship: OWH, BB, 140.
Hoar had successfully . . . "loving me": OWH to HJL, 4/5/25; OWH papers, HLSL.
"great satisfaction": Welch, "Opponents," 203.
349–50   Although Hoar . . . cost: Garraty, Henry, 53. Welch, "Opponents," 183.
350   informed . . . July: TR to George F. Hoar, 7/25/02; TR papers, LC.
"absolute" . . . rules: George F. Hoar to TR, 7/28/02; TR papers, LC.
"I hope . . . anyway": TR to HCL, 7/29/02; TR papers, LC.
350–51   his accomplishments . . . "able judge": George F. Hoar to HCL, 7/29/02; OWH papers, HLSL.
351   explaining . . . submit it: TR to George F. Hoar, 7/30/02; TR papers, LC.
"everything . . . possible": George F. Hoar to HCL, 8/15/02; OWH papers, HLSL.
"I dare . . . any more": George F. Hoar to HCL, 8/7/02; OWH papers, HLSL.
Roosevelt . . . Senate: NYT, 8/12/02, 1. TR to OWH, 8/19/02; TR papers, LC.
Holmes reacted . . . court: Beringause, Brooks, 204, 247–48.
351–52   newspaper . . . "interviewed": BG, 8/12/02, 2. NYT, 8/12/02, 1. BET, 8/12/02, 1. OWH to FP, 8/13/02; OWH papers, HLSL.
352   While . . . Experience: OWH to WJ, 7/8/02; OWH papers, HLSL.
Some day . . . forget: OWH to WJ, 8/15/02; OWH papers, HLSL.
"sadness" . . . feeling: OWH to NG, 8/17/02; OWH papers, HLSL.
Francis . . . accept: Biddle, Mr., 101.
Thomas . . . account: Corcoran, Rendezvous, 2.
352–53   Felix . . . "Boston": FF to Francis Biddle, 6/25/43; FF papers, LC.
353   Fanny . . . September: FDH to Annie H. Thwing, 8/12/02; Thwing papers, MHS.
"perhaps . . . nomination": FDH to Annie H. Thwing, 9/29/02; Thwing papers, MHS.
It was whispered . . . case: Follansbee, "Oliver", 10.

"more interesting . . . unions": 25 *Literary Digest* 214 (8/23/02).

"workingmen . . . rights": 54 *Independent,* 8/28/02, 205.

"The quality . . . laborer": *World,* 8/12/02, 8.

"Justice . . . organization": *BET,* 8/12/02, 8.

354   "extremely . . . improbable": *NYT,* 8/13/02, 8.

"they don't . . . lot of them": OWH to FP, n.d./23/02; OWH papers, HLSL.

"roomy . . . afterward": *World,* 8/17/02, 4.

"in natural . . . welcome": Melville W. Fuller to OWH, 8/12/02; Fuller papers, Chicago Historical Society.

"Holmes will . . . country": John M. Harlan to Melville W. Fuller, 8/18/02; Fuller papers, LC.

355   Holmes wanted no . . . confirmed him: OWH to HCL, 8/19/02, 8/23/02; OWH papers, HLSL.

Both Lodge . . . course: HCL to OWH, 8/18/02; OWH papers, HLSL. TR to OWH, 8/21/02; HCL to TR, 8/20/02; TR papers, LC.

"burning . . . to be": OWH to E.A. Curtis, 10/15/02; OWH papers, HLSL.

"mind . . . certain": OWH to NG, 10/10/02; OWH papers, HLSL.

he had unloaded . . . before: *Pittsfield Evening Journal,* 1/19/1895, unpaged clipping; OWH papers, HLSL.

"purged . . . flower": OWH to Clara Stevens, 10/17/02; OWH papers, HLSL.

"a fish" . . . confirmed his appointment: Belknap, "Some," 5. HCL to TR, 8/20/02; TR, *Selections,* i, 527. OWH to Melville W. Fuller, 10/14/02; Fuller papers, Chicago Historical Society.

In late . . . diverted him: *Chicago Record-Herald,* 10/21/02, 9. *Chicago Tribune,* 10/21/02, 3. *NYT,* 10/21/02, 9.

355–56   On December . . . it: *NYT,* 12/5/02, 5.

356   Senator . . . very day: telegram, George F. Hoar to OWH, 12/4/02; OWH papers, HLSL.

The night . . . farewell: *BET,* 12/4/02, 6.

To have . . . charge: OWH, speech, 12/3/02; FF papers, LC.

"There is . . . court": King, *Melville,* 287.

Three days . . . justice: Derby, "Recollections," 3.

Chapter 17: Settling In

357   On December 8 . . . Capitol: *WP,* 12/9/02, 10. *BG,* 12/9/02, 11. *World,* 12/17/02, 4.

Hardly anyone . . . that state: Butler, *Century,* 65–66.

358   "the best . . . machine": LDB to FF, conversations; FF papers, LC.

358–59   Biographical details are taken from Friedman and Israel, *The Justices; DAB;* Bickel, *The Judiciary;* Swindler, *Court.*

359   "frequently . . . colleagues": McDevitt, *Joseph,* 202.

360   Envious . . . comments: Bickel, *The Judiciary,* 238–42. OWH to FP, 2/6/26; OWH papers, HLSL.

no scholars . . . speculations: OWH to PAS, 4/1/11; OWH to CM, 5/16/12; OWH papers, HLSL.

"the most obscure . . . Justice": Friedman and Israel, *The Justices,* ii, 1479.

361   It was rumored . . . Hayes: Gresham, *Life,* ii, 459.

361–63   Court history is taken from Warren, Charles, *The Supreme*. National Geographic Society, *Equal*. Baker, Liva, *Felix*. Beck, *May*.

363   "kitchen-knives . . . stings": CEH, Autobiographical, 227; CEH papers, LC.
Holmes . . . sleep: Pusey, *Charles*, i, 285.
"my only . . . thoughts": OWH to LE, 4/7/05; OWH papers, HLSL.
"First . . . that night": 349 U.S. xliv (1954).

364   "held up . . . voting": FF to Charles Whittaker, 10/24/57; FF papers, LC.
"Why, Mr. . . . seasons": Butler, *Century*, 90.
"bored . . . me once": OWH to Alice S. Green, 12/8/14; FF papers, LC.
"Butler . . . law": Butler, *Century*, 18.

365   "cockfight": OWH to FP, 2/24/23; OWH papers, HLSL.
The good . . . cockfight: FF, *Of Law and Men*, 118.
Holmes . . . wife's death: Willard King to MDH, 4/n.d./49; MDH papers, HLSL.
"business . . . fingers' ends": OWH to Alice S. Green, 2/7/09; FF papers, LC.
"perfectly . . . laugh": OWH to W.L. Putnam, 7/7/10; OWH papers, HLSL.
"embarrass . . . much": FF, *Of Law and Men*, 137.
"had a tiny . . . now": OWH to FF, 10/24/20; OWH papers, HLSL.

368   The break . . . "real": FDH to Annie H. Thwing, 2/18/03; Thwing papers, MHS.
They intended . . . "of life": OWH to EJH, Jr., 12/26/02; OWH papers, HLSL.
"sit in the Bow . . . night": FDH to Annie H. Thwing, 2/18/03; Thwing papers, MHS.
"touch . . . shudder": OWH to EJH, Jr., 11/16/04; OWH papers, HLSL.
"a place . . . farewells": Meyer, Agnes E., diary, 5/18/1920; Meyer papers, LC.
Fanny had destroyed . . . embroideries: MDH, *Proving*, 255.
"closed . . . safe": OWH to John G. Palfrey, 12/17/02; OWH papers, HLSL.

369   "Chief . . . Justice"?: OWH to Melville W. Fuller, 12/28/02; OWH papers, HLSL.
the mud . . . head: OWH, speech, 12/3/02; OWH papers, HLSL.
Descriptions of Washington are taken from Bryce, *Nation's;* Maude Parker Child, "Capital"; Constance McLaughlin Green, *Washington;* Low, "Society" and "Washington."

369–70   Southerners . . . arrived: Pringle, *TR*, 248–50.

370   Not long . . . present: OWH to E.A. Curtis, 1/25/03; OWH papers, HLSL.
1947 . . . Gallery: *NYT*, 6/3/47, 27.
pumped . . . meeting: OWH to ES, 1/1/09; OWH papers, HLSL.
"suspect . . .'that' ": OWH to NG, 5/8/10; OWH papers, HLSL.
Every Mark . . . remarks: OWH to E.A. Curtis, 12/21/02; OWH papers, HLSL.
"delightful": OWH to E.A. Curtis, 1/12/03; OWH papers, HLSL.
"Gracious . . . demi-princess": OWH to NG, 2/8/04; OWH papers, HLSL.
"to make . . . of most": OWH to NG, 3/21/04; OWH papers, HLSL.
the way . . . one cares: OWH to Alice S. Green, 11/9/13; FF papers, LC.
"seeing . . . laugh": OWH to E.A. Curtis, 12/21/02; OWH papers, HLSL.

371   "relief . . . law": OWH to JTM, 2/8/07; OWH papers, HLSL.

"almost . . . task": OWH to Alice S. Green, 2/10/05; FF papers, LC.

"bumbling . . . another": FDH to Annie H. Thwing, 12/17/02; Thwing papers, MHS.

The Holmeses . . . "happens": HCL to JTM, 2/28/03; Morse papers, MHS. OWH to Alice S. Green, 2/6/10; FF papers, LC. OWH to NG, 2/15/03; OWH papers, HLSL.

the Holmeses gave . . . arrival: OWH to NG, 1/4/03; OWH papers, HLSL.

two extra places: Einstein, *Diplomat,* 108.

"so perfect . . . manners": Ely, Recollections, 7.

"terror": OWH to E.A. Curtis, 2/7/03; OWH papers, HLSL.

Some justices . . . placed: Meyer, Agnes E., diary, 1/6/18; Meyer papers, LC.

One's . . . country: OWH to E.A. Curtis, 2/7/03; OWH papers, HLSL.

372   "getting on well": FDH to Annie H. Thwing, 12/25/02; Thwing papers, MHS.

"ridiculous bore": OWH to NG, 2/15/03; OWH papers, HLSL.

"in future . . . that": OWH to Melville W. Fuller, 5/25/10; FF papers, LC.

"comfortable enough" . . . returning: FDH to Annie H. Thwing, 2/18/03; Thwing papers, MHS.

After deciding . . . home: OWH to NG, 2/15/03; OWH papers, HLSL.

Holmes sold . . . Street: OWH to EJH, Jr., 2/8/03, 2/12/03, 2/27/03; OWH papers, HLSL.

"every kind . . . town": OWH to NG, 12/25/03; OWH papers, HLSL.

The four . . . pieces: appraisal of 1720 I Street, 1935; OWH to Clara Stevens, 5/12/03; OWH papers, HLSL.

Callers . . . butcher's wax: Griswold, "Justices," 2.

"more at . . . mine": OWH to NG, 4/12/03; OWH papers, HLSL.

373   *"fecundissimus"*: OWH to LE, 11/23/03; OWH papers, HLSL.

"that belonged . . . great-granddaddies": OWH to LE, 11/23/03; OWH papers, HLSL.

Sunlight . . . "upon it": OWH to NG, 11/1/03; OWH papers, HLSL.

Only Fanny's . . . "body": Derby, "Recollections," 346–47.

"You will . . . novels": "Meeting of Holmes's"; OWH papers, HLSL.

Evenings . . . solitaire: OWH to CM, 4/9/08; OWH papers, HLSL.

"50 . . . doing": Wister, *Roosevelt,* 131.

"at home . . . leather": OWH, Sr., *Works,* i, 20–23.

373–74   At the end . . . Farms: Estate . . . Washington; Estate . . . Beverly Farms; LCRB.

374   The bulk . . . feet: LCRB.

"family shrine . . . *alteri*": OWH to LE, 11/23/03; OWH papers, HLSL.

"yard of product": OWH to NG, 10/19/05; OWH papers, HLSL.

"to have . . . discovered": OWH to FP, 11/5/23; OWH papers, HLSL.

He owned . . . editions: LCRB.

"Lord . . . (to me)": OWH to LE, 2/10/08; OWH papers, HLSL.

375   to familiarize . . . acquainted: OWH to FP, 4/15/1892; OWH papers, HLSL.

he believed . . . books read: Sutherland, Recollections, 14.

"rip[ped] . . . boy": OWH to NG, 9/17/24; OWH papers, HLSL.

D.H. . . . "about": interview with H. Chapman Rose. OWH to FF, 10/23/31; OWH papers, HLSL.

William . . . "eternal": Wister, *Roosevelt,* 132.

"great author . . . like him": Hale, Richard W., *Some,* 15.

"books . . . life": OWH to HJL, 5/8/18; OWH papers, HLSL.

"everywhere . . . soul": OWH to HJL, 8/12/23; OWH papers, HLSL.

Perhaps . . . taste: OWH to NG, 8/12/1897; OWH papers, HLSL.

Holmes . . . offered him: Belknap, "Some," 2–3.

376   *"can't help . . . worth"*: OWH to FP, 6/23/06; OWH papers, HLSL.

He cultivated . . . "slate": OWH to HJL, 3/27/23; OWH to LE, 3/31/32 and 12/1/17; OWH to NG, 12/10/19; OWH papers, HLSL. LCRB. Tittle, "Glimpses," 183.

To his . . . "today": OWH to FP, 12/27/17; OWH to LE, 12/1/17; OWH papers, HLSL.

"This . . . concur": Biddle, *Mr.,* 153.

376–77   "The birds . . . remember": OWH to CM, 6/7/20; OWH papers, HLSL.

Chapter 18: Holmes v. Roosevelt

378   demi-gods . . . swiftness: OWH to John G. Palfrey, 12/27/02; OWH papers, HLSL.

379   He never . . . Supreme Court: FF, *Of Law and Life,* 84.

Yes . . . these: OWH to FP, 12/28/02; OWH papers, HLSL.

379–80   "shudder . . . people": OWH to NG, 5/3/03; OWH papers, HLSL.

380   The variety . . . previous work: OWH to E.A. Curtis, 12/23/03; OWH to John H. Wigmore, 5/14/04; OWH papers, HLSL.

"There is . . . job": *NYT,* 10/5/86, iv, 2.

Benjamin . . . federal court: FF, *Of Law and Life,* 85.

"pretty . . . work": OWH to E.A. Curtis, 2/25/04; OWH papers, HLSL.

confidence . . . share: OWH to NG, 1/4/03; OWH papers, HLSL.

"as if . . . life": OWH to PAS, 11/19/09; OWH papers, HLSL.

"where . . . facts": Hale, Richard W., *Some,* 15.

"agreeable . . . aloud": OWH to Clara Stevens, 5/10/08; OWH papers, HLSL.

"free . . . spontaneity": OWH to J.C.H. Wu, 10/7/23; OWH papers, HLSL.

He was . . . "wills": WHT to Horace Taft, 10/21/27; WHT papers, LC.

"so that" . . . feeling: OWH to Albert J. Beveridge, 7/11/26; OWH papers, HLSL.

"sake . . . word": Leland B. Durer to FF, 2/16/38; OWH papers, HLSL.

"seem . . . shoulders": OWH to NG, 5/3/03; OWH papers, HLSL.

381   lawyers . . . brevity: CEH, Autobiographical, 224; CEH papers, LC.

"think . . . there": Duffus, "At Ninety," 16.

"first . . . wrong": OWH, *TCL,* 41.

"deep-seated . . . interfere": *Otis* v. *Parker,* 609 ff.

"I hope . . . sinners": Mr. Justice Holmes's opinions, O.T. 1902; OWH papers, HLSL.

382   The question . . . the judge: *Bleistein* v. *Donaldson Lithographing Co.,* 249–52.

The Court . . . pneumonia: OWH to E.A. Curtis, 3/3/03; OWH papers, HLSL.

382–83   He developed . . . disposition of a case: [Hiss], "Observations"; Gilmore papers, HLSL.

383   "fasting and prayer": OWH to HJL, 11/5/23; OWH papers, HLSL.

Holmes's votes . . . immediately: [Hiss], "Observations," 1–2; Gilmore papers, HLSL. Derby, "Recollections," 347–48. Wales, "Personal," 396.

"loom[ed] . . . immensity": OWH to NG, 6/5/27; OWH papers, HLSL.

it turned . . . skin: OWH to HJL, 1/7/24; OWH papers, HLSL.

"delirium": OWH to Margaret Clifford, 4/27/27; OWH papers, HLSL.

"miserable . . . done": CEH, Autobiographical, 223; CEH papers, LC.

"by . . . physically": OWH to Clara Stevens, 11/18/06; OWH papers, HLSL.

By Tuesday . . . tradition: OWH to Margaret Clifford, 4/27/27; OWH papers, HLSL.

He seldom . . . offered: [Hiss], "Observations"; Gilmore papers, HLSL.

"men . . . thought: OWH, speech, 1/17/1886; OWH papers, HLSL.

Why . . . me?: OWH to Melville W. Fuller, 2/9/09, 2/5/09; Fuller papers, LC.

384   "vice . . . him": FF-LDB Conversations; FF papers, LC.

"put . . . clouds": OWH to ES, 4/24/09; OWH papers, HLSL.

Shortly . . . "dear": Woollcott, "The Second," 50–51.

385   his customary . . . marshal: Harlan, Some Memories, 97–102.

A study . . . questions: Harris, *Quest,* 59.

386   "questions . . . character": *Brownfield* v. *South Carolina,* 429.

387   "Whenever . . . States": *Rogers* v. *Alabama,* 231.

*Ignorance . . . selection: Harris, *Quest,* 93–95, 110 ff.

387–88   "impossible . . . political rights": *Giles* v. *Harris,* 482 ff.

388   "actual . . . wrong": OWH, TCL, 41.

"little . . . form": *Giles* v. *Harris,* 487–88.

Brewer . . . be done: *Giles* v. *Harris,* 488 ff.

"inevitable . . . formula": OWH to Clara Stevens, 5/2/03; OWH papers, HLSL.

Holmes always claimed . . . opinions: Edward D. White to William R. Day, 3/9/16; Day papers, LC.

"representing . . . decision": OWH to Clara Stevens, 5/2/03; OWH papers, HLSL.

389   "demigods . . . swiftness": OWH to John G. Palfrey, 12/27/02; OWH papers, HLSL.

"Lord . . . dreamed": OWH to NG, 12/25/03; OWH papers, HLSL.

"profoundly . . . chance": OWH to Clara Stevens, 1/10/03; OWH papers, HLSL.

"flabby . . . hygiene": OWH to E.A. Curtis, 5/3/03; OWH papers, HLSL.

"lark" . . . cared to: OWH to NG, 5/3/03; OWH papers, HLSL.

"filled . . . lengths": OWH to NG, 8/14/03; OWH papers, HLSL.

He visited . . . Rye: Edel, Henry, v, 171. Henry James to OWH, 7/18/03, 7/27/03; OWH papers, HLSL.

the Castletowns . . . "or book": OWH to NG, 8/14/03, 9/2/03; OWH papers, HLSL.

389–90   Castletowns introduced . . . correspondence: PAS to OWH, 3/2/04; OWH papers, HLSL. Heuser, *Canon*, 185 ff.

390   "love[d]" . . . ideals: OWH to PAS, 2/n.d./04; OWH papers, HLSL.
          "interpretation . . . esteem": PAS to OWH, 3/2/04; OWH papers, HLSL.
          Roosevelt . . . time: TR to Arthur Lee, 12/7/03; TR papers, LC. Bailey, "Theodore," 127. Foster, *Diplomatic*, i, 198–99.
          "privately" . . . discussions: TR to OWH, 7/25/03; OWH papers, HLSL.
          "exactly . . . decision": TR to OWH, 10/20/03; OWH papers, HLSL.
          "extremely . . . history": OWH to TR, 10/21/03; TR papers, LC.
          Holmes sent . . . in: OWH to TR, 3/26/05, 10/24/03; TR papers, LC.
          best friends . . . "from him": OWH to ES, 12/11/08; OWH papers, HLSL.

390–91   "with" . . . Lodges: OWH to E.A. Curtis, 11/12/04, 2/7/03; OWH papers, HLSL.

391   "always . . . sayings": OWH to ES, 12/11/08; OWH papers, HLSL.
          "great-hearted": OWH to NG, 3/21/04; OWH papers, HLSL.
          "picturesqueness . . . him": OWH to Kentaro Kaneko, 6/22/28; OWH papers, HLSL.
          politically unscrupulous: OWH to FP, 2/9/21; OWH papers, HLSL.
          "it was . . . wanted": OWH to LE, 11/25/12; OWH papers, LC.

392   "The President . . . thought": Pringle, *TR*, 259.

393   "in the interests . . . people": TR, *Autobiography*, 443.

393–94   "great corporations . . . whole": TR, *Message*, xiv.

394   Early in 1902 . . . with it: Bishop, *Theodore*, 182. 5 *DAB* 478 ff.
          While . . . city: Wister, *Roosevelt*, 208–09.
          When on . . . sharply: Pringle, *Theodore*, 255. WP, 2/20/02, 3. Bishop, *Theodore*, 182–83.
          J.P. . . . "salary": Winkelman, *John*, 209.
          "an unknown . . . ended": Bishop, *Theodore*, 183.
          After all . . . House: Pringle, *Theodore*, 254.

394–95   If his company . . . "stop it": Bishop, *Theodore*, 184.

395   "cheerfully . . . with them": Philander C. Knox to John B. McPherson, 10/22/02; Knox papers, LC.
          He was the last . . . Holmes's: Sullivan, *Our*, iv, 340.
          "Christ, what dignity!": Biddle, *Mr.*, 112.
          Originally . . . elevated: Lowry, "The Men," 634.
          Chief . . . feet: King, *Melville*, 137.
          Henry . . . ailment: Henry Brown to Charles Kent, 12/7/03; Burton Historical Collection, Detroit Public Library. Winkelman, *John*, 213.

396   Richard Olney . . . Act: Swindler, *Court*, i, 98.
          Solicitor . . . government: Keller, *In Defense*, 172–173. Pringle, *Life and Times*, 1013–14. J.M. Beck to WHT, 5/16/22; WHT papers, LC.
          Johnson really . . . railroads: Winkelman, *John*, 210.

396–97   The courtroom . . . opened: NYT, 12/15/03, 1. WP, 12/15/03, 1. WS, 12/15/03, 1. Winkelman, *John*, 213.

397   He began . . . unconstitutional: NYT, 12/15/03, 2. Winkelman, *John*, 218–19.
          Attorney . . . hands: NYT, 12/16/03, 5.

397–98   gnawing . . . attention: Umbreit, *Our*, 385. Essary, "Human," 501–02.

398   Although . . . 5 to 4: NYT, 3/15/04, 1. WP, 3/15/04, 1.

"premature New Dealer": Friedman and Israel, *Justices,* ii, 1292.

398–99 "We must . . . Constitution": Harlan, John M., speech, 12/23/07, Harlan papers, LC.

399 "no reference . . . commerce": *Northern Securities* v. *United States,* 331.

"it is the history . . . the law": ibid., 351.

"like a vise . . . objects": Acheson, *Morning,* 65.

To Holmes . . . to deal: Pusey, *Charles,* 277; Swindler, *Court,* i, 34.

"That won't . . . away": FF, *Of Law and Men,* 118.

400 "simple . . . courage": OWH to E.A. Curtis, 3/3/03; OWH papers, HLSL.

one can say . . . else: OWH to HJL, 8/16/24; OWH papers, HLSL.

an appeal . . . betrayed: CEH, *Supreme,* 68.

worry . . . interest: OWH to Charles Owen, 2/5/12; OWH papers, HLSL.

401 "shut up": OWH to Alice S. Green, 2/6/10; FF papers, LC.

He sometimes . . . deliver it: *United States* v. *Vanderweide,* No. 642; Mr. Justice Holmes's Opinions, O.T. 1908; OWH papers, HLSL.

"I don't . . . dissenter": Pollard, "Opinions," 5.

"feelings . . . community": OWH, *TCL,* 41.

"painful . . . expecting": OWH to John G. Palfrey, 4/1/04; OWH papers, HLSL.

"no effect . . . impersonally": OWH to PAS, 9/6/04; OWH papers, HLSL.

he may . . . independence: Holmes, *Mind,* 219.

402 "government . . . events": OWH to Franklin Ford, 2/8/08; OWH papers, HLSL.

"monopolies . . . grounds": OWH to LE, 8/1/08; OWH papers, HLSL.

"humbug . . . striking way": OWH to FP, 4/3/10; OWH papers, HLSL.

"free competition means combination": *Vegelahn* v. *Guntner,* 108.

"growth . . . myself": OWH to NG, 8/30/04; OWH papers, HLSL.

you could . . . knife: Melville W. Fuller to Calista R. Fuller, 3/15/04; OWH papers, HLSL.

"called great . . . law": *Northern Securities* v. *United States,* 400.

"the great . . . combinations": OWH to FP, 8/10/08; OWH papers, HLSL.

402–3 He admired . . . meant: OWH to LE, 6/13/18; OWH papers, HLSL. *Vegelahn* v. *Guntner,* 108.

403 that legislation . . . desires: OWH to LE, 10/28/12; OWH papers, HLSL.

his thinking . . . twenty-five: Biddle, *Mr.,* 86–87.

"drove" . . . economics: OWH to HJL, 5/8/19; OWH papers, HLSL. Biddle, *Mr.,* 86–87.

"anyone . . . knows": OWH to HJL, 10/24/30; OWH papers, HLSL.

"imbecile . . . victorious": OWH to Alice S. Green, 1/10/11; FF papers, LC.

404 Much . . . Congress: *Northern Securities* v. *United States,* 403 ff.

Public . . . confidence: Winkelman, *John,* 220.

405 "return . . . management": WP, 3/15/04, 1.

Knox was besieged . . . printed: Philander C. Knox to OWH, 3/10/04; OWH papers, HLSL. James H. McKenney to OWH, 3/31/04; United States Supreme Court case files, NA.

"blow . . . enterprises": Jessup, *Elihu,* i, 415.

The president . . . decision: WP, 3/25/04, 1.

"care . . . goods": OWH to LE, 4/1/28; OWH papers, HLSL.

"carve . . . than that": Bowen, Catherine Drinker, *Yankee,* 370.

"will never . . . or two": H. Chapman Rose to FF, 7/17/32; FF papers, LC.

"spouting . . . 'wants' ": OWH to LE, 4/1/28; OWH papers, HLSL.

"cool . . . shall see": OWH to E.A. Curtis, 3/8/04; OWH papers, HLSL.

"political . . . way)": OWH to FP, 2/9/21; OWH papers, HLSL.

405–6   When shortly . . . wrong: Pringle, *Theodore,* 262–63.

406   "talked . . . that": OWH to FP, 2/9/21; OWH papers, HLSL.

406–7   Brooks . . . owned: Beringause, *Brooks,* 247.

407   could not . . . assigned: OWH to NG, 3/21/04; OWH papers, HLSL.

Chapter 19: "The Fourteenth Amendment does not enact Mr. Herbert Spencer's Social Statics"

408   "our . . . work": *NYT,* 7/25/86, B6.

"relief . . . of you": OWH to Clara Stevens, 6/14/04; OWH papers, HLSL.

Washingtonians . . . air: Low, "Washington," 770.

Women . . . "Slowly": Warner, "Transferred," 178.

"a good . . . rest": OWH to John H. Wigmore, 12/21/05; OWH papers, HLSL.

"Look at . . . it on!": OWH to E.A. Curtis, 1/24/04; OWH papers, HLSL.

409   "more" . . . dinners: OWH to E.A. Curtis, 12/30/04, 2/7/03; OWH papers, HLSL.

"Mr. . . . young": Monagan, "Enigmatic," 81.

When Mrs. . . . didn't go: Thomas Barbour to MDH, 12/2/45; OWH papers, HLSL.

"running amuck": Pringle, *Theodore,* 352.

In May . . . 1904: Bishop, *Theodore,* 186.

409–10 J.P. . . . $50,000: Pringle, *Theodore,* 354–58.

410   Fifty-two-year-old . . . trust-busting: Friedman and Israel, *Justices,* iii, 1801–02.

"a defendant . . . not do": *Swift* v. *United States,* 377.

"control . . . oppressive": *Swift* v. *United States,* 390.

Holmes . . . were not: *WP,* 1/7/05, 3.

410–11 Three weeks . . . support it: *Swift* v. *United States,* 390 ff.

411   that it . . . believe in: OWH to Franklin Ford, 6/30/12; OWH papers, HLSL.

"favorite author": Irving S. Olds to Catherine Drinker Bowen, 7/31/44; Bowen papers, LC.

component parts . . . such commerce: *Swift* v. *United States,* 396 ff.

411–12 That night . . . "first made": *NYT,* 1/30/05, 1.

414   "unwholesome . . . States": *Slaughter-House Cases,* 62.

Over the next . . . civil rights: Congressional Quarterly, *Guide,* 29.

Citing . . . rates: Warren, Charles, *The Supreme,* iii, 289–321.

"The liberty . . . above mentioned": *Allgeyer* v. *Louisiana,* 589.

416   At the urging . . . studied law: Butler, *Century,* 171.

"denies . . . law": *Lochner* v. *New York,* 48–50.

At the first . . . to Harlan: Butler, *Century,* 170–72.

"in order . . . labor": *Lochner* v. *New York,* 69.

At a later . . . vote: Butler, *Century,* 172.

Peckham owed . . . "shelf": Friedman and Israel, *Justices,* ii, 1694.

417   "emotional . . . damn it": OWH to FF, 3/28/22; OWH papers, HLSL.

"other motives": *Lochner* v. *New York,* 64.

"necessarily . . . the employés": *Lochner* v. *New York,* 53 ff.

418   "get rid . . . bearing it": [OWH], "Gas-Stokers,' " 528.

"agreement . . . in law": *Lochner* v. *New York,* 75.

"chafe . . . mind": OWH to Melville W. Fuller, n.d.; Fuller papers, Chicago Historical Society.

418–19   "which a large . . . our law": *Lochner* v. *New York,* 74 ff.

419   "What I . . . Statics": OWH to Alice S. Green, 7/11/05; FF papers, LC.

420   Henry . . . "success": Edel, *Henry,* v. 274–77. Henry James to OWH, 1/13/05, 1/14/05; OWH to PAS, 4/30/05; OWH papers, HLSL.

Holmes briefly . . . "*à deux*": OWH to LE, 4/7/05, 9/18/05; OWH to PAS, 4/30/05; OWH papers, HLSL. OWH to Alice S. Green, 7/11/05; FF papers, LC.

"admirable" . . . author: OWH to JTM, 8/25/05; OWH papers, HLSL.

420–21   "be much . . . school": OWH to NG, 11/5/05; OWH papers, HLSL.

421   "have . . . spirit": OWH to FF, 12/19/15; OWH papers, HLSL.

"reserved . . . resign": OWH to FF, 1/6/25; OWH papers, HLSL.

Discretion . . . discussion: John Lockwood to Alger Hiss, 6/15/29; OWH papers, HLSL.

The official . . . annually: Wales, "Some Aspects," 397. MDH, "Mr. Justice." Irving S. Olds to Catherine Drinker Bowen, 7/31/44; Bowen papers, LC.

You see . . . is done: Corcoran, Rendezvous, 7.

421–22   "jaw . . . Street": Acheson, *Morning,* 63.

422   By early . . . Court: *NYT,* 3/17/06, 7.

Roosevelt's . . . wishes: Pringle, *Life and Times,* 238 ff. Heffron, "Theodore," 551.

"Nothing . . . right": TR to HCL, 9/4/06; TR, *Selections,* ii, 228.

"why . . . secession": HCL to TR, 9/10/06; TR, *Selections,* ii, 229.

"felt . . . time": OWH, *TCL,* 1.

422–23   rationale . . . "source": *Georgia* v. *Tennessee Copper Co.,* 237–38.

423   "like a . . . problems": OWH to Clara Stevens, 4/28/07; OWH papers, HLSL.

"without . . . more": OWH to NG, 6/1/07; OWH papers, HLSL.

he did not . . . him: OWH to LE, 8/24/07; OWH papers, HLSL.

Once he . . . September 3: OWH, 1907 diary; OWH to CM, 7/17/07; OWH to LE, 8/24/07; OWH papers, HLSL.

"old . . . socket": OWH to NG, 10/20/07; OWH papers, HLSL.

424   Holmes . . . be upheld: *Employers' Liability Act Cases,* 541.

"a body . . . in": OWH to NG, 5/8/10; OWH papers, HLSL.

"most . . . say so": OWH to LE, 2/10/08; OWH papers, HLSL.

425   "within . . . free land": *Adair* v. *United States,* 174–75.

425–26   "I confess . . . at large": *Adair* v. *United States,* 191–92.

426   "few . . . grows": *Hudson County Water Co.* v. *McCarter,* 356.

That spring . . . house: OWH to LDB, 3/13/08; OWH papers, HLSL.

426–27   Brandeis brought . . . social workers: Baker, Leonard, *Brandeis,* 9–16.

427   "copious collection . . . injurious": *Muller* v. *Oregon*, 421.

"When I . . . retire": Ely, Recollections, 1.

Fanny appears . . . at home: FDH to OWH, 5/11/08; OWH to Clara Stevens, 5/10/08; OWH papers, HLSL.

427–28   Fanny's . . . Washington: OWH to ES, 8/22/08; OWH to EJH, Jr., 2/29/08; OWH to PAS, 8/26/08; OWH to JTM, 2/8/07; OWH papers, HLSL.

428   "confused" . . . five more: OWH to ES, 8/22/08; OWH papers, HLSL.

"I am . . . plutocracy": NYT, 3/20/08, 5.

Before . . . "finished": OWH to NG, 5/30/08; OWH papers, HLSL.

Holmes would . . . a change: OWH to FP, 2/21/09; OWH papers, HLSL.

"sneered . . . overworked": OWH to HJL, 9/15/16; OWH papers, HLSL.

429   "always . . . power": OWH to FP, 4/23/10; OWH papers, HLSL.

limited to enforcing . . . future: *Harriman* v. *Interstate Commerce Commission*, 418, 421.

"blood . . . boil": OWH to HJL, 9/15/16; OWH papers, HLSL.

Chapter 20: The Court Rejuvenated

430   "windswept platform": OWH to FP, 2/21/09; OWH papers, HLSL.

Shortly . . . Drive: NYT, 4/1/09, 2.

Chief . . . "discouraging": WHT to Horace H. Lurton, 5/22/09; WHT papers, LC.

"a good . . . grow": OWH to Clara Stevens, 3/6/09; OWH papers, HLSL.

430–31   Fanny . . . answered: MDH, memorandum, 8/10/64; OWH papers, HLSL.

431   "The only . . . act?": OWH, Review of *The Law Magazine*, 724.

"prediction . . . court": OWH, "Path," 458.

The case . . . figure: WP, 12/5/06, 1, 2; 5/25/09, 1. NYT, 12/6/06, 2; 12/5/06, 1. *Chattanooga Times*, 12/5/06, 1; 12/6/06, 3.

431–32   The day . . . mob: King, *Melville*, 324.

432   Peckham . . . strong: Mr. Justice Holmes's Opinions, O.T. 1906; OWH papers, HLSL.

"as a matter . . . or not": *United States* v. *Shipp* (1906), 565–67.

Holmes was . . . wrote it: OWH to Melville W. Fuller, 5/15/09; OWH papers, HLSL. King, *Melville*, 323–27.

"not admit . . . such": *United States* v. *Shipp*, 214 U.S. 386, 425 (1909).

"sore" . . . imprisonment: OWH to Melville W. Fuller, 5/13/09; OWH papers, HLSL.

After giving . . . defendants: *United States.* v. *Shipp*, 215 U.S. 580, 582 (1909).

432–33   The early . . . could help: *The Times of London*, 6/24/09, 9. OWH to C.K. Poe, misdated, 6/4/09; OWH to John H. Wigmore, 8/18/09; OWH to PAS, 9/13/09; OWH to Kentaro Kaneko, 8/2/09; OWH papers, HLSL.

433   The Pollocks . . . "work": OWH to CM, 8/15/09; OWH papers, HLSL.

When the Court . . . opinions: NYT, 10/12/09, 6; 10/21/09, 1.

"sunk . . . depression": HCL to TR, 10/20/09; TR, *Selections*, ii, 351.

Peckham . . . funeral: NYT, 10/25/09, 1; 10/26/09, 4. OWH to ES, 11/7/09; OWH papers, HLSL.

433–34   Lurton . . . federal power: 237 U.S. v (1915). Friedman and Israel, *Justices*, iii, 1847 ff. *Outlook*, 1/1/10, 2–3.

434   The seventy-three-year-old . . . "had gone": *NYT*, 3/29/10, 1. OWH to
       FF, 4/1/10; OWH papers, HLSL.
       "the most . . . life": *NYT*, 1/20/35, vi, 6.

434–35 As a young . . . Supreme Court: Pusey, *Charles*, vol. 1. Friedman and
       Israel, *Justices*, iii, 1893 ff.

435   "very . . . the law": OWH to CM, 5/12/08; OWH papers, HLSL. OWH
       to Alice S. Green, 4/26/10; FF papers, LC.
       During . . . dissents: Friedman and Israel, *Justices*, iii, 1897.
       "not been . . . interest": OWH to FP, 4/23/10; OWH papers, HLSL.

435–36 At April's . . . pending: OWH to Alice S. Green, 4/26/10; FF papers, LC.

436   Fanny had . . . "possibilities": OWH to CM, 6/7/10; OWH papers, HLSL.
       They went . . . "themselves": OWH to CM, 6/30/10; OWH papers, HLSL.
       On July 4 . . . Maine: *NYT*, 7/5/10, 1.
       "less rapid . . . Bench": OWH to W.L. Putnam, 7/12/10; OWH to CM,
       7/14/10; OWH papers, HLSL.
       William James . . . Hampshire: *DAB*, v, 600.
       The affectionate . . . communication: OWH to FP, 9/1/10; OWH papers,
       HLSL.
       "root . . . past": OWH to Alice S. Green, 9/4/10; FF papers, LC.
       The funeral . . . Chapel: Edel, *Henry*, v, 451.
       "deeply . . . distingue": OWH to CM, 8/31/10; OWH papers, HLSL.

436–37 "seemed . . . interests": OWH to Alice S. Green, 9/4/10; FF papers, LC.

437   A few weeks . . . buried: OWH to FP, 9/24/10; OWH papers, HLSL.
       "slowly dying . . . accustomed to": OWH to Alice S. Green, 9/4/10; FF
       papers, HLSL. OWH to ES, 7/30/10; OWH papers, HLSL.
       Lady . . . eye: OWH to CM, 12/16/10; OWH papers, HLSL.
       "used to . . . ghosts": OWH to Alice S. Green, 9/4/10; FF papers, LC.
       He cheered . . . gather: OWH to PAS, 9/3/10; OWH papers, HLSL.
       "encouraging" . . . satisfied: OWH to CM, 11/5/10; OWH papers, HLSL.
       "well not . . . doesn't he": OWH to ES, 9/13/10; OWH papers, HLSL.
       He dangled . . . later: Pusey, *Charles*, i, 278 ff.
       "round robin" . . . protest: FF, *Of Law and Man*, 121.

437–38 The seventy-seven-year-old . . . trade: Swindler, *Court*, i, 144–45.

438   "like [d] . . . place": OWH to PAS, 8/14/10; OWH papers, HLSL.
       "who didn't . . . [them]": OWH to HJL, 6/17/26; OWH papers, HLSL.
       "the ablest . . . appointments": OWH to FP, 9/24/10; OWH papers, HLSL.
       Each year . . . robe: Acheson, "Reminiscences," 4.

439   "My God . . . succeeded": Umbreit, *Our*, 372.
       "Both . . . again": Corcoran, Rendezvous, 29–30.
       "seeing . . . side": Baker, Leonard, *Brandeis*, 131.
       "obscurities" and generalities: Pusey, *Charles*, i, 286.
       "advent . . . decisions": OWH to Alice S. Green, 1/10/11; FF papers, LC.
       White . . . could wish: OWH to CM, 5/16/12; OWH papers, HLSL.

439–40 For this . . . alike: Friedman and Israel, *Justices*, iii, 1945 ff. CEH, Au-
       tobiographical, 220–21; CEH papers, LC. Adams, Mildred, "Three," 23.

440   "Van Devanter . . . politicians": LDB-FF Conversations; FF papers, LC.
       Moody was forced . . . fifty-seven: William H. Moody to William H. Taft,
       10/3/10; Taft papers, LC.
       His successor . . . statewide: Frank, "The Appointment," 376–78.

public record . . . all: W.G. Brantley to E.H. Callaway, 12/10/10; Lamar papers, University of Georgia.

441   Oh my . . . I do: OWH to PAS, 4/1/11; OWH papers, HLSL.
"sad and aged": OWH to LE, 12/19/10; OWH papers, HLSL.

442   cautious . . . power: *Noble State Bank* v. *Haskell*, 110.

442–43   "an ulterior . . . sides": *Noble State Bank* v. *Haskell*, 110, 112.

443   "feelings . . . community": OWH, *TCL*, 41.
"prima . . . defraud": Bickel, *Judiciary*, 857.
The judge . . . *Post:* ibid., 858.

444   "It is a curious . . . Land": *Bailey* v. *Alabama* (1908), 459.
"Hughes . . . unconstitutional": Pusey, *Charles*, i, 288.

444–45   "dismissed . . . Idaho": *Bailey* v. *Alabama* (1911), 231.

445   "a convenient . . . victims": ibid., 244–45.
"by which . . . 'otherwise' ": ibid., 243.
Hughes . . . Holmes's dissent: CEH, Autobiographical, 224; CEH papers, LC.
surprise: CEH, Autobiographical, 225; CEH papers, LC.
"service . . . will": *Bailey* v. *Alabama* (1911), 246.
"a promise . . . broken": OWH, *TCL*, 300.

445–46   "disagreeable . . . plainly was": *Bailey* v. *Alabama* (1911), 246–48.

446   "with prejudice . . . laboring man": *Bailey* v. *Alabama* (1911), 248.
"The distinctions . . . logic": OWH, *TCL*, 312.
"the men . . . plantation": *Bailey* v. *Alabama* (1911), 248.
The Progressive . . . finally: Bickel, *Judiciary*, 871.
"not a *promise* . . . pass": OWH to FP, 3/12/11; OWH papers, HLSL.
A little . . . justice: OWH to Alice S. Green, 10/14/11; FF papers, LC.
"to the future . . . keep on": OWH to Alice S. Green, 3/25/11; FF papers, LC.

446–47   "most of them . . . ourselves": OWH to ES, 9/9/11; OWH papers, HLSL.

447   "knew . . . unreason?": Acheson, *Morning*, 62.
it was no trick . . . competitors: *Standard Oil Co.* v. *United States*, 42–43.
"the roar . . . lion": Pusey, *Charles*, i, 283.
"our present . . . unreasonable": *Standard Oil Co.* v. *United States*, 96, 102, 105.

448   "most moderate . . . fools": OWH to CM, 5/26/11; OWH papers, HLSL.
"very . . . possible": Pringle, *Life and Times*, ii, 665–69.

448–49   "Every . . . case": Winkelman, *John*, 242.

449   In fact . . . 1920s: Swindler, *Court*, i, 154.
"hard . . . content": OWH to ES, 6/5/11; OWH papers, HLSL.
Added . . . friends: OWH to Alice S. Green, 9/4/10; OWH to PAS, 3/1/11, 3/25/11; OWH to LE, 12/19/10; OWH papers, HLSL.
"meddle . . . themes": OWH to Learned Hand, 1/17/23; OWH papers, HLSL.
"hate [d]" . . . event: OWH to Alice S. Green, 6/18/11; FF papers, LC.

449–50   In a nostalgic . . . ourselves: OWH, speech, 6/28/11; OWH papers, HLSL.

450–51   "beautiful . . . tea": Henry James to OWH, 7/6/11; OWH papers, HLSL.

451   During . . . 1911: Edward D. White to William R. Day, 10/16/11; Day papers, LC.
"fierce . . . negotiator": 222 U.S. xxiv (1911).

"the old . . . charming": OWH to Alice S. Green, 10/14/11; FF papers, LC.

tall . . . collars: Acheson, "Reminiscences," 4.

451–52   Back . . . safe: Friedman and Israel, *Justices,* iii, 2001 ff.

"emotional . . . thunderbolt": OWH to FP, 2/24/23; OWH papers, HLSL.

452   "flying . . . back": OWH to Alice S. Green, 7/29/12; FF papers, LC.

"did what . . . man": OWH to LE, 9/28/12; OWH papers, HLSL.

Finally . . . "believe": OWH to Alice S. Green, 12/8/12; FF papers, LC.

453   "unmixed . . . flagellations": OWH to CM, 1/22/18; OWH papers, HLSL.

He felt . . . turn in: OWH to Alice S. Green, 9/4/10; OWH papers, HLSL.

"Our business . . . life": OWH, speech, 9/28/12; OWH papers, HLSL.

"When I . . . bones": OWH to Alice S. Green, 5/17/15; FF papers, LC.

Chapter 21: "[T]he quiet of a storm center"

454   The first . . . School: OWH to NG, 10/28/14; OWH papers, HLSL.

The two . . . reverence: Baker, Liva, *Felix,* 36–41.

"a very . . . intimations": OWH to HJL, 5/8/18; OWH papers, HLSL.

455   One summer . . . second time: FF to Marion Frankfurter, 8/31/13; FF papers, LC.

Pre–World . . . legend: Baker, Liva, *Felix,* 36.

456   In January . . . Senate: *NYT,* 1/5/13, 3.

"the beginning . . . end": OWH to Alice S. Green, 3/15/13; FF papers, LC.

Olds . . . branch: Irving S. Olds to Catherine Drinker Bowen, 7/31/44; Bowen papers, LC.

As he rose . . . New York: OWH to Alice S. Green, 3/15/13; FF papers, LC.

He had . . . carefully: Irving S. Olds to Catherine Drinker Bowen, 7/31/44; Bowen papers, HLSL.

Henry . . . document: OWH to Alice S. Green, 3/15/13; FF papers, LC.

456–58   He spoke . . . stars: OWH, speech, 2/15/13; OWH papers, HLSL.

458   "sorry for Taft": OWH to PAS, 11/23/12; OWH papers, HLSL.

For . . . cast for Wilson: Swindler, *Court,* i, 164.

"the best . . . mistake": OWH to PAS, 11/23/12; OWH papers, HLSL.

"speak . . . soon": OWH to PAS, 3/9/13; OWH papers, HLSL.

"a good . . . respect": OWH to Alice S. Green, 3/9/13; OWH papers, HLSL.

459   When, at . . . "talk about": interview with Alger Hiss.

Holmes's birthday . . . "friendly": OWH to PAS, 3/9/13; OWH papers, HLSL.

"cataracts . . . me": OWH to PAS, 4/16/13; OWH papers, HLSL.

Fanny thought . . . "so much": OWH to Alice S. Green, 4/5/13; FF papers, LC. OWH to Anna K. Codman, 4/n.d./13; OWH papers, HLSL.

He had about . . . farther: OWH to FP, 4/20/13; OWH to John H. Wigmore, 5/19/13; OWH to LE, 5/18/13; OWH to FF, 6/15/13; OWH papers, HLSL.

460   "seem . . . to man": OWH to FP, 4/20/13, 8/13/13; OWH, 1913 diary; OWH to LE, 9/12/13; OWH papers, HLSL.

His encounters . . . attend him: OWH, 1913 diary; OWH to PAS, 6/20/

13; Henry James to OWH, 7/6/13, 7/9/13; OWH to LE, 9/12/13; OWH to John C. Gray, 9/4/13; OWH papers, HLSL.

mischievous . . . paper: OWH to LE, 10/2/13; OWH papers, HLSL.

His first . . . to begin: OWH to LE, 9/20/26; OWH papers, HLSL.

461   A bout . . . briefly: OWH to Alice S. Green, 11/9/13; OWH papers, HLSL.

The event . . . to *him*: BG, 5/23/13, 5.

Holmes's seventy-third . . . "strong": NYT, 3/11/14, 1. OWH to Alice S. Green, 3/13/14; FF papers, LC.

"ceased . . . bare": OWH to LE, 4/17/14; OWH papers, HLSL.

"an inward" . . . died: OWH to CC, 4/26/14; OWH papers, HLSL.

463   When Davis . . . to court: Harbaugh, *Lawyer's,* 91–92.

"persons . . . compensation": *The Pipeline Cases,* 554.

The period . . . 1914 term: FF, *Felix,* 341–46.

463–64   "Vanity . . . for months": OWH to William H. Moody, 9/30/14; FF papers, LC. Mr. Justice Holmes's Opinions, O.T. 1913; OWH papers, HLSL.

464–65   Solicitor . . . "dough": John W. Davis to MDH, 6/12/52; OWH papers, HLSL.

465   "wish[ed] . . . more": OWH to unnamed correspondent, 8/4/14; OWH papers, HLSL.

A new . . . began: MDH's interview with Mrs. Albert J. Beveridge, 7/42; OWH papers, HLSL.

Justice . . . July: Friedman and Israel, *Justices,* iii, 1863.

He was replaced . . . life-long bachelor: Friedman and Israel, *Justices,* iii, 2023 ff. FF to C.C. Burlingham, 3/18/57; FF papers, LC. Acheson, *Morning,* 85.

They . . . something: James C. McReynolds to unnamed aunt, 3/15/n.d.; McReynolds papers, University of Virginia.

466   "[W]ith . . . us all": James C. McReynolds to R.P. McReynolds, 3/11/27; McReynolds papers, University of Virginia.

His progress . . . upstairs to the Supreme Court: Friedman and Israel, *Justices,* iii, 2024–26.

What particularly . . . announce: OWH to HJL, 5/12/28, 2/18/28; OWH papers, HLSL.

"vanity . . . one off": James C. McReynolds to unnamed aunt, 3/15/n.d.; McReynolds papers, University of Virginia.

he wrote . . . robes: James C. McReynolds to Thomas E. Waggaman, 5/4/43; McReynolds papers, University of Virginia.

"poor" . . . Court: OWH to HJL, 6/4/26; OWH papers, HLSL.

467   "inevitable" . . . Castletown: OWH to ES, 9/5/15; OWH to LE, 10/12/14; OWH to CC, 10/30/14; OWH papers, HLSL.

war work . . . recruiting: Castletown, *Ego,* 221.

"simply . . . groan": OWH to ES, 9/5/15; OWH papers, HLSL.

When . . president: NYT, 10/13/14, 10.

467–69   Frank's story . . . ordinary Americans: Dinnerstein, *Leo.* Golden, *Lynching.* Samuels, Charles and Louise, *Night.*

469   Citing . . . too late: *Frank* v. *Mangum,* 311 ff.

469–70   They then . . . Lamar: WP, 11/27/14, 10.

470   "had not . . . Court": OWH to CC, 11/28/14; OWH papers, HLSL.

"in the presence . . . rendered": NYT, 11/27/14, 1.

"suggestion" . . . leaked: OWH to CC, 11/28/14; OWH papers, HLSL.

"human . . . case": *NYT,* 11/27/14, 10.

Heartened . . . Supreme Court: *NYT,* 12/25/14, 13.

470–71   now at the end . . . Frank's appeal: Lamar, Joseph R., In re Leo Frank; United States Supreme Court case files, NA. *In the matter of Leo Frank, Petitioner,* 694.

471   "legally . . . impregnable": Dinnerstein, *Leo,* 111.

Leo . . . "turning": *NYT,* 12/25/14, 13.

472   Solicitor . . . case: Harbaugh, *Lawyer's,* 98. Bickel, Judiciary, 135.

"to maintain . . . obligation": *United States* v. *Reynolds,* 143.

473   "impulsive . . . and by": ibid., 150.

"actual . . . wrong": OWH, *TCL,* 41.

473–74   "constitutional . . . invaded": *McCabe* v. *Atchison, Topeka & Santa Fe Railway Co.,* 161–62.

474   "insuperable . . . indefinite": ibid., 162–63.

474–75   The public . . . standpoint: *McCabe* v. *Atchison, Topeka & Santa Fe Railway Co., brief for appellees,* 6, 18.

475   "a black . . . race": CEH to OWH, 11/29/14; OWH papers, HLSL.

"The night . . . world": OWH to CC, 12/24/14; OWH papers, HLSL.

Chapter 22: The Young Turks

477   "Anti-Trust . . . common law": *Lawlor* v. *Loewe* (1907), 297.

"with a view . . . return": *Vegelahn* v. *Guntner,* 108.

Now, in January . . . damages: *Lawlor* v. *Loewe* (1915), 533–37.

The company . . . attached: Sklar, *Corporate,* 223 n. 60.

"felt . . . cents": OWH to E.R. Thayer, 1/13/15; OWH papers, HLSL.

478   "not unnaturally . . . Massachusetts": *Coppage* v. *Kansas,* 26–27.

Every seat . . . process of law: *NYT,* 2/26/15, 7; 2/27/15, 8; 4/20/15, 1. *Atlanta Constitution,* 2/26/15, 9; 2/27/15, 10.

479   "competent" . . . Constitution: *Frank* v. *Mangum,* 344–45.

He had no idea . . . care: OWH to CM, 7/6/15; OWH papers, HLSL.

"it would . . . not true": Mr. Justice Holmes's Opinions, O.T. 1914; OWH papers, HLSL.

"non-conformist . . . skepticism": OWH to CM, 7/6/15; OWH papers, HLSL.

480   Holmes seems . . . approached: OWH to ES, 7/13/15; OWH to CC, 11/28/15; OWH papers, HLSL.

The aroused . . . courtroom: *Frank* v. *Mangum,* 345 ff.

"farce": OWH to CM, 7/6/15; OWH papers, HLSL.

Whatever . . . on death: *Frank* v. *Mangum,* 345 ff.

relieved . . . letter: OWH to John H. Wigmore, 4/22/15; OWH to ES, 7/13/15; OWH papers, HLSL.

481   Georgia Governor . . . "barbarians": Dinnerstein, *Leo.* Golden, *Lynching.* Samuels, Charles and Louise, *Night.*

*In 1982 . . . pardon: *NYT,* 3/16/86, iv, 7.

481–82   Holmes had not seen . . . Society: OWH to ES, 3/7/15; OWH to NG, 2/28/15. 48 MHS *Proceedings,* 323 (1915).

482   "A very" . . . the end: OWH to CM, 2/28/15; OWH to LE, 12/20/17;
           OWH papers, HLSL. OWH to Alice S. Green, 5/17/15; FF papers, LC.
           "freshen . . . wiggle": OWH to Ellen Askwith, 3/3/15; OWH papers, HLSL.
           most . . . happier: OWH to LE, 12/20/17; OWH papers, HLSL.
482–83   *Mosley* involved . . . candidates: Bickel, *Judiciary,* 949 ff.
483   Both . . . term: ibid., 945.
           Solicitor . . . wise: Harbaugh, *Lawyer's,* 94.
           "consists . . . paper": *United States* v. *Mosley,* 384.
483–84   Although . . . affords: ibid., 388 ff.
484   Beveridge . . . publisher: Braeman, *Albert,* 244.
           "man of . . . birds": OWH to CM, 6/22/08; OWH papers, HLSL.
           agreed to read it: OWH to Albert J. Beveridge, 9/18/15; OWH papers, HLSL.
           Johnny Morse . . . island: JTM to Thomas Sergeant Perry, 9/16/15; Morse
           papers, MHS.
485   The summer . . . paralyzed: Bickel, *Judiciary,* 357–58.
           Brandeis had been making . . . radical: Baker, Leonard, *Brandeis,* chap-
           ter 3.
           Fanny Holmes . . . anti-Semitic: ibid., 190 n.
486   "good . . . admired": OWH to LE, 5/14/16; OWH papers, HLSL.
           "made aware . . . down on": OWH to unnamed correspondent, 5/13/16;
           OWH papers, HLSL.
           "misfortune . . . question": OWH to LE, 5/14/16; OWH papers, HLSL.
486–87   seventy-fifth . . . "punch": 29 *HLR* 703–04 (1916). OWH to LE, 3/10/16,
           7/11/16; OWH to CM, 10/23/16; OWH to ES, 3/10/16; OWH papers, HLSL.
487   "I want . . . bench": FF to Learned Hand, 4/22/46; FF papers, LC.
           "giggled . . . pleased": OWH to LE, 3/10/16; OWH papers, HLSL.
           The progress . . . lines: Bickel, *Judiciary,* 375 ff. Baker, Leonard, *Brandeis,*
           97–121.
           "Welcome": OWH to LDB, 6/2/16; LDB papers, University of Louisville.
           "loveableness" . . . aim: OWH to HJL, 1/12/21; OWH papers, HLSL.
488   "warm . . . at any age": OWH to HJL, 1/12/21; OWH papers, HLSL.
           OWH and HJL, *Holmes-Laski,* i, 3 n. 1; xiv. Martin, *Harold,* 23, 26–27.
           OWH to FP, 2/18/17; OWH papers, HLSL.
           the realisation . . . to live: HJL to OWH, 7/11/16; OWH papers, HLSL.
488–89   "much . . . so much": OWH to HJL, 7/21/21, 8/9/30, 8/1/25; OWH to
           LE, 3/24/23, 5/7/30; OWH papers, HLSL.
489   Shortly before . . . to Holmes: OWH and Cohen, Morris R., "Holmes-
           Cohen," 3 ff.
           "to have known . . . personality": 82 *NR* 206 (4/3/35).
           "few . . . so much": OWH to Morris R. Cohen, 1/30/21; OWH papers,
           HLSL.
           Lewis . . . to Holmes: OWH and LE, *Holmes-Einstein,* iii.
           "devilish . . . thinking": OWH to FP, 11/7/14; OWH papers, HLSL.
489–90   Much has . . . discipline: Wilson, Edmund, "Justice," 151–53. OWH to
           FP, 7/12/16, 4/5/19; OWH to CM, 4/9/n.d.; OWH to unnamed correspon-
           dent, 2/13/21; OWH papers, HLSL.
490   Not all . . . visits: Wu, *Beyond,* 87 ff. *NYT,* 2/10/86, B14. OWH-Roscoe
           Pound correspondence; OWH papers, HLSL. OWH-Kaneko correspon-
           dence; OWH papers, HLSL. HLS, *Quinquennial,* 158.

On his way . . . "consumedly": FF, *Felix,* 133 ff. O'Connell and Dart, "The House," 79 ff. OWH to HJL, 3/15/18; OWH papers, HLSL.

491   "life . . . free": MDH, "Mr. Justice," 71.

Henry . . . court: *NYT,* 2/1/25, iv, 10. OWH to HJL, 3/1/28; OWH to LE, 5/26/26; OWH papers, HLSL.

"most . . . lonely": OWH to Alice S. Green, 6/7/14; FF papers, LC.

491–92   "put" . . . circulation: OWH to LE, 8/12/26; OWH to FF, 4/19/16; OWH to LE, 1/15/15; OWH to CM, 2/25/12; OWH papers, HLSL. OWH to Alice S. Green, 7/5/14; FF papers, LC.

Chapter 23: *Child Labor*

493   Less than . . . Court: Bickel, *Judiciary,* 395 ff.

Hughes's . . . "conscience": OWH to FP, 7/12/16; OWH papers, HLSL.

They had enjoyed . . . *Mangum:* Pusey, *Charles,* i, 275 ff. CEH, Autobiographical, 224; CEH papers, LC.

494   "deeply—incumbent": OWH to Alfred E. Zimmern, 11/10/16; Zimmern papers, Bodleian Library, Oxford University.

Holmes did not . . . more: OWH to LE, 2/1/17; OWH papers, HLSL.

"in the old-fashioned" . . . for me: Slayden, *Washington,* 293.

The news . . . "world's": Mary Aldwort to OWH, 12/28/16; OWH to LE, 1/27/17; OWH papers, HLSL.

494–95   Felix . . . other states: Baker, Liva, *Felix,* 56. Baker, Leonard, *Brandeis,* 138 ff.

495   "Ten" . . . lawyer talked: FF, *Felix,* 128–29.

496   "mighty . . . wrongdoers": OWH to HJL, 1/8/17; OWH papers, HLSL.

He had told . . . before: OWH to FF, 8/14/16; OWH papers, HLSL.

"actual . . . community": OWH, *TCL,* 41.

497   "not convinced": Mr. Justice Holmes's Opinions, O.T. 1916; OWH papers, HLSL.

"darkly . . . ago": OWH to HJL, 5/8/17; OWH papers, HLSL.

During . . . America great: *WP,* 6/3/17, 4; 5/6/17, 5.

"*Damn . . . wrong*": OWH to HJL, 6/9/17; OWH papers, HLSL.

"the pleasure . . . season": OWH to FP, 6/1/17; OWH papers, HLSL.

"odd . . . safe": OWH to HJL, 7/23/17, 9/17/17; OWH to LE, 10/30/17; OWH papers, HLSL.

497–98   Following . . . areas of the city: Kluger, *Simple,* 108–09. Bickel, *Judiciary,* 789 ff. *Buchanan* v. *Warley,* 70 ff.

498   "disagreeable": Bickel, *Judiciary,* 798.

499   "attacks . . . question": *Buchanan* v. *Warley,* 72.

"entertained . . . else": draft of Holmes's dissent in *Buchanan* v. *Warley,* Mr. Justice Holmes's Opinions, O.T. 1916; OWH papers, HLSL.

"the right . . . process of law": *Buchanan* v. *Warley,* 74–75.

500   The Progressive . . . frustrated: Bickel, *Judiciary,* 801–02.

"matter . . . difficulty": OWH to HJL, 5/25/18; OWH papers, HLSL.

"there is no" . . . underneath: OWH to John H. Wigmore, 12/13/16; OWH papers, HLSL.

501   "I think . . . physically": Baker, Leonard, *Brandeis,* 198.

"securing . . . states": TR, *Message,* xiii.

502   No sooner . . . Supreme Court: Bickel, *Judiciary*, 449–50.

502–3   Eighteen . . . that day: *WP*, 4/16/18, 3.

503   Solicitor . . . "to the States": *Raleigh* (N.C.) *News & Observer*, 4/16/18, 3.
          WP, 4/17/18, 5. *Hammer* v. *Dagenhart*, 252–68.

504   "may be . . . Constitution": *Gibbons* v. *Ogden*, 196.
          "power to regulate . . . destroy": *Hammer* v. *Dagenhart*, 169–70.
          "power . . . void": OWH, *CLP*, 295–96.

505   "at the last . . . up": OWH to FF, 1/13/17; OWH papers, HLSL.

506   "the use . . . destroyed": *Hammer* v. *Dagenhart*, 270–76.

506–7   Holmes did not . . . reservations: Mr. Justice Holmes's Opinions, O.T.
          1917; OWH papers, HLSL.

507   The only . . . "United States": *Hammer* v. *Dagenhart*, 177–80.

507–8   The act . . . domain: Mr. Justice Holmes's Opinions, O.T. 1917; OWH
          papers, HLSL.

508   "You have . . . emphasize it": ibid.
          The public . . . command: *Hammer* v. *Dagenhart*, 281.
          "You have . . . purpose": Mr. Justice Holmes's Opinions, O.T. 1917; OWH
          papers, HLSL.
          "Flattered . . . reason": OWH to FP, 6/14/18; OWH papers, HLSL.

508–9   In Congress . . . "industry": 56 *CR*, 7431 ff. (6/6/18).

509   "Burleson . . . help you": Baker, Ray Stannard. *Woodrow Wilson, Life and
          Letters.* New York, 1939, viii, 187.
          Meanwhile . . . government: Bickel, *Judiciary*, 456–57.
          "not a . . . term": OWH to FP, 6/14/18; OWH papers, HLSL.
          Responding . . . eighty-seven years: Congressional Quarterly, *Guide*, 279.

510   "public . . . discussion": *Toledo Newspaper Co.* v. *United States*, 411.
          "however . . . wrong-doing": ibid., 419–20.
          "would go . . . unwarranted": *Toledo Newspaper Co.* v. *United States*, 425–
          26.
          "ordinary . . . justice": ibid., 424–25.
          "the last . . . courts": OWH to FP, 6/14/18; OWH papers, HLSL.

Chapter 24: "Clear and Present Danger"

511   With . . . its policies: O'Brian, *Civil*, 4–5.

511–12   For that . . . never existed: Chafee, *Free Speech*, 3–4, 39–40. Sullivan,
          Our, v, 472.

512   flu . . . briefly: OWH to LE, 10/31/18; OWH papers, HLSL.
          German operas . . . disloyalty: *NYT*, 3/11/19, 1. Swindler, *Court*, i, 201.
          "chief Bolshevik": Brooks Adams to HCL, 1/12/19; HCL papers, MHS.

513   May 3: *Schenck* v. *United States, Transcript of Record,* cover page.
          Johnny . . . trusteeships: Jaher, "Boston," 190.
          "essential . . . temerity": Blackstone, *Blackstone's,* iv, 15; v, 5, 15, 152.

514   Court's refusal . . . Newark: *NYT*, 11/1/18, 9.
          On the train . . . *Patten:* OWH to HJL, 6/25/18; OWH papers, HLSL.
          Gunther, "Learned," 732.
          *Masses . . . 1924: Gunther, "Learned," 731.

514–15   "urging . . . free government": *Masses Publishing Co.* v. *Patten*, 538–540.

515 Hand and Holmes . . . "counts": Gerald Gunther to Liva Baker, 8/21/89. OWH to Learned Hand, 4/19/18; OWH to FF, 12/6/16; OWH papers, HLSL.

"hard-bought . . . freedom": *Masses Publishing Co.* v. *Patten,* 540.

It seems . . . same thing: OWH, *TCL,* 44.

515–16 "gave up . . . nonsense": Learned Hand to OWH, 6/22/18; Hand papers, HLSL.

516 all the money . . . bonds: OWH to LE, 4/26/18; OWH papers, HLSL.

Opinions . . . our own: Learned Hand to OWH, 6/22/18; Hand papers, HLSL.

"Rarely" . . . Canst: OWH to Learned Hand, 6/24/18; OWH papers, HLSL.

"fortnight . . . work": OWH to LE, 7/11/18; OWH papers, HLSL.

516–17 In it . . . fashion: Mayda, *François,* 130–31.

517 Holmes was inspired . . . "way": OWH, "Natural," 40–41.

Holmes finished . . . loaned him: OWH to JTM, 9/7/18; OWH papers, HLSL.

On a visit . . . time: HJL to OWH, 8/27/18; OWH papers, HLSL. Martin, *Harold,* 25–26.

"in the attempt . . . art": OWH to HJL, 8/29/18; OWH papers, HLSL.

It had been . . . find out: Chafee, "Thirty-five," 2–3.

517–18 Chafee's . . . "punished": Chafee, "Freedom," *NR,* 66–68.

518 "A conscript . . . Constitution!": leaflet, "Long Live the Constitution of the United States"; United States Supreme Court case files, NA.

They took . . . former: *Brief for the Plaintiff in Error, Schenck* v. *United States,* 1–31.

518–19 Privately . . . society: OWH to Alice S. Green, 3/26/19; FF papers, LC.

519 "too far . . . or that": OWH to LE, 8/6/17; OWH papers, HLSL.

"little band . . . Society": OWH to HJL, 11/5/26; OWH papers, HLSL.

On Liberty: OWH, BB, 1919, 124.

" 'liberty' . . . act": Mill, *On,* 17, 53.

520 "force . . . result": OWH to Learned Hand, 2/25/19; OWH papers, HLSL.

"was the majority . . . others": OWH, "Natural," 40.

"demand . . . rationality": OWH to FF, 3/27/17; OWH papers, HLSL.

No society . . . rest: OWH, *TCL,* 43.

521 "so exactly . . . live[d]": OWH to Learned Hand, 6/24/18; OWH papers, HLSL.

"would go . . . favor": Mr. Justice Holmes's Opinions, O.T. 1918; OWH papers, HLSL.

522–23 The document . . . a crime: *Schenck* v. *United States,* 51, 52.

523 In Holmes's . . . haystack: OWH to Zechariah Chafee, 6/12/n.d.; Chafee papers, HLSL.

he loved . . . rang: Butler, *Century,* 178–79.

The reasoning . . . done: OWH, *TCL,* 67.

523–24 "many places" . . . degree: *Schenck* v. *United States,* 52.

524 An opinion . . . placard: Mill, *On,* 53.

"all . . . void": Kent, *Commentaries* (12th ed.), i, 67.

"when a nation . . . right": *Schenck* v. *United States,* 52.

Some years . . . somewhere: Zechariah Chafee to OWH, 6/9/n.d.; Chafee papers, HLSL.

"not helped . . . unhelped": OWH to Zechariah Chafee, 6/12/n.d.; Chafee papers, HLSL.

"ought . . . all": Chafee, "Freedom," *NR*, 67.

525   "the foothills" . . . Almighty": OWH to Esther Owen, 3/13/19; OWH papers, HLSL.

He felt . . . Marshall: OWH to Albert J. Beveridge, 1/19/19; OWH papers, HLSL.

"shake" . . . car: OWH to CM, 4/19/18; OWH papers, HLSL.

"for many . . . courage": OWH to LDB, 9/4/02; LDB papers, University of Louisville.

"some very . . . place": OWH to Alice S. Green, 3/26/19; FF papers, LC.

"greatly . . . hearing": OWH to HJL, 3/16/19; OWH papers, HLSL.

"should . . . could": OWH to FP, 4/27/19; OWH papers, HLSL.

"insubordination . . . States": *Debs* v. *United States,* 212.

525–26   "monumental . . . self-preservation": *Frohwerk* v. *United States,* 212–14.

526   He talked . . . "stood alone": *Debs* v. *United States,* 212–14.

*Debs served . . . sentence: 3 *DAB* 184.

"I agree . . . again": Mr. Justice Holmes's Opinions, O.T. 1918; OWH papers, HLSL.

526–27   "quite . . . quickly": LDB-FF Conversations, FF papers, LC.

527   "positively . . . popular feeling": Learned Hand to OWH, n.d.; OWH papers, HLSL.

"words . . . adieu": OWH to Learned Hand, 4/3/19; Hand papers, HLSL.

A few . . . asked: HJL to OWH, 5/11/19; OWH papers, HLSL.

previously . . . *Legislation* (1916): LCRB.

527–28   "actual . . . prudence": Freund, "Debs," 13 ff.

528   "some . . . burning": OWH to HJL, n.d.; OWH papers, HLSL.

Abrams . . . March 12: *Abrams* v. *United States, Transcript of Record,* cover page.

"guessing" . . . force: OWH to Herbert Croly, 5/12/19; OWH papers, HLSL.

528–29   "one of the most . . . even in wartime": Chafee, "Freedom . . . in Wartime," 944, 956–57, 968.

529   Laski gave . . . discussed it: Smith, Donald L., *Zechariah,* 30.

"a very wide latitude": Zechariah Chafee to Charles F. Amidon, 9/30/19; Chafee papers, HLSL.

"to have . . . country": OWH to John H. Wigmore, 6/7/19; OWH papers, HLSL.

"stupid . . . pretence": OWH to FP, 4/5/19; OWH papers, HLSL.

Not all . . . Palmer's home: *NYT,* 5/4/19, 1.

The one meant . . . "job": OWH to Kentaro Kaneko, 6/21/19; OWH to FP, 6/17/19; OWH to LE, 5/22/19; OWH papers, HLSL.

"general . . . liberal": Roscoe Pound to FF, 4/18/19; FF papers, HLSL.

530   Frankfurter, . . . Boston: Baker, Liva, *Felix,* 91.

"push" . . . accord: OWH to HJL, 6/1/19; Roscoe Pound to OWH, 5/29/19; OWH papers, HLSL.

Laski was still not . . . blood: Martin, *Harold,* 26, 31–36. OWH to FF, 4/5/19; OWH papers, HLSL. Wigdor, *Roscoe,* 193–94, 202–03.

530–31   Considerable . . . in that way: OWH to HJL, 6/1/19; OWH papers, HLSL.

531 uncertain . . . thought he should: LDB to Roscoe Pound, 5/15/20; Pound papers, HLSL.

Holmes did . . . has been lost: OWH to A. Lawrence Lowell, 6/2/19; OWH and HJL, *Holmes-Laski,* i, 211.

Lowell himself . . . faculty: Greenslet, *Lowells,* 399.

These were a group . . . scale would: *Arizona Employers' Liability Cases,* 417 ff.

532 "pauperism . . . crime": *Arizona Employers' Liability Cases,* 424.

"any . . . absurd": OWH to HJL, 5/24/19; OWH papers, HLSL.

no more certain . . . just: *Arizona Employers' Liability Cases,* 432–33.

533 Pitney, for one . . . next term: Mr. Justice Holmes's Opinions, O.T. 1918; OWH papers, HLSL. Acheson, *Morning,* 67–68.

In the interests . . . Court's opinion: Mr. Justice Holmes's Opinions, O.T. 1918; OWH papers, HLSL.

"we would . . . laws": LDB-FF Conversations; FF papers, LC.

"You talk . . . duties": OWH to FP, 5/26/19; OWH papers, HLSL.

"meditate . . . spin": OWH to HJL, 5/18/19; OWH papers, HLSL.

533–34 He protested . . . "understanding of it": LDB-FF Conversations; FF papers, LC.

534 Brandeis's little . . . hoped for: OWH to Kentaro Kaneko, 6/21/19; OWH to NG, 9/2/19; OWH to LE, 9/19/19; OWH papers, HLSL. FF to Marion D. Frankfurter, 9/20/19; FF papers, LC. Novick, *Honorable,* 32; Monagan, "Enigmatic," 81. LDB-FF Conversations; FF papers, LC.

Sandwiched . . . shapes: OWH, BB, 124.

"a little . . . discretion": HJL to OWH, 3/18/19; OWH papers, HLSL.

Laski had dedicated . . . "thingsters": HJL, dedication, *Authority.* HJL to OWH, 3/5/19; OWH to HJL, 3/7/19, 4/4/19, 4/8/19; OWH papers, HLSL.

534–35 We . . . insist . . . engage: HJL, *Authority,* 121–22.

535 Not long . . . "entire belief": OWH to HJL, n.d., 5/24/19; OWH papers, HLSL.

Laski had recently . . . fighting for: HJL to OWH, 2/8/19; OWH papers, HLSL. OWH, BB, 124. OWH to HJL, 9/19/19; OWH papers, HLSL.

Chapter 25: *"Free Trade in Ideas"*

536 "last . . . war": OWH to FP, 10/26/19; OWH papers, HLSL.

The most detailed account of events leading to the Abrams case is to be found in Richard Polenberg's *Fighting Faiths.*

537 "made to . . . avow": *Abrams* v. *United States,* 629.

I fear . . . accomplish it: OWH to HJL, 10/26/19; OWH papers, HLSL.

"be persuaded . . . expect it": OWH to FP, 11/6/19; OWH papers, HLSL.

537–38 In an unusual . . . unmoved: Acheson, *Morning,* 119.

538 fear of open . . . weakness: OWH, Sr., *Works,* ii, 109.

He simply . . . not press: Acheson, *Morning,* 119.

"heartily . . . gratefully": Mr. Justice Holmes's Opinions, O.T. 1919; OWH papers, HLSL.

"murderous": Friedman and Israel, *Justices,* iii, 2084.

coincidentally . . . spring: NYT, 11/11/19, 1.

"the language . . . war": *Abrams* v. *United States,* 624.

"Poor . . . anonymities": ibid., 629.

"duty . . . others": OWH to Albert J. Beveridge, 12/8/19; OWH papers, HLSL.

539   "rightly . . . prevent": *Abrams* v. *United States,* 627.

"the struggle . . . strongest": OWH, "Law in Science," 449.

539–40 [W]hen men . . . notion: *Abrams* v. *United States,* 630.

540   "greatly . . . hysteria": Learned Hand to OWH, 11/25/19; OWH papers, HLSL.

He was a little . . . "of one": Learned Hand to Zechariah Chafee, 12/3/19; Chafee papers, HLSL.

"fine . . . grateful": HJL to OWH, 11/12/19; OWH papers, HLSL.

"Respectable . . . out": OWH to E.A. Curtis, 12/7/19; OWH papers, HLSL.

Chafee . . . Milton: Chafee, *Free Speech,* 509.

For obvious reasons . . . air: *BET,* 1/1/20, 11.

"with barrels . . . time": Meyer, Agnes, diary, 3/4/18; Meyer papers, LC.

"lay in a good cellar": Corcoran, Rendezvous, 15.

541   Early indications . . . Pitney as well: LDB-FF Conversations; FF papers, LC.

"If only . . . that score": OWH to NG, 3/5/21; OWH papers, HLSL.

542   I have sent . . . "harmony": OWH to HJL, 11/30/17, 5/25/18, 11/17/20, 1/11/24, 3/9/24, 12/26/31, 12/13/18, 2/18/28; OWH papers, HLSL.

542–43 "letting . . . little": OWH to HJL, 1/16/18, 7/5/17; OWH papers, HLSL.

543   "loading . . . wagon": Edward D. White to W.R. Day, 3/9/16; Day papers, LC.

"to sit . . . Brandeis": OWH to LE, 10/14/17; OWH papers, HLSL.

"that cuss . . . gawping": OWH to HJL, 3/1/23; OWH papers, HLSL.

"bullie[d] . . . can go": OWH to HJL, 1/6/23; OWH papers, HLSL.

"as little . . . go on": OWH to FP, 12/3/25; OWH papers, HLSL.

544   Felix . . . Harvard: Baker, Liva, *Felix,* 91.

544–45 "Of course . . . martyrdom": OWH to FF, 12/4/19; OWH papers, HLSL.

545   The spat . . . delayed: Baker, Leonard, *Brandeis,* 221–22.

Luina: OWH to HJL, 1/15/20; OWH papers, HLSL.

"Dickie!" . . . that day: Kanin, "Trips," 56–57.

546   "no other . . . conducted": *Schaefer* v. *United States,* 472.

"harmless . . . impotent": ibid., 493–94.

"in times . . . passion": ibid., 482–83.

The constitutional . . . belief: ibid., 495.

547   "whether . . . century": Chafee, *Free Speech,* 94.

"heartily": OWH to LDB, notation on LDB's draft opinion; LDB papers, HLSL.

to educate . . . court: Acheson, *Morning,* 94.

Chapter 26: *"Still the dash of a D'Artagnan"*

548   records . . . himself: OWH to John H. Wigmore, 3/16/19; OWH papers, HLSL.

Brandeis . . . disqualify himself: Bickel, *Judiciary,* 161.

548–49   "deeply . . . law": OWH to HJL, 3/4/20; OWH papers, HLSL.
549   The steel case . . . example: Bickel, *Judiciary*, 170–71.
           "the Union . . . to end": OWH, speech, 2/15/13; OWH papers, HLSL.
           Wild birds . . . deal with: *Missouri* v. *Holland*, 434–35.
549–50   [W]hen we . . . nation: ibid., 433.
550   "blood . . . neck": OWH to HJL, 6/4/20; OWH papers, HLSL.
           "The exemption . . . others": *Evans* v. *Gore*, 265.
           "for four . . . example": Mr. Justice Holmes's Opinions, O.T. 1919; OWH
           papers, HLSL.
           "all . . . savage": LDB-FF Conversations; FF papers, LC.
550–51   "to make . . . be stated": OWH to HJL, 6/4/20; OWH papers, HLSL.
551   Abbott . . . 1895: Greenslet, *Lowells*, 394–95.
           Now . . . "slumber": Abbott Lawrence Lowell to OWH, 4/10/20; OWH
           papers, HLSL.
           Holmes did not . . . invitation: Harvard commencement program for 1920.
           In the summer . . . Company: OWH and HJL, *Holmes-Laski*, i, 215 n. 1.
           OWH to HJL, 10/16, 20/19, 1/15/20, 5/11/20, 11/17/20; HJL to OWH, 10/
           17/19, 10/28/19, 11/5/19, 1/14/20, 1/26/20, 4/2/20; OWH papers, HLSL.
           Holmes told . . . forty: OWH to Hampton L. Carson, 4/2/21; Carson pa-
           pers, Free Library of Philadelphia.
           "little . . . life": OWH, *CLP*, "Preface."
           In due . . . scholar: 34 *HLR* 449 (3/21); 21 *Columbia LR* 296 (3/21); 30
           YLJ 775 (3/21); 69 *University of Pennsylvania LR* 291 (3/21); 6 *Cornell LQR*
           353 (3/21); 112 *Nation* 237 (2/9/21); NYT, 4/4/21, iii, 9; 25 *NR* 294 (2/2/
           21).
551–52   "great pleasure . . . war": OWH, *CLP*, "Preface."
552   Between . . . his conviction: Chafee, *Free Speech*, 285–88.
           The Minnesota . . . authority: *Gilbert* v. *Minnesota*, 325.
           "disagreed . . . said": OWH to FF, 12/22/20; OWH papers, HLSL.
           White . . . state: *Gilbert* v. *Minnesota*, 334.
           whom sent . . . errors: LDB to FF, 12/6/20; FF papers, LC.
           Holmes lumped . . . "murder": OWH to FF, 12/22/20; OWH papers, HLSL.
553   "the most . . . to pass": OWH to NG, 3/5/21; OWH papers, HLSL.
           noted . . . "of Law": 34 *HLR* 553 (3/21).
           Fanny took . . . my heart: OWH to HJL, 3/10/21; OWH to ES, 3/25/21;
           OWH to E.A. Curtis, 3/17/21; OWH papers, HLSL. Biddle, "Friendship,"
           87.
554   In the following . . . achievement: 26 *NR* 34 (3/9/21).
           "put . . . happiness": OWH to HJL, 3/10/21; OWH papers, HLSL.
           Duplex . . . "Carta": Swindler, *Court*, i, 210.
           "legislative humbug": OWH to FF, 1/30/21; OWH papers, HLSL.
           Milwaukee Publishing . . . Espionage Act: Chafee, *Free Speech*, 298.
           "almost . . . one man": *Milwaukee Publishing Co.* v. *Burleson*, 437.
           "tangible . . . compensation": *Block* v. *Hirsh*, 155–56.
555   "question . . . smiled": OWH to Charles E. Clark, 12/23/21; FF papers,
           LC.
           "unquestionable . . . health": *Block* v. *Hirsh*, 156.
           Between them . . . "rendered?": ibid., 158, 161–63.

"bad form": OWH to FF, 4/20/21; OWH papers, HLSL.

555–56   Pleading . . . that day: NYT, 5/19/21, 1. Edward D. White to James C.
McReynolds, 5/13/21; McReynolds papers, University of Virginia.

556   "close . . . recovered": OWH to LE, 5/20/21; OWH papers, HLSL.
"with regard" . . . Hughes: OWH to HJL, 5/27/21; OWH papers, HLSL.
speculation . . . Taft: NYT, 5/20/21, 1.
And when . . . shoes: King, Melville, 304.
Now, in 1921 . . . retirement: Pringle, Life and Times, ii, 956.
"before . . . well": Edward D. White to James C. McReynolds, 5/13/21;
McReynolds papers, University of Virginia.

556–57   After . . . succeed him: Pringle, Life and Times, ii, 957–58.

557   "how . . . now": OWH to HJL, 5/27/21; OWH papers, HLSL.
endorsed . . . businessmen: Frank, "Appointment," 469.
"I can't . . . position": Pringle, Life and Times, ii, 959.
On the personal . . . "everyone": Hammond, Autobiography, 541, 547.
OWH to Joseph C. Hutcheson, 2/5/30; OWH papers, HLSL.

558   "indolent . . . with him": OWH to HJL, 5/27/21; OWH papers, HLSL.
"Cooperate . . . agreeable": OWH to WHT, 7/2/21; WHT papers, LC.
"two . . . judicial work": Hammond, Autobiography, 56. Pringle, Life and
Times, 961.
Taft liked . . . "making them": LDB-FF Conversations; FF papers, LC.
Adams, Mildred, "In the Supreme," 9.
"muckraker . . . evil": WHT to Gus Karger, 1/3/16; WHT papers, LC.
"to like . . . indeed": Pringle, Life and Times, ii, 970–71.

559   This is a most . . . WHT: WHT to LDB, notation on LDB's draft opinion
in St. Louis, Brownsville and Mexico Railway Co. v. United States, 268 U.S.
169 (1925); LDB papers, HLSL.
I congratulate . . . promptness: WHT to LDB, notation on LDB's draft
opinion in Southern Railway Co. v. Watts, 260 U.S. 519 (1923); LDB papers, HLSL.
I like . . . satisfactorily: WHT to LDB, 5/16/27; LDB papers, HLSL.
Taft soon found . . . honorary degree: Pringle, Life and Times, ii, 969–71.
Holmes's friend . . . hadn't: Bickel, Judiciary, 70.
"appointed . . . said it": Investors' Syndicate v. Porter, 52 Federal Reporter,
2d Series, 189, 196 (1931).

559–60   Holmes seemed . . . together: Pringle, Life and Times, ii, 969.

560   "fond . . . of one": WHT to Henry L. Stimson, 5/18/28; WHT papers,
LC.
"experience . . . questions": WHT to Charles P. Taft II, 3/7/26; WHT
papers, LC.

561   Afterwards, Holmes . . . he said: LDB-FF Conversations, FF papers, LC.
The Court voted . . . his vote: Acheson, Morning, 68.
"find no . . . with the vote": Mahlon Pitney, memorandum, n.d., 4, 1;
LDB papers, HLSL.
Taft had no . . . overprotecting labor: Pringle, Life and Times, ii, 1031–
42.

561–62   "The only . . . purpose": WHT to Horace Taft, 5/7/22; WHT papers, LC.

562   Beginning . . . other justices: WHT to Willis Van Devanter, 12/7/21; Van
Devanter papers, LC.

"At Brandeis's" . . . published it: OWH to HJL, 12/22/21; OWH papers, HLSL.

562–63   "Delusive" . . . most respect: *Truax* v. *Corrigan,* 342 ff.

563   "too . . . expanded": John H. Clarke, notation on LDB's draft of *Truax* v. *Corrigan;* LDB papers, HLSL.

The Arizona . . . second-guess them: *Truax* v. *Corrigan,* 352.

"the rules" . . . the law: ibid., 357.

564   Instigated . . . tones: OWH to FF, 12/22/22; OWH papers, HLSL. 33 *NR* 84 (12/20/22).

For . . . D'Artagnan: LDB to OWH, 12/8/22; OWH papers, HLSL.

"went to . . . hill": OWH to FF, 12/22/22; OWH papers, HLSL.

"half" . . . child: OWH to HJL, 2/17/22, 1/15/22; OWH papers, HLSL. WHT to Horace Taft, 4/17/22; WHT papers, LC.

The better . . . month later: *NYT,* 6/28/22, 25. OWH to HJL, 7/7/22; OWH to E.A. Curtis, 7/12/22; OWH papers, HLSL.

564–65   "suspended . . . serious": OWH to CM, 8/10/[22]; OWH to FF, 8/24/22; OWH to HJL, 7/7/22; OWH to E.A. Curtis, 7/26/22; OWH papers, HLSL.

565   All went . . . taxi: OWH to FF, 7/22/22; OWH to HJL, 7/7/22; OWH to JTM, 11/24/22; OWH to John H. Wigmore, 8/24/22; OWH to NG, 9/27/22; OWH papers, HLSL.

The Holmeses lived . . . youth: OWH to HJL, 9/28/22; OWH to FP, 11/19/22; OWH papers, HLSL. OWH to Pittsfield Library, 11/13/22; Berkshire Athenaeum.

He worried . . . "convalescing": OWH to NG, 12/26/22; OWH papers, HLSL. FF to Marion Frankfurter, 6/n.d./24; FF papers, LC.

"drop . . . product": OWH to HJL, 9/22/22; OWH papers, HLSL.

His young . . . "universal": OWH to J.C.H. Wu, 9/2/23; OWH papers, HLSL.

565–66   "as regularly . . . allowances": HJL to FF, 11/29/22; LDB to FF, 10/19/22; FF papers, LC. WHT to Horace Taft, 10/8/22; WHT papers, LC. OWH to FP, 11/19/22; OWH to ES, 5/21/23; OWH papers, HLSL.

566   Life at 1720 . . . "vehicle": LDB to FF, 10/30/22; FF papers, LC. OWH to NG, 12/26/22; OWH to LE, 5/31/23; OWH papers, HLSL.

While Holmes . . . "to pieces": WHT to Horace Taft, 4/17/22; WHT papers, LC. Pringle, *Life and Times,* ii, 1059.

566–67   "determining . . . public office": Levitan, "Jurisprudence," 47.

567   The "public" . . . United Nations: Friedman and Israel, *Justice,* iii, 2085–86.

Clarke was . . . welcome: Pringle, *Life and Times,* ii, 1058.

"Our views . . . prevail": WHT to George Sutherland, 9/10/22; Sutherland papers, LC.

567   Day was the . . . 1923: Friedman and Israel, *Justices,* 1789.

To all . . . capacities: LDB-FF Conversations; FF papers, LC.

567–68   This one involved . . . property?: Friedman, Lawrence, "Search," 2 ff.

568   "some values" . . . bought: *Pennsylvania Coal Co.* v. *Mahon,* 413–16.

568–69   "refined . . . injustice": LDB-FF Conversations; FF papers, LC.

569   imminent disaster . . . detail: Friedman, Lawrence, "Search," 22.

"heightened . . . to go whole hog": LDB-FF Conversations; FF papers, LC.

"the life . . . fellow-men": OWH, *TCL,* 1.

Predictably . . . "statesmanship": OWH to FP, 12/31/22; OWH papers, HLSL. 34 *NR* 136 (1/3/23).

Frankfurter . . . comments: OWH to HJL, 12/14/22, 12/22/22, 1/13/23; OWH papers, HLSL.

"more than" . . . dining out: LDB-FF Conversations; FF papers, LC. OWH to HJL, 12/14/22, 10/19/20; OWH papers, HLSL.

569–70   But Holmes . . . *"pro tem"*: OWH to FF, 4/10/22; OWH to Learned Hand, 1/17/23; OWH to NG, 12/26/22; OWH to HJL, 2/5/23; OWH to FP, 1/25/23; OWH papers, HLSL.

Chapter 27: *Upholding the "right of a donkey to talk drool"*

571   Holmes was ready . . . Brandeis: Corcoran, Rendezvous, 7. OWH to ES, 5/17/24, 12/26/29; OWH to HJL, 3/27/23; OWH papers, HLSL. LDB to FF, 1/3/23; FF papers, LC.

"everything . . . don't go": OWH to NG, 12/20/27; OWH papers, HLSL.

"general . . . *day*": JTM to Thomas Sergeant Perry, 12/20/27; Morse papers, MHS.

Holmes acknowledged . . . plot: OWH to ES, 12/26/29, 10/24/23; OWH to HJL, 11/10/23; OWH papers, HLSL.

On days . . . robin: Biddle, *Mr.*, 139–40.

571–72   informal . . . his rest [Sutherland]. "Sutherland's," 20.

572   "one of . . . bag": OWH to ES, 6/5/11; OWH papers, HLSL.

"Holmes!" . . . fidgeted: [Sutherland], "Sutherland's," 20.

Shortly . . . for work: interview with Alger Hiss. Corcoran, Rendezvous, 18–19.

On days . . . Saturday: Biddle, *Mr.*, 147. Interview with Alger Hiss.

"The goddam . . . yet": FF to Learned Hand, 3/22/60; FF papers, LC.

572–73   Afternoons . . . Park: Lockwood, "Justice," 4. OWH to NG, 3/28/20; OWH papers, HLSL. Francis Biddle to Catherine Drinker Bowen, 12/20/40; Bowen papers, LC. OWH to Margaret Clifford, 4/27/27; OWH papers, HLSL.

573   After dinner . . . "troubles": OWH to John H. Wigmore, 3/29/29; OWH papers, HLSL.

The total annual . . . law student: Hamilton, "On Dating," 8.

His eagerness . . . tolerantly: Lockwood, "Justice," 1. LDB to HJL, 3/20/24; Urofsky, *Letters*, v, 123. OWH to Charles E. Clark, 12/23/21; OWH papers, HLSL.

When the justices . . . known: MDH, memorandum of a talk with FF, 1/2/64; OWH papers, HLSL.

574   The make-up . . . stroke: LDB-FF Conversations; FF papers, LC.

"processes . . . subverted": *Frank* v. *Mangum*, 347.

"the whole . . . wrong": *Moore* v. *Dempsey*, 91.

"would almost . . . dissenter": Swindler, *Court*, i, 228.

574–75   The chief . . . "progressive": Pringle, *Life and Times*, ii, 1049–50. Swindler, *Court*, i, 228.

575   unsettling . . . "untried things": Paschal, *Mr. Justice*, 62.

"in the light . . . founded": Swindler, *Court*, i, 231.

576   Brandeis . . . in the case: Baker, Leonard, *Brandeis*, 239.

Heartened . . . constitutions: *Adkins* v. *Children's Hospital, Brief for appellants,* xx.

"one of" . . . to the justices: FF to Marion Frankfurter, 3/12/23; FF papers, LC.

577 "Sutherland" . . . laughter: Paschal, *Mr.*, 11.

He had been born . . . help from government: 323 U.S. v, vi, viii.

from which . . . observations: WHT to OWH, notation on draft of Holmes's dissent in *Adkins* v. *Children's Hospital*, Mr. Justice Holmes's Opinions, O.T. 1922; OWH papers, HLSL.

577–78 "judicial . . . degree": *Adkins* v. *Children's Hospital*, 544–60.

578 *"in every . . . invalid": *West Coast Hotel Co.* v. *Parrish*, 405.

Ultimately . . . own dissent: *Adkins* v. *Children's Hospital*, 562.

"the continuity . . . dissent": WHT to HFS, 1/26/27; HFS papers, LC.

578–79 "did not . . . see them": *Adkins* v. *Children's Hospital*, 567.

579 "absolutely . . . was worth": ibid., 567–71.

The C.J. . . . business: OWH to HJL, 4/14/23.

The Court's . . . required: *Adkins* v. *Children's Hospital*, *Brief for appellants*, iv, xxv, xxviii.

580 "jaw . . . joy": OWH to ES, 4/18/24; OWH papers, HLSL.

"joy of a child": LDB to FF, 6/3/24; FF papers, LC.

In peace . . . contributions: *NYT*, 6/3/24, 16.

For five . . . today: OWH to LE, 6/4/24; OWH papers, HLSL.

580–81 Summer . . . "downs": OWH to ES, 6/9/24; OWH to HJL, 5/22/24, 8/16/24; OWH to FF, 7/27/24; OWH papers, HLSL.

581 At Beveridge's . . . "Boys": OWH to Albert J. Beveridge, 8/3/24, 8/23/24; OWH papers, HLSL.

"Day of . . . I'd feel": OWH to HJL, 8/8/24, 7/31/24; OWH papers, HLSL. 51 *New Yorker* 30 (4/14/75).

"delighted . . . years": OWH to HJL, 8/16/24; OWH papers, HLSL. FF to Marion Frankfurter, 8/14/24; FF papers, LC.

"no impairment . . . fit him": LDB to HJL, 8/3/25; W. Bloch to FF, 5/31/38; OWH to FP, 5/7/25; LDB to OWH, 5/18/25; OWH to FF, 1/10/25; OWH papers, HLSL. FF to Marion Frankfurter, 6/11/24; FF papers, LC. *NYT*, 11/6/24, 21; 1/10/25, 2.

582 Unable . . . resign: Pringle, *Life and Times*, ii, 1059.

Descendant . . . Court: *NYT*, 1/11/25, viii, 5; 1/5/36, vii, 5. McCormack, "Law Clerk's," 710 ff. Friedman and Israel, *Justices*, iii, 2221 ff.

Progressives . . . confirmed: Frank, "Appointment," 489 ff.

"entirely . . . court": *NYT*, 1/11/25, viii, 4.

His stolidity . . . Court: McCormack, "Law Clerk's," 716 ff.

583 Don't make . . . thinker: OWH to HJL, 11/29/25; OWH papers, HLSL.

As to . . . wait: LDB to FF, 11/30/25; FF papers, LC.

Taft wooed . . . "legislation": Pringle, *Life and Times*, ii, 1043. Swindler, *Court*, i, 225.

584 Bootlegging . . . high: Longworth, *Crowded*, 313–15. Meyer, Agnes E., diary, 3/n.d./18; Meyer papers, LC. *NYT*, 4/2/19, ii, 1.

584–85 Like the rest . . . progress: Green, Constance McLaughlin, *Washington*, ii, 278 ff.

585 National . . . Washington: *NYT*, 3/4/28, iv, 2.

New government . . . open-air garage: Green, Constance McLaughlin, *Washington*, 278–81.

Holmes resisted . . . sued: OWH to ES, 8/9/25; OWH papers, HLSL. Interview with Alger Hiss.

586   "the Constitution . . . speech": *Prudential Insurance Co.* v. *Cheek,* 538.

587   "every . . . statute": *Gitlow* v. *New York,* 668.
A single . . . incipiency: ibid., 669.
Holmes's scheme . . . murder: OWH to FF, 12/22/20; OWH papers, HLSL.
"drool": OWH to HJL, 6/14/25; OWH papers, HLSL.

587–88   didn't believe . . . revolution: OWH to FP, 2/26/11; OWH papers, HLSL.
*Gitlow . . . Reports: Mason, *Harlan,* 518.
"humbug": OWH to HJL, 6/17/26; OWH papers, HLSL.

588–89   "chance" . . . their way: *Gitlow* v. *New York,* 673.

589   The victories . . . future: Chafee, *Free Speech,* 325.
"the right . . . shock *me*": OWH to Kentaro Kaneko, 6/16/25; OWH papers, HLSL.
As for . . . sentence: Chafee, *Free Speech,* 266 n. 25.

Chapter 28: *"Three generations of imbeciles are enough"*

590   Holmes celebrated . . ."[his] life": OWH to FP, 4/2/26; OWH to HJL, 11/29/24; OWH papers, HLSL. LDB to FF, 3/14/25, 3/21/26; FF papers, LC. *NYT,* 3/6/26, iv, 1. *WP,* 3/8/26, 18. *WS,* 3/7/26, 13. 46 *NR* 88 (3/17/26).

592   "actual . . . community": OWH, *TCL,* 41.
Myers's heirs . . . a half: Congressional Quarterly, *Guide,* 212.
"most important case": WHT to Edward T. Sanford, 11/7/25; WHT papers, LC.

593   Brandeis puts . . . obnoxious person: WHT to Horace Taft, 11/28/25; WHT papers, LC.
Taft was also . . . agree with it: WHT to Horace Taft, 11/28/25; WHT to Helen Taft Manning, 6/11/23; WHT papers, LC.

593–94   "to run . . . child": WHT to Edward T. Sanford, 11/7/25; WHT to Horace Taft, 10/15/26; WHT papers, LC. WHT to Willis Van Devanter, 11/1/26; Van Devanter papers, LC.

594   "the advance of Congress": WHT to Horace Taft, 10/28/26; WHT papers, LC.
"exhaustive research": *Myers* v. *United States,* 177.
"few words": OWH to LDB, 2/18/21; LDB papers, HLSL.
"spider's" . . . power: *Myers* v. *United States,* 177.

595   Dear . . . permits: OWH to JTM, 11/8/26; OWH papers, HLSL.
In 1927 . . . pathetic: correspondence files of the NAACP, LC.
The NAACP . . . Nixon: James Weldon Johnson, memorandum, 2/11/25; NAACP papers, LC.
Moorfield . . . tiring: Moorfield Storey to James Weldon Johnson, 4/20/26; NAACP papers, LC.

596   "simple . . . with": ibid.
"In no event . . . Texas": *NYT,* 3/8/27, 1.
"a pretty" . . . thought not: OWH to HJL, 4/25/27; OWH papers, HLSL.
Certainly . . . Tuesday: OWH to Margaret Clifford, 4/22/27; OWH papers, HLSL.

596–97   He announced . . . courtroom: *NYT,* 3/8/27, 1. LDB to FF, 3/9/27; FF papers, LC.
597   "unnecessary" . . . in this case: *Nixon* v. *Herndon,* 540–41.
    James . . . "to offer": *NYT,* 3/8/27, 1.
598   At the end . . . century: Kluger, *Simple,* 116–17.
    The justices . . . Constitution: *NYT,* 2/25/26, 2.
599   As March . . . months: Ethel St. Leger to OWH, 4/11/27; OWH papers, HLSL.
    "the other . . . joint": OWH to CC, 1/10/15; OWH papers, HLSL.
    "gap . . . horizon": OWH to Bernard Castletown, 11/3/26; OWH papers, HLSL.
    "Kindly . . . dead"; OWH to FF, 5/21/26; OWH papers, HLSL.
    "pleasure": OWH to LE, 5/19/27; OWH papers, HLSL.
    The case . . . "normal": the case history of *Buck* v. *Bell* is gathered from "Sterilization"; Kevles, "Annals"; Lombardo, "Three."
    "afflicted . . . society": *Buck* v. *Bell,* 206.
600   "fundamental . . . authority": OWH, "Path," 470–71.
601   When . . . creatures: OWH, Sr., *Works,* iii, 226.
    " 'not . . . criminal' ": OWH quoting Havelock Ellis in "Path," 471.
    When in 1914 . . . eagerly: LCRB. OWH, BB, 131.
601–2   "devout . . . build a race": OWH, Introduction to *Rational,* xxxi. OWH to HJL, 7/17/25; OWH to ES, 11/19/15, 5/17/12; OWH papers, HLSL. OWH, *CLP,* 306.
602   Some of . . . reasonableness: WHT to OWH, 4/23/27; OWH papers, HLSL.
    "admirably put": notation on Holmes's draft of *Buck* v. *Bell,* Mr. Justice Holmes's Opinions, O.T. 1926; OWH papers, HLSL.
    the rights . . . considered: *Buck* v. *Bell,* 207.
    no society . . . existence: OWH, *TCL,* 43.
603   We have seen . . . enough: *Buck* v. *Bell,* 207.
    "near to . . . getting near": OWH to HJL, 5/12/27; OWH papers, HLSL.
    Shortly after . . . "very bright": Lombardo, "Three," 60 ff.
603–4   Following . . . United States; Kevles, "Annals," 125.

Chapter 29: Sacco and Vanzetti

605   Holmes had avoided . . . six years: OWH to HJL, 9/1/27; OWH papers, HLSL. OWH to FF, 3/18/27; FF papers, LC.
605–6   "was part" . . . inconclusive: Frankfurter, *The Case,* 59, 65, 68.
606   "moved" . . . say more: OWH to FF, 3/18/27; FF papers, LC.
    "heroism . . . kicked up": OWH to LE, 5/19/27; OWH papers, HLSL.
    "self-sacrifice . . . martyr": OWH to HJL, 11/23/27; OWH papers, HLSL.
    The atmosphere . . . duty: *BH,* 8/1/27, 1; 8/5/27, 1; 8/7/27, 1; 8/17/27, 1. *NYT,* 8/8/27, 1.
    "Stirred" . . . Beverly Farms: OWH to HJL, 8/18/27; OWH papers, HLSL.
    "exciting . . . neighbors": OWH to LE, 8/14/27; OWH papers, HLSL.
606–7   They wanted Holmes . . . request: OWH to HJL, 8/18/27, 8/24/27, 9/1/27; OWH papers, HLSL.
607   I am . . . Governments: Musmanno, *After,* 300.

Fearing . . . weeks: OWH to HJL, 8/18/27; OWH to FF, 9/13/27; OWH papers, HLSL.

607–8   "But has justice" . . . carried out: Corcoran, *Rendezvous*, 23–26.

608   I have received . . . intervene: OWH, denial of petition for stay of execution pending certiorari in *Sacco and Vanzetti* v. *Massachusetts*, 487 O.T. 1927, dated 8/20/27; United States Supreme Court case files, NA.

Recalling . . . guns: OWH to HJL, 7/23/27; OWH papers, HLSL.

Far stronger . . . believe: OWH, denial of petition for stay of execution pending certiorari in *Sacco and Vanzetti* v. *Massachusetts*, 487 O.T. 1927, dated 8/20/27; United States Supreme Court case files, NA.

609   Undeterred . . . 9 P.M.: OWH to LE, 9/11/27; OWH papers, HLSL.

"an event . . . point": LDB to FF, 3/9/27; FF papers, LC.

The party . . . Stone was vacationing: Baker, Leonard, *Brandeis*, 269. *NYT*, 8/22/27, 1.

Mr. Justice . . . Vanzetti: FF to Leo H. Winters, 7/1/59; FF papers, LC.

*Some years . . . explained *his*: Baker, Liva, *Felix*, 280–82.

610   they had discussed it previously: OWH to LE, 12/13/22; OWH papers, HLSL.

Privately . . . criticisms: OWH to LE, 8/24/27; OWH to FF, 9/9/27; OWH papers, HLSL. OWH to FF, 11/23/27; FF papers, LC.

it has even . . . Massachusetts?: Wilson, Edmund, *Patriotic*, 786.

610–11   "the world . . . howl": OWH to LE, 8/14/27, 12/8/27, 9/11/27; OWH to FF, 9/9/27; OWH to HJL, 9/1/27, 11/23/27, 11/16/27; OWH papers, HLSL.

612   "the criminal . . . blundered": *People* v. *Defore*, 242 N.Y. 13, 21 (1926).

"The efforts . . . land": *Weeks* v. *United States*, 393.

"reduces . . . at all": *Silverthorne* v. *United States*, 392.

614   It is better . . . courts: *Olmstead* v. *United States*, *Brief for amicus curiae*, 8.

"rhetorical . . . difference": OWH to FP, 6/20/28; OWH papers, HLSL.

"great . . . society": WHT to Horace Taft, 4/3/25, 6/1/28; WHT papers, LC.

In putting . . . "change": WHT to Edward T. Sanford, 5/31/18; WHT to Horace Taft, 6/1/28; WHT papers, LC.

"consciously . . . within": James C. McReynolds to HFS, 4/2/30; HFS papers, LC.

Taft . . . unanimity: WHT to HFS, 1/26/27; HFS papers, LC.

615   "subservience . . . disappointed": WHT to Horace Taft, 6/8/28; WHT papers, LC.

Desperately . . . graciously: WHT to James C. McReynolds, 5/30/28, 5/31/28; WHT to Edward T. Sanford, 5/31/28; WHT papers, LC.

His health . . . 1927 term: *NYT*, 6/5/28, 9. *WP*, 6/5/28, 1,3.

615–16   the courts . . . obtained: *Olmstead* v. *United States*, 465–66.

616   Holmes confessed . . . him to: OWH to FP, 6/20/28; OWH papers, HLSL.

"scattered . . . regret[ted]": OWH to HJL, 6/12/28; OWH papers, HLSL.

"disdainful . . . hands": [Sutherland], "Sutherland's," 25.

"dirty business": *Olmstead* v. *United States*, 470.

616–17   He dismissed . . . ignoble part: ibid., 469–71.

617   "the nastiest . . . yes": WHT to Horace Taft, 6/12/28; WHT papers, LC.

"the academic . . . ideals": Mason, *William*, 259.

"the more . . . Holmes": WHT to George Sutherland, 7/25/28; Sutherland papers, LC.

I suppose . . . strictly: LDB to FF, 6/15/28; FF papers, LC.

Chapter 30: Duty Done

618 "near" . . . *Brunettes*: OWH to HJL, 6/16/28, 7/20/28; OWH papers, HLSL.

He found . . . ordinary day: OWH to Owen Wister, 7/16/28; OWH papers, HLSL.

When he returned . . . twenty-five days: *NYT*, 10/6/28, 4.

He was beginning . . . at times: John E. Lockwood to FF, 10/1/28; OWH papers, HLSL.

618–19 "stupid" . . . issues: OWH to FF, 10/23/21; OWH papers, HLSL.

619 "felt . . . noticed": OWH to HJL, 10/19/28; OWH papers, HLSL.

Rum . . . dough: OWH to LE, 6/17/28; OWH papers, HLSL.

In the spring . . . pain: OWH to LE, 2/28/29; OWH papers, HLSL.

"There seems . . . machinery": OWH to HJL, 5/30/29.

"slowly" . . . misfortune: OWH to HJL, 4/2/29; OWH to LE, 2/28/29; correspondence with FP, HJL, FF, LE, ES, NG, etc., spring 1929; OWH papers, HLSL.

"crushed . . . hard one": LDB to FF, 4/21/29, 4/22/29; FF papers, LC.

Finally . . . sleep: OWH to ES, n.d.; OWH papers, HLSL.

"Exhaustion . . . femur": District of Columbia death certificate number 320561.

619–20 "how to" . . . private: Pringle, *Life and Times*, ii, 970. *NYT*, 5/1/29, 31.

620 "How . . . spot": OWH to HJL, 6/15/29; OWH papers, HLSL.

In her . . . Justice: FF to Learned Hand, 4/22/46; FF papers, LC.

At the same . . . in hand: John E. Lockwood to FF, 5/7/29, 5/24/29; FF papers, LC.

"seemed like . . . anything": OWH to HJL, 5/23/29, 5/30/29; OWH papers, HLSL.

"reconciled . . . last[ed]": OWH to FP and Georgina Pollock, 5/24/29; OWH papers, HLSL.

If I . . . dead: OWH to John H. Wigmore, 5/29/29; OWH papers, HLSL.

It was better . . . "intimate": OWH to LE, 6/n.d./29.

620–21 One of the reasons . . . she could: FF to Learned Hand, 10/24/52; FF papers, LC. OWH to Nina Gray, 11/7/31; OWH papers, HLSL.

621 Following . . . callers: John E. Lockwood to HFS, 5/2/[29]; HFS papers, LC.

Before . . . lunch: OWH to Owen Wister, 5/20/29; OWH papers, HLSL.

He already . . . "of old": LDB to FF, 5/11/29; FF papers, LC.

"the boys . . . Christmas": *NYT*, 8/4/48, 21.

"a country . . . No": *United States* v. *Schwimmer*, 647–48.

(Ordinarily . . . answer.): Harbaugh, *Lawyers'*, 285.

"that a . . . allegiance": *United States* v. *Schwimmer*, 647.

621–22 Civic-minded . . . 1920s: ibid., 646–47.

622 Whatever . . . "principles of the Constitution": ibid., 650–52.

"anti-draft . . . flamboyant": OWH to HJL, 6/15/29; OWH papers, HLSL.

623   This is . . . quarters: Wister, *Roosevelt,* 143.
      Holmes always . . . birth: Mason, *Harlan,* 43.
      [S]ome persons . . . non-attendance: Putnam, *Memoir,* 108–09.
      "burnt . . . souls": [OWH], "Books," 410.
      If there . . . onward: OWH to ES, 11/19/15; OWH papers, HLSL.
624–25   He began . . . we hate: *United States* v. *Schwimmer,* 653–54.
625   Though he . . . "prescribed": HFS to Robert Hale, 6/3/29; HFS papers, LC.
      "a lot . . . understand": WHT to Willis Van Devanter, 7/3/29; Van Devanter papers, LC.
      It also inspired . . . citizenship: Mason, *Harlan,* 521.
      "At the risk . . . nation": Rosika Schwimmer to OWH, 1/28/30; OWH papers, HLSL.
625–26   "You are too . . . expression": OWH to Rosika Schwimmer, 1/30/30; OWH papers, HLSL.
626   Accompanied . . . year: Ex Rel OWH Holmes talking, 5/9/29; Bowen papers, LC.
      "memories" . . . gossip: OWH to NG, 6/28/31; OWH to ES, 10/24/29; OWH to LE, 7/27/29, 7/28/30; OWH to HJL, 7/9/29; OWH papers, HLSL.
      As the shadows . . . soldier: OWH to HJL, 9/9/29; OWH papers, HLSL.
      "one . . . glimpse": OWH to FF, 5/29/30; OWH papers, HLSL.
      Later that year . . . fellow: OWH to ES, 10/24/29; OWH papers, HLSL. FF, memorandum, 9/9/64; FF papers, LC.
627   From January 6 . . . Holmes: Charles E. Cropley to FF, 8/3/43; FF papers, LC.
      Over the past . . . fill in: ibid.
      "admirable . . . rapidity": HFS to FF, 1/27/30; HFS papers, LC.
      On March 8 . . . conference: *NYT,* 3/11/30, 8.
      The president shrewdly . . . "burdened": OWH to HJL, 2/27/30; OWH papers, HLSL.
      This time . . . justiceship: HJL, "Mr.," 415 ff. OWH to HJL, 2/27/30; OWH papers, HLSL.
628   The summer . . . "break": OWH to HJL, 9/14/30; OWH to ES, 8/28/30; OWH papers, HLSL.
      In September . . . felt up to: *BH,* 9/30/30, 2.
      In October . . . "much longer": OWH to CM, 10/17/30; OWH papers, HLSL.
      The year . . . "throw off": OWH to FF, 12/24/40; OWH papers, HLSL. FF to HFS, 9/30/31; FF papers, LC.
      Holmes himself . . . "to pieces": OWH to HJL, 10/9/31, 12/25/31, 11/21/31, 12/3/31; OWH to CM, 4/5/31; OWH to unnamed correspondent, 10/27/31; OWH to HFS, 7/27/31; OWH papers, HLSL. FF to Learned Hand, 11/10/31; LDB to FF, 11/8/31; FF papers, LC.
628–29   "all kind" . . . work: OWH to FF, 4/27/31; OWH papers, HLSL.
629   He suspected . . . judgment: OWH to unnamed correspondent, 12/19/31; OWH papers, HLSL. CEH, Autobiographical, 14; CEH papers, LC.
      As the 1931 . . . there: CEH, Autobiographical, 11–12; CEH papers, LC. Urovsky, *Letters,* v, 496.
      The time . . . inevitable: 284 U.S. vii (1932).
      He postdated . . . day: LDB to FF, 1/10/32; FF papers, LC.

630

When on . . . tomorrow: *WP*, 3/6/35, 1.
I know . . . people: 284 U.S. vii (1932).
The same mail . . . Holmes: 284 U.S. v–vi (1932).
*Retirement . . . pension: CEH, Autobiographical, 17–18; CEH papers, LC.
The following . . . brethren: *NYT*, 1/13/32, 3; 1/14/32, 15.

631

There are few . . . thought: *New York Herald Tribune*, 1/14/32, 21.
It is revolting . . . past: OWH, "Path," 469.
Certitude . . . not so: OWH, "Natural," 40.

631–32

The development . . . growth: OWH, "Path," 468.

632

resort . . . jury!: OWH, "Law in Science," 444–45.
An ideal . . . wisdom: OWH, speech, 6/25/1895; OWH papers, HLSL.
just as . . . true: OWH to HJL, 3/1/23; OWH papers, HLSL.

633–34

I have considered . . . present: OWH, speech, 12/3/02; OWH papers, HLSL.

635

Life seems . . . Goodbye: *WP*, 3/9/32, 1.

Part VIII: BENEDICTION

Chapter 31: Finishing Canter

639

Although . . . in writing: interview with H. Chapman Rose. H. Chapman Rose to Mrs. EJH, Jr., 1/13/32; MDH, diary, 1933–34; OWH papers, HLSL. HFS to FF, 2/2/32, 2/2/33; H. Chapman Rose to FF, 1/25/32; FF papers, LC. *NYT*, 3/9/32, 23.

639–40

He was seen . . . murder tale: *NYT*, 1/30/32, 8. Interview with H. Chapman Rose. OWH to LE, 5/15/32; OWH to Margaret Clifford, 10/24/27; OWH to E.A. Curtis, 10/1/31; FF, memorandum, 8/20/32; MDH to Albert Mordell, 1/16/50; OWH papers, HLSL. H. Chapman Rose to FF, 2/9/32, 3/24/32; FF, memorandum, n.d.; FF papers, LC. Meyer, Agnes, *Out of*, 172. Biddle, *Mr.*, 202. OWH, BB, 72.

640

"It's all . . . through me": FF, memorandum, 8/10/32; FF papers, LC.
His body . . . salute: C.C. Burlingham to MDH, 6/5/42; MDH papers, HLSL.
"hard case . . . affection": FF, memorandum, 8/10/32; FF papers, LC.
Johnny . . . "college days": JTM to OWH, 3/7/28, 3/5/31; Morse papers, MHS.
Brahmins . . . position: Jaher, "Boston," 210–11.

640–41

You had . . . well: JTM to OWH, 3/5/31; Morse papers, MHS.

641

"Mine . . . blood": MDH, diary, 11/20/33; MDH papers, HLSL.
On March . . . "fight": FF, memorandum, 3/15/33; FF, LC. *WS*, 3/9/33, A11. *BH*, 3/9/33, 1. *BG*, 3/9/33, 9. Laski, "Memories," 360. Monagan, *Great*, 1–2.

641–42

Holmes had . . . "tired": Arthur Sutherland, memorandum, n.d.; FF papers, LC. OWH to E.A. Curtis, 12/19/33; OWH papers, HLSL. MDH to HJL, 12/26/33; FF papers, LC.

642

Owen Wister came . . . "have to": Biddle, *Mr.*, 202.
After making . . . explanation: OWH, will, 10/24/33; OWH papers, HLSL.
*Unaccustomed . . . were set: *NYT*, 5/3/84, iv, 26.

By late . . . 1993: interview with John Hutson.

642–43   Through . . . *My Destination:* MDH to FF, 11/19/33, 1/1/34, 2/1/34, 2/17/ 34, 2/19/34, 3/9/34, 5/8/34, 7/31/34, 10/9/34, FF papers, LC. Benjamin N. Cardozo to cousin, 3/7/24; OWH papers, HLSL. Corcoran, Rendezvous, 39. OWH, BB, 74.

643   A Unitarian . . . taps: Knox, "Some Correspondence," 224.
"Soldiers . . . rain": James H. Rowe to FF, 3/22/35; FF papers, LC.